R.A. TORREY

ON THE CHRISTIAN LIFE

R.A. TORREY

ON THE CHRISTIAN LIFE

WHITAKER
HOUSE

Unless otherwise indicated, all Scripture quotations are taken from the King James Version of the Holy Bible. Scripture quotations marked (RV) are taken from the Revised Version of the Holy Bible. Scripture quotations marked (ASV) are taken from the American Standard Edition of the Revised Version of the Holy Bible.

R. A. Torrey on the Christian Life

Titles included in this anthology:
God, the Bible, and You
ISBN: 978-1-60374-191-0 © 1999 by Whitaker House
The Answer
ISBN: 978-0-88368-539-6 © 1999 by Whitaker House
How to Pray
ISBN: 978-0-88368-133-6 © 1984 by Whitaker House
How to Study the Bible
ISBN: 978-0-88368-164-0 © 1986 by Whitaker House
How Bring Men to Christ
ISBN: 978-0-88368-098-8 © 1984 by Whitaker House
Heaven or Hell
ISBN: 978-0-88368-610-2 © 1985 by Whitaker House
Your Life in God
ISBN: 978-0-88368-751-2 © 1984 by Whitaker House
The Presence and Work of the Holy Spirit
ISBN: 978-0-88368-177-0 © 1996 by Whitaker House

ISBN: 978-1-60374-835-3
Printed in the United States of America

Whitaker House
1030 Hunt Valley Circle
New Kensington, PA 15068
www.whitakerhouse.com

Library of Congress Cataloging-in-Publication Data (Pending)

1 2 3 4 5 6 7 8 9 10 11 ꟺ 20 19 18 17 16 15 14 13

CONTENTS

GOD, THE BIBLE, AND YOU

CONTENTS

1

IS THE BIBLE INSPIRED BY GOD?

For the prophecy came not in old time by the will of man:
but holy men of God spake as they were moved by the Holy Ghost.
—2 Peter 1:21

All scripture is given by inspiration of God,
and is profitable for doctrine, for reproof, for correction,
for instruction in righteousness: that the man of God may be perfect,
thoroughly furnished unto all good works.
—2 Timothy 3:16–17

To what extent is the Bible inspired by God? The answer to this question is of vital and fundamental importance. We must understand that the writers of the various books of the Bible were inspired by God in a sense that no other men were ever inspired by God. Indeed, they were so gifted and taught and led by the Holy Spirit in recording the words of the Bible that they taught the truth and nothing but the truth. Their teachings were absolutely without error. We have in the Bible a court of final appeal and of infallible wisdom to which we can go to settle every question of doctrine or duty.

However, many believe that the writers of the Bible were "inspired" only in the vague and uncertain sense that Shakespeare, Browning, and many other men of genius were inspired. In other words, they were inspired only to the extent that their minds were made more keen to see the truth than ordinary men, and they still made mistakes and chose the wrong words to express their thoughts. Those who believe this false but popular doctrine say that we must recast the Bible writers' thoughts by discovering, if we may, the inspired thoughts behind the uninspired words.

If this is the case, we are all lost at sea. We are in hopeless confusion, for each generation must then settle for itself what the Holy Spirit meant to say through the blundering Bible writers. However, since no generation can determine with any accuracy what the Spirit meant, no generation can arrive at the truth but must simply promote blunders for the next and wiser generation to correct, to be corrected in turn by the next generation. Thank God that this subtle doctrine can be proven to be utterly untrue!

There is a great need for crystal clear teaching on this subject. Our seminaries, pulpits, and Sunday schools, as well as our religious literature, are full of teaching that is vague, inaccurate, misleading, unscriptural, and often grossly false. Many people these days say, "I believe that the Bible is inspired," when by "inspired" they do not mean at all what we understand or what the mighty men of faith in the past meant by inspired. They often say that they "believe the Bible is the Word of God," when at the same time they believe it is full of errors.

But the Bible is as clear as crystal in its teachings and claims regarding itself. Either those claims are true, or the Bible is the biggest fraud in all the literature of the human race. The position held by so many today—that the Bible is a good book, perhaps the best book in the world, but at the same time is full of errors that must be corrected by the higher wisdom of our day—is utterly illogical and absolutely ridiculous. If the Bible is not what it claims to be, it is a fraud—an outrageous fraud.

What does the Bible teach and claim concerning itself? What does it teach and claim regarding the fact and extent of its own inspiration?

Previously Undiscovered Truth Was Revealed

The first thing taught in the Bible regarding the inspiration of the various authors of the books of the Bible is this: truth hidden from men for ages, which they had not discovered and could not have discovered by the unaided processes of human reasoning, was revealed to the Bible writers by the Holy Spirit. We find this very clearly taught in the Word of God:

> *If ye have heard of the dispensation of the grace of God which is given me to you-ward: how that by revelation he made known unto me the mystery; (as I wrote afore in few words, whereby, when ye read, ye may understand my knowledge in the mystery of Christ) which in other ages was not made known unto the sons of men, as it is now revealed unto his holy apostles and prophets by the Spirit.* (Ephesians 3:2–5)

The meaning of these words is unmistakable. Here Paul declared very plainly that God *"by the Spirit"* had revealed *"unto his holy apostles and prophets" "the mystery of Christ."* This mystery had not been made known to the sons of men in former generations. Men had not discovered it and could not discover it, except by revelation from God. But Paul and the other apostles and prophets knew it by direct revelation from God Himself through the Holy Spirit.

The Bible contains truth that men never had discovered and never could have discovered if left to themselves. The Father, in great grace, has revealed this truth to His children through His servants, the prophets and apostles. This teaching is inescapable.

We see the foolishness, a foolishness so common in our day, of seeking to test the statements of Scripture by the conclusions of human reasoning. The revelation of God transcends human reasoning; therefore, human reasoning cannot be its test. Furthermore, Christian reasoning is the *product* of studying the truth of the Bible; it is not the *test* of the truth of the Bible. If our reasoning differs from the statements of the Bible, the thing for us to do is not to try to pull God's revelation down to the level of our reasoning, but to elevate our reasoning to the level of God's Word.

The Revelation to the Prophet Was Independent of His Own Thinking

A second thing about the inspiration of the Bible writers that the Bible makes perfectly clear is this: the revelation made by God through His Holy Spirit to the prophets was independent of the prophets' own thinking. It was made to them by the Spirit of Christ, who was in them. They themselves often did not thoroughly understand the full meaning of what the Spirit was saying through them. In fact, they diligently searched and inquired in their own minds as to the meaning of what they themselves had said. This point comes out very plainly in 1 Peter:

> *Of which salvation the prophets have inquired and searched diligently, who prophesied of the grace that should come unto you: searching what, or what manner of time the Spirit of Christ which was in them did signify, when it testified beforehand the sufferings of Christ, and the glory that should follow. Unto whom it was revealed, that not unto themselves, but unto us they did minister the things, which are now reported unto you by them that have preached the gospel unto you with the Holy Ghost sent down from heaven; which things the angels desire to look into.*
>
> (1 Peter 1:10–12)

Here, again, the meaning is clear; it is inescapable. We are told that the prophets had a revelation made to them by the Holy Spirit, the meaning of which they did not thoroughly comprehend. They themselves "*inquired and searched diligently"* as to the meaning of this revelation that they had received and recorded. Through them the Spirit testified beforehand about *"the sufferings of Christ, and the glory that should follow."* (See, for example, Isaiah 53:3 and Psalm 22.) They recorded what the Spirit testified, but what it meant they did not thoroughly understand.

It was not merely that their minds were made keen to see things that they would not otherwise see and they therefore more or less accurately recorded them. No, there was a very definite revelation, arising not from their own minds at all, but from the Spirit of God. This they recorded. The revelation was not of themselves, for they themselves wondered about its meaning. What they recorded was not at all their own thoughts; it was the thoughts of the Holy Spirit who spoke through them. How utterly different this concept is from what is so persistently taught in many of our pulpits and theological seminaries!

Prophetic Utterances Were from God Himself

The third thing that the Bible makes perfectly clear is that not one single prophetic utterance was of the prophet's own will (that is, it was not in any sense merely what he wished to say). In every instance, the prophet's words were from God, and the prophet was "carried along" in the prophetic utterance by the Holy Spirit, regardless of his own will or thoughts. We find this stated in so many words in 2 Peter 1:21, where we read,

> *For the prophecy came* [literally, "was brought"] *not* [literally, "not a prophecy ever"] *in old time by the will of man: but holy men of God spake as they were moved* [literally, "carried along" or "borne"] *by the Holy Ghost.*

There can be no honest mistaking of the meaning of this language. The prophet never thought that there was something that needed to be said and therefore said it, but God took possession of the prophet and *carried him along* in his utterance by the power of the Holy Spirit. The prophet did not speak by his own reasoning or by his own intuition; he spoke *"by the Holy Ghost."* As God's messenger, he spoke what God told him to say.

The Holy Spirit Was the Real Speaker

The fourth thing that the Bible teaches regarding the inspiration of the Bible writers and their utterances is that the Holy Spirit was the real speaker in the prophetic utterances. What was said or written was the Holy Spirit's words, not the words of the prophet. This truth is revealed repeatedly in various Scriptures.

For example, in Hebrews 3:7–8, we read, *"Wherefore (as the Holy Ghost saith, To day if ye will hear his voice, harden not your hearts."* The author of the epistle to the Hebrews was quoting Psalm 95:7–8; he said that what the psalmist is recorded as saying is actually what *"the Holy Ghost saith."*

Again, in Hebrews 10:15–16, we read,

> *Whereof the Holy Ghost also is a witness to us: for...he had said before, This is the covenant that I will make with them after those days, saith the Lord, I will put my laws into their hearts, and in their minds will I write them.*

Now, the author of the epistle to the Hebrews is quoting Jeremiah 31:33, and he does not hesitate to say that the testimony that Jeremiah gave is *the testimony of the Holy Spirit,* that the Holy Spirit was the real speaker.

We read in Acts 28 that Paul said,

> *Well spake the Holy Ghost by Esaias the prophet unto our fathers, saying, Go unto this people, and say, hearing ye shall hear, and shall not understand; and seeing ye shall see, and not perceive: for the heart of this people is waxed gross, and their ears are dull of hearing, and their eyes have they closed; lest they should see with their eyes, and hear with their ears, and understand with their heart, and should be converted, and I should heal them.* (Acts 28:25–27)

Here Paul was quoting Isaiah's words as recorded in Isaiah 6:9–10, and he distinctly said that the real speaker was not Isaiah, but *"the Holy Ghost"* who spoke *"by Esaias* [Isaiah] *the prophet."*

Turning now to the Old Testament, we read in 2 Samuel 23:2 this assertion by David regarding the things that he said and wrote: *"The spirit of the LORD spake by me, and his word was in my tongue."* There can be no mistaking the meaning of these words on the part of anyone who goes to the Bible to find out what it really claims and teaches. The Holy Spirit was the real speaker in the prophetic utterances. It was the Holy Spirit's utterance that was upon the prophet's tongue. The prophet was simply the mouth by which the Holy Spirit spoke. Merely as a man, except as the Holy Spirit taught him and used him, the prophet was fallible as other men are fallible. But when the Spirit was upon him, when he was taken up and borne along by the Holy Spirit, he became infallible in his teachings; for his teachings were not his, but the teachings of the Holy Spirit. It was God who was then speaking, not the prophet.

For example, Paul, merely as a man, even as a Christian man, undoubtedly had mistaken notions on many things and was more or less subject to the ideas and opinions of his time. But when he taught as an apostle, under the power of the Holy Spirit, he was infallible; rather, the Spirit who taught through him was infallible, and the teachings that resulted from the Spirit's teaching through him were infallible, as infallible as God. Common sense demands that we carefully distinguish between what Paul may have thought as a man and what he actually taught as an apostle. In the Bible, we have the record of what he taught as an apostle.

Someone may cite as possible exceptions to this statement verses in 1 Corinthians 7, where Paul said,

> *But I speak this by permission, and not of commandment....Now concerning virgins I have no commandment of the Lord: yet I give my judgment, as one that hath obtained mercy of the Lord to be faithful.*
>
> (1 Corinthians 7:6, 25)

There are those who think that Paul does not seem to have been sure here that he had the word of the Lord in this particular matter, but that is not the meaning of the passage. The meaning of verse 6 is that his teaching that he had just given was by way of concession to their weakness, not a commandment as to what they must do. And the teaching of verse 25 is that the Lord, during His earthly life, had given no commandment on this subject, but that Paul was giving his judgment. But he said distinctly that he was giving it *"as one that hath obtained mercy of the Lord to be faithful."* Furthermore, in the fortieth verse of the chapter, he distinctly said that he had the Spirit of God in his judgment.

But even if we said that the other interpretation of this passage is the correct one—that Paul was not absolutely sure in this case that he had the word of the Lord and the mind of the Lord—that would only show that where Paul was not absolutely sure that he was teaching in the Holy Spirit he was careful to note the fact. This interpretation would only give additional certainty to all other passages that he wrote.

It is sometimes said that Paul taught in his earlier epistles that the Lord would return during his lifetime, and that in this matter he certainly was mistaken. But Paul never taught this in his earlier epistles or any other epistles—he never taught this anywhere. This assertion is contrary to fact. He did say in 1 Thessalonians, which was his first epistle,

> *Then we which are alive and remain shall be caught up together with them in the clouds, to meet the Lord in the air: and so shall we ever be with the Lord.* (1 Thessalonians 4:17)

In this verse, Paul did put himself in the same class with those who were still alive when he wrote the words. He naturally and necessarily did not include himself with those who had already died. But in speaking of the Lord's return, he did not say or even hint that he would still be alive when the Lord returned. It is quite probable that Paul did believe at this time that he might be alive when the Lord returned, *but he never taught that he would be alive.* The attitude of expectancy is the true attitude in all ages for every believer. This was the attitude that Paul took until it was distinctly revealed to him that he would depart before the Lord came. I think it is very probable that Paul was inclined to believe in the earlier part of his ministry that he would live until the coming of the Lord, but the Holy Spirit kept him from teaching this and also kept him from all other errors in his teachings.

The Very Words Were Given by the Holy Spirit

The fifth thing that the Bible makes clear about the inspiration of the Bible writers is that the Holy Spirit in them not only gave the thought, but also gave the words in which the thought was to be expressed. We find this very clearly stated in 1 Corinthians 2:13:

> *Which things also we speak, not in the words which man's wisdom teacheth, but which the Holy Ghost teacheth; comparing spiritual things with spiritual.*

One of the most popular of the false theories of inspiration in our day is that the Holy Spirit was the author of the thought but the Bible writers were left to their own choice of words in the expression of the thought. Therefore, according to this theory, we cannot emphasize the exact meaning of the Bible's words, but we must try to find the thought of God that was behind the words, which the writer more or less inaccurately expressed.

Many teachers in our pulpits and theological seminaries today speak very sneeringly and arrogantly of those who believe in verbal inspiration—that is, the doctrine that the Holy Spirit chose the very words in which the thought He was teaching was to be expressed. But regardless of how contemptuously they may speak of those who believe in verbal inspiration, certainly the Bible claims for itself that it was verbally inspired. The passage that I previously quoted makes it as plain as language can possibly make it that the "*words*" in which the apostle Paul spoke were not "*words which man's wisdom teacheth, but which the Holy Ghost teacheth.*"

Now, if this were not the fact, if only the *thought* that was given to Paul was from God and Paul clothed the thought in his own words, then Paul was thoroughly deceived on a fundamental point. In this case, we cannot depend on any point of his teachings. Or, Paul was a deliberate fraud, in which case the quicker we burn up his books, the better for us and all concerned.

Attempts to find a compromise between the two positions have landed those who have tried it in all kinds of absurdities. There is no possibility of finding any middle ground. If you have an exact and logical mind, you must make your choice between verbal inspiration and blatant unbelief. I, for one, must choose verbal inspiration, for Paul distinctly stated that the words in which he conveyed to others the truth that was revealed to him were the words that the Holy Spirit taught him.

The Holy Spirit Himself has anticipated all these ingenious but wholly unbiblical, utterly illogical, and entirely false theories regarding His own work in the Bible writers. The theory that "the concept" was inspired but the words in which the concept was expressed were not was anticipated by the Holy Spirit. He discredited it many centuries before our supposedly wise theological teachers conceived it and attempted to foist it upon an unsuspecting public.

Furthermore, the theory is absurd in itself. The only way thought can be conveyed from one mind to another—from one man's mind to another man's mind, or from the mind of God to the mind of man—is by words; therefore, if the words are imperfect, the thought expressed by those words is also imperfect. The theory is an absurdity on its very surface, and it is difficult to see how intelligent men could ever have deceived themselves into believing such a thoroughly illogical theory. If the words are not inspired, the Bible is not inspired. Let us not deceive ourselves; let us face facts.

In addition, the more carefully and minutely one studies the *wording* of the statements of this wonderful Book—the Bible—the more he will become convinced of the marvelous accuracy of *the very words* used to express the thought. To a superficial thinker, the doctrine of verbal inspiration may appear questionable or even absurd. But any regenerate and Spirit-taught individual who ponders the words of Scripture day by day, and year after year, will become thoroughly and immovably convinced that the wisdom of God is in *the very words* used as well as in the thought that is expressed in the words.

It is a significant and deeply impressive fact that our difficulties with the Bible rapidly disappear as we note the precise language used. The changing of a word or letter, or a tense, case, or number, would often land us in contradiction or untruth. But as we take the words *exactly as written in the original manuscripts,* difficulties disappear and truth shines forth. Countless times people have come to me with apparent difficulties and supposed contradictions in the Bible and have asked for a solution. I have pointed them to the exact words used, and the solution was found in taking the words exactly as written. It was because they changed in a slight degree the very words that God spoke that a difficulty had seemed to arise.

The divine origin of nature shines forth more clearly the closer we examine it under a microscope. By the use of a powerful microscope, we see the perfection of form in the minutest particles of matter. We are overwhelmingly convinced that God, a God of infinite wisdom and power, a wisdom extending down to the minutest parts of matter, is the author of the material universe. Likewise, the divine origin of the Bible shines forth more and more clearly under close inspection. The more intently we study the Bible, the more we note the perfection with which the turn of a word reveals the absolute thought of God.

An important question—and a question that has puzzled many writers at this point—is this: If the Holy Spirit is the author of the very words of Scripture, how do we account for the variations in style and wording? How is it, for example, that Paul always used Pauline language, that John always used Johannine language, and so on? The answer to this question is very simple and is twofold.

First, even if we could not account at all for this fact, it would have little weight against the explicit statements of God's Word. Anyone who is humble and wise will recognize that there are a great many things that he cannot account for at all that could be easily accounted for if he knew a little more. It is only the man who has such amazing and astounding conceit that he thinks he knows as much as God—in other words, that he is infinite in wisdom—who will reject an explicit statement of God's Word simply because he sees a difficulty within it that he in his limited knowledge cannot solve.

But there is a second answer, and an all-sufficient one, and it is this: these variations in style and wording are easily accounted for because the Holy Spirit is infinitely wise. He Himself is the creator of man and of man's power of speech; therefore, He is wise enough and has quite enough skill in the use of language that, when revealing truth to and through any individual, He uses words, phrases, and forms of expression that are in that person's ordinary vocabulary and forms of thought. He is also quite wise enough to make use of that person's individuality in revealing the truth through him. It is one of the marks of the divine wisdom of this Book that the same divine truth is expressed with absolute accuracy in such widely different forms of expression.

Every Scripture Is Inspired by God

The sixth thing that the Bible makes plain regarding the work of the Holy Spirit in the various writers of Scripture, is that all Scripture—that is, everything contained in all the books of the Old and New Testaments—is inspired by God. We are distinctly taught this truth in 2 Timothy 3. Here we read,

> *All Scripture* [more exactly, "every Scripture"] *is given by inspiration of God* [more literally, "is God-breathed"], *and is profitable for doctrine* [or teaching], *for reproof, for correction, for instruction in righteousness* [rather, "instruction that is in righteousness"], *that the man of God may be perfect, thoroughly furnished* [better, "equipped completely"] *unto all good works.* (2 Timothy 3:16–17)

In the Revised Version, an attempt has been made to obscure the full force of these words. In this translation, the words are rendered as follows:

> *Every Scripture inspired of God is also profitable for teaching, for reproof, for correction, for instruction which is in righteousness: that the man of God may be complete, furnished completely unto every good work.* (RV)

There is absolutely no warrant in the Greek text for changing "[Every] *Scripture is given by inspiration of God, and is profitable for* [teaching]" to *"Every Scripture inspired of God is also profitable for teaching." Every* is in the Greek. There is no *is* in the Greek. It must be supplied, as is often the case in translating from Greek into English. *Is* must be supplied somewhere, either before *"given by inspiration"* or after it. But if the *is* is placed after it, *and* must be changed to *also* (a change that is possible but very uncommon). Furthermore, there is not a single instance in the New Testament outside of this one in which two adjectives coupled by *and* are ripped apart and the *is* is placed between them and the *and* is changed to *also.* On the other hand, the other construction, "[Every] *Scripture is given by inspiration of God, and is profitable for* [teaching]," is not at all uncommon. So we see that the translation of the Revised Version does violence to all customary usage of the Greek language.

But we do not need to dwell on that, for, even if we accept the changes given in the Revised Version, the thought is not essentially changed. If Paul had said what the Revised Version makes him say, that *"Every Scripture inspired of God is also profitable for teaching,"* there can be no question that by *"every Scripture inspired of God"* he referred to every Scripture contained in the Old Testament. Here, then, taking whichever translation you will, we have the plain teaching that every Scripture of the Old Testament is "God-breathed" or *"inspired of God."* Certainly, if we can believe this about the Old Testament, there is no difficulty in believing it about the New.

Furthermore, there can be no question that Paul claimed for his own teaching an authority equal to that of Old Testament teaching. This we will see clearly in the next section of this chapter. And not only did Paul claim this, but the apostle Peter also classified the teaching of Paul with Old Testament teaching as being Scripture. Peter said in 2 Peter 3:15–16,

> *Even as our beloved brother Paul also according to the wisdom given unto him hath written unto you; as also in all his epistles, speaking in them of these things; in which are some things hard to be understood, which they that are unlearned and unstable wrest, as they do also the other scriptures, unto their own destruction.*

Here Peter clearly spoke of Paul's epistles as being Scripture.

The Bible Is God's Inerrant Word

The seventh thing that the Bible teaches concerning the extent of the inspiration of its writings is that, because of this inspiration of the writers of the Bible, the whole Bible as originally given is the absolutely inerrant Word of God. In the Old Testament, David said of his own writings, in a passage already referred to, "*The spirit of the Lord spake by me, and his word was in my tongue*" (2 Samuel 23:2).

In Mark 7:13, our Lord Jesus Himself called the Law of Moses "*the word of God.*" He said, "*making the word of God of none effect through your tradition, which ye have delivered.*" In the verses immediately preceding, He had been drawing a contrast between the teachings of the Mosaic Law (not merely the teachings of the Ten Commandments, but other parts of the Mosaic Law as well) and the traditions of the scribes and Pharisees. He had shown how the traditions of the scribes and Pharisees flatly contradicted the requirements of the Law as given through Moses. In summing up the matter, He said in the verse just quoted that the scribes and Pharisees invalidated "*the word of God*" by their traditions, thus calling the Law of Moses "*the word of God.*"

When I was in England, a high dignitary and scholar in the Church of England wrote me a private letter in which he tried to reprimand me by saying that the Bible nowhere claims to be the Word of God. I replied to him by showing him that not only does the Bible claim it, but the Lord Jesus Himself said in so many words that the Law given through Moses was "*the word of God.*"

In 1 Thessalonians 2:13, the apostle Paul claimed that his own epistles and teachings are *"the word of God."* He said,

> *For this cause also thank we God without ceasing, because, when ye received the word of God which ye heard of us, ye received it not as the word of men, but as it is in truth, the word of God, which effectually worketh also in you that believe.*

Here the apostle Paul claimed in the most absolute way that his own teachings are *"the word of God."*

When we read the words of Jeremiah, Isaiah, Paul, John, James, Jude, and the other Bible writers, we are reading what God says. We are not listening to the voice of man, but we are listening to the voice of God. The Word of God, which we have in the Old and New Testaments, is absolutely inerrant as originally given—down to the smallest word and smallest letter or part of a letter. In Matthew 5:18, our Lord Jesus Himself said of the Pentateuch (the first five books of the Bible), *"For verily I say unto you, Till heaven and earth pass, one jot or one tittle shall in no wise pass from the law, till all be fulfilled."* Now, a *"jot"* is the Hebrew character *yodh*, the smallest character in the Hebrew alphabet, less than half the size of any other letter in the Hebrew alphabet. A *"tittle"* is a part of a letter, the little horn put on some of the Hebrew consonants, less than the cross we put on a "t." Here our Lord said that the Law given through Moses is absolutely inerrant, down to its smallest letter or part of a letter. That certainly is verbal inspiration with a vengeance.

Again, Jesus said, as recorded in John 10:35, after having quoted from Psalm 82:6 as conclusive proof of a point, *"The scripture* ***cannot be broken****"* (emphasis added). Thus He asserted the absolute inerrancy and finality of the Scriptures. If the Scriptures as originally given are not the inerrant Word of God, then not only is the Bible a fraud, but Jesus Christ Himself was utterly misled and is therefore utterly unreliable as a teacher.

I have said that the Scriptures of the Old and New Testaments *as originally given* were absolutely inerrant. Of course, the following question arises: To what extent are the modern translations the inerrant Word of

God? The answer is simple: they are the inerrant Word of God just to the extent that they are an accurate rendering of the Scriptures of the Old and New Testaments as originally given. There are, it is true, many variations in the many manuscripts we possess—thousands of variations. But by a careful study of these variations, we are able to find with marvelous accuracy what the original manuscripts said. A very large share of the variations are of no importance whatsoever, since it is evident from a comparison of different manuscripts that they are the mistakes of a transcriber. Many other variations simply concern the order of the words used, and in translating into English, in which the order of words is often different from what it is in the Greek, the variation is not translatable. Many other variations are of small Greek particles, many of which are not translatable into English anyway. When all the variations of any significance have been reduced to the minimum to which it is possible to reduce them by a careful study of manuscripts, not one single variation is left that affects any doctrine held by the evangelical churches.

2

WHO IS THE GOD OF THE BIBLE?

God is a Spirit.
—John 4:24

God is light.
—1 John 1:5

God is love.
—1 John 4:8, 16

The texts above give three of the most remarkable statements that were ever uttered. In the clearest possible way, they set before us the Christian understanding of God as distinguished from every other understanding of God.

Many wrong ideas about God are being promoted today. The Christian Scientists are one group that is spreading falsehood. They constantly quote one of our texts: *"God is love"*; in fact, they quote it more than almost any other passage in the Bible. But by *"God is love"* they do not mean at all what 1 John 4:8 or 1 John 4:16 clearly mean when taken in their context. By *"love"* the Christian Scientists do not mean a personal attribute of God; they mean an impersonal, abstract quality that is itself God. Mary Baker Eddy, the founder of Christian Science, frankly and flatly denied that God is a person.

Not only do the Christian Scientists say, *"God is love,"* but they also say, "Love is God." Not only do they say, *"God is good"* (Psalm 73:1), but they also say, "Good is God." Saying "Love is God" is entirely different from saying *"God is love."* You might as well say, "Spirit is God," because the Bible says, *"God is Spirit."* However, we know that all spirit is not God. Or you might as well say, "Light is God," because the Bible says, *"God is light."* However, we know that light is not God. In the same way, love is not God, though *"God is love."*

What is meant by *"love"* in the inspired statement *"God is love"*? The answer is shown by the definition or description of love given in the context and in a passage in the immediately preceding chapter—1 John 3:13–18. These verses clearly show that the statement in 1 John 4:8 and 1 John 4:16, *"God is love,"* does not mean that God is an abstract quality called love and that the abstract quality of love is God. It means that God is a person whose whole being and conduct are dominated by the quality of love, that is, by a desire for and delight in the highest welfare of others. This fact will be evident to you if you read the passage from 1 John 3:

> *Marvel not, my brethren, if the world hate you. We know that we have passed from death unto life, because we love the brethren. He that loveth not his brother abideth in death. Whosoever hateth his brother is a murderer: and ye know that no murderer hath eternal life abiding in him. Hereby perceive we the love of God, because he laid down his life*

for us: and we ought to lay down our lives for the brethren. But whoso hath this world's good, and seeth his brother have need, and shutteth up his bowels of compassion from him, how dwelleth the love of God in him? My little children, let us not love in word, neither in tongue; but in deed and in truth. (1 John 3:13–18)

This fact is also evident from the context of the chapter of our text—1 John 4:

Beloved, let us love one another: for love is of God; and every one that loveth is born of God, and knoweth God. He that loveth not knoweth not God; for God is love. In this was manifested the love of God toward us, because that God sent his only begotten Son into the world, that we might live through him. Herein is love, not that we loved God, but that he loved us, and sent his Son to be the propitiation for our sins. Beloved, if God so loved us, we ought also to love one another. No man hath seen God at any time. If we love one another, God dwelleth in us, and his love is perfected in us. Hereby know we that we dwell in him, and he in us, because he hath given us of his Spirit. And we have seen and do testify that the Father sent the Son to be the Saviour of the world. Whosoever shall confess that Jesus is the Son of God, God dwelleth in him, and he in God. And we have known and believed the love that God hath to us. God is love; and he that dwelleth in love dwelleth in God, and God in him. Herein is our love made perfect, that we may have boldness in the day of judgment: because as he is, so are we in this world.

(1 John 4:7–17)

Along with Christian Science, modern philosophy also spreads false ideas about God. The God of modern philosophy is sometimes called "The Absolute." What is generally meant by "The Absolute" is a cold, abstract thing, not a dear, definite, warm Person who loves others and grieves, suffers, and works intelligently for them. Modern philosophy often teaches that not only is God *in* all things but God *is* all things and all things are God. Such a God is no God at all. However, the God of the Bible, as we will see as we proceed, is a divine Person who exists apart from the world that He created and who existed before the world that He created. The God of the Bible is actively involved in the world He has made, and He works along definite and clearly revealed lines.

In addition, many political leaders are fond of talking about God, but if anyone will carefully study their words, it often becomes plain that by "God" they do not mean the God and Father of our Lord Jesus Christ.

So we come face to face with the question, What sort of a being is the God of the Bible, the one true God, the only God whom we should worship, love, and obey?

God Is Spirit

First of all, "God is Spirit." The King James Version says, "*God is a Spirit*" (John 4:24). However, there is no indefinite article in the Greek language. Wherever an indefinite article is necessary in an English translation to fit the English idiom, it has to be supplied, and it is supplied in this case. But there is no more reason for supplying it here than for supplying it in 1 John 4:8 and saying "God is a love," or in 1 John 1:5 and saying "God is a light." The preferable translation is as I have given it: "God is Spirit."

What Is Meant by "*Spirit*"?

"God is Spirit" is a definition of the essential nature of God. What does it mean? Our Lord Jesus Himself defined what is meant by "*spirit*" in Luke 24:39, where He is recorded as saying after His resurrection, "*Behold my hands and my feet, that it is I myself: handle me, and see; for a spirit hath not flesh and bones, as ye see me have.*" It is evident from these words of our Lord that "*spirit*" is that which is contrasted with body. That is to say, "*spirit*" is invisible reality. To say that "God is Spirit" is to say that God is essentially incorporeal (without a material body) and invisible (see 1 Timothy 6:16), that God in His essential nature is not material but immaterial and invisible, but nevertheless real.

This thought is also found in the very heart of the revelation that God made of Himself to Moses in the Old Testament. We read in the book of Deuteronomy,

> *Take ye therefore good heed unto yourselves; for ye saw no manner of similitude on the day that the* Lord *spake unto you in Horeb out of the midst of the fire: lest ye corrupt yourselves, and make you a graven image, the similitude of any figure, the likeness of male or female, the likeness of any beast that is on the earth, the likeness of any winged fowl that flieth in the air, the likeness of any thing that creepeth on the ground, the likeness of any fish that is in the waters beneath the earth.*
> (Deuteronomy 4:15–18)

Fifteen centuries before Christ, this is a plain declaration of the spirituality of God in His essential nature. God is essentially invisible spirit.

Can God Be Seen with the Human Eye?

Spirit, however, may be manifested in visible, bodily form. This fact is clearly revealed in the Word of God. We read in John 1:32 these words of John the Baptist about what his own eyes had seen: "*And John bare witness, saying, I have beheld the Spirit descending as a dove out of heaven; and it abode upon him* [Jesus]" (RV). Here, then, we see God the Holy Spirit, who is essentially spirit, manifesting Himself in a bodily, visible form.

Furthermore, we are told in the Bible that God the Father has manifested Himself in visible form. We read in Exodus,

> *Then went up Moses, and Aaron, Nadab, and Abihu, and seventy of the elders of Israel: and they saw the God of Israel: and there was under his feet as it were a paved work of a sapphire stone, and as it were the body of heaven in his clearness.* (Exodus 24:9–10)

What they saw was not God in His essential nature as spiritual being. Indeed, what we see when we see one another is not our essential selves, but the houses we live in. Therefore, John could say, as he did in John 1:18: "*No man hath seen God at any time.*" Similarly, I could say that no one has ever seen me. Nevertheless, it was a real manifestation of God Himself that they saw. It could be said, and said truthfully, that they had seen God, even as it could be said truthfully that people have seen me.

Furthermore, though God is essentially spirit, He has a visible form. This is taught in the most unmistakable terms in Philippians 2:6, where we are told that our Lord Jesus existed originally "*in the form of God.*" The Greek word that is translated "*form*" in this passage means "visible form," "the form by which a person or thing strikes the vision," "the external appearance." It cannot mean anything else. This is the definition given in the best Greek-English lexicon of the New Testament. Now, since Jesus existed originally "*in the form of God,*" it is evident that God Himself must have a form, this form in which our Lord Jesus is said to have existed originally.

That God in His external form, though not in His invisible essence, is *seeable,* is also clear from Acts 7:55–56, where we read,

> *But he* [Stephen], *being full of the Holy Ghost, looked up stedfastly into heaven, and saw the glory of God, and Jesus standing on the right hand of God.*

Now, if God does not have a form that can be seen, then, of course, the Lord Jesus could not be seen standing at His right hand. As we will see later, God is everywhere, but God is not everywhere *in the same sense.* There is a place where God is visibly and clearly present in a way in which He is not present anywhere else.

Does God Live in Heaven?

Although in His spiritual presence God pervades the universe, the place of God's visible presence and full manifestation of Himself is heaven. This fact is evident from many passages in the Scriptures. For example, it is clear from the prayer that our Lord taught us—a portion of Scripture accepted by many who reject most of the Bible. Our Lord began the prayer that He taught His disciples with these words: "*Our Father which art in heaven"* (Matthew 6:9). If these words mean anything, they certainly mean that God our Father is in heaven in a way in which He is not elsewhere. That was where God was when Jesus was addressing Him. We read in Matthew 3:17, *"And lo a voice from heaven, saying, This is my beloved Son, in whom I am well pleased."* If these words mean anything, they mean that God is in heaven and that His voice came out of the heavens to the Lord Jesus who was here on earth.

Again, in John 14:28, Jesus is recorded as saying,

> *Ye have heard how I said unto you, I go away, and come again unto you. If ye loved me, ye would rejoice, because I said, I go unto the Father: for my Father is greater than I.*

Taken in the light of the events that were to follow, these words, if they mean anything, mean that Jesus was going away from the place where He was then—earth—to another place—heaven. Furthermore, in going to heaven, He was going to where God is, and He was leaving earth, where God is not present in the sense in which He is in heaven.

We read in Acts 11:9: *"But the voice answered me again from heaven, What God hath cleansed, that call not thou common."* Here, again, God is represented as speaking from heaven, where He was.

Again, our Lord Jesus Christ is recorded in John 20:17 as saying to Mary Magdalene after His resurrection,

> *Touch me not; for I am not yet ascended to my Father: but go to my brethren, and say unto them, I ascend unto my Father, and your Father; and to my God, and your God.*

From this it is unmistakably evident that there is a place where God is, a place to which Jesus was going after His resurrection. That place is in heaven. There is no possibility of explaining this away by saying that Jesus was using a figure of speech. The whole passage loses its meaning by any such interpretation, and to attempt to so explain it is a trick and a deception that will not bear close examination.

Moreover, the apostle Paul told us regarding our Lord Jesus Christ that God the Father *"raised him from the dead, and set him at his own right hand in the heavenly places"* (Ephesians 1:20). This verse makes it as clear as language can make anything that there is a place called heaven where God is in a sense that He is nowhere else, and where one can be placed at His right hand.

The same thing is evident from the verses that I already quoted when talking about God in His external form in the seventh chapter of Acts. Here we are told that Stephen,

> *Being full of the Holy Ghost, looked up stedfastly into heaven, and saw the glory of God, and Jesus standing on the right hand of God.*
> (Acts 7:55)

The meaning of these words—to anybody who wishes to know what words are intended to convey and does not merely wish to distort them to fit his own theories—is that God is, in a special sense, present in heaven. There is no escaping this truth by any fair, honest interpretation.

Men who are skillful in the art of discrediting truth by assigning it improper names—names that sound very scholarly—may call this precious truth found in Acts 7:55–56 *anthropomorphism* (which means "attributing qualities of personhood to something that is not a person"). That sounds very learned. Nevertheless, whether it is anthropomorphism or what not, this truth is the clear teaching of the Word of God, in spite of frightful terms used to scare immature college students. There is no mistaking that this truth that God is in heaven is the teaching of the Bible, and we have already proven that the Bible is God's Word. As such, it is to be taken at its face value, in spite of all the attempts to explain it away—attempts made by men and women who profess to be wise but have become fools. (See Romans 1:22.)

God Is a Person

The next thing that the Bible teaches about God is that God is a person. That is to say, He is a being who knows, feels, loves, speaks, acts, and hears.

He is a being who interacts intelligently with us and with whom we can interact.

While God is in all things, He is a person distinct from the persons and things in which He is. He has created these persons and things. The Bible, both in the Old and New Testaments, is full of this vital teaching of "a living God" as distinguished from the mere cold ideas of "The Absolute" or "The Infinite" or "The Supreme Being" or "The Great First Cause," all of which modern philosophy loves to promote.

For example, we read in Jeremiah,

> *But the LORD is the true God, he is the living God, and an everlasting king: at his wrath the earth shall tremble, and the nations shall not be able to abide his indignation. Thus shall ye say unto them, The gods that have not made the heavens and the earth, even they shall perish from the earth, and from under these heavens. He hath made the earth by his power, he hath established the world by his wisdom, and hath stretched out the heavens by his discretion. When he uttereth his voice, there is a multitude of waters in the heavens, and he causeth the vapours to ascend from the ends of the earth; he maketh lightnings with rain, and bringeth forth the wind out of his treasures. Every man is brutish in his knowledge: every founder is confounded by the graven image: for his molten image is falsehood, and there is no breath in them. They are vanity, and the work of errors: in the time of their visitation they shall perish. The portion of Jacob is not like them: for he is the former of all things; and Israel is the rod of his inheritance: the LORD of hosts is his name.*
>
> (Jeremiah 10:10–16)

In this passage, God is distinguished from idols, which are things and not persons—things that *"speak not," "cannot go," "cannot do evil, neither also is it in them to do good"* (verse 5). We are also told that Jehovah is wiser than *"all the wise men"* (verse 7). Is *"the living God," "an everlasting King,"* who has *"wrath"* and *"indignation"* (verse 10), separate from His creatures? The answer is found in the same verse: *"At his wrath the earth shall tremble, and the nations shall not be able to abide his indignation."*

In the New Testament, we find another example of the wonderful truth that God is a person. In the fourteenth chapter of Acts, the people of Lystra observed a miracle performed by Paul and supposed that he and Barnabas were gods. As the people were about to sacrifice to Paul and Barnabas, the two men cried out,

> *Sirs, why do ye these things? We also are men of like passions with you, and preach unto you that ye should turn from these vanities unto the living God, which made heaven, and earth, and the sea, and all things that are therein.* (Acts 14:15)

Here, also, we have the representation of God as a personal being distinct from His created work, and also clearly distinct from idols, which are not living gods. In addition, in 1 Thessalonians 1:9, the converts at Thessalonica are represented as turning from "*idols* [dead gods] *to serve the* ***living*** *and true God*" (emphasis added).

In 2 Chronicles 16:9, we are told that "*the eyes of the* L*ORD* *run to and fro throughout the whole earth, to show himself strong in the behalf of them whose heart is perfect toward him.*" In Psalm 94:9–10, we read, "*He that planted the ear, shall he not hear? He that formed the eye, shall he not see? He that chastiseth the heathen, shall not he correct?*" These are clearly descriptions of a personal God, not a mere abstract idea, such as "The Absolute" or "The Infinite" or "The Supreme Being."

The distinction between God, who is present in all things and dwells in all believers, and the things and persons in which He dwells, is brought out very clearly by our Lord Himself in John 14:10. Here Jesus revealed that He is one with the Father, but that the Father works within Him independently as a separate person:

> *Believest thou not that I am in the Father, and the Father in me? The words that I speak unto you I speak not of myself: but the Father that dwelleth in me, he doeth the works.*

In the twenty-fourth verse of the same chapter, our Lord Jesus again distinguished between His own personhood and that of the Father, who dwelt in Him, in these words: *"He that loveth me not keepeth not my sayings: and the word which ye hear is not mine, but the Father's which sent me."*

This understanding of God pervades the entire Bible. The view of God presented in the Bible is entirely different from the view of God presented in pantheism, Buddhism, Theosophy,[1] and Christian Science. The correct understanding of God is found in the opening words of the Bible: *"In the beginning God created the heaven and the earth"* (Genesis 1:1). Here the God of the Bible is clearly differentiated from the so-called God of pantheism and the so-called God of Christian Science. The proper understanding of God is also found in the last chapter of the Bible, and it is found in every chapter of the Bible between the first and the last. The God of the Bible is a personal being who, while He created all things and is in all things, is a distinct person, separate from the persons and things He has created.

God Is Actively Involved in the World

We turn now to a consideration of the present relationship of this personal God to the world that He has created and to the people whom He has created.

In the first place, we find that God sustains, governs, and cares for the world He has created. He shapes the whole present history of the world. This comes out in the Bible again and again. A few illustrations must suffice. We read in the book of Psalms,

> *These wait all upon thee; that thou mayest give them their meat in due season. That thou givest them they gather: thou openest thine hand, they are filled with good. Thou hidest thy face, they are troubled: thou takest away their breath, they die, and return to their dust. Thou sendest forth thy spirit, they are created: and thou renewest the face of the earth.*
> (Psalm 104:27–30)

1. Theosophy is the teaching of a movement that originated in the U.S. in 1875 and that follows primarily Buddhistic and Hindu theories, especially of pantheistic evolution and reincarnation.

We read in Psalm 75:6–7, "*For promotion cometh neither from the east, nor from the west, nor from the south. But God is the judge: he putteth down one, and setteth up another.*" These passages, along with others that could be cited, set forth God's present relationship to the world that He has created.

Now let us look at God's relationship to the concerns of people. We will find that God has a present, personal interest and an active hand in the concerns of people. He makes a path for His own people and leads them. He delivers, saves, and punishes.

To prove this point, four illustrations from the Bible will suffice. First of all, we read in Joshua,

> *And Joshua said, Hereby ye shall know that the living God is among you, and that he will without fail drive out from before you the Canaanites, and the Hittites, and the Hivites, and the Perizzites, and the Girgashites, and the Amorites, and the Jebusites.*
> (Joshua 3:10)

Now we will look at a passage in Daniel:

> *And when he* [the king] *came to the den, he cried with a lamentable voice unto Daniel: and the king spake and said to Daniel, O Daniel, servant of the living God, is thy God, whom thou servest continually, able to deliver thee from the lions? Then said Daniel unto the king, O king, live for ever. My God hath sent his angel, and hath shut the lions' mouths, that they have not hurt me: forasmuch as before him innocency was found in me; and also before thee, O king, have I done no hurt.... Then King Darius wrote....I make a decree, that in every dominion of my kingdom men tremble and fear before the God of Daniel: for he is the living God, and stedfast for ever, and his kingdom that which shall not be destroyed, and his dominion shall be even unto the end. He delivereth and rescueth, and he worketh signs and wonders in heaven and in earth, who hath delivered Daniel from the power of the lions.*
> (Daniel 6:20–22, 25–27)

First Timothy 4:10 provides the third illustration: "*For therefore we both labour and suffer reproach, because we trust in the living God, who is the Saviour of all men, specially of those that believe.*"

Now we will look at some verses in Hebrews:

> *He that despised Moses' law died without mercy under two or three witnesses: of how much sorer punishment, suppose ye, shall he be thought worthy, who hath trodden under foot the Son of God, and hath counted the blood of the covenant, wherewith he was sanctified, an unholy thing, and hath done despite unto the Spirit of grace? For we know him that hath said, Vengeance belongeth unto me, I will recompense, saith the Lord. And again, The Lord shall judge his people. It is a fearful thing to fall into the hands of the living God.*
>
> (Hebrews 10:28–31)

In all these passages, we have this same concept of God in His relationship to man, namely, that God has a personal interest and an active hand in the concerns of people. He makes a path for His own people and leads them. He delivers, saves, and punishes.

The God of the Bible is to be clearly distinguished, not merely from the God of the pantheists, who has no existence separate from His creation, but also from the God of the deists, who has created the world, put into it all the necessary powers of self-government and development, set it going, and left it to go by itself. The God of the Bible is a God who is personally and actively present in the affairs of the universe today. He sustains, governs, and cares for the world He has created; He shapes the whole present history of the world. He has a present, personal interest and an active hand in the concerns of people, and it is He who is behind all the events that are occurring today. He reigns and makes even the wrath of men to praise Him, and the remainder of wrath He restrains. (See Psalm 76:10.)

Armies may clash, force and violence and outrage may seem victorious for the passing hour, but God stands triumphant over all. Through all the confusion and the discord and the turmoil and the agony and the ruin, through all the outrageous atrocities that are making men's hearts stand still with horror, He is carrying out His own purposes of love and making all things work together for good to those who love Him. (See Romans 8:28.)

3

IS GOD PERFECT, AND IS HE ONE?

God is light, and in him is no darkness at all.
—1 John 1:5

God is love.
—1 John 4:8, 16

With God all things are possible.
—Matthew 19:26

His understanding is infinite.
—Psalm 147:5

In this chapter, we will continue to consider the Christian understanding of God. We saw in the previous chapter that God is spirit, that God is a person, and that God has a personal interest and an active hand in the concerns of people today. He sustains, governs, and cares for the world He has created, and He shapes the whole present history of the world.

The Infinite Perfection of God

The next thing to be observed about the Christian understanding of God is that God is perfect and infinite in power and in all His intellectual and moral attributes.

God Is Light

First of all, fix your attention on the first part of our first text: *"God is light"* (1 John 1:5). These three words form a marvelously beautiful and overwhelmingly impressive statement of the truth. They set forth the absolute holiness and perfect wisdom of God. These three words need to be meditated on rather than expounded. *"In him is no darkness at all"* (verse 5). That is to say, in God is no darkness of error, no darkness of ignorance, no darkness of sin, no darkness of moral imperfection or intellectual imperfection of any kind. The three words *"God is light"* form one of the most beautiful, one of the most striking, and one of the most stupendous statements of truth that has ever been penned.

God Is Omnipotent

Second, the God of the Bible is omnipotent, or all-powerful. This wonderful fact comes out again and again in the Word of God. One direct statement of this great truth, which is especially striking because of the context in which it is found, is in Jeremiah 32:17:

> *Ah Lord God! behold, thou hast made the heaven and the earth by thy great power and stretched out arm, and there is nothing too hard for thee.*

Here Jeremiah said that there is nothing too difficult for God, but in the twenty-seventh verse, Jehovah Himself said, *"Behold, I am the Lord, the God of all flesh: is there any thing too hard for me?"*

When at last Job had been brought to see and to recognize the true nature of Jehovah, he said, *"I know that thou canst do every thing, and that no thought can be withholden from thee"* (Job 42:2). In Matthew 19:26, our Lord Jesus said, *"With God all things are possible."*

So we are plainly taught by our Lord Himself and by others that God can do all things, that nothing is too hard for Him, that all things are possible with Him—in a word, that God is omnipotent.

Here is a very impressive passage from the book of Psalms that sets forth this same great truth:

> *By the word of the Lord were the heavens made; and all the host of them by the breath of his mouth. He gathereth the waters of the sea together as an heap: he layeth up the depth in storehouses. Let all the earth fear the Lord: let all the inhabitants of the world stand in awe of him. For he spake, and it was done; he commanded, and it stood fast.*
> (Psalm 33:6–9)

Here we see God, by the mere utterance of His voice, bringing to pass anything that He desires to be brought to pass.

We find this same majestic portrayal of God in the very first chapter of the Bible. So many people who imagine themselves to be scholarly are telling us this chapter is out-of-date, yet it contains some of the sublimest words that were ever written, unmatched by anything that any philosopher, scientist, or orator is saying today. The very first words of this chapter read, *"In the beginning God created the heaven and the earth"* (Genesis 1:1). This description of the origin of things has never been matched for simplicity, sublimity, and profundity. In the third verse, we read, *"And God said, Let there be light: and there was light."* These words need no comment. In this verse, there is a sublime thought about the omnipotence of God's mere word, before which any truly intelligent and alert soul will stand in wonder and awe. Nothing in poetry or in philosophical dissertation, ancient or modern, can for one moment compare with these sublime words.

Over and over again, the thought is brought out in the Word of God that all nature is absolutely subject to God's will and word. We see this, for example, in the book of Psalms:

> *For he commandeth, and raiseth the stormy wind, which lifteth up the waves thereof. They mount up to the heaven, they go down again to the depths: their soul is melted because of trouble. They reel to and fro, and stagger like a drunken man, and are at their wit's end. Then they cry unto the* Lord *in their trouble, and he bringeth them out of their distresses. He maketh the storm a calm, so that the waves thereof are still.* (Psalm 107:25–29)

A similar description is found in the book of Nahum:

> *The* Lord *is slow to anger, and great in power, and will not at all acquit the wicked: the* Lord *hath his way in the whirlwind and in the storm, and the clouds are the dust of his feet. He rebuketh the sea, and maketh it dry, and drieth up all the rivers: Bashan languisheth, and Carmel, and the flower of Lebanon languisheth. The mountains quake at him, and the hills melt, and the earth is burned at his presence, yea, the world, and all that dwell therein. Who can stand before his indignation? And who can abide in the fierceness of his anger? His fury is poured out like fire, and the rocks are thrown down by him.* (Nahum 1:3–6)

What a picture we have here of the omnipotence and awe-inspiring majesty of God!

Not only is nature shown to be absolutely subject to God's will and word, but men also are shown to be absolutely subject to His will and word. For example, we read in the book of James,

> *There is one lawgiver, who is able to save and to destroy: who art thou that judgest another? Go to now, ye that say, To day or to morrow we*

> *will go into such a city, and continue there a year, and buy and sell, and get gain: whereas ye know not what shall be on the morrow. For what is your life? It is even a vapour, that appeareth for a little time, and then vanisheth away. For that ye ought to say, If the Lord will, we shall live, and do this, or that.* (James 4:12–15)

Happy is the man who voluntarily subjects himself to God's will and word. But whether we voluntarily subject ourselves or not, we are subject. The angels are also subject to His will and word. (See Hebrews 1:13–14.) Even Satan himself, though entirely against his own will, is absolutely subject to the will and word of God, as is evident from Job 1:12 and Job 2:6.

The exercise of God's omnipotence is limited by His own wise and holy and loving will. God *can* do anything but *will* do only what infinite wisdom, holiness, and love dictate. This comes out, for example, in Isaiah 59:1–2:

> *Behold, the* LORD*'s hand is not shortened, that it cannot save; neither his ear heavy, that it cannot hear: but your iniquities have separated between you and your God, and your sins have hid his face from you, that he will not hear.*

God Is Omniscient

The God of the Bible is also omniscient, or all-knowing. In 1 John 3:20, we read, "*God...knoweth all things.*" Turning to the Old Testament, we read, "*Great is our Lord, and of great power: his understanding is infinite*" (Psalm 147:5). The literal translation of the last clause of this passage is "of His understanding there is no number." In these passages, it is plainly declared that God knows everything and that His understanding is inexhaustible.

In Job 37:16, Elihu, the messenger of God, said that Jehovah is "*perfect in knowledge.*" Along the same lines, in Acts 15:18, we read, "*Known unto God are all his works from the beginning of the world.*" In Psalm 147:4, we are told that "*He telleth the number of the stars; he calleth them all by their names,*" while in Matthew 10:29, we are told that "*one* [sparrow] *shall not fall on the ground without your Father.*" The stars in all their magnitude and the sparrows in all their insignificance are equally in His mind.

We are further told that everything has a part in God's purpose and plan. In Acts chapter 3, the apostle Peter said of the crucifixion of our Lord, the wickedest act in all the history of the human race,

> *And now, brethren, I wot that through ignorance ye did it, as did also your rulers. But those things, which God before had showed by the mouth of all his prophets, that Christ should suffer, he hath so fulfilled.* (Acts 3:17–18)

In addition, Peter had declared on the Day of Pentecost that the Lord Jesus was "*delivered* [up] *by the determinate counsel and foreknowledge of God*" (Acts 2:23). According to the words of the psalmist, God takes the acts of the wickedest men into His plans and causes the wrath of men to praise Him, and the remainder of wrath He restrains. (See Psalm 76:10.)

For example, even war with all its horrors, with all its atrocities, with all its abominations, is foreknown by God and taken into His own gracious plan of the ages. He will make every event, even the most shocking things designed by the vilest conspiracy of devil-inspired men, work together for the good of those who love God and are called according to His purpose. (See Romans 8:28.)

The whole plan of the ages—not merely of the centuries, but of the immeasurable ages of God—and every man's part in it, has been known to God from all eternity. This is made clear in the book of Ephesians, where we read,

> [God] *made known unto us the mystery of his will, according to his good pleasure which he hath purposed in himself: that in the dispensation of the fulness of times he might gather together in one all things in Christ, both which are in heaven, and which are on earth; even in him: in whom also we have obtained an inheritance, being predestinated according to the purpose of him who worketh all things after the counsel*

of his own will: that we should be to the praise of his glory, who first trusted in Christ. (Ephesians 1:9–12)

And later in Ephesians, we are told,

(Whereby, when ye read, ye may understand my knowledge in the mystery of Christ) Which in other ages was not made known unto the sons of men, as it is now revealed unto his holy apostles and prophets by the Spirit; that the Gentiles should be fellowheirs, and of the same body, and partakers of his promise in Christ by the gospel: whereof I was made a minister, according to the gift of the grace of God given unto me by the effectual working of his power. Unto me, who am less than the least of all saints, is this grace given, that I should preach among the Gentiles the unsearchable riches of Christ; and to make all men see what is the fellowship of the mystery, which from the beginning of the world hath been hid in God, who created all things by Jesus Christ. (Ephesians 3:4–9)

There are no afterthoughts with God. Everything is seen, known, purposed, and planned from the outset. We may well exclaim, "*O the depth of the riches both of the wisdom and knowledge of God! How unsearchable are his judgments, and his ways past finding out!*" (Romans 11:33). God knows from all eternity what He will do for all eternity.

God Is Omnipresent

Furthermore, not only is God perfect in His intellectual and moral attributes and in power, but He is also omnipresent, or all-present. In the second chapter of this book, we saw that God has a particular habitation, that there is a place where He exists and manifests Himself in a way in which He does not manifest Himself everywhere. But while we insist on this clearly revealed truth, we must also never lose sight of the fact that God is everywhere. We find this truth set forth by Paul in his sermon to the Epicurean and Stoic philosophers on Mars Hill:

God that made the world and all things therein, seeing that he is Lord of heaven and earth, dwelleth not in temples made with hands; neither

> *is worshipped with men's hands, as though he needed any thing, seeing he giveth to all life, and breath, and all things; and hath made of one blood all nations of men for to dwell on all the face of the earth, and hath determined the times before appointed, and the bounds of their habitation; that they should seek the Lord, if haply they might feel after him, and find him, though he be not far from every one of us: for in him we live, and move, and have our being; as certain also of your own poets have said, for we are also his offspring.* (Acts 17:24–28)

This thought about God also comes out in the Old Testament. In the book of Psalms, we read,

> *Whither shall I go from thy spirit? Or whither shall I flee from thy presence? If I ascend up into heaven, thou art there: if I make my bed in hell, behold, thou art there. If I take the wings of the morning, and dwell in the uttermost parts of the sea; even there shall thy hand lead me, and thy right hand shall hold me.* (Psalm 139:7–10)

There is no place where one can flee from God's presence, for God is everywhere. This great truth is set forth in a remarkable way in the book of Jeremiah:

> *Am I a God at hand, saith the* Lord, *and not a God afar off? Can any hide himself in secret places that I shall not see him? saith the* Lord. *Do not I fill heaven and earth? saith the* Lord. (Jeremiah 23:23–24)

From these passages, we see that God is all-present (omnipresent). He is in all parts of the universe, and He is near to each individual. In Him each individual, as God's offspring, lives and moves and has his being. (See Acts 17:28–29.) God is in every rose and lily and blade of grass.

God Is Eternal

There is one thought in the Christian understanding of God that needs to be placed alongside of His omnipresence, and that is His eternity. God is eternal. His existence had no beginning and will have no ending. He always was, always is, and always will be. God is not only everywhere present in space, but also everywhere present in time. This teaching about God appears constantly in the Bible. We are told in Genesis 21:33 that Abraham *"called there on the name of the Lord, the Everlasting God."* In Isaiah 40:28, we read this description of Jehovah:

> *Hast thou not known? Hast thou not heard, that the everlasting God, the Lord, the Creator of the ends of the earth, fainteth not, neither is weary? There is no searching of his understanding.*

Here, again, He is called *"the everlasting God."*

Habakkuk set forth the same picture of God. He said, *"Art thou not from everlasting, O Lord my God, mine Holy One?"* (Habakuk 1:12). The psalmist also gave us the same description of God:

> *Before the mountains were brought forth, or ever thou hadst formed the earth and the world, even from everlasting to everlasting, thou art God....For a thousand years in thy sight are but as yesterday when it is past, and as a watch in the night.* (Psalm 90:2, 4)

We have the same description of God later in the book of Psalms:

> *O my God, take me not away in the midst of my days: thy years are throughout all generations. Of old hast thou laid the foundation of the earth: and the heavens are the work of thy hands. They shall perish, but thou shalt endure:...they shall be changed: but thou art the same, and thy years shall have no end.* (Psalm 102:24–27)

The very name of God—His covenant name, *Jehovah*—sets forth His eternity. He is the eternal *"I Am"* (Exodus 3:14), the One who is, was, and ever will be. (See Revelation 1:8.)

God Is Holy

God is also absolutely and infinitely holy. This is a point of central and fundamental importance in the biblical understanding of God. It comes out in our first text: *"God is light, and in him is no darkness at all"* (1 John 1:5). When John wrote these words, he gave them as the summary of *"the message which we have heard of* [God]" (verse 5).

In the vision of Jehovah that was given to Isaiah in the year that King Uzziah died, the *"seraphims"* (Isaiah 6:2), or "burning ones," burning in their own intense holiness, are shown standing before Jehovah with covered faces and covered feet and constantly crying, *"Holy, holy, holy is the* Lord *of hosts"* (verse 3). And in 1 Peter 1:16, God cries to us, *"Be ye holy; for I am holy."*

This thought of the infinite and awe-inspiring holiness of God pervades the entire Bible. It underlies everything in it. The entire Mosaic system is built on and is about this fundamental and central truth. The instructions given to Moses, as well as the punishment of those who disobeyed, were intended to teach, emphasize, and burn into the minds and hearts of the Israelites the fundamental truth that God is holy, unapproachably holy. These instructions and punishments included the following: the system of washings; the divisions of the tabernacle; the divisions of the people into ordinary Israelites, Levites, priests, and high priests, who were all permitted different degrees of approach to God under strictly defined conditions; insistence on blood sacrifices as the necessary medium of approach to God; the strict orders to Israel in regard to approaching Mount Sinai when Jehovah came down upon it; God's directions to Moses in Exodus 3:5 and to Joshua in Joshua 5:15 to remove their shoes; the doom of Korah, Dathan, and Abiram in Numbers 16:1–34; the destruction of Nadab and Abihu in Leviticus 10:1–3; and the punishment of King Uzziah in 2 Chronicles 26:16–21.

The truth that God is holy is the fundamental truth of the Bible—of the Old Testament and the New Testament—and of the Jewish religion and the Christian religion. It is the preeminent factor in the Christian understanding of God. No fact in the Christian understanding of God needs to be more emphasized in our day than the fact of the absolute, unqualified, and uncompromising holiness of God. This is the chief note that is lacking in Christian Science, Theosophy, occultism, Buddhism, New Thought,[2] and

2. New Thought teaches that the power of the mind can achieve health and happiness. Its teachings are similar to those of Christian Science.

all the base but boasted cults of the day. The great truth of God's holiness underlies the fundamental doctrines of the Bible—atonement by shed blood and justification by faith. The doctrine of the holiness of God is the keystone in the arch of Christian truth.

God Is Love

God is also love. This truth is declared in one of our texts for this chapter: *"God is love."* These words are found twice in the same chapter of the Bible. (See 1 John 4:8, 16.) This truth is essentially the same truth as *"God is light"* (1 John 1:5) and *"God is holy"* (Psalm 99:9), for the very essence of true holiness is love. Light is love, and love is light.

The Unity of God

One more fact about the Christian understanding of God remains to be mentioned, and it is this: There is but one God. The unity of God comes out again and again in both the Old Testament and the New. For example, we read in Deuteronomy 4:35, *"The LORD he is God; there is none else beside him."* And in Deuteronomy 6:4, we read, *"Hear, O Israel: the LORD our God is one LORD."* Turning to the New Testament, we read, *"There is one God, and one mediator between God and men, the man Christ Jesus"* (1 Timothy 2:5). And in Mark 12:29, our Lord Jesus Himself said, *"Hear, O Israel; the Lord our God is one Lord."*

But we must bear in mind the character of the divine unity. It is clearly revealed in the Bible that in this divine unity, in this one Godhead, there are three persons. This reality is expressed in a variety of ways.

In the first place, the Hebrew word translated *"one"* in the various passages given denotes a compound unity, not a simple unity. (See also John 17:22–23; 1 Corinthians 3:6–8; 1 Corinthians 12:13; and Galatians 3:28.)

In the second place, the Old Testament word most frequently used for God is a plural noun. The Hebrew grammarians and lexicographers tried to explain this by saying that it was the *"pluralis majestatis"* (*we* in place of *I* in the speech of royalty). But the very simple explanation is that the Hebrews, in spite of their intense monotheism, used a plural name for God because there is a plurality of persons in the one Godhead.

More striking yet, as a proof of the plurality of persons in the one Godhead, is the fact that God Himself uses plural pronouns in speaking of Himself. For example, in the first chapter of the Bible, we read that God said, "*Let us make man in our image, after our likeness*" (Genesis 1:26). And in Genesis 11:7, He is further recorded as saying, "*Go to, let us go down, and there confound their language, that they may not understand one another's speech.*" In Genesis 3:22, we read, "*And the Lord God said, Behold, the man is become as one of us, to know good and evil.*" And in that wonderful vision to which I have already referred, in which Isaiah saw Jehovah, we read this statement of Isaiah: "*Also I heard the voice of the Lord, saying, Whom shall I send, and who will go for us? Then said I, Here am I; send me*" (Isaiah 6:8).

Another illustration of the plurality of persons in the one Godhead in the Old Testament understanding of God is found in Zechariah 2:10–11. Here Jehovah spoke of Himself as sent *by Jehovah* in these words:

> *Sing and rejoice, O daughter of Zion: for, lo, I come, and I will dwell in the midst of thee, saith the Lord. And many nations shall be joined to the Lord in that day, and shall be my people: and I will dwell in the midst of thee, and thou shalt know that the Lord of hosts hath sent me unto thee.*

Here Jehovah clearly spoke of Himself as sent *by Jehovah*, thus clearly indicating two persons of the Deity.

This same thought of the plurality of persons in the one Godhead is brought out in John 1:1, where we reach the very climax of this thought. Here we are told, "*In the beginning was the Word, and the Word was with God, and the Word was God.*" We will see later, when we come to study the deity of Christ and the personhood and deity of the Holy Spirit, that the Lord Jesus and the Holy Spirit are clearly designated as divine beings and, at the same time, are distinguished from one another and from God the Father. So it is clear that in the Christian understanding of God, while there is but one God, there are three persons in the one Godhead.

In these two chapters on the understanding of God, I have inadequately stated this understanding. This understanding of God runs throughout the whole Bible, from the first chapter of the book of Genesis to the last chapter of the book of Revelation. This is one of the many marvelous illustrations of the divine unity of the Bible. How wonderful is that Book! There is unity of thought on this profound doctrine pervading the whole Book! This is a clear indication that the Bible is the Word of God.

There is in the Bible a philosophy that is profounder than any human philosophy, ancient or modern. The only way to account for it is that God Himself is the author of this incomparable philosophy. What a wondrous God we have! How we ought to meditate on His person! With what awe and, at the same time, with what delight we should come into His presence and bow before Him, adoringly contemplating the wonder, beauty, majesty, and glory of His being.

4

IS JESUS CHRIST GOD?

While the Pharisees were gathered together, Jesus asked them, saying, What think ye of Christ? Whose son is he?
—Matthew 22:41–42

This question that our Lord Jesus asked the Pharisees is the most fundamental question concerning Christian thought and faith that can be asked of anybody in any age. Jesus Christ Himself is the center of Christianity, so the most fundamental questions of faith are those that concern the person of Christ. If a man holds right views concerning the person of Jesus Christ, he will sooner or later get right views on every other question. If he holds wrong views concerning the person of Jesus Christ, he is pretty sure to go wrong on everything else sooner or later. "*What think ye of Christ?*" That is the central, vital question.

The most fundamental question concerning the person of Christ is, Is Jesus Christ really God? Not merely, Is He divine? but, Is He actually God? When I was a boy, for a person to say that he believed in the divinity of Christ meant that he believed in the real deity of Christ, that he believed that Jesus is actually a divine person, that He is God. It no longer means that. The Devil is shrewd and subtle, and he knows that the most effective way to instill error into the minds of the uninformed and unwary is to take old and precious words and give them new meanings.

So when Satan's messengers, who masquerade as *"ministers of righteousness"* (2 Corinthians 11:15), seek to lead, if possible, the elect astray (see Matthew 24:24), they use the old precious words but with entirely new and entirely false meanings. They talk about "the divinity of Christ," but they do not mean at all by it what was meant in former days. In the same way, they talk about "the Atonement," but they do not mean at all by the Atonement the substitutionary death of Jesus Christ by which eternal life is secured for us. And often, when they talk about Christ, they do not mean at all our Lord and Savior Jesus Christ, the actual historical Jesus of the four gospels. They mean an "ideal Christ" or a "Christ principle."

Therefore, our subject in this chapter is not the divinity of Christ, but the deity of Christ. Our question is not, Is Jesus Christ divine? but, Is Jesus Christ God? Who was that person who was born at Bethlehem many centuries ago; who lived thirty-three or thirty-four years here on earth as recorded in the four gospels of Matthew, Mark, Luke, and John; who was crucified on Calvary's cross; who rose from the dead the third day; and who was exalted from earth to the right hand of the Father in heaven? Was He God manifested in the flesh? Was He God embodied in a human being? Was He and is He a being worthy of our absolute faith, our supreme love, our unhesitating obedience, and our wholehearted worship, just as God the Father is worthy of our absolute faith, supreme love, unhesitating obedience, and wholehearted worship? Should all men honor Jesus Christ even as they honor God the Father? (See John 5:23.) The question is not merely whether He is an example that we can wisely follow or a master whom we can wisely serve, but whether He is a God whom we can rightly worship.

I presume that most of you, my readers, do believe that Jesus was God manifested in the flesh and that He is God today at the right hand of the Father. But why do you believe this? Are you so well-informed in your faith, and therefore so well-grounded, that no silver-tongued talker, no Unitarian[3] or Jehovah's Witness or Christian Scientist or Theosophist or other errorist, can confuse you and upset you and lead you astray? It is important that we be thoroughly sound in our faith on this point, and thoroughly well-informed, wherever else we may be in ignorance or error. For we are distinctly told in John 20:31 that *"these* [things] *are written, that ye might believe that Jesus is the Christ, the Son of God; and that believing ye might have life through his name."* It is evident from these words of the inspired apostle John that this question is not merely a matter of theoretical opinion, but a matter that concerns our salvation. I am writing this chapter to strengthen and instruct you in your blessed faith, your saving faith in Jesus Christ as a divine person.

When I studied the subject of the deity of Christ in a theological seminary, I got the impression that there are a few proof texts in the Bible that conclusively prove that He is God. Years later, I found that there are not merely a few proof texts that prove this fact, but that the Bible in many ways and in countless passages clearly teaches that Jesus Christ was God manifest in the flesh. Indeed, I found that the doctrine of the deity of Jesus Christ forms the very foundation of the Bible.

Jesus' Divine Names Prove His Deity

The first proof of the absolute deity of our Lord Jesus is that many names and titles clearly implying deity are used of Jesus Christ in the Bible, some of them repeatedly. In fact, the total number of passages reaches far into the hundreds. Of course, I can give you only a few illustrations. First of all, look at Revelation 1:17:

> *And when I saw Him* [Jesus], *I fell at his feet as dead. And he laid his right hand upon me, saying unto me, Fear not; I am the first and the last.*

3. Unitarianism denies the Christian doctrine of the Trinity and the Christian doctrine of the deity of Jesus Christ.

The context clearly shows that our Lord Jesus is the speaker, and here our Lord Jesus distinctly called Himself "*the first and the last.*" Now, beyond a question, this is a divine name, for we read in Isaiah,

> *Thus saith the* Lord, *the King of Israel, and his redeemer the* Lord *of hosts; I am the first, and I am the last; and beside me there is no God.* (Isaiah 44:6)

In Revelation 22, our Lord Jesus said that He is "*the Alpha and the Omega*" (verse 12). His words are,

> *Behold, I come quickly; and my reward is with me, to give every man according as his work shall be. I am Alpha and Omega, the beginning and the end, the first and the last.* (Revelation 22:12–13)

Now, in Revelation 1:8, "*the Lord God*" declared that *He* is "*the Alpha and the Omega.*" His words are, "*I am the Alpha and the Omega, saith the Lord God, which is and which was and which is to come, the Almighty*" (rv).

In 1 Corinthians 2:8, the apostle Paul spoke of our crucified Lord Jesus as "*the Lord of glory.*" His exact words are, "*Which none of the princes of this world knew: for had they known it, they would not have crucified the Lord of glory.*" There can be no question that "*the Lord of glory*" is Jehovah God, for we read in Psalm 24,

> *Who is this King of glory? The* Lord *strong and mighty, the* Lord *mighty in battle. Lift up your heads, O ye gates; even lift them up, ye everlasting doors; and the King of glory shall come in. Who is this King of glory? The* Lord *of hosts, he is the King of glory.* (Psalm 24:8–10)

We are told in the passage already referred to that our crucified Lord Jesus is "*the Lord* [the King] *of glory*"; therefore, He must be Jehovah.

In John 20:28, Thomas addressed the Lord Jesus as his Lord and his God: "*And Thomas answered and said unto him, My Lord and my God.*"

Unitarians have endeavored to get around the force of this statement of Thomas by saying that Thomas was excited and that he was not addressing the Lord Jesus at all, but was saying, *"My Lord and my God."* as an exclamation of astonishment, just in the way that the ungodly sometimes use these exclamations today. This interpretation is impossible, and it shows to what desperate measures the Unitarians are driven, for Jesus Himself commended Thomas for seeing the truth and saying it. Our Lord Jesus' words immediately following those of Thomas are, *"Thomas, because thou hast seen me, thou hast believed: blessed are they that have not seen, and yet have believed"* (John 20:29).

In Titus 2:13, our Lord Jesus is spoken of as *"God"*: *"Looking for that blessed hope, and the glorious appearing of the great God and our Saviour Jesus Christ."* In Romans 9:5, Paul told us that *"Christ…is over all, God blessed for ever."* Unitarians have desperately tried to overcome the force of these words, but the only fair translation and interpretation of the words that Paul wrote in Greek are the translation and interpretation just given.

To the person who goes to the Bible to find out what it actually teaches—not to read his own thoughts into it—there can be no honest doubt that Jesus is spoken of by various names and titles that beyond a question imply deity, and that He is in so many words called God. In Hebrews 1:8, it is said of the Son, *"But unto the Son he* [God] *saith, Thy throne, O God, is for ever and ever: a sceptre of righteousness is the sceptre of thy kingdom."* If we were to go no further, it is clearly the plain and often repeated teaching of the Bible that Jesus Christ is truly God.

Jesus' Divine Attributes Prove His Deity

But there is a second proof that Jesus Christ is God, one that is equally convincing. It is this: all the distinctively divine attributes are ascribed to Jesus Christ, and in Him is said to dwell *"all the fullness of the Godhead"* (Colossians 2:9). There are five distinctively divine attributes, that is, five attributes that God alone possesses. These are omnipotence, omniscience, omnipresence, eternity, and immutability. Each one of these distinctively divine attributes is ascribed to Jesus Christ.

First of all, omnipotence is ascribed to Jesus Christ. We are taught that Jesus had power over disease, death, winds, the sea, and demons; they were all subject to His word. In fact, He is "*far above all principality, and power, and might, and dominion, and every name that is named, not only in this world, but also in that which is to come*" (Ephesians 1:21). In addition, the Bible says that He upholds "*all things by the word of his power*" (Hebrews 1:3).

Omniscience is also ascribed to Jesus Christ. We are taught in the Bible that Jesus knew men's lives, even their secret histories (see John 4:16–19), that He knew the secret thoughts of men, knew all men, knew what was in man. (See Mark 2:8; Luke 5:22; and John 2:24–25.) Significantly, we are distinctly told in 2 Chronicles 6:30 and Jeremiah 17:9–10 that only God possesses this knowledge. In addition, we are told in so many words in John 16:30 that Jesus knew "*all things*," and in Colossians 2:3 that in Him "*are hid all the treasures of wisdom and knowledge.*"

Omnipresence is also ascribed to Jesus Christ. We read in Matthew 18:20 that "*where two or three are gathered together in* [His] *name,*" He is "*in the midst of them.*" And in Matthew 28:20, we are told that wherever His obedient disciples would go, He would be with them, "*even unto the end of the world.*" In John 14:20 and 2 Corinthians 13:5, we see that He dwells in each believer, in all the millions of believers scattered over the earth. In Ephesians 1:23, we are told that He "*filleth all in all.*"

Eternity is also ascribed to Jesus Christ. John 1:1 states that "*in the beginning was the Word, and the Word was with God, and the Word was God.*" In John 8:58, Jesus Himself said, "*Verily, verily, I say unto you, Before Abraham was, I am.*" Note that the Lord Jesus did not merely say that "before Abraham was, I *was*," but "*before Abraham was, I am*," thus declaring Himself to be the eternal "*I Am*" (Exodus 3:14), Even in the Old Testament, we have a declaration of the eternity of the Christ who was to be born in Bethlehem. In Micah 5:2, we read,

> *But thou, Bethlehem Ephratah, though thou be little among the thousands of Judah, yet out of thee shall he come forth unto me that is to be ruler in Israel; whose goings forth have been from of old, from everlasting.*

And in Isaiah 9:6, we learn of the Child who was to be born,

> *Unto us a child is born, unto us a son is given: and the government shall be upon his shoulder: and his name shall be called Wonderful, Counsellor, the mighty God, the everlasting Father, the Prince of Peace.*

In Hebrews 13:8, we are told that *"Jesus Christ the same yesterday, and to day, and for ever."*

His immutability is also taught in the passage just quoted from Hebrews. In addition, in Hebrews 1:11–12, we see that while even the heavens change, the Lord Jesus does not change. The exact words are,

> *They* [the heavens] *shall perish; but thou remainest; and they all shall wax old as doth a garment; and as a vesture shalt thou fold them up, and they shall be changed: but thou art the same, and thy years shall not fail.*

So we see that each one of the five distinctly divine attributes is ascribed to our Lord Jesus Christ. And in Colossians 2:9, we are told, *"In him dwelleth all the fulness of the Godhead bodily"* (that is, in a bodily form). Here, again, we might rest our case, for what has been said about His divine attributes, even if taken alone, clearly proves the absolute deity of our Lord Jesus Christ. It shows that He possesses every perfection of nature and character that God the Father possesses.

Jesus' Divine Offices Prove His Deity

But we do not need to rest the case here. There is a third indisputable proof that Jesus Christ is God; namely, all the distinctively divine offices are attributed to Jesus Christ. The seven distinctively divine offices—seven things that God alone can do—are creation, preservation, forgiveness of sin, the raising of the dead, the transformation of bodies, judgment, and the bestowal of eternal life. Each of these distinctly divine offices is ascribed to Jesus Christ.

Creation is ascribed to Him. In Hebrews 1:10, these words are spoken to our Lord: *"Thou, Lord, in the beginning hast laid the foundation of the earth; and the heavens are the works of thine hands."* The context clearly shows that the Lord addressed here is the Lord Jesus. In John 1:3, we are told that *"all things were made by him* [Jesus Christ]*; and without him was not any thing made that was made."*

Preservation of the universe and of everything in it is also ascribed to Him in Hebrews 1:3, where it is said of the Lord Jesus,

> *Who being the brightness of his* [God's] *glory, and the express image of* [God's] *person, and* ***upholding all things by the word of his power,*** *when he had by himself purged our sins, sat down on the right hand of the Majesty on high.* (emphasis added)

The forgiveness of sin is ascribed to Jesus Christ as well. Jesus Himself said in Mark 2:10, when His power to forgive sins was questioned because that was recognized as a divine power, *"The Son of man hath power on earth to forgive sins."*

The future raising of the dead is distinctly ascribed to Him in John, where Jesus said,

> *This is the Father's will which hath sent me, that of all which he hath given me I should lose nothing, but should raise it up again at the last day....No man can come to me, except the Father which hath sent me draw him: and I will raise him up at the last day.*
> (John 6:39, 44)

The transformation of our bodies is ascribed to Him in Philippians 3:20–21: *"The Lord Jesus Christ ...shall change our vile body, that it may be fashioned like unto his glorious body."*

In 2 Timothy 4:1, judgment is ascribed to Him. We are told that He *"shall judge the quick and the dead."* Jesus Himself declared that He would be the judge of all mankind and emphasized the fact of the divine character of that office. In John chapter 5, He said,

> *For the Father judgeth no man, but hath committed all judgment unto the Son: that all men should honour the Son, even as they honour the Father. He that honoureth not the Son honoureth not the Father which hath sent him.* (John 5:22–23)

The bestowal of eternal life is ascribed to Jesus Christ again and again. In John 10:28, He Himself said, *"I give unto them eternal life; and they shall never perish, neither shall any man pluck them out of my hand."* And in John 17, Jesus said,

> *Father, the hour is come; glorify thy Son, that thy Son also may glorify thee: as thou hast given him power over all flesh, that he should give eternal life to as many as thou hast given him.* (John 17:1–2)

Here, then, we have the seven distinctively divine offices all attributed to Jesus Christ. This evidence alone would prove that He is God, and we could rest the case here. But there are even more proofs of His absolute deity.

A Comparison of Old and New Testament Verses Proves His Deity

The fourth proof of the absolute deity of Jesus Christ is found in the fact that over and over again statements that in the Old Testament are made distinctly of Jehovah are taken in the New Testament to refer to Jesus Christ. Many illustrations could be given, but I will give only one illustration here. In Jeremiah 11:20, the prophet said,

> *O Lord of hosts, that judgest righteously, that triest the reins and the heart, let me see thy vengeance on them: for unto thee have I revealed my cause.*

Here the prophet Jeremiah distinctly said that it is Jehovah of Hosts who "judgest" and *"triest the reins and the heart."* And in Jeremiah 17:10, the prophet represented Jehovah Himself as saying the same thing in these words: *"I the LORD search the heart, I try the reins, even to give every man according to his ways, and according to the fruit of his doings."*

But in the New Testament, the Lord Jesus said, *"I am he which searcheth the reins and hearts: and I will give unto every one of you according to your works"* (Revelation 2:23). We are distinctly told in the context that it is *"the Son of God"* (verse 18) who is speaking here. So Jesus claimed for Himself in the New Testament what Jehovah in the Old Testament said is true of Himself and of Himself alone.

In many other instances, statements that in the Old Testament are made distinctly of Jehovah are taken in the New Testament to refer to Jesus Christ. This is to say, Jesus Christ occupies the place in New Testament thought and doctrine that Jehovah occupies in Old Testament thought and doctrine.

The Names of the Father and the Son Coupled Together Prove Christ's Deity

The fifth proof of the absolute deity of our Lord is found in the way in which the name of Jesus Christ is coupled with that of God the Father. In numerous passages, His name is coupled with the name of God the Father in a way in which it would be impossible to couple the name of any finite being with that of Deity. I will give only a few of the many illustrations that could be given.

A striking instance is in the words of our Lord Himself in John 14, where we read,

> *Jesus answered and said unto him, If a man love me, he will keep my words: and my Father will love him, and we will come unto him, and make our abode with him.* (John 14:23)

Here our Lord Jesus did not hesitate to couple Himself with the Father in such a way as to say "*We*"—that is, "God the Father and I"—"*will come... and make our abode with him.*"

In John 14:1, Jesus said, "*Let not your heart be troubled: ye believe in God, believe also in me.*" If Jesus Christ is not God, this is shocking blasphemy. There is absolutely no middle ground between admitting the deity of Jesus Christ and charging Christ with the most daring and appalling blasphemy of which any man in all history was ever guilty.

Christ's Acceptance of Worship Proves His Deity

There is a sixth proof of the absolute deity of our Lord Jesus. The proofs already given have been decisive—each one of the five has been decisive—but this, if possible, is the most decisive of them all. It is this: we are taught that Jesus Christ should be worshiped as God, both by angels and men. In numerous places in the gospels, we see Jesus Christ accepting without hesitation a worship that good men and angels declined with fear and that He Himself taught should be rendered only to God. (See Matthew 14:33; Matthew 28:9; and Luke 24:52. Compare Matthew 4:9–10; Acts 10:25–26; and Revelation 22:8–9.)

A curious and very misleading comment is made in the margin of the American Standard Revision on the meaning of the word translated "*worship*" in these passages. It says, "The Greek word translated 'worship' denotes an act of reverence, *whether paid to a creature* or to the Creator" (emphasis added). Now, this is true, but it is utterly misleading. While this word is used to denote an act of reverence paid to a creature by *idolaters*, our Lord Jesus Himself distinctly said, using exactly the same Greek word, "*Thou shalt worship the Lord thy God, and him only shalt thou serve*" (Matthew 4:10).

Furthermore, Jesus said in John 5:23 that "*all men should honour the Son, even as they honour the Father.*" And in Revelation 5:8–9, 12–13, the four living creatures and the twenty-four elders are shown falling down before the Lamb and offering worship to Him just as worship is offered to

Him who sits on the throne, that is, God the Father. In Hebrews 1:6, we are told, *"And again, when He* [God] *bringeth in the firstbegotten* [Jesus] *into the world, he saith, And let all the angels of God worship him."*

One night, in a church in Chicago, I stepped up to an intelligent-looking man and asked him, "Are you a Christian?" He replied, "I do not suppose you would consider me a Christian." "Why not?" I asked. He said, "I am a Unitarian." I said, "What you mean, then, is that you do not think that Jesus Christ is a person who should be worshiped." He replied, "That is exactly what I think," and added, "The Bible nowhere says we ought to worship Him." I said, "Who told you that?" He replied, "My pastor," mentioning a prominent Unitarian minister in the city of Boston. I said, "Let me show you something," and I opened my Bible to Hebrews 1:6 and read, *"And again, when He* [God] *bringeth in the firstbegotten* [Jesus] *into the world, he saith, And let all the angels of God worship him."*

The Unitarian man said, "Does it say that?" I handed him the Bible and said, "Read it for yourself." He read it and said, "I did not know that was in the Bible." I said, "Well, it is there, isn't it?" "Yes, it is there." Language could not make it any plainer. The Bible clearly teaches that Jesus, the Son of God, is to be worshiped as God by angels and men, even as God the Father is worshiped.

Additional Verses Amazingly Prove Christ's Deity

The six proofs of the deity of Jesus Christ that I have given leave no possibility of doubting that Jesus Christ is God, that Jesus of Nazareth is God manifest in a human person, that He is a being to be worshiped, even as God the Father is worshiped. But there are also incidental proofs of His absolute deity that, if possible, are in some ways even more convincing than the direct assertions of His deity.

First, our Lord Jesus said in Matthew 11:28, *"Come unto me, all ye that labour and are heavy laden, and I will give you rest."* Now, anyone who makes a promise like that must either be God, a lunatic, or an impostor. No one can give rest to all the weary and burdened who come to him unless he is

God, yet Jesus Christ offers to do it. If He offers to do it and fails to do it when men come to Him, then He is either a lunatic or an impostor. If He actually does it, then beyond a question He is God. And thousands can testify that He actually does it. Thousands and tens of thousands who were weary and burdened and crushed, and for whom there was no help in man, have come to Jesus Christ, and He has given them rest. Surely, then, He is not merely a great man—He is God.

Second, in John 14:1, Jesus Christ demanded that we put the same faith in Him that we put in God the Father, and He promised that in such faith we will find a cure for all troubles and anxieties. His words are, *"Let not your heart be troubled: ye believe in God, believe also in me."* It is clear that He demanded that the same absolute faith be put in Him that is to be put in God Almighty. Now, in Jeremiah 17:5, a Scripture with which our Lord Jesus was perfectly familiar, we read, *"Thus saith the LORD; Cursed be the man that trusteth in man."* Yet regardless of this clear curse pronounced upon all who trust in man, Jesus Christ demanded that we put trust in Him just as we put trust in God. It is the strongest possible assertion of deity on His part. No one but God has a right to make such a demand, and Jesus Christ, when He made this demand, must either have been God or an impostor. Furthermore, thousands and tens of thousands have found that when they have believed in Him just as they believe in God, their hearts have been delivered from trouble no matter what their bereavement or circumstances have been.

Third, the Lord Jesus demanded supreme and absolute love for Himself. It is as clear as day that no one but God has a right to demand such a love, but there can be no question that Jesus did demand it. In Matthew 10:37, He said to His disciples, *"He that loveth father or mother more than me is not worthy of me: and he that loveth son or daughter more than me is not worthy of me."* And in Luke 14:26, 33, He said,

> *If any man come to me, and hate not his father, and mother, and wife, and children, and brethren, and sisters, yea, and his own life also, he cannot be my disciple....So likewise, whosoever he be of you that forsaketh not all that he hath, he cannot be my disciple.*

There can be no question that this is a demand on Jesus' part of supreme and absolute love for Himself, a love that puts even the dearest loved ones in an entirely secondary place. No one but God has a right to make such a demand, but our Lord Jesus made it; therefore, He is God.

Fourth, the Lord Jesus claimed absolute equality with the Father. He said, "*I and my Father are one*" (John 10:30).

Fifth, our Lord Jesus went so far as to say, "*He that hath seen me hath seen the Father*" (John 14:9). He claimed here to be so absolutely God that to see Him is to see the Father who dwells in Him.

Sixth, Jesus said, "*And this is life eternal, that they might know thee the only true God, and Jesus Christ, whom thou hast sent*" (John 17:3). In other words, He claimed that knowledge of Himself is as essential a part of eternal life as knowledge of God the Father.

Christ's Deity: A Glorious Truth

There is no room left to doubt the absolute deity of Jesus Christ. It is a glorious truth. The Savior in whom we believe is God—a Savior for whom nothing is too hard, a Savior who can save *from* the uttermost and *to* the uttermost. (See Hebrews 7:25.) Oh, how we should rejoice that we have no merely human Savior, but a Savior who is absolutely God.

On the other hand, how black is the guilt of rejecting such a Savior as this! Whoever refuses to accept Jesus as his divine Savior and Lord is guilty of the enormous sin of rejecting a Savior who is God. Many a man thinks he is good because he has never stolen or committed murder or cheated. "Of what great sin am I guilty?" he complacently asks. Have you ever accepted Jesus Christ? "No." Well, then, you are guilty of the awful and damning sin of rejecting a Savior who is God. "But," he answers, "I do not believe that He is God." That does not change the fact or lessen your guilt. Questioning a fact or denying a fact never changes it, regardless of what anyone may say to the contrary.

Suppose a man has a wife who is one of the noblest, purest, truest women who has ever lived. Would her husband's bringing baseless charges against her, questioning her purity and loyalty, change the fact? It would not. It would simply make that husband guilty of awful slander; it would simply prove that man to be an outrageous scoundrel. Likewise, denying the deity of Jesus Christ does not make His deity any less a fact, but it does make the denier of His deity guilty of awful, incredible, blasphemous slander.

5

IS JESUS CHRIST TRULY MAN?

And the Word [Jesus Christ] *was made flesh, and dwelt among us, (and we beheld his glory, the glory as of the only begotten of the Father,) full of grace and truth.*
—John 1:14

[Jesus], *being in the form of God, thought it not robbery to be equal with God: but made himself of no reputation, and took upon him the form of a servant, and was made in the likeness of men: and being found in fashion as a man, he humbled himself, and became obedient unto death, even the death of the cross.*
—Philippians 2:6–8

There is one God, and one mediator between God and men, the man Christ Jesus.
—1 Timothy 2:5

In the preceding chapter, we saw many things about Jesus Christ. First, we saw that *"in him dwelleth all the fulness of the Godhead bodily"* (Colossians 2:9). He possesses all the distinctively divine attributes and exercises all the distinctively divine offices. He occupies the position in New Testament thought that Jehovah occupies in Old Testament thought. He is a being worthy of our absolute faith, supreme love, unhesitating obedience, and wholehearted worship. In summary, we saw that He was God and is God.

But in this chapter's three texts, we are told that this Divine One, who had existed from all eternity with God the Father and who was God, became a man. In becoming a man, He did not cease to be God; however, the Word, the Eternal Word, which was *"with God"* and *"was God"* (John 1:1), took human nature upon Himself. While Jesus was very God of very God, He was also a real man, as truly and completely a man as any man who has ever walked on this earth.

The doctrine of the real humanity of Christ is as essential a part of the Christian faith as the doctrine of His real deity. There is a very large group of people who do not accept the real deity of Jesus Christ. They are in fundamental error. Another large group of people accept only His deity and do not accept the reality of His humanity. They also are in error. A doctrine of a Savior who is only man is a false doctrine, and a doctrine of a Savior who is only God is an equally false doctrine. The doctrine of the Bible is that One who from all eternity was God became man in the person of Jesus of Nazareth. There are many passages in the Bible that set forth the deity of our Lord Jesus in a way that is unmistakable and inescapable. Many other passages in the Bible set forth the complete humanity of our Lord Jesus in a way that is equally unmistakable and inescapable. It is with the doctrine of His real humanity that we are concerned in this chapter.

The Human Parentage of Jesus Christ

First of all, the Bible teaches that Jesus Christ had a human parentage. We read in Luke,

> *And she* [Mary] *brought forth her firstborn son, and wrapped him in swaddling clothes, and laid him in a manger; because there was no room for them in the inn.* (Luke 2:7)

Here we are told that our Lord Jesus Christ, though supernaturally conceived, was Mary's son. Mary was as truly His mother as God was His Father. He had a human parentage as truly as He had a divine parentage.

In Luke 1:35, we read,

> *And the angel answered and said unto her* [Mary], *The Holy Ghost shall come upon thee, and the power of the Highest shall overshadow thee: therefore also that holy thing which shall be born of thee shall be called the Son of God.*

He was called *"the Son of God"* because He was begotten directly by the power of the Holy Spirit. But the Holy Spirit came upon Mary, and she became the mother of this One who was to be called *"the Son of God."*

Jesus' human parentage was not only reflected in the fact that He descended from Mary; we are also clearly told in Romans 1:3 that God's Son *"was made of the seed of David according to the flesh."* In Acts 2:30, we are told that He was *"the fruit of his* [David's] *loins, according to the flesh."* And in Hebrews 7:14, we are told that *"our Lord sprang out of Juda."* While we read in Galatians 4:4 that *"when the fulness of the time was come, God sent forth his Son,"* we are also told with equal plainness in the same verse that this Son of God was *"made of a woman."* The human parentage of our Lord and Savior Jesus Christ is just as real and just as essential a part of Him as His divine parentage.

The Human Physical Nature of Jesus Christ

Not only did Jesus Christ have a human parentage, but He had a human physical nature, a human body. This comes out in the first of our texts: *"The Word was made flesh"* (John 1:14). In Hebrews 2:14, we are taught that...

> *Forasmuch then as the children are partakers of flesh and blood, he also himself likewise took part of the same; that through death he might destroy him that had the power of death, that is, the devil.*

Words could not make it any plainer that our Lord Jesus had a real human body, a real human physical nature. Indeed, the apostle John taught us that not to believe in the actuality of His human body is a mark of the Antichrist. He said,

> *Hereby know ye the Spirit of God: every spirit that confesseth that Jesus Christ is come in the flesh is of God: and every spirit that confesseth not that Jesus Christ is come in the flesh is not of God: and this is that spirit of antichrist, whereof ye have heard that it should come; and even now already is it in the world.* (1 John 4:2–3)

There were those in John's day who denied the reality of Jesus' human nature, who asserted that His body was only a seeming or apparent body, that it was an illusion, or, as the Christian Scientists now put it, "mortal thought." John, speaking in the wisdom and power of the Holy Spirit, asserted that this doctrine is a mark of the Antichrist. It is the one supreme mark today that Christian Science is of the Antichrist.

Not only did Jesus Christ have a human body during His life here on earth, but He still had a human body after His resurrection. The Millennial Dawnists[4] tell us that this is not so. They say that before His incarnation He was wholly a spiritual being, at His incarnation He became wholly a human being, and after His death and resurrection He became wholly a divine being. All of this is unscriptural and is therefore untrue. Jesus Himself said to His disciples after His resurrection,

> *Behold my hands and my feet, that it is I myself: handle me, and see; for a spirit hath not flesh and bones, as ye see me have. And when he had thus spoken, he showed them his hands and his feet.* (Luke 24:39–40)

---

4. Also known as the Dawn Bible Students, this cult sprang from the teachings of Charles Taze Russell, whose teachings also led to the formation of the cult known as the Jehovah's Witnesses.

And Jesus said to Thomas, after Thomas had doubted the reality of His resurrection, *"Reach hither thy finger, and behold my hands; and reach hither thy hand, and thrust it into my side: and be not faithless, but believing"* (John 20:27).

Not only did Jesus have a real human body after His resurrection while He was still here on earth, but He retains His human body in heaven. Of that wonderful view into heaven that was given to Stephen at the time he was stoned and killed, we read,

> *But he, being full of the Holy Ghost, looked up stedfastly into heaven, and saw the glory of God, and Jesus standing on the right hand of God, and said, Behold, I see the heavens opened, and the Son of man standing on the right hand of God.* (Acts 7:55–56)

Furthermore, when Christ comes again to take His rightful authority on this earth, He will come with a human body. He will come as *"the Son of Man."* He Himself said to the high priest when He stood before him on trial, *"Hereafter shall ye see the Son of man sitting on the right hand of power, and coming in the clouds of heaven"* (Matthew 26:64). In these words of our Lord, we have both a clear declaration of His deity and an equally clear declaration that He was a real man and will come again as a real man with a human, though glorified, body. Indeed, we are told in Philippians 3:20–21 that when He does come in this way, He is going to transform our present human bodies into the likeness of His own *"glorious body"* (verse 21)—His glorified human body.

The Human Limitations of Jesus Christ

The reality and completeness of our Lord's human nature come out in the fact that He had a human parentage and a human body, but that is not all. We are also clearly taught that, while as God He possessed all the attributes and exercised all the offices of Deity, as a man He was subject to human limitations.

His Physical Limitations

Jesus was subject to the physical limitations that are inherent to humanity. In John 4:6, we read that Jesus Christ was weary. The words are, "*Jesus therefore, being wearied with his journey, sat thus on the well: and it was about the sixth hour.*" But God is never weary. We read explicitly in Isaiah 40:28,

> *Hast thou not heard, that the everlasting God, the* Lord*, the Creator of the ends of the earth, fainteth not, neither is weary?*

We are told in Matthew 8:24 that Jesus Christ slept. But God never sleeps. Psalm 121:4–5 says, "*Behold, he that keepeth Israel shall neither slumber nor sleep. The* Lord *is thy keeper: the* Lord *is thy shade upon thy right hand.*" By comparing these two verses, we see distinctly that Jehovah never sleeps, yet Jesus did sleep. So Jesus was Jehovah, but He was not Jehovah only. He was man as truly as He was God.

In Matthew 21:18 and John 19:28, we read that Jesus Christ was hungry and thirsty. In Luke 22:44, we see that Jesus Christ suffered physical agony. His agony was so great that He was on the point of dying with agony.

In 1 Corinthians 15:3, we read that Christ died. This passage reveals that Jesus' death is an essential part of the gospel. Paul wrote,

> *Moreover, brethren, I declare unto you the gospel which I preached unto you, which also ye have received, and wherein ye stand; by which also ye are saved, if ye keep in memory what I preached unto you, unless ye have believed in vain. For I delivered unto you first of all that which I also received, how that Christ died for our sins according to the scriptures.* (1 Corinthians 15:1–3)

Christ's death was not merely an "apparent" death; it was a real death. It was no illusion. Our salvation depends on the reality of His death.

Christian Science cuts the very heart out of the gospel by denying the reality of His death. I am often asked, "Was it the human nature of Jesus Christ that died, or was it the divine nature that died?" It was neither the one nor the other. Natures do not die; persons die. It was *Jesus* who died, the Person who was at once God and man. We are told in 1 Corinthians 2:8 that they *"crucified the Lord of glory,"* and we saw in the last chapter that *"the Lord of glory"* is unquestionably a divine title. It was the one person Jesus, at once human and divine, who died on the cross of Calvary.

His Intellectual and Moral Limitations

Jesus Christ was also, as a man, subject to intellectual and moral limitations. We read in Luke 2:52, *"Jesus increased in wisdom and stature, and in favour with God and man."* Since we are told here that He grew in wisdom, He must have been more perfect in wisdom after He grew than before He grew. And since He grew in favor with God and man, He must have attained to a higher type of moral perfection when He grew than He had attained to before He grew. God was incarnate in the Babe of Bethlehem; nevertheless, Jesus was a real babe and grew not only in stature, but in wisdom and in favor with God and man.

As a man, Jesus was limited in knowledge. He Himself said in Mark 13:32,

> *But of that day and that hour* [that is, the day and the hour of His own return] *knoweth no man, no, not the angels which are in heaven, neither the Son, but the Father.*

Of course, His knowledge was *self-limited.* To set an example for you and me to follow, He voluntarily *as a man* put away His knowledge of the time of His own return.

Furthermore, we are definitely and explicitly taught in Hebrews 4:15 that Jesus Christ was *"in all points tempted like as we are."* We should bear in mind that this is a clear and complete proof of the reality of His humanity—not only physical but mental and moral. We should also bear in mind what is stated in the same verse, that He was *"without sin"*; that is, there was not the slightest taint or tinge of sin in His temptations, not one moment's yielding to them in thought or desire or act. He was tempted and overcame temptation in the same way that we may overcome it—by the Word of God and prayer. He Himself voluntarily placed Himself under the basic moral limitations that man is under, in order to redeem man.

His Limitations in Obtaining and Exercising Power

As a man, Jesus was also subject to limitations in the ways in which He obtained power and exercised power. Jesus Christ obtained power for the divine work that He did while here on earth, not by His incarnate deity, but by prayer. We read in Mark 1:35, *"And in the morning, rising up a great while before day, he went out, and departed into a solitary place, and there prayed."* And we read also that before He raised Lazarus from the dead—before He called him forth from the tomb by His word—He lifted up His eyes to God and said, *"Father, I thank thee that thou hast heard me"* (John 11:41). By this He showed conclusively that the power by which He raised Lazarus from the dead was not His inherent, inborn, divine power, but was power obtained by prayer. It is mentioned not less than twenty-five times in the New Testament that Jesus prayed. He obtained power for work and for moral victory as other men do—by prayer.

Again, Jesus was subject to human conditions for obtaining what He desired. He obtained power for the divine works and miracles that he did by the anointing of the Holy Spirit as well as by prayer. We read in Acts 10:38,

> *God anointed Jesus of Nazareth with the Holy Ghost and with power: who went about doing good, and healing all that were oppressed of the devil; for God was with him.*

We are taught, furthermore, that Jesus was subject, during His earthly life, to limitations in the exercise of power. He Himself said just before His crucifixion and subsequent glorification,

> *Verily, verily, I say unto you, He that believeth on me, the works that I do shall he do also; and greater works than these shall he do; because I go unto my Father.* (John 14:12)

The evident meaning of this Scripture is that during the days of His earthly existence there was a limitation to His exercise of power. But then He was glorified with the Father with the glory that He had with Him before the world was. (See John 17:5.) After His glorification, there were no more limitations to the exercise of His power. Therefore, we, being united to our Lord Jesus, not as He was on earth but as He is in His exaltation and restoration to divine glory, will do greater works than He did during the days of His earthly existence.

The Human Relationship That Jesus Had with God

The completeness of the humanity of Jesus Christ comes out in still another matter, that is, the relationship that He had with God. God was His God. He Himself said to Mary in John 20:17,

> *Touch me not; for I am not yet ascended to my Father: but go to my brethren, and say unto them, I ascend unto my Father, and your Father; and to my God, and your God.*

The evident meaning of this verse is that Jesus Christ's relationship to God the Father was the relationship between a man and God. He spoke of God the Father as "*my God.*" Though possessing all the attributes and exercising all the functions of Deity, Jesus Christ the Son was subordinate to the Father.

This truth explains statements of our Lord that have puzzled many who believe in His deity. One example of a puzzling statement is in John 14:28, where Jesus said,

> *Ye have heard how I said unto you, I go away, and come again unto you. If ye loved me, ye would rejoice, because I said, I go unto the Father: for my Father is greater than I.*

The question is often asked, "If Jesus Christ is God, how could the Father be greater than He?" The very simple answer to this is that He, *as the Son,* is subordinate to the Father. He is equal to the Father in the possession of all the distinctively divine attributes, in the exercise of all the divine offices, and as an object of our wholehearted worship, but He is subordinate to the Father in His position as Son. Jesus Christ's relationship to the Father is like the relationship of the wife to the husband in this respect. The wife may be fully the equal of the husband; nevertheless, *"the head of the woman is the man"* (1 Corinthians 11:3). This means that she is subordinate to the man. We are told in the same verse that *"the head of every man is Christ."* This means that Jesus Christ the Son is subordinate to the Father.

Jesus Christ: A Real Man in Every Way

It is evident from what we have read from God's Word that Jesus Christ in every respect was a true man, a real man, a complete man. He was made *"in all things...like unto his brethren"* (Hebrews 2:17). He was subject to all the physical, mental, and moral conditions of existence inherent to human nature. He was in every respect a real man. He became this way voluntarily in order to redeem men. From all eternity He had existed *"in the form of God"* (Philippians 2:6) and could have remained *"in the form of God,"* but if He had remained that way, we would have been lost. Therefore, out of love for us, the fallen race, He,

> *Thought it not robbery to be equal with God: but made himself of no reputation, and took upon him the form of a servant, and was made in the likeness of men: and being found in fashion as a man, he humbled himself, and became obedient unto death, even the death of the cross.*
> (Philippians 2:6–8)

Oh, wondrous love! Out of love for us, He took our nature upon Himself, turning His back on the glory that had been His from all eternity. He took upon Himself all the shame and suffering that was involved in our redemption and became one of us so that He could die for us and redeem us. Oh, the wondrous grace of our Lord Jesus Christ! *"Though he was rich, yet for your sakes he became poor, that ye through his poverty might be rich*" (2 Corinthians 8:9). He partook of human nature so that we might become partakers of the divine nature. (See 2 Peter 1:4.) The philosophy of the divine and human natures of Christ, which is the philosophy of the New Testament, is a most wonderful philosophy—the most wonderful philosophy the world has ever heard. And, thank God, it is true.

Reconciling Two Apparently Contradictory Doctrines

Someone may ask, "How can we reconcile the biblical doctrine of the true deity of Jesus Christ with the biblical doctrine of the true humanity of Jesus Christ? How can we reconcile the doctrine that He was truly God with the doctrine that He was equally truly man?" The answer to this question is very simple. Reconciling doctrines is not our main business. Our first business is to find out what the various passages in the Bible mean, taken in their natural, grammatical interpretation. Then, if we can reconcile them, well and good. If not, we should still believe them. We should leave the reconciliation of the two apparently conflicting doctrines to our increasing knowledge, as we go on communing with God and studying His Word. It is an utterly foolish and wrong idea that we must interpret every passage of the Bible in such a way that we can readily reconcile it with every other passage. It is this idea of interpretation that gives rise to one-sided, and therefore untrue, theology.

One man, for example, takes the passages in the Bible concerning the sovereignty of God, which Calvinists emphasize, and believes them. Then he twists and distorts the other passages that teach the freedom of man to make them fit with those that teach the sovereignty of God. In this way, he becomes a one-sided Calvinist. Another man sees only the passages that clearly teach man's power of self-determination, which Arminians emphasize. Then he seeks to twist all the passages that teach the sovereignty of God and the foreordaining wisdom and will of God. In this way, he becomes a one-sided Arminian. And so it is with the whole gamut of doctrine.

It is utter foolishness, to say nothing of presumption, to thus handle the Word of God deceitfully. Our business is to find out the plainly intended sense of a passage that we are studying, as determined by the usage of words, grammatical construction, and context. When we have discovered the plainly intended meaning, we are to believe it whether we can reconcile it with something else that we have found out and believe or not.

Two truths that seem to be utterly irreconcilable or flatly contradictory often, with increased knowledge, are seen to beautifully harmonize. We should always remember this point. Then we will have no difficulty in recognizing the fact that truths that still seem to be contradictory to us do perfectly harmonize in the infinite wisdom of God. Moreover, they will perfectly harmonize in our minds when we more closely approach God's omniscience.

Setting Christ's Deity and His Humanity Side by Side

The Bible, in the most fearless way, puts the absolute deity of Jesus Christ in closest juxtaposition with the true humanity of Jesus Christ. For example, we read in Matthew 8:24, "*And, behold, there arose a great tempest in the sea, insomuch that the ship was covered with the waves: but* [Jesus] *was asleep.*" Here we have a plain statement of the real humanity of our Lord. But two verses later, in the twenty-sixth verse, we read,

> *And he saith unto them, Why are ye fearful, O ye of little faith? Then he arose, and rebuked the winds and the sea; and there was a great calm.*

Here we have a clear shining forth of His deity, even the winds and the waves being subject to His word. No wonder the disciples asked one another, "*What manner of man is this, that even the winds and the sea obey him!*" (verse 27). The answer is plain: a divine Man.

Again, we read in Luke 3:21, "*Now when all the people were baptized, it came to pass, that Jesus also being baptized, and praying, the heaven was opened.*" Here we see Jesus in His humanity, baptized and praying. Surely this is a man. But in the next verse we read,

> *And the Holy Ghost descended in a bodily shape like a dove upon him, and a voice came from heaven, which said, Thou art my beloved Son; in thee I am well pleased.* (Luke 3:22)

Here, with an audible voice, God declared Him to be divine, to be His Son.

In John 11:38 we read, "*Jesus therefore again groaning in himself cometh to the grave. It was a cave, and a stone lay upon it.*" Here we see Jesus in His humanity, but five verses further down, we read, "*And when he thus had spoken, he cried with a loud voice, Lazarus, come forth. And he that was dead came forth*" (verses 43–44). Here His deity shines forth.

In Luke 9:28, we read, "*And it came to pass about an eight days after these sayings, he took Peter and John and James, and went up into a mountain to pray.*" Here we very clearly see Jesus' humanity, His limitation, His dependence on God. But in the very next verse, we read, "*And as he prayed, the fashion of his countenance was altered, and his raiment was white and glistering.*" Here we see His divinity shining forth. Then, again, in the thirty-fifth verse, we read of the voice coming out of the cloud, saying, "*This is my beloved Son: hear him.*" Jesus' deity is unmistakably revealed again.

In Matthew 16, we read,

> *Simon Peter answered and said, Thou art the Christ, the Son of the living God. And Jesus answered and said unto him, Blessed art thou, Simon Barjona: for flesh and blood hath not revealed it unto thee, but my Father which is in heaven.* (Matthew 16:16–17)

Here is a clear declaration by Jesus Himself of His deity. But four verses further down, we read,

> *From that time forth began Jesus to show unto his disciples, how that he must go unto Jerusalem, and suffer many things of the elders and chief priests and scribes, and be killed, and be raised again the third day.* (Matthew 16:21)

Here we have the clear declaration of the reality and completeness of His humanity.

In Hebrews 1:6, we read of our Lord Jesus, "*When he* [God the Father] *bringeth in the firstbegotten into the world, he saith, And let all the angels of God worship him.*" Here is a most unmistakable and inescapable declaration that Jesus Christ is a divine person, to be worshiped as God by angels as well as by men. In verse 8, we read this further declaration of His absolute deity: "*But unto the Son he* [God] *saith, Thy throne, O God, is for ever and ever.*" Here, again, the Son is declared to be God. But in the very next chapter, we read, "*For in that he himself hath suffered being tempted, he is able to succour them that are tempted*" (Hebrews 2:18). Here we have the clearest possible declaration of the reality of His human nature.

In Hebrews 4:14, we read, "*Seeing then that we have a great high priest, that is passed into the heavens, Jesus the Son of God, let us hold fast our profession.*" Here we have a plain declaration of His deity. But in the very next verse, we read, "*For we have not an high priest which cannot be touched with the feeling of our infirmities; but was in all points tempted like as we are, yet without sin*"—one of the Bible's plainest declarations of the fullness and completeness of His humanity.

The doctrine of the deity of Jesus Christ and the doctrine of the humanity of Jesus Christ go hand in hand in the Bible. What kind of a Savior, what kind of a Lord Jesus, do you believe in? Do you believe in a Savior who is man and man only? Then you do not believe in the Savior who is presented in the Bible. On the other hand, do you believe in a Savior who is God and God only? Then you do not believe in the Savior of the Bible. The Lord Jesus, our Lord and Savior, presented to us in the Bible, is very God of very God and, at the same time, is our brother, our fellowman, and is not ashamed to call us brethren. (See Hebrews 2:11.)

Oh, I thank God that I have a Savior who is God, possessing all the attributes and powers of Deity, all the perfections of Deity—a Savior for whom nothing is too hard. I thank God that my Savior is One who made the heavens and the earth, and who holds all the powers of nature and of history in His control. But I equally thank God that my Savior is my brother man, One who was tempted in all points as I am. (See Hebrews 4:15.) I truly thank God that my Savior was in a position to bear my sins (see Hebrews 9:28), on the one hand because He is God, on the other hand because He is man. A merely divine Savior could not be a Savior for me. A merely human Savior could not be a Savior for me. But a Savior in whom Deity and humanity meet, a Savior who is at once God and man, is just the Savior I need, and just the Savior you need. He is a Savior who "*is able also to save them to the uttermost*" (Hebrews 7:25) all who come to God through Him.

6

IS THE HOLY SPIRIT A PERSON?

The communion of the Holy Ghost, be with you all.
—2 Corinthians 13:14

The doctrine of the personhood of the Holy Spirit is both fundamental and vital. Anyone who does not know the Holy Spirit as a person has not arrived at a complete and well-rounded Christian experience. Anyone who knows God the Father and God the Son but does not know God the Holy Spirit has not arrived at the Christian understanding of God. At first glance, it may seem to you that the doctrine of the personhood of the Holy Spirit is a purely technical and apparently impractical doctrine, but it is not. As we will see shortly, the doctrine of the personhood of the Holy Spirit is a doctrine of utmost practical importance.

The Importance of the Doctrine of the Personhood of the Holy Spirit

From the Standpoint of Worship

This doctrine is vital from the standpoint of worship. If we do not know the Holy Spirit as a divine person, if we think of Him as only an impersonal influence or power, then we are robbing a divine person of the worship that is His due, and the love that is His due, and the trust and surrender and obedience that are His due.

May I stop at this point to ask you, "Do you worship the Holy Spirit?" Theoretically, we all do, every time we sing the doxology,

> Praise God from whom all blessings flow,
> Praise Him all creatures here below.
> Praise Him above, ye heavenly hosts,
> Praise Father, Son, *and Holy Ghost.*

Theoretically, we all do, every time we sing the Gloria Patri: "Glory be to the Father and to the Son *and to the Holy Ghost,* as it was in the beginning, is now, and ever shall be, world without end. Amen." But it is one thing to do a thing theoretically and quite another thing to do it in actuality. It is one thing to sing words and quite another thing to realize the meaning and the force of the words that we sing.

I had a striking illustration of this some years ago. I was going to a Bible conference in New York State. I had to pass through a city four miles from the place where the conference was being held. A relative of mine lived in that city, and on the way to the conference I stopped to see my relative, who went with me to the conference. This relative was much older than I and had been a Christian much longer than I. She was a member of the Presbyterian Church and was thoroughly orthodox. That morning at the conference, I spoke on the personhood of the Holy Spirit. After the meeting was over, we were standing on the veranda of the hotel when she turned to me and said, "Archie, I never thought of *it* before as a person." Well, I had never thought of *it* as a person, but thank God I had come to know *Him* as a person.

From a Practical Standpoint

In the second place, it is of the highest importance from a practical standpoint that we know the Holy Spirit as a person. If you think of the Holy Spirit, as even so many Christians do, as a mere influence or power, then your thought will be, "How can I get hold of the Holy Spirit and use it?" But if you think of Him in the biblical way, as a divine person, your thought will be, "How can the Holy Spirit get hold of me and use me?" There is a great difference between man—the worm—using God to thresh the mountain, and God using man, the worm, to thresh the mountain. (See Isaiah 41:14–15.) The former concept is heathenish; essentially, it is no different from the concept of primitive tribes in Africa using magical charms and trying to control their gods. On the other hand, the concept of God the Holy Spirit getting hold of and using us is sublime and Christian.

Again, if you think of the Holy Spirit merely as an influence or power, your thought will be, "How can I get more of the Holy Spirit?" But if you think of Him in the biblical way as a person, your thought will be, "How can the Holy Spirit get more of me?"

The concept of the Holy Spirit as a mere influence or power inevitably leads to self-confidence, self-exaltation, and the parade of self. If you think of the Holy Spirit as an influence or power, and then fancy that you have received the Holy Spirit, the inevitable result will be that you will strut around as if you belonged to a superior order of Christians. I remember a woman who came to me one afternoon at the Northfield Bible Conference and said to me, "Brother Torrey, I want to ask you a question. But before I do, I want you to understand that I am a Holy Spirit woman." Her words made me shudder.

On the other hand, if you think of the Holy Spirit in the biblical way, as a divine person of infinite majesty who comes to dwell in our hearts and take possession of us and use us, you are led to self-renunciation, self-denial, and deep humility. I know of no thought that is more calculated to induce meekness than this great biblical truth about the Holy Spirit.

From the Standpoint of Experience

The doctrine of the personhood of the Holy Spirit is of the highest importance from the standpoint of experience. Thousands and tens of thousands of Christian men and women can testify to an entire transformation in their lives through coming to know the Holy Spirit as a person. In fact, this subject of the personhood of the Holy Spirit, which I have covered in almost every city in which I have held a series of meetings, is in some respects the deepest and most technical subject that I have ever attempted to handle before a public audience. Yet, notwithstanding that fact, more men and women have come to me or written to me at the close of the meetings, testifying to personal blessing received, than after covering any other subject that God has permitted me to speak on.

Four Proofs of the Personhood of the Holy Spirit

There are four separate and distinct proofs of the personhood of the Holy Spirit.

The Holy Spirit Has Characteristics That Only a Person Could Have

The first proof of the personhood of the Holy Spirit is that all the distinctive marks or characteristics of personhood are ascribed to the Holy Spirit in the Bible. What are the distinctive characteristics of personhood? Knowledge, will, and feeling. Any being who knows and wills and feels is a person. Often, when I say that the Holy Spirit is a person, people think that I mean that the Holy Spirit has hands and feet and fingers and toes and eyes and ears and so on. But these are not the marks of personhood;

these are the marks of bodily existence. Any being who knows, wills, and feels is a person, whether he has a body or not. Now, all three characteristics of personhood are ascribed to the Holy Spirit in the Bible.

Knowledge

Read, for instance, 1 Corinthians 2:11:

> *For what man knoweth the things of a man, save the spirit of man which is in him? Even so the things of God knoweth no man, but the Spirit of God.*

Here knowledge is ascribed to the Holy Spirit. In other words, the Holy Spirit is not a mere illumination that comes to our minds whereby our minds are cleared and strengthened to see truth that they would not otherwise discover. The Holy Spirit is a person who Himself knows the things of God and reveals to us what He knows.

Will

We read in 1 Corinthians 12:11, *"But all these worketh that one and the selfsame Spirit, dividing to every man severally as he will."* In this verse, will is ascribed to the Holy Spirit. Clearly the thought is not that the Holy Spirit is a divine power that we get hold of and use according to our will, but that the Holy Spirit is a person who gets hold of us and uses us according to His will. This is one of the most fundamental facts about the Holy Spirit that we must bear in mind if we are to get into right relationship with Him.

More people are going astray at this point than almost any other. They are trying to acquire some divine power that they can use according to their own will. I thank God that there is no divine power that I can possess and use according to my will. What could I, in my foolishness and ignorance, do with a divine power? What evil I might work! On the other hand, I am even gladder that while there is no divine power that I can get hold of and use according to my foolish will, there is a divine person who can get hold of me and use me according to His infinitely wise and loving will.

Romans 8:27 tells us, *"And he that searcheth the hearts knoweth what is the mind of the Spirit, because he maketh intercession for the saints according to the will of God."* What I wish you to notice here is the expression *"the mind of the Spirit."* The Greek word here translated *"mind"* is a comprehensive word that has in it the ideas of both thought and purpose. It is the same word that is used in the seventh verse of the chapter, where we read, *"The carnal mind is enmity against God."* This does not mean merely that the thought of the flesh is against God, but that the whole moral and intellectual life of the flesh is against God.

Feeling

Now let us look at a most remarkable passage:

> *Now I beseech you, brethren, for the Lord Jesus Christ's sake, and for the love of the Spirit, that ye strive together with me in your prayers to God for me.* (Romans 15:30)

What I wish you to notice in this verse are the words *"the love of the Spirit."* That the Holy Spirit loves us is a wonderful thought. It teaches us that the Holy Spirit is not a mere blind influence or power that comes into our hearts and lives. He is a divine person, loving us with the tenderest love.

I wonder how many believers have ever thought much about *"the love of the Spirit."* I wonder how many ministers have ever preached a sermon on *"the love of the Spirit."* Every day of your life you kneel down before God the Father, at least I hope you do, and say, "Heavenly Father, I thank You for Your great love that led You to give Your Son to come down to this world and die on the cross of Calvary in my place." Every day of your life you kneel down before Jesus Christ the Son and say, "Blessed Son of God, I thank You for that great love of Yours that led You to come down to this world in obedience to the Father and die in my place on the cross of Calvary." But have you ever knelt down and looked to the Holy Spirit and said to Him, "Holy Spirit, I thank You for that great love of Yours"?

We owe our salvation as much to the love of the Holy Spirit as we do to the love of the Father and of the Son. If it had not been for the love of

God the Father looking down on me in my lost state, yes, anticipating my fall and ruin and sending His Son down to this world to die on the cross, to die in my place, I would be in hell today. If it had not been for the love of Jesus Christ the Son, who came down to this world in obedience to the Father to lay down His life, who was a perfect atoning sacrifice on the cross of Cavalry in my place, I would be in hell today. But if it had not been for the love of the Holy Spirit, who came down to this world in obedience to the Father and the Son and sought me out in my lost condition, I would be in hell today.

The Holy Spirit continued to follow me when I would not listen to Him, when I deliberately turned my back on Him, when I insulted Him. He followed me into places where it must have been agony for One so holy to go. He followed me day after day, week after week, month after month, year after year, until at last He succeeded in bringing me to my senses. He brought me to realize my utterly lost condition and revealed the Lord Jesus to me as just the Savior I needed. He induced me and enabled me to receive the Lord Jesus as my Savior and my Lord. I repeat: if it had not been for this patient, long-suffering, never-wearying love of the Spirit of God for me, I would be in hell today.

Now let us consider Ephesians 4:30: *"And grieve not the holy Spirit of God, whereby ye are sealed unto the day of redemption."* Here grief is ascribed to the Holy Spirit. In other words, the Holy Spirit is not a mere blind impersonal influence or power that comes to dwell in your heart and mine. He is a person—a person who loves us, a person who is holy and intensely sensitive toward sin, a person who recoils from sin in what we call its slightest forms as the holiest person on earth never recoiled from sin in its grossest and most repulsive forms.

The Holy Spirit sees whatever we do; He hears whatever we say; He knows our very thoughts. Not a wandering thought is allowed a moment's lodging in our minds without His knowing it. If there is anything impure, unholy, immodest, untrue, harsh, or unChristlike in any way, He is grieved beyond expression. This truth about the Holy Spirit is a wonderful thought. It is the strongest incentive of which I know to walk a Christian walk.

How many a young man is kept back from doing things that he would otherwise do by the thought that, if he did do them, his mother might hear of his actions and be grieved beyond expression? Many a young man has come to the big city and, in a time of temptation, has been about to go into a place that no self-respecting man ought ever to enter. But just as his hand has been on the doorknob and he has been about to open the door, the thought has come to him, "If I go in, Mother might hear about it. If she did, it would nearly kill her," and he has turned away without entering.

There is One holier than the holiest mother that any of us has ever known, One who loves us with a tenderer love than the love with which our own mothers love us, One who sees everything we do, not only in the daylight but under the cover of night. He hears every word we utter, every careless word that escapes our lips. He knows our every thought; yes, He knows every fleeting notion that we allow a moment's entertainment in our minds. If there is anything unholy, impure, immodest, improper, unkind, harsh, or unChristlike in any way, in act or word or thought, He sees it and is grieved beyond expression.

Oh, how often there has come into my mind some thought or imagination—I do not know from what source—that I ought not to entertain. Just as I have been about to dwell on it, the thought has come, "The Holy Spirit sees that and will be grieved by it," and the improper thought has left.

Keeping this truth about the Holy Spirit in our minds will help us to solve all the questions that perplex the young believer today. Take, for example, the question, "Should I as a Christian go to the movies?" Well, if you go, the Holy Spirit will go, for He dwells in the heart of every believer and goes wherever the believer goes. Would the atmosphere of the place be congenial to the Holy Spirit? If not, do not go. "Should I as a Christian go to a dance?" Well, here again, if you go, the Holy Spirit will surely go. Would the atmosphere of the place be congenial to the Holy Spirit? If not, do not go. "Should I as a Christian go somewhere with my friends to play cards?" Would the atmosphere of the place be congenial to the Holy Spirit? If not, do not go.

With the questions that come up and that some of us find so hard to settle, this thought of the Holy Spirit will help you to settle them all, and to settle them right—if you really desire to settle them right and not merely to do the thing that pleases you.

Characteristics Revealed in the Old Testament

Now let us look at a passage in the Old Testament:

> *Thou gavest also thy good spirit to instruct them, and withheldest not thy manna from their mouth, and gavest them water for their thirst.*
> (Nehemiah 9:20)

In this verse, both intelligence and goodness are ascribed to the Holy Spirit. This passage does not add anything to what I have already said on this matter; I include it simply because it is from the Old Testament. There are those who say that the doctrine of the personhood of the Holy Spirit is in the New Testament but is not in the Old Testament. But here we find it as clearly in the Old Testament as in the New. Of course, we do not find it as frequently in the Old Testament, for the dispensation of the Holy Spirit began in the New Testament. But the doctrine of the personhood of the Holy Spirit is most certainly in the Old Testament.

The Holy Spirit Performs Actions That Only a Person Could Perform

The second proof of the personhood of the Holy Spirit is this: many actions are ascribed to the Holy Spirit that only a person could perform. Many biblical examples illustrate this point, but I will limit our consideration to three instances.

The Holy Spirit Searches the Deep Things of God

We will first consider 1 Corinthians 2:10: *"But God hath revealed them unto us by his Spirit: for the Spirit searcheth all things, yea, the deep things of God."* Here the Holy Spirit is represented as searching the deep things of

God. In other words, as I have already said, the Holy Spirit is not a mere illumination whereby our minds are made clear and strong to comprehend truth that we would not otherwise discover. The Holy Spirit is a person who searches the deep things of God and reveals to us the things that He discovers. Such words could only be spoken of a person.

The Holy Spirit Prays

In Romans, we read,

> *Likewise the Spirit also helpeth our infirmities: for we know not what we should pray for as we ought: but the Spirit itself maketh intercession for us with groanings which cannot be uttered.* (Romans 8:26)

Here the Holy Spirit is represented as doing what only a person could do—praying. The Holy Spirit is not a mere influence that comes to impel us to prayer. He is not a mere guidance to us in offering our prayers. He is a person who Himself prays. Every believer in Christ has two divine Persons praying for him. First, the Son, our Advocate with the Father, who always lives to make intercession for us at the right hand of God in the place of power. (See 1 John 2:1 and Hebrews 7:25.) Second, the Holy Spirit, who prays through us on earth. Oh, what a wonderful thought, that we have these two divine Persons praying for us every day! What a sense it gives us of our security.

The Holy Spirit Teaches

Now let us consider two other closely related passages. Both are found in John's gospel:

> *But the Comforter, which is the Holy Ghost, whom the Father will send in my name, he shall teach you all things, and bring all things to your remembrance, whatsoever I have said unto you.* (John 14:26)

Here the Holy Spirit is represented as doing what only a person could do, namely, teaching. We have the same thought in John 16:12–14:

> *I have yet many things to say unto you, but ye cannot bear them now. Howbeit when he, the Spirit of truth, is come, he will guide you into all truth: for he shall not speak of himself; but whatsoever he shall hear, that shall he speak: and he will show you things to come. He shall glorify me: for he shall receive of mine, and shall show it unto you.*

Here, again, the Holy Spirit is represented as a living, personal teacher. It is our privilege to have the living person of the Holy Spirit today as our Teacher. Every time we study our Bibles, it is possible for us to have this divine Person, the author of the Book, interpret it for us and teach us its meaning.

This truth about the Holy Spirit is a precious thought. When we have heard some great human teacher whom God has made a special blessing to us, many of us have thought, "Oh, if I could only hear that person every day, then I might make some progress in my Christian life." But every day we can have a teacher far more competent than the greatest human teacher who has ever spoken—the Holy Spirit.

The Holy Spirit Is Treated in Ways That Only a Person Could Be Treated

There is another proof of the personhood of the Holy Spirit: the Bible describes the Holy Spirit as being treated in ways that only a person could be treated. In Isaiah 63:10, we are taught that the Holy Spirit is "*rebelled* [against]" and "*vexed.*" You cannot rebel against or grieve a mere influence or power. Only a person can be rebelled against and grieved. In Acts 5:3, we are taught that people can "*lie to the Holy Ghost.*" One can only lie to a person. In Matthew 12:31, we read that there was a "*blasphemy against the Holy Ghost.*" We are told that blasphemy against the Holy Spirit is more serious than blasphemy against the Lord Jesus (see verse 32), and this certainly could only be said of a person, and a divine person.

The Holy Spirit Fills an Office That Only a Person Could Fill

The fourth proof of the personhood of the Holy Spirit is that an office is attributed to the Holy Spirit that could only be attributed to a person. Look, for example, at John 14:16–17. Here we read,

> *And I will pray the Father, and he shall give you another Comforter, that he may abide with you for ever; even the Spirit of truth; whom the world cannot receive, because it seeth him not, neither knoweth him: but ye know him; for he dwelleth with you, and shall be in you.*

Here the Holy Spirit is represented as *"another Comforter"* who was coming to take the place of our Lord Jesus. Up to this time, our Lord Jesus had always been the Friend at hand to help the disciples in every emergency that arose. But now He was leaving, and their hearts were filled with consternation. He told them that although He was going, Another was coming to take His place. Can you imagine our Lord Jesus saying this if the One who was coming to take His place had been a mere impersonal influence or power? If the One who was coming to take His place had not been another person but a mere influence or power, I could not imagine our Lord Jesus saying what He said in John 16:7,

> *Nevertheless I tell you the truth; it is expedient for you that I go away: for if I go not away, the Comforter will not come unto you; but if I depart, I will send him unto you.*

Is it conceivable for one moment for our Lord to say that it was to their advantage for Him, a divine person, to leave and for a mere influence or power, no matter how divine, to come to take His place? No! What our Lord said was that He, one divine Person, was going, but that another Person, just as divine, was coming to take His place.

To me, this promise is one of the most precious promises in the whole Word of God. During the absence of my Lord, until that glad day when He will come back again, another Person, just as divine as He, is by my side—yes, dwells in my heart every moment to commune with me and to help me in every emergency that can possibly arise.

The Meaning of the Word "Helper"

I suppose you know that the Greek word translated *"Helper"* in these verses means helper plus a whole lot besides. The Greek word so translated is *parakletos*. This word is a compound word, made up of the word *para*, which means "alongside," and *kletos*, which means "one called." So *parakletos* means "one called to stand alongside another"—to take his part and help him in every emergency that arises.

Parakletos is the word that is translated *"Advocate"* in 1 John 2:1: *"If any man sin, we have an advocate with the Father, Jesus Christ the righteous."* But the word *"advocate"* does not give the full force of the word *parakletos*. Etymologically, it means about the same. *Advocate* is a Latin word transliterated into the English. The word is a compound word made up of *ad*, meaning "to," and *vocatus*, meaning "one called," that is to say, "one called to another to take his part, to help him." But in our English usage, the word *advocate* has obtained a restricted sense. The Greek word, as I have already said, means "one called alongside another," and the thought is of a helper always at hand with his counsel and his strength and any form of help needed.

Up to this time, the Lord Jesus Himself had been the disciples' Paraclete, or their Friend always at hand to help. Whenever they got into any trouble, they simply turned to Jesus. For example, on one occasion they were perplexed about the subject of prayer. They said to Him, *"Lord, teach us to pray"* (Luke 11:1), and He taught them to pray. On another occasion, Jesus was coming to them by walking on the water. When their first fear was over and He had said, *"It is I; be not afraid"* (Matthew 14:27), Peter said to Him, *"Lord, if it be thou, bid me come unto thee on the water"* (verse 28). The Lord said to him, *"Come"* (verse 29). Then Peter clambered over the side of the fishing boat and started to go to Jesus by walking on the water. Seemingly, he turned around, took his eyes off the Lord, and looked at the fishing boat to see if the other disciples were noticing how well he was doing. But no sooner had he taken his eyes off the Lord and focused on his fears than he began to sink. He cried out, *"Lord, save me"* (verse 30), and Jesus reached out His hand and held him up.

In the same way, when the disciples got into any other emergency, they turned to the Lord, and He delivered them. Now He was leaving, and, as I said, consternation filled their hearts. But the Lord said to them, "Yes, I am going, but Another just as divine, just as able to help, is coming to take my place." This other Paraclete is with us wherever we go, every hour of the day or night. He is always by our side.

The Cure for Fear

If this thought gets into your heart and stays there, you will never have another moment of fear no matter how long you live. How can we fear in any circumstance if He is by our side? You may be surrounded by a howling mob, but what of it if He walks between you and the mob? This thought will banish all fear.

I had a striking illustration of this truth in my own experience some years ago. I was speaking at a Bible conference at Lake Kenka in New York State. A cousin of mine had a cottage four miles up the lake, and I went there and spent my day off with him. The next day he brought me down in his boat to where the conference was being held. As I stepped off the boat onto the pier, he said to me, "Come back again tonight and spend the night with us," and I promised him that I would. But I did not realize what I was promising.

That night, after the meeting, as I left the hotel and started on my walk, I found that I had undertaken a very difficult task. The cottage was four miles away, and a four-mile walk or an eight-mile walk was nothing under ordinary circumstances. But a storm was brewing; the whole sky was overcast. The path led along a cliff bordering the lake, and the path was near the edge of the cliff. Sometimes the lake was perhaps not more than ten or twelve feet below; at other times it was some thirty or forty feet below. I had never traveled on the path before, and since there was no starlight, I could not see the path at all. Furthermore, there had already been a storm that had torn out deep ditches across the path into which one might fall and break his leg. I could not see these ditches except when there was a sudden flash of lightning. I would see one, and then my surroundings would be darker and I would be blinder than ever.

As I walked along this path with all its furrows, so near the edge of the cliff, I felt it was perilous to make the trip and thought of going back. Then the thought came to me, "You promised that you would come tonight, and they might be sitting up waiting for you." So I felt that I must go on. But it seemed creepy and uncanny to walk along the edge of that cliff on a path that I could not see. I could only hear the sobbing and wailing and moaning of the lake at the foot of the cliff. Then the thought came to me, "What was it that you told the people there at the conference about the Holy Spirit being a person always by our side?" At once I realized that the Holy Spirit walked between me and the edge of the cliff, and that four miles through the dark was four miles without a fear—a cheerful instead of a fearful walk.

I once explained this thought in the Royal Albert Hall in London one dark, dismal February afternoon. There was a young lady in the audience who was very much afraid of the dark. It simply seemed impossible for her to go into a dark room alone. After the meeting was over, she hurried home and rushed into the room where her mother was sitting and cried, "Oh, Mother, I have heard the most wonderful message this afternoon about the Holy Spirit always being by our side as our ever present Helper and Protector. I will never be afraid of the dark again." Her mother was a practical Englishwoman and said to her, "Well, let us see how real this is. Go upstairs to the top floor, into the dark room; shut the door, and stay in there alone in the dark." The daughter went bounding up the stairs, went into the dark room, and closed the door. It was pitch dark. "Oh," she wrote me the next day, "it was dark, utterly dark, but that room was bright and glorious with the presence of the Holy Spirit."

The Cure for Insomnia

In this thought is also the cure for insomnia. Have you ever had insomnia? I have. For two dark, awful years. Night after night, I would go to bed, almost dead, as it seemed to me, for lack of sleep, and I thought I would certainly sleep since I could hardly stay awake. But scarcely had my head touched the pillow when I knew I would not sleep. I would hear the clock strike twelve, one, two, three, four, five, six, and then it was time to get up. It seemed as though I did not sleep at all, though I have no doubt I did, for I believe that people who suffer from insomnia sleep more than they think they do, or else they would die. But it seemed as if I did not sleep at all. This went on for two whole years, until I thought that if I could not get sleep, I would lose my mind.

Then I received deliverance. For years thereafter, I would retire and fall asleep about as soon as my head touched the pillow. But one night I went to bed in the Bible Institute in Chicago, where I was then staying. I expected to fall asleep almost immediately, as had become my custom, but scarcely had my head touched the pillow when I knew I was not going to sleep. Insomnia was back. If you have ever had it, you will always recognize it. It seemed as if Insomnia were sitting on the foot of my bed looking like an imp, grinning at me and saying, "I'm back for two more years."

"Oh," I thought, "two more years of this awful insomnia." But that very morning I had been teaching the students in the lecture room on the floor below about the personhood of the Holy Spirit, and the thought came to me almost immediately, "What was that you were telling the students downstairs this morning about the Holy Spirit always being with us?" And I said, "Why don't you practice what you preach?" I looked up and said, "O blessed Holy Spirit of God, You are here. If You have anything to say to me, I will listen." And He opened to me some of the sweet and precious things about Jesus Christ, filling my soul with calm and peace and joy. The next thing I knew I was asleep, and then it was the next morning. Whenever Insomnia has come around since and sat on the foot of my bed, I have done the same thing, and relying on the Holy Spirit has never failed.

The Cure for Loneliness

Also in this thought of the Holy Spirit as our Helper is a cure for all loneliness. If the thought of the Holy Spirit as an ever present friend once enters your heart and stays there, you will never have another lonely moment as long as you live. For the majority of the last sixteen years, my life has been a lonely life. I have often been separated from my whole family for months at a time. Sometimes I have not seen my wife for two or three months, and for eighteen months I was with my wife but did not see any other member of my family.

One night I was walking the deck of a ship in the South Seas between New Zealand and Tasmania. It was a stormy night. Most of the other passengers were below, sick; none of the officers or sailors could walk with me because they had their hands full looking after the boat. I walked the deck alone. Four of the five other members of my family were on the other side of the globe, seventeen thousand miles away by the nearest route that I could get to them. And the one member of my family who was nearer was not with me that night. As I walked the deck alone, I got to thinking about my four children seventeen thousand miles away and was about to get lonesome when the thought came to me of the Holy Spirit by my side. I knew that as I walked He took every step with me, and all loneliness was gone.

I expressed this thought some years ago in the city of Saint Paul. At the close of the meeting, a physician came to me and said, "I wish to thank you for that thought. I am often called to go out alone at night, through darkness and storm, to attend to a sick patient, and I have been very lonely. But I will never be lonely again, for I will know that every mile of the way the Holy Spirit is beside me."

The Cure for a Broken Heart

In this same precious truth there is a cure for a broken heart. Oh, how many brokenhearted people there are in the world today! Many of us have lost loved ones. But we need not have a moment's heartache if we only know *"the communion of the Holy Ghost"* (2 Corinthians 13:14). There is perhaps some woman who a year ago, or a few months ago, or a few weeks ago, or a few days ago, had by her side a man whom she dearly loved, a man so strong and wise that she was freed from all sense of responsibility and care, for all the burdens were on him. How bright and happy life was in his companionship! But the dark day came when that loved one was taken away, and how lonely, empty, barren, and full of burden and care life is today! Listen! There is One who walks right by your side, wiser and stronger and more loving than the wisest and strongest and most loving husband who has ever lived, ready to bear all the burdens and responsibilities of life. Yes, He is ready to do far more. He is ready to come and dwell in your heart and fill every nook and corner of your empty, aching heart, and thus banish all loneliness and heartache forever.

I made this statement one afternoon in Saint Andrews Hall in Glasgow. At the close of the meeting, when I went to the reception room, a lady who had hurried along to meet me approached me. She wore the customary clothing of a widow, her face bore the marks of deep sorrow, but now there was a happy look in her face. She hurried to me and said, "Doctor Torrey, this is the anniversary of my dear husband's death," (her husband was one of the most highly esteemed Christian men in Glasgow) "and I came to Saint Andrews Hall today saying to myself, 'Doctor Torrey will have something to say that will help me.' Oh," she continued, "you have said just the right thing! I will never be lonesome again, never have a heartache again. I will let the Holy Spirit come in and fill every aching corner of my heart."

Eighteen months passed. I was in Scotland again, taking a short vacation on the Clyde River on the private yacht of a friend. One day, when we stopped, a little boat came alongside the yacht. The first one who clambered up the side of the yacht and onto the deck was this widow. Seeing me standing on the deck, she hurried across and took my hand in both of hers, and with a radiant smile on her face she said, "Oh, Doctor Torrey, the thought you gave me in Saint Andrews Hall that afternoon stays with me still, and I have not had a lonely or sad hour from that day to this."

Help in Our Christian Work

It is in our Christian work that this thought comes to us with the greatest power and helpfulness. Take my own experience as an example. I became a minister simply because I had to or be forever lost. I do not mean that I am saved by preaching the gospel. I am saved simply on the ground of Christ's atoning blood and that alone, but my becoming a Christian and accepting Him as my Savior depended on my preaching the gospel. For six years I refused to become a Christian because I was unwilling to preach, and I felt that if I became a Christian I must preach. The night that I was converted I did not say, "I will accept Christ" or "I will give up my sins." I said, "I will preach."

But if there was ever a man who by natural temperament was unfit to preach, it was I. I was an abnormally bashful boy. A stranger could scarcely speak to me without my blushing to the roots of my hair. Of all the tortures I endured at school, none was so great as that of reciting in front of the class. To stand up on the platform and have all the other students looking at me—I could scarcely endure it. When I had to recite and my own mother and father asked me to recite to them before I went to school, I simply could not recite in front of my own parents. Think of a man like that going into the ministry!

Even after I started attending Yale College, when I would go home on a vacation and my mother would have visitors and send for me to come in and meet them, I could not say a word. After they were gone, my mother would say to me, "Archie, why didn't you say something to Mrs. So-and-So," and I would say, "Why, Mother, I did!" She would reply, "You didn't utter a sound." I thought I had, but the sound would come no farther than my throat and would there be smothered.

I was so bashful that I would never even speak in a church prayer meeting until after I entered the theological seminary. Then I thought that if I was to be a preacher, I must at least be able to speak in my own church prayer meeting. Making up my mind that I would, I learned a little message by heart. I remember some of it now, but I think I forgot much of it when I got up to speak that night. As soon as the meeting started, I grasped the back of the seat in front of me, pulled myself up to my feet, and held on to that seat so that I would not fall. I tremblingly repeated as much of my little message as I could remember and then dropped back into my seat. At the close of the meeting, a dear old lady, a lovely Christian woman, came to me and encouragingly said, "Oh, Mr. Torrey, I want to thank you for what you said tonight. It did me so much good. You spoke with so much feeling." Feeling! The only feeling I had was that I was scared nearly to death. Think of a man like that going into the ministry!

My first years in the ministry were torture. I would preach three times each Sunday. I would commit my sermons to memory, and then I would stand up and twist the top button of my coat until I had twisted the sermon out. Then, when the third sermon was preached and finished, I would drop back into my seat with a great sense of relief that that was over for another week. Then the thought would take hold of me, "Well, you have to begin tomorrow morning to get ready for next Sunday!"

But a glad day came when the truth I am trying to teach you took possession of me. That truth is this: when I stood up to preach, though people saw me, there was Another who stood by my side whom they did not see, but upon whom was all the responsibility for the meeting. All that I had to do was to get as far back out of sight as possible and let Him do the preaching. From that day, preaching has been the joy of my life. I would rather preach than eat. Sometimes, when I rise to preach, before I have uttered a word, the thought of Him standing beside me, able and willing to take charge of the whole meeting and do whatever needs to be done, has so filled my heart with exultant joy that I have felt like shouting.

The same thought applies to Sunday school teaching. Perhaps you worry about your Sunday school class for fear that you will say something that ought not to be said, or leave unsaid something that ought to be said. The thought of the burden and responsibility almost crushes you. Listen! Always remember this as you teach your class: there is One right beside you who knows just what ought to be said and just what ought to be done. Instead of carrying the responsibility of the class, let Him carry it; let Him do the teaching.

One Monday morning I met one of the most faithful laymen I have ever known, and a very gifted Bible teacher. He was deep in the blues over his failure with his class the day before—at least, what he regarded as failure. He unburdened his heart to me. I said to him, "Mr. Dyer, did you not ask God to give you wisdom as you went before that class?" He said, "I did." I said, "Did you not expect Him to give it?" He said, "I did." Then I said, "What right have you to doubt that He did?" He replied, "I never thought of that before. I will never worry about my class again."

The same thought applies to personal ministry. At the close of a meeting, when the pastor urges those who are saved to go and speak to someone about his soul's salvation, oh, how many of you want to go, but you do not stir. You think to yourself, "I might say the wrong thing." You will if *you* say it. You will certainly say the wrong thing. But trust the Holy Spirit—He will say the right thing. Let Him have your lips to speak through. It may not appear the right thing at the time, but sometime you will find out that it was just the right thing.

One night in Launceston, Tasmania, as Mrs. Torrey and I left the meeting, my wife said to me, "Archie, I wasted my whole evening. I have been talking to the most frivolous girl. I don't think that she has a serious thought in her head." I replied, "Clara, how do you know? Did you not trust God to guide you?" "Yes." "Well, leave it with Him." The very next night at the close of the meeting, the same seemingly frivolous girl came up to Mrs. Torrey, leading her mother by the hand, and said, "Mrs. Torrey, won't you speak to my mother? You led me to Christ last night; now please lead my mother to Christ."

Conclusion

So we see by these many examples that the Holy Spirit is a person. Theoretically, you probably believed this before, but do you, in your real thoughts of Him, in your practical attitude toward Him, treat Him as a person? Do you really regard Him as just as real a person as Jesus Christ is—as loving, as wise, as strong, as worthy of our confidence and love and surrender? Do you see Him as a divine person always by your side?

After our Lord's departure, the Holy Spirit came into this world to be to the disciples, and to be to us, what Jesus Christ had been to them during the days of His personal companionship with them. Is He that to you today? Do you know *"the communion of the Holy Ghost"* (2 Corinthians 13:14)—the companionship of the Holy Spirit, the partnership of the Holy Spirit, the fellowship of the Holy Spirit, the comradeship of the Holy Spirit? To put it simply, the whole purpose of this chapter—I say it reverently—is to introduce you to my Friend, the Holy Spirit.

7

IS THE HOLY SPIRIT GOD, AND IS HE SEPARATE FROM THE FATHER AND SON?

The grace of the Lord Jesus Christ, and the love of God, and the communion of the Holy Ghost, be with you all.
—2 Corinthians 13:14

In the previous chapter, I wrote about the personhood of the Holy Spirit. We saw clearly that the Holy Spirit is a person. I referred to His deity in passing but did not dwell on it; so the question remains, Is the Holy Spirit a divine person? And still another question remains: If the Holy Spirit is a divine person, is He separate and distinct from the Father and the Son? In this chapter, we will consider what the Bible teaches on these subjects.

Proofs of the Deity of the Holy Spirit

First, let us examine the question of the deity of the Holy Spirit. The fact that the Holy Spirit is a person does not prove that He is divine. There are spirits who are persons but are not God. However, there are five distinct proofs of the deity of the Holy Spirit.

The Holy Spirit's Divine Attributes Prove His Deity

The first proof that the Holy Spirit is God is that four distinctively divine attributes are ascribed to the Holy Spirit in the Bible. As I mentioned in the chapter on the deity of Christ, when I speak of distinctively divine attributes, I am speaking of attributes that God alone possesses. Any person who has these attributes must therefore be God. These four distinctively divine attributes are omnipotence, omniscience, omnipresence, and eternity.

Omnipotence

First of all, omnipotence is ascribed to the Holy Spirit. Take, for example, this verse in Luke:

> *And the angel answered and said unto her, The Holy Ghost shall come upon thee, and the power of the Highest shall overshadow thee: therefore also that holy thing which shall be born of thee shall be called the Son of God.* (Luke 1:35)

This passage plainly declares that the Holy Spirit has the power of the Highest, that He is omnipotent.

Omniscience

In the second place, omniscience is ascribed to the Holy Spirit. This is done, for example, in 1 Corinthians 2:10–11:

But God hath revealed them unto us by his Spirit: for the Spirit searcheth all things, yea, the deep things of God. For what man knoweth the things of a man, save the spirit of man which is in him? Even so the things of God knoweth no man, but the Spirit of God.

Here we are distinctly told that the Holy Spirit searches all things and knows all things, even the deep things of God.

We find the same thought again in the fourteenth chapter of John:

But the Comforter, which is the Holy Ghost, whom the Father will send in my name, he shall teach you all things, and bring all things to your remembrance, whatsoever I have said unto you. (John 14:26)

Here we are distinctly told that the Holy Spirit teaches all things; therefore, He must know all things.

This truth is stated even more explicitly in John 16:12–13:

I have yet many things to say unto you, but ye cannot bear them now. Howbeit when he, the Spirit of truth, is come, he will guide you into all truth: for he shall not speak of himself; but whatsoever he shall hear, that shall he speak: and he will show you things to come.

In all these passages, it is either directly declared or unmistakably implied that the Holy Spirit knows all things, that He is omniscient.

Omnipresence

Thirdly, omnipresence is ascribed to the Holy Spirit. We find this in the Psalms:

Whither shall I go from thy spirit? or whither shall I flee from thy presence? If I ascend up into heaven, thou art there: if I make my bed in hell, behold, thou art there. If I take the wings of the morning, and dwell in the uttermost parts of the sea; even there shall thy hand lead me, and thy right hand shall hold me. (Psalm 139:7–10)

Here we are told in the most explicit and unmistakable way that the Spirit of God, the Holy Spirit, is everywhere. There is no place in heaven, earth, or Hades, where we can go from His presence.

Eternity

Eternity is also ascribed to the Holy Spirit. This we find in Hebrews 9:14, where we read,

> *How much more shall the blood of Christ, who through the eternal Spirit offered himself without spot to God, purge your conscience from dead works to serve the living God?*

Here we find the words *"the eternal Spirit"* just as elsewhere we find the words *"the eternal God"* (Deuteronomy 33:27).

Putting these different passages together, we see clearly that each of four distinctively divine attributes, four attributes that no one but God possesses, is ascribed to the Holy Spirit.

The Holy Spirit's Divine Works Prove His Deity

The second proof of the true deity of the Holy Spirit is found in the fact that three distinctively divine works are ascribed to the Holy Spirit. That is to say, the Holy Spirit is said to do three things that God alone can do.

Creation

The first of these distinctively divine works is the one that we always think of first when we think of God's work—the work of creation. We find creation ascribed to the Holy Spirit in Job 33:4: *"The spirit of God hath made me, and the breath of the Almighty hath given me life."* We find the same thing implied in Psalm 104:30: *"Thou sendest forth thy spirit, they are created: and thou renewest the face of the earth."* In these two passages, the most distinctively divine of all works—the work of creation—is ascribed to the Holy Spirit.

Impartation of Life

The impartation of life is also ascribed to the Holy Spirit. This we find, for example, in John 6:63: *"It is the spirit that quickeneth; the flesh profiteth nothing."* We find the same thing again in Romans 8:11:

> *But if the Spirit of him that raised up Jesus from the dead dwell in you, he that raised up Christ from the dead shall also quicken your mortal bodies by his Spirit that dwelleth in you.*

In this passage, we do not have merely the impartation of life to the spirit of man, but the impartation of life to the body of man in the resurrection.

Man's creation and the impartation of life to man are ascribed to the operation of the Holy Spirit in Genesis, where we read,

> *And the Lord God formed man of the dust of the ground, and breathed into his nostrils the breath of life; and man became a living soul.*
>
> (Genesis 2:7)

Here we are told that man was created and became a living soul through God's breathing into him the breath of life. These words clearly imply that man's creation was through the instrumentality of the Holy Spirit, for the Holy Spirit is the breath of God going out in a personal way.

Authorship of Divine Prophecies

The third divine work ascribed to the Holy Spirit is the authorship of divine prophecies. We find this, for example, in 2 Peter 1:21: *"For the prophecy came not in old time by the will of man: but holy men of God spake as they were moved by the Holy Ghost."* Here we are distinctly told that it was through the operation of the Holy Spirit that men were made the mouthpiece of God and uttered God's truth. We find this same thought in 2 Samuel:

> *The spirit of the Lord spake by me, and his word was in my tongue. The God of Israel said, the Rock of Israel spake to me.*
>
> (2 Samuel 23:2–3)

In this passage, the authorship of God's prophecies is ascribed to the Holy Spirit.

Putting all these passages together, we see that three distinctively divine works are ascribed to the Holy Spirit.

A Comparison of Old Testament and New Testament Verses Proves His Deity

The third proof of the deity of the Holy Spirit is found in the fact that passages that refer to Jehovah in the Old Testament are taken to refer to the Holy Spirit in the New Testament. There are numerous instances of this—not as numerous as in the case of Jesus Christ the Son, yet enough to make it perfectly clear that the Holy Spirit occupies the same place in New Testament thought that Jehovah occupies in Old Testament thought.

Isaiah 6:8–10 and Acts 28:25–27

A striking illustration of this is found in Isaiah 6:8–10, where we read,

> *Also I heard the voice of the Lord, saying, Whom shall I send, and who will go for us? Then said I, Here am I; send me. And he said, Go, and tell this people, Hear ye indeed, but understand not; and see ye indeed, but perceive not. Make the heart of this people fat, and make their ears heavy, and shut their eyes; lest they see with their eyes, and hear with their ears, and understand with their heart, and convert, and be healed.*

Here we are distinctly told it is *"the Lord"*—and the context shows that *"the Lord"* is the Lord Jehovah—who is speaking. But when we turn to Acts 28:25–27, we read these words:

> *And when they agreed not among themselves, they departed, after that Paul had spoken one word, Well spake the Holy Ghost by Esaias the prophet unto our fathers, saying, Go unto this people, and say, Hearing ye shall hear, and shall not understand; and seeing ye shall see, and not perceive: for the heart of this people is waxed gross, and their ears are*

> *dull of hearing, and their eyes have they closed; lest they should see with their eyes, and hear with their ears, and understand with their heart, and should be converted, and I should heal them.*

In the Old Testament, we are told that the Lord Jehovah is the speaker; in the New Testament, we read that the Holy Spirit is the speaker. The Holy Spirit occupies the place in New Testament thought that the Lord Jehovah occupies in Old Testament thought.

It is notable that this same passage is applied to Jesus Christ in John 12:39–41. In the same chapter of Isaiah, in the threefold "*holy*" (Isaiah 6:3) in the seraphic cry, do we not have a hint of the tri-personhood of Jehovah of Hosts? Is it then not proper to have a threefold application of Isaiah's vision?

Exodus 16:7 and Hebrews 3:7–9

Another illustration of a statement that in the Old Testament refers to Jehovah but in the New Testament refers to the Holy Spirit, is found by a comparison of Exodus 16:7 with Hebrews 3:7–9. In Exodus 16:7, we read,

> *And in the morning, then ye shall see the glory of the LORD; for that he heareth your murmurings against the LORD; and what are we, that ye murmur against us?*

Here we are told that the murmuring and provocation of the children of Israel in the wilderness were against Jehovah. But in the third chapter of Hebrews, we read,

> *Wherefore (as the Holy Ghost saith, To day if ye will hear his voice, harden not your hearts, as in the provocation, in the day of temptation in the wilderness: when your fathers tempted me, proved me, and saw my works forty years.* (Hebrews 3:7–9)

In this New Testament passage, we are told that it was the Holy Spirit whom they provoked in the wilderness. It is clear that the Holy Spirit occupies here in New Testament thought the position Jehovah occupies in Exodus 16:7 in Old Testament thought.

To sum up the passages in this section, we see that statements that in the Old Testament distinctly name the Lord, God, or Jehovah as their subject are applied to the Holy Spirit in the New Testament. That is to say, the Holy Spirit occupies the position of deity in New Testament thought.

The Name of the Holy Spirit Coupled with That of the Father and of the Son Proves His Deity

The fourth way that the deity of the Holy Spirit is clearly taught in the New Testament is that the name of the Holy Spirit is coupled with that of the Father and of the Son in a way in which it would be impossible for a reverent and thoughtful mind to couple the name of any finite being with that of Deity. There are numerous illustrations of this point. Three will suffice for our present purpose.

We read, for example, in 1 Corinthians 12:4–6:

> *There are diversities of gifts, but the same Spirit. And there are differences of administrations, but the same Lord. And there are diversities of operations, but it is the same God which worketh all in all.*

In this passage, we see the name of the Holy Spirit coupled with that of God and of the Lord on a ground of equality.

We see the same thing again in Matthew 28:19: "*Go ye therefore, and teach all nations, baptizing them in the name of the Father, and of the Son, and of the Holy Ghost.*" If the Holy Spirit were not God, it would be shocking to couple His name in this way with that of God the Father and of the Lord Jesus His Son.

Another striking illustration is found in 2 Corinthians 13:14: "*The grace of the Lord Jesus Christ, and the love of God, and the communion of the Holy Ghost, be with you all.*" Here the name of the Holy Spirit is coupled on a ground of equality with that of the Father and of the Son.

In all these passages, as we have seen, the name of the Holy Spirit is coupled with that of God in a way in which it would be impossible for an intelligent worshiper of the Lord to couple the name of any finite being with that of Deity.

The Fact That the Holy Spirit Is Called God Proves His Deity

The fifth way, and perhaps the most decisive way, in which the deity of the Holy Spirit is taught in the Bible, is that the Holy Spirit in so many words is called God. This we find in Acts 5:3–4:

> *But Peter said, Ananias, why hath Satan filled thine heart to lie to the Holy Ghost, and to keep back part of the price of the land? Whiles it remained, was it not thine own? And after it was sold, was it not in thine own power? Why hast thou conceived this thing in thine heart? Thou hast not lied unto men, but unto God.*

In the third verse, we are distinctly told that it was the Holy Spirit to whom Ananias had lied, while in the fourth verse, we are told that it was God to whom Ananias had lied. Putting the two statements together, we clearly see that the Holy Spirit is God.

All These Facts about the Holy Spirit Combined Prove His Deity

Allow me to sum up all that I have said about the deity of the Holy Spirit. We see that the Holy Spirit is a divine person by the following: several distinctively divine attributes are ascribed to the Holy Spirit; several distinctively divine works are ascribed to the Holy Spirit; statements that in the Old Testament distinctly name Jehovah, the Lord, or God as their subject distinctly name the Holy Spirit in the New Testament; the name of the Holy Spirit is coupled with that of God in a way in which it would be impossible to couple the name of any finite being with that of Deity; the Holy Spirit is called God.

In all these unmistakable ways, God distinctly proclaims in His Word that the Holy Spirit is a divine person. It is absolutely impossible for anyone who goes to the Bible to find out what it actually teaches—and not merely to twist and distort it to fit into his own preconceived notions—to come to any other conclusion than that the Holy Spirit is God.

Proofs of the Distinction between the Father, the Son, and the Holy Spirit

Now we come to the question: Is the Holy Spirit a person who is distinct from the Father and from the Son? He might be a person, as we have clearly seen that He is, and He might be a divine person, as we have just seen that He is. But at the same time, He might be only the same person who manifested Himself at times as the Father and at other times as the Son. In this case, there would not be three divine Persons in the Godhead, but one divine Person who variously manifested Himself as Father, Son, and Holy Spirit. So, again, the question that confronts us is, Is the Holy Spirit a person who is separate and distinct from the Father and the Son? This question is plainly answered in various passages in the New Testament.

Verses That Prove the Distinctiveness of the Person of the Holy Spirit

In the first place, we find this question answered in John 14:26 and John 15:26. In John 14:26, we read,

> *But the Comforter, which is the Holy Ghost, whom the Father will send in my name, he shall teach you all things, and bring all things to your remembrance, whatsoever I have said unto you.* (John 14:26)

In John 15:26, we read,

> *But when the Comforter is come, whom I will send unto you from the Father, even the Spirit of truth, which proceedeth from the Father, he shall testify of Me.*

In both of these passages, we are told that the Holy Spirit is a person entirely distinct from the Father and the Son, that He is sent from the

Father by the Son. Elsewhere we are taught that Jesus Christ was sent by the Father. (See John 6:29; 8:29, 42.) In these passages, it is as clear as language can make it that Father, Son, and Holy Spirit are not one and the same Person manifesting Himself in three different forms, but that they are three distinct Persons.

We find clear proof that the Father, Son, and Holy Spirit are three distinct Persons in John 16:13, where we read,

> *Howbeit when he, the Spirit of truth, is come, he will guide you into all truth: for he shall not speak of himself; but whatsoever he shall hear, that shall he speak: and he will show you things to come.* (John 16:13)

In this passage, the clearest possible distinction is drawn between the Holy Spirit who speaks and the One from whom He speaks. We are told in so many words that this One from whom the Spirit speaks is not Himself, but Another.

In the next verse, the same thought is brought out in still another way. In this verse, Jesus said, *"He shall glorify me: for he shall receive of mine, and shall show it unto you"* (John 16:14). Here the clearest distinction is drawn between *"He,"* the Holy Spirit, and *"me,"* Jesus Christ. It is the work of the Holy Spirit not to glorify Himself, but Another, and this Other is Jesus Christ. The Holy Spirit takes what belongs to Another—that is, to Christ—and declares it to believers. It would be impossible to express in human language a distinction between two persons more plainly than the distinction between the Son and the Holy Spirit that is expressed in this verse.

The distinction between the Father and the Son and the Holy Spirit is very clearly brought out in Luke 3:

> *Now it came to pass, when all the people were baptized, that, Jesus also having been baptized, and praying, the heaven was opened, and the Holy Ghost descended in a bodily form, as a dove, upon him, and a voice came out of heaven, Thou art my beloved Son; in thee I am well pleased.* (Luke 3:21–22 RV)

Here a clear distinction is drawn between Jesus Christ, who was on the earth; the Father, who spoke to Him from heaven; and the Holy Spirit, who descended from the Father upon the Son in bodily form as a dove.

Still another striking illustration is found in Matthew 28:19: "*Go ye therefore, and teach all nations, baptizing them in the name of the Father, and of the Son, and of the Holy Ghost.*" Here a clear distinction is drawn between the name of "*the Father*" and the name of "*the Son*" and the name of "*the Holy Ghost.*"

A very clear distinction between the Father, Son, and Holy Spirit is found in John 14:16–17:

> *And I will pray the Father, and he shall give you another Comforter, that he may abide with you for ever; even the Spirit of truth.*

Here the clearest possible distinction is drawn between the Son who prays, the Father to whom He prays, and "*another Comforter*" who is given in response to the Son's prayer. Nothing could possibly be plainer than the distinction that Jesus Christ made in this passage between Himself and the Father and the Holy Spirit.

We find the same thing again in John 16:7:

> *Nevertheless I tell you the truth; it is expedient for you that I go away: for if I go not away, the Comforter will not come unto you; but if I depart, I will send him unto you.*

Here, once more, the Lord Jesus Himself made a clear distinction between Himself, who was about to go away, and the Holy Spirit, the other Helper who was coming to take His place after He had gone away.

The same thing is brought out again in Acts 2 in Peter's sermon on the day of Pentecost, in which Peter is recorded as saying about Jesus,

> *Therefore being by the right hand of God exalted, and having received of the Father the promise of the Holy Ghost, he hath shed forth this, which ye now see and hear.* (Acts 2:33)

Here a clear distinction is drawn between the Son, who was exalted to the right hand of the Father, the Father Himself, and the Holy Spirit, whom the Son received from the Father and poured out on the church.

The Doctrine of the Trinity

In summary, let me say that again and again the Bible draws the clearest possible distinction between the Holy Spirit, the Father, and the Son. They are three separate Persons who have mutual relationships with one another, who speak of or to one another, and who apply the pronouns of the second and third persons to one another.

We have seen that the Bible makes it plain that the Holy Spirit is a divine person and that He is an entirely separate person from the Father and from the Son. In other words, there are three divine Persons in the Godhead. It has often been said that the doctrine of the Trinity is not taught in the Bible. It is true that the doctrine of the Trinity is not directly taught in the Bible in so many words, but this doctrine is simply the putting together of truths that are distinctly and unmistakably taught in the Bible. The Bible clearly states that there is but one God. (See Deuteronomy 6:4.) But it teaches with equal clearness, as we have seen in this chapter, that there are three divine Persons—the Father, the Son, and the Holy Spirit. The doctrine of the Trinity, therefore, is the putting together of these truths, which are taught with equal plainness.

Many people say that the doctrine of the Trinity is in the New Testament but not in the Old Testament. But it is in the very first chapter of the Bible. In Genesis 1:26, we read, *"And God said, Let us make man in our image, after our likeness.'"* Here the plurality of the persons in the Godhead comes out clearly. God did not say, "I will" or "Let Me make man in My image." He said, *"Let us make man in our image, after our likeness."*

Moreover, the three persons of the Trinity are found in the first three verses of the Bible. *"In the beginning God created the heaven and the earth"* (Genesis 1:1). There you have God the Father. *"And the earth was without form, and void; and darkness was upon the face of the deep. And the Spirit of God moved upon the face of the waters"* (verse 2). There you have the Holy

Spirit. *"And God said"*—there you have the Word—*"Let there be light: and there was light."* (verse 3). Here we have the three persons of the Trinity in the first three verses of the Bible.

In fact, the doctrine of the Trinity is found hundreds of times in the Old Testament. In the Hebrew Bible, it is found every place where you find the word *God* in your English Bible, for the Hebrew word for *God* is a plural noun. Literally translated, it would be "Gods," not "God."

The Unitarians and the Jews reject the deity of Christ. They often refer to Deuteronomy 6:4 as conclusive proof that the deity of Christ cannot be true: *"Hear, O Israel: the LORD our God is one LORD."* But the very doctrine that they are seeking to disprove is found in Deuteronomy 6:4, for the literal translation of the verse is, "Hear, O Israel: Jehovah our Gods is one Jehovah."

Why did the Hebrews, with their intense monotheism, use a plural name for God? This question puzzled the Hebrew grammarians and lexicographers. The best explanation they could find was that the plural for God used in the Bible was the *"pluralis majestatis"* (*we* in place of *I* in the speech of royalty). This explanation is entirely inadequate, to say nothing of the fact that its validity is very doubtful. Another explanation is far nearer at hand, and far more adequate and satisfactory: the inspired Hebrew writers used a plural name for God in spite of their intense monotheism because there is a plurality of persons in the one Godhead.

Someone may ask, "How can God be three and one at the same time?" The answer to this question is very simple and easily understandable. He cannot be three and one in the same sense, nor does the Bible teach that He is. In what sense can He be one and three? A perfectly satisfactory answer to this question is clearly impossible from the very nature of the case. In the first place, *"God is a spirit"* (John 4:24), and numbers belong primarily to the physical world. Difficulty always arises when we attempt to conceive of spiritual being in the forms of physical thought. In the second place, a perfectly satisfactory answer is impossible because God is infinite and we are finite. God dwells *"in the light which no man can approach unto"* (1 Timothy 6:16). Our attempts at a philosophical explanation of the triune nature of God are attempts to put the facts of infinite being into the forms of finite thought, and of necessity such attempts can at the very best be only partially successful.

This much we know, that God is essentially one, and also that there are three Persons in this one Godhead. There is but one God, but this one God makes Himself known to us as three distinct Persons—Father, Son, and Holy Spirit. There is one God, eternally existing, and manifesting Himself in three Persons.

If we were to go into the realm of philosophy, it could be shown from the very necessities of the case that, if God was to be God, He had to exist as more than one person. Before the creation of finite beings, there had to be a multiplicity of persons in the eternal Godhead. Otherwise, God could not love, for there would be no one to love, and therefore, God could not be God.

The ease with which one can grasp the Unitarian concept of God is not in its favor but against it.[5] Any God who could be thoroughly comprehended by a finite mind would not be an infinite God. It would be impossible for a thoroughly intelligent mind to really worship a God whom he could thoroughly understand. If God is to be truly God, He must be beyond our complete understanding.

The doctrine of the Trinity is not merely a speculative doctrine. It is a doctrine of tremendous daily practical importance. It enters into the very foundation of our experience, if our experience is a truly Christian one. For example, in our prayers, we need God the Father, to whom we pray; we need God the Son, through whom we pray; and we need God the Holy Spirit, in whom we pray. Also, in our worship, we need God the Father, the very center of our worship; we need the Son, through whom we approach the Father in our worship; and we need the Holy Spirit, by whom we worship. But all three—Father, Son, and Holy Spirit—are the objects of our worship. The following doxology is thoroughly Christian in its worship:

---

5. Unitarianism denies the Christian doctrine of the Trinity and instead teaches that God exists in only one person.

Praise God from whom all blessings flow,
Praise Him all creatures here below.
Praise Him above, ye heavenly hosts,
Praise Father, Son, and Holy Ghost.

So, also, is the Gloria Patri, the words of which we so often sing, but the thought of which we so seldom grasp: "Glory be to the Father and to the Son and to the Holy Ghost, as it was in the beginning, is now, and ever shall be, world without end. Amen."

THE ANSWER

CONTENTS

1

WHY DID JESUS DIE?

Without shedding of blood there is no remission.
—Hebrews 9:22

One of the most fundamental, central, and vital doctrines of the Christian faith is the doctrine of the Atonement. Without the biblical doctrine of the Atonement, there is no real Christianity—you have only the Devil's substitute. Without the biblical doctrine of the Atonement, you have no real Gospel but, instead, an entirely false and soul-destroying philosophy.

In the past, I have said, "If a person holds right views about the person of Jesus Christ, he will sooner or later get right views on every other question. But if he holds wrong views about the person of Jesus Christ, he is pretty sure to go wrong on everything else, sooner or later." The same thing can be said about the doctrine of the Atonement. If a person holds right views about the atonement made by Jesus Christ on Calvary's cross, he will sooner or later get right views on every other question. But if he holds wrong views about the Atonement, he is pretty sure to go wrong on everything else, sooner or later.

In this day, we are in great need of teaching on the Atonement—teaching that is definite, clear, accurate, exact, and complete. Not only in Unitarian and Christian Science circles[1], but also in circles that are nominally Bible-based—in outwardly Christian colleges, seminaries, pulpits, Sunday school classes, magazines, pamphlets, and books—there is much teaching that is vague, inaccurate, misleading, unscriptural, and often absolutely false and devilish. Much of so-called Christian teaching is essentially the same as that of Unitarianism or Christian Science. Men and women use the old words—such as *divinity* and *atonement*—with a new meaning, in order *"to deceive, if* [it were] *possible, even the elect"* (Matthew 24:24).

Even the Christian Scientist will tell you that he believes in the Atonement and that the founder of Christian Science, Mary Baker Eddy, taught the Atonement. But when you begin to ask direct and pointed questions regarding his belief and teaching, you will find that by "Atonement" he means, and Mrs. Eddy meant, something entirely different from what you mean and what the Bible teaches. Paul told us that the Devil camouflages himself as *"an angel of light"* (2 Corinthians 11:14), but never has he done it more successfully and dangerously than in the teaching about the Atonement that he inspired in Mary Baker Eddy and in Unitarian teachers, and also in the teachers in many supposedly Christian pulpits.

Some years ago, I taught a Bible class in Minneapolis, which was attended by people from all the churches in the area. I happened to remark that Christian Science denies the doctrine of the atonement through the shed blood of Jesus Christ. A very intelligent lady, a lady perfect in her manners, came to me at the close of the class and said, "Mr. Torrey, you should

1. Unitarianism denies the Christian doctrine of the Trinity and the Christian doctrine of the deity of Jesus Christ. Christian Science falsely teaches that disease, sin, death, etc., do not really exist but are the cause of mental error. Its official name is Church of Christ, Scientist.

not have said that about Christian Science, for you do not understand its teachings. Christian Scientists do teach the Atonement." I replied, "I said that Christian Science denies the doctrine of the Atonement *through the shed blood of Jesus Christ.* Do you believe, as the Bible states in 1 Peter 2:24, that Jesus Christ bore your sins in His own body on the cross?" She answered, "I think Christian Science is a beautiful system of teaching." I said, "That is not what I asked you. Do you believe that Jesus Christ bore your sins in His own body on the cross?" She replied, "Christian Science has done me a great deal of good." "That is not what I asked you. Do you believe that Jesus Christ bore your sins in His own body on the cross?" "I think that Jesus Christ's life was the most beautiful life ever lived here on earth." "That is not what I asked you. Do you believe that Jesus Christ bore your sins in His own body on the cross?" "The Christian Scientists are lovely people." "But do you believe that Jesus Christ bore your sins in His own body on the cross?" "I believe in following the Lord Jesus Christ." "Do you believe that Jesus Christ bore your sins in His own body on the cross?" "Oh," she said, "that is a doctrinal question." "Now," I said, "you yourself are an illustration of the truth of the very thing I said. You do not believe in the Atonement *through the shed blood of Jesus Christ.*"

The Christian Scientist uses the word *atonement,* but he means something entirely different from what the Bible teaches regarding the atoning death of Jesus Christ. So does the Unitarian, and so do many of the ministers from supposedly Christian denominations. A pastor in Los Angeles said recently, "I have my own kind of religion. It works for me, but I hope I have enough sense to see that it would not work for everybody. I imagine that if the pastor down the street preached my kind of religious doctrine—without a devil, without a hell, without an *atonement of blood* and retribution, without an infallible Bible—his audience would melt away like snow in the rain. Is his doctrine truer than mine, or is mine truer than his? Why, neither. His is true for him, and mine is true for me."

Now, his thinking may sound tolerant and lovely, but it is utter nonsense. Any doctrine that is not true for everybody is not true for anybody, and any doctrine that is true is true for everybody. If a doctrine that leaves out an atonement of blood is not true for the pastor down the street—and it certainly is not—then it is not true for anybody else. Truth is not relative; it is absolute. What is true is true, and what is false is false. So we come face to face with the question, What does the Bible teach about this great fundamental doctrine of the Atonement?

The Necessity and Importance of Christ's Death

The first thing that the Bible plainly teaches on this question is the absolute necessity and fundamental importance of the death of Jesus Christ and the shedding of His blood. The tendency in our day in Unitarian circles—and in Christian circles that have been corrupted by Unitarianism—is to minimize the importance of the death of our Lord Jesus Christ. The tendency is to make His life and character, His teaching and leadership, the main thing. Christian Science even goes so far as to deny the fact of His death. To them His death is "an illusion"; it is only "mortal thought." But the Bible puts its emphasis on His atoning death.

Christ's Death Is Referred to Many Times in the Bible

The death of Jesus Christ is mentioned directly more than 175 times in the New Testament. Besides this, there are very many prophetic and typological references to the death of Jesus Christ in the Old Testament.

When I was holding some meetings in the Royal Albert Hall in London, someone took one of our hymnbooks, went through it, and cut out every reference to the blood. Then he sent it back to me through the mail, saying, "I have gone through your hymnbook and cut out every reference to the blood. These references to the blood are foolish. Now sing your hymns with the blood left out, and there will be some sense in them." If you were to take your Bible and go through it that way, cutting out of the New Testament and Old Testament every passage that refers to the death of Christ or to His atoning blood, you would have a sadly torn and tattered Bible—a Bible without a heart, and a gospel without saving power.

If I were a member of a church where the pastor preached a system of religious doctrine "without a Devil, without a hell, without an atonement of blood and retribution, without an infallible Bible," he would see his own audience "melting away like snow in the rain" as far as I was concerned. Either the pastor would get out of the pulpit, or I would get out of that church, for I would know that he was not preaching God's pure, saving Gospel, but the Devil's poisonous substitute.

Christ's Death Was His Reason for Becoming Man

Not only are the references to the death of Christ so numerous in the Old and New Testaments, but we are taught distinctly in Hebrews that Jesus Christ became a man for the specific purpose of dying. He became a partaker of flesh and blood so that He could die. In this verse, we read,

> *Inasmuch then as the children have partaken of flesh and blood, He Himself likewise shared in the same, that through death He might destroy him who had the power of death, that is, the devil.*
>
> (Hebrews 2:14)

The meaning of these words is as plain as day. They tell us that the Incarnation was for the purpose of Christ's death. They tell us that His death was not a mere accident or incident of His human life (as many would have us believe) but that it was the supreme purpose of it. He became man in order to die as man and for man. This is the doctrine of the Bible, and it is true for anybody and for everybody.

Furthermore, Jesus Christ died for a specific purpose. He died as a ransom for us. He Himself said so in Matthew 20:28: *"The Son of Man did not come to be served, but to serve, and to give His life a ransom for many."*

Christ's Death Was the Topic of Conversation at the Transfiguration

One of the most remarkable scenes recorded in the New Testament is that of the Transfiguration, when Moses and Elijah came back from the other world to commune with Jesus. And what did they talk about in that great moment of human history? Luke 9:30–31 tells us:

> *And behold, two men talked with Him* [Jesus], *who were Moses and Elijah, who appeared in glory and spoke of His decease which He was about to accomplish at Jerusalem.*

His atoning death was the one subject that engrossed the attention of these two men who came back from the glory world.

We are also told in 1 Peter 1:10–12 that the death of Jesus Christ is a subject of intense interest and earnest inquiry on the part of the angels. We are told that it is something that *"angels desire to look into"* (1 Peter 1:12).

Christ's Death Is the Theme of Heaven's Song

The death of Christ is the central theme of heaven's song. Revelation 5:8–13 gives us a picture of heaven with its wonderful choir of *"ten thousand times ten thousand, and thousands of thousands,"* and this is a description of the song they sing:

> *Now when He* [the Lamb] *had taken the scroll, the four living creatures and the twenty-four elders fell down before the Lamb* [Jesus], *each having a harp, and golden bowls full of incense, which are the prayers of the saints. And they sang a new song, saying: "You are worthy to take the scroll, and to open its seals; for You were slain, and have redeemed us to God by Your blood out of every tribe and tongue and people and nation, and have made us kings and priests to our God; and we shall reign on the earth." Then I looked, and I heard the voice of many angels around the throne, the living creatures, and the elders; and the number of them was ten thousand times ten thousand, and thousands of thousands, saying with a loud voice: "Worthy is the Lamb who was slain to receive power and riches and wisdom, and strength and honor and glory and blessing!" And every creature which is in heaven and on the earth and under the earth and such as are in the sea, and all that are in them, I heard saying: "Blessing and honor and glory and power be to Him who sits on the throne, and to the Lamb, forever and ever!"*
>
> (Revelation 5:8–13)

So, it is evident that the great central theme of heaven's song is the atoning death of Jesus Christ, and the shed *"blood"* by which He redeemed people *"out of every tribe and tongue and people and nation."* If the Unitarian or the Christian Scientist were to go to heaven, he would have no song to sing. The glorious song of that wondrous choir would sound to him like a gruesome hymn. He would be very lonesome and feel that he had sat in the wrong pew.

The Purpose of Christ's Death

We have seen the fundamental and central importance of Christ's death, of the shedding of His blood. But what was its purpose?

Christ Died as a Vicarious Offering for Sin

First of all, the Bible distinctly and repeatedly tells us by direct statement, and by countless typological references in the Old Testament, that He died as a vicarious offering for sin. He, an absolutely perfect, righteous One who deserved to live, died in the place of unrighteous men who deserved to die. For example, we read in Isaiah 53:5,

> *But He was wounded for our transgressions, He was bruised for our iniquities; the chastisement for our peace was upon Him, and by His stripes we are healed.*

And in the eighth verse, we read,

> *He was taken from prison and from judgment, and who will declare His generation? For He was cut off from the land of the living; for the transgressions of My people He was stricken.*

And in the eleventh and twelfth verses, we read,

> *He shall see the labor of His soul, and be satisfied. By His knowledge My righteous Servant shall justify many, for He shall bear their iniquities.*

> *Therefore I will divide Him a portion with the great, and He shall divide the spoil with the strong, because He poured out His soul unto death, and He was numbered with the transgressors, and He bore the sin of many, and made intercession for the transgressors.*

In 1 Peter 3:18, we read,

> *For Christ also suffered once for sins, the just for the unjust, that He might bring us to God, being put to death in the flesh but made alive by the Spirit.*

And in 1 Peter 2:24, we read,

> *Who Himself bore our sins in His own body on the tree, that we, having died to sins, might live for righteousness; by whose stripes you were healed.*

Now, the meaning of these verses and many others is inescapable. No one can misunderstand their message unless he is determined not to see. These verses teach that the death of Jesus Christ was a vicarious atonement. That is, a just One who deserved to live died in the place of unjust ones who deserved to die. His death was, to use the language of the Los Angeles minister who denied any belief in the atonement, "an atonement of blood and retribution." This is God's doctrine of the atonement versus the Unitarian and Christian Science doctrine of the atonement.

Christ Died as a Ransom

But this is not all. We are further taught that Jesus Christ died as a ransom; that is, His death was the price paid to redeem others from death. He Himself said so. His own words are, "*The Son of Man did not come to be served, but to serve, and to give His life a ransom for many*" (Matthew 20:28). If His life was not a ransom—that is to say, if He did not redeem others from death by dying in their place—then He was the greatest fool in the whole history of this universe. Was He a fool, or was He a ransom? No one who in any real sense can be said to believe on the Lord Jesus Christ can hesitate as to his answer.

Christ Died as a Sin Offering

But even this is not all. The Bible distinctly tells us that He died as a sin offering. That is, it was on the ground of His death—and on this ground alone—that forgiveness of sin was made possible for and offered to sinners. This we are told in the fifty-third chapter of Isaiah, to which I have already referred. In the tenth verse, it is written,

> *Yet it pleased the LORD to bruise Him;* [Jehovah] *has put Him to grief* [literally, "made Him sick"]. *When You make His soul an offering for sin, He shall see His seed, He shall prolong His days, and the pleasure of the LORD shall prosper in His hand.*

Now, the meaning of *"an offering for sin"* is unquestionable to anyone who has studied the Old Testament offerings. *"An offering for sin,"* or "a guilt offering"—which is the exact meaning of the Hebrew word translated *"an offering for sin"*—was the death of a sacrificial victim on the ground of which pardon was offered to sinners. (See Leviticus 6:6–7.)

The Holy Spirit said explicitly in Hebrews 9:22, *"Without shedding of blood there is no remission."* The meaning of these words is unmistakable, and their force is inescapable. The whole context of Hebrews 9:22 shows that the *"blood,"* to which all the blood of the Old Testament types as sacrifices pointed, is the blood of Jesus Christ. So then, the Word of God declares that apart from the shedding of the blood of Jesus Christ, there is absolutely no pardon for sin. There is absolutely no forgiveness outside of the atoning blood of Christ. If it were not for Christ's atoning blood, every member of the human race would forever perish.

Christ Died as a Propitiation for Our Sins

Fourth and further yet, the Bible teaches that Jesus Christ died as a *"propitiation for our sins."* God the Father gave Christ the Son to be a *"propitiation by His blood."* That is to say, Jesus Christ, through the shedding of His blood, is the means by which God's holy wrath at sin is appeased. We read in 1 John 4:10, *"In this is love, not that we loved God, but that He loved us and sent His Son to be the propitiation for our sins."* And we read in Romans 3:25–26,

> *Whom God set forth as a propitiation by His blood, through faith, to demonstrate His righteousness, because in His forbearance God had passed over the sins that were previously committed, to demonstrate at the present time His righteousness, that He might be just and the justifier of the one who has faith in Jesus.*

The meaning of these words is also as plain as day. The two Greek words used for *"propitiation"* in these two passages are not exactly the same word, but they are from the same root. The word used for *"propitiation"* in 1 John 4:10 is *hilasmos,* and the word used for *"propitiation"* in Romans 3:25 is *hilasterion.* The definition of *hilasmos* given in *Thayer's Greek-English Lexicon of the New Testament,* which is the standard work, is "the means of appeasing." The definition of *hilasterion* given in the same dictionary is "an expiatory sacrifice." Of course, an expiatory sacrifice is one that makes atonement or satisfaction, one that removes guilt and cancels the obligation to punish the offender. So the thought that is in both passages is that the death of Jesus Christ was a *"propitiation,"* "an expiatory sacrifice," the "means of appeasing" God's holy wrath at sin. In other words, Jesus, through the shedding of His blood, is the means by which the wrath of God against us as sinners is appeased.

God's holiness and consequent hatred of sin, like every other attribute of His character, is real and must manifest itself. His wrath at sin must strike somewhere, either upon the sinner himself or upon a lawful substitute. It struck upon Jesus Christ, a lawful substitute.

As we read in Isaiah 53:6, *"All we like sheep have gone astray; we have turned, every one, to his own way; and the* LORD ***has laid on Him*** [the Lord Jesus] *the iniquity of us all"* (emphasis added). The word translated *"has laid,"* according to the marginal note of the Revised Version, means literally, "has made to light." More literally still, it means, "has made to strike." If we read it in this way, what God said through Isaiah is, *"All we like sheep have gone astray; we have turned, every one, to his own way; and the* L*ORD* [has made to strike] *on Him the iniquity of us all."* In the eighth verse of the same chapter, we are taught that the stroke due to others fell upon Jesus Christ, and He was consequently *"cut off from the land of the living."* The first cause of the death of Jesus Christ is the demands of God's holiness.

This is the biblical doctrine versus the Unitarian and Christian Science doctrine of atonement. The biblical doctrine is often misrepresented and distorted as follows: God, a holy first person, took the sins of man, the guilty second person, and put them on Jesus Christ, an innocent third person. Those who believe this false viewpoint often say, "This is not just." No, this would not be just, and it is not for a moment the doctrine of the Bible. The Bible clearly teaches that Jesus Christ was not a third person but was Himself God, and was also man. So He was not a third person at all, but both the first person and the second person. The true doctrine of the Atonement is that God, instead of punishing the sinner for his sins, took the punishment upon Himself. This act certainly is something more than justice—it is wondrous love.

Christ Died to Redeem Us from the Curse of the Law

Further yet, the Bible teaches us that Jesus Christ died to redeem us from the curse of the law by bearing that curse Himself. We read in Galatians 3:10,

> *As many as are of the works of the law are under the curse; for it is written, "Cursed is everyone who does not continue in all things which are written in the book of the law, to do them."*

So then, every one of us is under the curse of the broken law, for not one of us has continued *"in all things which are written in the book of the law, to do them."* But we read in the thirteenth verse,

> *Christ has redeemed us from the curse of the law, having become a curse for us* [literally, "in our behalf"] *(for it is written, "Cursed is everyone who hangs on a tree").*

By His crucifixion and death, Christ redeemed us from the curse that we deserved by taking that curse upon Himself. This certainly is "an atonement of blood and retribution."

Christ Died as Our Passover Sacrifice

The Bible puts essentially the same truth in still another way, namely, that Jesus Christ died as our Passover Sacrifice. That is, He died so that His shed blood would serve as the ground upon which God would pass over us and spare us. We read in 1 Corinthians 5:7, *"Christ, our Passover, was sacrificed for us."* Now, what a Passover sacrifice was and what it signified to the Israelites we learn from Exodus 12:12–13. Here the Lord told the children of Israel at the inauguration of the Passover,

> *I will pass through the land of Egypt on that night, and will strike all the firstborn in the land of Egypt, both man and beast; and against all the gods of Egypt I will execute judgment: I am the Lord. Now the blood shall be a sign for you on the houses where you are. And when I see the blood, I will pass over you; and the plague shall not be on you to destroy you when I strike the land of Egypt.*

Again, we read in the twenty-third verse of the same chapter,

> *For the Lord will pass through to strike the Egyptians; and when He sees the blood on the lintel and on the two doorposts, the Lord will pass over the door and not allow the destroyer to come into your houses to strike you.*

Paul wrote his words in 1 Corinthians 5:7 with all this in mind. When Paul said that Christ is our Passover Sacrifice, beyond a question he meant that the shed blood of Jesus Christ serves as a ground—the only ground—upon which God passes over and spares us.

The Results of Christ's Death

We have seen, then, the gracious and glorious purposes of the atoning death of Jesus Christ. What are the results of that death? They are even more glorious. I can speak of them only in part.

God Can Deal in Mercy with the Whole World

The first result of the atoning death of Jesus Christ is that a propitiation is provided for the whole world. We read in 1 John 2:2, *"He Himself is the propitiation for our sins, and not for ours only but also for the whole world."* This plainly means that, by the death of Jesus Christ, a basis is provided upon which God can deal in mercy and does deal in mercy with the whole world. All God's merciful dealings with man are on the ground of Christ's death. Only on the ground of Christ's death could God deal in mercy with any man. God's merciful dealings with the most ungodly blasphemer or the most blatant atheist are on the ground of the atoning death of Jesus Christ.

Every Person Will Be Raised from the Dead

In the second place, through the atoning death of Jesus Christ, all people will obtain resurrection from the dead. We read in Romans 5:18,

> *Therefore, as through one man's offense* [the trespass of Adam] *judgment came to all men, resulting in condemnation, even so through one Man's righteous act* [Christ's righteous act in dying on the cross in obedience to the will of God] *the free gift came to all men, resulting in justification of life.*

Also, we are told in 1 Corinthians 15:22, *"As in Adam all die, even so in Christ all shall be made alive."* In the entire fifteenth chapter of 1 Corinthians, the apostle Paul was speaking about the resurrection of the body, not about eternal life. Here he distinctly taught that even as every child of Adam loses life (physical life—see Genesis 3:19) in the First Adam, so also he obtains resurrection from the dead through the atoning death of Jesus Christ, the Second Adam.

Every person, the most ungodly infidel as well as the most devout believer, will someday be raised from the dead because Christ died in his place. Whether the resurrection that he obtains through the death of Jesus Christ will be a *"resurrection of life"* or a *"resurrection of condemnation"* (John 5:29), of *"shame and everlasting contempt"* (Daniel. 12:2), will depend entirely on what attitude the individual takes toward the Christ in whom he receives the resurrection.

Every Believer Is Forgiven of Every Sin

By the atoning death of Jesus Christ, all believers in Jesus Christ have forgiveness of all their sins. We read in Ephesians 1:7, *"In Him* [Jesus Christ] *we have redemption through His blood, the forgiveness of sins, according to the riches of His grace."* Because Jesus Christ died as a full satisfaction for our sins, forgiveness of sin is not something that believers can do something to secure. It is something that the blood of Jesus Christ has already secured and that our faith has already taken hold of. We *have* forgiveness; we *are* forgiven. Every believer in Jesus Christ is forgiven of every sin he has ever committed or ever will commit, because Jesus Christ shed His blood in his place.

As we read in Romans 5:10, *"When we were enemies we were reconciled to God through the death of His Son."* Through Christ's atoning death, all believers in Him, although they once *"were enemies,"* are now *"reconciled to God through the death of His Son."* That is to say, the enmity between God and the sinner is done away with, or, as Paul put it in Colossians 1:20, Christ has *"made peace through the blood of His cross."* Or, as he put it in the next two verses, Christ *"has reconciled* [believers] *in the body of His flesh through death"* (verses 21–22).

The story is told of a faithful English minister in the 1800s who was told that one of his parishioners was dying. She was a good woman, and he hurried to her side to talk with her. As he sat down beside the dying woman, he said to her very gently but solemnly, "They tell me you do not have long to live." "No," she replied, "I know I do not." "They tell me you will probably not live through the night." "No," she replied, "I do not expect to live through the night." Then he said very earnestly, "Have you made your peace with God?" She replied, "No, I have not." "And are you not afraid to meet God without having made your peace with Him?" "No, not at all," she calmly replied.

Again, he said to her, "Do you understand what I am saying? Do you realize that you are at the point of death?" "Yes." "Do you realize you probably will not live through the night?" "Yes." "And you have not made your peace with God?" "No." "And you are not afraid to meet Him?" "No, not at all."

Something about the woman's manner made him think there was something behind her words, and so he asked, "What do you mean?" She replied, "I know I am dying and will not live through the night. I know I must soon meet God, and I am not at all disturbed. I did not need to make my peace with God, because Jesus Christ made peace with God for me more than eighteen hundred years ago by His death on the cross of Calvary. I am resting in the peace that Jesus Christ has already made."

The woman was right. No one needs to make his or her peace with God; Jesus Christ has already made peace by His atoning death, and all we have to do is enter into the peace that Jesus Christ has made for us. We enter into that peace by simply believing in the One who made peace by His death on the cross. Jesus Christ's work was a complete and perfect work. There is nothing to be added to it. We cannot add anything to it, and we do not need to. Jesus Christ has *"made peace through the blood of His cross"* (Colossians 1:20).

Every Believer Is Justified

The fourth result of the atoning death of Jesus Christ is that all believers in Him are justified. We read in Romans 5:9, *"Having now been justified by His blood."*

Justification is more than forgiveness. Forgiveness is the putting away of our sins, which is manifested in God's treating us as if we had never sinned. Justification means to count us as positively righteous, to impute to us the perfect righteousness of God in Jesus Christ. God does not merely treat us as if we had never sinned, but He sees us as clothed with perfect righteousness.

Because of Jesus Christ's atoning death, there is an absolute exchange of position between Jesus Christ and His people. In His death on the cross, Jesus Christ took our place of condemnation before God; and the moment we accept Him, we step into His place of perfect acceptance before God. As Paul put it in 2 Corinthians 5:21, *"He made Him who knew no sin to be sin for us, that we might become the righteousness of God in Him."* Jesus Christ stepped into our place in the curse and rejection, and the moment we accept Him, we step into His place of perfect acceptance.

This truth has been expressed by one poet as follows:

Near, so very near to God,
  Nearer I cannot be;
For in the person of His Son,
  I'm just as near as He.

Dear, so very dear to God,
  Dearer I cannot be;
For in the person of His Son,
  I'm just as dear as He.

Every Believer Has Bold Access into God's Presence

Furthermore, because of the full atonement that Jesus Christ has made by the shedding of His blood, every believer can enter boldly into the Holy Place, into the very presence of God. As it is put in Hebrews 10:19–22,

> *Therefore, brethren, having boldness to enter the Holiest* [the very presence of God] *by the blood of Jesus, by a new and living way which He consecrated for us, through the veil, that is, His flesh, and having a High*

> *Priest over the house of God, let us draw near with a true heart in full assurance of faith.*

Some of us hesitate to come into the presence of God when we think of the greatness and the number of our sins and when we think of how holy God is. Even the seraphim (the "burning ones," burning in their own intense holiness) veil their faces and feet in His presence and unceasingly cry, *"Holy, holy, holy is the LORD of hosts"* (Isaiah 6:3).

We say to ourselves, "God is holy." Yes. "And I am a sinner." Yes. But by the wondrous offering of Christ *"once for all"* (Hebrews 10:10), I am *"perfected forever"* (verse 14). On the ground of that blood—so precious and so sufficient in God's eyes—I can march boldly into the very presence of God, look up with unveiled face into His face, call Him Father, and pour out before Him every desire of my heart. (See Hebrews 4:16.) Oh, wondrous blood!

Every Believer Obtains Eternal Life and an Eternal Inheritance

But this is not all. Because of the atoning death of Jesus Christ, those who believe in Him will live with Him forever. How plainly Paul put it in 1 Thessalonians 5:9–10: *"Our Lord Jesus Christ…died for us, that…we should live together with Him."*

Further yet, because of the atoning death of Jesus Christ, all those who believe in Him *"receive the promise of the eternal inheritance."* This is what we are told in Hebrews 9:15:

> *And for this reason He is the Mediator of the new covenant, by means of death, for the redemption of the transgressions under the first covenant, that those who are called may receive the promise of the eternal inheritance.*

If I had more time, I would go into greater detail about this wonderful promise.

The Material Universe Is Reconciled to God

There are results of the atoning death and resurrection of Jesus Christ regarding His victory over the Devil and his angels, which we are not able to cover here. I will cover just one more thing: the results of His atoning death concerning the material universe. God teaches us that, through the death of Jesus Christ, the material universe—*"all things,...whether things on earth or things in heaven"*—is reconciled to God. These are His words:

> *For it pleased the Father that in* [Jesus Christ] *all the fullness should dwell, and by Him to reconcile all things to Himself, by Him, whether things on earth or things in heaven, having made peace through the blood of His cross.* (Colossians 1:19–20)

These are wonderful words. They tell us that the death of Jesus Christ is related to the material universe, to things on earth and to things in heaven, as well as to us and to our sins.

The material universe has fallen away from God in connection with sin. (See Genesis 3:17–18; Romans 8:20.) Both earth and heaven have been invaded and polluted by sin. (See Ephesians 6:12; Hebrews 9:23–24.) Through the death of Jesus Christ, this pollution is put away. Just as the blood of the Old Testament sacrifice was taken into the Most Holy Place of the temple, the type of heaven, so Christ has taken the blood of the better sacrifice into heaven itself and cleansed it. *"All things,...whether things on earth or things in heaven"* (Colossians 1:20), are now reconciled to God. *"The creation itself also will be delivered from the bondage of corruption into the glorious liberty of the children of God"* (Romans 8:21). *"We...look for new heavens and a new earth in which righteousness dwells"* (2 Peter 3:13).

The atonement of Jesus Christ has an immense sweep, far beyond the reach of our human philosophies. We have just begun to understand what the blood that was spilled on Calvary means. Sin is a far more awful, ruinous, and far-reaching evil than we have been accustomed to thinking, but the blood of Christ has power and effectiveness, the fullness of which only eternity will disclose.

2

AM I JUSTIFIED BY MY GOOD WORKS?

Therefore let it be known to you, brethren, that through this Man is preached to you the forgiveness of sins; and by Him everyone who believes is justified from all things from which you could not be justified by the law of Moses.
—Acts 13:38–39

But to him who does not work but believes on Him who justifies the ungodly, his faith is accounted for righteousness.
—Romans 4:5

These are two remarkable passages, and I will explain them both in this chapter. Our subject is justification by faith, which is the distinctive doctrine of Protestantism, for it was the central tenet of the Reformation. Today, this teaching is one of the vital doctrines of evangelicalism. The first biblical writer to fully explain and repeatedly emphasize this teaching was Paul. However, it can be found throughout the entire Bible, from Genesis to Revelation. In the first book of the Bible, we read, "[Abraham] *believed in the LORD, and He accounted it to him for righteousness*" (Genesis 15:6). In these words, we have the seed of the gracious and precious doctrine of justification by faith.

What Is Justification?

The first thing for us to understand is what justification is. At this point, many people go astray in their study of this great truth. There are two fundamentally different definitions of the words *justify* and *justification*. One definition of justify is "to make righteous," and of justification, "being made righteous." The other definition of justify is "to count, declare, or show to be righteous," and of justification, "being declared or counted righteous." Based on these two different definitions, two different schools of thought depart from one another. Which is the true definition?

The way to settle the meaning of any word in the Bible is by examining all the passages in which that word and its derivatives are found. If anyone will go through the Bible, the Old Testament and the New, and carefully study all the passages in which the word *justify* and its derivatives are found, he will discover that, beyond a question, the biblical definition of justify is not "to make righteous," but "to count righteous, declare righteous, or show to be righteous." A person is justified before God when God counts him righteous.

This truth appears, for example, in Romans 4:

For if Abraham was justified by works, he has something to boast about, but not before God. For what does the Scripture say? "Abraham believed God, and it was accounted to him for righteousness." Now to him who

> *works, the wages are not counted as grace but as debt. But to him who does not work but believes on Him who justifies the ungodly, his faith is accounted for righteousness, just as David also describes the blessedness of the man to whom God imputes righteousness apart from works: "Blessed are those whose lawless deeds are forgiven, and whose sins are covered; blessed is the man to whom the Lord shall not impute sin."*
> (verses 2–8)

It is plain from this passage, and from many others, that a person is justified when God counts him righteous, no matter what his character and conduct may have been. Of course, as we saw in the previous chapter and will see again later in this chapter, justification means more than mere forgiveness.

How Are We Justified?

Now we come to the second question, which is the all-important question: How are we justified? In general, there are two opposing views of justification. The first view states that people are justified by their own works, that is, on the ground of something that they themselves do. This view may be expressed in various ways. The good works that people speak of as the ground of their justification may be their good moral conduct or their keeping of the Golden Rule or something of that sort. Or, they may be works of religion, such as doing penance, saying prayers, joining the church, going to church, being baptized, partaking of the Lord's Supper, or performing some other religious duty. But these all amount to the same thing: in their view, it is something that they themselves do that brings justification.

The other view of justification is that we are justified not by our own works in any sense, but entirely by the work of Another, that is, by the atoning death of Jesus Christ on the cross of Calvary. This view states that our own works have nothing to do with our justification but that we are justified entirely by Christ's finished and complete work of atonement. Furthermore, all that we have to do to receive our justification is merely to take hold of it by simply trusting in the One who made the atonement.

Which is the correct view? We will go directly to the Bible for the answer to this all-important question.

We Are Not Justified by Our Own Works

We find the first part of the answer in Romans 3:20: "*Therefore by the deeds of the law no flesh will be justified in His sight, for by the law is the knowledge of sin.*" Here it is very plainly stated that we are not justified by keeping the law of God, either the Mosaic Law or any other law. The law is given, not to bring us justification, but to bring us a knowledge of sin, that is, to bring us to the realization of our need of justification by grace. In the above verse, it is plainly stated that no one is justified by the works of the law. The same great truth is found in Galatians 2:16:

> *Knowing that a man is not justified by the works of the law but by faith in Jesus Christ, even we have believed in Christ Jesus, that we might be justified by faith in Christ and not by the works of the law; for by the works of the law no flesh shall be justified.*

Justification by any works of our own is an impossibility. Why? Because in order to be justified by the works of the law, or by anything we can do, we must keep the law of God perfectly. The law demands perfect obedience as the ground of justification. It says, "*Cursed is everyone who does not continue in all things which are written in the book of the law, to do them*" (Galations 3:10). But not one of us has perfectly kept the law of God, and the moment we break the law of God at any point, justification by works becomes an absolute impossibility. Therefore, as far as the law of God is concerned, every one of us is under the curse, and if we are to be justified at all, we must find some other way of justification than by keeping the law of God.

God did not give mankind the law with the expectation or intention that they would keep it and be justified by it. He gave them the law in order to produce conviction of sin and to lead them to Christ. Or, as Paul put it in Romans 3:19–20,

> *Now we know that whatever the law says, it says to those who are under the law, that every mouth may be stopped, and all the world may become guilty before God. Therefore by the deeds of the law no flesh will be justified in His sight, for by the law is the knowledge of sin.*

These words of God are plain. But strangely enough, many people today are preaching the law as a way of salvation. When they preach this message, they are preaching another way of salvation than the one laid down in God's own Word.

We Are Justified Freely by God's Grace

The answer to the question of how we are justified has a second part. We find it in Romans 3:24: "*Being justified freely by His grace through the redemption that is in Christ Jesus.*" The word translated "*freely*" in this passage means "as a free gift." This verse tells us that justification is a free gift by God's grace (God's unmerited favor) "*through* [on the ground of] *the redemption that is in Christ Jesus.*" In other words, justification is not on the ground of any merit that is in us or anything that we have done. We are justified neither by our own doing nor by our own character. Justification is an absolutely free gift; God bestows it without asking for payment. The channel through which this free gift is bestowed is "*the redemption that is in Christ Jesus.*" Christ paid the purchase price of our redemption by shedding His blood on Calvary's cross.

We Are Justified by Christ's Shed Blood

The third part of the answer is found in Romans 5:9: "*Much more then, having now been justified by His blood, we shall be saved from wrath through Him.*" Here we are told in so many words that we are "*justified,*" or counted righteous, "*by,*" or more literally, "in," Christ's "*blood*"—that is, on the ground of Christ's propitiatory death. We were all under the curse of the broken law of God, for we had all broken it. But by dying in our place on the cross of Calvary, our Lord Jesus Christ *"has redeemed us from the curse of the law, having become a curse for us (for it is written, 'Cursed is everyone who hangs on a tree')"* (Galatians 3:13).

Peter put it this way in 1 Peter 2:24: "[Christ] *Himself bore our sins in His own body on the tree.*" Paul put it this way in 2 Corinthians 5:21: "[God] *made* [Christ] *who knew no sin to be sin for us, that we might become the righteousness of God in Him.*" We will have the opportunity to come back to this passage later. All that I want you to notice in it right now is that it is on the ground of Jesus Christ's becoming a substitute for us, on the ground of His taking the place we deserved on the cross, that we are counted righteous. The one and only ground of justification is the shed blood of Jesus Christ.

Of course, this doctrine is entirely different from the teaching of Christian Science, and entirely different from the teaching of New Thought and Theosophy,[2] and entirely different from the teaching of Unitarianism. But it is the teaching of the Word of God. We find this same teaching clearly given by the prophet Isaiah seven hundred years before our Lord was born:

> *All we like sheep have gone astray; we have turned, every one, to his own way; and the Lord has laid* [literally, "made to strike"] *on* [the Lord Jesus] *the iniquity of us all.* (Isaiah 53:6)

Get this point clearly settled in your mind: the sole but all-sufficient ground upon which people are justified before God is the shed blood of Jesus Christ. He offered His blood as an atonement for our sins, and God the Father accepted it as an all-sufficient atonement.

We Are Justified by Faith in Jesus

The fourth part of the answer to the question of how we are justified is in Romans 3:26:

2. New Thought teaches that the power of the mind can achieve health and happiness. Its teachings are similar to those of Christian Science. Theosophy is the teachings of a movement that originated in the U.S. in 1875 and that follows primarily Buddhistic and Hindu theories, especially of pantheistic evolution and reincarnation.

> *To demonstrate at the present time His* [God's] *righteousness, that He* [God] *might be just and the justifier of the one who has faith in Jesus.*

Here we are taught that we are justified on the condition of faith in Jesus. If possible, Romans 4:5 makes this even plainer: "*To him who does not work but believes on Him who justifies the ungodly, his faith is accounted for righteousness.*" Here the Holy Spirit, speaking through the apostle Paul, tells us that the faith of those who believe in Jesus "*is accounted for righteousness.*" In other words, faith makes Christ's shed blood, which is the ground of justification, ours. We are justified when we believe.

Every person is *potentially* justified by the death of Christ on the cross, but believers are *actually* justified by taking hold of the justifying value in His shed blood by faith. Simple faith in Jesus Christ is the sole condition of justification. God asks nothing else of the sinner than that he believe in His Son, Jesus Christ. When he believes, he is justified, whether he has any works to offer or not. As Paul put it in Romans 3:28, "*Therefore we conclude that a man is justified by faith apart from the deeds of the law.*" Or, as Paul put it in the verse already quoted, "*To him who does not work but believes on Him who justifies the ungodly, his faith is accounted for righteousness*" (Romans 4:5).

A person is justified entirely apart from the works of the law. That is, he is justified on the condition that he believe in Jesus Christ, even though he has no works to offer as the ground upon which to claim justification. When we cease to work for justification and simply believe "*on Him who justifies the ungodly,*" our faith is "*accounted for righteousness,*" and therefore we are accounted righteous.

The question, then, is not, Do you have any works to offer? but, Do you believe in the One who justifies the ungodly? Works have nothing to do with justification, except to hinder it when we trust in them. The blood of Jesus Christ secures justification; faith in Jesus Christ takes hold of it. We are justified not by our works, but by His work. We are justified on the simple and single ground of His shed blood and on the simple and single condition of our faith in the One who shed the blood.

So great is the pride of the natural heart that it is extremely difficult to hold people to this doctrine of justification by faith apart from the works of the law. We are constantly seeking to bring in our own works somewhere.

We Are Justified by a Heart-Faith That Confesses Christ

But I have not yet completely answered the question of how we are justified. There is another side to the truth, and if our doctrine of justification is to be complete and well-balanced, we must look at this other side. We will find part of it in Romans 10:9–10:

> *If you confess with your mouth the Lord Jesus and believe in your heart that God has raised Him from the dead, you will be saved. For with the heart one believes unto righteousness, and with the mouth confession is made unto salvation.*

Here God tells us that the faith that takes hold of justification is a faith of the heart. This faith is not a mere idea or opinion; this faith leads to action. This faith leads to open, verbal confession of Jesus as Lord.

If a person has a faith, or what he calls a faith, that does not lead him to an open confession of Christ, he has a faith that does not justify; it is not a faith of the heart. Our Lord Jesus Christ Himself told us that heart-faith leads to open confession, for He said in Matthew 12:34, *"Out of the abundance of the heart the mouth speaks."* Heart-faith in Jesus Christ inevitably leads to a verbal confession of Jesus as Lord. If you are not confessing Jesus as your Lord with your mouth, you do not have justifying faith, and you are not justified.

We Are Justified by a Faith That Works

Let us examine the rest of this other side of the truth. James 2:14 says, *"What doth it profit, my brethren, if a man say he hath faith, but have not works? can that faith save him?"* (RV). We see here that a faith that a person merely says he has, but that does not lead to works consistent with what he claims to believe, cannot justify. James went on to say...

> *But someone will say, "You have faith, and I have works." Show me your faith without your works, and I will show you my faith by my works. You believe that there is one God. You do well. Even the demons believe; and tremble! But do you want to know, O foolish man, that faith without works is dead? Was not Abraham our father justified by works when he offered Isaac his son on the altar? Do you see that faith was working together with his works, and by works faith was made perfect?* [That is, in the works to which Abraham's faith led, faith had its perfect manifestation.] *And the Scripture was fulfilled which says, "Abraham believed God, and it was accounted to him for righteousness." And he was called the friend of God. You see then that a man is justified by works, and not by faith only.* (James 2:18–24)

Some see in these verses a contradiction between the teaching of James and the teaching of Paul, but there is no contradiction whatsoever. Here James taught us an important truth, namely, that the faith that one says he has, but that does not manifest itself in action, will not justify. The faith that justifies is real faith that leads to actions consistent with the truth we profess to believe. It is true that we are justified simply by faith apart from the works of the law, *but our faith must be real faith;* otherwise, it does not justify. As someone once put it, "We are justified by faith without works, but we are not justified by a faith that is without works."

The faith that God sees and upon which He justifies leads inevitably to works that others can see. God saw the faith of Abraham the moment Abraham believed, before there was any opportunity to work, and He accounted that faith to Abraham for righteousness. But the faith that God saw was a real faith, and it led Abraham to works that all could see. These works proved the reality of his faith. To us, the proof of the faith is the works, and we know that he who does not work does not have justifying faith.

On the one hand, we must not lose sight of the truth that Paul emphasized to combat legalism, namely, that we are justified on the single and simple condition of a real faith in Christ. But on the other hand, we must not lose sight of the truth that James emphasized to combat lawless living, namely, that a justifying faith is a real faith that proves its genuineness by works. To the legalist who is seeking to do something to merit justification, we must say, "Stop working, and believe in the One who justifies the ungodly." (See Romans 4:5.) To the one who thinks he can live a lawless, careless, unseparated, sinful life and still be justified—the one who boasts that he has faith and is justified by it but does not show his faith by his works—we must say, "*What doth it profit, my brethren, if a man* ***say*** *he hath faith, but have not works? can* ***that*** *faith save him?*" (James 2:14 RV, emphasis added). We are justified by faith alone; however, we are not justified by a faith that is alone, but by a faith that is demonstrated by works.

To What Extent Are We Justified?

I think that the above Scriptures have made it plain just how a person is justified. Now we come to another question: To what extent is an individual who believes in the Lord Jesus justified? This question is plainly, wonderfully, and gloriously answered in Acts 13:38–39:

> *Therefore let it be known to you, brethren, that through this Man is preached to you the forgiveness of sins; and by Him everyone who believes is justified from all things from which you could not be justified by the law of Moses.*

These words very plainly declare to us that every believer in Jesus Christ is "*justified from all things.*" In other words, the old account against the believer is totally wiped out. No matter how bad and how black the account is, the moment a person believes in Jesus Christ, the account is wiped out. God has absolutely nothing that He counts against the one who believes in Jesus Christ. Even if he is still a very imperfect believer, a very young and immature Christian, he is perfectly justified. As Paul put it in Romans 8:1, "*There is therefore now no condemnation to those who are in Christ Jesus.*" Or, as he put it further along in the chapter,

> *Who shall bring a charge against God's elect? It is God who justifies. Who is he who condemns? It is Christ who died, and furthermore is also risen, who is even at the right hand of God, who also makes intercession for us.* (verses 33–34)

Suppose the world's most brutal murderer were to hear the gospel of God's grace, believe in the Lord Jesus Christ, and accept Him as his Savior, surrendering to Him and confessing Him as his Lord. The moment he did so, every sin he ever committed would be blotted out, and his record would be as white in God's sight as that of the purest angel in heaven. God counts absolutely nothing against the believer in Jesus Christ.

But this is not all. Paul went beyond this in 2 Corinthians 5:21: "[God] *made Him* [Jesus Christ] *who knew no sin to be sin for us, that we might become the righteousness of God in Him.*" Here we are explicitly told that the believer in Jesus Christ is made the "*righteousness of God*" in Christ. In Philippians 3:9, we are told that when one is in Christ, he has a righteousness not his own, a "*righteousness which is from God by faith.*" In other words, there is an absolute exchange of positions between Christ and the justified believer. Christ took our place, the place of the curse on the cross (Galatians 3:13). He was "*made to be sin on our behalf*" (2 Corinthians 5:21 RV). God counted Him a sinner and dealt with Him as a sinner, causing Him to cry out as He died in the sinner's place, "*My God, My God, why have You forsaken Me?*" (Matthew 27:46). And when we are justified, we step into Christ's place, the place of perfect acceptance before God. In the exact words of Scripture, we "*become the righteousness of God in Him*" (2 Corinthians 5:21).

To be justified is more than to be forgiven. Forgiveness is the putting away of sin. Justification is the attributing of perfect righteousness to the one justified. Jesus Christ is so united to the believer that God attributes the believer's sins to Christ. On the other hand, the believer is so united to Christ that God attributes Christ's righteousness to him. God sees us, not as we are in ourselves, but as we are in Him. God considers us to be as righteous as Christ is.

When Christ's work in us has been completed, we will be in actual fact what we are already in God's eyes. However, the moment one believes, as far as God's estimation is concerned, he is as perfect as he ever will be. Our present standing before God is absolutely perfect, though our present state may be very imperfect. Allow me to use again the words of the poet:

Near, so very near to God,
  Nearer I cannot be;
For in the person of His Son,
  I'm just as near as He.

Dear, so very dear to God,
  Dearer I cannot be;
For in the person of His Son,
  I'm just as dear as He.

When Are We Justified?

One question still remains, though it has really been answered in what has already been said. It concerns the time of justification. When is a believer justified? This question is answered plainly in one of our texts: *"And by Him everyone who believes is justified from all things from which you could not be justified by the law of Moses"* (Acts 13:39). What I want you to particularly notice now in this verse is the word *"is"*: *"Everyone who believes is justified from all things."* This verse plainly answers the question as to when a believer is justified. In Christ Jesus, everyone who believes in Him is justified from all things the moment he believes. The moment a person believes in Jesus Christ, that moment he becomes united to Christ, and God attributes His righteousness to him.

I repeat: if the world's most brutal murderer were to believe in the Lord Jesus Christ, the moment that he did so, not only would every sin he ever committed be blotted out, but all the perfect righteousness of God in Christ would be put in his account. His standing before God would be as perfect as it would be after being in heaven ten million years.

I was preaching one Sunday morning in D. L. Moody's church in Chicago on Romans 8:1, "*There is therefore now no condemnation to those who are in Christ Jesus.*" In the course of my preaching, I said, "If the wickedest woman in Chicago were to come into the Chicago Avenue Church this morning and here and now accept Jesus Christ as her Savior, the moment she did so, every sin she ever committed would be blotted out, and her record would be as white in God's sight as that of the purest woman in the auditorium."

Unknown to me, one of the members of my congregation had gone down that very morning into a low den of iniquity near the river and had invited a woman who was an outcast to come and hear me preach. The woman replied, "I never go to church. Church is not for the likes of me. I would not be welcome at the church if I did go." The saintly woman's reply was, "You would be welcome at our church," which, thank God, was true. "No," the woman insisted, "it would not do for me to go to church. Church is not for the likes of me." But the saintly woman urged the sinful woman to go. She offered to accompany her to the church, but the sinful woman said, "No, that would never do. The policemen know me, and the boys on the street know me and sometimes throw stones at me. If they saw you going up the street with me, they would think that you are what I am." But the saintly woman had the Spirit of the Master and said, "I don't care what they think of me. If you will accompany me to hear Mr. Torrey preach, I will go along with you." The other woman refused. But the saved woman was so insistent that the woman who was an outcast finally said, "If you will go up the street a few steps ahead, I will follow you."

Up La Salle Avenue they went, the woman who was a saint a few steps ahead, and the woman who was a sinner a few steps behind. Block after block they went, until they reached the corner of La Salle Avenue and Chicago Avenue. The saved woman entered the tower door at the corner, went up the steps, and entered the church, and the woman who was a sinner followed her. Upon reaching the door, the sinful woman looked in, saw a vacant seat under the balcony in the very last row at the back, and slipped into it. Scarcely had she taken her seat, when I made the remark that I just quoted: "If the wickedest woman in Chicago were to come into the Chicago Avenue Church this morning and here and now accept Jesus Christ as her Savior, the moment she did so, every sin she ever committed would be blotted out, and her record would be as white in God's sight as that of the purest woman in the auditorium." My words went floating down over the audience and dropped into the heart of the sinful woman. She believed them. She believed that Jesus died for her. She believed that by the shedding of His blood she could be saved. Believing, she found pardon and peace and justification then and there. When the meeting was over, she came up the aisle to the front as I stepped down from the pulpit, tears streaming down her face, and thanked me for the blessing that she had received.

I repeat it right now, not knowing who may be reading this, not knowing what may be the secret life of anyone who is reading, not knowing what may be the sins that are hidden in the heart: Even if you are the wickedest man or woman on earth, if you were to here and now accept Jesus Christ as Savior, the moment you did so, every sin you ever committed would be blotted out. In an instant, your record would be as white in God's sight, not only as that of the purest person in the world, but as that of the purest angel in heaven. Not only that, but all the perfect righteousness of God that clothed our Lord Jesus Christ would be put in your account, and you would be just as near and just as dear to God as the Lord Jesus Christ Himself is. That is the doctrine of justification by faith. Wondrous doctrine! Glorious doctrine!

3

HAVE I BEEN BORN AGAIN?

Jesus answered and said to him, "Most assuredly, I say to you, unless one is born again, he cannot see the kingdom of God....Most assuredly, I say to you, unless one is born of water and the Spirit, he cannot enter the kingdom of God."
—John 3:3, 5

Our subject in this chapter is regeneration, or the new birth. What I have to say will be covered under four main questions: What does it mean to be born again? What are the results of being born again? Why is it necessary to be born again? How can a person be born again?

What Does It Mean to Be Born Again?

Many people speak of the new birth or of regeneration without any definite idea of just what the new birth is. As a result, they are never sure whether they themselves have been born again or not. In 2 Peter 1:4, we find as clear a definition of the new birth as can be found in the Word of God:

> *Exceedingly great and precious promises* [have been given to us], *that through these you may be partakers of the divine nature, having escaped the corruption that is in the world through lust.*

From these words of Peter, it is evident that the new birth means that a new nature is given to the one who is born again—God's own nature. By being born again, we become actual partakers of the divine nature.

We are all born into this world with a corrupted intellectual and moral nature. The natural person, or unregenerate person, is intellectually blind—blind to the truth of God. He cannot see or receive *"the things of the Spirit"* (1 Corinthians 2:14). *"They are foolishness to him; nor can he know them"* (verse 14). His inclinations are corrupt; he loves the things he ought to hate and hates the things he ought to love. A definite description of the inclinations and tastes and desires of the unregenerate person is found in Galatians 5:19–21. He is also perverse in his will, as Paul put it in Romans 8:7: *"The carnal mind is enmity against God; for it is not subject to the law of God, nor indeed can be."* This state of spiritual blindness and moral corruption is the condition of every unregenerate person. No matter how cultured or refined or moral he may be outwardly, his inner life is radically wrong.

In the new birth, God imparts His own wise and holy nature, a nature that thinks as God thinks. The one who is born again *"is renewed in knowledge according to the image of Him who created him"* (Colossians 3:10). He feels as God feels (see 1 Corinthians 2:16), loves what God loves (see 1 John 3:14; 4:7–8), hates what God hates (see Revelation 2:6), and wills as God wills (see Philippians 2:13). It is evident, then, that regeneration is a deep, thorough change in the deepest springs of thought, feeling, and action. It is a change so thorough that Paul said in 2 Corinthians 5:17, *"If anyone is in Christ, he is a new creation; old things have passed away; behold, all things have become new."*

In the inspired language of the apostle John, regeneration is a passing *"out of death into life"* (1 John 3:14 RV). Until we are born again, we are in a condition of moral and spiritual death. When we are born again, we are made alive, we who *"were dead in* [our] *trespasses and sins"* (Ephesians 2:1).

There is a profound contrast between true regeneration and a mere conversion experience. Conversion is an outward thing, a turning around. A person is facing the wrong way, facing away from God, and he turns around and faces toward God. That is conversion. But regeneration is not a mere outward change; it is a thorough change in the deepest depths of one's being. It leads to a genuine conversion, or genuine outward change. Many an apparently thorough conversion is a temporary thing because it did not go deep enough; but regeneration is a permanent thing. When God imparts His nature to a person, that nature abides in the person. When he is born again, he cannot be unborn, or as John put it in 1 John 3:9, *"Whoever has been born of God does not sin, for His* [God's] *seed remains in him."* A person may be "converted" a thousand times, but he can be regenerated only once.

What Are the Results of Being Born Again?

Now we come to the second question, which is closely related to the first. It will help us to understand even more clearly what the new birth is. The question is, What are the results of being born again? They are numerous.

We Become the Temple of the Holy Spirit

The first of these results is found in 1 Corinthians 6:19: *"Do you not know that your body is the temple of the Holy Spirit who is in you, whom you have from God?*" These words were spoken to believers, to regenerated individuals, and they plainly tell us that when one is born again, the Holy Spirit comes to take up His permanent dwelling in the person. In this way, the person who is born again becomes a "*temple of the Holy Spirit.*" It is true that he may not always be conscious of this indwelling of the Holy Spirit; nevertheless, He dwells in him.

We Are Free from the Law of Sin and Death

The second result of the new birth is found in Romans 8:2–4:

> *For the law of the Spirit of life in Christ Jesus has made me free from the law of sin and death. For what the law could not do in that it was weak through the flesh, God did by sending His own Son in the likeness of sinful flesh, on account of sin: He condemned sin in the flesh, that the righteous requirement of the law might be fulfilled in us who do not walk according to the flesh but according to the Spirit.*

In the seventh chapter of Romans, we have a picture of the person who is awakened by the law of God. He approves God's law in the "*inward man*" (Romans 7:22) and sees it as "*holy and just and good*" (verse 12). He tries to keep it in his own strength but utterly fails. At last he comes to the end of himself and is filled with despair—he despairs of ever being able to keep the law of God that is outside him because of the law of sin and death that is inside him. The law of sin and death says, "The good that you want to do you cannot do, and the evil that you hate and do not want to do, you must keep on doing." (See verse 15.)

When a person sees his own utter helplessness, turns to God, and accepts Jesus Christ, the Holy Spirit sets him free from this law of sin and death. By the power of the indwelling Spirit, whom Jesus Christ gives to the one who dwells in Him, the believer is enabled to obey the law of God. He gets victory over the evil things that he does not want to do, and he is enabled to do the things that he wants to do. In a person merely awakened by the law of God, "*the law of sin and death*" (Romans 8:2) gets a perpetual victory. But in a regenerate person, *"the law of the Spirit of life in Christ Jesus"* (verse 2) gets a perpetual victory.

Undoubtedly, many of you reading this are still struggling to keep the law of God and are utterly failing in your attempt to do so. What you need is to be born again and thus have the Holy Spirit come to dwell in you. Then you need to walk by the Spirit. (See Romans 8:1, 4.) By the power of this indwelling Spirit, you can get victory every day and every hour over the law of sin and death that wars in your members against the law of God. (See Romans 7:22–23.)

We Are Transformed

The third result of the new birth is found in Romans 12:2: *"And do not be conformed to this world, but be transformed by the renewing of your mind."* From this we see that the third result of the new birth is an outward transformation of our lives by an inward renewing of our minds. We are no longer conformed to this world.

Of course, the regenerated person does not immediately have a perfect manifestation of all that is in him in seed form. He begins the new life just as we begin our natural lives, as a babe, and he must grow. As Peter put it in 1 Peter 2:2, we must *"as newborn babes, desire the pure milk of the word, that* [we] *may grow thereby."* This new life must be fed and developed.

It is irrational and unwarranted by the Word of God to expect someone who has just been born again—someone who is a babe in Christ—to be as perfect in character as someone who was born again years ago and has grown to maturity. But the moment we are born again, we receive in seed all the moral perfection that is to be ours when this seed is fully developed within us and comes to its perfect manifestation.

We Believe That Jesus Is the Christ

The fourth result of the new birth is found in 1 John 5:1: *"Whoever believes that Jesus is the Christ is born of God."* The fourth result of being born again is a belief that Jesus is the Christ. Of course, this faith that comes from the new birth is a real faith. The faith that John spoke of here is not a faith that is a mere opinion, but a real faith that Jesus is the anointed of God—a faith that leads us to enthrone Jesus as King in our lives. If you are not making Jesus the King of your heart and life, you have not been born again. But if you are making Jesus the King of your heart and life, and absolute Ruler of your thoughts and conduct, then you are born again, for *"whoever believes that Jesus is the Christ is born of God."*

We Have Victory over the World

We find the fifth result of being born again three verses further down in this same chapter: *"For whatever is born of God overcomes the world"* (1 John 5:4). The fifth result of being born of God is victory over the world.

The world is in conflict with God. *"The whole world lies under the sway of the wicked one"* (1 John 5:19). It is under the dominion of the Evil One, ruled by his ambitions and ideas. The world fights against God in its economic life, social life, domestic life, and in all the phases of intellectual and educational life. It is constantly exercising a power over each of us, to draw us into disobedience to God.

But the person who is born of God by the power of faith gets victory over the world. (See 1 John 5:4.) He gets victory over the world's ideas, purposes, plans, and ambitions. Every day, he gets victory over the world in his personal life, domestic life, economic life, political life, and intellectual life.

We Do Not Make a Practice of Sin

The sixth result of being born of God is found in 1 John 3:9:

> *Whoever has been born of God does not sin, for His* [God's] *seed remains in him; and he cannot sin* [more literally, cannot be sinning], *because he has been born of God.*

The sixth result, then, in the one who is born of God is that the seed of God remains in him. Therefore, the one born of God is not making a practice of sin. Some people ask, Just what does this mean? It means exactly what it says if we look carefully at the exact definitions of the words and give due emphasis to the tense of the verbs.

First of all, let us look at the exact meaning of the word translated *"sin."* What does *"sin"* mean? John himself was careful to define it in the verse itself and in the context in which our verse is found. The first thing that is evident from 1 John 3:9 is that *"sin"* is something that a person does, not merely something that he leaves undone, and not merely sinful thoughts and desires. What kind of "something" is defined five verses back in verse 4: *"Whoever commits sin also commits lawlessness, and sin is lawlessness."* Here, by John's own definition (and we have no right to bring the definition of anyone else into the verse we are studying), *"sin is lawlessness."* That is, sins are acts that reveal conscious disregard for the will of God as revealed in His Word.

So we see that sin, as used here, means a conscious, intentional violation of the law of God. The regenerate individual will not be doing what he knows is contrary to the will of God. He may do what is contrary to God's will when he does not know it is contrary to God's will. In that case, his action is not, therefore, *"lawlessness."* Perhaps he ought to have known that it was contrary to God's will, and when he is led to see that it is, he will confess his guilt to God.

Furthermore, we should note the tense of the verb used in 1 John 3:9. It is the present tense, which denotes progressive or continuous action. A literal translation of the passage would be, "Whoever has been born of God is not doing sin, because His (God's) seed in him is remaining; and he cannot be sinning, because he has been born of God." It is not taught here that a born-again believer never sins in a single act, but it is taught that he is not going on sinning or making a practice of sin. We see what he is practicing in 1 John 2:29: *"If you know that He is righteous, you know that everyone who practices righteousness is born of Him."*

The result, then, in a born-again believer is that he does not go on consciously, day after day, doing what he knows is contrary to the will of God. But he does make a practice of "doing righteousness," that is, doing God's will as revealed in His Word. The new nature imparted in regeneration renders the continuous practice of sin impossible and renders the practice of righteousness inevitable.

We Love Our Fellow Believers

The seventh result of the new birth is found in 1 John 3:14: "*We know that we have passed from death to life, because we love the brethren. He who does not love his brother abides in death.*" The seventh result of being born again is that we love our brothers and sisters in Christ. We should note carefully what the meaning of "*love*" is as brought out in the context. It is not love as a mere sentiment. It is love in that higher and deeper sense of a desire for and delight in the welfare of others, the sort of love that leads us to make sacrifices for those we love. As we read further down in this same chapter,

> *By this we know love, because He laid down His life for us. And we also ought to lay down our lives for the brethren. But whoever has this world's goods, and sees his brother in need, and shuts up his heart from him, how does the love of God abide in him? My little children, let us not love in word or in tongue, but in deed and in truth.*
>
> (verses 16–18)

This passage makes it very evident that what the Holy Spirit means by "*love*" here is not a mere affection or fondness for others, not a mere delight in their company. It means a deep and genuine interest in their welfare that leads us to dig into our pockets when they are in need and supply their need. It leads us to sacrifice our own interests for the sake of their interests, even to the point of laying down our lives for them.

The objects of this love are "*the brethren,*" that is, all those who are born of God. We read in 1 John 5:1: "*Whoever believes that Jesus is the Christ is born of God, and everyone who loves Him who begot also loves him who is begotten of Him.*" Any person who is born again will love every other person who is born again. The other individual may be an American, a German, an Englishman, an African-American, or an Indian; the individual may be educated or uneducated; but the person is a child of God and a brother or a sister. As such, he or she will be the object of your love if you are born of God. This is a searching test of whether or not a person is born again.

We Are New

The final result that we will consider is found in 2 Corinthians 5:17: *"Therefore, if anyone is in Christ, he is a new creation; old things have passed away; behold, all things have become new."* The eighth result of being born again is that in the regenerate person, *"old things have passed away"* and *"all things have become new."* In the place of the old ideas, old desires, old purposes, and old choices are new ideas, new desires, new purposes, and new choices.

Why Is It Necessary to Be Born Again?

For just a few paragraphs, let us look at the necessity of the new birth. This is set forth in the following verses:

> *Most assuredly, I say to you, unless one is born of water and the Spirit, he cannot enter the kingdom of God. That which is born of the flesh is flesh, and that which is born of the Spirit is spirit.* (John 3:5–6)

We see here that the new birth is a universal necessity, and we see why it is a universal necessity. Verse 6 tells us that all that one gets by natural birth is *"flesh,"* and the kingdom of God is spiritual. Therefore, to enter it, one must be *"born of the Spirit."*

No matter how refined and intelligent our ancestry is, no matter how godly our fathers and mothers may have been, we do not get the Holy Spirit from them. All we get is *"flesh."* It may be refined flesh, moral flesh, upright flesh, and very attractive flesh, but it is flesh. We know that *"those who are in the flesh cannot please God"* (Romans 8:8) or *"inherit the kingdom of God"* (1 Corinthians 15:50). We also know that the flesh is incapable of improvement. *"Can… the leopard* [change] *its spots?"* (Jeremiah 13:23). Of course not. Nor can a person who is unregenerate change his life in such a way that it will be pleasing to God. He must be born again.

The new birth is absolutely imperative, so imperative that Jesus said to Nicodemus—though he was a man of most exemplary morality, a man of high moral and spiritual education, a leader in Israel's religious life—*"You must be born again"* (John 3:7). Nothing else will take the place of the new birth. People are trying to substitute education, morality, religion, orthodoxy, baptism, outward reform, New Thought, Theosophy, the knowledge of God, and other such things; but none of these, nor all of them put together, are sufficient. You *must* be born again. There is absolutely no exception to this rule. As Jesus said in John 3:3, *"Most assuredly, I say to you, unless one is born again, he cannot see the kingdom of God."*

How Can a Person Be Born Again?

This question, therefore, confronts each one of us: Have you been born again? There is no more important question that you could possibly face. Face it in these pages, and don't dodge it.

This brings us to the immediately practical question: How are individuals born again? Or, What must anyone reading this who is not born again do in order to be born again right now? This question is plainly answered in the Word of God. I can answer it in very few paragraphs and in a way that anyone reading this can understand. There are three parts to the answer.

By God's Working

You will find the first part of the answer in Titus 3:5:

> *Not by works of righteousness which we have done, but according to His mercy He* [God] *saved us, through the washing of regeneration and renewing of the Holy Spirit.*

These words tell us very plainly that it is God who regenerates and that He does it through the power of His Holy Spirit.

The same thought is found in John 3:5–6:

> *Jesus answered, "Most assuredly, I say to you, unless one is born of water and the Spirit, he cannot enter the kingdom of God. That which is born of the flesh is flesh, and that which is born of the Spirit is spirit."*

Regeneration is God's work, performed by Him by the power of His Holy Spirit working in the mind, feelings, and will of the one born again—in your heart and mine.

By Getting in Contact with God's Word

Someone might infer from the fact that regeneration is God's work that all we have to do is wait until God sees fit to work. But we see plainly from other passages in the Word that this is not true. In James 1:18, we are taught the second thing concerning how regeneration is brought about: *"Of His own will He brought us forth by the word of truth, that we might be a kind of firstfruits of His creatures."* Here we are taught that the Word of Truth, the Word of God, is the instrument that God uses in regeneration. The same thought is found in 1 Peter 1:23: *"Having been born again, not of corruptible seed but incorruptible, through the word of God which lives and abides forever."* And Paul gave voice to the same great thought in 1 Corinthians 4:15, where he said,

> *For though you might have ten thousand instructors in Christ, yet you do not have many fathers; for in Christ Jesus I have begotten you through the gospel.*

From these passages, it is evident that the new birth is brought about by God through the instrument of His Word. It is God who works through the power of His Holy Spirit, but the Holy Spirit works through the Word. Thus God makes individuals new by the Word of Truth, or the Word of God—that is, the Word that is preached by the Gospel. So then, if you or I wish to be born again, we should get in contact with the Word of God by studying the Bible and asking God that the Holy Spirit would make the Word that we are studying a living thing in our own hearts. We should get in contact especially with the gospel of John, for John told us in John 20:31,

> *These* [that is, these things in the gospel of John] *are written that you may believe that Jesus is the Christ, the Son of God, and that believing you may have life in His name.*

If we wish to see others born again, we should use the Word of God effectively to touch their minds and hearts, either by preaching the Word, teaching the Word, or using the Word in our personal ministry. We should look to the Holy Spirit to make that Word alive in the hearts of people as we sow it there. In this way, the new birth will result.

By Trusting in Jesus

The third, last, and decisive truth as to how we are born again is found in Galatians 3:26 and John 1:12–13. In Galatians 3:26, we read, *"For you are all sons of God through faith in Christ Jesus."* This verse tells us plainly that we become born again through putting our faith in Christ Jesus. This is even more explicitly stated in John 1:12–13:

> *But as many as received* [the Lord Jesus], *to them He gave the right to become children of God, to those who believe in His name: who were born, not of blood, nor of the will of the flesh, nor of the will of man, but of God.*

Here we are told that the decisive thing in our becoming children of God is that we believe in, or receive, Jesus Christ. We must (1) receive Jesus Christ as our personal Savior and trust God to forgive us because Jesus Christ died in our place, (2) receive Him as our Lord and King and surrender our thoughts and lives to His absolute control, and (3) be willing to confess Jesus Christ as Lord before the world. Anyone who does these things is immediately a child of God, is immediately born again, is immediately made a partaker of the divine nature. (See 2 Peter 1:4.)

The same thought was illustrated by Jesus Himself in John 3:14–15, where our Lord Jesus is recorded as saying,

> *And as Moses lifted up the serpent in the wilderness, even so must the Son of Man be lifted up, that whoever believes in Him should not perish but have eternal life.*

The reference is to the Old Testament story of how the Israelites were bitten by *"fiery serpents."* (Numbers 21:6.) The dying Israelite, with the poison of the fiery serpent coursing through his veins, was saved by simply looking at the bronze serpent on the pole, a serpent that looked like the one that had bitten him. He had new life as soon as he looked. In the same way, we dying individuals, with the poison of sin coursing through our veins, are saved by looking at Jesus Christ, who was made *"in the likeness of sinful flesh"* (Romans 8:3) and lifted up on the cross. We have new life the moment we look. The only part we have to play in our regeneration is to receive Christ as He is presented to us in the Word, by which we are born again. *"Therefore, if anyone is in Christ, he is a new creation; old things have passed away; behold, all things have become new"* (2 Corinthians 5:17).

In the new birth, the Word of God is the seed, and the human heart is the soil. The preacher of the Word is the sower who drops the seed of the Word into the soil of the human heart. (See Luke 8:11–15.) God, by His Spirit, opens the heart to receive the seed. (See Acts 16:14.) The hearer believes, and the Spirit gives life to the seed in the receptive heart. The heart closes around the seed by faith. The new nature, the divine nature, springs up out of the divine Word, and the believer is *"born again"* (1 Peter 1:23), is *"made alive"* (Ephesians 2:1), has *"passed out of death into life"* (1 John 3:14 RV).

You Can Be Born Again

Have you been born again? I ask this question of everyone reading this book. I do not ask whether you are a church member. I do not ask whether you have been baptized. I do not ask whether you have gone regularly to communion. I do not ask whether you have turned over a new leaf. I do not ask whether you are a likable, cultured, intelligent, moral, or popular person. I ask you, Have you been born again? If not, you are outside of the kingdom of God and are headed for an everlasting hell.

But you can be born again today. You can be born again before you put this book down. You can be born again right now, for the Word of God says,

> *But as many as received Him, to them He gave the right to become children of God, to those who believe in His name: who were born, not of blood, nor of the will of the flesh, nor of the will of man, but of God.* (John 1:12–13)

And it says again in Romans 10:9–10,

> *If you confess with your mouth the Lord Jesus and believe in your heart that God has raised Him from the dead, you will be saved. For with the heart one believes unto righteousness, and with the mouth confession is made unto salvation.*

These verses make it as plain as day just what you must do right here and now to become a child of God. It is up to you to say whether or not you will do it.

4

WHAT IS SANCTIFICATION, AND HOW CAN IT BE MINE?

Now may the God of peace Himself sanctify you completely; and may your whole spirit, soul, and body be preserved blameless at the coming of our Lord Jesus Christ.
—1 Thessalonians 5:23

The subject of sanctification is of great importance. Not only is there much ignorance and error and misconception about the subject, but there is also, strange to say, much bitter controversy over it. Some years ago, there were two rival "holiness conventions" held at the same time in Chicago at different hours of the day, in the same church. The animosity between these two groups of "holiness brethren" was so intense that on one occasion they came close to having a fistfight at the altar of the church.

The subject of sanctification has given rise to such bitterness and such extremes in some places that many even dread the use of the word. But *sanctification* is a Bible word and a deeply significant word, a word full of precious meaning. It would not be wise to give up this good Bible word simply because it is so often abused.

On one occasion, at the Bible Institute of Chicago, a man said to me, "Aren't you afraid of holiness?" Of course, what the man wanted to know was whether I was afraid of certain aspects of so-called holiness doctrine. I replied that I was not nearly as afraid of holiness as I was of unholiness.

The teaching of the Bible on this subject is very plain and very precious. What I have to say about it will come under three main questions: What is sanctification? How are we sanctified? When does sanctification take place?

What Is Sanctification?

Before we consider what sanctification is, it is important to see what sanctification is not. There are many things that it is not, but I would like to discuss two of them.

What Sanctification Is Not

In the first place, let me make it clear that sanctification is not the baptism with the Holy Spirit. These two experiences are constantly confused. There is an intimate relationship between the two, but they are not one and the same thing at all. Only confusion and misconception can arise when we combine two experiences that God keeps separate. Sanctification is not the baptism with the Holy Spirit, and the baptism with the Holy Spirit is not sanctification. This fact will become clear as we proceed.

In the second place, let me say that sanctification is not the eradication of the carnal nature. We will see this when we examine God's definition of sanctification, for God has very clearly defined what sanctification is and when it takes place. Those who teach the eradication of the carnal nature are grasping after a great and precious truth, but they have expressed that truth in a very inaccurate, unfortunate, and unscriptural way. Their way of stating it leads to grave misunderstandings, errors, and abuses.

The whole controversy about the eradication of the carnal nature comes from a misunderstanding, and from using terms for which there is no warrant in the Bible. The Bible nowhere speaks about "the carnal nature," and so it certainly does not speak about the eradication of the carnal nature. There is such a thing as a carnal nature, but it is not a material thing or substance. It is not something that can be eradicated in the same way that a doctor can pull a tooth or remove an appendix. A carnal nature is a nature controlled by the flesh (the sinful tendencies of man). Certainly, it is a believer's privilege not to have his nature governed by the flesh. His nature may be and should be under the control of the Holy Spirit, and then it is not a carnal nature. But one nature has not been eradicated and then replaced by another nature. The believer's nature is taken out from under the control of the flesh and put under the control of the Holy Spirit.

Furthermore, while it is the Christian's privilege to have his nature under the control of the Holy Spirit and to have it delivered from the control of the flesh, he still has the flesh, and he will have the flesh as long as he is in this body. But if he "*walk*[s] *in the Spirit,*" he does not "*fulfill the lust of the flesh*" (Galatians 5:16).

The eighth chapter of Romans describes the life of victory, just as the seventh chapter, in verses 9–24, describes the life of defeat, the life of being "*carnal, sold under sin*" (verse 14). It is in the eighth chapter, where life "*in the Spirit*" (verse 9) is described, that we are told that we still have the flesh, but that it is our privilege not to "*live according to the flesh*" (verse 12) but to "*by the Spirit...put to death the deeds of the body*" (verse 13). So we see that the flesh is there, but in the power of the Spirit, we do day by day (and if we live up to our privilege, hour by hour and minute by minute) "*put to death the deeds of the body.*"

What Sanctification Is

That will suffice as an explanation of what sanctification is not. Now we will see exactly what it is by looking at God's definition. The word *sanctification* is used in the Bible in a twofold sense.

We find the first meaning of sanctification in Leviticus 8:10–12:

> *Also Moses took the anointing oil, and anointed the tabernacle and all that was in it, and consecrated ["sanctified" KJV] them. He sprinkled some of it on the altar seven times, anointed the altar and all its utensils, and the laver and its base, to consecrate ["sanctify" KJV] them. And he poured some of the anointing oil on Aaron's head and anointed him, to consecrate ["sanctify" KJV] him.*

Now, it is perfectly clear in this passage that "*sanctify*" means "to separate or set apart for God" and that sanctification is "the process of setting apart or the state of being set apart for God."

The word *sanctify* is used in this sense over and over again in the Bible. Another illustration is Leviticus 27:14, 16:

> *And when a man dedicates his house to be holy to the LORD, then the priest shall set a value for it, whether it is good or bad; as the priest values it, so it shall stand....If a man dedicates ["shall sanctify" KJV] to the LORD part of a field of his possession, then your valuation shall be according to the seed for it.*

Still another instance of this same use of the word *sanctify* is found in Numbers 8:17:

> *For all the firstborn among the children of Israel are Mine, both man and beast; on the day that I struck all the firstborn in the land of Egypt I sanctified them to Myself.*

This verse, of course, does not mean that at the time that God smote the firstborn in Egypt, He eradicated the carnal nature from the firstborn of Israel. It does mean that He set apart all the firstborn to be uniquely His own.

Another very significant illustration of the same usage of the word is found in Jeremiah's statement of his own case:

> *Then the word of the* Lord *came to me, saying: "Before I formed you in the womb I knew you; before you were born I sanctified you; I ordained you a prophet to the nations."* (Jeremiah 1:4–5)

This passage plainly means that before Jeremiah's birth, God set him apart for Himself. There would still be much imperfection and weakness in him, but he was set apart for God.

Another thought-provoking instance of the same use of the word *sanctify* is found in Matthew 23:17, in the words of our Lord Jesus Himself: *"Fools and blind! For which is greater, the gold or the temple that sanctifies the gold?"* But perhaps the most striking illustration of all is in what our Lord said about His own sanctification in John 17:19: *"And for their sakes I sanctify myself, that they themselves also may be sanctified in truth"* (RV). Here the plain meaning is that our Lord Jesus set Himself apart for this work for God, and He did it in order that believers might be set apart for God *"in truth,"* or "in the truth."

This is the most frequent use of the word *sanctify*. There are numerous illustrations of it in the Bible. So sanctify means "to separate or to set apart for God," and sanctification is "the process of setting apart or the state of being set apart for God." This is the primary meaning of the words.

But sanctification, as used in the Bible, also has a secondary definition closely related to this primary meaning. We find an illustration of this secondary definition in 2 Chronicles 29:5:

> *Hear me, Levites! Now sanctify yourselves, sanctify the house of the* Lord *God of your fathers, and carry out the rubbish from the holy place.*

When we bear in mind the parallelism that is the chief characteristic of Hebrew poetry, it is plain that to sanctify here is synonymous with "[to] *carry out the rubbish from the holy place.*" So here, to sanctify means "to separate from ceremonial or moral defilement; to cleanse"; and sanctification is "the process of separating, or the state of being separated, from ceremonial or moral defilement."

The same use of the word is found in Leviticus:

> *For I am the Lord your God: ye shall therefore sanctify yourselves, and ye shall be holy; for I am holy: neither shall ye defile yourselves with any manner of creeping thing that creepeth upon the earth.*
> (Leviticus 11:44 KJV)

Here again, it is clear that "*sanctify yourselves*" is synonymous with "*ye shall be holy*" and is contrasted with "*defile yourselves.*"

The same meaning of sanctification is found in the New Testament in 1 Thessalonians 5:23:

> *Now may the God of peace Himself sanctify you completely; and may your whole spirit, soul, and body be preserved blameless at the coming of our Lord Jesus Christ.*

Here we see the close relationship between entire sanctification and being preserved wholly, without blame. To sanctify here clearly means "to separate from moral defilement," and sanctification, here again, is "the process of separating, or the state of being separated, from moral defilement."

The same thing is evident from 1 Thessalonians 4:7: "*For God called us not for uncleanness, but in sanctification*" (RV). Here our "*sanctification*" is set in direct contrast to "*uncleanness*"; hence, it is evident that here sanctification means "the state of being separated from all moral defilement." The same concept is clear from the third verse of this same chapter: "*For this is the will of God, your sanctification: that you should abstain from sexual immorality.*" Here again, it is evident that sanctification means "separation from impurity or moral defilement."

The two meanings, then, of sanctification are as follows: first, "the process of separating or setting apart, or the state of being separated or set apart, for God"; and second, "the process of separating, or the state of being separated, from ceremonial or moral defilement." These two meanings of the word are closely allied. One cannot be truly separated unto God without being separated from sin.

How Are We Sanctified?

We now come to the second question: How are we sanctified? There are several parts to the complete answer to this question.

God Sanctifies Us

The first part of the answer is found in the text of this chapter:

> *Now may the God of peace Himself sanctify you completely; and may your whole spirit, soul, and body be preserved blameless at the coming of our Lord Jesus Christ.* (1 Thessalonians 5:23)

It appears from this verse that God sanctifies us, that sanctification is God's work. Both our separation from sin and our separation unto God is God's work. As it was God who in the Old Testament set apart the firstborn of Israel unto Himself, so it is God who in the New Testament sets apart the believer unto Himself and separates him from sin. Sanctification primarily is not ours, but God's.

Christ Sanctifies Us

The second part of the answer is found in Ephesians 5:25–26:

> *Husbands, love your wives, just as Christ also loved the church and gave Himself for her, that He might sanctify and cleanse her with the washing of water by the word.*

Here we are taught that Christ sanctifies the church and that sanctification is Christ's work. Of course, we are faced with the question,

In what sense does Christ sanctify the church? The answer is found in Hebrews 10:10: "*By that will we have been sanctified through the offering of the body of Jesus Christ once for all.*" Here it appears that Jesus Christ sanctified the church by giving Himself up as a sacrifice for it. In this way, Christ set the church apart for God. Just as the blood of the Passover lamb, referred to in the eleventh and twelfth chapters of Exodus, made a difference between Israel and Egypt (see Exodus 11:7), so our Lord Jesus, by the offering of His own body, has forever made a difference between the believer and the world. He has forever set every believer apart for God. The cross of Christ stands between the believer and the world, and the shed blood of Christ separates the believer from the world and purchases him for God, thus making him belong to God.

The Holy Spirit Sanctifies Us

The third part of the answer to the question of how we are sanctified is found in 2 Thessalonians 2:13:

> *But we are bound to give thanks to God always for you, brethren beloved by the Lord, because God from the beginning chose you for salvation through sanctification by the Spirit and belief in the truth.*

It appears from this passage, as well as from other passages in the Bible, that it is the Holy Spirit who sanctifies the believer. Sanctification is the Holy Spirit's work.

Here the question arises: In what sense does the Holy Spirit sanctify the believer? Just as, in the Old Testament, tabernacle, altar, and priest were set apart for God by the anointing oil (see Leviticus 8:10–12), so in the New Testament, the believer, who is both tabernacle and priest, is set apart for God by the anointing of the Holy Spirit. Furthermore, it is the Holy Spirit's work in the heart that overcomes the flesh and its defilement, and thus separates the believer from sin and clothes him with divine graces of character and makes him fit to be God's own.

As Paul put it in Galatians 5:22–23, "*The fruit of the Spirit is love, joy, peace, longsuffering, kindness, goodness, faithfulness, gentleness, self-control.*" In direct contrast to this work of the Holy Spirit, we read in the immediately preceding verses about "*the works of the flesh*" (verse 19), an awful catalog of vileness and sin. However, we are told in the sixteenth verse, "*Walk in the Spirit, and you shall not fulfill the lust of the flesh.*"

The Blood of Jesus Sanctifies Us

The fourth part of the answer to the question of how we are sanctified is found in Hebrews 13:12: "*Therefore Jesus also, that He might sanctify the people with His own blood, suffered outside the gate.*" It is plain from this passage that believers are sanctified through the blood of Jesus Christ. But in what sense does the blood of Jesus sanctify? The answer is plain: the blood of Jesus Christ cleanses us from all the guilt of sin, and thus it separates us from all the people who are under the curse of the broken law and sets us apart for God. (See 1 John 1:7, 9.) In the Old Testament, the blood of the sacrifice cleansed the Israelites from the guilt of ceremonial offenses and set them apart for God. In the New Testament fulfillment of this Old Testament type, the blood of Christ cleanses the believer from the guilt of moral offenses and sets him apart for God.

The Word of God Sanctifies Us

The fifth part of the answer to the question of how we are sanctified is found in John 17:17: "*Sanctify them by Your truth. Your word is truth.*" Here in our Lord Jesus' prayer, He indicated that we are sanctified by the truth and that the Word of God is the truth. In what sense does the Word of God sanctify us? This question is plainly answered in different parts of the Bible, where we are taught that the Word of God cleanses us from the presence of sin and thus separates us from it and sets us apart unto God. (See Psalm 119:9, 11; John 15:3.) As we bring our lives into daily contact with the Word, the sins and imperfections of our lives and hearts are disclosed and put away, and thus we are more and more separated from sin unto God. (See John 13:10.)

Taking Hold of Christ Sanctifies Us

The sixth part of the answer is found in 1 Corinthians 1:30: *"But of Him you are in Christ Jesus, who became for us wisdom from God; and righteousness and sanctification and redemption."* In this passage, we are taught that Jesus Christ became for us sanctification from God. Just what does this mean? Simply this: separation from sin and separation unto God are provided for us in Christ Jesus. By taking hold of Jesus Christ, we obtain this sanctification that has been provided. The more completely we take hold of Christ, the more completely we are sanctified. Perfect sanctification is provided for us in Him, just as perfect wisdom is provided for us in Him. (See Colossians 2:3). We take hold of wisdom, sanctification, or anything else that is provided for us in Christ, in ever increasing measure. Through the indwelling Christ presented to us by the Spirit in the Word, we are made Christlike, and we bear fruit.

Our Pursuit of Holiness Sanctifies Us

The seventh part of the answer to the question of how we are sanctified is found in Hebrews 12:14: *"Follow after peace with all men, and the sanctification without which no man shall see the Lord"* (RV). Here we are taught that we have our own part in sanctification. If we are to be sanctified in the fullest sense, sanctification is something that we must pursue, or seek earnestly. While sanctification is God's work, we have our part in it, namely, to make it the object of our earnest desire and eager pursuit.

Presenting Ourselves to God Sanctifies Us

The eighth part of the answer is found in Romans:

> *As ye presented your members as servants to uncleanness and to iniquity unto iniquity, even so now present your members as servants to righteousness unto sanctification....But now being made free from sin, and become servants to God, ye have your fruit unto sanctification.*
>
> (Romans 6:19, 22 RV)

The meaning of these words is plain, and the teaching is important and practical. We are taught here that we attain to sanctification through presenting our members as servants (bondservants or slaves) to righteousness. In other words, if we want to attain to sanctification, we should present our whole bodies and every member of them to God to be His servants, belonging wholly to Him. We should present our whole selves to God as His servants, to be His property entirely. This is the practical method of attaining to sanctification, a method that is available to each one of us, no matter how weak we are in ourselves.

Faith in Christ Sanctifies Us

The ninth and final part of the answer to the question of how we are sanctified is found in Acts 26:18, where Jesus said,

> *To open their eyes, in order to turn them from darkness to light, and from the power of Satan to God, that they may receive forgiveness of sins and an inheritance among those who are sanctified by faith in Me.*

Here we are told that we are sanctified by faith in Christ. Sanctification—just like justification, regeneration, and adoption—is dependent on faith. Faith is the hand by which we take hold of the blessing of sanctification that God has provided for us through His Son's death on the cross, and through the Holy Spirit's power working in us. We claim sanctification by simple faith in the One who shed His blood and by surrendering ourselves to the control of the Holy Spirit, whom Jesus Christ gives.

When Does Sanctification Take Place?

We now come to the question about which there has been the most discussion, the most differences of opinion, the most controversy: When does sanctification take place? If we go to our Bibles to get the answer to this question, there does not need to be any difference of opinion. The answer has three parts.

The Moment We Believe

First, we find part of the answer in 1 Corinthians 1:2:

> *To the church of God which is at Corinth, to those who are sanctified in Christ Jesus, called to be saints, with all who in every place call on the name of Jesus Christ our Lord, both theirs and ours.*

Here the Holy Spirit, speaking through the apostle Paul, plainly declared that all the members of the church of God are already sanctified in Christ Jesus. Sanctification in this sense is not something that we are to look for in the future; it is something that has already taken place. The moment anyone becomes a member of the church of God by simple faith in Christ Jesus (for all who have faith in Christ Jesus are members of the church of God), in that moment, the person is sanctified. Every saved man, woman, and child, everyone who has a living faith in Jesus Christ, is sanctified.

In other words, our sanctification is involved in our salvation. But in what sense are all believers already sanctified? The answer to this question is found in Hebrews:

> *By which will we have been sanctified through the offering of the body of Jesus Christ once for all....For by one offering he hath perfected for ever them that are sanctified.* (Hebrews 10:10, 14 RV)

The meaning of this is plain. By *"the offering of the body of Jesus Christ once for all"* on the cross of Calvary as a perfect atonement for sin, every believer is cleansed forever from the guilt of sin. We are *"perfected for ever"* as far as our standing before God is concerned, and we are set apart for God. The sacrifice of Christ does not need to be repeated as the Jewish sacrifices were. (See Hebrews 10:1, 11.) The work was done *"once for all"* (verse 10); sin is put away, and put away forever. (See Hebrews 9:26.) We are set apart forever as God's special and eternal possession.

If you are a believer in Jesus Christ—that is, if you have a living faith in Jesus Christ—you have a right to say, "I am sanctified." Every believer in

Christ is a saint—not a saint in the sense that the word is often used these days, but in the biblical sense, as being set apart for God, belonging to God, and being God's special property.

But there is another sense in which every believer may be fully sanctified today. This is found in Romans 12:1:

> *I beseech you therefore, brethren, by the mercies of God, that you present your bodies a living sacrifice, holy, acceptable to God, which is your reasonable service.*

In this passage, we see that it is the believer's present and blessed privilege, as well as his important and solemn duty, to present his body to God as *"a living sacrifice"*—not some part or parts of his body, but his whole body with its every member and every ability. When we do present our whole bodies to God as living sacrifices, then we are wholly sanctified. Such an offering is well-pleasing to God. In the Old Testament, God sometimes showed His pleasure in an offering by sending down fire to take it to Himself. (See 1 Kings 18:36–39.) Likewise, when the whole body is thus offered to God, He will send down fire again, the fire of the Holy Spirit, and take to Himself what is presented.

The moment a believer presents himself as a living sacrifice to God, then, as far as his will—the governing purpose of his life, the very center of his being—is concerned, he is wholly God's, or "perfectly sanctified." He may and will still daily discover, as he studies the Word of God and is enlightened by the Holy Spirit, aspects of his life that are not in conformity with this new central purpose of his will. These habits, feelings, words, and actions must be confessed to God as blameworthy and must be put away. These areas of the believer's being and life must be brought, by God's Spirit and the indwelling Christ, into conformity with God's will as revealed in His Word.

The victory in this newly discovered and unclaimed territory may be instantaneous. For example, I may discover in myself an irritability that is clearly displeasing to God. I can go to God, confess it, renounce it, and then instantly—not by my own strength but by looking to Jesus and claiming

His patience and gentleness—overcome it and never have another failure in that area. So it is with every other sin and weakness in my life that I am brought to see is displeasing to God.

As We Progress in Our Walk with God

But this is not the whole answer to the question of when we are sanctified. The second part of the answer is found in the following passages:

> *May the Lord make you increase and abound in love to one another and to all, just as we do to you.* (1 Thessalonians 3:12)

> *Finally then, brethren, we urge and exhort in the Lord Jesus that you should abound more and more, just as you received from us how you ought to walk and to please God....Indeed you do so toward all the brethren who are in all Macedonia. But we urge you, brethren, that you increase more and more.* (1 Thessalonians 4:1, 10)

> *Grow in the grace and knowledge of our Lord and Savior Jesus Christ.* (2 Peter 3:18)

> *But we all, with unveiled face, beholding as in a mirror the glory of the Lord, are being transformed into the same image from glory to glory, just as by the Spirit of the Lord.* (2 Corinthians 3:18)

> *But, speaking the truth in love,* [we] *may grow up in all things into Him who is the head; Christ; from whom the whole body, joined and knit together by what every joint supplies, according to the effective working by which every part does its share, causes growth of the body for the edifying of itself in love.* (Ephesians 4:15–16)

From these passages, we see that there is a progressive work of sanctification—an increasing in love; an abounding more and more in a godly walk and in pleasing God; a growing in the grace and the knowledge of our Lord and Savior Jesus Christ; a being transformed into the image of our Lord from glory to glory, each new gaze at Him making us more like Him; a growing up into Christ in all things, until we attain to a full-grown man, *"to the measure of the stature of the fullness of Christ"* (Ephesians 4:13).

At the Coming of Our Lord Jesus Christ

Even yet, we have not found the whole answer to the question of when we are sanctified. We find the remainder of the answer in our text:

> *Now may the God of peace Himself sanctify you completely; and may your whole spirit, soul, and body be preserved blameless at the coming of our Lord Jesus Christ.* (1 Thessalonians 5:23)

Here we are plainly told that the complete sanctification of believers, complete in the fullest sense, is something that is to be sought in prayer and that is to be accomplished by God in the future and perfected at the coming of our Lord Jesus Christ.

The same thought is found again in 1 Thessalonians:

> *And may the Lord make you increase and abound in love to one another and to all, just as we do to you, so that He may establish your hearts blameless in holiness before our God and Father at the coming of our Lord Jesus Christ with all His saints.* (1 Thessalonians 3:12–13)

It is *"at the coming of our Lord Jesus Christ with all His saints"* that He is to establish our hearts *"blameless in holiness before our God and Father."* It is at Christ's coming that our whole spirits and souls and bodies are to be preserved without blame.

The same thought is found in 1 John 3:2:

> *Beloved, now we are children of God; and it has not yet been revealed what we shall be, but we know that when He is revealed, we shall be like Him, for we shall see Him as He is.*

It is not in the life that now is, and it is not at death, that we are entirely sanctified, spirit, soul, and body. It is at the coming of our Lord Jesus Christ. This fact is one of the many reasons that the well-instructed believer constantly cries, *"Even so, come, Lord Jesus!"* (Revelation 22:20). Moreover, he cries, "Come quickly!"

5

WHAT WILL MY RESURRECTED BODY BE LIKE?

Remember that Jesus Christ, of the seed of David, was raised from the dead according to my gospel.
—2 Timothy 2:8

For I delivered to you first of all that which I also received: that Christ died for our sins according to the Scriptures, and that He was buried, and that He rose again the third day according to the Scriptures.
—1 Corinthians 15:3–4

The resurrection of Christ was a resurrection of the body of Christ. What appeared to the disciples on the first resurrection day was not merely the indwelling Spirit of Jesus Christ, clothed with a new and entirely different body. Appearing before their eyes was the body that had been buried and raised again.

For us, this truth involves not merely the immortality of our own souls, but also the resurrection and eternal existence of our own bodies. Yet many people who say that they are doctrinally sound, Bible-believing Christians and believe in the immortality of the soul, do not believe in the resurrection of the body. In this chapter, we will examine what the Bible has to say about bodily resurrection.

The Fact of the Resurrection

First, we will consider the fact of the resurrection of the body of Jesus Christ and of our bodies.

Second Timothy 2:8, one of the texts of this chapter, says, "*Remember that Jesus Christ, of the seed of David, was raised from the dead according to my gospel.*" Here Paul explicitly declared that Jesus Christ was raised from the dead according to the gospel that he preached. Now, what was raised? Certainly not Christ's soul. That did not die. Turning to the second chapter of Acts, we find that the soul of the Lord Jesus went into hades, the abode of the dead. These are Peter's words, spoken on the Day of Pentecost:

> *For David says concerning* [Jesus]: "*...For You* [God] *will not leave my* [Jesus'] *soul in Hades, nor will You allow Your Holy One to see corruption* [that is, to undergo bodily corruption]. *You have made known to me the ways of life; You will make me full of joy in Your presence." Men and brethren, let me speak freely to you of the patriarch David, that he is both dead and buried, and his tomb is with us to this day. Therefore, being a prophet, and knowing that God had sworn with an oath to him that of the fruit of his body, according to the flesh, He would raise up the Christ to sit on his throne, he, foreseeing this, spoke concerning the resurrection of the Christ, that His soul was not left in Hades, nor did His flesh see corruption. This Jesus God has raised up, of which we are all witnesses.* (Acts 2:25, 27–32)

Here Peter declared that the soul of Jesus went to Hades and that it was *"His flesh,"* that is, His body, that was kept from corruption and afterward raised.

Turning now to 1 Corinthians 15:3–4, the other text of this chapter, we read these words of Paul:

> *For I delivered to you first of all that which I also received: that Christ died for our sins according to the Scriptures, and that He was buried, and that He rose again the third day according to the Scriptures.*

Here Paul declared that Jesus Christ *"died"* and *"was buried"* and *"rose again."* What was raised? Paul said that what was buried was raised. But what was buried? Not the soul of the Lord Jesus, but His body.

Peter made this even plainer, if possible, in this passage:

> *Christ also suffered for sins once, the righteous for the unrighteous, that he might bring us to God; being put to death in the flesh, but quickened in the spirit; in which also he went and preached unto the spirits in prison, which aforetime were disobedient, when the longsuffering of God waited in the days of Noah.* (1 Peter 3:18–20 RV)

These words clearly mean that it was the body of Jesus that was put to death, but that the spirit still lived and went into Hades. So it was the body that was raised; and the spirit, which had not died or become unconscious, came back to the body.

First Corinthians 15:12–19 removes all possibility of doubt on this point—that is, for anyone who goes to the Bible to find out what it actually teaches, not merely to see how he can twist and distort it to fit into his own preconceived opinions. Paul's Spirit-given words are:

> *Now if Christ is preached that He has been raised from the dead, how do some among you say that there is no resurrection of the dead?* [Notice, he does not say "no immortality of the soul," but *"no resurrection of the dead."*] *But if there is no resurrection of the dead, then Christ is*

> *not risen. And if Christ is not risen, then our preaching is empty and your faith is also empty. Yes, and we are found false witnesses of God, because we have testified of God that He raised up Christ, whom He did not raise up; if in fact the dead do not rise. For if the dead do not rise, then Christ is not risen. And if Christ is not risen, your faith is futile; you are still in your sins! Then also those who have fallen asleep in Christ have perished. If in this life only we have hope in Christ, we are of all men the most pitiable.*

There is no honest mistaking the plain meaning of these words. By the "*resurrection of the dead,*" Paul plainly meant a resurrection of the body. In the whole chapter, beyond a doubt, he is not talking about the immortality of the soul, but the resurrection of the body. The whole argument hinges on that fact. Here Paul clearly said that if the body of Jesus was not raised, then Christianity is a sham, our faith is in vain, and we Christians are to be pitied more than all other people. For if the body of Jesus was not raised, and if our bodies are not to be raised, then we Christians are making tremendous sacrifices for a lie. Paul further said that if our bodies are not to be raised, then Christ's body has not been raised, and Christianity is a fraud.

Christianity, as it is taught in the New Testament, stands or falls with the resurrection of the body of Jesus and the resurrection of our bodies. There is no room in Paul's argument for Charles Taze Russell's doctrine.[3] Russell taught that the resurrection of Jesus Christ was not a resurrection of the body that was crucified and laid in the grave. He said that the body of Jesus Christ was carried away and preserved somewhere, or else dissolved into gases. But Paul said here that if the body that was laid in the sepulcher was not raised, "*then our preaching is empty and your faith is also empty.*"

In Luke 24:5–6, the angels at Jesus' tomb are recorded as saying to the women who came there, "*Why do you seek the living among the dead? He is not here, but is risen!*" Now, what were the women seeking? They were

---

3. Charles Taze Russell was the founder of the Jehovah's Witnesses.

seeking the body of Jesus to embalm it. The angels said that what they were seeking was not there but was risen.

Furthermore, in the second part of verse 6 and in verse 7, the angels said,

> *Remember how He spoke to you when He was still in Galilee, saying, "The Son of Man must be delivered into the hands of sinful men, and be crucified, and the third day rise again."*

Here they plainly told the women that what was crucified, which of course was the body of Jesus, had been raised. If the actual, literal body of Jesus had not been raised, these angels were liars.

These verses are only a few of the many passages that contain the clear-cut teaching that the very body of Jesus was raised from the dead. Either this teaching is true, and it is also true that our bodies will be raised from the dead, or Christianity is a lie from start to finish. But Christ was raised from the dead, and we will be raised. Or, as Paul put it in 1 Corinthians 15:20, *"Christ is risen from the dead, and has become the firstfruits of those who have fallen asleep."* The resurrection of our bodies will be the harvest that follows the resurrection of Christ's body, which was *"the firstfruits."*

The Characteristics of Our Resurrection Bodies

Since we have clearly settled the fact of the resurrection of the body of Jesus Christ and of our bodies, next we will consider the characteristics of our resurrection bodies.

Different from Our Earthly Bodies

First of all, we know that the body that is raised will not be identical to the body that was laid in the grave. This is apparent from 1 Corinthians 15:35–38:

> *But someone will say, "How are the dead raised up? And with what body do they come?" Foolish one, what you sow is not made alive unless*

> *it dies. And what you sow, you do not sow that body that shall be, but mere grain; perhaps wheat or some other grain. But God gives it a body as He pleases, and to each seed its own body.*

Here we are told that when our bodies are raised, they will not be exactly the same as when they were buried, any more than the wheat that springs up is the same as the seed that was planted. However, just as the wheat comes from the seed and bears the most intimate relationship to it, so our resurrection bodies will come from the bodies that are buried and bear the most intimate relationship to them. The resurrection body will be the outcome of the body that is buried. It will be the old body made alive and transformed; or, as Paul put it in Philippians 3:20–21,

> *Jesus Christ...will transform our lowly body that it may be conformed to His glorious body, according to the working by which He is able even to subdue all things to Himself.*

Similar to Christ's Glorified Body

The next thing that the Bible teaches about our resurrection bodies is that they will be like the glorified body of Jesus Christ. This fact is apparent from the verses just quoted, Philippians 3:20–21. Let us read them again:

> *Jesus Christ...will transform our lowly body that it may be conformed to His glorious body, according to the working by which He is able even to subdue all things to Himself.*

Christ's resurrection body was not the same body that was laid in the sepulcher. It was the old body transformed and delivered from the limitations that He had while living here among men. It had new qualities imparted to it. Our bodies will also be transformed to be like this glorious body of Christ and will thus be delivered from the limitations to which they are subjected now. They will have new qualities imparted to them. The resurrected body will be a transformed body.

The character of its transformation is indicated by the transformation that took place in the body of Jesus Christ. A hint as to what that transformed body of Jesus Christ is like is found in that preview of His resurrection that was seen by Peter, James, and John on the Mount of Transfiguration. In Matthew's description of the appearance of Jesus at His transfiguration, he told us that *"His face shone like the sun, and His clothes became as white as the light"* (Matthew 17:2). Luke told us that *"the appearance of His face was altered, and His robe became white and glistening"* (Luke 9:29). Mark told us that *"He was transfigured before them. His clothes became shining, exceedingly white, like snow, such as no launderer on earth can whiten them"* (Mark 9:2–3).

Not Composed of Flesh and Blood

The next thing that we are told about our resurrection bodies is that they will not be flesh and blood. In 1 Corinthians 15:50–51, we read, *"Now this I say, brethren, that flesh and blood cannot inherit the kingdom of God."* Here Paul was talking about our resurrection bodies. It is in the resurrection chapter that he said this, and he distinctly told us that our resurrection bodies will not be *"flesh and blood."*

Composed of Flesh and Bones

But while our resurrection bodies will not be flesh and blood, they will have flesh and bones. This is apparent from what our Lord Himself said about His own resurrection body in Luke 24:39: *"Behold My hands and My feet, that it is I Myself. Handle Me and see, for a spirit does not have flesh and bones as you see I have."* Since our bodies are to be transformed to be like His, our resurrection bodies will have *"flesh and bones."* Some have objected that there is a contradiction between what our Lord said here and what Paul said in the passage quoted above (see 1 Corinthians 15:50–51), but there is no contradiction. *"Flesh"* we will have, but not *"flesh and blood,"* that is, not the flesh that has blood as its animating principle.

So we are faced with the question, What will take the place of blood in our resurrection bodies? The answer seems to be that in our present existence, *"blood is the life"* (Deuteronomy 12:23) of the natural body; but in our future existence, our bodies are to be, as we are told in 1 Corinthians 15:44, *"spiritual"* bodies. That is, our bodies will have the Spirit of God as their animating principle, not their own blood. Although I cannot delve into the specifics of this truth, let me just say that our not having blood in our resurrection bodies involves many great and glorious possibilities.

Not Subject to Corruption

The fifth point, which is closely connected with the third and fourth points, is that our resurrection bodies will be incorruptible. We read in 1 Corinthians 15:42, *"So also is the resurrection of the dead. The body is sown in corruption, it is raised in incorruption."* The idea behind this word *"incorruption"* is that the body is not subject to decay; it is imperishable. Our present bodies are decaying all the time. We are perishing every day and every minute. My present body is disintegrating even as I write this chapter. But the bodies that we will receive in the resurrection will be absolutely free from corruption or decay. They *cannot* disintegrate or suffer decay or deterioration of any kind.

Glorious in Beauty

The next thing that we are taught about the resurrection body is that it is a glorious body. This comes out in the following verse: *"It is sown in dishonor, it is raised in glory"* (1 Corinthians 15:43). We have some idea of the glory, the glorious beauty, of that body from the description of our glorified Lord in Revelation 1:13–17:

> *And in the midst of the seven lampstands One like the Son of Man, clothed with a garment down to the feet and girded about the chest with a golden band. His head and hair were white like wool, as white as snow, and His eyes like a flame of fire; His feet were like fine brass, as if refined in a furnace, and His voice as the sound of many waters; He had in His right hand seven stars, out of His mouth went a sharp two-edged sword, and His countenance was like the sun shining in its strength. And when I saw Him, I fell at His feet as dead. But He laid*

> *His right hand on me, saying to me, "Do not be afraid; I am the First and the Last."*

Our resurrection bodies will be like that.

Complete and Powerful

Furthermore, the resurrection body will be powerful; or, as we read in the last half of 1 Corinthians 15:43, *"It is sown in weakness, it is raised in power."* Then all our weariness and weakness will be forever at an end. Our present bodies are often a hindrance to our highest aspirations. They thwart the carrying out of our loftiest purposes. *"The spirit indeed is willing, but the flesh is weak"* (Matthew 26:41). But the resurrection body will be able to accomplish all that the spirit purposes. The redeemed body will be a perfect counterpart of the redeemed spirit that inhabits it. There will be no deafness, nearsightedness, or blindness; no tired hands and feet; no lameness or missing limbs.

Heavenly in Nature

The resurrection body will be a heavenly body. This truth is apparent from 1 Corinthians 15:47–49:

> *The first man was of* [literally, "out of"] *the earth, made of dust; the second Man is the Lord from* [literally, "out of"] *heaven. As was the man of dust, so also are those who are made of dust; and as is the heavenly Man, so also are those who are heavenly. And as we have borne the image of the man of dust, we shall also bear the image of the heavenly Man.*

The thought plainly is that our present bodies are of an earthly origin and an earthly character, but that our transformed bodies will be of a heavenly origin and a heavenly character. Paul explained this at length in 2 Corinthians 5:1–4, where he said,

> *For we know that if our earthly house, this tent, is destroyed, we have a building from God, a house not made with hands, eternal in the heavens.*

> *For in this* [in these present earthly houses, or earthy bodies] *we groan, earnestly desiring to be clothed with our habitation which is from heaven* [that is, our heavenly bodies], if indeed, having been clothed, we shall not be found naked. For we who are in this tent [in these present earthy bodies] *groan, being burdened, not because we want to be unclothed, but further clothed* [that is, with our heavenly bodies], *that mortality may be swallowed up by life.*

Bright and Shining

Our transformed bodies will be luminous, shining, dazzling, bright like the sun. This fact is seen in many passages. Take, for example, Matthew 13:43: "*Then the righteous will shine forth as the sun in the kingdom of their Father.*" This sentence is to be taken literally, for it is in the *interpretation* of one of the parables found in this chapter, not in the parable itself. This verse suggests what we have already seen about the transfigured body of Jesus in Matthew 17:2, where we are told that "*His face shone like the sun, and His clothes became as white as the light.*"

We also have the same thought in the Old Testament in Daniel 12:3, where we are told, "*Those who are wise shall shine like the brightness of the firmament, and those who turn many to righteousness like the stars forever and ever.*" They will shine literally as well as figuratively.

A hint of the luminous glory of our resurrection bodies is revealed in the light that Paul saw beaming from the person of Jesus Christ. In Paul's description of his encounter with the glorified Jesus on the Damascus road, we read,

> *As I journeyed to Damascus with authority and commission from the chief priests, at midday, O king, along the road I saw a light from heaven, brighter than the sun, shining around me and those who journeyed with me.* (Acts 26:12–13)

The light that Paul saw, as is evident from the whole account, was the light that shone from the person of our glorified Lord. In our resurrection bodies, we will be like Him.

Like the Angels

Three interesting facts regarding our resurrection bodies are stated in Matthew 22:30 and Luke 20:35–36. In Matthew 22:30, we read, "*For in the resurrection they neither marry nor are given in marriage, but are like angels of God in heaven.*" In Luke 20:35–36, we read,

> *But those who are counted worthy to attain that age, and the resurrection from the dead, neither marry nor are given in marriage; nor can they die anymore, for they are equal to the angels and are sons of God, being sons of the resurrection.*

Taking these two passages together, we learn that in our resurrected state we will be like the angels, that in our resurrection bodies we will not marry, and that in our resurrection bodies we cannot die anymore.

Unique in Their Glory

Though all our resurrection bodies will be glorious, they will differ from one another, each one having its own particular glory. This is apparent from 1 Corinthians 15:41–42:

> *There is one glory of the sun, another glory of the moon, and another glory of the stars; for one star differs from another star in glory. So also is the resurrection of the dead.*

As glorious as all our bodies will be, there will be no tiresome uniformity, even of glory, in the world of resurrection bodies. Each body will have its own unique glory.

An Outward Manifestation of Our Sonship

In regard to the characteristics of our resurrection bodies, I would like to make one more point. The resurrection of our bodies will be the culmination of our adoption, that is, the completion of our being established as sons, or of our manifestation as sons of God. In Romans 8:23, we read,

> *We also who have the firstfruits of the Spirit, even we ourselves groan within ourselves, eagerly waiting for the adoption* [that is, our manifestation as sons], *the redemption of our body.*

When I say that the resurrection body will reveal the completion of our being established as sons, I mean that it will be outwardly manifested in the resurrection body that we are sons of God. Before His incarnation, Christ was "*in the form* [visible appearance] *of God*" (Phil. 2:6). So will we be also in the resurrection, for our bodies will be like His.

This truth sheds light on what Paul meant when he said in Colossians 3:4, "*When Christ, who is our life, shall be manifested, then shall ye also with him be manifested in glory*" (RV). It also sheds light on what John meant when he said in 1 John 3:2,

> *Beloved, now we are children of God; and it has not yet been revealed what we shall be, but we know that when He is revealed, we shall be like Him, for we shall see Him as He is.*

The Timing of the Resurrection of Our Bodies

There remains only one question to be considered in this chapter, and we can deal with it briefly. This question is, When will the resurrection of the body take place? The Bible plainly answers this question time and time again. Read, for example, Philippians 3:20–21:

> *For our citizenship is in heaven, from which we also eagerly wait for the Savior, the Lord Jesus Christ, who will transform our lowly body that it may be conformed to His glorious body, according to the working by which He is able even to subdue all things to Himself.*

Here it is plainly declared that the transformation of our bodies into the likeness of Christ's glorious body will take place when the One whom we are awaiting appears from heaven. The same thought is given in 1 Thessalonians 4:16–17:

> *For the Lord Himself will descend from heaven with a shout, with the voice of an archangel, and with the trumpet of God. And the dead in Christ will rise first. Then we who are alive and remain shall be caught up together with them in the clouds to meet the Lord in the air. And thus we shall always be with the Lord.*

Perhaps you are wondering, What will happen to us in the meantime if we happen to die before the coming of the Lord? This question is also plainly answered:

> *For we know that if our earthly house, this tent* [our present bodies], *is destroyed* [dies and decays], *we have a building from God, a house not made with hands* [our resurrection bodies that we are to receive at the coming of the Lord], *eternal in the heavens. For in this* [that is, while living in this present body] *we groan, earnestly desiring to be clothed with our habitation which is from heaven* [our resurrection bodies], *if indeed, having been clothed, we shall not be found naked. For we who are in this tent* [this present earthy body] *groan, being burdened, not because we want to be unclothed* [that is, not because we would merely like to get rid of our present bodies], *but further clothed* [that is, we want to receive our resurrection bodies], *that mortality may be swallowed up by life. Now He who has prepared us for this very thing is God, who also has given us the Spirit as a guarantee* [that is, the Holy Spirit, whom we have received as a deposit guaranteeing the full redemption in our resurrection bodies, which are to be obtained at the coming of the Lord]. *So we are always confident, knowing that while we are at home in the body* [that is, while we are still living our earthly lives in these present earthly bodies] *we are absent from the Lord. For we walk by faith, not by sight. We are confident, yes, well pleased rather to be absent from the body* [that is, to have our present earthly bodies die even before we get our resurrection bodies, which we will not receive until the return of the Lord] *and to be present with the Lord.*
>
> (2 Corinthians 5:1–8)

The plain teaching of this passage is that if we die before the return of the Lord and therefore before we obtain our resurrection bodies, our spirits will be unclothed, that is, they will be unclothed from these present bodies, and will not yet be clothed with our resurrection bodies. Nevertheless, we will be at home with the Lord in conscious blessedness—in a condition that is far better than that of this present life (see Philippians 1:23), but not as perfect as the condition that will exist when our redeemed spirits are clothed with our resurrection bodies. It will be at the return of the Lord Jesus that we will receive our full redemption. That is one reason that we *"eagerly wait for the Savior"* (Philippians 3:20).

There are many reasons that we long for the return of our Lord. All the great problems that are confronting us at this present time in national and international life, in social, economic, and political life, will be solved when He comes—and not until He comes. For this reason, we eagerly wait for Him. But we long for Him also because, while this present body serves many a useful purpose for the redeemed spirit that inhabits it, it is often a hindrance. The human body is often subject to aches, pains, and frailties, and it is constantly subject to temptations. But when our Lord Jesus comes again, He will transform these lowly bodies of ours into the likeness of His own glorious body. (See Philippians 3:21.) At that time, we will know what "full salvation" means. Then we will shine forth like the sun in the kingdom of our Father. (See Matthew 13:43.)

6

HOW CAN I DEFEAT THE DEVIL?

The devil…is.
—John 8:44

The devil has sinned.
—1 John 3:8

The biblical doctrine concerning the Devil—his existence, nature, character, work, and destiny—is a fundamental doctrine of the Christian faith and is of vital importance. The teaching of the Bible on this subject is not a matter of mere theory or useless philosophy, but it is a matter of truths that have practical, everyday importance. Experience shows that if people are in error on this subject, they are pretty sure to be in error on other fundamental doctrines. When men and women begin to question the existence of a personal Devil—one that has the qualities of a person, such as a personality and a will—before long, they will likely challenge a good many other things that a true child of God should not question.

Doubt about the existence of a literal Devil is widespread today. The absolute denial of Satan's existence is one of the main points in Christian Science, a system that is doing much evil. Partly because of its denial of him, Christian Science has appropriately been called "The Devil's Masterpiece."

In addition, many supposedly sound preachers do not hesitate to say, "I do not believe in the existence of a real Devil." As I mentioned in the first chapter of this book, a well-known and popular pastor in Los Angeles proclaimed to his congregation that he was going to preach a gospel "without a Devil, without a hell, without an atonement of blood and retribution, without an infallible Bible." If he does omit any of these elements, he is preaching a system of doctrine that is different from what is contained in the Bible, which our Lord Jesus Christ has endorsed as the Word of God.

The Existence of the Devil

The first point I want to make clear is that there is a Devil. This fact is plain from our first text, John 8:44: "*The devil...is.*" The verse in its entirety reads,

> *You are of your father the devil, and the desires of your father you want to do. He was a murderer from the beginning, and does not stand in the truth, because there is no truth in him. When he speaks a lie, he speaks from his own resources, for he is a liar and the father of it.*

These are the words of Jesus Christ. With anyone who has any right to call himself a Christian, the words of Jesus Christ have infinitely more weight than the words of Mary Baker Eddy or anyone else, or everyone else put together. Here Jesus said, "*The devil...is.*"

By no means is this the only passage in which our Lord Jesus asserted in the most emphatic and unmistakable terms the existence of the Devil. We read these words in Matthew 13:19:

> *When anyone hears the word of the kingdom, and does not understand it, then the wicked one comes and snatches away what was sown in his heart.*

This verse is found in the interpretation of a parable—the parable of the sower. It is impossible to say that these words are figurative. In parables, we have symbolic language; in the explanation of the parables, we have the literal facts that the symbolic language represents. The words of Matthew 13:19 are not taken from the parable, but from our Lord's own explanation of the parable. In this verse, we are distinctly told that there is a person called "*the wicked one*" who "*snatches away*" the Word of God from hearts that do not understand and heed it.

If Satan were not a real person, and if our Lord had only been referring to evil forces or even human influences as snatching away the Word from hearts, His words in Matthew 13:19 would not make any sense. But Jesus Christ believed that there is a person called Satan. He referred to him here as "*the wicked one,*" and He referred to him elsewhere, as we will soon see, as "the Devil." If we grant that the Lord Jesus was an honest man, we can have no doubt that He believed there is a literal Devil. Therefore, if we believe in the Lord Jesus, we must also believe that there is a Devil. We can deny his existence only by questioning either the honesty or the intelligence of our Lord.

I could also easily show from the teachings of Peter (see 1 Peter 5:8–9; Acts 5:3) and from the teachings of John (see John 13:2) and from the teachings of Paul (see Ephesians 6:10–12) that there is a Devil. However, that is unnecessary for anyone who has any right to call himself a Christian, for if the Lord said it, that settles it, and the Lord Jesus did say, "*The devil...is.*" If there is no Devil, then our Lord Jesus was either a fool or a fraud.

Clearly, the question of believing in the existence of a literal Devil involves the honor of our Lord Jesus. If His teaching is not to be trusted on this point, it is not to be trusted on any other point. To deny a literal Devil is to deny the trustworthiness of the Lord Jesus as a Teacher and as a Savior at every point. So we see that the question of the existence of the Devil is of fundamental and vital importance.

The Nature of the Devil

Having settled that there is a Devil, we now face the question of the nature of the Devil.

The Devil Is a Person

First of all, the Bible teaches us that the Devil is a person. This truth comes out in our second text, 1 John 3:8: "*The devil has sinned.*" Only a person can sin. When I say that the Devil is a person, I do not mean that he necessarily has a body—and I certainly do not mean that he has the kind of body that he is pictured as having in various paintings. The definition of a person is "any being who knows and feels and wills." When I say that the Devil is a person, I mean that he is a being who has intelligence, feeling, and will—that he is not a mere "principle of evil."

The personhood of the Devil is taught over and over again in the Bible. I will give just a few illustrations in addition to our texts. Looking again at Matthew 13:19, we read,

> *When anyone hears the word of the kingdom, and does not understand it, then the wicked one comes and snatches away what was sown in his heart.*

The entity spoken of in this passage is a person. He is called by the name "*the wicked one*"—not merely "wickedness," but "*the wicked one*"—which of course represents a person.

The personhood of the Devil is shown again very clearly and very forcibly in Ephesians 6:10–12:

> *Finally, my brethren, be strong in the Lord and in the power of His might. Put on the whole armor of God, that you may be able to stand against the wiles of the devil. For we do not wrestle against flesh and blood, but against principalities, against powers, against the rulers of the darkness of this age, against spiritual hosts of wickedness in the heavenly places.*

Here Paul distinctly told us that the big reason that we need to be *"strong in the Lord"* and to *"put on the whole armor of God"* is that there is a being of great cunning, subtlety, and power, a person named *"the devil."* Furthermore, this being has under him a multitude of other persons, who have such rank and power that they are called by the titles *"principalities," "powers," "rulers," "spiritual hosts of wickedness."*

Beyond a question, our Lord Jesus, along with the apostles Peter, John, and Paul, believed in and taught the existence of a literal Devil. If there is not a literal Devil, we may as well give up the Bible, for in that case it is a book that is full of foolishness and fraud. If there is not a real Devil, we must give up our belief in the inspired authority of the apostles Peter, John, and Paul, and we must give up our faith in the Lord Jesus Christ. No intelligent student of the Bible can retain his faith in the inspiration and authority of that Book, or his faith in the Lord Jesus Christ, if he gives up his belief in the existence of a literal Devil. As intelligent men and women, we must make our choice between believing in the existence of a literal Devil and giving up our faith in Jesus Christ and Christianity. Any system of doctrine that denies the existence of a real Devil is radically unchristian, no matter what name it may claim for itself.

The Devil Is Powerful

The second thing that the Bible teaches about the nature of the Devil is that the Devil is a being of great power and authority. This fact comes out in two of the verses we have just read, Ephesians 6:10–11:

> *Finally, my brethren, be strong in the Lord and in the power of His might. Put on the whole armor of God, that you may be able to stand against the wiles of the devil.*

These words make it clear that the Devil is so mighty that God's people cannot resist his power and cunning schemes without being clothed with the armor of God and being strengthened with the strength of God.

This is not all. In the twelfth verse, we read,

> *For we do not wrestle against flesh and blood, but against principalities, against powers, against the rulers of the darkness of this age, against spiritual hosts of wickedness in the heavenly places.*

These are tremendous words. If they mean anything, they certainly mean that there are beings of great authority and rank who are under the leadership of the one supreme being of evil, the Devil.

The conflict that we have on hand as believers in Christ is terrific. Any international military conflict that could arise is nothing in comparison with the battle that we have on hand with the Devil and his hosts. We are fools if we underestimate the fight.

On the other hand, we must not overestimate it. While our conflict is with the Devil, and while our wrestling is against the *"principalities,"* the *"powers,"* the *"rulers,"* and the *"spiritual hosts of wickedness,"* He who is for us is far mightier than they (1 John 4:4). The Devil is mighty, but our Savior is almighty. It is quite possible for a person to become morbid over this subject of the Devil, and to become utterly discouraged and even deranged. This extreme is entirely unnecessary and unwarranted. While our conflict is with the Devil and his mighty hosts, God has provided for us a strength and an armor whereby we may *"quench all the fiery darts of the wicked one"* (Ephesians 6:16) and *"withstand in the evil day, and having done all, to stand"* (verse 13).

The Devil Has an Exalted Position

The third thing that the Bible teaches about the nature of the Devil is that the Devil is a being of grandeur and rank. We read in Jude 8–9,

> *Likewise also these dreamers defile the flesh, reject authority, and speak evil of* dignitaries [the literal translation of the Greek word rendered "dignitaries" is "glories"]. *Yet Michael the archangel, in contending with the devil, when he disputed about the body of Moses, dared not bring against him a reviling accusation, but said, "The Lord rebuke you!"*

From these words, it is evident that the position of the Devil was so exalted that even Michael the archangel did not dare to bring *"a reviling accusation"* against him. The context seems to imply that the position of the Devil was more exalted than that of Michael the archangel himself.

The Devil in God's Word is not at all the Devil that is commonly portrayed. He is not hideous in appearance, with hooves and horns and tail. He is not even the being pictured by Milton or Bunyan. He is a being of great original majesty and dignity, a being of great wisdom and power. When people talk lightly and contemptuously of the Devil, they display gross ignorance of what the Bible teaches about him. It is true that he is wicked in character and is therefore called *"the wicked one"* (1 John 5:19). It is true that he is a liar and a murderer (John 8:44). It is true that he is full of malignity. (See 2 Corinthians 4:4.) But he is a being of grandeur and rank, so that even Michael the archangel did not dare to bring an abusive accusation against him.

The Devil Is the Ruler of the Present World Order

Furthermore, the Bible teaches that the Devil is *"the prince of this world."* Our Lord Jesus Himself taught this fact. He said in John 12:31, *"Now is the judgment of this world: now shall the prince of this world be cast out"* (KJV). The Greek word translated *"world"* in this passage is *kosmos,* which refers to the present world order. Our Lord's teaching is that the Devil is the prince of this present world order.

Jesus taught the same thing in John 14:30, on the evening before His crucifixion: *"I will no longer talk much with you, for the ruler of this world is coming, and he has nothing in Me."* These words of Jesus Christ are found in what many people regard as the most precious chapter in the Bible, the fourteenth chapter of John. If we give up this teaching of our Lord regarding Satan, we must give up this most precious chapter and, indeed, the entire Bible. We find Jesus teaching the same thing again on that same night, the night before His crucifixion, in John 16:11: *"The ruler of this world is judged,"* the evident reference being to Satan.

How the Devil came to be *"the prince of this world"* it may be impossible for us to say, but if we are to accept the teaching of Jesus Christ, there is no question that he is so. To anyone who studies the ruling principles of economic life, political life, social life, and above all, international relations, it becomes perfectly evident that the Devil is the one who is the master of the present order of things. If we ever doubted before that there is a Devil, and just such a Devil as the Bible describes, we can scarcely doubt it now, when we consider the actions of the rulers of this earth. How could beings so intelligent in matters of science and philosophy and economics, ever be guilty of plunging the nations of the earth into war? There is only one reasonable answer: because there is a Devil who rules the present kosmos, or world order, and he controls the evil rulers of the world and will continue to control them until the true Prince comes, the Prince of Peace, our Lord Jesus Christ.

The Character of the Devil

As for the character of the Devil, the Bible teaches us that he is a being who is absolutely wicked. In Matthew 13:19, he is called *"the wicked one"*; that is, he is the person who is the embodiment of absolute wickedness. First John 5:19 also calls him *"the wicked one."* God, on the other hand, is called *"the Holy One"* throughout the Bible; that is, He is the Person who is the embodiment of perfect holiness. Simply put, the Devil is the opposite of God. The Devil is to evil what God is to good.

In 1 John 3:8, we read,

> *He who sins is of the devil, for the devil has sinned from the beginning. For this purpose the Son of God was manifested, that He might destroy the works of the devil.*

This verse does not mean that the Devil has sinned from the very origin of all things and that he was created sinful, for we learn from Ezekiel 28:15 that the Devil was created upright. The expression "*from the beginning*" is characteristic of the epistle from which these words are taken and does not necessarily mean from the origin of things. (See, for example, 1 John 3:11.) This verse does mean, however, that Satan is the original sinner.

In a similar way, we are told in John 8:44 that the Devil "*was a murderer from the beginning,*" and that "*he is a liar and the father of it.*" There is absolutely "*no truth in him*" (verse 44). This is the character of the Devil.

The Work of the Devil

We now come to the question of the work of the Devil, or how the Devil manifests himself and what he does.

The Devil Is the Tempter

First of all, we are taught that the Devil tempts people to sin. We have a most striking illustration of this in his temptation of our Lord. There are three accounts of this temptation in the Bible. We will look at Matthew's account:

> *Then Jesus was led up by the Spirit into the wilderness to be tempted by the devil. And when He had fasted forty days and forty nights, afterward He was hungry. Now when the tempter came to Him, he said, "If You are the Son of God, command that these stones become bread." But He answered and said, "It is written, 'Man shall not live by bread alone, but by every word that proceeds from the mouth of God.'" Then the devil took Him up into the holy city, set Him on the pinnacle of the temple, and said to Him, "If You are the Son of God, throw Yourself down. For it is written: 'He shall give His angels charge over you,' and, 'In their hands they shall bear you up, lest you dash your foot against a stone.'" Jesus said to him, "It is written again, 'You shall not tempt the* LORD *your God.'" Again, the devil took Him up on an exceedingly high mountain, and showed Him all the kingdoms of the world and their*

> *glory. And he said to Him, "All these things I will give You if You will fall down and worship me." Then Jesus said to him, "Away with you, Satan! For it is written, 'You shall worship the* Lord *your God, and Him only you shall serve.'" Then the devil left Him, and behold, angels came and ministered to Him.* (Matthew 4:1–11)

Of course, it would require a long study to go into the whole matter of our Lord's temptation, but this much is certainly plain: the Devil is represented as the Tempter. If there is no literal Devil, as so many would have us believe, or if he is not the Tempter, there would be absolutely no reason for bringing him into this account.

As the Devil tempted our Lord, so he tempts us today. Notice that he does not tempt us merely with gross animal lusts and vile sins, but with subtle spiritual temptations. Above all, he tempts us to doubt God's Word. It was with this form of temptation that he first assaulted Jesus. God had just said to our Lord at His baptism, "*You are My beloved Son; in You I am well pleased*" (Luke 3:22). Satan tried to cause Christ to doubt what God had said by beginning his temptation with these words: "*If You are the Son of God....*" Again, later on in his temptation of Christ, he repeated the doubt, saying to the Lord Jesus, "*If You are the Son of God....*"

In exactly the same way, Satan began his assault on Eve in the Garden of Eden. He introduced a doubt of God's Word and God's goodness. He began by saying, "*Has God indeed said...?*" (Genesis 3:1), and later on, when Eve stated exactly what God had said, the Devil flatly contradicted Him and said, "*You will not surely die* [literally, "dying, you will not die"]" (verse 4), when God had said, "*You shall surely die* ["dying, you will die"]" (Genesis 2:17).

Satan's favorite and most effective method of attack today is to get us to doubt God's Word, to lead us into doubt and error on fundamental points. The bars, the casinos, and the houses of prostitution are not the chief spheres of Satan's activities. His primary fields are the schools, colleges, and theological seminaries, where he is inducing men, women, and children to doubt the truth of God's Word. The Devil tempts them to reject the fundamental truths of God's Word and to accept his errors in their place. He knows very well that if he can get people to doubt God's Word, it is easy to lead them into the vilest of sins. False doctrine has been a more prolific source of the vilest sins than even the barrooms.

The Devil Uses Churches and Ministers

Not only does Satan tempt people to sin by introducing doubts of God's Word, but he also has his churches and ministers to do his work. We find this fact in Revelation 3:9:

> *Indeed I will make those of the synagogue of Satan, who say they are Jews and are not, but lie; indeed I will make them come and worship before your feet, and to know that I have loved you.*

What I want you to notice here are the words *"the synagogue of Satan."* In this case, Satan's tool was a Jewish synagogue, but nowadays, it is often a so-called Christian church.

In 2 Corinthians 11:14–15, we have an even more remarkable passage:

> *For Satan himself transforms himself into an angel of light. Therefore it is no great thing if his ministers also transform themselves into ministers of righteousness, whose end will be according to their works.*

Here we are told that Satan has his ministers. They do not advertise themselves as such. Oftentimes they are not even aware that they are Satan's ministers; instead, they promote themselves as *"ministers of righteousness."* Satan's ministers advocate a system of salvation without atoning blood. They are frequently men and women with very attractive personalities and great intelligence, but they are doing the Devil's work.

Satan is never so dangerous as when he *"transforms himself into an angel of light."* Furthermore, no ministers of his are so dangerous as the men and women with pleasing personalities and brilliant minds who are undermining the faith of God's children. Many of Satan's ministers are teaching various forms of seductive and alluring error through Christian Science, New Thought, Theosophy, occultism (Spiritualism), and other cults.

The Devil Blinds People to the Truth about Jesus

Satan is also the author of sickness (see Acts 10:38; Luke 13:16) and the author of death (see Hebrews 2:14). But I must also tell about another task of the Devil. It is found in 2 Corinthians 4:3–4:

> *But even if our gospel is veiled, it is veiled to those who are perishing, whose minds the god of this age has blinded, who do not believe, lest the light of the gospel of the glory of Christ, who is the image of God, should shine on them.*

We read here that it is the work of Satan to blind the minds of unbelievers *"lest the light of the gospel of the glory of Christ, who is the image of God, should shine on them."*

It is evident, then, that the Devil is the originator of false views, especially false views of the person of Christ. He is the author of Unitarianism, along with all the various forms of the denial of Christ's deity. He so blinds the minds of men who submit to his working that the divine *"glory of Christ,"* who is the very *"image of God,"* is hidden from them. This fact explains why Unitarianism persists in all its various forms, even after its foolishness has been so often exposed.

Satan's work along these lines will culminate at the appearing of the Antichrist:

> *The coming of the lawless one* [the Antichrist] *is according to the working of Satan, with all power, signs, and lying wonders, and with all unrighteous deception among those who perish, because they did not receive the love of the truth, that they might be saved.*
>
> (2 Thessalonians 2:9–10)

The Destiny of the Devil

We now come to the fifth topic of our subject—the Devil's destiny.

First, we will look at Revelation 20:1–3:

> *Then I saw an angel coming down from heaven, having the key to the bottomless pit and a great chain in his hand. He laid hold of the dragon, that serpent of old, who is the Devil and Satan, and bound him for a thousand years; and he cast him into the bottomless pit, and shut him up, and set a seal on him, so that he should deceive the nations no more till the thousand years were finished. But after these things he must be released for a little while.*

At the second coming of our Lord Jesus Christ, Satan will be bound with a great chain and cast into "*the bottomless pit*" for a thousand years. "*The bottomless pit*" does not mean hell, but we will soon see that Satan will later be cast into hell.

Second, let us consider Revelation 20:7–8:

> *Now when the thousand years have expired, Satan will be released from his prison and will go out to deceive the nations which are in the four corners of the earth, Gog and Magog, to gather them together to battle, whose number is as the sand of the sea.*

In these verses, we are taught that at the end of the Millennium, the thousand-year reign of Christ on earth, Satan will be loosed for a short season from his bondage and from the bottomless pit into which he has been cast. He will come forth to deceive the nations, but the time of his power will be brief.

Third, in Revelation 20:10, we find the ultimate destiny of the Devil:

> *The devil, who deceived them, was cast into the lake of fire and brimstone where the beast and the false prophet are. And they will be tormented day and night forever and ever.*

Here is one of the points at which the theories of the Universalists[4] generally break down. The argument of the Universalists, by which they attempt to prove that everyone must ultimately be saved, carried to its logical conclusion, would also prove the salvation of Satan. Many of them do plainly say that the Devil will ultimately be brought to repentance and be saved. Indeed, that is what I believed and taught in my early ministry. But the passage that we have just read shows the impossibility of this being true, for the Devil will go to the lake of fire.

Our Lord Himself said that when He comes back to judge this world, He will say to the unbelievers, *"Depart from Me, you cursed, into the everlasting fire prepared for the devil and his angels"* (Matthew 25:41). Hell was not prepared for people but for the Devil and his angels. The only reason that any person will go there will be that he has chosen to cast in his lot with the Devil rather than with God. Therefore, he will go where the Devil goes. Everyone who rejects Jesus Christ is throwing in his lot with Satan.

How to Be Victorious over the Devil

Now let me briefly show you from the Word of God how to get the victory over the Devil in practical, everyday life. There are four things to keep in mind.

First, James 4:7 says, *"Therefore submit to God. Resist the devil and he will flee from you."* This teaches us that we are first of all to surrender to God and then resist the Devil. In spite of all Satan's cunning and power, if we do resist him, he will flee from us. Although the Devil is strong, it is our privilege in God's strength to withstand him and overcome him.

Second, we read in 1 John 2:14,

> *I have written to you, fathers, because you have known Him who is from the beginning. I have written to you, young men, because you are*

4. The main tenet of Universalism is that eventually everyone will be saved. Universalism began in the eighteenth century and later united with Unitarianism.

> *strong, and the word of God abides in you, and you have overcome the wicked one.*

This passage teaches us that when we feed upon the Word of God and store the Word of God in our hearts, thus having it abide in us, we will be able to overcome the Devil. If we neglect the study of the Bible for a single day, we leave an open door for the Devil. I have been a Christian for forty-three years, but I would not dare to neglect the study of God's Word for one single day. Why not? Because there is a Devil; and if I neglect the study of the Word of God for a single day, I leave a window open through which he can enter, and I leave myself too weak to cope with him and to conquer him. But if we will feed upon the Word of God daily and trust in God, we can resist the Devil at every point. Though the Devil is cunning and strong, God is stronger, and God imparts His strength to us through His written Word.

Third, we are told in Ephesians 6:11, *"Put on the whole armor of God, that you may be able to stand against the wiles of the devil."* Here we are taught that in order to stand against Satan's schemes, we must *"put on the whole armor of God."* We find what that armor is in the verses that immediately follow.

This armor, this panoply of God, is at our disposal. The fact that there is a Devil, that he is a being of such grandeur, dignity, cunning, and power, that he is incessantly plotting to ruin us and to undermine our faith, is no reason for fear or discouragement. By taking *"the shield of faith,"* we *"will be able to quench all the fiery darts of the wicked one"* (Ephesians 6:16). By taking *"the helmet of salvation, and the sword of the Spirit, which is the word of God"* (verse 17), and by *"praying always with all prayer and supplication in the Spirit"* (verse 18), it is our privilege to have victory over the Devil every day of our lives—every hour of the day, and every minute of the hour.

The fourth and final step in the plan to get victory over Satan is found in Ephesians 6:10: *"Finally, my brethren, be strong in the Lord and in the power of His might."* The way to get victory over Satan is to give up all confidence in our own strength, to believe in the almighty strength of Jesus

Christ, and to claim that strength for ourselves. It is in the strength of Jesus Christ's might that we will get the victory over the Evil One. In the strength of His might, as I have already said, it is our privilege to have victory over the Devil every minute of our lives. Hallelujah!

7

IS THERE A LITERAL HELL?

In danger of hell fire.
—Matthew 5:22

I wish that the things that I am going to write in this chapter were not true. God wishes so, too. "*The Lord...is longsuffering toward us, not willing that any should perish but that all should come to repentance*" (2 Peter 3:9). But God has made us in His own image—with a moral nature, with a capacity for decision, with a power of choice. People can, if they want, choose darkness instead of light. They can choose to trample God's saving love underfoot. They can choose to reject the One who was "*wounded for* [their] *transgressions*" and "*bruised for* [their] *iniquities*" (Isaiah 53:5).

Some people will make this choice. I am sorry that they will—so sorry that I would be willing to die to save them. The Lord Jesus did die to save them, but they spurn Him.

The things that I am about to tell you about hell are true, and I am going to explain them in order that you may be certain of them. I am writing about hell in order to keep as many of you as possible from going there.

Is there a literal hell? Almost all intelligent people who believe that there is a future life at all believe that there is future punishment. They agree that men and women who sin in the present life and who die impenitent will be punished in the future life, at least to some extent. They admit that whoever sins must suffer, and that the suffering that sin causes will not be limited to our earthly existence.

But while almost all intelligent people who believe in the afterlife believe that there is some kind of future punishment, many of them do not believe in a literal hell, that is, a place of awful and unutterable torment.

Is there a hell? Is there a place to which impenitent men and women will go sometime after death and suffer agonies far beyond those that anyone suffers here on earth? Some say, "Yes, there is a hell." Yet many preachers, even supposedly sound preachers, say, "No, the only hell is the inward hell in a man's heart." So how are we to settle this question? How are we to determine who is right?

We cannot settle it as some are trying to do, by consensus. Majorities are not always right, especially in matters of science, philosophy, and theology. What the majority of scientists firmly believed a century ago, the majority of scientists laugh at today. What the majority of philosophers once believed, the majority of philosophers today regard as ridiculous. Therefore, we cannot settle this question by asking what the majority believe.

Nor can we settle it by our own human reasoning. How can finite and foolish man judge what an infinitely holy and infinitely wise God would do? Man never appears more foolish than when he tries to use his own thoughts to reach conclusions in this matter. All these arguments about hell that result from reasoning as to what God must or must not do are stupid. A child of seven cannot reason infallibly as to what a wise and good man of fifty would do. Much less can puny creatures of the dust (such as you and I, such as the most educated philosophers and theologians) reason infallibly as to what a wise and good God must do.

However, with the wars and atrocities happening around us in the world, it is far easier today to believe in a literal and everlasting hell from the standpoint of pure reasoning than it was in past centuries. Nevertheless, even today we cannot settle this matter by reasoning as to what such a being as God must do.

There is only one way to settle this question properly, and that is by going to the Bible, finding out what it says, and taking our stand firmly and unhesitatingly upon that. We know that the Bible is, beyond a doubt, God's Word,[5] so whatever the Bible says on this subject, or any other subject, is true and certain.

It is especially true that we must go to the Bible to find what it says in the matter of future punishment and future blessedness. All we know about the future is what the Bible tells us. All reasoning about the future outside of what the Bible tells us is pure guessing; it is a waste of time. We know nothing about heaven except what God's Word says, and we know nothing about hell except what God's Word says. On a subject like this, one ounce of God's revelation is worth a thousand tons of man's speculation. The whole question is, What does the Bible say about hell?

Not only are we dependent entirely on the Bible, but the Bible clearly reveals all that we need to know. The Bible tells us a great deal about heaven and still more about hell. It is an interesting fact that the Lord Jesus Himself, whose words many are ready to accept even though they may reject the authority of the rest of the Bible, is the One who told us the most about hell—and the One who told us the most clearly about hell. Indeed,

---

5. For an in-depth discussion on the inspiration of the Bible, see Torrey's book *God, the Bible, and You* (New Kensington, PA: Whitaker House, 1999).

most of what I am going to show you is what the Lord Jesus Himself said on this subject.

What Is the Difference between Hell and Hades?

First of all, in order to clear the way for our study of what Jesus said on this subject, let me call your attention to the fact that hell and Hades are not the same. The word that is translated *hell* in many verses in the King James Version is translated *hades* in these verses in other Bible versions. These other versions are right on this point, as every Greek scholar knows. Hades is not hell. Hades is the Greek equivalent of the Old Testament Hebrew word *sheol*. This Hebrew word *sheol* is frequently translated in the King James Version of the Old Testament as *grave*. It should never be translated in this way, since it never means grave. I have taken the pains to look up every passage where this Hebrew word is used, and in not a single instance does it mean grave. There is an entirely different Hebrew word that can properly be translated in that way. *Sheol*, or the New Testament word *hades*, means "the place of departed spirits."

Before the birth, life, death, resurrection, and ascension of our Lord, Sheol (or Hades) was the place where all the spirits of the dead—both good and bad—went. Before the ascension of Christ, Hades contained both paradise, the abode of the blessed dead, and the *"place of torment"* (Luke 16:28), the abode of the wicked dead. At His ascension, Christ emptied the paradise of Hades and took its inhabitants up to heaven with Him, as we read in Ephesians 4:8: *"When He ascended on high, He led captivity captive, and gave gifts to men."*

Before Christ ascended, paradise was in sheol; now it is in heaven. Christ said to the repentant thief on the cross, *"Assuredly, I say to you, today you will be with Me in Paradise"* (Luke 23:43), and Jesus Himself taught us that He went down into *"the heart of the earth"* (Matthew 12:40). The dying thief went down with Him into this subterranean paradise. I think Jesus Himself also went into that part of Hades where the lost spirits were (see 1 Peter 3:18–20), but that is another story. All that is important now is that the repentant, dying thief went *down* into paradise with Christ but was taken to heaven when Christ ascended there. Note that, after the ascension of the Lord, when Paul wrote that he had gone to paradise, he said that he had been *"caught **up** to the third heaven…into Paradise"* (2 Corinthians 12:2, 4, emphasis added).

No blessed dead are now left in Hades, and ultimately, *"Death"* and *"Hades"* (that is, all the dead who have not been caught up into the celestial paradise—all of whom are still in Hades) will be *"cast into the lake of fire"* (Revelation 20:14). This *"lake of fire"* into which death and Hades are to be cast is the true and ultimate hell.

Is There a Literal Hell?

Having cleared the way by removing the misunderstanding so common in the minds of people today that Hades and hell are the same, let me say next that there is a literal hell. The Bible says so. Jesus said in Matthew 5:22,

> *I say to you that whoever is angry with his brother without a cause shall be in danger of the judgment. And whoever says to his brother, "Raca!"* [a strong term of derision] *shall be in danger of the council. But whoever says, "You fool!" shall be in danger of hell fire.*

In the twenty-ninth verse of the same chapter, the Lord Jesus said,

> *If your right eye causes you to sin, pluck it out and cast it from you; for it is more profitable for you that one of your members perish, than for your whole body to be cast into hell.*

And in the thirtieth verse, He said,

> *And if your right hand causes you to sin, cut it off and cast it from you; for it is more profitable for you that one of your members perish, than for your whole body to be cast into hell.*

Mark 9:45, 47–48 repeats this teaching of Jesus:

> *And if your foot causes you to sin, cut it off. It is better for you to enter life lame, rather than having two feet, to be cast into hell....And if your eye causes you to sin, pluck it out. It is better for you to enter the kingdom of God with one eye, rather than having two eyes, to be cast into hell fire; where "Their worm does not die, and the fire is not quenched."*

Someone may say that these words of our Lord are figurative, but there is not the slightest hint that this is so. The context of each of these passages is against their being taken figuratively. It is indeed wrong to interpret figurative language as if it were literal, but it is just as wrong to interpret literal language as if it were figurative.

Of course, the word *gehenna*, which is translated "*hell*" in these passages, is derived from the name of a valley of Jerusalem, the valley of Hinnom, where in ancient times human sacrifices were offered. But the *use* of the word is literal throughout the New Testament, even though its *derivation* is figurative. Many words that are figurative in their derivation are literal in their use, and the meaning of words is never determined by derivation but by usage. For example, our word *eclipse* is a figure of speech. Figuratively, it means a "leaving" or "failing" or "fainting" of the moon or sun, whichever it may be that is eclipsed. But though the word is figurative in its derivation, the ordinary usage of it is literal.

In the New Testament, the universal use of *gehenna*, or "*hell*," is literal. *Gehenna* is found twelve times in the New Testament, and eleven of these twelve times it is used by our Lord Jesus Himself. He uniformly used it, as in the passages that I have just read, concerning a literal hell.

If we go to Christ's words to discover their natural meaning, there can be no doubt that He meant to convey the impression that there is a literal hell. If there is no literal hell, then either Jesus thought there was one when there is not, in which case He was a fool; or He thought that hell does not exist but tried to make men think that it does, in which case He was a fraud. There is no other alternative. We must believe that there is a literal hell or else believe that Jesus of Nazareth, our Lord and Savior, was a fool or a fraud.

I know that Jesus was not senseless or deceptive. I know that He was the *"only begotten Son"* (John 3:16) of God, that *"in Him dwells all the fullness of the Godhead bodily"* (Colossians 2:9), that He and the Father are one (John 10:30), that *"all should honor the Son just as they honor the Father"* (John 5:23). I know that He spoke the very words of God; therefore, I know that there is a literal hell.

Furthermore, it is noteworthy that most of these words about hell that I have quoted from Scripture are taken from the Sermon on the Mount, the one part of Scripture that most people who are familiar with the Bible claim to believe. There are many who say that they do not know about the reliability of the Bible as a whole but who do accept the Sermon on the Mount. Since most of these passages are from the Sermon on the Mount, we must either accept these parts of the Sermon or throw the whole thing overboard as the utterance of a fool or a fraud. There is no other choice possible for anyone who is willing to think things through.

Is the Fire of Hell Literal Fire?

The next question that confronts us is, Is the hellfire mentioned in some of the passages we have read literal fire? This is not as vital a question as, Is there is a literal hell? but it is nevertheless important. I believe the question is plainly answered in the Bible by Jesus Christ Himself. Referring again to Matthew 5:22, we read,

> *I say to you that whoever is angry with his brother without a cause shall be in danger of the judgment. And whoever says to his brother, "Raca!"* [a strong term of derision] *shall be in danger of the council. But whoever says, "You fool!" shall be in danger of hell fire.*

These are Christ's own words. He speaks not only of hell, but *"hell fire,"* and this verse, too, is from the Sermon on the Mount.

In Matthew 18:9, the Lord Jesus said again,

> *And if your eye causes you to sin, pluck it out and cast it from you. It is better for you to enter into life with one eye, rather than having two eyes, to be cast into hell fire.*

And in Mark 9:43, 45, 47–48, most of which I quoted earlier in this chapter, we read,

> *If your hand causes you to sin, cut it off. It is better for you to enter into life maimed, rather than having two hands, to go to hell, into the fire that shall never be quenched....And if your foot causes you to sin, cut it off. It is better for you to enter life lame, rather than having two feet, to be cast into hell....And if your eye causes you to sin, pluck it out. It is better for you to enter the kingdom of God with one eye, rather than having two eyes, to be cast into hell fire; where "Their worm does not die, and the fire is not quenched."*

Here again, some may say the fire is figurative. But in Matthew 13:30, we read these words:

> *Let both grow together until the harvest, and at the time of harvest I will say to the reapers, "First gather together the tares and bind them in bundles to burn them, but gather the wheat into my barn."*

Now, this verse is part of a parable, which has symbolic language. There would be warrant, if this verse were all that we had, for saying that the fire is figurative, just as the other things in the verse are figurative. But in the forty-first and forty-second verses of the same chapter, we read,

> *The Son of Man will send out His angels, and they will gather out of His kingdom all things that offend, and those who practice lawlessness, and will cast them into the furnace of fire. There will be wailing and gnashing of teeth.*

Here we have the *interpretation* of the parable.

Now, in parables, as I have already said, we have symbols; but in the interpretation of parables, we have the literal facts that the symbols represent. We see clearly that here in the interpretation, as well as in the parable, we have fire. Everything else in the parable is explained—every item in the parable except the fire. The fire in the parable remains fire in the interpretation.

We find the same teaching in another parable, in Matthew 13:47–50—the parable of the net:

> *Again, the kingdom of heaven is like a dragnet that was cast into the sea and gathered some of every kind, which, when it was full, they drew to shore; and they sat down and gathered the good into vessels, but threw the bad away. So it will be at the end of the age. The angels will come forth, separate the wicked from among the just, and cast them into the furnace of fire. There will be wailing and gnashing of teeth.*

Here also, in the interpretation of the parable, we have fire.

Furthermore, we read in Revelation 20:15 that at the judgment of the Great White Throne, "*anyone not found written in the Book of Life was cast into the lake of fire.*" There is nothing in the whole context that suggests that the lake of fire is a symbol. And in Revelation 21:8, we read,

> *But the cowardly, unbelieving, abominable, murderers, sexually immoral, sorcerers, idolaters, and all liars shall have their part in the lake which burns with fire and brimstone, which is the second death.*

In light of these facts, we cannot deny the literal fire of hell without doing violence to every reasonable law of interpretation.

Will People in Hell Have Bodies?

The wicked in the eternal world will not be mere disembodied spirits. This fact is plain from both the Old Testament and the New.

We read in Daniel 12:2, "*And many of* ***those who sleep in the dust of the earth*** *shall awake, some to everlasting life, some to shame and everlasting contempt*" (emphasis added). The soul of the wicked departs into Hades; it is the *body* that crumbles into dust. So this verse is referring to the physical bodies that are going to be raised.

In the New Testament, in John 5:28–29, our Lord is recorded as saying,

> *Do not marvel at this; for the hour is coming in which all who are in the graves will hear His voice and come forth; those who have done good, to the resurrection of life, and those who have done evil, to the resurrection of condemnation.*

Now, it is not souls that are in the graves—it is bodies. This passage teaches the resurrection of bodies, both of the good and of the wicked.

In 1 Corinthians 15:22, we read, "*For as in Adam all die, even so in Christ all shall be made alive.*" What Paul was talking about in this entire chapter is the resurrection of the *body*, not merely the immortality of the soul. Here we are distinctly told that every child of Adam will receive the resurrection of his body in Christ.

Furthermore, in Matthew 5:30, Jesus said,

> *And if your right hand causes you to sin, cut it off and cast it from you; for it is more profitable for you that one of your members perish, than for your whole body to be cast into hell.*

Here, in the plainest possible terms, the body is spoken of as going to hell.

In a similar way, in Matthew 10:28, the Lord Jesus said, "*Do not fear those who kill the body but cannot kill the soul. But rather fear Him who is able to destroy both soul and body in hell.*" From these clear and definite words of our Lord, it is as plain as day that in the future life we are to have bodies, and that the bodies of the lost are to have a place in hell.

The bodily torments of hellfire are not the most appalling feature of hell. The mental agony—the agony of remorse, the agony of shame, and the agony of despair—is worse, immeasurably worse. Nevertheless, physical suffering—a physical suffering with which no pain on earth is anything in comparison—is a feature of hell.

Is the Lake of Fire a Place of Continued, Conscious Torment?

One other question remains to be answered: Is the lake of fire a place of conscious torment, a place of unconscious existence, or a place of annihilation—that is, a place of nonexistence? There are those who believe in a literal hell but do not believe that those who are consigned to it will consciously suffer for any great length of time. They believe either that those who are sent to hell will be annihilated or that they will exist there in a unconscious state.

Of course, this would still be an everlasting hell, and everlasting punishment, but is it the hell that is taught in the Bible? Is the lake of fire a place of continued, conscious torment? In answer to this question, let me call your attention to the fact that the punishment of the wicked is spoken of in the Bible most frequently as "death" and "destruction." But what do these words mean in biblical usage?

The Biblical Meaning of "Death"

First, let us look at the word *death*. I have been told by people time and time again that death means nonexistence, or at least unconscious existence, and that therefore this is what it must mean in the passages where it is spoken of as the future punishment of the impenitent. But does death *as used in the Bible* mean either unconscious existence or annihilation?

First of all, look at 1 Timothy 5:6: *"She who lives in pleasure is dead while she lives."* Death here certainly does not mean either nonexistence or unconscious existence. The woman who lives in pleasure still exists, and she certainly exists consciously, but she is *"dead."* In a similar way, we are told in Ephesians 2:1 that until people are made alive by the power of God, they are *"dead in trespasses and sins."*

Death means wrong existence rather than nonexistence. It is just the opposite of life, and life in New Testament usage does not mean mere existence—it means a right, Godlike, holy existence, the elevation and ennoblement and glorification of existence. Death means just the opposite. It means a wrong and debased existence—the ruin, the shame, the ignominy, and the despair of existence. It is perfectly clear, then, that when the Bible speaks of death, it does not mean either annihilation or unconscious existence.

But even more decisive than these examples is the fact that God Himself has defined death very exactly and very fully in Revelation 21:8:

> *But the cowardly, unbelieving, abominable, murderers, sexually immoral, sorcerers, idolaters, and all liars shall have their part in the lake which burns with fire and brimstone, which is the second death.*

Here we are told in so many words that the *"death"* that is the final outcome of persistent sin and unbelief is a portion in the place of torment, the lake of fire. That this lake of fire is a place of conscious suffering is made clear in the preceding chapter, in Revelation 20:10, where we are told,

> *The devil, who deceived them, was cast into the lake of fire and brimstone where the beast and the false prophet are. And they will be tormented day and night forever and ever.*

The Beast and False Prophet will have already been in the lake of fire for a thousand years when the Devil is thrown there (see Revelation 19:20–20:3, 7–10), and they will have been tormented all that time. Then they will continue to be tormented consciously without rest, and Satan will be punished in the same way.

The Biblical Meaning of "Destruction"

Now let us look at what the word *destruction* means in the Bible. We are told by a certain school of religious thought that the biblical meaning of destruction is simply destruction. Yes, but what does destruction mean? They say it means annihilation, or ceasing to exist, but the Greek word so translated never means that in the Bible or even outside of the Bible. When we look at the root meaning, we see that the noun that is commonly translated *destruction* and *perdition* is derived from a verb that means "to perish." Therefore, we need to find out what the word *perish* means in the Bible. For this task, let us turn to the best Greek-English dictionary of the New Testament that exists—*Thayer's Greek-English Lexicon of the New Testament* (a translation of Grimm's great work). Here we are told that when a thing is said to "perish," it does not cease to exist, but it is "so ruined that it no longer subserves the use for which it was designed."

Furthermore, here again, God has been careful to define His terms. He Himself has given us in the Bible a definition of the term *destruction*. We read in Revelation 17:8, "*The beast that you saw was, and is not, and will ascend out of the bottomless pit and go to perdition.*" Here we are told that the Beast will go "*to perdition.*" The word here translated "*perdition*" is precisely the same word that is elsewhere translated *destruction,* and it should be so translated here. Or, in the other instances, it should be translated "*perdition.*" Now, if we can find what the Beast will go into, we will know exactly what destruction means, for we are told that he will go "into destruction."

As we have already seen, Revelation 19:20 tells us exactly where the Beast will go:

> *Then the beast was captured, and with him the false prophet who worked signs in his presence, by which he deceived those who received the mark of the beast and those who worshiped his image. These two were cast alive into the lake of fire burning with brimstone.*

So then, we see that the destruction into which the Beast will go is a place in the lake that burns with fire and brimstone. As we saw earlier, the Beast and the False Prophet will be consciously tormented for a thousand years before they are joined by the Devil, and then they will continue to exist in conscious torment forever and ever. So then, the word *destruction* is clearly defined in the New Testament in the same way in which *death* is defined, as the condition of beings in a place of conscious torment.

In Revelation 14:10–11, we read regarding the person who worships the Beast and his image, and who receives his mark on his forehead or on his hand:

> *He himself shall also drink of the wine of the wrath of God, which is poured out full strength into the cup of His indignation. He shall be tormented with fire and brimstone in the presence of the holy angels and in the presence of the Lamb. And the smoke of their torment ascends forever and ever; and they have no rest day or night, who worship the beast and his image, and whoever receives the mark of his name.*

The Bible makes it as clear as language can make it that the lake of fire, to which "*anyone not found written in the Book of Life*" (Revelation 20:15) will be consigned, is a place of continued, conscious torment. There is no escaping the clear teaching of the Word of God, unless we throw our Bibles away and discredit the teaching of the apostles and the teaching of Jesus Christ Himself.

General Sherman said, "War is hell." Of course, in the way that Sherman meant this statement, it is true. In fact, it is far more true of war today than it was in the worst and most inexcusable phases of our Civil War. But even war today is not literally hell, for hell is incomparably more awful than the worst war.

This dreadful hell that we have been studying is the destiny of some of you reading this, unless you repent and accept the Lord Jesus Christ. Other appalling facts about hell we will examine in the next chapter, in which we will consider the question, Is the punishment of the wicked everlasting? But we have already seen enough to make any true Christian determine to work with all his might to save others from this awful hell. And we have seen enough to make every honest and sensible person reading this determine to escape this terrible hell at any cost.

8

IS FUTURE PUNISHMENT EVERLASTING?

And these will go away into everlasting punishment,
but the righteous into eternal life.
—Matthew 25:46

Jesus Christ plainly taught that there is a literal hell and that this hell is a place of conscious suffering, suffering far beyond that experienced by anyone here in this present life. But we are faced with another issue of great importance: Is this future conscious suffering of the impenitent going to be endless?

Many who believe in a severe future punishment, and who indeed believe in a literal hell, nevertheless deny, or at least doubt, that this future hell will be endless. They usually acknowledge and teach that the suffering may go on for a long time, and perhaps for thousands of years, but they believe that it will end at last and that all people will ultimately come to repentance, accept Jesus Christ, and be saved.

What is the precise truth about this matter? Like the question, Is there a literal hell? we cannot decide this question by asking what the majority of supposedly reliable theologians believe, for majorities are often wrong, and minorities are often right. Nor can we use our reasoning to determine what such a being as God must do. As we have seen, it is impossible for finite and foolish humans such as we are, and such as the wisest philosophers and theologians are, to judge what an infinitely wise and infinitely holy God must do. All such reasonings are utterly futile and an absolute waste of time.

What the Bible Teaches about the Endlessness of Future Punishment

What I said about the Bible in the previous chapter, I will say again, for it bears repeating. All that we know about the future is what God has been pleased to tell us in His Word. The Bible is, beyond a question, the Word of God; therefore, what it has to say is true and absolutely sure. In this matter, as well as in all others, one ounce of God's revelation is worth more than a thousand tons of man's speculation. The whole question is, What does the Bible teach regarding future punishment?

What Does "Everlasting" Mean?

Let us turn, first of all, to the words of our Lord Jesus Himself in Matthew 25:46: *"And these* [the wicked] *will go away into everlasting punishment, but the righteous into eternal life."* The first question that confronts us in studying this passage is what the word *aionios,* which is here translated *"everlasting,"* means. Thayer carefully studied Greek words, their derivation, and their usage, and in *Thayer's Greek-English Lexicon of the New Testament,* he gave these three definitions of the word, and these three only:

(1) "Without beginning or end, that which always has been and always will be"; (2) "Without beginning"; and (3) "Without end; never to cease; everlasting."

Some say that the word *aionios*, according to its derivation, means "age-lasting," and therefore may refer to a limited period of time. Even admitting this to be true, we should again bear in mind that the meaning of words is not determined by their derivation but by their usage. The most important question is not what the derivation of this word may be, but how the word is used in the New Testament.

Aionios is used seventy-two times in the New Testament. Forty-four of these seventy-two times it is used in the phrase "eternal life" or in the phrase "everlasting life." No one questions that everlasting life is endless. In connection with the word *life*, the word *age-lasting* (if that is the proper derivation of *aionios*) means "lasting through all ages; never ending."

Below I will list fourteen more instances of the Greek word *aionios* in the Bible:

1. Once *"eternal"* is used of the *"salvation"* Christ brings (Hebrews 5:9), which is indisputably never ending.

2. Once the term *"everlasting home"* is used (Luke 16:9), referring to the home that the blessed are to have in the world to come; and, of course, this also is never ending.

3. Once *"eternal"* is used to describe the *"weight of glory"* that awaits the believer who endures affliction for Christ in the present life (2 Corinthians 4:17). In this case, again, by universal consent, *"eternal"* means endless.

4. Once *"eternal"* is used to describe the *"house not made with hands"* that believers in Christ are to receive at the coming of the Lord Jesus (2 Corinthians 5:1). Of course, this *"house not made with hands"* is everlasting. In fact, the very point that is being explained in 2 Corinthians 5:1–8 is the contrast between our present bodies,

which are only for a brief time, and our resurrection bodies, which are to exist throughout all eternity.

5. Once *"eternal"* is used to illustrate the future unseen things that will never end, contrasted with the present seen things that are for a season (2 Corinthians 4:18). That these unseen things are unending is the very point that is being brought out in this verse.

6. Once *"everlasting"* is used of the *"consolation"* given to us by *"our Lord Jesus Christ Himself, and our God and Father"* (2 Thessalonians 2:16), and this is certainly endless.

7. Once *"eternal"* is used of the *"redemption"* that Jesus Christ secured for us by His blood (Hebrews 9:12). This redemption is never ending. In fact, the chief point of contrast in the context in this case is between the *temporary* redemption secured by the constantly repeated sacrifices of the Mosaic ritual and the *never ending* redemption secured by the perfect sacrifice of Christ *"once for all"* (verse 12).

8. Once *"eternal"* is used of the *"inheritance"* that those who are in Christ receive (Heb. 9:15). Here again, beyond a question, it is unending.

9. Once *"everlasting"* is used of the *"covenant"* through Christ's blood (Hebrews 13:20), which is contrasted with the *temporary* covenant, based on the blood of bulls and goats, given through Moses. Here again, *"everlasting"* necessarily and emphatically means never ending. This is the very point being discussed in the book of Hebrews.

10. Once *"everlasting"* is used of the *"kingdom of our Lord and Savior Jesus Christ"* (2 Peter 1:11), and we are told in Luke 1:33, *"Of His kingdom there will be no end."*

11. Once *"everlasting"* is used of *"gospel"* (or Good News), and this, of course, never ends (Revelation 14:6).

12. Once *"everlasting"* is used of *"God"* (Romans 16:26), and He certainly endures, not merely through long ages, but without end.

13. Once *"eternal"* is used of the *"Spirit"* (Hebrews 9:14), and He also certainly endures throughout an absolutely endless eternity.

14. Twice *"eternal"* is used of the *"glory"* that those in Christ obtain (2 Timothy 2:10; 1 Peter 5:10). This, of course, by universal consent, is endless.

We have covered fifty-nine of the seventy-two times the Greek word *aionios* is used in the Bible. In these fifty-nine instances, the idea of endlessness is absolutely necessary to the meaning, and in not a single one of the thirteen remaining places where the word is used is it used of anything that is known to end. If usage can determine the meaning of any word, certainly the New Testament use of this word determines it to mean "never ending," or, as Thayer defined it, "without end; never to cease; everlasting."

Nor is this all. God Himself defines *aionios* as never ending by specifically using it in contrast with that which does end. One example that we have already noticed is 2 Corinthians 4:18, where we read,

> *While we do not look at the things which are seen, but at the things which are not seen. For the things which are seen are temporary* [literally, "for a season"], *but the things which are not seen are eternal.*

Here the whole point is that the unseen things—as distinct from the seen, which are for a season—are for a never ending duration.

But suppose we conceded that the word *aionios* could be used to describe that which, though it may last throughout an age, or ages, has an end. Even if that were true (which it is not), the meaning of the word in any given instance would have to be determined by the context in which it is found.

Now, what is the context in the passage that we are studying? Let us read it again: *"And these will go away into everlasting* [aionios] *punishment, but the righteous into eternal* [aionios] *life"* (Matthew 25:46). The same Greek adjective, *aionios*, is used in connection with "*punishment*" and with "*life*." Certainly, this qualifying adjective must have the same meaning in the one half of the sentence that it has in the other half of the sentence.

We must at least admit that Jesus Christ was an honest man, and He certainly was too honest to juggle with words. He would not use a word to mean one thing in one half of a sentence and something entirely different in the other half. He obviously sought to convey the impression that the punishment of the unsaved is of the same duration as the life of the saved.

No one questions that the life of the saved is endless. If it were not endless, all our hopes would be destroyed. Therefore, if we are to deal honestly with our Lord's words, we must believe that He taught that the punishment of the unsaved is going to be endless. We have exactly the same reason in God's Word for believing in unending punishment that we have for believing in unending life. If you give up the one, you must give up the other, or else deal dishonestly with the words of Jesus Christ.

What Does "Forever and Ever" Mean?

We could rest the case here and call it proven, but let us turn to another passage, Revelation 14:9–11:

> *Then a third angel followed them, saying with a loud voice, "If anyone worships the beast and his image, and receives his mark on his forehead or on his hand, he himself shall also drink of the wine of the wrath of God, which is poured out full strength into the cup of His indignation. He shall be tormented with fire and brimstone in the presence of the holy angels and in the presence of the Lamb. And the smoke of their torment ascends forever and ever; and they have no rest day or night, who worship the beast and his image, and whoever receives the mark of his name."*

Here we have another expression for the duration of the suffering of the impenitent, the expression rendered "*forever and ever.*" In the Greek, there are two slightly different forms of expression that are translated in this way. The one form of expression, rendered literally, is "unto the ages of the ages"; the other form is "unto ages of ages."

What thought do these expressions convey? Those who seek to escape the fact that these words refer to absolute endlessness say that the expressions are a Hebraism[6] for "the supreme one of its class." As illustrations of the same alleged Hebraism, they cite the names *Lord of Lords* and *Holy of Holies*.

But their theory is not true. In the first place, neither of these two names have the same form as "unto the ages of the ages." In the second place, the definition they give is not even the meaning of the names *Lord of Lords* and *Holy of Holies*. The expression *Lord of Lords* does not mean merely the *greatest* Lord, but One who is Himself Lord of all other lords. Likewise, this expression *unto the ages of the ages* never means merely the ages that are the supreme ages as distinct from other ages (nor, as someone else put it, "the ages that *come out of* the other ages," that is, the closing ages before eternity). The expression, according to its form, means ages that are themselves composed of ages. It represents not years tumbling upon years, nor centuries tumbling upon centuries, but ages tumbling upon ages in endless procession. It is the strongest possible form of expression for absolute endlessness.

Furthermore, the way to determine conclusively what "*forever and ever*" means is by considering its usage. Usage is always the decisive thing in determining the meaning of words and phrases. What is the usage of this expression in the book from which we have taken our passage? The expression "*forever and ever*" is used thirteen times in the book of Revelation. In nine of the thirteen times, it refers to the duration of the existence, reign, or glory of God and of His Son, Jesus Christ our Lord. Of course, in these instances, it must not represent merely the supreme ages, or any individual ages—it must refer to absolute eternity and endlessness. Once it is used of the duration of the blessed reign of the righteous, and, of course, here again it refers to an endless eternity. In the three remaining instances, it is used of the duration of the torment of the Devil, the Beast, the False Prophet, and the persistently impenitent.

---

6. A Hebraism is a feature that is characteristic of Hebrew and that occurs in another language.

Those who deny that *"forever and ever"* means an absolutely endless eternity use the following argument. They point out that the phrase is used in Revelation 11:15, where we are told *"the kingdoms of this world have become the kingdoms of our Lord and of His Christ, and He shall reign forever and ever* ["unto the ages of the ages"]!" They add that we are told in 1 Corinthians 15:24 that Christ *"delivers the kingdom to God the Father."* Therefore, His kingdom must come to an end, and consequently, *"forever and ever"* in this passage cannot mean without end.

There are two answers to this objection, either of which is sufficient. The first is that the *"He"* in *"He shall reign forever and ever"* does not necessarily refer to the Christ, but rather to the Lord Jehovah. In this case, their argument falls to the ground.

The second answer is that while we are taught in 1 Corinthians 15:24, and elsewhere, that Jesus Christ will deliver up His *mediatorial* kingdom to the Father, we are distinctly taught that He will rule with the Father. We are told in Luke 1:33 that *"of His kingdom there will be no end."* Therefore, even if the *"He"* in Revelation 11:15 refers to the Christ and not to the Lord Jehovah, the statement is exactly correct. He, the Christ, is to reign *"forever and ever,"* that is, without end.

There is not a single passage in the whole book of Revelation in which *"forever and ever"* is used of anything except what is absolutely endless. So the question is answered again, and answered decisively, that the conscious suffering of the persistently impenitent is absolutely endless.

What Does "Everlasting Destruction" Mean?

Now, let us look at another passage, 2 Thessalonians 1:7–9:

> *The Lord Jesus [will be] revealed from heaven with His mighty angels, in flaming fire taking vengeance on those who do not know God, and on those who do not obey the gospel of our Lord Jesus Christ. These shall be punished with everlasting destruction from the presence of the Lord and from the glory of His power.*

Here we are told that the punishment of those who *"do not know God"* and *"do not obey the gospel"* is *"everlasting destruction."*

What does *"everlasting destruction"* mean? In the previous chapter, "Is There a Literal Hell?" we saw that the biblical meaning of *"destruction"* is a portion in the lake of fire. We saw, moreover, that the inhabitants of the lake of fire *"will be tormented day and night forever and ever"* (Revelation 20:10). It is clear, then, that those who do not know God and do not obey the gospel of our Lord Jesus Christ will be punished with never ending, conscious suffering.

What Does "Everlasting Fire" Mean?

Let us look at one more passage, Matthew 25:41, where Jesus said,

> *Then He* [the Lord Jesus Himself] *will also say to those on the left hand, "Depart from Me, you cursed, into the everlasting fire prepared for the devil and his angels."*

What I want you to notice here is that the punishment into which the impenitent are sent is the *"everlasting fire"* that is *"prepared for the devil and his angels."* In Revelation 20:10, we have an exact description of just what the eternal fire prepared for the Devil and his angels is:

> *The devil, who deceived them, was cast into the lake of fire and brimstone where the beast and the false prophet are. And they will be tormented day and night forever and ever.*

By a comparison of these two statements, we have another explicit declaration of our Lord that the punishment of the impenitent is to be a conscious agony. They will be punished *"day and night"* without rest *"forever and ever."*

From any one of these passages, and especially from all of them put together, we see that the Scriptures make it as plain as language can make it that the future punishment of the persistently impenitent will be absolutely endless.

Arguments against the Endlessness of Future Punishment

Those who believe that all people will ultimately repent, accept Christ, and be saved urge several Scriptures against what seems to be the plain teaching of the passages we have been studying.

Christ Preached to the Spirits in Prison

The first of these is 1 Peter 3:18–20:

> *For Christ also suffered once for sins, the just for the unjust, that He might bring us to God, being put to death in the flesh but made alive by the Spirit, by whom also He went and preached to the spirits in prison, who formerly were disobedient, when once the Divine longsuffering waited in the days of Noah, while the ark was being prepared, in which a few, that is, eight souls, were saved through water.*

It is urged that since Christ went and preached to the spirits in prison, there will be another chance for people to be saved after they have died. But the passage in question does not assert or imply this idea in any way.

First of all, there is no proof that *"the spirits in prison"* refers to the departed spirits of people who once lived here on earth. In the Bible, departed spirits of people are not spoken of in this way. These words are used of other spirits, but not of disembodied human spirits. There is every reason for supposing that these *"spirits in prison"* were not the sinful people who were on the earth when the ark was being prepared, but the angels referred to in Genesis 6:1–2 who sinned at that time. (See also Jude 6–7.)

Furthermore, even if *"the spirits in prison"* here spoken of were the spirits of people who were disobedient in the time of Noah, there is not a hint in the passage that they were saved through the preaching of Christ to them, or that they had another chance. There are two words commonly used in the New Testament for preaching. One is *kerusso,* and the other is *euaggelizo*. The first of these means "to herald," as in heralding a king, or heralding a kingdom. It may, however, be used of preaching a message—the gospel message or some other message. The second word, *euaggelizo*, means "to preach the Gospel." In the passage that we are studying, the word *kerusso* is used, and there is not a hint that Christ preached the Gospel to these spirits in prison. His message was not a saving message; He simply heralded the triumph of the kingdom. So there is nothing in this passage that contradicts the plain, direct statements regarding the destiny of the wicked found in the passages we have been studying.

Those "*under the earth*" Will Bow to Christ

The second passage that is appealed to by those who deny the endlessness of future punishment is Philippians 2:9–11:

> *Therefore God also has highly exalted Him and given Him the name which is above every name, that at the name of Jesus every knee should bow, of those in heaven, and of those on earth, and of those under the earth, and that every tongue should confess that Jesus Christ is Lord, to the glory of God the Father.*

Here it is said that all those "*under the earth,*" as well as all those in heaven and on earth, will bow the knee at the name of Jesus and confess that Jesus Christ is Lord. Some people say that this verse implies that all those "*under the earth*" will be saved. But it does not imply this idea at all. Every knee of every lost individual—and of the Devil and of his angels, too—will be forced someday to bow at the name of Jesus, and every tongue will be forced to confess that He is Lord. If anyone does that in the present life of his own free choice, he will be saved; otherwise, he will do it by compulsion in the age to come. Everyone has to choose between doing it now willingly and gladly, and being saved, or doing it in the hereafter by compulsion, and being lost. There is absolutely nothing in this passage that teaches universal salvation or that even implies anything that weakens the plain statements we have been studying.

All Things Will Be Restored

The third passage that is appealed to is Acts 3:19–21:

> *Repent therefore and be converted, that your sins may be blotted out, so that times of refreshing may come from the presence of the Lord, and that He may send Jesus Christ, who was preached to you before, whom heaven must receive until the times of restoration of all things, which God has spoken by the mouth of all His holy prophets since the world began.*

Here we are told of a coming *"restoration of all things."* Those who contend for the doctrine of universal salvation believe that this means the restoration to righteousness of all persons. But that is not what this passage says, and that is not what it refers to.

We are taught in Old Testament prophecy, and also in the book of Romans, that in connection with the return of our Lord Jesus, there is going to be a restoration of all nature—of the whole physical universe—from its fallen state. For example, in Romans 8:19–21, we read,

> *For the earnest expectation of the creation eagerly waits for the revealing of the sons of God. For the creation was subjected to futility, not willingly, but because of Him who subjected it in hope; because the creation itself also will be delivered from the bondage of corruption into the glorious liberty of the children of God.*

In Isaiah 55:13, we read,

> *Instead of the thorn shall come up the cypress tree, and instead of the brier shall come up the myrtle tree; and it shall be to the* Lord *for a name, for an everlasting sign that shall not be cut off.*

In Isaiah 65:25, we are told,

> *"The wolf and the lamb shall feed together, the lion shall eat straw like the ox, and dust shall be the serpent's food. They shall not hurt nor destroy in all My holy mountain," says the* Lord.

And in Isaiah 32:15, we read,

> *The Spirit is poured upon us from on high, and the wilderness becomes a fruitful field, and the fruitful field is counted as a forest.*

It is to this restoration of the physical universe, plainly predicted here in Romans 8:19–21 and these Old Testament prophecies, that the "*restoration of all things*" spoken of in Acts 3:21 refers. There is not a hint, not the slightest suggestion, of a restoration of impenitent sinners.

All Things in Heaven and on Earth Will Be Summed Up in Christ

Still another passage that is urged is Ephesians 1:9–10, where we read,

> [God] *made known to us the mystery of His will, according to His good pleasure which He purposed in Himself, that in the dispensation of the fullness of the times He might gather together in one all things in Christ, both which are in heaven and which are on earth; in Him.*

Here it is urged that things in heaven and things on earth are to be summed up in Christ. This is true, but it should be noticed that the Holy Spirit has specifically omitted here the phrase that is found in Philippians 2:10, "*those under the earth,*" that is, the abode of the lost. So this passage, far from suggesting that the lost ones in hell will be restored, suggests exactly the opposite. There is, then, certainly nothing in this passage to contradict the plain doctrine of the eternal punishment of the unsaved.

All Will Be Made Alive in Christ

One more passage that is urged against the truth we have been studying remains to be considered: 1 Corinthians 15:22. Here we read, "*For as in Adam all die, even so in Christ all shall be made alive.*" Some say that we are distinctly told here that all who die in Adam, that is, every human being, will be made alive in Christ, and that "*made alive*" means "to obtain eternal life" or "to be saved."

For years I thought that this was the true interpretation of this passage. For this reason, in part, I believed and preached that all people ultimately—sometime, somewhere, somehow—would be brought to accept Jesus Christ and be saved. But when I came to study this verse more carefully, I saw that this was a misinterpretation of the passage.

Every passage in the Bible, or in any other book, must be interpreted in its context. The whole subject that Paul was talking about in this chapter is not the immortality of the soul, but *the resurrection of the body*. All this passage declares is that, just as all lose physical life in Adam, so also all will obtain a resurrection of the body in Christ. Whether that resurrection of the body is a resurrection to *"everlasting life"* or a resurrection to *"shame and everlasting contempt"* (Daniel 12:2) depends entirely on what people do with Jesus Christ. Absolutely nothing in 1 Corinthians 15:22 teaches universal salvation. It only teaches a universal resurrection—a resurrection of the wicked as well as a resurrection of the righteous.

So these are the passages that are so often urged to prove universal salvation. We have seen that there is nothing in any one of them, or in all of them put together, to teach that all people will ultimately be saved. Furthermore, nothing in them conflicts with what we have seen to be the honest meaning of the passages studied earlier in this chapter, namely, that the future punishment of sin is absolutely endless. Not one passage in the Bible teaches that all people will ultimately come to repentance and be saved. I wish that there were one, but there is not. Though I have been searching diligently for such a passage for nearly forty years, I have not found it, and it cannot be found.

Is There a Chance to Be Saved after Death?

One other important question remains: Where are the issues of eternity settled? Some who believe that the punishment of the persistently impenitent is everlasting, that it has no end, nevertheless believe that the issues of eternity are not settled in this present life. They believe that many people settle these issues after death, and that when people die impenitent, they will have another chance. So we see that if someone believes in endless punishment, he does not necessarily believe that there is no chance to be saved after death. Many believe that there will be a chance after death, that many will accept it, and that some will not accept it and will therefore be punished forever and ever.

Now, what is the teaching of the Word of God on this point? Let me call your attention to four passages, any one of which settles the question. Taken together, they leave no possible room for doubt for any honest person who is willing to take the Bible as meaning what it says and who is not merely trying to support a theory.

The first passage is 2 Corinthians 5:10:

> *For we must all appear before the judgment seat of Christ, that each one may receive the things done in the body, according to what he has done, whether good or bad.*

In this passage, we are plainly told that the basis of judgment in the world to come is *"the things done in the body,"* that is, the things done before the spirit leaves the body, the things done before we exit this world. Of course, this particular passage has to do primarily with the judgment of the believer, but it shows what the basis of future judgment is, namely, the things done this side of the grave.

The second passage is Hebrews 9:27: *"It is appointed for men to die once, but after this the judgment."* Here we are distinctly told that after death there is to be, not an opportunity to prepare for judgment, but judgment itself, and that therefore our destiny is settled *at death*. There is no chance of salvation after death.

The third passage is John 5:28–29:

> *Do not marvel at this; for the hour is coming in which all who are in the graves will hear His voice and come forth; those who have done good, to the resurrection of life, and those who have done evil, to the resurrection of condemnation.*

Here, also, it is clearly implied that the resurrection of the good and the bad is for the purpose of judgment regarding the things they did before their bodies were laid in the grave.

A fourth passage—and, if possible, a more decisive passage than any of these—is John 8:21: *"Then Jesus said to them* [the Pharisees] *again, 'I am going away, and you will seek Me, and will die in your sin. Where I go you cannot come.'"* Here our Lord distinctly declared that the question of whether people will go to be with Him or not depends on what they do *before* they die. If they die in their sins, they will not go to be with Him.

We see from these passages that the issues of eternity—the issues of eternal blessedness and glory or eternal agony and shame—are settled in the life that now is.

Do You Believe in Eternal Punishment?

The future state of those who, in this life, reject the redemption offered to them in Christ Jesus is a state of conscious, unutterable, endless torment and anguish. This concept is appalling, but it is scriptural. It is the unmistakable, inescapable teaching of God's own Word.

I wish that all people would repent and accept Christ. If anyone could show me one single passage in the Bible that clearly teaches that every individual will ultimately repent, accept Christ, and be saved, it would be the happiest day of my life, but it cannot be found. I once thought it could, and I believed and taught according to this line of reasoning. These ideas that are so widely circulated today—these theories of Charles Taze Russell and many others—are not at all new to me. I held and taught substantially the same views regarding ultimate universal salvation nearly forty years ago. I was familiar with the arguments that others now urge, and other more persuasive arguments that they do not seem to know.

But the time came, as I studied the Bible more carefully, when I could not reconcile my teaching with what I found to be the unmistakable teaching of God's Word. I had three choices: to give up my belief that the Bible is the Word of God, to twist the words of Jesus (and others in the New Testament) to mean something other than what they clearly teach, or to give up my doctrine of ultimate universal restoration and salvation.

I could not give up my belief that the Bible is the Word of God, for I had found absolutely overwhelming proof that it is God's Word. I could not twist the words of Jesus and of others to mean something other than their clearly intended meaning, for I was an honest man. There was only one thing left to do, and that was to give up my doctrine of universal restoration and salvation. I gave it up with great reluctance, but I was compelled to give it up or to be untrue to my own reason and conscience. It is the inescapable teaching of the Word of God that all who leave this world without having accepted Jesus Christ will spend eternity in hell—a hell of unutterable, conscious anguish.

This biblical concept is a reasonable one when we come to see the appalling nature of sin, and especially the sin of trampling underfoot God's mercy toward sinners and rejecting God's glorious Son, whom in His love He has provided as a Savior. (See Hebrews 10:29.)

Shallow views of sin, God's holiness, and the glory of Jesus Christ lie at the bottom of weak theories of the doom of the impenitent. When we see sin in all its hideousness and enormity, the holiness of God in all its perfection, and the glory of Jesus Christ in all its infinity, nothing will satisfy the demands of our own moral intuitions but the doctrine of the endless, conscious suffering of the lost. Those who persist in the choice of sin, who love darkness rather than light (John 3:19), and who persist in the rejection of the Son of God, will endure everlasting anguish. Nothing but the fact that we dread suffering more than we loathe sin, that we avoid sorrow more than we love the glory of Jesus Christ, makes us reject the thought that beings who eternally choose sin should eternally suffer.

In spite of people's sin, God offers them mercy in this life. In fact, He made the tremendous sacrifice of His Son to save them. However, many despise that mercy and trample God's Son underfoot. (See Hebrews 10:29.) If, then, they are consigned to everlasting torment, I cannot help but say, "Amen! Hallelujah! '*True and righteous are Your judgments*' (Revelation 16:7)!"

At any rate, the doctrine of conscious, eternal torment for impenitent individuals is clearly revealed in the Word of God. Whether we can defend it on philosophical grounds or not, it is our business to believe it and to leave it to the clearer light of eternity to explain what we cannot now understand. We must realize that God may have many infinitely wise reasons for doing things for which we, in our ignorance, can see no sufficient reason at all. It is the most ludicrous pride for beings so limited and foolish as the wisest of men are, to attempt to dogmatize how a God of infinite wisdom must act. All we know about how God is to act is what God has seen fit to tell us.

In conclusion, two things are certain. First, the more closely people walk with God and the more devoted they become in His service, the more likely they are to believe this doctrine. Many people say that they love their fellowmen too much to believe it. But the people who show their love in more practical ways than by sentimental protests about this doctrine, the people who show their love for their fellowmen as Jesus Christ showed His, by laying down their lives for them—these people believe this doctrine, even as Jesus Christ Himself believed it.

As Christians become worldly and lazy, they grow loose in their doctrine concerning the doom of the impenitent. The fact that loose doctrines are spreading so rapidly and widely in our day, and that worldliness is also spreading in the church, testifies against them. (See 1 Timothy 4:1–2; 2 Timothy 3:1–5; 4:2–4.) Increasing laxity of life and increasing laxity of doctrine go hand in hand.

The second thing that is certain is that people who accept a loose doctrine regarding the ultimate penalty of sin lose their power for God. I have seen this fact proven over and over again. These people are very clever at argument and are very zealous in proselytizing, but they are seldom found pleading with others to be reconciled to God. (See 2 Corinthians 5:20.) They are far more likely to be found trying to upset the faith of people already won by the efforts of those who do believe in everlasting punishment than trying to win people who have no faith at all.

If you really believe the doctrine of the endless torment of the impenitent, if the doctrine really gets hold of you, you will work as you have never worked before for the salvation of the lost. Lessening the doctrine in any way will lessen your zeal. Time and time again, I have come to this awful doctrine and tried to find some way of escape from it. But when I have failed—as I have always done at last when I have determined to be honest with the Bible and myself—I have returned to my work with an increased burden for souls and an intensified determination to *"spend and be spent"* for their salvation. (See 2 Corinthians 12:15.)

Eternal, conscious suffering—suffering without the least hope of relief—awaits every one of you reading this who goes on persistently rejecting Jesus Christ and who passes out of this world having rejected Him. In that world of never ending gloom, there will be no possibility of repentance. As you look out into the future, there will not be one single ray of hope. *"Forever and ever"* will be the unceasing wail of that restless sea of fire. After you have been there ten million years and look out toward the future, you will see eternity still stretching on and on and on, with no hope.

Oh, men and women outside of Christ, why will you risk such a doom for a single year, or a month, or a week, or a day? Hell is too awful to risk for five minutes the chance of going there. There is but one rational thing for you to do, and that is to accept Christ right now as your Savior, surrender to Him as your Lord and Master, confess Him as such before the world, and strive from this time on to please Him in everything, day by day. Any other choice is absolute madness.

HOW TO PRAY

CONTENTS

1

THE IMPORTANCE OF PRAYER

In Ephesians 6:18, the tremendous importance of prayer is expressed with startling and overwhelming force: *"Praying always with all prayer and supplication in the Spirit, being watchful to this end with all perseverance and supplication for all the saints."* When the perceptive child of God stops to weigh the meaning of these words, then notes the connection in which they are found, he or she is driven to say, "I must pray, pray, pray. I must put all my energy and heart into prayer. Whatever else I do, I must pray."

Notice the *alls*: *"all prayer and supplication...all perseverance...for all the saints."* Note the piling up of strong words: *"prayer," "supplication,"* "*perseverance.*" Also notice the strong expression, "*being watchful,*" more literally, "in this, be not lazy." Paul realized the natural apathy of man, especially his natural neglect in prayer. How seldom we pray things through! How often the church and the individual get right up to the verge of a great blessing in prayer and then let go, become lazy, and quit. I wish that these words "in this, be not lazy" might burn into our hearts. I wish that the whole verse would burn into our hearts.

The Necessity of Persistent Prayer

Why is this constant, persistent, sleepless, overcoming prayer so necessary? Because there is a Devil. He is cunning; he is mighty; he never rests; he is continually plotting the downfall of the children of God. If the children of God relax in prayer, the Devil will succeed in ensnaring them.

Ephesians 6:12–13 reads:

> *For we do not wrestle against flesh and blood, but against principalities, against powers, against the rulers of the darkness of this age, against spiritual hosts of wickedness in the heavenly places. Therefore take up the whole armor of God, that you may be able to withstand in the evil day, and having done all, to stand.*

Next follows a description of the different parts of the Christian's armor that we are to put on if we are to stand against Satan and his mighty schemes. Paul brings his message to a climax in Ephesians 6:18, telling us that to all else we must add prayer—constant, persistent, untiring, sleepless prayer in the Holy Spirit—or all will be in vain.

Prayer is God's appointed way for obtaining things. The reason we lack anything in life is due to a neglect of prayer. James pointed this out very forcibly: "*You do not have because you do not ask*" (James 4:2). The secret behind the poverty and powerlessness of the average Christian is neglect of prayer.

Many Christians are asking, "Why is it that I progress so little in my Christian life?"

"Neglect of prayer," God answers. "You do not have because you do not ask."

Many ministers are asking, "Why is it I see so little fruit from my labors?"

Again, God answers, "Neglect of prayer. You do not have because you do not ask."

Many Sunday school teachers are asking, "Why is it that I see so few converted in my Sunday school class?"

Still, God answers, "Neglect of prayer. You do not have because you do not ask."

Both ministers and churches are asking, "Why is it that the church of Christ makes so little headway against unbelief, error, sin, and worldliness?"

Once more, we hear God answering, "Neglect of prayer. You do not have because you do not ask."

Those men whom God set forth as a pattern of what He expected Christians to be—the apostles—regarded prayer as the most important business of their lives. When the multiplying responsibilities of the early church crowded in upon them, this was the response of the twelve disciples:

> [They] *summoned the multitude of the disciples and said, "It is not desirable that we should leave the word of God and serve tables. Therefore, brethren, seek out from among you seven men of good reputation, full of the Holy Spirit and wisdom, whom we may appoint over this business; but we will give ourselves continually to prayer and to the ministry of the word."* (Acts 6:2–4)

From what Paul wrote to both churches and individuals, it is evident that much of his time, strength, and thought were devoted to prayer for them. (See Romans 1:9; Ephesians 1:15–16; Colossians 1:9;

1 Thessalonians 3:10; and 2 Timothy 1:3.) All the mighty men of God outside the Bible have been men of prayer. They have differed from one another in many things, but in this practice of faithful praying, they have been alike.

The Ministry of Intercession

Prayer occupied a very prominent place and played a very important part in the earthly life of our Lord. Turn, for example, to Mark 1:35. *"In the morning, having risen a long while before daylight, He went out and departed to a solitary place; and there He prayed."* The preceding day had been a very busy and exciting one, but Jesus shortened the hours of needed sleep so that He could rise early and give Himself to more sorely needed prayer.

Turn to Luke 6:12, where we read: *"Now it came to pass in those days that He went out to the mountain to pray, and continued all night in prayer to God."* Our Savior occasionally found it necessary to spend a whole night in prayer.

The words *pray* and *prayer* are used at least twenty-five times in connection with our Lord in the brief record of His life in the four Gospels, and His praying is mentioned in places where these words are not used. Evidently prayer took much of Jesus' time and strength. A man or woman who does not spend much time in prayer cannot properly be called a follower of Jesus Christ.

Praying is the most important part of the present ministry of our risen Lord. This reason for constant, persistent, sleepless, overcoming prayer seems, if possible, even more forcible than the others.

Christ's ministry did not end with His death. His atoning work was finished then, but when He rose and ascended to the right hand of the Father, He entered into other work for us, work just as important in its place as His atoning work. It cannot be separated from His Atonement because it rests on that as its basis and is necessary to our complete salvation.

We read what that great, present work is by which He carries our salvation on to completeness: *"Therefore He is also able to save to the uttermost those who come to God through Him, since He always lives to make intercession for them*" (Hebrews 7:25). This verse tells us that Jesus is able to save us to the uttermost, not merely *from* the uttermost, but *to* the uttermost—to entire completeness and absolute perfection. He is able to do this not only because He died, but also because He "*always lives.*"

The verse also tells us why He now lives: "*to make intercession*"—to pray. Praying is the principal thing He is doing in these days. It is by His prayers that He is saving us.

The same thought is found in Paul's remarkable, triumphant challenge: "*Who is he who condemns? It is Christ who died, and furthermore is also risen, who is even at the right hand of God, who also makes intercession for us*" (Romans 8:34).

If we are to have fellowship with Jesus Christ in His present work, we must spend much time in prayer. We must give ourselves to earnest, constant, persistent, sleepless, overcoming prayer.

I know of nothing that has so impressed me with a sense of the importance of praying at all seasons—being much and constantly in prayer—as the thought that this is the principal occupation of my risen Lord even now. I want to have fellowship with Him. For that reason I have asked the Father, whatever else He may make me, to make me an intercessor. I pray that He will make me a man who knows how to pray and who spends much time in prayer.

This ministry of intercession is glorious and mighty, and we can all have a part in it. The man or woman who cannot attend a prayer meeting because of illness can have a part in it. The busy mother and the woman who works outside the home can have a part. They can mingle prayers for the saints, for their pastor, for the unsaved, and for missionaries with their day's work. The hard-driven man of business can have a part in it, praying as he hurries from duty to duty. But we must, if we want to maintain this spirit of constant prayer, take time—and plenty of it—when we shut ourselves up in the secret place alone with God for nothing but prayer.

Receiving Mercy, Grace, and Joy

Prayer is the means that God has appointed for our receiving mercy and obtaining grace. Hebrews 4:16 is one of the simplest, sweetest verses in the Bible: *"Let us therefore come boldly to the throne of grace, that we may obtain mercy and find grace to help in time of need."* These words make it very clear that God has appointed a way by which we can seek and obtain mercy and grace. That way is prayer—a bold, confident, outspoken approach to the throne of grace, the Most Holy Place of God's presence. There our sympathizing High Priest, Jesus Christ, has entered in our behalf. (See Hebrews 4:14–15.)

Mercy is what we need, and grace is what we must have; otherwise, all our lives and efforts will end in complete failure. Prayer is the way to obtain mercy and grace. Infinite grace is at our disposal, and we make it ours by prayer. It is ours for the asking. Oh, if we only realized the fullness of God's grace—its height, depth, length, and breadth—I am sure we would spend more time in prayer. The measure of our appropriation of grace is determined by the measure of our prayers.

Who does not feel that he needs more grace? Then ask for it. Be constant and persistent in your asking. Be diligent and untiring in your asking. God delights in our persistence in prayer, for it shows our faith in Him, and He is mightily pleased with faith. Because of our perseverance, He will rise and give us as much as we need. (See Luke 11:8.) What little streams of mercy and grace most of us know when we might know rivers overflowing their banks!

Prayer in the name of Jesus Christ is the way He Himself has appointed for His disciples to obtain fullness of joy. He states this simply and beautifully: *"Until now you have asked nothing in My name. Ask, and you will receive, that your joy may be full"* (John 16:24). Who does not wish for joy? Well, the way to have full joy is by praying in the name of Jesus. We all know people who are full of joy. Indeed, it is just running over, shining from their eyes, bubbling out of their very lips, and running off their fingertips when they shake your hand. Coming in contact with them is like coming in contact with an electrical machine charged with gladness. People of that sort are always people who spend much time in prayer.

Why is it that prayer in the name of Christ brings such fullness of joy? In part, because we get what we ask. But that is not the only reason, nor is it the greatest. Prayer makes God real. When we ask something definite of God, and He gives it, how real God becomes! He is right there! It is blessed to have a God who is real and not merely an idea. I remember once when I suddenly and seriously fell ill all alone in my study. I dropped on my knees and cried to God for help. Instantly, all pain left me, and I was perfectly well. It seemed as if God stood right there, reached out His hand, and touched me. The joy of the healing was not as great as the joy of meeting God.

No joy on earth or in heaven is greater than communion with God. Prayer in the name of Jesus brings us into communion with God. The psalmist was surely not speaking only of future blessedness, but also of present blessedness, when he said, *"In Your presence is fullness of joy"* (Psalm 16:11). Oh, the unutterable joy of those moments when, in our prayers, we really enter into the presence of God!

Does someone say, "I have never known joy like that in prayer"? Do you take enough leisure for prayer to actually sense God's presence? Do you really give yourself up to prayer in the time that you do take?

Freedom from Anxiety

In every care, anxiety, and need of life, prayer with thanksgiving is the means that God has appointed for our obtaining freedom from all anxiety and the peace of God that passes all understanding. Paul said:

> *Be anxious for nothing, but in everything by prayer and supplication, with thanksgiving, let your requests be made known to God; and the peace of God, which surpasses all understanding, will guard your hearts and minds through Christ Jesus.* (Philippians 4:6–7)

To many, this initially seems like the picture of a life that is beautiful but beyond the reach of ordinary mortals. This is not so at all. The verse tells us how this life of peace is attainable by every child of God: *"Be anxious for nothing"* (verse 6). The remainder of the verse tells us how to do this. It is very simple: *"But in everything by prayer and supplication, with thanksgiving, let your requests be made known to God."*

What could be plainer or more simple than that? Just keep in constant touch with God. When troubles or afflictions—great or small—occur, speak to Him about it, never forgetting to return thanks for what He has already done. What will the result be? *"The peace of God, which surpasses all understanding, will guard your hearts and minds through Christ Jesus"* (verse 7).

That is glorious, and it is as simple as it is glorious! Thank God, many are trying it. Do you know anyone who is always serene? Perhaps this person has a very temperamental nature. Nevertheless, when troubles, conflicts, opposition, and sorrow sweep around him, the peace of God that is beyond all understanding will keep his heart and his thoughts in Christ Jesus.

We all know people like that. How do they do it? By prayer, that is how. They know the deep peace of God, the unfathomable peace that surpasses all understanding, because they are men and women of much prayer.

Some of us let the hurry of our lives crowd prayer out; what a waste of time, energy, and emotion there is in this constant worry! One night of prayer will save us from many nights of insomnia. Time spent in prayer is not wasted; it is time invested at a big interest.

Vehicle for the Holy Spirit

Prayer is the method that God Himself has appointed for our obtaining the Holy Spirit. The Bible is very plain on this point. Jesus said, *"If you then, being evil, know how to give good gifts to your children, how much more will your heavenly Father give the Holy Spirit to those who ask Him!"* (Luke 11:13).

I know this as definitely as I know that my thirst is quenched when I drink water. Early one morning in the Chicago Avenue Church prayer room, where several hundred people had been assembled a number of hours in prayer, the Holy Spirit fell so fully that no one could speak or pray. The whole place was so filled with His presence that sobs of joy filled the place. Men left that room and went to different parts of the country, taking trains that very morning, and the effects of the outpouring of God's Holy Spirit in answer to prayer were soon reported. Others went into the city with the blessing of God on them. This is only one instance among many that might be cited from personal experience.

If we would only spend more time in prayer, there would be more fullness of the Spirit's power in our work. Many who once worked unmistakably in the power of the Holy Spirit now fill a room with empty shoutings, beating the air with meaningless gestures, because they have neglected prayer. We must spend much time on our knees before God if we are to continue in the power of the Holy Spirit.

Be Ready for His Return

Prayer is the means that Christ has appointed so that our hearts will not be overcome with indulgences, drunkenness, and the cares of this life, so that the day of Christ's return will not come upon us suddenly as a snare. (See Luke 21:34–35.) We are warned in Scripture: "*Watch therefore, and pray always that* [we] *may be counted worthy to escape all these things that will come to pass, and to stand before the Son of Man*" (verse 36). According to this passage, there is only one way that we can be prepared for the coming of the Lord when He appears: through much prayer.

The second coming of Jesus Christ is a subject that is awakening much interest and discussion in our day. It is one thing to be interested in the Lord's return and to talk about it, but it is another thing to be prepared for it. We live in an atmosphere that has a constant tendency to make us unsuitable for Christ's coming. The world tends to draw us down by its self-indulgences and cares. There is only one way by which we can triumphantly rise above these things—by constant watching in prayer, that is, by sleeplessness in prayer. "*Watch*" in this passage is the same strong word used in Ephesians 6:18, and "*always*" means to pray at all times. The man who spends little time in prayer, who is not steadfast and constant in prayer, will not be ready for the Lord when He comes. But we can be ready. How? Pray! Pray! Pray!

We Need to Pray

Prayer is necessary because of what it accomplishes. Much has been said about that already, but more should be added. Prayer promotes our spiritual growth as almost nothing else, indeed, as nothing else except Bible study. Prayer and Bible study go hand in hand.

Through prayer, my sin—my most hidden sin—is brought to light. As I kneel before God and pray, "*Search me, O God, and know my heart; try me, and know my anxieties; and see if there is any wicked way in me*" (Psalm 139:23–24), God directs the penetrating rays of His light into the innermost recesses of my heart. The sins I never suspected to be present are brought to light. In answer to prayer, God washes away my iniquity and cleanses my sin. (See Psalm 51:2.) My eyes are opened to behold wondrous things out of God's Word. (See Psalm 119:18.) I receive wisdom to know God's way (see James 1:5) and strength to walk in it. As I meet God in prayer and gaze into His face, I am changed into His image "*from glory to glory*" (2 Corinthians 3:18). Each day of true prayer life finds me more like my glorious Lord.

John Welch, the son-in-law of John Knox, was one of the most faithful men of prayer this world has ever seen. He counted any day in which seven or eight hours were not devoted solely to God in prayer and the study of His Word as wasted time. An old man speaking of him after his death said, "He was a type of Christ." How did he become so like his Master? His prayer life explains the mystery.

Prayer also brings power into our work. If we wish power for any work to which God calls us, whether it is preaching, teaching, personal work, or the raising of our children, we can receive it by earnest prayer.

A woman, with a little boy who was perfectly incorrigible, once came to me in desperation and said, "What should I do with him?"

I asked, "Have you ever tried prayer?"

She said that she had prayed for him, she thought. I asked if she had made his conversion and his character a matter of specific, expectant prayer. She replied that she had not been definite in the matter. She began that day, and at once there was a marked change in the child. As a result, he grew up into Christian manhood.

How many Sunday school teachers have taught for months and years and seen no real fruit from their labors. Then, they learn the secret of intercession; by earnest pleading with God, they see their students, one by one, brought to Christ! How many poor teachers have become mighty people of God by casting away their confidence in their own abilities and gifts and giving themselves up to God to wait on Him for the *"power from on high"* (Luke 24:49)! Along with other believers, the Scottish evangelist John Livingstone spent a night in prayer to God. When he preached the next day, five hundred people were either converted or marked some definite uplift in their spiritual lives. Prayer and power are inseparable.

Prayer avails for the conversion of others. Few people are converted in this world in any other way than in connection with someone's prayers. I previously thought that no human being had anything to do with my own conversion, for I was not converted in church or Sunday school or in personal conversation with anyone. I was awakened in the middle of the night and converted. As far as I can remember, I did not have the slightest thought of being converted, or of anything of that nature, when I went to bed and fell asleep. But I was awakened in the middle of the night and converted probably within five minutes. A few minutes before, I was about as near eternal damnation as one gets. I had one foot over the brink and was trying to get the other one over. As I said, I thought no human being had anything to do with it, but I had forgotten my mother's prayers. Later, I learned that one of my college classmates had decided to pray for me until I was saved.

Prayer often avails where everything else fails. How utterly all of Monica's efforts and entreaties failed with her son! But her prayers prevailed with God, and the immoral youth became St. Augustine, the mighty man of God. By prayer, the bitterest enemies of the Gospel have become its most valiant defenders, the most wicked the truest sons of God, and the most contemptible women the purest saints. Oh, the power of prayer to reach down, where hope itself seems vain, and lift men and women up into fellowship with and likeness to God! It is simply wonderful! How little we appreciate this marvelous weapon!

Prayer brings blessings to the church. The history of the church has always been full of grave difficulties to overcome. The Devil hates the church and seeks in every way to block its progress by false doctrine, by division, and by inward corruption of life. But by prayer, a clear way can be made through everything. Prayer will root out heresy, smooth out misunderstanding, sweep away jealousies and animosities, obliterate immoralities, and bring in the full tide of God's reviving grace. History abundantly proves this. In the darkest hour, when the state of the church has seemed beyond hope, believing men and women have met together and cried to God, and the answer has come.

It was so in the days of Knox, and in the days of Wesley, Whitefield, Edwards, and Brainerd. It was so in the days of Finney and in the days of the great revival of 1857 in this country and of 1859 in Ireland. And it will be so again in your day and mine! Satan has organized his forces. Some people, claiming great apostolic methods, are merely covering the rankest dishonesty and hypocrisy with their loud and false assurance. Christians equally loyal to the great fundamental truths of the Gospel are scowling at one another with a Devil-sent suspicion. The world, the flesh, and the Devil are holding a merry carnival. It is a dark day, but now *"it is time for You to act, O Lord, for they have regarded Your law as void"* (Psalm 119:126). He is getting ready to work, and now He is listening for the voice of prayer. Will He hear it? Will He hear it from you? Will He hear it from the church as a body? I believe He will.

2

PRAYING TO GOD

After having seen some of the tremendous importance and irresistible power of prayer, we now come directly to the lesson—how to pray with power.

In the Acts 12, we have the record of a prayer that prevailed with God and also brought about great results. In the fifth verse of this chapter, the manner and method of this prayer are described in a few words: "*Constant prayer was offered to God for him by the church*" (Acts 12:5). The first thing to notice in this verse is the brief expression "*to God.*" The prayer that has power is the prayer that is offered to God.

But some will say, "Is not all prayer offered to God?" No. Much of so-called prayer, both public and private, is not directed to God. In order for a prayer to really be to God, there must be a definite and conscious approach to Him when we pray. We must have an explicit and vivid realization that He is bending over us and listening as we pray. In too many of our prayers, God is thought of too little. Our minds are taken up with thoughts of what we need and are not occupied with thoughts of the mighty and loving Father from whom we are seeking our requests. Often, we are neither occupied with the need nor with the One to whom we are praying. Instead, our minds are wandering here and there. There is no power in that sort of prayer. But when we really come into God's presence, really meet Him face-to-face in the place of prayer, really seek the things that we desire from Him, then there is power.

Coming into God's Presence

If we want to pray correctly, the first thing we should do is to make sure that we really seek an audience with God—that we really come into His very presence. Before a word of petition is offered, we should have the definite and vivid consciousness that we are talking to God. Also, we should believe that He is listening to our requests and is going to grant the things that we ask of Him. This is only possible by the Holy Spirit's power, so we should look to the Holy Spirit to lead us into the presence of God. And we should not be hasty in words until He has actually brought us there.

One night, a very active Christian man dropped into a prayer meeting that I was leading. Before we knelt to pray, I said something like the above, telling all the friends to be sure that before they prayed, they were really in God's presence. I also explained that while they were praying, they should have thoughts of God definitely in mind and be more taken up with Him than with their petitions. A few days later, I met this same gentleman. He said that this simple thought was entirely new to him. It had made prayer a completely new experience for him. If we want to pray correctly, these two little words must sink deep into our hearts: "*to God*."

Pray without Ceasing

The second secret of effective praying is found in the same verse in the words, *"constant prayer."* The word *constant* does not convey the full force of the original Greek. The word literally means "stretched-out-ed-ly." It is a pictorial word and wonderfully expressive. It represents the soul on a stretch of earnest and intense desire. *Intensely* would perhaps be as close a translation as any English word. It is the same word used to speak of our Lord in Luke 22:44, where it is said, *"He prayed more earnestly. Then His sweat became like great drops of blood falling down to the ground."*

We read in Hebrews 5:7 that Christ *"in the days of His flesh...offered up prayers and supplications, with vehement cries and tears."* In Romans 15:30, Paul begged the saints in Rome to *"strive together"* with him in their prayers. The word translated *strive* means primarily to contend as in athletic games or in a fight. In other words, prayer that prevails with God is prayer into which we put our whole souls, stretching out toward God in intense and agonizing desire. Much of our modern prayer lacks power because it lacks heart. We rush into God's presence, run through a string of petitions, jump up, and go out. If someone asks us an hour later what we prayed for, often we cannot remember. If we put so little heart into our prayers, we cannot expect God to put much heart into answering them.

We hear much in our day about the *rest* of faith, but there is not much said about the *fight* of faith in prayer. Those who want us to think that they have attained to some great height of faith and trust because they have never known any agony or conflict in prayer have surely gone beyond their Lord. They have even gone beyond the mightiest victors for God, both in effort and prayer, that the ages of Christian history have known. When we learn to come to God with an intensity of desire that wrings the soul, then we will know a power in prayer that most of us do not yet know.

Prayer and Fasting

How will we achieve this earnestness in prayer? Not by trying to work ourselves up into it. The true method is explained in Romans 8:26:

> *Likewise the Spirit also helps in our weaknesses. For we do not know what we should pray for as we ought, but the Spirit Himself makes intercession for us with groanings which cannot be uttered.*

The earnestness that we work up in the energy of the flesh is a repulsive thing. The earnestness created in us by the Holy Spirit is pleasing to God. Here again, if we desire to pray correctly, we must look to the Spirit of God to teach us how to pray.

It is in this connection that fasting enters in. In Daniel 9:3, we read that Daniel set his face *"toward the Lord God to make request by prayer and supplications, with fasting, sackcloth, and ashes."* There are those who think that fasting belongs to the old dispensation. But when we look at Acts 14:23 and Acts 13:2–3, we find that it was practiced by earnest men of the apostolic day.

If we want to pray with power, we should pray with fasting. This, of course, does not mean that we should fast every time we pray. But there are times of emergency or special crisis, when sincere believers will withdraw even from the gratification of natural appetites that would be perfectly proper under other circumstances in order to give themselves up solely to prayer. There is a mysterious power in such prayer. Every great crisis in life and work should be met in that way. There is nothing pleasing to God in our giving up things that are pleasant in a purely Pharisaic or legalistic way. But there is power in that downright earnestness and determination to obtain, in prayer, the things that we strongly feel are needs. This feeling of urgency leads us to put away everything, even things that are normal and necessary, that we may set our faces to find God and obtain blessings from Him.

Unity in Prayer

Another secret of proper praying is found in Acts 12:5. It appears in the three words: *"by the church."* There is power in united prayer. Of course, there is power in the prayer of an individual, but there is much more power in united prayer. God delights in the unity of His people and seeks to emphasize it in every way. Thus, He pronounces a special blessing on corporate prayer. We read in Matthew 18:19: *"If two of you agree on earth concerning anything that they ask, it will be done for them by My Father in heaven."* This unity, however, must be real. The passage just quoted does not say that if two will agree in asking, but if two will agree as *"concerning anything that they ask."* Two people might agree to ask for the same thing, and yet there may be no real agreement concerning the thing they asked. One might ask it because he really desired it; the other might ask simply to please his friend. But where there is real agreement, where the Spirit of God brings believers into perfect harmony concerning what they ask of God, where the Spirit lays the same burden on two or more hearts, there is absolutely irresistible power in prayer.

3

OBEYING AND PRAYING

One of the most significant verses in the Bible on prayer is 1 John 3:22. John said, *"And whatever we ask we receive from Him, because we keep His commandments and do those things that are pleasing in His sight."* What an astounding statement! John said, in so many words, that he received everything he asked for. How many of us can say the same? But John explains why this was so: *"Because we keep His commandments and do those things that are pleasing in His sight."* In other words, the one who expects God to do as he asks Him must do whatever God bids him. If we give a listening ear to all God's commands to us, He will give a listening ear to all our petitions to Him. If, on the other hand, we turn a deaf ear to His precepts, He will be likely to turn a deaf ear to our prayers. Here we find the secret of much unanswered prayer. We are not listening to God's Word; therefore, He is not listening to our petitions.

I was once speaking to a woman who had been a professed Christian but had given it all up. I asked her why she was not a Christian any longer. She replied, because she did not believe the Bible. I asked her why she did not believe the Bible.

"Because I have tried its promises and found them untrue."

"Which promises?"

"The promises about prayer."

"Which promises about prayer?"

"Does it not say in the Bible, '*Whatever things you ask in prayer, believing, you will receive*'" (Matthew 21:22)?

"It does say that."

"Well, I asked fully expecting to get and did not receive, so the promise failed."

"Was the promise made to you?"

"Why, certainly, it is made to all Christians, is it not?"

"No, God carefully defines who the *yous* are whose believing prayers He agrees to answer."

I then directed her to 1 John 3:22, and read the description of those whose prayers had power with God.

"Now," I said, "were you keeping His commandments and doing those things that are pleasing in His sight?"

She frankly confessed that she was not, and she soon came to see that the real difficulty was not with God's promises, but with herself. That is the reason for many unanswered prayers today—the one who offers them is not obedient.

Knowing and Doing God's Will

If we want power in prayer, we must be earnest students of His Word to find out what His will regarding us is. Then having found it, we must do it. One unconfessed act of disobedience on our part will shut the ear of God against many petitions. But this verse goes beyond the mere keeping of God's commandments. John tells us that we must *"do those things that are pleasing in His sight"* (1 John 3:22).

There are many things that would please God, but which He has not specifically commanded. A true child is not content with merely doing those things that his father specifically commands him to do. He tries to know his father's will, and if he thinks that there is anything that he can do that would please his father, he does it gladly. He does so even if his father has never given him any specific order to do it. So it is with the true child of God. He does not merely ask whether certain things are commanded or certain things forbidden. He tries to know his Father's will in all things.

Many Christians today are doing things that are not pleasing to God. Many also neglect to do things that would be pleasing to God. When you speak to them about these things, they will confront you at once with the question, "Is there any command in the Bible not to do this thing?" If you cannot show them the verse in which their action is plainly forbidden, they think they are under no obligation whatever to give it up. But a true child of God does not demand a specific command. If we make it our desire to find out and do the things that are pleasing to God, He will make it His desire to do the things that are pleasing to us. Here again we find the explanation of much unanswered prayer. We are not making it our desire to know what pleases our Father; thus, our prayers are not answered.

Praying in Truth

Psalm 145:18 throws a great deal of light on the question of how to pray: *"The Lord is near to all who call upon Him, to all who call upon Him in truth*." That little expression "*in truth*" is worthy of further study. If you take your concordance and go through the Bible, you will find that this expression means "in reality," "in sincerity." The prayer that God answers is the prayer that is real, the prayer that asks for something that is sincerely desired.

Much of our prayer is insincere. People ask for things that they do not wish. Many women pray for the conversion of their husbands, but do not really wish their husbands to be converted. They think they do, but if they knew what would be involved in the conversion of their husbands, they would think again. It would necessitate an entire revolution in their manner of doing business and would consequently reduce their income, making it necessary to change their entire way of living. If they were sincere with God, the real prayer of their hearts would be: "O God, do not convert my husband." Some women do not wish their husbands' conversion at so great a cost.

Many churches are praying for a revival but do not really desire a revival. They think they do, for in their minds, a revival means an increase of membership, income, and reputation among the churches. But if they knew what a real revival meant, they would not be so eager. Revival brings the searching of hearts on the part of professed Christians, a radical transformation of individual, home, and social life, when the Spirit of God is poured out in reality and power. If all this were known, the real cry of the church would be: "O God, keep us from having a revival."

Many ministers are praying for the filling with the Holy Spirit, yet they do not really desire it. They think they do, for the filling with the Spirit means new joy and power in preaching the Word, a wider reputation among men, and a larger prominence in the church of Christ. But if they understood what a filling with the Holy Spirit really involved, they would think less about its rewards. They would think more of how it would necessarily bring them into antagonism with the world, with unspiritual Christians, how it would cause their name to be "cast out as evil" (see Luke 6:22), and how it might necessitate their leaving a good, comfortable living to go to work in the slums or even in some foreign land. If they understood all this, their prayer most likely would be—if they were to express the real wish of their hearts—"O God, save me from being filled with the Holy Spirit."

When we do come to the place where we really desire the conversion of friends at any cost, really desire the outpouring of the Holy Spirit whatever it may involve, really desire anything *"in truth"* and then call upon God for it *"in truth,"* God is going to hear.

4

PRAYING IN THE NAME OF CHRIST

Jesus spoke a wonderful word about prayer to His disciples on the night before His crucifixion: *"Whatever you ask in My name, that I will do, that the Father may be glorified in the Son. If you ask anything in My name, I will do it"* (John 14:13–14). Prayer in the name of Christ has power with God. God is well pleased with His Son Jesus Christ. He always hears Him, and He also always hears the prayer that is really in His name. There is a fragrance in the name of Christ that makes every prayer that bears it acceptable to God. But what is it to pray in the name of Christ?

Many explanations have been attempted that make little sense to the average person. But there is nothing mystical or mysterious about this expression. If you go through the Bible and examine all the passages in which the expressions "in My name" or "in His name" are used, you will find that they mean just about what they do in everyday language.

If I go to a bank and hand in a check with my name signed to it, I ask of that bank in my own name. If I have money deposited in that bank, the check will be cashed; if not, it will not be. If, however, I go to a bank with somebody else's name signed to the check, I am asking in his name, and it does not matter whether I have money in that bank or any other. If the person whose name is signed to the check has money there, the check will be cashed. For example, if I were to go to the First National Bank of Chicago and present a check that I had signed for $500, the teller would say to me: "Why, Mr. Torrey, we cannot cash that. You have no money in this bank."

But if I were to go to the First National Bank with a check for $500 made payable to me and signed by one of the large depositors in that bank, they would not ask whether I had money in that bank or in any bank. Instead, they would honor the check at once.

When I go to God in prayer, it is like going to the bank of heaven. I have nothing deposited there. I have absolutely no credit there. If I go in my own name, I will get absolutely nothing. But Jesus Christ has unlimited credit in heaven, and He has granted me the privilege of going to the bank with His name on my checks. When I thus go, my prayers will be honored to any extent.

To pray in the name of Christ is to pray on the ground of His credit, not mine. It is to renounce the thought that I have any claims on God whatever and approach Him on the ground of Christ's claims. Praying in the name of Christ is not done by merely adding the phrase, "I ask these things in Jesus' name," to my prayer. I may put that phrase in my prayer and really be resting in my own merit all the time. On the other hand, I may omit that phrase but really be resting in the merit of Christ all the time. When I really do approach God on the ground of Christ's merit and His atoning blood (see Hebrews 10:19), God will hear me. Many of our prayers are in vain because men approach God imagining that they have some claim that obligates Him to answer their prayers.

Forgiveness in His Name

Years ago when D. L. Moody was young in Christian work, he visited a town in Illinois. A judge in the town was not a Christian. This judge's wife asked Mr. Moody to call on her husband, but he replied: "I cannot talk with your husband. I am only an uneducated, young Christian, and your husband is a scholarly non-believer."

But the wife would not take no for an answer, so Mr. Moody made the call. The clerks in the outer office giggled as the young salesman from Chicago went in to talk with the scholarly judge. The conversation was short. Mr. Moody said, "Judge, I can't talk with you. You are an educated non-Christian, and I have no learning. I simply want to say that if you are ever converted, I want you to let me know."

The judge replied: "Yes, young man, if I am ever converted, I will let you know."

The conversation ended. The clerks snickered louder when the zealous, young Christian left the office, but the judge was converted within a year. Mr. Moody, visiting the town again, asked the judge to explain how it came about. The judge said:

> One night, when my wife was at prayer meeting, I began to grow very uneasy and miserable. I did not know what was the matter with me, but I finally retired before my wife came home. I could not sleep all that night. I got up early, told my wife that I would eat no breakfast, and went down to the office. I told the clerks they could take a holiday and shut myself up in the inner office. I kept growing more and more miserable, and finally I got down and asked God to forgive my sins. But I would not say "for Jesus' sake" because I was a Unitarian and did not believe in the Atonement. I kept praying,

> "God forgive my sins," but no answer came. At last, in desperation, I cried, "O God, for Christ's sake, forgive my sins" and found peace at once.

The judge had no access to God until he came in the name of Christ. When he finally came in the name of Jesus, he was heard and answered at once.

Knowing God's Will through His Word

Great light is thrown on the subject "How to Pray" by 1 John 5:14–15:

> *Now this is the confidence that we have in Him, that if we ask anything according to His will, He hears us. And if we know that He hears us, whatever we ask, we know that we have the petitions that we have asked of Him.*

This passage clearly teaches that if we are to pray correctly, we must pray according to God's will. Then, we will, beyond a shadow of a doubt, receive the thing we ask of Him. But can we know the will of God? Can we know that any specific prayer is according to His will?

We most surely can. How? First by the Word. God has revealed His will in His Word. When anything is definitely promised in the Word of God, we know that it is His will to give that thing. If, when I pray, I can find some definite promise of God's Word and lay that promise before God, I know that He hears me. And if I know that He hears me, I know that I have the petition that I have asked of Him. For example, when I pray for wisdom, I know that it is the will of God to give me wisdom, for He said so in James 1:5: "*If any of you lacks wisdom, let him ask of God, who gives to all liberally and without reproach, and it will be given to him.*" So when I ask for wisdom, I know that the prayer is heard and that wisdom will be given to me. In like manner, when I pray for the Holy Spirit, I know that it is God's will, that my prayer is heard, and that I have the petition that I have asked of Him: "*If you then, being evil, know how to give good gifts to your children, how much more will your heavenly Father give the Holy Spirit to those who ask Him!*" (Luke 11:13).

Some years ago, a minister came to me at the close of an address on prayer at a YMCA Bible school and said, "You have given those young men the impression that they can ask for definite things and get the very things that they ask."

I replied that I did not know whether that was the impression I had given or not, but that was certainly the impression I desired to give.

"But," he replied, "that is not right. We cannot be sure, for we don't know God's will."

I turned at once to James 1:5, read it to him, and said, "Is it not God's will to give us wisdom, and if you ask for wisdom do you not know that you are going to get it?"

"Ah!" he said, "we don't know what wisdom is."

I said, "No, if we did, we would not need to ask. But whatever wisdom may be, don't you know that you will get it?"

Certainly it is our privilege to know. When we have a specific promise in the Word of God, if we doubt that it is God's will or if we doubt that God will do what we ask, we make God a liar. (See 1 John 5:10.)

Here is one of the greatest secrets of prevailing prayer: Study the Word to find what God's will is as revealed there in the promises. Then, simply take these promises and claim them before God in prayer with the absolutely unwavering expectation that He will do what He has promised in His Word.

Knowing God's Will by His Spirit

Another way in which we may know the will of God is by the teaching of His Holy Spirit. There are many things that we need from God that are not covered by any specific promise. But we are not in ignorance of the will of God even then. In Romans 8:26–27, we are told:

> *Likewise the Spirit also helps in our weaknesses. For we do not know what we should pray for as we ought, but the Spirit Himself makes intercession for us with groanings which cannot be uttered. Now He who searches the hearts knows what the mind of the Spirit is, because He makes intercession for the saints according to the will of God.*

Here we are distinctly told that the Spirit of God prays in us, draws out our prayers, according to God's will. When we are thus led out by the Holy Spirit in any direction, to pray for any given object, we may do it in all confidence that it is God's will. We are to be assured that we will receive the very thing we ask of Him, even though there is no specific promise to cover the case. Often, by His Spirit, God lays a heavy burden of prayer for some given individual on our hearts. We cannot rest. We pray for him "*with groanings which cannot be uttered.*" Perhaps the man is entirely beyond our reach, but God hears the prayer. And, in many cases, it is not long before we hear of his definite conversion.

The passage in 1 John 5:14–15 is one of the most abused passages in the Bible:

> *This is the confidence that we have in Him, that if we ask anything according to His will, He hears us. And if we know that He hears us, whatever we ask, we know that we have the petitions that we have asked of Him.*

Undoubtedly, the Holy Spirit put this passage into the Bible to encourage our faith. It begins with "*this is the confidence that we have in Him,*" and closes with "*we know that we have the petitions that we have asked of Him.*" But one of the most frequent usages of this passage, which was so clearly given to bring confidence, is to introduce an element of uncertainty into our prayers. Often, when a person is confident in prayer, some cautious brother will come and say, "Now, don't be too confident. If it is God's will, He will do it. You should add, 'If it be Your will.'"

Doubtless, there are many times when we do not know the will of God, and submission to the excellent will of God should be the basis for all prayer. But when we know God's will, there need be no *ifs*. This passage was not put into the Bible so that we could introduce *ifs* into all our prayers, but so that we could throw our *ifs* to the wind and have *"confidence"* and *"know that we have the petitions that we have asked of Him."*

5

PRAYING IN THE SPIRIT

Over and over again, we have seen our dependence on the Holy Spirit in prayer. This is stated very clearly in Ephesians 6:18, *"Praying always with all prayer and supplication in the Spirit,"* and in Jude 20, *"Praying in the Holy Spirit."* Indeed, the whole secret of prayer is found in these three words, *"in the Spirit."* God the Father answers the prayers that God the Holy Spirit inspires.

The disciples did not know how to pray as they should, so they came to Jesus and said, *"Lord, teach us to pray"* (Luke 11:1). We also do not know how to pray as we should, but we have another Teacher and Guide right at hand to help us. (See John 14:16–17.) *"The Spirit also helps in our weaknesses"*

(Romans 8:26). He teaches us how to pray. True prayer is prayer in the Spirit; that is, the prayer the Spirit inspires and directs. When we come into God's presence, we should recognize our infirmities, our ignorance of what we should pray for or how we should pray for it. In the consciousness of our utter inability to pray properly, we should look to the Holy Spirit, casting ourselves completely on Him to direct our prayers. He must lead our desires and guide our expressions of them.

Nothing can be more foolish in prayer than to rush heedlessly into God's presence and ask the first thing that comes into our minds. When we first come into God's presence, we should be silent before Him. We should look to Him to send His Holy Spirit to teach us how to pray. We must wait for the Holy Spirit and surrender ourselves to the Spirit. Then, we will pray correctly.

Often, when we come to God in prayer, we do not feel like praying. What should we do in such a case? Stop praying until we feel like it? Not at all. When we feel least like praying is the time when we most need to pray. We should wait quietly before God and tell Him how cold and prayerless our hearts are. We should look to Him, trust Him, and expect Him to send the Holy Spirit to warm our hearts and draw us out in prayer. It will not be long before the glow of the Spirit's presence will fill our hearts. We will begin to pray with freedom, directness, earnestness, and power. Many of the most blessed seasons of prayer I have ever known have begun with a feeling of utter deadness and prayerlessness. But in my helplessness and coldness, I have cast myself on God and looked to Him to send His Holy Spirit to teach me to pray. And He has always done it.

When we pray in the Spirit, we will pray for the right things in the right way. There will be joy and power in our prayers.

Praying with Faith

If we are to pray with power, we must pray with faith. In Mark 11:24, Jesus said, *"Therefore I say to you, whatever things you ask when you pray, believe that you receive them, and you will have them."* No matter how positive any promise of God's Word may be, we will not enjoy it unless we confidently expect its fulfillment. James said, *"If any of you lacks wisdom, let him ask of God, who gives to all liberally and without reproach, and it will be given to him"* (James 1:5). Now, that promise is as positive as a promise can be. The next two verses add:

> *But let him ask in faith, with no doubting, for he who doubts is like a wave of the sea driven and tossed by the wind. For let not that man suppose that he will receive anything from the Lord.* (verses 6–7)

There must then be confident, unwavering expectation.

But there is a faith that goes beyond expectation. It believes that prayer is heard and that the promise is granted. This comes out in Mark 11:24: *"Therefore I say to you, whatever things you ask when you pray, believe that you receive them, and you will have them."* But how can one have this kind of faith?

Let us say with all emphasis, it cannot be forced. A person reads this promise about the prayer of faith and then asks for things that he desires. He tries to make himself believe that God has heard the prayer. This only ends in disappointment. It is not real faith, and the thing is not granted. At this point, many people lose faith altogether by trying to create faith by an effort of their will. When the thing they made themselves believe they would receive is not given, the very foundation of faith is often undermined.

But how does real faith come? Romans 10:17 answers the question: *"So then faith comes by hearing, and hearing by the word of God."* If we are to have real faith, we must study the Word of God and discover what is promised. Then, we must simply believe the promises of God. Faith must have God's sanction. Trying to believe something that you want to believe is not faith. Believing what God says in His Word is faith. If I am to have faith when I pray, I must find some promise in the Word of God to rest my faith on.

Furthermore, faith comes through the Spirit. The Spirit knows the will of God. If I pray in the Spirit and look to the Spirit to teach me God's will, He will lead me in prayer according to the will of God. He will give me faith that the prayer is to be answered. But in no case does real faith come by simply determining that you are going to receive what you want. If there is no promise in the Word of God and no clear leading of the Spirit, there can be no real faith. There should be no scolding for your lack of faith in such a case. But if the thing desired is promised in the Word of God, we may well scold ourselves for lack of faith if we doubt, for we are making God a liar by doubting His Word.

6

ALWAYS PRAYING AND NOT FAINTING

In the Gospel of Luke, Jesus emphasized the lesson that men should always pray and not faint. (See Luke 18:1.) The first parable is found in Luke 11:5–8 and the other in Luke 18:1–8.

> *And He said to them, "Which of you shall have a friend, and go to him at midnight and say to him, 'Friend, lend me three loaves; for a friend of mine has come to me on his journey, and I have nothing to set before him'; and he will answer from within and say, 'Do not trouble me; the door is now shut, and my children are with me in*

> *bed; I cannot rise and give to you'? I say to you, though he will not rise and give to him because he is his friend, yet because of his persistence he will rise and give him as many as he needs."*
>
> (Luke 11:5–8)

> *Then He spoke a parable to them, that men always ought to pray and not lose heart, saying: "There was in a certain city a judge who did not fear God nor regard man. Now there was a widow in that city; and she came to him, saying, 'Get justice for me from my adversary.' And he would not for a while; but afterward he said within himself, 'Though I do not fear God nor regard man, yet because this widow troubles me I will avenge her, lest by her continual coming she weary me.'" Then the Lord said, "Hear what the unjust judge said. And shall God not avenge His own elect who cry out day and night to Him, though He bears long with them? I tell you that He will avenge them speedily. Nevertheless, when the Son of Man comes, will He really find faith on the earth?"*
>
> (Luke 18:1–8)

In the former of these two parables, Jesus sets forth in a startling way the necessity of persistence in prayer. The word translated "*persistence*" literally means *shamelessness*. Jesus wants us to understand that God desires us to draw near to Him with a determination to obtain the things we seek that will not be put to shame by any seeming refusal or delay on God's part. God delights in the holy boldness that will not take no for an answer. It is an expression of great faith, and nothing pleases God more than faith.

Jesus seemed to deal with the Syro-Phoenician woman almost with rudeness. But she would not give up that easily, and Jesus looked on her shameless persistence with pleasure. He said, "*O woman, great is your faith! Let it be to you as you desire*" (Matthew 15:28). God does not always give us things at our first efforts. He wants to train us and make us strong by compelling us to work hard for the best things. Likewise, He does not always give us what we ask in answer to the first prayer. He wants to train us and make us strong people of prayer by compelling us to pray hard for the best things. He makes us pray through.

I am glad that this is so. There is no more blessed training in prayer than what comes through being compelled to ask again and again, over long periods of time, before obtaining what we seek from God. Many people call it submission to the will of God when God does not grant them their requests at the first or second asking. They say, "Well, perhaps it is not God's will."

As a rule, this is not submission but spiritual laziness. We do not call it submission to the will of God when we give up after one or two efforts to obtain things by action. We call it lack of strength of character. When the strong man or woman of action starts out to accomplish a thing and does not accomplish it the first or second or one hundredth time, he or she keeps hammering away until it is accomplished. The strong person of prayer keeps on praying until he prays through and obtains what he seeks. We should be careful about what we ask from God. But when we do begin to pray for a thing, we should never give up praying for it until we receive it or until God makes it very clear and very definite that it is not His will to give it.

Some people like us to believe that it shows unbelief to pray twice for the same thing. They think we ought to claim the answer the first time we ask. Doubtless, there are times when we are able, through faith in the Word or the leading of the Holy Spirit, to claim the first time what we have asked of God. But beyond question, there are other times when we must pray again and again for the same thing before we receive our answers. Those who are beyond praying twice for the same thing are beyond following their Master's example. (See Matthew 26:44.)

George Müller prayed for two men daily for more than sixty years. Although both were eventually converted, one turned to the Lord shortly before George Müller's death, I think at the last service that George Müller held. The other was converted within a year after Müller's death. One of the great needs of the present day is for men and women who will not only start out to pray for things, but will pray on and on until they obtain what they seek from the Lord.

7

ABIDING IN CHRIST

The whole secret of prayer is found in these words of our Lord: *"If you abide in Me, and My words abide in you, you will ask what you desire, and it shall be done for you"* (John 15:7). Here is prayer that has unbounded power: *"Ask what you desire, and it shall be done for you."*

There is a way, then, of asking and receiving precisely what we ask. Christ gives two conditions for this all-prevailing prayer. The first condition is *"If you abide in Me."* What does it mean to abide in Christ? Some explanations are so mystical or so profound that many children of God think they mean practically nothing at all. But what Jesus meant was really very simple.

He had been comparing Himself to a vine and His disciples to the branches in the vine. Some branches continued in the vine in living union so that the sap or life of the vine constantly flowed into the branches. They had no independent life of their own. Everything in them was simply the outcome of the life of the vine flowing into them. Their buds, leaves, blossoms, and fruit were not really theirs, but the buds, leaves, blossoms, and fruit of the vine. Other branches were completely severed from the vine, or the flow of the sap or life of the vine was in some way hindered.

For us to abide in Christ is to bear the same relationship to Him that the first sort of branches bear to the vine. That is to say, to abide in Christ is to renounce any independent lives of our own. We must give up trying to think our own thoughts, form our own resolutions, or cultivate our own feelings. We must simply and constantly look to Christ to think His thoughts in us, to form His purposes in us, to feel His emotions and affections in us. It is to renounce all life independent of Christ and constantly look to Him for the inflow of His life into us and the outworking of His life through us. When we do this, our prayers will obtain what we seek from God.

This must necessarily be so, for our desires will not be our own desires but Christ's. And our prayers will not in reality be our own prayers, but Christ praying in us. Such prayers will always be in harmony with God's will, and the Father always hears Him. When our prayers fail, it is because they are indeed our prayers. We have conceived the desire and offered our own petitions, instead of looking to Christ to pray through us.

To abide in Christ, one must already be in Christ through the acceptance of Christ as an atoning Savior from the guilt of sin. Christ must be acknowledged as a risen Savior from the power of sin and as Lord and Master over all the believer's life. Once we are in Christ, all that we have to do to abide in Christ is simply to renounce our self-life. We must utterly renounce every thought, purpose, desire, and affection of our own and continually look for Jesus Christ to form His thoughts, purposes, affections, and desires in us. Abiding in Christ is really a very simple matter, though it is a wonderful life of privilege and of power.

Christ's Words in Us

Another condition is stated in John 15:7, though it is really involved in the first: *"and My words abide in you."* If we are to receive from God all we ask from Him, Christ's words must abide in us. We must study His words and let them sink into our thoughts and hearts. We must keep them in our memories, obey them constantly in our lives, and let them shape and mold our daily lives and all our actions.

This is really the method of abiding in Christ. It is through His words that Jesus imparts Himself to us. The words He speaks to us are spirit and life. (See John 6:63.) It is vain to expect power in prayer unless we meditate on the words of Christ and let them sink deeply and find a permanent abode in our hearts. Many wonder why they are so powerless in prayer. The very simple explanation of it all is found in their neglect of the words of Christ. They have not hidden His words in their hearts (see Psalm 119:11); His words do not abide in them. It is not by moments of mystical meditation and rapturous experiences that we learn to abide in Christ. It is by feeding on His Word, His written word in the Bible, and looking to the Spirit to implant these words in our hearts to make them a living thing in our hearts. If we thus let the words of Christ abide in us, they will stir us up to prayer. They will be the mold in which our prayers are shaped. And our prayers will necessarily be consistent with God's will and will prevail with Him. Prevailing prayer is almost an impossibility where there is neglect of the study of God's Word.

Mere intellectual study of the Word of God is not enough; there must be meditation on it. The Word of God must be revolved over and over in the mind with a constant looking to God and His Spirit to make that Word a living thing in the heart. The prayer that is born of meditation on the Word of God is the prayer that soars upward to God's listening ear.

George Müller, one of the mightiest men of prayer, would begin praying by reading and meditating on God's Word until a prayer began to form itself in his heart. Thus, God Himself was the real Author of the prayer, and God answered the prayer that He Himself had inspired.

The Word of God is the instrument through which the Holy Spirit works. It is the *"sword of the Spirit"* (Ephesians 6:17) in more senses than one. The person who wants to know the work of the Holy Spirit in any direction must feed on the Word. The person who desires to pray in the Spirit must meditate on the Word so that the Holy Spirit may have something through which He can work. The Holy Spirit works His prayers in us through the Word. Neglect of the Word makes praying in the Holy Spirit an impossibility. If we seek to feed the fire of our prayers with the fuel of God's Word, all our difficulties in prayer will disappear.

8

PRAYING WITH THANKSGIVING

Two words are often overlooked in the lesson about prayer that Paul gives us in Philippians 4:6–7:

Be anxious for nothing, but in everything by prayer and supplication, with thanksgiving, let your requests be made known to God; and the peace of God, which surpasses all understanding, will guard your hearts and minds through Christ Jesus.

The two important words often disregarded are "*with thanksgiving.*"

In approaching God to ask for new blessings, we must never forget to thank Him for blessings already granted. If we would just stop and think about how many prayers God has answered and how seldom we have thanked Him, I am sure we would be overwhelmed. We should be just as definite in returning thanks as we are in making our requests. We come to God with very specific petitions, but when we thank Him, our thanksgiving is indefinite and general.

Doubtless one reason why so many of our prayers lack power is because we have neglected to thank God for blessings already received. If anyone were to constantly ask us for help and never say "Thank you" for the help given, we would soon get tired of helping one so ungrateful. Indeed, our respect for the one we were helping would stop us from encouraging such rank ingratitude. Doubtless our heavenly Father, out of wise regard for our highest welfare, often refuses to answer our prayers in order to bring us to a sense of our ingratitude. We must be taught to be thankful.

God is deeply grieved by the thanklessness and ingratitude of which so many of us are guilty. When Jesus healed the ten lepers and only one came back to give Him thanks, in wonderment and pain, He exclaimed, *"Were there not ten cleansed? But where are the nine?"* (Luke 17:17). How often He looks down on us in sadness at our forgetfulness of His repeated blessings and frequent answers to prayer.

Returning thanks for blessings already received increases our faith and enables us to approach God with new boldness and new assurance. Doubtless the reason so many have so little faith when they pray is because they take so little time to meditate on and thank God for blessings already received. As one meditates on the answers to prayers already granted, faith grows bolder and bolder. In the very depths of our souls, we come to feel that nothing is too hard for the Lord. As we reflect on the wondrous goodness of God on the one hand and on the little thanksgiving offered on the other hand, we may well humble ourselves before God and confess our sins.

The mighty men of prayer in the Bible, and those throughout the ages of the church's history, have been men who were devoted to offering thanksgiving and praise. David was a mighty man of prayer, and his psalms abound with thanksgiving and praise. The apostles were mighty men of prayer. We read that they *"were continually in the temple praising and blessing God"* (Luke 24:53). Paul was a mighty man of prayer. Often in his epistles, he burst out in specific thanksgiving to God for definite blessings and definite answers to prayers.

Jesus is our model in prayer as in everything else. In the study of His life, His manner of returning thanks at the simplest meal was so noticeable that two of His disciples recognized Him by this act after His resurrection. Thanksgiving is one of the inevitable results of being filled with the Holy Spirit. One who does not learn *"in every thing give thanks in all circumstances"* (1 Thessalonians 5:18) cannot continue to pray in the Spirit. If we want to learn to pray with power, we would do well to let these two words sink deeply into our hearts: *"with thanksgiving."*

9

HINDRANCES TO PRAYER

We have very carefully studied the positive conditions of prevailing prayer, but there are some things that hinder prayer. God has made these obstacles very plain in His Word.

Selfish Prayers

The first hindrance to prayer is found in James 4:3: "*You ask and do not receive, because you ask amiss, that you may spend it on your pleasures.*" A selfish purpose in prayer robs prayer of power. Many prayers are selfish. These may be prayers for things for which it is perfectly proper to ask, for things which it is the will of God to give, but the motive of the prayer is entirely wrong, so the prayer falls powerless to the ground. The true purpose in prayer is that God may be glorified in the answer. If we ask any petition merely to receive something to use for our pleasure or gratification, we *"ask amiss"* and should not expect to receive what we ask. This explains why many prayers remain unanswered.

For example, a woman is praying for the conversion of her husband. That certainly is a most proper thing to ask. But her motive in asking for the conversion of her husband is entirely improper; it is selfish. She desires that her husband may be converted because it would be so much more pleasant for her to have a husband who sympathized with her. Or it is so painful to think that her husband might die and be lost forever. For some such selfish reason as this, she desires to have her husband converted. The prayer is purely selfish. Why should a woman desire the conversion of her husband? First and above all, that God may be glorified. It should be her desire because she cannot bear the thought that God the Father would be dishonored by her husband.

Many pray for a revival. That certainly is a prayer that is pleasing to God and in line with His will. But many prayers for revivals are purely selfish. Some churches desire revivals so that their membership may be increased or so that their church may have more power and influence in the community. Some churches want revival so that the church treasury may be filled or so that a good report may be made at the presbytery, conference, or association. For such low purposes as these, churches and ministers are often praying for a revival, and God does not answer the prayer.

We should pray for a revival because we cannot endure the dishonor of God caused by the worldliness of the church, the sins of unbelievers, and the proud unbelief of the day. We should pray for revival because God's Word is being made void. We should pray for revival so that God may be glorified by the outpouring of His Spirit on the church of Christ. For these reasons, first and above all, we should pray for revival.

Many prayers for filling by the Holy Spirit are selfish requests. It certainly is God's will to give the Holy Spirit to those who ask Him. He has told us so plainly in His Word. (See Luke 11:13.) But many prayers for filling by the Holy Spirit are hindered by the selfishness of the motive behind the prayer. Men and women pray for the Holy Spirit so that they may be happy, saved from the wretchedness of their lives, have power as Christian workers, or for some other self-centered reason. We should pray for the Holy Spirit in order that God may no longer be dishonored by the low level of our Christian lives and by our ineffective service. We should pray for the Holy Spirit so that God may be glorified in the new beauty that comes into our lives and the new power that comes into our service.

Sin Hinders Prayer

The second hindrance to prayer is seen in Isaiah 59:1–2:

> *Behold, the Lord's hand is not shortened, that it cannot save; nor His ear heavy, that it cannot hear. But your iniquities have separated you from your God; and your sins have hidden His face from you, so that He will not hear.*

Sin hinders prayer. Perhaps a man prays and prays and receives no answer to his prayers. Perhaps he is tempted to think that it is not the will of God to answer, or he may think that the days when God answered prayer are over. This is what the Israelites seem to have thought. They thought that the Lord's hand was shortened, that it could not save, and that His ear could no longer hear.

"Not so," said Isaiah. "God's ear is just as open to hear as ever; His hand is just as mighty to save. But there is a hindrance. That hindrance is your own sins. Your iniquities have separated you and your God. Your sins have hid His face from you so that He will not hear."

It is the same today. A man is crying to God in vain, simply because of sin in his life. It may be some sin in the past that has been unconfessed and unjudged. It may be some sin in the present that is cherished. Very likely, it is not even looked on as sin. But the sin is there, hidden away somewhere in the heart or in the life, and God "*will not hear.*"

Anyone who finds his prayers unanswered should not think that what he asks of God is not according to His will. Instead, he should go alone to God with the psalmist's prayer, *"Search me, O God, and know my heart; try me, and know my anxieties; and see if there is any wicked way in me"* (Psalm 139:23–24). He should wait before Him until He puts His finger on the thing that is displeasing in His sight. Then, this sin should be confessed and renounced.

I well remember a time in my life when I was praying for two definite things that I thought I must have, or God would be dishonored. But the answer did not come. I awoke in the middle of the night in great physical suffering and distress of soul. I cried to God for these things, reasoned with Him as to how necessary it was that I get them, and get them at once. Still no answer came. I asked God to show me if there was anything wrong in my own life. Something came to my mind that had often come to it before—something definite, which I was unwilling to confess as sin. I said to God, "If this is wrong, I will give it up." Still no answer came. Though I had never admitted it, in my innermost heart, I knew it was wrong.

At last I said, "This is wrong. I have sinned. I will give it up." I found peace, and in a few moments, I was sleeping like a child. In the morning, the money that was needed so much for the honor of God's name came.

Sin is an awful thing. One of the most awful things about it is the way it hinders prayer. It severs the connection between us and the source of all grace, power, and blessing. Anyone who desires power in prayer must be merciless in dealing with his own sins. *"If I regard iniquity in my heart, the Lord will not hear"* (Ps. 66:18). As long as we hold on to sin or have any controversy with God, we cannot expect Him to heed our prayers. If there is anything that is constantly coming up in your moments of close communion with God, that is the thing that hinders prayer. Put it away.

Who Comes First?

The third hindrance to prayer is found in Ezekiel 14:3: *"Son of man, these men have set up their idols in their hearts, and put before them that which causes them to stumble into iniquity. Should I let Myself be inquired of at all by them?"* Idols in the heart cause God to refuse to listen to our prayers.

What is an idol? An idol is anything that takes the place of God, anything that is the ultimate object of our affections. God alone has the right to the supreme place in our hearts. Everything and everyone else must be subordinate to Him.

Suppose a man makes an idol of his wife. Not that a man can love his wife too much, but he can put her in the wrong place. He can put her before God. When a man regards his wife's pleasure before God's pleasure, when he gives her first place and God second place, his wife is an idol. God cannot hear his prayers.

Suppose a woman makes an idol of her children. Not that we can love our children too much. The more dearly we love Christ, the more dearly we love our children. But we can put our children in the wrong place; we can put them before God and their interests before God's interests. When we do this, our children become our idols.

Many make an idol of their reputations or careers. If these things come before God, God cannot hear the prayers of such people.

If we really desire power in prayer, we must answer the question: "Is God absolutely first?" Is He before our wives, before our children, before our reputations, before our careers, before our own lives? If not, prevailing prayer is impossible.

God often calls our attention to the fact that we have an idol by not answering our prayers. Thus, He leads us to inquire as to why our prayers are not answered. And so, we discover the idol, renounce it, and then God hears our prayers.

Give in order to Receive

The fourth hindrance to prayer is found in Proverbs 21:13: "*Whoever shuts his ears to the cry of the poor will also cry himself and not be heard.*" There is perhaps no greater hindrance to prayer than stinginess, the lack of generosity toward the poor and toward God's work. It is the one who gives generously to others who receives generously from God:

> *Give, and it will be given to you: good measure, pressed down, shaken together, and running over will be put into your bosom. For with the same measure that you use, it will be measured back to you.* (Luke 6:38)

The generous man is the mighty man of prayer. The stingy man is the powerless man of prayer.

One of the most wonderful statements about prevailing prayer is made in direct connection with generosity toward the needy: "*And whatever we ask we receive from Him, because we keep His commandments and do those things that are pleasing in His sight*" (1 John 3:22). We are told in the context of the verse that when we love, not "*in word or in tongue, but in deed and in truth*" (verse 18), when we open our hearts toward the "*brother in need*" (verse 17), that God hears us. It is only then that we have confidence toward God in prayer.

Many men and women are seeking to find the secret of their powerlessness in prayer. They need not seek far. It is nothing more nor less than downright stinginess. George Müller was a mighty man of prayer because he was a mighty giver. What he received from God never stuck to his fingers. He immediately passed it on to others. He was constantly receiving because he was constantly giving. When one thinks of the selfishness of the professing church today, it is no wonder that the church has so little power in prayer. If we want to receive from God, we must give to others. Perhaps the most wonderful promise in the Bible in regard to God's supplying our needs is Philippians 4:19, "*And my God shall supply all your need according to His riches in glory by Christ Jesus.*" This glorious promise was made to the Philippian church and made in immediate connection with their generosity.

An Unforgiving Spirit

The fifth hindrance to prayer is found in Mark 11:25: "*And whenever you stand praying, if you have anything against anyone, forgive him, that your Father in heaven may also forgive you your trespasses.*"

An unforgiving spirit is one of the most common hindrances to prayer. Prayer is answered on the basis that our sins are forgiven. However, God cannot deal with us on the basis of forgiveness while we are harboring ill will against those who have wronged us. Anyone who is nursing a grudge against another has closed the ear of God against his own petition. How many are crying to God for the conversion of their husband, children, or friends and are wondering why it is that their prayers are not answered. The whole secret to their dilemma is some grudge that they have in their hearts against someone who has injured them. Many mothers and fathers allow their children to go through to eternity unsaved for the miserable gratification of hating somebody.

Husband and Wife Relationship

The sixth hindrance to prayer is found in 1 Peter 3:7:

> *Husbands, likewise, dwell with* [your wives] *with understanding, giving honor to the wife, as to the weaker vessel, and as being heirs together of the grace of life, that your prayers may not be hindered.*

Here we are plainly told that a wrong relationship between husband and wife is a hindrance to prayer.

In many cases, the prayers of husbands are hindered because of their failure in duty toward their wives. On the other hand, without a doubt, it is true that the prayers of wives are hindered because of their failure in duty toward their husbands. If husbands and wives diligently seek to find the cause of their unanswered prayers, they will often find it in their relationship to one another.

Many men make great claims of holiness and are very active in Christian work but show little consideration in the treatment of their wives. It is often unkind, if not brutal. Then they wonder why their prayers are not answered. The verse that we have just read explains the seeming mystery. On the other hand, many women are very devoted to the church and very faithful in attendance, yet they treat their husbands with the most unpardonable neglect. They are cross and peevish toward them and wound them by the sharpness of their speech and unruly temper. Then they wonder why they have no power in prayer.

Other things in the relationship between husbands and wives cannot be spoken of publicly but are often hindrances in approaching God in prayer. There is much sin covered up under the holy name of marriage. This sin is a cause of spiritual deadness and of powerlessness in prayer. Men or women whose prayers seem to bring no answer should spread their whole married life out before God. They should ask Him to put His finger on anything that is displeasing in His sight.

Believe His Word Absolutely

The seventh hindrance to prayer is found in James 1:5–7:

> *If any of you lacks wisdom, let him ask of God, who gives to all liberally and without reproach, and it will be given to him. But let him ask in faith, with no doubting, for he who doubts is like a wave of the sea driven and tossed by the wind. For let not that man suppose that he will receive anything from the Lord.*

Prayers are hindered by unbelief. God demands that we believe His Word absolutely. To question it is to make Him a liar. (See 1 John 5:10.) Many of us do that when we plead His promises. Is it any wonder that our prayers are not answered? How many prayers are hindered by our wretched unbelief? We go to God and ask Him for something that is positively promised in His Word, and then we only half expect to get it. *"Let not that man suppose that he will receive anything from the Lord."*

10

WHEN TO PRAY

If we want to know the fullness of blessing in our prayer lives, it is important not only to pray in the right way but also at the right time. Christ's own example is full of suggestions as to the right time for prayer. In the first chapter of Mark, we read: "*Now in the morning, having risen a long while before daylight, He went out and departed to a solitary place; and there He prayed*" (verse 35).

Prayer in the Morning

Jesus chose the early morning hour for prayer. Many of the mightiest men of God have followed the Lord's example in this. In the morning hour, the mind is fresh and at its very best. It is free from distraction. That absolute concentration that is essential to the most effective prayer is most easily possible in the early morning hours. Furthermore, when the early hours are spent in prayer, the whole day is sanctified. Power is then obtained for overcoming life's temptations and for performing its duties. More can be accomplished in prayer in the first hours of the day than at any other time. Every child of God who wants to make the most out of his life for Christ should set apart the first part of the day to meet with God in the study of His Word and in prayer. The first thing we do each day should be to get alone with God. We can then face the duties, the temptations, and the service of that day and receive strength from God for all. We should get victory before the hour of trial, temptation, or service comes. The secret place of prayer is the place to fight our battles and gain our victories.

Nights of Prayer

In Luke, we find further light regarding the right time to pray: *"Now it came to pass in those days that He went out to the mountain to pray, and continued all night in prayer to God"* (Luke 6:12). Here we see Jesus praying at night, spending the entire night in prayer. Of course, we have no reason to suppose that this was the constant practice of our Lord, nor do we even know how common this practice was. But there were certainly times when the whole night was given up to prayer. Here, too, we would do well to follow in the footsteps of the Master.

Of course, there is a way of setting apart nights for prayer in which there is no profit. It is pure legalism. But the abuse of this practice is no reason for neglecting it altogether. One should not say, "I am going to spend a whole night in prayer," thinking that there is any merit that will win God's favor in such an exercise. That is legalism. But we often do well to say, "I am going to set apart this night for meeting God and obtaining His blessing and power. If necessary, and if He so leads me, I will give the whole night to prayer." Often, we will have prayed things through long before the night has passed. Then we can retire and enjoy more refreshing and invigorating sleep than if we had not spent the time in prayer. At other times, God will keep us in communion with Himself way into the morning. When He does this in His infinite grace, these hours of night prayer are blessed indeed.

Nights of prayer to God are followed by days of power with men. In the night hours, the world is hushed in slumber. We can easily be alone with God and have undisturbed communion with Him. If we set apart the whole night for prayer, there will be no hurry. There will be time for our own hearts to become quiet before God. There will be time for the whole mind to be brought under the guidance of the Holy Spirit. There will be plenty of time to pray things through. A night of prayer should be put entirely under God's control. We should lay down no rules as to how long we will pray or what we will pray about. Be ready to wait on God for as short or as long a time as He may lead. Be ready to be led in one direction or another as He sees fit.

Prayer before and after a Crisis

Jesus Christ prayed before all the great crises in earthly life. He prayed before His entrance into His public ministry. (See Luke 3:21–22.) He prayed before choosing the twelve disciples. (See Luke 6:12–13.) He prayed during His public ministry. (See, for example, Mark 1:35–38.) He prayed before announcing to the Twelve His approaching death (see Luke 9:18, 21–22) and before the great consummation of His life on the cross. (See Luke 22:39–46.) He prepared for every important crisis by a lengthy season of prayer. We should do likewise. When any crisis of life is seen to be approaching, we should prepare for it by a season of very definite prayer to God. We should take plenty of time for this prayer.

Christ prayed not only before the great events and victories of His life, but also after its great achievements and important crises. When He had fed the five thousand with the five loaves and two fishes, the multitude desired to take Him and make Him king. Having sent them away, He went up into the mountain to pray and spent hours there alone with God. (See Matthew 14:23; John 6:15.) So He went on from victory to victory.

It is more common for most of us to pray before the great events of life than it is to pray after them. But the latter is as important as the former. If we prayed after the great achievements of life, we might go on to still greater accomplishments. As it is, we are often either exalted or exhausted by the things that we do in the name of the Lord, and so we advance no further. Often, a man, in answer to prayer, has been endued with power and has thus worked great things in the name of the Lord. When these great things were accomplished, instead of going alone with God and humbling himself before Him, giving God the glory, he has congratulated himself. He has become arrogant, and God has been obliged to lay him aside. The great things done were not followed by humility and thanks to God. Thus, pride entered, and the man was stripped of his power.

Never Too Busy

Jesus Christ gave special time to prayer when He was unusually busy. He would withdraw from the multitudes that thronged about Him and go into the wilderness to pray. For example, we read in Luke 5:15–16:

> *However, the report went around concerning Him all the more; and great multitudes came together to hear, and to be healed by Him of their infirmities. So He Himself often withdrew into the wilderness and prayed.*

Some men are so busy that they find no time for prayer. Apparently, the busier Christ's life was, the more He prayed. Sometimes He had no time to eat. (See Mark 3:20.) Sometimes He had no time for needed rest and sleep. (See Mark 6:31, 33, 46.) But He always took time to pray. The more the work increased, the more He prayed.

Many mighty followers of God have learned this secret from Christ. And when the work has increased more than usual, they have set an unusual amount of time apart for prayer. Other people of God, once mighty, have lost their power because they did not learn this secret. They allowed increasing work to crowd out prayer.

Years ago, it was my privilege, with other theological students, to ask questions of one of the most helpful Christian men of the day. I was led to ask, "Will you tell us something of your prayer life?"

The man was silent a moment, and then, turning his eyes earnestly upon me, replied: "Well, I must admit that I have been so swamped with work lately that I have not given the time I should to prayer."

Is it any wonder that man lost power? The great work he was doing was curtailed in a very marked degree. Let us never forget that the more work pressures us, the more time we must spend in prayer.

Pray at All Times

Jesus Christ prayed before the great temptations of His life.

As He drew nearer and nearer to the cross and realized that the great final test of His life was imminent, Jesus went out into the Garden to pray. He came *"to a place called Gethsemane, and said to the disciples, 'Sit here while I go and pray over there'"* (Matthew 26:36). The victory of Calvary was won that night in the Garden of Gethsemane. The calm majesty with which He bore the awful onslaughts of Pilate's Judgment Hall and Calvary resulted from the struggle, agony, and victory of Gethsemane. While Jesus prayed, the disciples slept. He stood fast while they fell dishonorably.

Many temptations come on us suddenly and unannounced. All we can do is lift a cry to God for help then and there. But many temptations of life we can see ahead of time, and in such cases, the victory should be won before the temptation really reaches us.

In 1 Thessalonians 5:17, we read: *"Pray without ceasing,"* and in Ephesians 6:18: *"Praying always."* Our whole lives should be lives of prayer. We should walk in constant communion with God. There should be a constant looking upward to God. We should walk so habitually in His presence that even when we awake in the night, it would be the most natural thing for us to speak to Him in thanksgiving or petition.

11

THE NEED FOR A GENERAL REVIVAL

If we are to pray correctly in such a time as this, many of our prayers should be for a general revival. If there was ever a need to cry to God in the words of the psalmist, "*Will You not revive us again, that Your people may rejoice in You?*" (Psalm 85:6), it is now. It is surely time for the Lord to work, for men have nullified His law. The voice of the Lord given in the written Word is made void both by the world and the church. This is not a time for discouragement: the man who believes in God and the Bible should never be discouraged. But it is a time for Jehovah Himself to step in and work. The intelligent Christian, the alert watchman on the walls of Zion, may well cry with the psalmist, *"It is time for You to act, O Lord, for they have regarded Your law as void"* (Psalm 119:126). The great need of the day is for a general revival. Let us consider first what a general revival is.

A revival is a time of quickening or impartation of life. As God alone can give life, a revival is a time when God visits His people. By the power of His Spirit, He imparts new life to them. Through them, He gives life to sinners *"dead in trespasses and sins"* (Ephesians 2:1). We have spiritual enthusiasm contrived by the cunning methods and hypnotic influence of the professional evangelist. But these are not revivals and are not needed. They are the Devil's imitations of a revival. New life from God—that is a revival. A general revival is a time when this new life from God is not confined to scattered localities. It is general throughout Christendom and the earth.

The reason why a general revival is needed is that spiritual desolation and death affect everyone. They are not confined to any one country, though they may be more manifest in some countries than in others. They are found in mission fields as well as at home. We have had local revivals. The life-giving Spirit of God has breathed on this minister and that, this church and that, this community and that, but we sorely need a widespread, general revival.

Let us look at the results of a revival. These results are apparent in ministers of the church and in the unsaved.

Revival in Ministers

When ministers experience revival, they have a new love for souls. We ministers, as a rule, have an inadequate love for souls. We fall short of loving people as Jesus does or even Paul did. But when God visits His people, the hearts of ministers are heavily burdened for the unsaved. They go out in great longing for the salvation of their fellowmen. They forget their ambition to preach great sermons and to acquire fame; they simply long to see sinners brought to Christ.

Along with a renewed love for others, ministers receive a new love for and faith in God's Word. They cast away their doubts and criticisms of the Bible and start preaching it. They especially preach Christ crucified. Revivals make ministers who have become lax in their doctrines orthodox. A genuine, widespread revival is needed to set things right.

Revivals bring new liberty and power in preaching to ministers. It is no weeklong grind to prepare a sermon, and no nerve-consuming effort to preach it after it has been prepared. Preaching is a joy and refreshment. There is power in preaching during times of revival.

Revival in Christians

The results of a revival in Christians generally are as noticeable as its results on the ministry. In times of revival, Christians come out from the world and live separated lives. Christians who have been amused with the world and its pleasures give them up. These things are found to be incompatible with increasing life and light.

In times of revival, Christians receive a new spirit of prayer. Prayer meetings are no longer a duty but become the necessity of a hungry, persistent heart. Private prayer is followed with new zest. The voice of earnest prayer to God is heard day and night. People no longer ask, "Does God answer prayer?" They know He does, and they besiege the throne of grace day and night.

In times of revival, Christians go to work to find lost souls. They do not go to meetings simply to enjoy themselves and get blessed. They go to meetings to watch for souls and to bring them to Christ. They talk to people on the street and in their homes. The cross of Christ, heaven, and hell become the subjects of conversation. Politics, the weather, news, and the latest novels are forgotten.

In times of revival, Christians have new joy in Christ. Life is joy, and new life is new joy. Revival days are glad days, days of heaven on earth.

In times of revival, Christians receive a new love for the Word of God. They want to study it day and night. Revivals are bad for bars and theaters, but they are good for bookstores and Bible publishers.

Revival's Influence on the Unsaved

Revivals also have a decided influence on the unsaved world. First of all, they bring deep conviction of sin. Jesus said that when the Spirit comes, He convicts the world of sin (John 16:8). Revival is a coming of the Holy Spirit; therefore, there must be a new conviction of sin, and there always is. If you see something that people call a revival and there is no conviction of sin, you may know immediately that it is not a revival. A lack of Holy Spirit conviction is a sure sign that there is no revival.

Revivals also bring conversion and regeneration. When God refreshes His people, He always converts sinners as well. The first result of Pentecost was new life and power to the one hundred and twenty disciples in the Upper Room. The second result was three thousand conversions in a single day. It is always so. I am constantly reading of revivals where Christians were greatly encouraged but there were no conversions. I have my doubts about that kind of revival. If Christians are truly refreshed, they will influence the unsaved by prayer, testimony, and persuasion. And there will be conversions.

Why General Revival Is Needed

We know what a general revival is and what it does. Let us now face the question of why it is needed at the present time. I think that the mere description of what it is and what it does shows why it is sorely needed. Let us look at some specific conditions that exist today that demonstrate the need for revival. In showing these conditions, one is likely to be called a pessimist. If facing the facts is pessimistic, I am willing to be called a pessimist. If in order to be an optimist one must shut his eyes and call black white, error truth, sin righteousness, and death life, I do not want to be an optimist. But I am an optimist all the same. Pointing out the real conditions will lead to better conditions.

Look again at the ministry. Many of us who profess to be orthodox ministers are practically non-believers. That is plain speech, but it is also indisputable fact. There is no essential difference between the teachings of the liberal Tom Paine and the teachings of some of our theological professors. The latter are not so blunt and honest about it. They phrase their beliefs in more elegant and studied sentences, but they mean the same. Much of the so-called new learning and higher criticism is simply Tom Paine's infidelity sugarcoated. A German professor once read a statement of some positions, then asked if they fairly represented the scholarly criticism of the day. When it was agreed that they did, he startled his audience by saying: "I am reading from Tom Paine's *Age of Reason*."

There is little new in the higher criticism. Some of our future ministers are being educated under immoral professors. Being immature when they enter college or the seminary, they naturally come out non-believers in many cases. Then they go forth to poison the church.

Even when our ministers are orthodox—as, thank God, so very many are—they are not always people of prayer. How many modern ministers know what it is to wrestle in prayer, to spend a good share of a night in prayer? I do not know how many, but I do know that many do not.

Some ministers have no love for souls. How many preach because they must preach? How many preach because they feel that men everywhere are perishing, and by preaching they hope to save some? How many follow up their preaching, as Paul did, by beseeching men everywhere to be reconciled to God?

Perhaps enough has been said about us ministers. But it is evident that a revival is needed for our sakes. If not, some of us will have to stand before God overwhelmed with confusion in an awful day of reckoning that is surely coming.

Look now at the doctrinal state of the church. It is bad enough. Many do not believe in the whole Bible. They think that the book of Genesis is a myth, Jonah is an allegory, and even the miracles of the Son of God are questioned. The doctrine of prayer is old-fashioned, and the work of the Holy Spirit is scorned. Conversion is unnecessary, and hell is no longer believed in. Look at the fads and errors that have sprung up out of this loss of faith. Christian Science, Unitarianism, Spiritualism, Universalism, Metaphysical Healing, etc., a perfect pandemonium of the doctrines of the Devil.

Look at the spiritual state of the church. Worldliness is rampant among church members. Many church members are just as eager as any to become rich. They use the methods of the world in their efforts to accumulate wealth. And they hold on to it just as tightly once they have gotten it.

Prayerlessness abounds among church members on every hand. Someone has said that Christians, on the average, do not spend more than five minutes a day in prayer. Neglect of the Word of God goes hand in hand with neglect of prayer to God. Many Christians spend twice as much time everyday engrossed in the daily papers as they do bathing in the cleansing Word of God. How many Christians average an hour a day in Bible study?

A lack of generosity goes along with neglect of prayer and the Word of God. Churches are rapidly increasing in wealth, but the treasuries of missionary societies are empty. Christians do not average a dollar a year for missions. It is simply appalling.

Then, there is the increasing disregard for the Lord's Day. It is fast becoming a day of worldly pleasures, instead of a day of holy service. The Sunday newspaper with its mundane rambling and scandals has replaced the Bible. Recreational activities have replaced Sunday school and church services. Christians mingle with the world in all forms of questionable amusements. The young man or young woman who does not believe in wearing immodest clothing, participating in wild parties, and attending the theater with its ever increasing appeal to lewdness is considered an old fogy.

How small a proportion of our membership has really entered into fellowship with Jesus Christ in His burden for souls! Enough has been said of the spiritual state of the church. Now look at the state of the world. Note how few conversions there are. Here and there a church has a large number of new members joining by confession of faith, but these churches are rare. Where there are such new members, in very few cases are the conversions deep, thorough, and satisfactory.

There is lack of conviction of sin. Seldom are men overwhelmed with a sense of their awful guilt in dishonoring the Son of God. Sin is regarded as a misfortune, infirmity, or even as good in the making. Seldom is it considered an enormous wrong against a holy God.

Unbelief is rampant. Many regard it as a mark of intellectual superiority to reject the Bible as well as faith in God and immortality. It is often the only mark of intellectual superiority many possess. Perhaps that is the reason they cling to it so dearly.

Hand in hand with this widespread atheism goes gross immorality, as has always been the case. Atheism and immorality are Siamese twins. They always exist and increase together. This prevailing immorality is found everywhere.

Look at the legalized adultery that we call divorce. Men marry one wife after another and are still admitted into good society, and women do likewise. Thousands of supposedly respectable men in America live with other men's wives. And there are thousands of supposedly respectable women living with other women's husbands.

This immorality is found in much modern theater. Many questionable characters of the stage rule the day. And the individuals who degrade themselves by appearing in such off-color plays are defended in the newspapers and welcomed by supposedly respectable people.

Much of our literature is rotten, but decent people will read bad books because they are popular. Art is often a mere covering for shameless indecency. Women are induced to cast modesty to the wind so that the artist may perfect his art and defile his morals.

Greed for money has become an obsession with the rich and poor. The multimillionaire will often sell his soul and trample the rights of his fellowmen in the hope of becoming a billionaire. The working man will often commit murder to increase the power of the union and keep up wages. Wars are waged and men shot down like dogs to improve commerce and to gain political prestige for unprincipled politicians who parade as statesmen.

The licentiousness of the day lifts its serpent head everywhere. You see it in the newspapers, on the billboards, in advertisements for cigars, shoes, bicycles, medicines, and everything else. You see it on the streets at night. You see it just outside the church door. You find it in the awful ghettos set apart for it in great cities. And it is crowding farther and farther up our business streets and into the residential portions of our cities. Alas! Every so often you find it, if you look closely, in supposedly respectable homes. Indeed it will be borne to your ears by the confessions of brokenhearted men and women. The moral condition of the world is disgusting, sickening, and appalling.

Pray for Revival

We need a revival—deep, widespread, and general—in the power of the Holy Spirit. It is either a general revival or the dissolution of the church, of the home, and of the state. A revival, new life from God, is the cure—the only cure. Revival will halt the awful tide of immorality and unbelief. Mere argument will not do it. But a wind from heaven, a new outpouring of the Holy Spirit, a true God-sent revival will. Atheism, higher criticism, Christian Science, Spiritualism, Universalism, all will go down before the outpouring of the Spirit of God. It was not discussion but the breath of God that banished non-believers of old to the limbo of forgetfulness. We need a new breath from God to send the current, radical non-Christians to keep those non-believers of old company. I believe that breath from God is coming.

The great need of today is a general revival. The need is clear. It allows no honest difference of opinion. What then must we do? Pray. Take up the psalmist's prayer, "*Will You not revive us again, that Your people may rejoice in You?"* (Psalm 85:6). Pray Ezekiel's prayer, *"Come from the four winds, O breath* [breath of God], *and breathe on these slain, that they may live"* (Ezekiel 37:9). Hark, I hear a noise! Behold a shaking! I can almost feel the breeze on my cheek. I can almost see the great living army rising to their feet. Will we not pray and pray and pray until the Spirit comes, and God revives His people?

12

PRAYER BEFORE AND DURING REVIVALS

No treatment of the subject "How to Pray" would be at all complete if it did not consider the place of prayer in revivals. The first great revival of Christian history had its origin on the human side in a ten-day prayer meeting. We read of that handful of disciples: "*These all continued with one accord in prayer and supplication*" (Acts 1:14). The result of that prayer meeting is in the second chapter of the Acts of the Apostles: "*They were all filled with the Holy Spirit and began to speak with other tongues, as the Spirit gave them utterance*" (verse 4). Further in the chapter, we read that on "*that day about three thousand souls were added to them*" (verse 41).

This revival proved genuine and permanent. The converts *"continued steadfastly in the apostles' doctrine and fellowship, in the breaking of bread, and in prayers"* (Acts 1:42). *"And the Lord added to the church daily those who were being saved"* (verse 47).

Testimonies of Answered Prayer

Every true revival from that day to this has had its earthly origin in prayer. The great revival under Jonathan Edwards in the eighteenth century began with his famous call to prayer. The marvelous work of grace among the Indians under Brainerd began in the days and nights that he spent before God in prayer for an anointing of *"power from on high"* (Luke 24:49) for this work.

A most remarkable and widespread display of God's reviving power was the revival in Rochester, New York, in 1830, under the labors of Charles G. Finney. It spread not only throughout the state, but ultimately to Great Britain as well. Mr. Finney himself attributed the power of this work to the spirit of prayer that prevailed. He described it in his autobiography in the following words:

> When I was on my way to Rochester, as we passed through a village, some thirty miles east of Rochester, a brother minister whom I knew, seeing me on the canal-boat, jumped aboard to have a little conversation with me, intending to ride but a little way and return. He, however, became interested in conversation, and upon finding where I was going, he made up his mind to keep on and go with me to Rochester. We had been there but a few days when this minister became so convicted that he could not help weeping aloud at one time as we passed along the street. The Lord gave him a powerful spirit of prayer, and his heart was broken. As he and I prayed together, I was struck with his faith in regard to what the Lord was going to do there. I recollect he would say, "Lord, I do not know how it is; but I seem to know that Thou art going to do a great work in this city." The spirit of prayer was poured out powerfully,

so much so that some people stayed away from the public services to pray, being unable to restrain their feelings under preaching.

And here I must introduce the name of a man, whom I shall have occasion to mention frequently, Mr. Abel Clary. He was the son of a very excellent man, and an elder of the church where I was converted. He was converted in the same revival in which I was. He had been licensed to preach; but his spirit of prayer was such, he was so burdened with the souls of men, that he was not able to preach much, his whole time and strength being given to prayer. The burden of his soul would frequently be so great that he was unable to stand, and he would writhe and groan in agony. I was well acquainted with him, and knew something of the wonderful spirit of prayer that was upon him. He was a very silent man, as almost all are who have that powerful spirit of prayer.

The first I knew of his being in Rochester, a gentleman who lived about a mile west of the city called on me one day and asked me if I knew a Mr. Abel Clary, a minister. I told him that I knew him well.

"Well," he said, "he is at my house, and has been there for some time. I don't know what to think of him."

I said, "I have not seen him at any of our meetings."

"No," he replied, "he cannot go to meetings, he says. He prays nearly all the time, day and night, and in such agony of mind that I do not know what to make of it. Sometimes he cannot even stand on his knees, but will lie prostrate on the floor, and groan and pray in a manner that quite astonishes me."

I said to the brother, "I understand it: please keep still. It will come out right; he will surely prevail."

I knew at the time a considerable number of men who were exercised in the same way....This Mr. Clary and many others among the men, and a large number of women, partook of the same spirit, and spent a great part of their time in prayer. Father Nash, as we called him who in several of my fields of labor came to me and aided me, was another of those men that had such a powerful spirit of prevailing prayer. This Mr. Clary continued in Rochester as long as I did, and did not leave it until after I had left. He never, that I could learn, appeared in public, but gave himself wholly to prayer.

I think it was the second Sabbath that I was at Auburn at this time, I observed in the congregation the solemn face of Mr. Clary. He looked as if he was borne down with an agony of prayer. Being well acquainted with him, and knowing the great gift of God that was upon him, the spirit of prayer, I was very glad to see him there. He sat in the pew with his brother, a doctor, who was also a professor of religion, but who had nothing by experience, I should think, of his brother Abel's great power with God.

At intermission, as soon as I came down from the pulpit, Mr. Clary and his brother met me at the pulpit stairs and invited me to go home with them and spend the intermission and get some refreshments. I did so.

After arriving at his house we were soon summoned to the dinner table. We gathered about the table, and Dr. Clary turned to his brother and said, "Brother Abel, will you ask the blessing?" Brother Abel bowed his head and began, audibly, to ask a blessing. He had uttered but a sentence or two when he broke instantly down, moved suddenly back from the table, and fled to his chamber. The doctor supposed he had been taken suddenly ill, and rose up and followed him. In a few moments he came down and said, "Mr. Finney, Brother Abel wants to see you."

Said I, "What ails him?"

Said he, "I do not know but he says you know. He appears in great distress, but I think it is the state of his mind."

I understood it in a moment, and went to his room. He lay groaning upon the bed, the Spirit making intercession for him, and in him, with groanings that could not be uttered. I had barely entered the room, when he made out to say, "Pray, Brother Finney." I knelt down and helped him in prayer, by leading his soul out for the conversion of sinners. I continued to pray until his distress passed away, and then I returned to the dinner table.

I understood that this was the voice of God. I saw the Spirit of prayer was upon him, and I felt His influence upon myself, and took it for granted that the work would move on powerfully. It did so. The pastor told me afterward that he found that in the six weeks that I was there, five hundred souls had been converted.

Persistent Prayer Results

Mr. Finney in his lectures on revivals told of other remarkable awakenings in answer to the prayers of God's people. He said:

> A clergyman...told me of a revival among his people, which commenced with a zealous and devoted woman in the church. She became anxious about sinners, and went to praying for them; she prayed, and her distress increased; and she finally came to her minister, and talked with him, and asked him to appoint an anxious meeting, for she felt that one was needed. The minister put her off, for he felt nothing of it. The next week she came again, and besought him to appoint an anxious meeting; she knew there would be somebody to come, for she felt as if God was going to pour out His Spirit. He put her off again. And finally she said to him, "If you do not appoint an anxious meeting I shall die, for there is certainly going to be a revival." The next Sabbath he appointed a meeting, and said that if there were any who wished to converse with him about the salvation of their souls, he would meet them on such an evening. He did not know of one, but when he went to the place, to his astonishment he found a large number of anxious inquirers.

In still another place, Finney said:

> The first ray of light that broke in upon the midnight which rested on the churches in Oneida county, in the fall of 1825, was from a woman in feeble health, who I believe had never been in a powerful revival. Her soul was exercised about sinners. She was in agony for the land. She did not know what ailed her, but she kept praying more and more, till it seemed as if her agony would destroy her body. At length she became full of joy and exclaimed, "God has come! God has come! There is no mistake about it, the work is begun, and is going over all the region!" And sure enough, the work began, and her family was almost all converted, and the work spread all over that part of the country.

The great revival of 1857 in the United States began in prayer and was carried on by prayer more than by anything else. Dr. Cuyler in an article in a religious newspaper some years ago said:

> Most revivals have humble beginnings, and the fire starts in a few warm hearts. Never despise the day of small things. During all my own long ministry, nearly every work of grace has had a similar beginning. One commenced in a meeting gathered at a few hours' notice in a private house. Another commenced in a group gathered for Bible study by Mr. Moody in our mission chapel. Still another—the most powerful of all—was kindled on a bitter January evening at a meeting of young Christians under my roof. That profound Christian, Dr. Thomas H. Skinner of the Union Theological Seminary, once gave me an account of a remarkable coming together of three earnest men in his study when he was the pastor of the Arch Street church in Philadelphia. They wrestled in prayer. They made a clean breast in confession of sin, and humbled themselves before God. One and another church officer came in and joined them. The heaven-kindled flame soon spread through the whole congregation in one of the most powerful revivals ever known in that city.

Prayer Knows No Boundaries

In the early part of the sixteenth century, there was a great religious awakening in Ulster, Ireland. The lands of the rebel chiefs, which had been forfeited to the British crown, were settled by a class of colonists who were governed by a spirit of wild adventure. Authentic righteousness was rare. Seven ministers, five from Scotland and two from England, settled in that country, the earliest arrivals being in 1613. A contemporary of one of these ministers named Blair recorded: "He spent many days and nights in prayer, alone and with others, and was vouchsafed great intimacy with God." Mr. James Glendenning, a man of very meager natural gifts, was a man similarly minded in regard to prayer. The work began under this man Glendenning. The historian of the time said:

> He was a man who never would have been chosen by a wise assembly of ministers, nor sent to begin a reformation in this land. Yet this was the Lord's choice to begin with him the admirable work of God which I mention on purpose that all may see how the glory is only the Lord's in making a holy nation in this profane land, and that it was "*not by might, nor by power, but by my spirit, saith the* Lord *of hosts*" (Zechariah 4:6).

In his preaching at Oldstone, multitudes of hearers felt great anxiety and terror of conscience. They looked on themselves as altogether lost and damned and cried out, "Men and women, what will we do to be saved?" They were stricken and became faint by the power of His Word. In one day, a dozen were carried out of doors as dead. These were not cowards, but some of the boldest spirits of the neighborhood, "some who had formerly feared not with their swords to put a whole market town into a fray." Concerning one of them, the historian wrote, "I have heard one of them, then a mighty strong man, now a mighty Christian, say that his end in coming into church was to consult with his companions how to work some mischief."

This work spread throughout the whole country of Ireland. By the year 1626, a monthly concert of prayer was held in Antrim. The work spread beyond the bounds of Down and Antrim to the churches of the neighboring counties. The spiritual interest became so great that Christians would come thirty or forty miles to the communions. They would continue from the time they came until they returned without wearying or making use of sleep. Many of them neither ate not drank, and yet some of them professed that they "went away most fresh and vigorous, their souls so filled with the sense of God." This revival changed the whole character of northern Ireland.

Another great awakening in Ireland in 1859 had a somewhat similar origin. By many who were unaware, it was thought that this marvelous work came without warning and preparation. But Rev. William Gibson, moderator of the General Assembly of the Presbyterian church in Ireland in 1860, in his history of the awakening, told how there had been two years of preparation. There had been constant discussion in the General Assembly of the low state of spiritual fervor and the need of a revival. There had been special sessions for prayer. Finally, four young men, who became leaders in the origin of the great work, began to meet together in an old schoolhouse. Around the spring of 1858, a work of power began to manifest itself. It spread from town to town, from county to county. The congregations became too large for the buildings, and the meetings were held outside. They were often attended by many thousands of people. Many hundreds of people were frequently convicted of sin in a single meeting. In some places, the criminal courts and jails were closed for lack of occupation. There were manifestations of the Holy Spirit's power of a most remarkable character. This clearly proves that the Holy Spirit is as ready to work today as in apostolic days. He will do so when ministers and Christians really believe in Him and begin to prepare the way by prayer.

Mr. Moody's wonderful work in England, Scotland, and Ireland, then afterwards in America, originated in prayer. Moody made little impression until men and women began to cry to God. Indeed, his going to England at all was in answer to the persistent cries to God by a bedridden saint. While the spirit of prayer continued, the revival grew in strength. But in the course of time, less and less was made of prayer, and the work fell off in power. One of the great secrets of the superficiality and unreality of many of our modern, so-called revivals is that more dependence is put on man's machinery than on God's power. His power must be sought and obtained by earnest, persistent, believing prayer. We live in a day characterized by the multiplication of man's machinery and the decrease of God's power. The great cry of our day is work, new organizations, new methods, and new machinery. The great need of our day is prayer.

Church—Wake Up!

It was a masterstroke of Satan when he got the church to so generally lay aside this mighty weapon of prayer. Satan is perfectly willing that the church multiply its organizations and contrive machinery for the conquest of the world for Christ if it will only give up praying. He laughs as he looks at the church today and says to himself, "You can have your Sunday schools and your Young People's Societies. Enjoy your Young Men's and Women's Christian Associations. Continue your institutional churches, your industrial schools, and your Boys' Brigades. Worship with your grand choirs, your fine organs, your brilliant preachers, and your revival efforts, too. But don't bring the power of almighty God into them by earnest, persistent, believing, mighty prayer." Prayer could work as marvelously today as it ever could, if the church would only take up the call.

There seem to be increasing signs that the church is awaking to this fact. God is laying a burden of prayer on individual ministers and churches like they have never known before. Less dependence is being placed on human instrumentality and more on God. Ministers are crying to God day and night for power. Churches and groups are meeting together in the early morning and the late night hours crying to God for the "*latter rain*" (Deut. 11:14). There is every indication of the coming of a mighty, widespread revival. There is every reason why, if a revival should come in any country at this time, it should be more widespread in its extent than any revival of history. There is the closest and swiftest communication among all parts of the world. A true fire of God kindled in America would soon spread to the uttermost parts of the earth. The only thing needed to bring this fire is prayer.

It is not necessary that the whole church begins praying at first. Great revivals always begin in the hearts of a few men and women whom God arouses by His Spirit to believe in Him as a living God. They believe He is a God who answers prayer. He lays a burden on their hearts from which no rest can be found except in persistent crying to God.

May God use this book to arouse many others to pray so that the greatly needed revival will come, and come quickly. Let us pray!

HOW TO STUDY THE BIBLE

CONTENTS

INTRODUCTION

The Bible contains golden nuggets of truth, and anyone willing to dig for biblical truth is certain to find it.

Those reading this book for the first time must not become frightened at the elaborate methods I will suggest. They are not difficult. Their fruitfulness has been tested with those who have varying degrees of education, and the results have been found to be practical. As you use the methods I will recommend, you will soon find your ability to study the Bible rapidly increasing, until you will accomplish more in fifteen minutes than you once could in an hour.

Although the Bible is read much, comparatively, it is studied little. The methods you will learn are the same methods being used in highly technical fields, such as science and medicine. First, you will make a careful analysis of the facts. Then, you will learn how to classify those facts. While we cannot all be students of technology, we can all be profound students of Scripture. No other book than the Bible offers the opportunity for intellectual development by its study. People who have studied few books besides the Scriptures have astonished and amazed scholars and theologians.

The truths you will find as you study Scripture will far transcend any other study in inspiration, helpfulness, and practical value. They will, in fact, become life-changing.

1

CONDITIONS FOR PROFITABLE BIBLE STUDY

While you will be learning profitable methods for Bible study, there is something more important than the best procedures. The secret lies in meeting certain fundamental conditions before you begin to study God's Word. If you meet these conditions, you will get more out of the Bible, even while pursuing the poorest methods, than the one who does not meet them while he pursues the best methods. What you will need is far deeper than a new and better technique.

Obtaining Spiritual Understanding

The most essential of these conditions is that *"you must be born again"* (John 3:7). The Bible is a spiritual book. It combines spiritual concepts with spiritual words. Only a spiritual man can understand its deepest and most precious teachings. *"The natural man does not receive the things of the Spirit of God, for they are foolishness to him; nor can he know them, because they are spiritually discerned"* (1 Corinthians 2:14).

Spiritual discernment can be obtained in only one way: by being born again—*"Unless one is born again, he cannot see the kingdom of God"* (John 3:3). No mere knowledge of the human languages in which the Bible was written, however extensive and accurate it may be, will qualify one to understand and appreciate the Bible. One must comprehend the divine language in which it was written as well as the language of the Holy Spirit.

A person who understands the language of the Holy Spirit but who does not understand a word of Greek, Hebrew, or Aramaic will get more out of the Bible than one who knows all about ancient languages but is not born again. Many ordinary men and women who possess no knowledge of the original languages in which the Bible was written have a knowledge of the real contents of the Bible. Their understanding of its actual teaching and its depth, fullness, and beauty far surpasses that of many learned professors in theological seminaries.

One of the greatest follies today is to allow an unregenerate person to teach the Bible. It would be just as unreasonable to allow someone to teach art because he had an accurate, technical knowledge of paints. An aesthetic sense is required to make a person a competent art teacher. Likewise, it requires spiritual sense to make a person a competent Bible teacher.

One who has aesthetic discernment but little or no technical knowledge of paint would be a far more competent critic of works of art than one who has extensive technical knowledge of paint but no aesthetic discernment. Similarly, the person who has no technical knowledge of biblical languages but who has spiritual discernment is a far more competent critic of the Bible than the one who has a rare knowledge of Greek and Hebrew but no spiritual discernment.

It is unfortunate that more emphasis is often placed on a knowledge of Greek and Hebrew in training for the ministry than is placed on the spiritual life and its consequent spiritual discernment. Unregenerate people should not be forbidden to study the Bible because the Word of God is the instrument the Holy Spirit uses in the new birth. (See 1 Peter 1:23; James 1:18.) But it should be distinctly understood that while there are teachings in the Bible that the natural man can understand, its most distinctive, characteristic teachings are beyond his grasp. Its highest beauties belong to a world in which he has no vision.

The first fundamental condition for profitable Bible study, then, is *"You must be born again"* (John 3:7). You cannot study the Bible to the greatest profit if you have not been born again. Its best treasures are sealed to you.

Gaining a Spiritual Appetite

The second condition for profitable study is to have a love for the Bible. A person who eats with an appetite will get far more good out of his meal than one who eats from a sense of duty. A student of the Bible should be able to say with Job, *"I have treasured the words of His mouth more than my necessary food"* (Job 23:12), or with Jeremiah, *"Your words were found, and I ate them, and Your word was to me the joy and rejoicing of my heart; for I am called by Your name, O Lord God of hosts"* (Jeremiah 15:16).

Many come to the table God has spread in His Word with no appetite for spiritual food. Instead of getting their fill of the feast God has prepared, they grumble about everything. Spiritual indigestion results from much of the modern criticism of the Bible.

But how can one acquire a love for the Bible? First of all, by being born again. Where there is life, there is likely to be appetite. A dead man never hungers. But going beyond this, the more there is of vitality, the more there is of hunger. Abounding life means abounding hunger for the Word.

Study of the Word stimulates love for the Word. I remember when I had more appetite for books about the Bible than I had for the Bible itself; but with increasing study, there has come increasing love for the Book. Bearing in mind who the Author of the Book is, what its purpose is, what its power is, and what the riches of its contents are will go far toward stimulating a love and appetite for the Book.

Digging for Treasures

The third condition is a willingness to work hard. Solomon gave a graphic picture of the Bible student who receives the most profit from his study:

> *My son, if you receive my words, and treasure my commands within you, so that you incline your ear to wisdom, and apply your heart to understanding; yes, if you cry out for discernment, and lift up your voice for understanding, if you seek her as silver and search for her as for hidden treasures; then you will understand the fear of the* Lord, *and find the knowledge of God.* (Proverbs 2:1–5)

Seeking for silver and searching for hidden treasure mean hard work, and the one who wishes to get not only the silver but also the gold out of the Bible must make up his mind to dig. It is not glancing at the Word but studying the Word, meditating on the Word, and pondering the Word that will bring the richest yield.

The reason many people get so little out of their Bible reading is simply that they are not willing to think. Intellectual laziness lies at the heart of a large percent of fruitless Bible reading. People are constantly crying for new methods of Bible study, but what many of them want is simply some method of Bible study where they can get the most without much work.

If someone could tell lazy Christians some method of Bible study whereby they could use the sleepiest ten minutes of the day, just before they go to bed, for Bible study and get the most profit that God intends, that would be what they desire. But it can't be done. We must be willing to work and work hard if we wish to dig out the treasures of infinite wisdom, knowledge, and blessing that He has stored up in His Word.

A business friend once asked me in a hurried call to tell him "in a word" how to study his Bible. I replied, "Think." The psalmist pronounced that the man who *"meditates day and night"* *"in the law of the LORD"* is *"blessed."* (See Psalm 1:1–2.) The Lord commanded Joshua to *"meditate in it day and night"* and assured him that as a result of this meditation, *"you will make your way prosperous, and then you will have good success"* (Josh. 1:8). In this way alone can one study the Bible to the greatest profit.

One pound of beef well-chewed, digested, and assimilated will give more strength than tons of beef merely glanced at; and one verse of Scripture chewed, digested, and assimilated will give more strength than whole chapters simply skimmed. Weigh every word you read in the Bible. Look at it. Turn it over and over. The most familiar passages take on new meaning in this way. Spend fifteen minutes on each word in Psalm 23:1 or Philippians 4:19, and see if it is not so.

Finding the Treasure's Keys

The fourth condition is a will wholly surrendered to God: *"If anyone wants to do His will, he shall know concerning the doctrine"* (John 7:17). A surrendered will gives that clearness of spiritual vision necessary to understand God's Book. Many of the difficulties and obscurities of the Bible arise simply because the will of the student is not surrendered to the will of the Author of the Book.

It is remarkable how clear, simple, and beautiful passages that once puzzled us become when we are brought to that place where we say to God, "I surrender my will unconditionally to Yours. I have no will but Yours. Teach me Your will." A surrendered will does more than a university education to make the Bible an open book. It is simply impossible to get the most profit out of your Bible study until you surrender your will to God. You must be very definite about this.

Many will say, "Oh, yes, my will is surrendered to God," but it is not. They have never gone alone with God and said intelligently and definitely to Him, "O God, I here and now give myself to You, for You to command me, lead me, shape me, send me, and do with me absolutely as You will." Such an act is a wonderful key to unlock the treasure-house of God's Word. The Bible becomes a new Book when a person surrenders to God. Doing this brought a complete transformation in my own theology, life, and ministry.

Use It or Lose It

The fifth condition is very closely related to the fourth. The student of the Bible who desires to receive the greatest profit out of his studies must be obedient to its teachings as soon as he sees them. It was good advice James gave to early Christians and to us: *"Be doers of the word, and not hearers only, deceiving yourselves"* (James 1:22).

Many who consider themselves Bible students are deceiving themselves in this way today. They see what the Bible teaches, but they do not do it; soon, they lose their power to see it. Truth obeyed leads to more truth. Truth disobeyed destroys the capacity for discovering truth.

There must be not only a general surrender of the will but also a specific, practical obedience to each new word of God discovered. In no place is the law more joyously certain on the one hand and more sternly inexorable on the other than in the matter of using or refusing the truth revealed in the Bible: *"To everyone who has, more will be given, and he will have abundance; but from him who does not have, even what he has will be taken away"* (Matthew 25:29). Use and you get more; refuse and you lose all.

Do not study the Bible for the mere gratification of intellectual curiosity but to find out how to live and how to please God. Whatever duty you find commanded in the Bible, do it at once. Whatever good you see in any Bible character, imitate it immediately. Whatever mistake you note in the actions of Bible men and women, scrutinize your own life to see if you are making the same mistake; if you find you are, correct it immediately.

James compared the Bible to a mirror. (See James 1:23–24.) The chief purpose of a mirror is to show you if anything is out of place about you. If you find there is, you can set it right. Use the Bible in that way.

You already see that obeying the truth will solve the enigmas in the verses you do not yet understand. Disobeying the truth darkens the whole world of truth. This is the secret of much of the skepticism and error of the day. People saw the truth but did not do it, and now it is gone.

I once knew a bright and promising young minister who made rapid advancement in the truth. One day, however, he said to his wife, "It's nice to believe this truth, but we do not need to speak so much about it." He began to hide his testimony. Not long after this, his wife died, and he began to drift. The Bible became a sealed book to him. His faith reeled, and he publicly renounced his belief in the fundamental truths of the Bible. He seemed to lose his grip even on the doctrine of immortality. What was the cause of it all? Truth flees when it is not lived and stood for. That man was admired by many and applauded by some, but light gave place to darkness in his soul.

Come as a Child

The sixth condition is a childlike mind. God reveals His deepest truths to babes. No time more than our own needs to take to heart the words of Jesus: *"I thank You, Father, Lord of heaven and earth, that You have hidden these things from the wise and prudent and have revealed them to babes"* (Matthew 11:25).

How can we be babes if God is to reveal His truth to us, and we are to understand His Word? By having a childlike spirit. A child is not full of his own wisdom. He recognizes his ignorance and is ready to be taught. He does not oppose his own notions and ideas to those of his teachers.

It is in this spirit that we should come to the Bible if we are to get the most profit out of our study. Do not come to the Bible seeking confirmation for your own ideas. Come rather to find out what God's ideas are as

He has revealed them. Do not come to find confirmation for your own opinions but to be taught what God may be pleased to teach. If a person comes to the Bible just to find his own ideas taught there, he will find them. But if he comes, recognizing his own ignorance just as a little child seeks to be taught, he will find something infinitely better than his own ideas; he will find the mind of God.

Thus, we see why many people cannot see things that are plainly taught in the Bible. They are so full of their own ideas that there is no room left for what the Bible actually teaches.

An illustration of this is given in the lives of the apostles at one stage in their training. In Mark 9:31, we read: *"For He taught His disciples and said to them, 'The Son of Man is being betrayed into the hands of men, and they will kill Him. And after He is killed, He will rise the third day.'"* Now this is as plain and definite as language can make it, but it was utterly contrary to the apostles' ideas of what would happen to Christ.

We read in the next verse: *"They did not understand this saying"* (verse 32). Is this any different than our own inability to comprehend plain statements in the Bible when they run counter to our preconceived notions?

You must come to Christ like a child to be taught what to believe and do, rather than coming as a full-grown person who already knows it all and must find some interpretations of Christ's words that will fit into his mature and infallible philosophy. Many people are so full of unbiblical theology that it takes a lifetime to get rid of it and understand the clear teaching of the Bible. "Oh, what can this verse mean?" many bewildered individuals cry. It means what it clearly says. But these people are not after the meaning God has clearly put into it, but the meaning they can, by some ingenious tricks of explanation, twist to make fit into their own interpretations.

Don't come to the Bible to find out what you can make it mean but to find out what God intended it to mean. People often miss the real truth of a verse by saying, "But that can be interpreted this way." Oh, yes, so it can, but is that the way God intended it to be interpreted?

We all need to pray, "O, God, make me like a little child. Empty me of my own notions. Teach me Your own mind. Make me ready to receive all that You have to say, no matter how contrary it is to what I have thought before." How the Bible opens up to one who approaches it in this way! How it closes to the fool who thinks he knows everything and imagines he can give points to Peter, Paul, and even to God Himself!

I was once talking with a ministerial friend about what seemed to be the clear teaching of a certain passage. "Yes," he replied, "but that doesn't agree with my philosophy." This man was sincere, yet he did not have the childlike spirit essential for productive Bible study. We have reached an important point in Bible study when we realize that an infinite God knows more than we, that our highest wisdom is less than the knowledge of the most ignorant babe compared with His, and that we must come to Him to be taught as children.

We are not to argue with Him. But we so easily and so constantly forget this point that every time we open our Bibles, we should bow humbly before God and say, "Father, I am but a child; please teach me."

Believing God's Word

The seventh condition of studying the Bible for the greatest profit is that we study it as the Word of God. The apostle Paul, in writing to the Thessalonians, thanked God "*without ceasing*" (1 Thessalonians 2:13) that when they received the Word of God, they "*welcomed it not as the word of men, but as it is in truth, the word of God*" (verse 13). Paul thanked God for that, and so may we thank God when we get to the place where we receive the Word of God as *the* Word of God.

He who does not believe the Bible is the Word of God should be encouraged to study it. Once I doubted that the Bible was the Word of God, but the firm confidence that I have today that the Bible is the Word of God has come more from the study of the Book itself than from anything else. Those who doubt it are more usually those who study about the Book rather than those who dig into the actual teachings of the Book.

Studying the Bible as the Word of God involves four things. First, it involves the unquestioning acceptance of its teachings when they are definitely understood, even when they may appear unreasonable or impossible. Reason demands that we submit our judgment to the statements of infinite wisdom. Nothing is more irrational than rationalism. It makes finite wisdom the test of infinite wisdom and submits the teachings of God's omniscience to the approval of man's judgment. Conceit says, "This cannot be true, even though God says it, for it does not approve itself to my reason." *"O man, who are you to reply against God?"* (Romans 9:20).

Real human wisdom, when it finds infinite wisdom, bows before it and says, "Speak what You will and I will believe." When we have once become convinced that the Bible is God's Word, its teachings must be the end of all controversy and discussion. A "Thus says the Lord" will settle every question. Yet many who profess to believe that the Bible is the Word of God will shake their heads and say, "Yes, but I think so and so," or "Doctor ——— or Professor ——— or our church doesn't teach it that way." There is little advantage to that sort of study.

Second, studying the Bible as the Word of God involves absolute reliance on all its promises in all their length and breadth. The person who studies the Bible as the Word of God will not discount any one of its promises one iota. A student who studies the Bible as the Word of God will say, "God who cannot lie has promised," and he will not try to make God a liar by trying to make one of His promises mean less than it says. (See 1 John 5:10.) The one who studies the Bible as the Word of God will be on the lookout for promises. As soon as he finds one, he should seek to discover what it means and then place his entire trust on its full meaning.

This is one of the secrets of profitable Bible study. Hunt for promises and appropriate them as fast as you find them by meeting the conditions and risking all upon them. This is the way to make all the fullness of God's blessing your own. This is the key to all the treasures of God's grace. Happy is the one who has learned to study the Bible as God's Word and is ready to claim for himself every new promise as it appears and to risk everything on it.

Next, studying the Bible as the Word of God involves prompt obedience to its every precept. Obedience may seem hard and impossible; but God has commanded it, and you have nothing to do but to obey and leave the results with God. To get results from your Bible study, resolve that from this time on, you will claim every clear promise and obey every plain command. When the meaning of promises and commands is not yet clear, try to discern their meaning immediately.

Finally, studying the Bible as the Word of God involves studying it in God's presence. When you read a verse of Scripture, hear the voice of the living God speaking directly to you in these written words. There is new power and attractiveness in the Bible when you have learned to hear a living, present Person—God our Father—talking directly to you in these words.

One of the most fascinating and inspiring statements in the Bible is *"Enoch walked with God"* (Genesis 5:24). We can have God's glorious companionship any moment we please by simply opening His Word and letting the living, ever present God speak to us through it. With what holy awe and strange and unutterable joy one studies the Bible if he studies it in this way! It is heaven come down to earth.

The Key to Understanding

The last condition for profitable Bible study is prayerfulness. The psalmist prayed, *"Open my eyes, that I may see wondrous things from Your law"* (Psalm 119:18). Everyone who desires productive study needs to offer a similar prayer each time he undertakes to study the Word. A few keys open many treasure chests of prayer. A few clues unravel many difficulties. A few microscopes disclose many beauties hidden from the eye of the ordinary observer. What new light often shines from familiar texts as you bend over them in prayer!

I believe in studying the Bible many times on your knees. When you read an entire book through on your knees—and this is easily done—that book takes on a new meaning and becomes a new book. You should never open the Bible without at least lifting your heart to God in silent prayer that He will interpret it and illumine its pages by the light of His Spirit. It is a rare privilege to study any book under the immediate guidance and instruction of the author, and this is the privilege of us all in studying the Bible.

When you come to a passage that is difficult to understand or interpret, instead of giving up or rushing to some learned friend or some commentary, lay that passage before God and ask Him to explain it. Plead God's promise, *"If any of you lacks wisdom, let him ask of God, who gives to all liberally and without reproach, and it will be given to him. But let him ask in faith, with no doubting"* (James 1:5–6).

Harry Morehouse, one of the most remarkable Bible scholars among unlearned men, used to say that whenever he came to a passage in the Bible that he could not understand, he would search through the Bible for another passage that threw light on it and place it before God in prayer. He said he had never found a passage that did not yield to this treatment.

Some years ago, I took a tour of Switzerland with a friend, visiting some of the more famous caves. One day, the country letter carrier stopped us and asked if we would like to see a cave of rare beauty and interest away from the beaten tracks of travel. Of course, we said yes. He led us through the woods and underbrush to the mouth of the cave. As we entered, all was dark and eerie. He expounded greatly on the beauty of the cave, telling us of altars and fantastic formations, but we could see absolutely nothing. Now and then he uttered a note to warn us to be careful since near our feet lay a gulf whose bottom had never been discovered. We began to fear that we might be the first discoverers of its depth.

There was nothing pleasant about the whole affair. But as soon as a magnesium taper was lit, all became different. Stalagmites rose from the floor to meet the stalactites descending from the ceiling. The great altar of nature that has been ascribed to the skill of ancient worshippers and the beautiful and fantastic formations on every hand all glistened in fairylike beauty in the brilliant light.

I have often thought it was like a passage of Scripture. Others tell you of its beauty, but you cannot see it. It looks dark, intricate, forbidding, and dangerous; but when God's own light is kindled there by prayer, how different it all becomes in an instant! You see a beauty that language cannot express. Only those who have stood there in the same light can appreciate it. He who desires to understand and love the Bible must pray much. Prayer will do more than a college education to make the Bible an open and glorious book.

2

INDIVIDUAL BOOK STUDY

The first method of Bible study that we will consider is the study of individual books. This method of study is the most thorough and the most difficult, but the one that yields the most permanent results. We examine it first because, in my opinion, it should occupy the greater portion of our time.

How to Begin

The first step is selecting the correct book of the Bible to study. If you make an unfortunate selection, you may become discouraged and give up a method of study that might have been most fruitful.

For your first book study, choose a short book. Choosing a long book to begin with leads to discouragement. The average student will give up before the final results are reached.

Choose a comparatively easy book. Some books of the Bible are harder to understand than others. You may want to meet and overcome these later, but they are not recommended work for a beginner. When you are more familiar with Scripture as a whole, then you can tackle these books successfully and satisfactorily. You will find yourself floundering if you begin the more difficult books too soon.

The first epistle of Peter is an exceedingly precious book, but a few of the most difficult passages in the Bible are in it. If it were not for these hard passages, it would be a good book to recommend to the beginner. In view of these difficulties, it is not wise to undertake it until later.

Choose a book that is rich enough in its teaching to illustrate the advantage of this method of study and thus give a keen appetite for further studies of the same kind. Once you have gone through one reasonably large book by the method of study about to be described, you will have an eagerness that will encourage you to find time for further studies.

A book that meets all the conditions stated is the first epistle of Paul to the Thessalonians. It is quite short, has no great difficulties in interpretation, and is exceedingly rich in its teaching. It has the further advantage of being the first of the Pauline Epistles. The first epistle of John is also a good book to begin with and is not difficult.

Possessing the Truths

The second step is to master the general contents of the book. The method is very simple. It consists in merely reading the book through without stopping, then reading it through again and again, say a dozen times in all, at a single sitting. To one who has never tried this, it does not seem as if that would amount to much. But any thoughtful man who has ever tried it will tell you quite differently.

It is simply wonderful how a book takes on new meaning and beauty. It begins to open up. New relationships between different parts of the book begin to disclose themselves. Fascinating lines of thought running through the book appear. The book is grasped as a whole, and a foundation is laid for an intelligent study of those parts in detail.

Rev. James M. Gray of Boston, a prominent teacher and a great lover of the Bible, said that for many years of his ministry he had "an inadequate and unsatisfactory knowledge of the Bible." The first practical idea he received in the study of the Bible was from a layman. The brother possessed an unusual serenity and joy in his Christian experience, which he attributed to his reading of the letter to the Ephesians.

Gray asked him how he read it. The man said that he had taken a pocket copy of the Scriptures into the woods one Sunday afternoon and read Ephesians through at a single sitting, repeating the process a dozen times before stopping. When he arose, he had gained possession of the epistle or, rather, its wondrous truths had gained possession of him. This was the secret, simple as it was, that Gray had been waiting and praying for. From that time on, he studied his Bible in this way, and it became a new Book to him.

Practical Principles for Study

The third step is to prepare an introduction to the book. Write down at the top of separate sheets of paper or cards the following questions:

- Who wrote this book?
- To whom was it written?
- Where did the author write it?
- When did he write it?
- What was the occasion of his writing?
- What was the purpose for which he wrote?
- What were the circumstances of the author when he wrote?

- What were the circumstances of those to whom he wrote?
- What glimpses does the book give into the life and character of the author?
- What are the leading ideas of the book?
- What is the central truth of the book?
- What are the characteristics of the book?

Having prepared your sheets of paper with these headings, lay them side by side on your study table. Go through the book slowly, and as you come to an answer to any one of these questions, write it down on the appropriate sheet of paper. It may be necessary to go through the book several times to do the work thoroughly and satisfactorily, but you will be amply rewarded. After you have completed this process, and not until then, it would be good to refer to commentaries to compare your results with those reached by others.

The introduction you prepare for yourself will be worth many times more to you than anything you can gain from the research of others. Your study will be a rare education of the facilities of perception, comparison, and reasoning.

Seeing the Big Picture

Sometimes the answers to our questions will be found in a related book. For example, if you are studying one of the Pauline Epistles, the answers to your questions may be found in the Acts of the Apostles or in another letter. Of course, all the questions given will not apply to every book in the Bible.

If you are not willing to give the time and effort necessary, this introductory work can be omitted but only at a great sacrifice. Single passages in an epistle can never be correctly understood unless we know to whom they were written. Much false interpretation of the Bible arises from taking a local application and applying it as universal authority. Also, false interpretations often arise from applying to the unbeliever what was intended for the believer.

Note the occasion of the writing. It will clear up the meaning of a passage that would otherwise be obscure. Bearing in mind the circumstances of the author as he wrote will frequently give new force to his words. The jubilant epistle to the Philippians contains repeated phrases, such as *"rejoice in the Lord"* (Philippians 3:1; 4:4), *"trust in the Lord"* (Philippians 2:19, 24), and *"be anxious for nothing"* (Philippians 4:6). Remember that these words were written by a prisoner awaiting a possible sentence of death, and then they will become more meaningful to you.

If you will remember the main purpose for which a book was written, it will help you to interpret its incidental exhortations in their proper relationship. In fact, the answers to all the questions will be valuable in all the work that follows, as well as valuable in themselves.

Divide and Conquer

The fourth step is to divide the book into its proper sections. This procedure is not indispensable, but still it is valuable. Go through the book, and notice the principal divisions among the thoughts. Mark them. Then go through these divisions, find if there are any natural subdivisions, and mark them. In organizing your studies, work from a version of the Bible that is divided according to a logical plan.

Having discovered the divisions of the book, proceed to give each section an appropriate caption. Make this caption as precise a statement of the general contents of the section as possible. Also, make it as brief and as impressionable as you can so that it will fix itself in your mind. Create captions for the subdivisions to connect with the general caption of the division. Do not attempt too complicated a division at first.

The following division of 1 Peter, without many marked subdivisions, will serve as a simple illustration:

1 Peter 1:1–2: Introduction and salutation to the pilgrims and sojourners in Pontus, etc.

1 Peter 1:3–12: The inheritance reserved in heaven and the salvation ready to be revealed for those pilgrims who, in the midst of manifold temptations, are kept by the power of God through faith.

1 Peter 1:13–25: The pilgrim's conduct during the days of his pilgrimage.

1 Peter 2:1–10: The high calling, position, and destiny of the pilgrim people.

1 Peter 2:11–12: The pilgrim's conduct during the days of his pilgrimage.

1 Peter 2:13–17: The pilgrim's duty toward the human governments under which he lives.

1 Peter 2:18–3:7: The duty of various classes of pilgrims.

1 Peter 2:18–25: The duty of servants toward their masters—enforced by an appeal to Christ's conduct under injustice and reviling.

1 Peter 3:1–6: The duty of wives toward their husbands.

1 Peter 3:7: The duty of husbands toward their wives.

1 Peter 3:8–12: The conduct of pilgrims toward one another.

1 Peter 3:13–22: The pilgrim suffering for righteousness' sake.

1 Peter 4:1–6: The pilgrim's separation from the practices of those among whom he spends the days of his pilgrimage.

1 Peter 4:7–11: The pilgrim's sojourning drawing to a close and his conduct during the last days.

1 Peter 4:12–19: The pilgrim suffering for and with Christ.

1 Peter 5:1–4: The duty and reward of elders.

1 Peter 5:5–11: The pilgrim's walk—humble, trustful, watchful, and steadfast—and a doxology.

1 Peter 5:12–14: Conclusion and benediction.

Taking Bite-Size Pieces

The fifth step is to take each verse in order and study it. In this verse-by-verse study of the book, derive the exact meaning of the verse. How is this to be done? Three steps lead to the meaning of a verse.

First, try to get the exact meaning of the words used. You will find two classes of words: those whose meaning is perfectly apparent and those whose meaning is doubtful. It is quite possible to find the precise meaning of these doubtful words. This is not done, however, by consulting a dictionary. That is an easy, but dangerous, method of finding the scriptural significance of a word. The only safe and sure method is to study the usage of the word in the Bible itself and particularly by the Bible writer whom you are studying.

To study the Bible usage of words, you must have a concordance. In my opinion, the best concordance is *Strong's Exhaustive Concordance of the Bible*. The next best is *Young's Analytical Concordance*. *Cruden's Complete Concordance* will also do if you are on a limited budget. When you are studying a particular word, all the passages in which the word occurs should be found and examined. In this way, the precise meaning of the word will be determined.

Many important Bible doctrines will change the meaning of a word. For example, two schools of theology are divided on the meaning of the word *justify*. The critical question is, does the word *justify* mean "to make righteous," or does it mean "to count or declare righteous"? The correct interpretation of many passages of Scripture hinges on the sense that we give to this word. Look up all the passages in the Bible in which the word is found, and then you will have no doubt as to the Bible usage and meaning of the word. Deuteronomy 25:1; Exodus 23:7; Isaiah 5:23; Luke 16:15; Romans 2:13, 3:23–24, 4:2–8; and Luke 18:14 will serve to illustrate the biblical usage of the word *justify*.

By using *Strong's* or *Young's Concordance*, you will see that the same word may be used in the English version for the translation of several Greek or Hebrew words. Of course, in determining the biblical usage, we should give special attention to those passages in which the English word examined is the translation of the same word in Greek or Hebrew. Either of these concordances will enable you to do this, even though you are not acquainted with Greek or Hebrew. It will be much easier to do, however, with *Strong's Concordance* than with *Young's*.

It is surprising how many knotty problems in the interpretation of Scripture are solved by the simple examination of the biblical usage of words. For example, one of the burning questions of today is the meaning of 1 John 1:7. Does this verse teach that *"the blood of Jesus Christ"* cleanses us from all the guilt of sin; or does it teach us that *"the blood of Jesus Christ"* cleanses us from the very presence of sin so that, by the blood of Christ, indwelling sin is itself eradicated?

Many of those who read this question will answer it offhand at once, one way or the other. But the spur-of-the-moment way of answering questions of this kind is a bad way. Take your concordance and look up every passage in the Bible in which the word *cleanse* is used in connection with blood, and the question will be answered conclusively and forever.

Never conclude that you have the right meaning of a verse until you have carefully determined the meaning of all doubtful words in it by an examination of Bible usage. Even when you are fairly sure you know the meaning of the words, it is good not to be too sure until you have looked them up.

Look Behind and Ahead

Now try to ascertain the meaning of a verse by carefully noticing the context (what goes before and what comes after). Many verses, if they stood alone, might be capable of several interpretations. But when the context is considered, all the interpretations except one are seen to be impossible.

For example, in John 14:18, Jesus said, *"I will not leave you orphans; I will come to you."* What did Jesus mean when He said, *"I will come to you"*? One commentator said, "He refers to His reappearance to His disciples after His resurrection to comfort them." Another said, "He refers to His second coming." Another said, "He refers to His coming through the Holy Spirit's work to manifest Himself to His disciples and make His abode with them."

So what did Jesus mean? When doctors disagree, can an ordinary layman decide? Yes, very often. Certainly in this case. If you will carefully note what Jesus was talking about in the verses immediately preceding (see verses 15–17) and immediately following (see verses 19–26), you will have no doubt as to what coming Jesus referred to in this passage. You can see this by trying it for yourself.

Look at Comparison Verses

To ascertain the correct and precise meaning of a verse, examine parallel passages—passages that deal with the same subject. For example, study other verses that give another account of the same event or passages that are evidently intended as a commentary on the passage at hand.

Very often, after having carefully studied the context, you may still be in doubt as to which interpretation the writer intended. In this case, there is probably a passage somewhere else in the Bible that will settle this question. In John 14:3, Jesus said, *"I will come again and receive you to Myself; that where I am, there you may be also."* A careful consideration of the words used in their relation to one another will help to determine the meaning of this passage.

Still, among commentators, we find four different interpretations. First, the coming referred to here is explained as Christ's coming at death to receive the believer to Himself, as in the case of Stephen. Another commentator interprets this as the coming again at the Resurrection. A third sees the coming again through the Holy Spirit. The last defines this passage to be when Christ returns personally and gloriously at the end of the age.

Which of these four interpretations is the correct one? What has already been said about verse eighteen might seem to settle the question, but it does not. It is not at all clear that the coming in verse three is the same as in verse eighteen. What is said in connection with the two comings is altogether different. In the one case, it is a coming of Christ to *"receive you to Myself; that where I am, there you may be also"* (John 14:3). In the other case, it is a coming of Christ to manifest Himself to us and make His abode with us.

Fortunately, there is a passage that settles the question. It is found in 1 Thessalonians 4:16–17. This will be clearly seen if we arrange the two passages in parallel columns.

John 14:3	***1 Thessalonians 4:16–17***
"I will come again..."	*"The Lord Himself will descend from heaven..."*
"...and receive you to Myself;..."	*"we...shall be caught up... to meet the Lord..."*
"...that where I am, there you may be also."	*"...thus we shall always be with the Lord."*

The two passages clearly match exactly in the three facts stated. Beyond a doubt, they refer to the same event. Look closely at 1 Thessalonians 4:16–17. There can be no doubt as to what coming of our Lord is referred to here.

These three steps lead us to the meaning of a verse. They require work, but it is work that anyone can do. When the meaning of a verse is settled, you can arrive at conclusions that are correct and fixed. After taking these steps, it is wise to consult commentaries to compare your conclusions to those of others.

Before we proceed to the next step, let me say that God intended to convey definite truth in each verse of Scripture. With every verse, we should ask what it was *intended* to teach, not what it can be *made* to teach; we should not be satisfied until we have settled this question. Of course, I admit a verse may have a primary meaning and then other more remote meanings. For example, a prophecy may have its primary fulfillment in some personage or event near at hand, such as Solomon, with a more remote and complete fulfillment in Christ.

Analyzing the Verse

We are not finished with a verse when we have determined its meaning. The next thing to do is to analyze the verse. The way to do it is this: Look steadfastly at the verse and ask yourself, "What does this verse teach?" Then begin to write down: This verse teaches first ———, second ———, third ———, etc. At first glance, you will see one or two things the verse teaches; but as you look again and again, the teachings will begin to multiply. You will wonder how one verse could teach so much, and you will have an ever growing sense of the divine Author of the Book.

I was once told the story of a professor who had a young man come to him to study ichthyology. The professor gave him a fish to study and told him to come back to get another lesson when he had mastered that fish. In time the young man came back and told the professor what he had observed about the fish. When he had finished, to his surprise, he was given the same fish again and told to study it further. He came back again, having observed new facts about the fish. But again he was given the same fish to study; and so it went on, lesson after lesson, until that student had been taught what his perceptive faculties were for and also how to do thorough work.

We should study the Bible in the same way. We ought to come back to the same verse of the Bible again and again until we have examined, as far as it is possible to us, all that is in the verse. The probability is that when we come back to the same verse several months later, we will find something we did not see before.

An illustration of this method of analysis will be helpful. Look at 1 Peter 1:1–2. (Here is an instance in which the verse division of the King James Version is so clearly illogical that in our analysis we cannot follow it but must take the two verses together. This will often be the case.)

These verses teach:

1. This epistle was written by Peter.
2. The Peter who wrote this epistle was an apostle of Jesus Christ. (*Apostle* is Greek for the word *missionary*.)
3. Peter delighted to think and speak of himself as one sent by Jesus Christ. (Compare 2 Peter 1:1.)
4. The name Jesus Christ is used twice in these two verses. Its significance:

    a. Savior.

    b. Anointed One.

    c. Fulfiller of the messianic predictions of the Old Testament. It has special reference to the earthly reign of Christ.

5. This epistle was written to the elect, especially to the elect who are sojourners of the dispersion in Pontus, i.e., Paul's old field of labor.
6. Believers are:

    a. Elect or chosen by God.

    b. Foreknown by God.

    c. Sanctified by the Spirit.

    d. Sprinkled by the blood of Jesus Christ.

    e. Sojourners or pilgrims on earth.

    f. Subjects of multiplied grace.

    g. Possessors of multiplied peace.

7. Election. Who are the elect? Believers. (Compare verse five.) To what are they elect? Obedience and the sprinkling of the blood of Jesus. According to what are they elect? The foreknowledge of God. (Compare Romans 8:29–30.) In what are they elect?

Sanctification of the Spirit. The test of election is obedience. (Compare 2 Peter 1:10.) The work of the three persons of the Trinity in election is this: the Father foreknows, Jesus Christ cleanses sin by His blood, and the Spirit sanctifies.

8. God is the Father of the elect.

9. The humanity of Christ is seen in the mention of His blood.

10. The reality of the body of Jesus Christ is seen in the mention of His blood.

11. It is by His blood and not by His example that Jesus Christ delivers from sin.

12. Peter's first and great wish and prayer for those to whom he wrote was that grace and peace might be multiplied.

13. It is not enough to have grace and peace. One should have multiplied grace and peace.

14. That one already has grace and peace is no reason to cease praying for them but rather an incentive to pray that they may have more grace and peace.

15. Grace precedes peace. Compare all passages where these words are found together.

This is simply an illustration of what is meant by analyzing a verse. The whole book should be gone through in this way.

Three rules must be observed, however, in this analytical work. First, do not put anything into your analysis that is not clearly in the verse. One of the greatest faults in Bible study is reading into passages what God never put into them. Some people have their pet doctrines; they see them everywhere, even where God does not see them. No matter how true, precious, or scriptural a doctrine is, do not put into your analysis what is not in the verse. Considerable experience in this kind of study leads me to emphasize this rule.

Second, find all that is in the verse. This rule can only be carried out relatively. Much will escape you because many of the verses of the Bible are so deep. But do not rest until you have dug and dug and dug, and there seems to be nothing more to find.

Then, state what you do find just as accurately and exactly as possible. Do not be content with putting into your analysis something similar to what is in the verse, but state in your analysis precisely what is in the verse.

Classifying Your Results

Through your verse-by-verse analysis, you have discovered and recorded a great number of facts. The work now is to get these facts organized. To do this, go carefully through your analysis, and note the various subjects in the epistle. Write these subjects down as fast as you find them. Having made a complete list of the subjects dealt with in the book, write these subjects on separate cards or sheets of paper. Then, go through the analysis again and copy each point in the analysis on its appropriate sheet of paper. For example, write every point regarding God the Father on one card or sheet of paper.

This general classification should be followed by a more thorough and minute subdivision. Suppose that you are studying 1 Peter. Having completed your analysis of the epistle and gone over it carefully, you will find that the following subjects are dealt with in this epistle:

- God
- Jesus Christ
- The Holy Spirit
- The Believer
- Wives and Husbands
- Servants
- The New Birth
- The Word of God

- Old Testament Scripture
- The Prophets
- Prayer
- Angels
- The Devil
- Baptism
- The Gospel
- Salvation
- The World
- Gospel Preachers and Teachers
- Heaven
- Humility
- Love

These will serve as general headings. After the material found in the analysis is arranged under these headings, you will find it easier to divide it into numerous subdivisions. For example, the material under the heading *God* can be divided into these subdivisions:

1. His names: The material under this heading is quite rich.
2. His attributes: This should be subdivided again into His holiness, His power, His foreknowledge, His faithfulness, His longsuffering, His grace, His mercy, His impartiality, and His severity.
3. God's judgments.
4. God's will.
5. What is acceptable to God?
6. What is due to God?
7. God's dwelling place.

8. God's dominion.
9. God's work or what God does.
10. The things of God: For example, *"the mighty hand of God"* (1 Peter 5:6), *"the house of God"* (1 Peter 4:17), *"the gospel of God"* (verse 17), *"the flock of God"* (1 Peter 5:2), *"the people of God"* (1 Peter 2:10), the *"bondservants of God,"* (verse 16), *"the word of God"* (1 Peter 1:23), *"the oracles of God"* (1 Peter 4:11), etc.

To illustrate the classified arrangement of the teaching of a book on one doctrine will probably show you better how to do this work than any abstract statement. It will also illustrate in part how fruitful this method of study is. Look again at 1 Peter and its teachings regarding the believer.

I. The Believer's Privileges

A. His election

1. He is foreknown by the Father, 1:2.
2. He is elect or chosen by God, 1:2.
3. He is chosen by God according to His foreknowledge, 1:2.
4. He is chosen to obedience, 1:2.
5. He is chosen for the sprinkling of the blood of Jesus, 1:2.
6. He is chosen in sanctification by the Spirit, 1:2.

B. His calling

1. By whom called: God, 1:15; and the God of all grace, 5:10.
2. To what called: the imitation of Christ in the patient taking of suffering for well doing, 2:20–21; to render blessing for reviling, 3:9; out of darkness into God's marvelous light, 2:9; to God's eternal glory, 5:10.

3. In whom called: in Christ, 5:10.

4. The purpose of his calling: that he may show forth the praises of Him who called, 2:9; that he may inherit a blessing, 3:9.

C. His regeneration

1. Of God, 1:3.

2. To a living hope, 1:3.

3. To an inheritance incorruptible, undefiled, and that does not fade away, reserved in heaven, 1:4.

4. By the resurrection of Jesus Christ, 1:3.

5. Of incorruptible seed by the Word of God that lives, 1:23.

D. His redemption

1. Not with corruptible things, such as silver and gold, 1:18.

2. With precious blood, even the blood of Christ, 1:19.

3. From his vain manner of life, handed down from his father, 1:18.

4. His sins have been borne by Christ, in His own body, on the tree, 2:24.

E. His sanctification by the Spirit, 1:2.

F. His cleansing by the blood, 1:2.

G. His security

1. He is guarded by the power of God, 1:5.

2. He is guarded to a salvation ready, or prepared, to be revealed in the last time, 1:5.

3. God cares for him, 5:7.

4. He can cast all his anxiety upon God, 5:7.

5. The God of all grace will perfect, establish, and strengthen him after a brief trial of suffering, 5:10.

6. None can harm him if he is zealous of what is good, 3:13.

7. He will not be put to shame, 2:6.

H. His joy

1. The character of his joy. Presently, it is an unspeakable joy, 1:8; a joy full of glory, 1:8. This present joy cannot be hindered by being put to grief because of many temptations, 1:6. His future joy is exceeding, 4:13.

2. He rejoices in the salvation prepared to be revealed in the last time, 1:5; in his faith in the unseen Jesus Christ, 1:8; and in fellowship in Christ's sufferings, 4:13.

3. What he will rejoice in: the revelation of Christ's glory, 4:13. Present joy in fellowship with the sufferings of Christ is the condition of exceeding joy at the revelation of Christ's glory, 4:13.

I. His hope

1. Its character: a living hope, 1:3; a reasonable hope, 3:15; an inward hope, 3:15.

2. In whom his hope lies: God, 1:21.

3. The foundation of his hope is in the resurrection of Jesus Christ, 1:3–21.

J. His salvation

1. A past salvation: he has been redeemed, 1:18–19; and he has been healed, 2:24. By baptism, like Noah by the flood, the believer has passed out of the old life of nature into the new resurrection life of grace, 3:21.

2. A present salvation: he is now receiving the salvation of his soul, 1:9.

3. A *growing* salvation: through feeding on His Word, 2:2.
4. A *future* salvation: ready or prepared to be revealed in the last time, 1:5.

K. The believer's possessions

1. God as his Father, 1:17.
2. Christ as his Sin-Bearer, 2:24; example, 2:21; fellow sufferer, 4:13.
3. A living hope, 1:3.
4. An incorruptible, undefiled, and unfading inheritance reserved in heaven, 1:4.
5. Multiplied grace and peace, 1:2.
6. Spiritual milk without guile for his food, 2:2.
7. Gifts for service—each believer has some gift, 4:10.

L. What believers are

1. Sojourners or strangers, 1:1.
2. A sojourner on his way to another country, 2:1.
3. A holy priesthood, 2:5.
4. Living stones, 2:5.
5. A spiritual house, 2:5.
6. A chosen generation, 2:9.
7. A royal priesthood, 2:9.
8. A holy nation, 2:9.
9. Partakers of, or partners in, Christ's sufferings, 4:13.
10. Representatives of Christ, 4:16.

11. The house of God, 4:17.

12. Partakers of, or partners in, the glory to be revealed, 5:1.

13. The flock of God, 5:2.

M. The believer's possibilities

1. He may die to sin, 2:24.

2. He may live for righteousness, 2:24.

3. He may follow in Christ's steps, 2:21.

4. He may cease from sin, 4:1.

5. He may cease from living for the lusts of men, 4:2.

6. He may live for the will of God, 4:2.

N. What was for the believer

1. The ministry of the prophets was in his behalf, 1:12.

2. The preciousness of Jesus is for him, 2:7.

O. Unclassified

1. The Gospel has been preached to him in the Holy Spirit, 1:12.

2. Grace is to be brought to him at the revelation of Jesus Christ, 1:3. (Compare Ephesians 3:7.)

3. He has tasted that the Lord is gracious, 2:3.

II. The Believer's Sufferings and Trials

A. The fact of the believer's sufferings and trials, 1:6.

B. The nature of the believer's sufferings and trials.

1. He endures grief, suffering wrongfully, 2:19.

2. He suffers for righteousness' sake, 3:14.

3. He suffers for doing good, 3:17; 2:20.
4. He suffers as a Christian, 4:16.
5. He is subjected to many temptations, 1:6.
6. He is put to grief in manifold temptations, 1:6.
7. He is spoken against as an evildoer, 2:12.
8. His good manner of life is reviled, 3:16.
9. He is spoken evil of because of his separated life, 4:4.
10. He is reproached for the name of Christ, 4:14.
11. He is subjected to fiery trials, 4:12.

C. Encouragement for believers undergoing fiery trials and suffering.

1. It is better to suffer for doing good than for doing evil, 3:17.
2. Judgment must begin at the house of God. The present judgment of believers through trial is not comparable to the future end of those who do not obey the Gospel, 4:17.
3. Blessed is the believer who suffers for righteousness' sake, 3:14. (Compare Matthew 5:10–12.)
4. Blessed is the believer who is reproached for the name of Christ, 4:14.
5. The Spirit of Glory and of God rests upon the believer who is reproached for the name of Christ, 4:14.
6. The believer's grief is for a little while, 1:6.
7. Suffering for a little while will be followed by God's glory in Christ, which is eternal, 5:10.
8. The suffering endured for a little while is for the testing of faith, 1:7.

9. The fiery trial is for a test, 4:12.
10. The faith thus proved is more precious than gold, 1:7.
11. Faith proven by manifold temptations will be found to praise and honor and glory at the revelation of Jesus Christ, 1:7.
12. His proved faith may result in praise, glory, and honor at the revelation of Jesus Christ, when the believer is for a little while subjected to many temptations, 1:7.
13. It is pleasing to God when a believer takes persecution patiently, when he does well and suffers for it, 2:20.
14. Through suffering in the flesh, we cease from sin, 4:1.
15. Those who speak evil of us will give account to God, 4:5.
16. Sufferings are being shared by fellow believers, 5:9.
17. Christ suffered for us, 2:21.
18. Christ suffered for sins once for all, the righteous for the unrighteous, so that He might bring us to God, being put to death in the flesh, but enlivened by the spirit, 3:18.
19. Christ left the believer an example that he should follow in His steps, 2:21.
20. In our fiery trials, we are made partakers of, or partners in, Christ's sufferings, 4:13.
21. When His glory is revealed, we will be glad with exceeding joy, 4:13.

D. How the believer should meet his trial and sufferings

1. The believer should not regard his fiery trial as a strange thing, 4:12.
2. The believer should expect fiery trials, 4:12.

3. When the believer suffers as a Christian, he should not be ashamed, 4:16.

4. When the believer suffers as a Christian, he should glorify God in this matter, 4:16.

5. When the believer suffers, he should not return reviling with reviling, or suffering with threatening, but commit himself to God who judges righteously, 2:23.

6. When the believer suffers, he should commit the keeping of his soul to God, as to a faithful Creator, 4:19.

III. The Believer's Dangers

A. The believer may fall into fleshly lusts that war against the soul, 2:11.

B. The believer may sin, 2:20.

C. The believer may fall into sins of the gravest character, 4:15. (Note in this verse the awful possibilities that lie dormant in the heart of a sincere, professed believer.)

D. The believer's prayers may be hindered, 3:7.

E. The believer is in danger that his high calling and destiny may tempt him to despise human laws and authority, 2:13.

F. The believer is in danger that his high calling may lead him to lose sight of his lowly obligations to human masters, 2:18.

G. Young believers are in danger of disregarding the will and authority of older believers, 5:5.

IV. The Believer's Responsibility

A. Each believer has an individual responsibility, 4:10.

B. Each believer's responsibility is for the gift he has received, 4:10.

V. The Believer's Duties

A. What the believer should be

1. Be holy in all manner of living because God is holy, 1:15; and because it is written, *"Be holy, for I am holy"* (verse 16).
2. Be like Him who called him, 1:15–16.
3. Be sober, or of a calm, collected, thoughtful spirit, 1:13; 4:7; 5:8.
4. Be serious in prayer, 4:7.
5. Be of a sound mind; the end of all things is approaching, 4:7.
6. Be watchful, 5:8.
7. Be steadfast in the faith, 5:9.
8. Be subject to every ordinance of man for the Lord's sake, 2:13; to the king as supreme, 2:13; to government officials who are sent by the king to punish evildoers and to praise those who do well, 2:14; because this is God's will, 2:15.
9. Be of one mind, 3:8.
10. Be compassionate, 3:8.
11. Be tenderhearted, 3:8.
12. Be courteous, 3:8.
13. Be ready always to give an answer to everyone who asks a reason for the hope that is in him, with meekness and fear, 3:15; in order to put to shame those who revile his good conduct in Christ, 3:16.
14. Be not troubled, 3:14.

B. What the believer should not do

1. The believer should not conform himself to the lusts of the old life of ignorance, 1:14.

2. The believer should not return evil for evil, 3:9.

3. The believer should not return reviling for reviling, 3:9.

4. The believer should not be afraid of the world's threats, 3:14.

5. The believer should not live his remaining time in the flesh for the lusts of men, 4:2.

C. What the believer should do

1. Live as a child of obedience, 1:14.

2. Pass the time of his sojourning here in fear of the Lord, 1:17.

3. Abstain from fleshly lusts that war against the soul, 2:11.

4. Observe God's will as the absolute law of life, 2:15.

5. Let his conscience be governed by the thought of God and not by the conduct of men, 2:19.

6. Sanctify Christ in his heart as Lord, 3:15. (Compare Isaiah 8:13.)

7. Live his remaining time in the flesh to the will of God, 4:2.

8. Put away all malice, 2:1; all deceit, 2:1; hypocrisy, 2:1; envy, 2:1; all evil speaking, 2:1.

9. Come to the Lord as to a living stone, 2:4.

10. Proclaim the praises of Him who called him out of darkness into His marvelous light, 2:9.

11. Arm himself with the mind of Christ, i.e., to suffer in the flesh, 4:1.

12. Cast all his care upon God because He cares for him, 5:7.

13. Stand fast in the true grace of God, 5:12.

14. Resist the Devil, 5:9.

15. Humble himself under the mighty hand of God: because God resists the proud and gives grace to the humble, 5:5; so that God may exalt him in due time, 5:6.

16. Glorify God when he suffers as a Christian, 4:16.

17. See to it that he does not suffer as a thief, an evildoer, or a meddler in other people's matters, 4:15.

18. Rejoice in fiery trials, 4:13.

19. Toward various persons: toward God—fear, 2:17; toward the king—honor, 2:17; toward masters—be in subjection with all fear (not only to the good and gentle, but also to the harsh) 2:18; toward the brethren—love, 1:22; 2:17; 4:8; toward his revilers—blessing for reviling, 3:9; toward the Gentiles—honorable conduct, 2:12 (that God may be glorified); toward foolish men—by doing good, put to silence their ignorance, 2:15; and toward all people—honor, 2:17.

20. Desire the pure milk of the Word, 2:2.

21. Gird up the loins of his mind, 1:13.

22. Grow, 2:2.

23. Hope fully on the grace that is to be brought to him at the revelation of Jesus Christ, 1:13.

VI. The Believer's Characteristics

A. His faith and hope are in God, 1:21.

B. He believes in God through Jesus Christ, 1:21.

C. He calls on God as Father, 1:17.

D. He believes in Christ, though he has never seen Him, 1:8.

E. He loves Christ, though he has never seen Him, 1:8.

F. He has returned to the Shepherd and Overseer of his soul, 2:25.

G. He has purified his soul in obedience to the truth, 1:22.

H. He has sincere love for the brethren, 1:22.

I. He has good conduct, 3:16.

J. He does not run with the Gentiles among whom he lives, to the same excess of riot, but lives a separated life, 4:4.

K. He refrains his tongue from evil, 3:10, and refrains his lips so that they speak no deceit, 3:10.

L. He turns away from evil, 3:11.

M. He does good, 3:11.

N. He seeks peace, 3:11.

O. He pursues peace, 3:11.

VII. The Believer's Warfare

A. The believer has a warfare before him, 4:1.

B. The mind of Christ is the proper armament for this warfare, 4:1.

C. The warfare is with the Devil, 5:8–9.

D. Victory is possible for the believer, 5:9.

E. Victory is won through steadfastness in the faith, 5:9.

How to Retain Your Studies

At first thought, it may seem that when we had completed our classification of results, our work was finished, but this is not so. These results are for use: first, for personal enjoyment and appropriation, and afterward to give to others. To obtain results, you must meditate on them.

We are no more through with a book when we have carefully and fully classified its contents than we are through with a meal when we have arranged it in an orderly way on the table. It is there to eat, digest, and assimilate.

One of the greatest failures in Bible study today is at this point. There is observation, analysis, classification, but no meditation. Perhaps nothing is as important in Bible study as meditation. (See Joshua 1:8; Psalm 1:2–3.)

Take your classified teachings and go slowly over them. Ponder them, point by point, until these wonderful truths live before you, sink into your soul, and become part of your life. Do this again and again. Nothing will go further than meditation to make you become a great, fresh, and original thinker and speaker. Very few people in this world are great thinkers.

The method of study outlined in this chapter can be shortened to suit the time and vocation of the student. For example, you can omit the verse-by-verse study and proceed at once to go through the book as a whole and note its teachings on different doctrines. This will greatly shorten and lighten the work. It will also greatly detract from the richness of the results, however, and will not be as thorough, accurate, or as scholarly. But anyone can be, if he will, a scholar, at least in the most important work: that of biblical study.

3

TOPICAL STUDY

A second method of Bible study, perhaps the most fascinating, is the topical method. This consists in searching through the Bible to find out what its teaching is on various topics. The only way to master any subject is to go through the Bible and find what it has to teach on that topic. Almost any great subject will take a remarkable hold on the heart of a Christian, if he will take time to go through the Bible from Genesis to Revelation and note what it has to say on that topic. He will have a fuller, more correct understanding of that specific area than he ever had before.

D. L. Moody once said that he studied the word *grace* in this way. Day after day, he went through the Bible, studying what it had to say about *grace*. As the Bible doctrine unfolded before his mind, his heart began to burn, until at last, full of the subject and on fire with the subject, he ran onto the street. Taking hold of the first man he met, he said, "Do you know grace?"

"Grace who?" was the reply.

"The grace of God that brings salvation."

Then he poured out his soul on that subject.

If any child of God will study grace, love, faith, prayer, or any other great Bible doctrine in this way, his soul, too, will become filled with it. Jesus evidently studied the Old Testament Scriptures in this way. *"Beginning at Moses and all the Prophets, He expounded to them in all the Scriptures the things concerning Himself"* (Luke 24:27). This method of study made the hearts of the two who walked with Him burn within them. (See Luke 24:32.) Paul seemed to have followed his Master in this method of study and teaching. (See Acts 17:2–3.)

Watch Out for Imbalance

This method of topical study has its dangers, however. Many are drawn by the fascination of this method to give up all other methods of study, and this is a great misfortune. A well-rounded, thorough knowledge of the Bible is not possible by one method of study alone.

But the greatest danger lies in this: everyone is almost certain to have some topics in which he is especially interested. If he studies his Bible topically, unless he is warned, he is more than likely to focus on certain topics repeatedly. Thus, he will be very strong in certain areas of truth, but other topics of equal importance may be neglected, and he may become one-sided.

We never know one truth correctly until we know it in its proper relationship to other truths. I know of people, for example, who are interested in the great doctrine of the Lord's second coming. Therefore, almost all their Bible studies are on that line. Now this is a precious doctrine, but there are other doctrines in the Bible that a person needs to know; it is folly to study this doctrine alone.

I know others whose whole interest and study seem to focus on the subject of divine healing. One man confided to a friend that he had devoted years to the study of the number seven in the Bible. This is doubtless an extreme case, but it illustrates the danger in topical study. It is certain that we will never master the whole range of Bible truth if we pursue the topical method alone. A few rules concerning topical study will probably be helpful to you.

Don't follow your fancy in the choice of topics. Don't take up any topic that happens to suggest itself. Make a list of all the subjects you can think of that are touched on in the Bible. Make it as comprehensive and complete as possible. Then study these topics one by one in logical order. The following list of subjects is given as a suggestion. Each person can add to the list for himself and separate the general subjects into proper subdivisions.

List of Topics

God

God as a Spirit

The unity of God

The eternity of God

The omnipresence of God

The personality of God

The omnipotence of God

The omniscience of God

The holiness of God

The love of God

The righteousness of God

The mercy or lovingkindness of God

- The faithfulness of God
- The grace of God

Jesus Christ

- The divinity of Christ
- The subordination of Christ to God
- The human nature of Jesus Christ
- The character of Jesus Christ
    - His holiness
    - His love for God
    - His love for man
    - His love for souls
    - His compassion
    - His prayer life
    - His meekness and humility
- The death of Jesus Christ
    - The purpose of Christ's death
    - Why did Christ die?
    - For whom did Christ die?
    - The results of Christ's death
- The resurrection of Jesus Christ
    - The fact of the resurrection
    - The results of the resurrection
    - The importance of the resurrection
    - The manner of the resurrection
- The ascension and exaltation of Christ
- The return or coming again of Christ

- The fact of His coming again
- The manner of His coming again
- The purpose of His coming again
- The result of His coming again
- The time of His coming again

The reign of Jesus Christ

The Holy Spirit

The personality of the Holy Spirit

The deity of the Holy Spirit

The distinction of the Holy Spirit

The subordination of the Holy Spirit

The names of the Holy Spirit

The work of the Holy Spirit

- In the universe
- In man in general
- In the believer
- In the prophet and apostle
- In Jesus Christ

Man

His original condition

His fall

His standing before God

The future destiny of unbelievers

Justification

The new birth

Adoption

The believer's assurance of salvation

The flesh

Sanctification

Cleansing

Consecration

Faith

Repentance

Prayer

Thanksgiving

Praise

Worship

Love for God

Love for Jesus Christ

Love for man

The future destiny of believers

Angels

Their nature and position

Their number

Their abode

Their character

Their work

Their destiny

Satan or the Devil

His existence

His nature and position

His abode

His work

Our duty regarding him

His destiny

Demons

Their existence

Their nature

Their work

Their destiny

For the student who has the perseverance to carry it through, it might be recommended to begin with the first topic on a list like this and go right through to the end, searching for everything the Bible has to say on these topics. I have done this and, thereby, gained a fuller knowledge of truth than I ever obtained by extended studies in systematic theology.

Many, however, will stagger at the seeming immensity of the undertaking. To such, it is recommended to begin by selecting those topics that seem more important, but sooner or later, settle down to a thorough study of what the Bible has to teach about God and man.

Be Thorough

Whenever you are studying any topic, do not be content with examining some of the passages in the Bible that pertain to the subject. As far as possible, find every passage in the Bible that relates to this subject. As long as there is a single passage in the Bible on any subject that you have not considered, you have not yet acquired a thorough knowledge of that subject.

How can you find all the passages in the Bible that relate to any subject? First, by the use of a concordance. Look up every passage that has the word in it. Then look up every passage that has synonyms of that word in it. If, for example, you are studying the subject of prayer, look up every passage that has the word *pray* and its derivatives in it and also every passage that has such words as *cry, call, ask, supplication, intercession,* etc.

You may also use a topical Bible, such as *Nave's Topical Bible: A Digest of the Holy Scriptures.* This book arranges the passages of Scripture by the subjects discussed.

Finally, passages not discovered by the use of either a concordance or topical guide will come to light as you study by books or as you read the Bible through. In this way, the number of topics we deal with will be ever broadening.

Getting the Exact Meaning

Study each passage in its context and find its meaning in the way suggested in the chapter on "Individual Book Study."

Topical study is frequently carried on in a very careless fashion. Passages taken out of context are strung or huddled together because of some superficial connection with one another without regard to their real sense and teaching.

This has brought the whole method of topical study into disrepute. But it is possible to be as exact and scholarly in topical study as in any other method when the results are instructive and gratifying and not misleading. But the results are sure to be misleading and unsatisfactory if the work is done in a careless, inexact way.

How to Arrange Your Notes

In studying any large subject, you will obtain a large amount of written material. Having obtained it, it must now be organized into a logical study form. As you look it over carefully, you will soon see the facts that belong together. Arrange them together in a logical order. For instance, perhaps you have accumulated much material on the deity of Jesus Christ. An example of topical study may be arranged as follows:

Jesus Christ: His Deity

I. Divine names

A. "The Son of God." (See Luke 22:70.) This name is given to Christ forty times. Additionally, the synonymous expression, *His Son* or *My Son* frequently occur. This name of Christ is a distinctly divine name that indicates Jesus' relationship with God, His Father. (See John 5:18.)

B. "The only begotten Son." (See John 1:18.) This name occurs five times. It is not true when people say that Jesus Christ is the Son of God only in the same sense that all men are sons of God. (Compare Mark 12:6.) Here Jesus Himself, having spoken of all the prophets as servants of God, speaks of Himself as *"one son, his beloved."*

C. "The First and the Last." (See Revelation 1:17.) (Compare Isaiah 41:4; 44:6.) In these latter passages, it is *"the Lord of hosts,"* who is *"the First and the Last"* (Isaiah 44:6).

D. "The Alpha and the Omega" or *"the Beginning and the End"* (Revelation 22:13). In Revelation 1:8, it is the Lord who is *"the Alpha and the Omega."*

E. "The Holy One." (See Acts 3:14.) In Hosea 11:9 and many other passages, it is God who is *"The Holy One."*

F. "The Lord." (See, for example, Malachi 3:1; Luke 2:11; Acts 9:17; John 20:28; Hebrews 1:10.) This name or title is used of Jesus several hundred times. He is spoken of as "the Lord" just as God is. (Compare Acts 4:26 with 4:33. Note also Matthew 22:43–45, Philippians 2:11, and Ephesians 4:5.) If anyone doubts the attitude of the apostles of Jesus toward Him as divine, they would do well to read one after another the passages that speak of Him as Lord.

G. "Lord of all." (See Acts 10:36.)

H. "The Lord of glory" (See 1 Corinthians 2:8,) In Psalm 24:10, it is *"the Lord of hosts"* who is *"the King of glory."*

I. "Wonderful," "Counselor," "Mighty God," "Everlasting Father," and "Prince of Peace." (See Isaiah 9:6.)

J. "God" (See Hebrews 1:8.) In John 20:28, Thomas calls Jesus *"my God"* and is gently rebuked for not believing it before. (See verse 29.)

K. "God with us." (See Matthew 1:23.)

L. "Our great God." (See Titus 2:13.)

M. "Eternally blessed God." (See Romans 9:5.)

Conclusion: Sixteen names clearly implying deity are used of Christ in the Bible, some of them over and over again, the total number of passages reaching into the hundreds.

II. Divine Attributes

A. Omnipotence

1. Jesus has power over disease. It is subject to His word. (See Luke 4:39.)
2. The Son of God has power over death. It is subject to His word. (See Luke 7:14–15; 8:54–55; John 5:25.)
3. Jesus has power over the winds and sea. They are subject to His word. (See Matthew 8:26–27.)
4. Jesus the Christ, the Son of God, has power over demons. They are subject to His word. (See Matthew 8:16; Luke 4:35–36, 41.)
5. Christ is far above *all* principality, power, might, dominion, and every name that is named, not only in this world but also in the one to come. All things are in subjection under His feet. All the hierarchies of the angelic world are under Him. (See Ephesians 1:20–23.)

6. The Son of God upholds *all* things by the word of His power. (See Hebrews 1:3.)

Conclusion: Jesus Christ, the Son of God, is omnipotent.

B. Omniscience

1. Jesus knows men's lives, even their secret histories. (See John 4:16–19.)

2. Jesus knows the secret thoughts of men. He knew all men. He knew what was in man. (See Mark 2:8; Luke 5:22; John 2:24–25.)

3. Jesus knew from the beginning that Judas would betray Him. Not only men's present thoughts, but also their future choices were known to Him. (See John 6:64.)

4. Jesus knew what men were doing at a distance. (See John 1:48.)

5. Jesus knew the future regarding not only God's acts, but also the minute, specific acts of men. (See Luke 5:4–6; Luke 22:10–12; John 13:1.)

6. Jesus knew all things. In Him are hidden all the treasures of wisdom and knowledge. (See John 16:30; 21:17; Colossians 2:3.)

Conclusion: Jesus Christ is omniscient.

C. Omnipresence

1. Jesus Christ is present in every place where two or three are gathered together in His name. (See Matthew 18:20.)

2. Jesus Christ is present with everyone who goes forth into any part of the world to make disciples, etc. (See Matthew 28:19–20.)

3. Jesus Christ is in each believer. (See John 14:20; 2 Corinthians 13:5.)

4. Jesus Christ fills all in all. (See Ephesians 1:23.)

Conclusion: Jesus Christ is omnipresent.

D. Eternal

1. Jesus is eternal. (See Isaiah 9:7; Micah 5:2; John 1:1; John 17:5; Colossians 1:17; Hebrews 13:8.)

Conclusion: The Son of God was from all eternity.

E. Immutable

1. Jesus Christ is unchangeable. He not only always is, but always is *the same*. (See Hebrews 1:12; 13:8.)

Conclusion: Five or more distinctively divine attributes are ascribed to Jesus Christ, and all the fullness of the Godhead is said to dwell in Him. (See Colossians 2:9.)

III. Divine Offices

A. The Son of God, the eternal Word, the Lord, is Creator of all created things. (See John 1:3; Colossians 1:16; and Hebrews 1:10.)

B. The Son of God is the preserver of all things. (See Hebrews 1:3.)

C. Jesus Christ had power on earth to forgive sins. (See Mark 2:5–10; Luke 7:48–50.)

D. Jesus Christ raised the dead. (See John 6:39–44; 5:28–29.) Question: Did not Elijah and Elisha raise the dead? No, God raised the dead in answer to their prayers, but Jesus Christ will raise the dead by His own word. During the days of His humiliation, it was by prayer that Christ raised the dead.

E. Jesus Christ will fashion anew the body of our humiliation into the likeness of His own glorious body. (See Philippians 3:21.)

F. Christ Jesus will judge the living and the dead. (See 2 Timothy 4:1.)

G. Jesus Christ is the giver of eternal life. (See John 10:28; 17:2.)

Conclusion: Seven distinctively divine offices belong to Jesus Christ.

IV. Old Testament Statements Made Distinctly about Jehovah God Refer to Jesus Christ in the New Testament

A. Numbers 21:6–7. Compare 1 Corinthians 10:9.

B. Psalm 23:1; Isaiah 40:10–11. Compare John 10:11.

C. Psalm 102:24–27. Compare Hebrews 1:10–12.

D. Isaiah 3:10; 6:1. Compare John 12:37–4 1.

E. Isaiah 8:12–13. Compare I Peter 3:14–15.

F. Isaiah 8:13–14. Compare 1 Peter 2:7–8.

G. Isaiah 40:3–4. Compare Matthew 3:3; Luke 1:68–69, 76.

H. Isaiah 60:19; Zechariah 2:5. Compare Luke 2:32.

I. Jeremiah 11:20; 17:10. Compare Revelation 2:23.

J. Ezekiel 34:11–12, 16. Compare Luke 19:10.

K. "Lord" in the Old Testament always refers to God except when the context clearly indicates otherwise. "Lord" in the New Testament always refers to Jesus Christ except where the context clearly indicates otherwise.

Conclusion: Many statements in the Old Testament made distinctly of Jehovah God are taken in the New Testament to refer to Jesus Christ. In New Testament thought and doctrine, Jesus Christ occupies the place that Jehovah occupies in Old Testament thought and doctrine.

V. Names of God the Father and Jesus Christ the Son Coupled Together

A. 2 Corinthians 13:14.

B. Matthew 28:19.

C. 1 Thessalonians 3:11.

D. 1 Corinthians 12:4–6.

E. Titus 3:4–5. Compare Titus 2:13.

F. Romans 1:7. (See all the Pauline Epistles.)

G. James 1:1.

H. John 14:23, "We," i.e., God and Jesus Christ.

I. 2 Peter 1:1.

J. Colossians 2:2.

K. John 17:3.

L. John 14:1. Compare Jeremiah 17:5–7.

M. Revelation 7:10.

N. Revelation 5:13. Compare John 5:23.

Conclusion: The name of Jesus Christ is coupled with that of God the Father in numerous passages in a way in which it would be impossible to couple the name of any finite being with that of the deity.

VI. Divine Worship Is to Be Given to Jesus Christ

A. Jesus Christ accepted without hesitation a worship that good men and angels declined with fear (horror). (See Matthew 4:9–10; Matthew 14:33; Matthew 28:8–9; Luke 24:52. Compare Acts 10:25–26 and Revelation 22:8–9.)

B. Prayer is to be made to Christ. (See Acts 7:59; 1 Corinthians 1:2; and 2 Corinthians 12:8–9.)

C. It is God the Father's will that all men pay the same divine honor to the Son as to Himself. (See Psalm 45:11; John 5:23. Compare Revelation 5:8–9, 12–13.)

D. The Son of God, Jesus, is to be worshipped as God by angels and men.

Conclusion: Jesus Christ is a person to be worshipped by angels and men even as God the Father is worshipped.

General Conclusion: By the use of numerous divine names, by attributing all the distinctively divine attributes, by the affirmation of several divine offices, by referring statements that in the Old Testament distinctly name Jehovah God as their subject to Jesus Christ in the New Testament, by coupling the name of Jesus Christ with that of God the Father in a way in which it would be impossible to couple that of any finite being with that of the deity, and by the clear teaching that Jesus Christ should be worshipped even as God the Father is worshipped—in all these unmistakable ways—God's Word distinctly proclaims that Jesus Christ is a divine being and is indeed God.

One suggestion remains in regard to topical study: choose further subjects for topical study from your own book studies.

4

BIOGRAPHICAL STUDY

A third method of study is the biographical study, which consists in studying the life, work, and character of various people mentioned in Scripture. It is a special form of topical study that can be particularly useful to ministers as they prepare their sermons. The following suggestions will help those who are not already experienced in this line of work.

1. Using *Strong's Concordance*, collect all the passages in the Bible that mention the person to be studied.

2. Analyze the character of the person. This will require a repeated reading of the passages in which he is mentioned. This should be done with pen in hand so that any characteristic may be noted at once.

3. Note the elements of power and success.

4. Note the elements of weakness and failure.

5. Note the difficulties overcome.

6. Note the helps to success.

7. Note the privileges abused.

8. Note the opportunities neglected.

9. Note the opportunities improved.

10. Note the mistakes made.

11. Note the perils avoided.

12. Make a sketch of the life in hand. Make it as vivid, living, and realistic as possible. Try to reproduce the subject as a real, living person. Note the place and surroundings of the different events, e.g., Paul in Athens, Corinth, or Philippi. Note the time relationships of different events. Very few people take notice of the rapid passage of time when they read the Acts of the Apostles. They regard events that are separated by years as following one another in close sequence. In this connection, note the age or approximate age of the subject at the time of the events recorded.

13. Summarize the lessons we should learn from the story of this person's life.

14. Note the person's relationship to Jesus as a type of Christ (Joseph, David, Solomon, and others), a forerunner of Christ, a believer in

Christ, an enemy of Christ, a servant of Christ, a brother of Christ (James and Jude), or a friend, etc.

Begin with some person who does not occupy too much space in the Bible, such as Enoch or Stephen. Of course many of the points mentioned above cannot be applied to some characters.

5

STUDY OF TYPES

A fourth method is the study of types. Both an interesting and instructive method, it shows us precious truths buried away in seemingly dry and meaningless portions of the Bible. This method of study is, however, greatly abused and overdone by some people. But that is no reason why we should neglect it altogether, especially when we remember that not only Paul, but also Jesus, was fond of this method of study. The following principles may guide us in this study.

Be sure you have a biblical authority for your supposed type. If one gives free rein to his suppositions, he can imagine types everywhere, even in places that neither the human nor the divine Author of the book intended.

Never say something is a type unless you can point to some clear passage of Scripture where types are definitely taught.

Begin with simple and evident types, such as the Passover (compare Exodus 12 with 1 Corinthians 5:7), the high priest, or the tabernacle.

Guard against an overstrained imagination. Anyone blessed with imagination and quickness of typical discernment will find his imagination running away unless he holds it in check.

In studying any passage where types may be suggested, look up all scriptural references in a reliable concordance. Study carefully the meaning of the names of people and places mentioned. Bible names often have a deep and far-reaching suggestiveness. For example, Hebron, which means "joining together," "union," or "fellowship," is deeply significant when taken in connection with its history, as are all the names of the cities of refuge. Was it accidental that Bethlehem, the name of the place where the Bread of Life was born, means "house of bread"?

6

STUDY OF BIBLICAL AND CHRONOLOGICAL ORDER

A fifth method of Bible study is the old-fashioned method of biblical order, beginning at Genesis and going right on through to Revelation. This method has some advantages that no other methods of study possess. Start at the beginning of this library of sixty-six books and read right through. It is important to master the Bible as a whole in order to understand the separate books in it.

There are advantages to studying the Bible in scriptural order. First, it is the only method by which you will get an idea of the Book as a whole. The more you know of the Bible as a whole, the better prepared you will be to understand any individual portion of it. Second, it is the only method by which you are likely to cover the whole Book and so take in the entire scope of God's revelation. This is a time-consuming but rewarding way to study the Bible.

Every part of God's Word is precious. Hidden away in the most unexpected places, such as 1 Chronicles 4:10, you will find priceless gems. It is also the best method to enable one to get hold of the unity of the Bible and its organic character.

The Bible is a many-sided book. It clearly teaches the deity of Christ and insists on His real humanity. It exalts faith and demands works. It urges to victory through conflict and asserts most vigorously that victory is won by faith.

If you become too one-sided with any line of truth, the daily, orderly study of the Bible will soon bring you to some contrasted line of truth and back to proper balance. Some people have become mentally distracted through too much occupation with a single line of truth. Thoughtful study of the whole Bible is a great corrective to this tendency.

It would be good to have three methods of study in progress at the same time: first, the study of a particular book; second, the study of topics (perhaps topics suggested by the book being studied); third, the study of the Bible in a progressive and organized fashion. Every other method of study should be supplemented by studying the Bible in biblical order. Some years ago I determined to read a different version of the Bible and the New Testament in Greek through every year. It proved exceedingly profitable in my own studies.

Studying by Chronological Order

Another method of study closely related to the above method has advantages of its own. It is studying the various portions of the Bible in their chronological order. In this way, the Psalms are read in their historical settings, as are prophecies, epistles, and so on.

7

STUDY FOR PRACTICAL USE IN DEALING WITH PEOPLE

The last method of Bible study is for use in dealing with people. To study the Bible in this way, make as complete a classification as possible of all the different personalities that you find in the world today. Write the names of these various types at the head of separate sheets of paper or cards. Then begin reading the Bible through slowly. When you come to a passage that seems likely to prove useful in dealing with a certain personality type, write it down on the appropriate sheet. Go through the entire Bible in this way. Use special Bible markers in different colored inks or use different letters or symbols to represent the personalities. The best book is the one you organize yourself. My book entitled *How To Bring Men To Christ* may give you some suggestions on how to begin.

The following list of types of people are suggestions to which you can add.

1. The careless and indifferent.

2. Those who wish to be saved but do not know how.

3. Those who know how to be saved but have difficulties. They may be further categorized with statements, such as:

   "I am too great a sinner."

   "My heart is too hard."

   "I must become better before I become a Christian."

   "I am afraid I can't hold out."

   "I am too weak."

   "I have tried before and failed.

   "I cannot give up my evil ways."

   "I will be persecuted if I become a Christian."

   "It will hurt my business."

   "There is too much to give up."

   "The Christian life is too hard."

   "I am afraid of ridicule."

   "I will lose my friends."

   "I have no feeling."

   "I have been seeking Christ but cannot find Him."

   "God won't receive me."

   "I have committed the unpardonable sin."

   "It is too late."

   "Christians are so inconsistent."

"God seems to me unjust and cruel."

"There are so many things in the Bible that I can't understand."

"There is someone I can't forgive."

Perhaps you will meet people who are cherishing false hopes. Their hope lies in being saved by a righteous life or by being saved by "trying to be a good Christian." They may "feel saved" because of a profession of religion or church membership.

Others on your list may include those who wish to put off the decision to be saved, such as Jews, Spiritualists, or Christian Scientists. You may also add to your list: the sorrowing, the persecuted, the discouraged, the despondent, or the worldly Christian.

The results of this work will be of incalculable value. You will get a new view of how perfectly the Bible is adapted to everyone's need. Familiar passages of the Bible will take on new meaning as you see their relationship to people's needs. In seeking food for others, you will get a vast amount of material to use in sermons, in teaching, and in personal work. You will acquire a rare working knowledge of the Bible.

8

FINAL SUGGESTIONS

Some suggestions remain to be given before I close this book. First of all, study the Bible regularly. Regularity counts more in Bible study than most people can imagine. The spasmodic student who sometimes gives a great deal of time to the study of the Word and at other times neglects it for days does not achieve the same results as the one who plods on faithfully day by day. The Bereans were wise as well as *"fair-minded"* in that they *"searched the Scriptures daily"* (Acts 17:11).

A well-known speaker among Christian college students once remarked that he had been at many conventions and had received great blessings from them, but the greatest blessing he had ever received was from a convention where only three people gathered together with him. These four had covenanted together to spend a certain portion of every day in Bible study. Since that day, much of his time had been spent in cars, in hotels, and at conventions, but he had kept that covenant. The greatest blessing that had come to him in his Christian life had come through this daily study of the Word.

Anyone who has tried it realizes how much can be accomplished by setting apart a fixed portion of each day for Bible study. You may study as little as fifteen or thirty minutes, but it is better to have an hour kept sacredly for that purpose under all circumstances.

Many will say, "I cannot spare the time." It will not do to study the Bible only when you feel like it or when you have leisure. You must have fixed habits if you are to study the Bible profitably. Nothing is more important than daily Bible study, and less important things must not take its place. What regularity in eating is to physical life, regularity in Bible study is to spiritual life. Decide upon some time, even if it is no more than fifteen minutes to start with, and hold to it until you are ready to set a longer period.

Select the Correct Time

Don't put off your Bible study until nearly bedtime when your mind is drowsy. It is good to meditate on God's Word as you retire, but this is not the time for study. Bible study demands a clear mind. Don't take the time immediately after a heavy meal when you are mentally and physically sluggish. It is almost the unanimous opinion of those who have given this subject careful attention that the early hours of the day are the best for Bible study, if they can be free from interruption. Wherever possible, lock yourself in and lock the world out to concentrate fully on the Word of God.

Look for Jesus

We read of Jesus that "*beginning at Moses and all the Prophets, He expounded to them in all the Scriptures the things concerning Himself*" (Luke 24:27). Jesus Christ is the subject of the whole Bible, and He pervades the entire Book. Some of the seemingly driest portions become infused with a new life when we learn to see Christ in them. I remember in my early reading what a dull book Leviticus seemed, but it all became different when I learned to see Jesus in the various offerings and sacrifices, in the high priest and his garments, in the tabernacle and its furniture, and indeed everywhere. Look for Christ in every verse you study, and even the genealogies and the names of towns will begin to have beauty and power.

Memorize Scripture

The psalmist said, *"Your word I have hidden in my heart, that I might not sin against You!"* (Psalm 119:11). There is nothing better to keep one from sinning than this. By the Word of God hidden in His heart, Jesus overcame the Tempter. (See Matthew 4:4, 7, 10.)

But the Word of God hidden in the heart is good for other purposes than victory over sin. It is good to meet and expose error. It is good to enable one *"to speak a word in season to him who is weary"* (Isaiah 50:4). It is good for manifold uses, even *"that the man of God may be complete, thoroughly equipped for every good work"* (2 Timothy 3:17).

Memorize Scripture by chapter and verse. It is just as easy as memorizing a few words, and it is immeasurably more useful for practical purposes. Memorize Scripture in systematic form. Do not have a chaotic heap of texts in your mind, but pigeonhole the Scripture you store in memory under appropriate titles. Then you can bring it out when you need it, without racking your brain. Many can stand up without a moment's warning and speak coherently and convincingly on any vital theme because they have a vast fund of wisdom in Scripture texts stored away in their mind in systematic form.

Utilize Spare Moments

Most of us waste too much time. Time spent traveling, waiting for appointments, or waiting for meals can be utilized in Bible study if you will carry a pocket Bible or pocket Testament. You can also utilize the time to meditate on texts already stored away in memory.

Henry Ward Beecher read one of the larger histories of England through while waiting day after day for his meals to be brought to the table. How many books of the Bible could be studied in the same way? A friend once told me about a man who had, in some respect, the most extraordinary knowledge of the Bible of any man he knew. This man was a junk dealer in a Canadian city. He kept a Bible open on his shelves; during intervals of business, he pondered the Book of God. His Bible became black from handling in such surroundings, but I have little doubt his soul became correspondingly white. No economy pays as does the economy of time, but there is no way of economizing time so thriftily as putting wasted moments into the study of or meditation on the Word of God.

HOW TO BRING MEN TO CHRIST

CONTENTS

1

YOU CAN BE A SOULWINNER

Certain requirements must be fulfilled for real success in leading lost souls to Christ. Fortunately these are few and simple, and anyone can meet them.

The one who desires real success in bringing others to Christ must himself be a thoroughly converted person. Jesus said to Peter, *"When thou art converted, strengthen thy brethren"* (Luke 22:32). Peter was in no position to help his brethren until he himself, after his cowardly denial, had turned again to his Lord with his whole heart.

If we desire to bring others to Christ, we must turn away from all sin, worldliness, and selfishness with our whole hearts, yielding to Jesus the absolute lordship over our thoughts, purposes, and actions. If we are seeking to have our own way and not letting Him have His way in our lives, our power will be crippled, and souls that might have been saved may be lost. This principle can be applied to the numerous questions that every young Christian asks as to whether he should do this or that. Each individual can find answers for himself if Christ's honor and not his own pleasure is uppermost in his mind.

Loving Others into the Kingdom

The one who desires real success in bringing others to Christ must truly love others and long for their salvation. If we have no love for other souls, our efforts will be mechanical and powerless. We may know how to approach men and what to say to them, but there will be no power in what we say. It will not touch the heart. But if like Paul we have *"great heaviness"* and unceasing pain in our hearts for the unsaved (see Romans 9:2), there will be an earnestness in our tone and manner that will impress even the most disinterested. Furthermore, if we have a love for souls, we will be watching constantly for opportunities to speak with the unsaved. We will find opportunities on the street, in the store, in the home, on buses and streetcars, and everywhere that would otherwise have entirely escaped our notice.

But how does one acquire a love for souls? Like every other grace of Christian character, a love for souls is the work of the Holy Spirit. If we are conscious that we do not have the love for souls that we should have, the first thing to do is to go to God and humbly confess this lack in our lives. We can ask Him by His Holy Spirit to supply what we need and expect Him to do it. (See 1 John 5:14–15; Philippians 4:19.) Jesus Christ had an intense love for souls. (See Matthew 23:37; Luke 19:10.) Intimate and constant companionship with Him will impart to our lives this grace that was so prominent in Him.

Feelings are the outcome of thoughts. If we desire any given feeling to develop in our lives, we should dwell on thoughts that produce that feeling.

If any saved person will concentrate long enough on the peril and misery of any man separated from Christ, he will realize the worth of his soul in God's sight because of the death of God's Son to save him. An intense desire for that man's salvation is almost certain to follow. Reflection on our own ruined, unhappy condition without Christ and on the great sacrifice He made to save us is sure to fill our hearts with a desire to bring others to the Savior we have found.

Using the Word and Prayer

The one who desires to have real success in bringing men and women to Christ must have a working knowledge of the Bible. The Word of God is *"the sword of the Spirit"* (Ephesians 6:17) that God uses to convict of sin, to reveal Christ, and to regenerate men. If we wish to work together with God, the Bible is the instrument we must rely on and use in bringing people to Christ. We must know how to use the Bible to show people their need of a Savior, to show them Jesus as the Savior they need, to show them how to make this Savior their own Savior, and to show them how to meet the difficulties that stand in the way of their accepting Christ. A large part of the following pages will be devoted to imparting this knowledge.

The one who desires to have real success in bringing people to Christ must pray frequently. Solid work in soulwinning must be accompanied by prayer at every step. We must first ask God to lead us to the right people to approach. God does not intend that we speak to everyone we meet. If we try to do this, we will waste much valuable time speaking to those whom we cannot help—time we might have used speaking to those for whom we could have done much good. God alone knows the one to whom He intends us to speak. We must ask Him to point him or her out to us and expect Him to do it. (See Acts 8:27–29.)

We must ask God to show us what to say to those to whom He leads us. We will need God's guidance to know which Bible passage to use in each case. Every experienced worker will testify to the many instances in which God has led him to use some text of Scripture that he would not otherwise have used but which proved to be just the one needed.

We must also ask God to give power to what He has given us to say. We not only need a message from God but power from God to send the message home. Most workers have to learn this lesson by experience. They sit down beside an unsaved man, reasoning, pleading, and citing texts from the Word of God, but the man does not accept Christ. At last it dawns on them that they are trying to convert the man in their own strength. When they lift an earnest and humble prayer to God for His strength, God hears. In a short time this "very difficult case" is rejoicing in Christ.

We must then ask God to carry on the work after our part of it has come to an end. After having done our whole duty in any given instance—whatever may have been our apparent successful or unsuccessful work—we should definitely commit the case to God in prayer. If there is anything the average worker in this hurrying age needs to have impressed on him, it is the necessity of more prayer. By praying more, we will not work any less, but we will accomplish much more.

The one who would have real success in bringing people to Christ must be *"baptized with the Holy Ghost"* (Acts 1:5). *"Ye shall receive power, after that the Holy Ghost is come upon you"* (verse 8). Jesus said this to His disciples after giving them the Great Commission to go out and bring men to Himself. The supreme condition of soulwinning power is the same today: *"After that the Holy Ghost is come upon you."* A later chapter will be devoted to a study of the baptism in the Holy Spirit and how any Christian can obtain it.

2

TAKING THE FIRST STEP

When God leads us to believe that He wants us to make an effort to lead someone to Christ, the first question that confronts us is, "How will I begin?" Regardless of who the person is, it is comparatively easy. Ask him whether he is a Christian, or ask some other direct and simple question that will inevitably lead to a conversation along this line. Even if the person is a total stranger, it is not difficult. The person can be engaged in conversation on some general topic or on something suggested by passing events and soon be brought around to the great subject of spiritual things. Christ's conversation with the woman of Samaria in the fourth chapter of John is an excellent illustration of this.

Many times, even with strangers, it is best to bring up the subject at once. Ask them if they are Christians, if they are saved, or some similar question. If this is done courteously and earnestly, it will frequently make even disinterested people start thinking, and it may result in their conversion. It is astonishing how often one who undertakes this work in humble dependence upon God and under His direction finds the way prepared, and how seldom he receives any rebuff.

One day I met a man on one of the most crowded streets of Chicago. As I passed him, the impulse came to speak to him about the Savior. Stopping a moment and asking God to show me if the impulse was from Him, I turned around and followed the man. I overtook him in the middle of the street, laid my hand on his shoulder, and said, "My friend, are you a Christian?"

He was startled and said, "That's a strange question to ask a man."

I said, "I know it, and I do not ask that question of every stranger; but God put it into my heart to ask it of you."

He then told me that his cousin was a minister and had been urging this very matter upon him. He said he was a prosperous businessman but had been drinking excessively. After further conversation we separated, but later I discovered the man had accepted Christ as his Savior.

It is often best to win a person's confidence and friendship before bringing up the subject. It is good to select someone first and then plan to win him to Christ. Cultivate his acquaintance, be kind to him, and when the right moment arrives, ask him the great question. An old man in Chicago was won to Christ in this way by a young woman who found him sick and alone. She called day after day and showed him many kindnesses. After a time, she spoke to him of the Savior and had the joy of seeing him accept Christ.

A wisely chosen tract placed in the hand of the one with whom you wish to speak will often lead easily and naturally to the subject. One day I was riding on a train and praying that God would use me to lead someone to His Son. A young daughter of a minister with whom I had had some conversation on this subject came in with a friend and took the seat in front of me. I took out a little bundle of tracts, selected one that seemed appropriate, handed it to her, and asked her to read it. As she read, I prayed. When she had finished, I leaned over and asked her what she thought about it. She was deeply moved, and I asked her if she would accept Christ right there, which she did. As she left the train, she thanked me heartily for what I had done for her.

You will often meet someone whose face tells the story of unhappiness or discontent. In such a case, it is easy to ask the person if he is happy. If he answers, "No," you can say, "I can tell you about Someone who will make you happy if you will only receive Him." Skill in beginning a conversation will come with practice. You may be rather awkward about it at first, but it will become easier.

Introducing Someone to Jesus

Once the subject is opened, the first thing to find out is where the person stands. Then you will know how to treat his case wisely. The following chapters describe different types of individuals you are likely to meet. To ascertain these "types," simply ask questions such as: "Are you a Christian?" "Are you saved?" "Do you know that your sins are forgiven?" "Do you have eternal life?" "Are you confessing Christ openly before the world?" "Are you a friend of Jesus?" "Have you been born again?"

These questions can be answered untruthfully either through ignorance or a desire to mislead you. You can, nevertheless, still learn a great deal from how the question is answered. A man's face will often reveal what his words try to conceal. In many instances, anyone who studies faces will soon be able to tell people's exact states, regardless of anything they may say.

Above all, be open to the leading of the Holy Spirit. If we only look to Him to do it, the Holy Spirit will often reveal the man's position and the exact Scripture he needs.

When we have learned where the person stands, the next thing to do is to lead him to accept Jesus Christ as his personal Savior and Master. We must always bear in mind that the primary purpose of our work is not to get people to join a church, to give up their bad habits, or to do anything other than to accept Jesus Christ as their Savior. He is the One who bore their sins in His own body on the tree, and through Him they can have immediate and entire forgiveness. He is to become their Master to whom they surrender absolutely the guidance of their thoughts, feelings, purposes, and actions.

After leading anyone to accept Christ, the next step will be to show him from God's Word that he has forgiveness of sin and eternal life. Acts 10:43, Acts 13:39, John 3:36, and John 5:24 give proof of this. Next, show him how to make a success of the Christian life that he has entered. How to do this will be explained later.

Each person is to be led to accept Christ through use of the Word of God. In the chapters that immediately follow, we will try to show what specific portions of the Word to use in certain cases and how to use them.

3

DEALING WITH THE INDIFFERENT

We make frequent contact with indifferent or careless people. There are several ways of dealing with them. One is to show them their need of a Savior. A good verse to use for this purpose is Romans 3:23. Get the person to read the verse, *"For all have sinned, and come short of the glory of God."* Ask him, "Who has sinned?" Then ask him what it is that he has done and pursue it until he plainly says, "I have sinned and come short of the glory of God." This is likely to make him realize his need of a Savior.

Another good verse to use is Isaiah 53:6: *"All we like sheep have gone astray; we have turned every one to his own way; and the* Lord *hath laid on him the iniquity of us all."* After the verse has been read, ask him who has gone astray. By a series of questions, bring him to the point where he will say, "I have gone astray." Then ask him what kind of a sheep one is that has gone astray, and hold him to it until he says, "A lost sheep." "What are you, then?" should be your next question. His only answer can be, "Lost." Ask him what the Lord has done with his sin, and help him to see the truth of the verse—God has laid his sin on Jesus Christ. Now he is in a position for you to ask him the direct question, "Will you accept this Savior upon whom the Lord has laid your sin?"

Recognize the Problem

In dealing with the indifferent, I use Matthew 22:37–38: *"Jesus said unto him, Thou shalt love the Lord thy God with all thy heart, and with all thy soul, and with all thy mind. This is the first and great commandment."* Before having the person read the verse, it is good to ask him, "Do you know that you have committed the greatest sin that a man can commit?" In all probability, he will answer, "No, I have not." Then ask him what he thinks the greatest sin a man can commit is. When he has answered, say to him, "Now let us see what God considers the greatest sin." Read the verses and ask him, "What is the first and greatest of the commandments?" Then ask him, "What, then, is the greatest sin?" He will soon answer that the violation of the first and greatest of the commandments must be the greatest sin. Ask him if he has kept the commandment. When he confesses—as sooner or later he must—that he has not, ask him of what he is guilty in the sight of God. Hold him to that point until he admits that he is guilty of committing the greatest sin that a man can commit.

I was once dealing with a very bright young man who evidently had no deep sense of sin or of his need of a Savior. When I asked if he was a Christian, he said promptly that he always had been. But there was something in his manner that showed he had no clear understanding of what it meant to be a Christian. I asked if he had been born again, and he did not even understand what I was talking about. I then asked if he knew that he had committed the greatest sin a man could possibly commit.

He at once answered, "No, I never did in my life." I asked what he considered to be the greatest sin. He replied, "Murder."

Opening my Bible to Matthew 22:37–38, I asked him to read the verses. I then asked him, "If this is the first and greatest commandment, what is the greatest sin?"

He answered, "I suppose the breaking of that commandment."

I then asked if he had always kept that commandment, if he had always loved God with all his heart, with all his soul, and with all his mind, and if he had always put God first in everything. He replied that he had not.

I then asked him, "Of what, then, are you guilty?"

The Spirit of God convicted him, and with great earnestness, he replied, "I have committed the greatest sin that a man can commit, but I never saw it before in my life."

Personalize the Message

Another verse that can be used with effect is John 8:34. After the person has read the verse, *"Whosoever committeth sin is the servant of sin,"* ask him, "What is one who commits sin?" Then ask him if he commits sin. Ask him the direct question, "What are you, then?" Hold him to it until he says, "The servant of sin." Ask him if he desires to be delivered from that awful bondage. Hold him to this point until he sees his need of Jesus Christ as a Deliverer from the slavery of sin.

The Holy Spirit has used Isaiah 57:21 for the salvation of many people who have been indifferent to the claims of the Gospel. After the verse, *"There is no peace, saith my God, to the wicked,"* has been read slowly, thoughtfully, and earnestly, ask the person, "Do you have peace?"

One night a rebellious young man was going out of one of our tent meetings in Chicago. As he passed by me, I took him by the hand and said to him, "You need the Savior." He wanted to know why I thought so. I replied, "Because you have no peace. "

He said, "Yes, I have."

"No, you have not," I replied with conviction. He asked me how I knew that. I told him God said so, and I quoted the above passage. He tried to laugh it off and say the verse was not true in his case. Then he became angry and went out of the tent in a rage. But the next night, I saw him kneeling with one of our workers in prayer.

When he arose from his knees, the worker came over and said that the man wished to speak with me. As I approached him, he held out his hand and said, "I want to beg your pardon for what I said last night. What you said was true. I did not have peace." I asked him if he had now accepted the Savior. He said he had.

Point to the Penalties

Galatians 3:10 is a verse we frequently use in our work in dealing with indifference. Allow the one with whom you are speaking to read the verse,

> *For as many as are of the works of the law are under the curse: for it is written, Cursed is every one that continueth not in all things which are written in the book of the law to do them.*

Then ask him the question, "What is everyone who does not keep the law?"

When he answers, "Cursed," ask him if he has continued "*in all things which are written in the book of the law to do them.*" When he replies, "No, I have not," ask him the direct question, "What are you, then?" Hold him to that point until he says, "I am under the curse." In many cases, he will be ready at once to be led to the thirteenth verse of the same chapter, which shows how he may be saved from that curse.

Romans 6:23 can often be used with good effect. "*For the wages of sin is death.*" Ask, "What are the wages of sin?" Then, "Who earns those wages?"

Then, "Are you a sinner? What wages have you earned? Do you wish to take your wages?"

John 3:36 is a verse that can be used in a similar way. *"He that believeth on the Son hath everlasting life: and he that believeth not the Son shall not see life; but the wrath of God abideth on him."* Ask the question, "Upon whom is it that the wrath of God abides?" Then, "Do you believe on the Son? What, then, abides upon you?" Finally ask the decisive question, "Are you willing to go away with the wrath of God abiding upon you?"

Second Thessalonians 1:7–9, John 8:24, and Revelation 14:10–11; 20:15; and 21:8 set forth in a most impressive way the awful consequences of sin. If these verses are used, they should be read with deep earnestness to reveal the severity of their truth.

His Suffering—Our Salvation

Another way to rouse a person from his indifference is to show him what Jesus has done for him. I have found Isaiah 53:5–6 more effective for this purpose than any other passage in the Bible.

A lady had asked for prayer for her daughter, a young woman of about twenty years of age. At the close of the service, I stepped up to the daughter and asked her if she would accept Jesus Christ as her Savior at once.

She stamped her foot in anger and said, "My mother should have known better than to do that. She knows it will only make me worse."

I asked her if she would sit down for a few minutes. As soon as we were seated, I opened my Bible to this passage and began to read,

> *But he was wounded for our transgressions, he was bruised for our iniquities: the chastisement of our peace was upon him; and with his stripes we are healed. All we like sheep have gone astray; we have turned every one to his own way; and the LORD hath laid on him the iniquity of us all.* (Isaiah 53:5–6)

I made no comment on the verses whatever, but the Spirit of God touched the young woman's heart, and tears began to roll down her cheeks. She became a Christian that same day.

It is a good idea in using these verses to get the inquirer to change the pronoun from the plural to the singular wherever possible. "He was wounded for my transgressions; He was bruised for my iniquities," and so forth.

John 3:16 can be used in a similar way. I was talking one night to someone who was apparently indifferent and hardened. She told me the story of her sin with seemingly little sense of shame. When I urged her to accept Christ, she simply refused. I put a Bible in her hands and asked her to read this verse. She began to read, "*God so loved the world, that he gave his only begotten Son....*" Before she had finished reading the verse, she broke into tears, softened by the thought of God's wondrous love for her.

First Peter 2:24 is a verse of similar character. "*Who his own self bare our sins in his own body on the tree, that we, being dead to sins, should live unto righteousness: by whose stripes ye were healed.*" Ask the inquirer whose sins Jesus bore in His own body on the tree, pursuing it until he says, "My sins." First Peter 1:18–19, Luke 22:44, and Matthew 27:46 are useful to bring out in detail what Christ has suffered for us.

Still another way to challenge indifferent people is to show them that they are guilty of this one sin: the sin of rejecting Jesus Christ. Hebrews 10:28–29 is very effective for this purpose.

> *He that despised Moses' law died without mercy under two or three witnesses: of how much sorer punishment, suppose ye, shall he be thought worthy, who hath trodden under foot the Son of God, and hath counted the blood of the covenant, wherewith he was sanctified, an unholy thing, and hath done despite unto the Spirit of grace?*

John 3:18–20, John 16:8–9, and Acts 2:36 can also be used.

Many times you will meet someone who is not willing to sit down and let you deal with him in this way. In that case, the only thing to do is to look to God for guidance and power and read him verses such as Hebrews 10:28–29, Romans 6:23, John 3:36, or Isaiah 57:21. Pray for the Spirit of God to carry the truth home to his heart. A passing comment of this kind has often resulted in the salvation of a soul. The passages given above can be wisely used with one who is not completely indifferent or careless but who does not have a sufficiently deep sense of sin or a desire to accept the Gospel.

4

DEALING WITH THE OPENHEARTED

Many people are ready to be saved but simply do not know how. It is not difficult to lead these people to Christ. Perhaps no other passage in the Bible is used for this purpose more than Isaiah 53:6. It makes the way of salvation very plain. Read the first part of the verse to the inquirer, "*All we like sheep have gone astray; we have turned every one to his own way.*" Then ask, "Is this true of you?" When he has thought it over and said, "Yes," then say to him, "Now let us see what God has done with your sins." Read the remainder of the verse, "*And the LORD hath laid on him the iniquity of us all.*" Ask him, "What, then, is necessary for you to do to be saved?" He can be led to see that all that is necessary for him to do is to accept the Sin-Bearer whom God has provided.

Some years ago, I noticed a white-haired man in a meeting who did not stand up to acknowledge that he was a Christian. At the close of the service, I walked over to him and said, "Are you a Christian?" He said he was not. I was sure he was interested, so I asked him the direct question, "Would you become a Christian tonight if I would show you the way?" He replied that he would.

I opened my Bible to Isaiah 53:6 and read the first part of the verse, *"All we like sheep have gone astray; we have turned every one to his own way."*

I then said to him, "Is that true of you?" and he answered, "Yes."

"Now," I said, "let us read the rest of the verse, *'And the LORD hath laid on him the iniquity of us all.'* What has the Lord done with your sins?"

He thought a moment and said, "He has laid them on Christ."

"What, then," I said, "is all that you have to do to be saved?"

He replied promptly, "Accept Him."

"Well," I said, "will you accept Him tonight?"

He said, "I will."

"Let us kneel down and tell God so." We knelt down, and I led in prayer. He followed in a simple way, telling God that he was a sinner, but that he believed that God had laid his sins on Jesus Christ.

He then asked God for Christ's sake to forgive his sins.

When he had finished, I asked him if he thought God had heard his prayer and that his sins were forgiven. He said, "Yes." I then asked him if he would begin to lead a Christian life at once, set up the family altar, and openly confess Christ before the world. He replied that he would. Some months later, I met his pastor and found that he had gone to his home in a distant city, set up the family altar, and united with the church. Apparently, all that this man was waiting for was for someone to make the way of salvation plain to him.

Knowing and Doing

Two things must be known, and one thing must be done, for a person to be saved. What he needs to know is, first, that he is a lost sinner and, second, that Christ is an all-sufficient Savior. What he needs to do is simply to accept this all-sufficient Savior whom God has provided. John 1:12 brings out this thought very clearly: *"As many as received him, to them gave he power to become the sons of God, even to them that believe on his name."* After the verse has been read, you can ask the one with whom you are dealing, "To whom is it that God gives the power to become the sons of God?"

"As many as receive Him."

"What must you then do to become a son of God?"

"Receive Him."

"Well, will you receive Him as your Savior and Master now?"

Isaiah 55:7, Acts 16:31, John 3:16; 36 are all useful in making the way of salvation plain. John 3:16 compared with Numbers 21:8–9 can often be used with good effect. When these verses are used, you should lead the inquirer to see what the serpent-bitten Israelite had to do to be saved—he simply had to look at the bronze serpent lifted up on the pole. Show him that the sin-bitten man simply has to do the same thing—look at Christ lifted up on the cross for his sins.

Romans 1:16 is another excellent verse to use. It makes the way of salvation very clear. You can ask the inquirer whom it is, according to this verse, that the Gospel saves. He will see that it is *"every one that believeth."* Then ask him, "What, then, is all that is necessary for one to do in order to be saved?" He will see that it is simply to believe. Ask him, "Believe what?" The answer is the Gospel.

What Is the Gospel?

This question is answered by 1 Corinthians 15:3–4. These verses show *"that Christ died for our sins according to the scriptures; and that he was buried, and that he rose again the third day according to the scriptures.*" This is what the inquirer must believe in order to be saved. He must believe from his heart that Christ died for his sins and that He rose again. Ask the inquirer, "Do you believe that Christ died for your sins? Do you believe that He rose again?" If he says that he does, ask him if he will ask God by faith to forgive his sins for Christ's sake. He must believe it is done because God says so, and He must trust in the living Savior to save him day by day from the power of sin. Romans 10:9–10 also makes the way of salvation clear to many minds where other verses fail.

Romans 10:13 makes it, if possible, simpler still. This shows that all a man has to do to be saved is to "*call upon the name of the Lord.*" You can ask the inquirer, "Are you ready now to call upon the name of the Lord for salvation and believe that God saves you because He says He will?"

The way of salvation can also be made plain by the use of Exodus 12:7, 13, 23. These verses show that it was the blood that made the Israelites safe. It is just the same today—the blood makes us safe. When God sees the blood, He passes over us. The only thing for us to do is to get under the blood. Show the inquirer that the way to be under the blood is by simple faith in Jesus Christ.

A Cry for Mercy

Luke 18:10–14 is useful in showing what a person may have and yet be lost (the Pharisee) and what a person may lack and yet be saved (the publican). Man simply must do as the publican did, that is, take the sinner's place and cry to God for mercy. Then he will go down to his house justified.

This passage can be used in the following manner to make the meaning clearer. Ask the inquirer, "Which one of these two (the Pharisee or the publican) went down to his house justified?" Ask him, "What did the publican do that the Pharisee did not do that brought him the forgiveness of his sins while the Pharisee went out of the temple unforgiven?"

When he studies the passage, he will soon see that the publican simply took the sinner's place before God and cried for mercy. As soon as he did this, he was "justified" or forgiven. Then you can ask him, "What must you do to find forgiveness? Will you do it here and now?" When he has done so, ask him if he believes God's Word and is now justified.

Saving faith is beautifully illustrated by Luke 7:48–50. The fiftieth verse tells us that this woman had saving faith. Now ask the inquirer, "What was the faith she had?" Show him that her faith was simply faith that Jesus could and would forgive her sins if she came to Him to do it. This is saving faith.

Galatians 3:10–13 also makes the way of salvation very simple. The tenth verse shows the sinner's position before accepting Christ: *"under the curse."* The thirteenth verse shows what Christ has done: He has been *"made a curse for us."* What the sinner has to do is simply accept Christ.

5

DEALING WITH DIFFICULTIES

Many are anxious to be saved, and they know how to be saved, but they are confronted with difficulties that they think are insurmountable. One of the difficulties is, "I am too great a sinner." First Timothy 1:15 answers this objection fully.

One Sunday morning, a man who had led a reckless life and had lost $35,000 came to talk with me after church. He had been separated from his wife. I asked him why he was not a Christian.

"I am too great a sinner to be saved," he replied.

I turned at once to 1 Timothy 1:15: "*This is a faithful saying, and worthy of all acceptation, that Christ Jesus came into the world to save sinners; of whom I am chief.*"

He quickly replied, "Well, I am the chief of sinners."

"Well," I said, "that verse means you, then."

He replied, "It is a precious promise."

I said, "Will you accept it now?"

"I will."

We knelt down, and he confessed his sins to God and asked God for Christ's sake to forgive him. I asked him if he had really accepted Christ, and he said he had. I asked him if he really believed that he was saved, and he said he did. He took an early opportunity to confess Christ. He left the city in a short time, but I kept in touch with him. A most active Christian, he worked at his business during the day but engaged in some form of Christian work every night of the week. He was reunited with his wife, adopted a child, and had a happy Christian home.

Luke 19:10 is also a useful passage when a person says, "I am lost." You can say, "I have a passage intended especially for you. If you really mean what you say, you are just the person Jesus is seeking. '*For the Son of man is come to seek and to save that which was lost.*'"

Romans 5:6–8 is an effective passage. I stopped a man one night as he was hurrying out of a meeting. Laying my hand on his shoulder, I said, "Did you not hold your hand up tonight for prayer?"

He said, "Yes."

I said, "Why, then, are you hurrying away? Do you know God loves you?"

He replied, "You do not know who you are talking to."

"I do not care who I am talking to, but I know God loves you."

He said, "I am the meanest thief in Minneapolis."

I said, "If you are the meanest thief in Minneapolis, then I know God loves you." I opened my Bible to Romans 5:8 and read, "*But God commendeth his love toward us, in that, while we were yet sinners, Christ died for us.*"

"Now," I said, "if you are the meanest thief in Minneapolis, you are a sinner, and this verse says that God loves sinners."

The man began to weep. Going into another room with me, he told me his story. He was just out of prison and had started out that night to commit one of the most daring burglaries ever in the city of Minneapolis. With his two companions in crime, he was passing a corner where he happened to hear an open-air meeting going on and stopped for a few minutes to listen. In spite of the protests and curses of his companions, he stayed through the meeting and went with us to the church.

After he told me his story, we knelt in prayer. Through tears, he cried to God for mercy, having been led by God's precious promise to believe that God loved a sinner even as vile as he.

Other useful passages are: Matthew 9:12–13, Romans 10:13 (emphasize "*whosoever*"), John 3:16 (emphasize "*whosoever*"), Isaiah 1:18, 1 John 4:14, Isaiah 44:22, and Isaiah 43:25. Isaiah 1:18 and Psalm 51:14 are especially useful in dealing with men who have committed murder. Never tell anyone that his sins are not great. It is better to say, "Yes, your sins are great, greater than you think, but they have all been settled." Then show him Isaiah 53:6 and 1 Peter 2:24.

A woman once came to me who was very upset. After many ineffectual attempts, she was at last able to unburden her heart. Fourteen years earlier, she had killed a man and had borne the memory of the act upon her conscience until it had almost driven her crazy. When she told the story to another Christian and myself, we turned to Isaiah 53:6.

After reading the verse carefully to her, I asked her what the Lord had done with her sin. After a few moments of deep and anxious thought, she said, "He has laid it on Christ."

I took a book in my hand. "Now," I said, "let my right hand represent you, and my left hand Christ, and this book your sin." I laid the book upon my right hand, and I said, "Where is your sin now?"

She said, "On me."

"Now," I said, "what has God done with it?"

She said, "Laid it on Christ."

I laid the book over on the other hand. "Where is your sin now?" I asked.

It was a long time before she could summon courage to answer; and then with a desperate effort, she said, "On Christ."

I asked, "Then, is it on you any longer?"

Slowly the light came into her face, and she burst out with a cry, "No, it is on Him! It is on Christ."

John 1:29, Acts 10:43, and Hebrews 7:25 are also helpful in similar cases.

Facing Failure and Weakness

Another difficulty we frequently meet with is "I am afraid of failure." First Peter 1:5 is useful in showing that we are not to keep ourselves in the faith but are *"kept by the power of God."* John 10:28–29 shows that the safety of the one who accepts Christ does not depend on his "holding out" but on the keeping power of the Father and the Son.

Second Timothy 1:12 shows that it is Christ's business and not ours to keep that which is entrusted to Him, and that He is able to do it. Isaiah 41:10, 13 is also helpful. Jude 24 shows that Christ is able to keep us from falling. Second Chronicles 32:7–8 and Romans 14:4, 8 are also good texts to use. First Corinthians 10:13 is especially useful when one is afraid that some great temptation will overtake him and he will fall.

"I am too weak" is a similar difficulty. With such a person, use 2 Corinthians 12:9–10. Ask him, "Where is it that Christ's strength is made perfect?" When he answers, "In weakness," tell him, "Then, the weaker you are in your own strength, the better." Philippians 4:13 shows that however weak we may be, we can do all things through Christ who strengthens us. First Corinthians 10:13 will show that God knows all about our weakness and will not permit us to be tempted above our strength.

Others say, "I cannot give up my evil ways or bad habits." Galatians 6:7–8 will show them that they must give them up or perish, because we reap what we sow. Philippians 4:13 will show that they can give up their sin in Christ's strength. Point the one who fears that he cannot give up his bad habits to Christ as a risen Savior in 1 Corinthians 15:3–4.

A man once came to me and said, "I come to you to know if there is any way I can get power to overcome my evil habits." He told me his story. He had been converted in childhood, but he had come to Chicago, fallen in with evil companions, and now could not break away from his sins.

I said to him, "You know only half of the Gospel—the Gospel of a crucified Savior. Through trusting in the crucified Savior, you found forgiveness. But Jesus Christ is also a risen Savior. Matthew 28:18 says, '*All power is given unto* [Him].' Read First Corinthians 15:4. He has power to give you victory over your evil habits. Do you believe that?"

He said, "Yes."

"You trusted," I continued, "in the crucified Christ and found forgiveness, did you not?"

"Yes," he replied.

"Now," I said, "will you trust the risen Christ to save you from the power of your sins?"

"Yes, I will."

"Let us kneel down then and tell Him so." We knelt and talked it all over with the Savior. When he stood up, his countenance was changed.

"I am so glad I came," he said. Some time later I received a letter from him telling me how he found constant victory through trusting in the risen Christ.

What Will Others Say?

"I will be persecuted if I become a Christian," people will say. Never tell anyone that he will not be persecuted, but show him from such passages as 2 Timothy 2:12 and 2 Timothy 3:12, Matthew 5:10–12, Mark 8:35, and Acts 14:22 that persecution is the only path to glory. Show him from Romans 8:18 that *"the sufferings of this present time are not worthy to be compared with the glory which shall be revealed in us."* Show him from Acts 5:41 and 1 Peter 2:20–21 that it is a privilege to be persecuted for Christ's sake. Hebrews 12:2–3 is useful in showing him where to look for victory in persecution.

Others will say, "It will hurt my business" or, "I cannot be a Christian in my present job." Point such a person to Mark 8:36. This will show him that it is better to lose his business than to lose his soul. After this thought has been sufficiently impressed upon his mind, show him Matthew 6:32–33. It contains God's promise that, if we put God and His kingdom first, He will provide for all our real and temporal needs. Matthew 16:24–27, Luke 12:16–21, and Luke 16:19–26 are also very effective passages to use here.

Some people will say, "I am afraid of my ungodly companions" or, "I will lose my friends if I accept Christ." Proverbs 29:25 will show them the consequences of yielding to the fear of man and the security of the one who trusts in the Lord. Proverbs 13:20 will show them the results of holding on to their companions, and Psalm 1:1 will show the blessedness of giving up evil companions. First John 1:3–4 shows how much better companionship one gets than loses by coming to Christ.

"I have too much to give up." Mark 8:36 will show people that they had better give up everything rather than lose their souls. Philippians 3:7–8 and Psalm 16:11 will show them that what they give up is nothing compared with what they get. Psalm 84:11 and Romans 8:32 will show them that God will not ask them to give up any good thing. In other words, the only things God asks them to give up are the things that are hurting them.

A young woman once refused to come to the Savior, saying, "There is too much to give up."

"Do you think God loves you?" I asked.

"Certainly," she replied.

"How much do you think He loves you?"

She thought for a moment and answered, "Enough to give His Son to die for me."

"Do you think, if God loved you enough to give His Son to die for you, that He will ask you to give up anything that is good for you?"

"No."

"Do you wish to keep anything that is not good for you?"

"No.

"Then, you had better come to Christ at once."

She did.

First John 2:17 and Luke 12:16–21 will show people how worthless the things that they are trying to keep really are.

"The Christian life is too hard." Say to the inquirer, "Let me show you from God's Word that you are mistaken about the Christian life being hard." Turn to Matthew 11:30, Proverbs 3:17, Psalm 16:11, and 1 John 5:3 to show him that a Christian life is not hard but exceedingly pleasant. Then turn to Proverbs 13:15 and show him that it is the sinner's life that is hard.

Relying upon Feelings

Some will say, "I don't feel anything." Ask the inquirer what kind of feeling he thinks he must have before he comes to Christ. If it is the peace of which Christians speak, show him from Galatians 5:22–23, Ephesians 1:13, 1 Peter 1:8, and Matthew 10:32 that this feeling is the result of accepting Christ and confessing Him. He cannot expect the feeling until he accepts and confesses Christ.

If the feeling he thinks he must have is the feeling that he is a sinner, show him by Isaiah 55:7 that it is not the feeling that we are sinners that God demands but a turning away from sin. Or, from Acts 16:31 and John 1:12, show him that God does not ask us to feel that we are sinners but to confess that we are sinners and trust in Christ as Savior. Isaiah 55:1 and Revelation 22:17 will show the inquirer that all the feeling he needs is a desire for salvation. Passages recommended for use with indifferent inquirers could be used here if you are talking with someone who does not believe he is a sinner.

"I am seeking Christ but cannot find Him." Jeremiah 29:13 shows that when we seek Him with our whole heart, we will find Him. One evening after a meeting, a woman said to me, "I have been seeking Christ for two years and cannot find Him."

I replied, "I can tell you when you will find Him." She looked at me in surprise, and I turned to Jeremiah 29:13 and read, *"And ye shall seek me, and find me, when ye shall search for me with all your heart."* I said, "This shows you when you will find Christ. You will find Him when you search for Him with all your heart. Have you done that?"

After a little thought, she answered, "No."

"Well, then," I said, "let us kneel down right now."

She did so, and in a few moments, she was rejoicing in Christ.

You can point one who has this difficulty to Luke 15:1–10 and Luke 19:10. These passages show that Jesus is seeking the sinner, and you can say, "If you are really seeking Christ, it will not take a seeking Savior and a seeking sinner very long to find each other."

Excuses, Excuses

"I cannot believe." In most cases where one says this, the real difficulty lies in his unwillingness to forsake sin. John 5:44 and Isaiah 55:7 are good passages to use. When using the latter passage, hold the person's attention to the fact that all God asks of him is that he turn away from sin and turn to Him.

"My heart is too hard." Ezekiel 36:26–27 says that although people's hearts are as hard as stone, it will make no difference because God will give them a new heart.

"God will not receive me" or, "I am afraid I have committed the unpardonable sin." The people who honestly say this are, as a rule, about the most difficult to deal with of any that you will meet. John 6:37 is the great text to use with them, for it shows that Jesus will receive anyone who will come to Him. Hold the person continually to this point: "*Him that cometh to me I will in no wise cast out.*" If he keeps saying, "He will not receive me," repeat the text, looking to the Spirit of God to make the truth real to him. Many utterly despondent souls have found light and peace through this verse in God's Word.

Revelation 22:17 is also useful because it shows that anyone who desires it can have the water of life freely. Isaiah 55:1 shows that anyone who desires salvation can have it. Isaiah 1:18 shows that no matter how great a man's sins are, they can still be forgiven. Acts 10:43 and John 3:16 say that "*whosoever*" will believe upon Christ will find pardon and eternal life. Romans 10:13 shows that anyone, no matter who or what he is, who will "*call upon the name of the Lord shall be saved.*"

It is sometimes helpful to turn to Hebrews 6:4–6 and Matthew 12:31–32 to show the inquirer just what the unpardonable sin is and what its results are. Matthew 12:31–32 says that the unpardonable sin is blasphemy against the Holy Spirit. Ask him squarely, "Have you ever blasphemed against the Holy Spirit?" Hebrews 6:4–6 shows that the difficulty is not in God's unwillingness to forgive, but in man's unwillingness to repent. Anyone who is concerned about his salvation evidently has not committed the unpardonable sin nor sinned away his day of grace. A little instruction along this line is often all that is needed.

"It is too late." When an inquirer says this, use 2 Corinthians 6:2 and tell him that God says the time is right. Luke 23:39–43 is useful in showing that, even at the last hour, Jesus will listen to the sinner's cry. Second Peter 3:9 will show that His will is that none should perish, and that He is delaying the judgment to save as many as will come. Deuteronomy 4:30–31 is an especially helpful passage, as it promises, "*Even in the latter days,*" if you turn to the Lord, He will be merciful.

Isaiah 1:18 and Revelation 22:17 can also be used here.

6

DEALING WITH THE SELF-RIGHTEOUS

Among those who entertain false hopes, perhaps the largest class are those who expect to be saved by their righteous lives. These persons are easily recognized by such sayings as these: "I am doing the best I can," "I do more good than evil," "I am not a great sinner," or "I have never done anything very bad." Galatians 3:10 is an excellent passage to use here, for it shows that all those who are trusting in their works are under the curse of the law. No hope is available on the ground of the law for anyone who does not continue *"in all things which are written in the book of the law to do them"* (verse 10). James 2:10 is also useful. Galatians 2:16 and

Romans 3:19–20 are very effective by showing that *"by the deeds of the law there shall no flesh be justified in* [God's] *sight"* (Romans 3:20).

All these passages show the kind of righteousness God demands. No man's righteousness comes up to God's standard. If a person wishes to be saved, he must find some other means of salvation than by his own deeds. It is sometimes wise to use these passages to say to the inquirer, "You do not understand the kind of righteousness that God demands, or you would not talk as you do. Now, let us turn to His Word and see what kind of righteousness God demands."

The Searching Eye of God

Another way of reaching this type of individual is by the use of such passages as Luke 26:15, Romans 2:16, and 1 Samuel 26:7. These passages show that God looks at the heart. Hold the inquirer right to that point. Everyone, when brought face to face with that, must tremble because he knows that whatever his outward life may be, his heart will not stand the scrutiny of God's eye.

No matter how self-righteous a person is, somewhere in the depths of his heart is the consciousness of sin. All we have to do is to work until we touch that point. Every man's conscience is on our side.

Matthew 22:37–38 can be used when a person says, "I am doing the best I can, and I do more good than evil." Say to him, "You are greatly mistaken about that. Do you know that you have broken the first and greatest of God's laws?" Then show him Hebrews 6:6 or John 6:29. The one thing God demands is faith; without that, it is impossible to please Him.

John 16:9 shows that unbelief in Christ is the greatest sin. John 3:36 shows that the question of eternal life depends solely on a person's accepting or rejecting Jesus Christ. Hebrews 10:28–29 reveals that the sin that brings the heaviest punishment is that of treading *"under foot the Son of God."*

Before using this last passage, you might say, "Do you know that you are committing the most awful sin in God's sight that a person can commit?"

If he replies, "No," then say, "Well, let me show you from God's Word that you are." Turn to this passage and read it with great solemnity and earnestness.

Understanding God's Judgment

Those who think "God is too good to damn anyone" are also entertaining false hopes. When anyone says this, you can reply, "We know nothing of God's goodness except what we learn from the Bible, so we must go to that Book to find out the character of God's goodness. Let us turn to Romans 2:4–5." Having read the verses, you can say something like this, "The purpose of God's goodness is to lead you to repentance, not to encourage you to sin. When we trample His goodness, we are treasuring up *'wrath against the day of wrath and revelation of the righteous judgment of God.'"* John 8:21, 24 and John 3:36 will show the person that however good God may be, He will reject all who reject His Son.

Still another way to approach this subject is to use John 5:40, 2 Peter 3:9–11, or Ezekiel 33:11, and show them that it is not so much God who damns men as men who damn themselves. This happens in spite of God's goodness because they will not come to Christ and accept the life freely offered. You can say, "God is not willing that any should perish. He offers life freely to you, but there is one difficulty in the way. Let us turn to John 5:40 to see what the difficulty is." Then read the passage, *"Ye will not come to me that ye might have life,"* and say, "My friend, your difficulty is that you won't come. Life is freely offered to you, but if you will not accept it, you must perish. "

Second Peter 2:4–6, 9 and Luke 13:3 show how the "good" God deals with those who persist in sin. Sometimes the latter passage can be effectively used in this way: "You say God is too good to damn anyone. Now let us see what God Himself says in His Word." Then turn to the passage and read, *"Except ye repent, ye shall all likewise perish."* Repeat the passage over and over again until the person understands this.

Trusting versus Trying

A third type of those who entertain false hopes are those who say, "I am trying to be a Christian." John 1:12 will show them that it is not "trying" to be a Christian or "trying" to live a better life or "trying" to do anything that God asks of us, but simply to receive Jesus Christ who did it all.

You can ask the inquirer, "Will you now stop your trying and simply receive Jesus as Savior?" Acts 16:31 shows that God does not ask us to try what we can do, but to trust Jesus and what He has done and will do.

Romans 3:23–25 shows that we are not to be justified by trying but "*freely by his grace through the redemption that is in Christ Jesus,*" on the simple condition of faith.

Still another group who entertain false hope are those who say, "I feel I am going to heaven " or "I feel I am saved. " Show them from John 3:36 that it is not a question of what they feel but what God says. God says distinctly in His Word, *"He that believeth not on the Son, shall not see life, but the wrath of God abideth on him."*

One afternoon I was talking with a lady who a few weeks before had lost her only child. At the time of the child's death, she had been deeply interested in salvation through Christ. But her serious desire to serve Him had since left her. I asked her the question, "Do you not wish to go where your little one has gone?"

She replied at once, "I expect to."

"What makes you think you will?" I said.

She replied, "I feel it. I feel that I will go to heaven when I die."

I asked her if she could point to anything in the Word of God that gave her reason to believe that she was going to heaven when she died.

"No," she said, "there is not." Then she turned and questioned me, saying, "Do you expect to go to heaven when you die?"

"Yes," I replied, "I know I will."

"How do you know it?" she said. "Have you any word from God for it?"

"Yes," I answered, and I turned to John 3:36. She was thus led to see the difference between a faith that rested on her feelings and a faith that rested on the Word of God.

Luke 18:9–14 can be used in the following way. You can say, "There was a man in the Bible who felt he was all right but was really all wrong. Let me read to you about him." Then read about the Pharisee who was sure that he was all right, but who was all the time an unforgiven sinner. Make the inquirer see how untrustworthy our feelings are and what the ground of assurance is—God's Word. Proverbs 14:12 can also be used to show that *"there is a way which seemeth right unto a man, but the end thereof are the ways of death."*

The last group of people who entertain false hopes are those who say they are saved even though they are leading sinful lives. In the case of many forms of sin, a good passage to use is 1 Corinthians 6:9–10. First John 2:29 will also, in many cases, sweep away people's false hope. First John 5:4–5 is useful to show that those who are born of God overcome the world. The fact that they are living in sin and are not overcoming the world is evidence that they have not been born of God.

7

DEALING WITH THE UNCERTAIN

Sometimes lack of assurance is caused by ignorance. Scripture tells us that we may know we have eternal life. Often, when you ask people if they know they are saved or if they know their sins are forgiven or if they know they have eternal life, they will reply, "Why, no one knows that." You can say to them, "Yes, the Bible says that all who believe may know this." Then show them 1 John 5:13:

> *These things have I written unto you that believe on the name of the Son of God; that ye may know that ye have eternal life, and that ye may believe on the name of the Son of God.*

John 1:12 shows that Christ gives, to as many as receive Him, power to become the sons of God. A good way to use this verse is to ask the inquirer questions regarding it: "What does everyone who receives Him receive power to become?" If the inquirer is attentively looking at the verse, he will answer, "A son of God." Then, ask the next question, "Have you received Him?" If he replies, "Yes," then ask him, "What are you, then?" It will probably be necessary to go over it several times, but at last the inquirer will see it and say, "I am a son of God."

John 3:36 can be used in a similar way. Ask the inquirer, "Who do these verses say has everlasting life?"

"He that believeth on the Son."

"Do you believe on the Son? What do you have, then?" In a little while, he will see it and say, "Everlasting life." Then have him say over and over again, "I have everlasting life," and have him kneel down and thank God for giving him everlasting life.

One night I found a young man on his knees in great distress at the close of the service. I showed him from the Bible how Jesus Christ had borne his sins and asked him if he would accept Christ as his Savior. He said he would, but he seemed to have no joy and went out of the meeting in deep distress. The next night he was there again, professing to have accepted Christ, but with no assurance that his sins were forgiven. I tried to show him from God's Word what God said of those who accepted the Savior, but the understanding did not come. Finally he rose to leave the meeting. I had just shown him from John 3:36 that God said, *"He that believeth on the Son hath everlasting life."*

As he turned to leave, he said, "Will you pray for me?"

I said, "Yes."

He walked a little way down the aisle, and I called to him and said, "Do you believe I will pray for you?"

He turned with a look of astonishment and replied, "Yes, of course."

"Why do you think I will pray for you?" I asked.

"Because you said so," he replied.

I said, "Isn't God's Word as good as mine?" He saw immediately that, while he had been willing to believe my word, he had not been willing to believe God's Word. He received assurance immediately and knew that he had everlasting life. John 5:24 and 1 John 5:12 can be used in a similar way. Acts 13:39 can be very useful. Ask the inquirer, "What does this verse say that all who believe are?" Then ask him, "Do you believe? What are you, then?" It will probably take two or three times going over it before he answers, "I am justified." Tell him to thank God for justifying him and to confess Christ.

The Witness of the Spirit

Many inquirers stumble over not having the witness of the Holy Spirit. Show them from 1 John 5:10 that the witness of the Word concerning their acceptance is sufficient. If they do not believe this witness of God in His Word, tell them this makes Him a liar. Show them further from Ephesians 1:13 that, after we believe the testimony of the Word, we are *"sealed with that holy Spirit of promise."*

The natural order in the assurance of salvation is this: first, assurance of our justification, resting on the Word of God; second, public confession of Christ with the mouth; third, the witness of the Holy Spirit.

The trouble with many is that they wish to invert this order and have the witness of the Holy Spirit before they confess Christ with their mouths. From Matthew 10:32–33 we learn that when we confess Christ before men, He confesses us before the Father. We cannot expect the witness of the Spirit from the Father until we are confessed before the Father. So confession of Christ logically precedes the witness of the Spirit.

It is very important in using these texts to make clear what saving faith is. Many may say that they believe when they do not, in the sense of these texts. They get a false assurance and entertain false hopes, never finding deliverance. Often, those who lack assurance are dealt with carelessly by workers who urge them on to assurance before they have really accepted Christ.

John 1:12 and 2 Timothy 1:12 clarify that believing means receiving Jesus or committing oneself to Him. Romans 10:10 serves a similar purpose by showing that *"with the heart man believeth unto righteousness."*

Often, those who lack assurance are involved in some sin or questionable practice that they should confess and give up. John 8:12, Isaiah 55:7, Proverbs 28:13, and Psalm 32:1–5 are useful passages in dealing with this situation. When sin is confessed and forsaken, and we follow Christ, we receive pardon, light, and assurance. Sometimes it works best to bluntly ask, "Do you know of any sin or anything in your life your conscience troubles you about?"

How to Deal with Backsliders

Many backsliders have no desire to come back to the Savior. With such people use Jeremiah 2:5 and drive the question home. "What iniquity have you found in the Lord?" Show them their ingratitude and folly in forsaking such a Savior and Friend. They may have wandered away because of unkind treatment by professed Christians. But hold them right to the point of how the Lord treated them and how they are now treating Him.

Use Jeremiah 2:13 to show them what they have forsaken. Have them read the verse, and then ask, "Is this verse true? When you forsook the Lord, did you not forsake the *'fountain of living waters'* and turn to *'broken cisterns, that can hold no water'*?" Illustrate the text by showing how foolish it would be to turn from a fountain of pure, living water to a broken cistern or muddy pool. God has used this verse many times to bring backsliders back to Himself.

Turn to Jeremiah 2:19 and ask the backslider whether he has found it *"an evil thing and bitter"* to have forsaken the Lord his God. Proverbs 14:14, 1 Kings 11:9, Amos 4:11–12, and Luke 15:13–17 can often be used effectively with an impenitent backslider to show him the result of his wandering.

Other backsliders are sick of their wanderings and sin, and they desire to come back to the Lord. These are perhaps as easy a group to deal with as we ever find. Jeremiah 3:12–13, 22 will show them how ready the Lord is to receive them back. All He asks of them is that they acknowledge their sin and return to Him. Hosea 14:1–4 is full of tender invitation to penitent backsliders and also shows the way back to God. Isaiah 43:22, 24–25, Isaiah 44:20–22, Jeremiah 29:11–13, Deuteronomy 4:28–31, 2 Chronicles 7:14, 1 John 1:9, and 1 John 2:1–2 set forth God's unfailing love for the backslider and His willingness to receive him back.

Mark 16:7, 2 Chronicles 15:4, and 2 Chronicles 33:1–9, 12–13 give illustrations of backsliders who returned to the Lord and how lovingly they were received. First John 1:9, Jeremiah 3:12–13, 2 Chronicles 15:12, 15, and 2 Chronicles 7:14 show the actual steps the backslider must take to come back to the Lord and be restored to His favor: humble himself, confess his sin, and turn from his sin.

Luke 15:11–24 is perhaps the most useful passage of all in dealing with a backslider who wishes to return. It illustrates both the steps that the backslider must take and the kind of reception he will receive. When a backslider has returned, he should always be given instructions on how to live so that he will not backslide again.

8

DEALING WITH SKEPTICS

Some skeptics simply take the Word of God lightly. If a man says the Bible is foolishness to him, you can say, "Yes, that is what the Bible says about itself." He will probably be surprised at this reply. Then you can show him the verse, "*The preaching of the cross is to them that perish foolishness*" (1 Corinthians 1:18). You can say to him, "You see that the Bible says that it is foolishness to some—"*them that perish*"—and the reason it is foolishness to you is because you are perishing."

One night a man said to a worker who was trying to persuade him to come to Christ, "All that you are saying is foolishness to me." The worker quickly replied, "Yes, that is what the Bible says." The man looked at him in astonishment and said, "What?" The worker turned to 1 Corinthians 2:14 and read, *"But the natural man receiveth not the things of the Spirit of God: for they are foolishness unto him: neither can he know them, because they are spiritually discerned."* The man said, "I never saw that before."

Second Corinthians 4:3–4 shows the doubter that he is lost and that his skepticism arises from the fact that the *"god of this world hath blinded"* his mind. Second Thessalonians 2:10–12 reveals the origin of skepticism, *"because they received not the love of the truth,"* and the consequences of skepticism—delusion and damnation. John 8:21–24 shows the terrible consequences of unbelief. John 5:44 and John 3:18–20 expose the origin of skepticism. Psalm 14:1 is useful in some cases, although one needs to be cautious to use it only when it can be done with earnestness and tenderness. Second Thessalonians 1:7–8 can also be used with good results.

Skepticism or Sin?

A large number of men and women in our day sincerely long to know the truth but are in an utter fog of skepticism. John 7:17 is a helpful passage to show the way through skepticism to faith. Get the skeptic to read that verse. Ask him, "Will you surrender your will to God and promise to search honestly and earnestly to find out what God's will is so that you can do it? Will you ask God to show you whether you need a Savior and whether Jesus is a divine Savior, the Son of God? And will you promise that, if God shows you that Jesus is the Son of God, you will accept Him as your Savior and confess Him before the world?" Have him make his promise definite by writing it down. If you get him to do this, his skepticism will soon take wings.

One evening at the close of a service I asked a gentleman why he was not a Christian. He replied, "I will tell you. I do not talk much about it, for I am not proud of it as some are, but I am a skeptic. I have lain awake nights thinking about this matter."

I asked him, "Do you believe there is a God?"

"Yes," he answered, "I never gave up my faith that there is a God."

"Well, if there is a God, you ought to obey Him. Tonight, will you take your stand to follow His will wherever it carries you, even if it carries you to the ends of the earth?"

"I will try to do as well as I know how," he said slowly.

"That is not what I asked. Will you follow God's will wherever it carries you?"

"I have never thought about it that way."

"Will you consider it tonight?"

"I will."

"Do you believe God answers prayer?"

"I don't know. I am afraid not."

"Well, since this is a possible clue to the truth, will you ask God to show you whether Jesus is His Son, and what your duty concerning Him is?"

"I will."

Not long after that, the man came into a meeting with a new look on his face. He stood up and said, "I was in a fog of doubt. I believed nothing." Then he told us he had done as he promised. "And now," he continued, "my doubts are all gone. I don't know where they have gone, but they are gone."

Knowing Right from Wrong

If the skeptic will not act in this way, you can silence him by showing him that he is not an honest skeptic. His trouble is not his skepticism but his sin. If the man does not believe there is a God, ask him if he believes there is an absolute difference between right and wrong. If he does not, he is merely foolish. If he says he does, ask him if he will take his stand for right and follow it wherever it carries him. He may try to put you off by saying, "What is right?" or, "I am doing right as nearly as I know how." Get him to promise that he will take his stand for right, whatever he may find it to be. Then show him that if he is honest in this promise, he will find out what the truth is.

Say to him, "You do not know whether God answers prayer or not. I know He does, and you must admit that here is a possible clue to knowledge. If you are honest in your desire to know the truth, you will follow this clue. You can at least pray, 'O my God, if You are real, teach me Your will, and I will do it. Show me whether Jesus is Your Son or not. If You show that He is, I will accept Him as my Savior and confess Him before the world.'"

Tell the man to begin reading the gospel of John, slowly and thoughtfully, only a few verses at a time. He should ask God for the light of understanding each time he begins reading and promise God that he will follow the light the moment He makes it clear. If the skeptic will follow this rational course, he will come into the clear light of faith in the Bible as the Word of God and Jesus Christ as the Son of God. If the man is not an honest skeptic, it will become obvious. You can then show him that the difficulty is not with his skepticism but with his rebellious heart.

One afternoon I asked anyone who wished to talk with me to remain after the meeting. A young man with whom I had dealt some months before stayed behind. I asked him what his trouble was. He replied, "The same trouble that I told you in the spring. I cannot believe there is a God." I asked him if he had taken his stand to follow what was right regardless of the consequences. He replied that he did not know whether there was any difference between right and wrong.

I looked him in the eye and said, "Is there some sin in your life?"

He said, "Yes."

I asked, "What is it?"

He replied, "The same that I told you last spring."

I said, "You promised to give it up. Have you?"

"No, I have not."

"Well," I said, "the problem is not with your skepticism. Give up that sin, and your skepticism will take care of itself."

In some confusion he replied, "I guess that is the trouble."

Questioning God and His Word

The previously mentioned passages can also be used with those who do not believe in God. Three other passages are often effective with this type of skeptic. Before using Psalm 14:1, you can say, "Let me read to you from God's own Word what He says about those who deny His existence." Often, it is sufficient to let the passage do its own work. Sometimes, however, it is wise to dwell a little on it. Call attention to the fact that it is *"in his heart"* that the fool says, *"There is no God."* He does not believe there is a God because he does not want to believe it.

You can add that the folly of saying in one's heart that there is no God is seen in two points: first, there is a God, and it is folly to say there is not one; second, the doctrine that there is not a God always brings misery and wretchedness. Ask the man if he ever knew a happy atheist. Psalm 19:1–2 and Romans 1:19–22 are also effective passages.

Romans 3:3–4 makes it plain that questioning the fact does not alter the fact. Matthew 24:35 is often used by the Spirit to convince the heart of the skeptic of the certainty and immutability of God's Word. Mark 7:13, Matthew 5:18, John 10:35, and Luke 24:27, 44 give Christ's testimony that the Old Testament is the Word of God. These passages are especially helpful in dealing with those who say that they accept the authority of Christ but not that of the Old Testament. Christ sets His seal on the Old Testament Scriptures. If we accept His authority, we must accept that of the Old Testament, as well. Along the same line, John 14:26 and John 16:12–13 also contain Christ's endorsement of the New Testament.

First Thessalonians 2:13 answers the skeptic's objection that Paul did not claim that his teaching is the Word of God. Second Peter 1:21, John 8:47, and Luke 16:30–31 can also be used. Second John 5:10 is very effective in showing the guilt of those who do not believe the record that God has given. Before using this passage, you can say, "You doubt that the Bible is the Word of God? Now let us see what God says about those who do not believe His testimony." Turn to the passage and have them read it.

Is There Life after Death?

Read 1 Corinthians 15:35–36, John 5:28–29, and Daniel 12:2. Some doubt the doctrine of future punishment or the conscious, endless suffering of the lost. Revelation 21:8 defines what death means when it is used in Scripture. Revelation 17:8, compared with Revelation 19:20, shows what perdition or destruction means in Scripture. Revelation 20:10 shows that those cast into the lake of fire do not cease to exist. The beast and false prophet are still there at the end of a thousand years. Far from being annihilated or losing conscious existence, they are tormented night and day forever. Revelation 13:7–8 shows that those subjected to terrible punishment are those whose names are not written in the Book of Life.

Matthew 10:28 refers to a destruction of the soul apart from the destruction of the body. Luke 12:5 shows that after one is dead, there can be punishment in hell. Mark 3:28–29 describes eternal sin. Luke 16:23–26 shows that the condition of the unsaved is one of conscious torment for eternity. Mark 14:21 shows that the retribution visited on the wicked is so severe that it would have been better for them never to have been born.

Second Peter 2:4 and Jude 6 show that hell is not a place where the inhabitants cease to exist, but where they are kept alive for the purpose of God. Hebrews 10:28–29 shows that while the punishment of transgression under the Mosaic Law was death, greater punishment awaits those who have *"trodden under foot the Son of God."* Matthew 25:41 sheds more light on the subject. The wicked go to the same place as the Beast, False Prophet, and the Devil mentioned in Revelation 19:20 and Revelation 20:10. They share the same endless, conscious torment.

Is Jesus the Son of God?

In Acts 10:36, 1 Corinthians 2:8, Psalm 24:8–10, Hebrews 1:8, John 20:28, Romans 9:5, Revelation 1:17, and Isaiah 44:6, several divine titles are applied to Christ. These same titles applied to Christ in the New Testament were applied to Jehovah in the Old.

In Hebrews 1:10, 13, we find divine offices attributed to Christ. In Revelation 5:13, John 5:22–23, Hebrews 1:6, Philippians 2:10, and Philippians 5:22–23, it is taught that Jesus Christ should be worshipped as God.

In John 5:22–23, Jesus claimed the same honor as His Father. Either He was divine or He was the most blasphemous impostor who ever lived. One who denies Christ's divinity puts Him in the place of a blasphemous impostor. Mark 14:61–62 can be used in a similar way.

First John 2:22–23 and 1 John 5:1, 5 show that the one who denies the divinity of Christ, no matter who he may be, is a liar and an antichrist. First John 5:10–12 shows that he who does not believe that Jesus is divine makes God a liar, *"because he believeth not the record that God gave of his Son."*

Hebrews 10:28–29 shows the folly, guilt, and punishment of rejecting Christ as the Son of God. John 8:24 shows beyond a question that he who wants to be saved must believe in the divinity of Jesus Christ. John 20:31 shows that we have life through believing that Jesus is the Christ, the Son of God.

There may be no need to take up specific questions, as for example, future punishment, until the inquirer has first decided whether he will accept Christ as his Savior.

9

DEALING WITH OBJECTIONS

Many that you wish to lead to Christ will try to suggest that God is unjust and cruel. Job 40:2 and Romans 9:20 are very pointed passages to use in this situation and need no comment. It may be wise to preface the reading of the passages with some remarks like this: "Do you know the enormous sin you are guilty of in accusing God of being unjust and cruel? Let me read what God says about it in His Word." Then read the passages.

Romans 11:33 will show the complaining person that the reason God's ways seem unjust and cruel is that His ways are so deep and unsearchable. The trouble is not with God's ways but with the limitations of human understanding. Hebrews 12:5, 7 and Hebrews 12:10–11 are especially useful in cases where the inquirer complains because of his own misfortunes or sorrow. Isaiah 55:8–9 can often prove helpful.

You will often meet someone who will say, "God is unjust to create men and then damn them." Refer them to Ezekiel 33:11. This passage meets this complaint by showing that God has no pleasure in the death of the wicked but desires their welfare. The wicked bring damnation on themselves by their stubborn refusal to repent. First Timothy 2:3–4 shows that God—far from creating man to damn him—desires that all men be saved. Second Peter 3:9 teaches that God is not willing that any should perish and is delaying His purposes in order that all may come to repentance. John 5:40 and Matthew 23:37 show that the whole cause of man's damnation is his own willful and persistent refusal to come to Christ. John 3:36 and John 3:16 are also helpful in many cases.

Is the Bible Reliable?

The Bible is often criticized as being contradictory and absurd. Scriptures that answer such criticisms are 1 Corinthians 1:18, 1 Corinthians 2:14, 2 Corinthians 4:3–4, Daniel 12:10, and Romans 11:33–34. In extreme cases, 2 Thessalonians 2:10–12, John 7:17, Psalm 25:14, and Matthew 11:25 will also help.

Sometimes the best thing to do with a person who says the Bible is full of contradiction is to hand him your Bible and ask him to show you one contradiction. In most cases, he will not attempt to do it. People who complain about the Bible usually know nothing about its contents.

One day I asked a certain man why he was not a Christian, and he replied, "The Bible is full of contradictions." I asked him to show me one. "Oh," he said, "it's full of them."

I said, "If it is full of them, you ought to be able to show me one. "

He said, "Well, there is one in Psalms."

I said, "Show it to me." He began looking in the back of the New Testament for the book of Psalms. I said, "You are not looking in the right part of the Bible for Psalms. Let me find it for you." I found the book of Psalms and handed it to him. After fumbling around, he said, "I could find it if I had my own Bible here."

"Well," I said, "will you bring your Bible tonight?" He promised he would and agreed to meet me at a certain place in the church. The appointed hour came, but he did not.

Some months afterward, in another series of meetings in the same church, one of the workers stopped me and said, "Here's a man I wish you would deal with. He is a skeptic." I looked at him and recognized him as the same man. "Oh," I said, "you are the man who lied to me." He admitted that he was, but he was still playing his old game of saying that the Bible is full of contradictions. In nine cases out of ten, men who say this know nothing about the Bible. When you ask them to show you a contradiction in the Bible, they are filled with confusion.

Why Did Jesus Have to Die?

A great many men will say, "I do not see why God could not save men in some other way than by the death of His Son." Isaiah 55:8–9 and Romans 11:33 are useful in answering them. Romans 9:20 is also effective.

One night I asked a young student why he was not a Christian. He answered that he did not see why it was necessary for Christ to die for him, and why God did not save him in some other way. I opened my Bible and read Romans 9:20, asking him directly, "*Who art thou that repliest against God?*" Then I said to him, "Do you realize what you are doing? You are condemning God!"

The confused young man said, "I did not mean to do that."

"Well," I said, "that is what you are doing."

"If that is so," he replied, "I will take it back."

Using the passages given in the chapter "Dealing with the Indifferent" may also help. When anyone is led to see that he is a lost sinner, God's way of salvation will prove itself to be just the thing needed.

Too Many Hypocrites

Frequently when we try to persuade men to accept Christ as their Savior, they reply, "There are too many hypocrites in church." Romans 14:4, 12 effectively deals with this remark. Romans 2:1 and Matthew 7:1–5 are also excellent. John 21:21–22 is useful in showing the objector that he is solely responsible for his own relationship to Christ, and what others do is none of his concern.

Sometimes the inquirer will complain of the way Christian people have treated him. In such a case turn the attention of the inquirer from the people to the way God has treated him. For this purpose use Jeremiah 2:5, Isaiah 53:5, and Romans 5:6–8. Then ask him if the fact that Christians have treated him badly is any excuse for his treatment of a heavenly Father who has treated him so well.

One night I asked an elderly man if he was a Christian. He replied that he was a backslider. I asked him why he turned away from the Lord. He replied that Christian people had treated him badly. I opened my Bible and read Jeremiah 2:5 to him: *"Thus saith the Lord, What iniquity have your fathers found in me, that they are gone far from me, and have walked after vanity, and are become vain?"* I said, "Did you find any iniquity in God? Did God not treat you well?" In a voice that shook with emotion, the man admitted that God had not treated him badly. I held him right to this point of God's treatment of him and his treatment of God. Matthew 18:23–35, Ephesians 4:30–32, and Matthew 6:14–15 are also useful in showing the absolute necessity of forgiving others.

Now Is the Time

Many people want to put off making a decision. They say, "I want to wait," "Not tonight," or "I will think about it." Read Isaiah 55:6 to the inquirer. Then ask him when he is to seek the Lord. When he answers, "While He may be found," ask him if he is sure that he will be able to find God tomorrow if he does not seek Him today.

You could also use Proverbs 29:1. After reading the verse, ask what becomes of the one who *"being often reproved hardeneth his neck."* When your inquirer answers, "He shall be destroyed," ask him how he shall be destroyed. When he answers, "Suddenly," ask him if he is willing to run the risk.

Another good Scripture to use is Matthew 25:10, 12. Ask the inquirer who could attend the Marriage Feast. When he answers, "Those who were ready," ask him if he is ready. Have him tell you what happened after those who were ready went in. Then ask him, "Are you willing to be on the outside?"

Luke 12:19–20 might be used. Ask the inquirer for how long a time the man in the passage thought he had made provision. Then ask him, "If God called you tonight, would you be ready?" Matthew 24:44 is especially effective in dealing with those who say, "I am not ready." An excellent way to use 1 Kings 18:21 is by asking the person whether he would be willing to wait a year with no opportunity to accept Christ. When he answers, "No, I might die within a year," ask him if he would be willing to wait a month, bringing it down to a week and finally to a day. Ask him if he wants God, the Holy Spirit, and all Christians to leave him alone for a day without any opportunity to accept Christ.

Almost any thoughtful person will say, "No." Tell him that, if that is the case, he had better accept Christ at once. This method has been used by many with great success. Proverbs 27:1, James 4:13–14, Job 36:18, Luke 13:24–28, Luke 12:19–20, John 8:21, John 12:35, and John 7:33–34 can also be used for further reference. "I must get set up in business first, and then I will become a Christian" or, "I must do something else first." Matthew 6:33 is the great passage to use in such cases, because it shows that we must seek the kingdom of God first.

Others say, "I am waiting for God's time." If one says this, ask him if he will accept Christ in God's time if you will show him when God's time is. Then turn to 2 Corinthians 6:2 or Hebrews 3:15.

To the objection, "I am too young" or, "I want to wait until I am older," Ecclesiastes 12:1 is a sufficient answer. Matthew 19:14 and Matthew 18:3

are also good passages to use, because they show that youth is the best time to come to Christ. All people must become like little children before they can enter into the kingdom of heaven. It is sometimes wise in dealing with persons who wish to put off a decision to use the passages given for the indifferent, until a deep impression is made of their need for Christ. Then they will not be willing to postpone accepting Him.

In some cases, using only one passage and driving it home by constant repetition works best. One night I was dealing with a man who was quite interested, but he kept saying, "I cannot decide tonight." I quoted Psalm 29:1, "*Give unto the LORD, O ye mighty, give unto the LORD glory and strength.*" To every answer he made, I would come back to this passage. I must have repeated it a great many times in the course of the talk. Finally the man realized not only his need of Christ but also the danger of delaying and the necessity of a prompt decision. He tried to get away from the passage, but I held him to this one point. Later that night he was assaulted and seriously injured. The next night, he came to accept Christ. The pounding he received from his assailant would probably have done him little good if the Scripture had not been pounded into his mind beforehand.

10

DEALING WITH EXCUSES

Many people are willful or headstrong. They will say, "I do not want you to talk to me." In such a case, it is usually best to recommend a passage of Scripture. Then leave the person alone to reflect on it, allowing the Word to speak for itself. Romans 6:23, Hebrews 10:28–29; Hebrews 12:25, Mark 16:16, Proverbs 29:1, and Proverbs 1:24–33 are good passages for this purpose.

Others may protest, "I cannot forgive someone." Matthew 6:15 and Matthew 18:23–35 show that they must forgive or be lost. Philippians 4:13 and Ezekiel 36:26 will teach them how to forgive. Many people are kept from Christ by an unforgiving spirit. Sometimes this difficulty can be removed by getting the person to kneel in prayer and ask God to take away their unforgiving spirit.

I once reasoned for a long time with an inquirer who was under deep conviction but was held back from accepting Christ by a hatred toward someone who had wronged her. She kept insisting that she could not forgive. Finally I said, "Let us tell God about this matter." She agreed, and the moment we knelt down, she burst into a flood of tears. The difficulty was removed, and she accepted Christ immediately.

Some will admit, "I love the world too much." Mark 8:36 is a great text to use with these people. Luke 14:33 shows the absolute necessity that the world be given up. Also see Luke 12:16–20. First John 2:15–17 shows the folly of holding onto the world. Psalm 84:11 and Romans 8:32 promise that the Lord will hold back no good thing from His children.

Another excuse is, "I cannot acknowledge a wrong that I have done." Proverbs 28:13 will show the misery that is sure to follow unless the wrong is confessed. Others will say, "I do not want to make a public confession." Romans 10:10 and Matthew 10:32–33 show that God will accept nothing else. Mark 8:38, John 12:42–43, and Proverbs 24:25 show the peril of not making a public confession.

Still others say, "I want to have my own way." Isaiah 55:8–9 shows how much better God's way is, and Proverbs 14:12 shows the consequences of having our own way. Finally, some refuse to take a stand, and they say, "I neither accept Christ nor reject Him." Matthew 12:30 shows that they must do one or the other. This verse has been used to convict many people.

More than Religion

Under this heading comes the churchgoer who believes he is saved through mere church membership. A good way to deal with this person is to show him the necessity of the new birth. The new birth is described in Ezekiel 36:25–27, 2 Corinthians 5:17, and 2 Peter 1:4. John 3:3, 5, 7 shows the necessity of the new birth.

Many people who have always attended church understand the new birth to mean baptism, but it obviously means more than that. In 1 Corinthians 4:15, Paul told the Corinthian Christians that he had begotten them through the Gospel. If the new birth meant baptism, he must have baptized them. But in 1 Corinthians 1:14, he declared he had not baptized them. Acts 9:13, 21, 23 shows that a person may be baptized while his heart is still not right in the sight of God, so that he has *"neither part nor lot in this matter."*

It is good to go a step further and show the inquirer the evidence of the new birth. First John 2:29, 1 John 3:9–17, and 1 John 5:1–4 give the biblical evidence of the new birth. The next question that will arise is, "How can I be born again?" This question is answered in John 1:12, 1 Peter 1:23, and James 1:18.

Acts 3:19 is a good text to use with churchgoers because it shows the necessity of repentance and conversion. Examples of repentance are found in Isaiah 55:7 and Jonah 3:10.

Another approach is to show people that it is the believer's privilege to know that he has eternal life. Nominal churchgoers almost always lack assurance of salvation. They do not know that they are forgiven, but they hope to be forgiven some day. If you can show them that we can know we are forgiven and that we have eternal life, a great many of them will want this assurance. First John 5:13 states that it is the believer's privilege to know that he has everlasting life. Acts 13:38–39, Acts 10:43, and John 3:36 are useful in leading people to this assurance.

Still another approach, to be used after you have already made some progress, is to show people the advantage of Bible study. Good texts for this purpose are John 5:39, 1 Peter 2:1–2, 2 Timothy 3:13–17, James 1:21–22, Psalm 1:1–2, Joshua 1:8, Mark 7:7–8, 13, and Matthew 22:29.

You may want to deal with a churchgoer in the same way you would deal with any sinner—awaken the realization in him that he is a sinner who needs Christ. For this purpose, use Matthew 22:37–38, Galatians 3:10–13, and Isaiah 53:6.

Some people think there is no use talking with those who believe they are saved through church membership. This is a great mistake. Many churchgoers are longing for something they do not find in their dry churches. If you can show them from the Word of God how to find it, they will come to Christ very easily and become strong Christians. Do not attack their particular church. Give them the truth, and the errors will take care of themselves in time. Often our attacks only expose our ignorance.

We always have a particular advantage in dealing with a churchgoer. We have peace and power in Christianity that they do not have, and they can see and appreciate the difference.

The best way to deal with a Jew is to show him that his own Bible points to Christ. The most helpful passages are Isaiah 53, Daniel 9:26, and Zechariah 12:10. The whole book of Hebrews relates to the Jews, especially chapters 7, 9, and 10, along with the whole gospel of Matthew. Many Jews today are inquiring into the claims of Jesus of Nazareth and are open to talking about Him. The great difficulty in their accepting Christ as the Messiah is the severe persecution a Jew must endure if he does. This difficulty can be met by the passages already given under the subject of persecution.

We also should be prepared to deal with spiritualists. Leviticus 19:31; Leviticus 22:6; Deuteronomy 18:10–12; 2 Kings 21:1, 2, 6; 1 Chronicles 10:13; Isaiah 8:19–20; 1 John 4:1–3; and 2 Thessalonians 2:9–12 are passages to be used here.

In dealing with people who are deceived, it is wise to begin with John 7:17 and bring them to the place where they heartily desire to know the truth. A man cannot be brought out of his deception unless he wants to know the truth.

11

HELPFUL SOULWINNING HINTS

1. Deal with people of your own sex and about your own age.

There are exceptions to this rule. One should always look to the Holy Spirit for His guidance concerning whom to approach. He may lead us to someone of the opposite sex. But unless there is clear guidance in the matter, experienced Christian workers agree that men do the most satisfactory work with men, and likewise women with women. This is especially true of the young. Many unfortunate complications can arise when young men try to lead young women to Christ or vice versa. Of course, an elderly, motherly woman may do excellent work with a young man or boy, and an elderly, fatherly man may do good work with a young woman or girl. It is not ordinarily wise for a young and inexperienced person to approach one much older and wiser than himself.

2. *Whenever it is possible, talk to the person alone.*

No one likes to open his heart freely to another on this personal and sacred subject when others are present. Many who would defend themselves out of pride when their friends are with them would admit their sin and need if they were alone with you. One worker can deal better with one unconverted person than several workers can deal with a single inquirer. A single worker cannot deal effectively with several people at once. But you may succeed in leading them one by one to Christ when you take the individuals off by themselves.

3. *Rely wholly on the Spirit and the Word of God.*

4. *Do not merely quote or read passages from the Bible, but have the one with whom you are speaking read them himself.*

The truth may enter his heart through the eye as well as the ear.

5. *It is best to emphasize a single passage of Scripture, repeating and discussing it until the inquirer cannot forget it. He will hear it ringing in his memory long after you have ceased talking.*

A friend of mine who was dealing with a young man who had many doubts and fears kept quoting the passage, "*Now is the accepted time; behold, now is the day of salvation*" (2 Corinthians 6:2). The young man tried to get my friend to talk about something else, but he just kept repeating the words. The next day the young man returned rejoicing in Christ. He thanked my friend for hammering him with that text. The words kept ringing in his ears during the night, and he could not rest until he had settled the matter by accepting Christ.

A person may want to point to some definite verse in the Word of God and say, "I know on the authority of this verse that my sins are forgiven and I am a child of God." Sometimes, however, a powerful effect is produced by grouping together passages along a particular subject until the mind is convinced and the heart conquered.

6. *Always hold the person with whom you are dealing to the main point of accepting Christ.*

If he wishes to discuss the claims of various denominations, the question of baptism, theories of future punishment, or any question other than the central one of his need of a Savior, tell him that the time to settle those questions is after he has decided to accept or reject Christ. Many opportunities for repentance have been lost by an inexperienced worker allowing himself to become involved in an argument over some side issue.

7. *Be courteous.*

Many well-meaning but indiscreet Christians, by their rudeness and impertinence, repel those whom they desire to win to Christ. We can be perfectly frank and perfectly courteous at the same time. You can point out to people their sin without insulting them. The more gentle our manner is, the deeper our words will go, for they will not stir up opposition in the hearts of others. Some overzealous workers cause the people they approach to become defensive and to clothe themselves with an armor that is impossible to penetrate.

8. *Be earnest.*

Only the earnest Christian can make the unsaved person realize the truth of God's Word. We should let the passages we want to use with others first sink into our own souls. I know of a very successful worker who for a long time used the one passage, *"Prepare to meet thy God"* (Amos 4:12), whenever she witnessed for Christ. That passage had taken such complete possession of her heart and mind that she used it with tremendous effect.

A few passages that have become real to us are better than many passages memorized from some textbook.

Take time to kneel and ponder some of the passages suggested in this book until you feel their power. Paul "*ceased not to warn every one night and day with tears*" (Acts 20:31). Genuine earnestness means more than any skill learned in a training class or even from the study of such a book as this.

9. Never lose your temper when trying to lead a soul to Christ.

Some people are exasperating, but even they can be won by patience and gentleness. They certainly cannot be won if you lose your temper. Nothing will delight them more or give them more comfort in their sins. The more irritating they are in their words and actions, the more impressed they will be if you answer their insults with kindness. Often, the one who has been most insufferable will come back in penitence.

One of the rudest men I ever met later became one of the most patient, persistent, and effective workers for Christ.

10. Never have a heated argument with anyone you desire to lead to Christ.

This always comes from the flesh and not from the Spirit. (See Galatians 5:19–20, 22–23.) It arises from pride and unwillingness to let the other person get the best of you in an argument. Refuse to argue. If the one with whom you are talking has mistaken notions that must be removed before he can be led to Christ, quietly and pleasantly show him his error. If the error is not essential to the doctrine of salvation, refuse to discuss it and hold the person to the main question.

11. Never interrupt anyone else who is leading someone to Christ.

You may think he is not doing it in the best way, but if you can do any better, wait quietly, and you will have the opportunity. Many unskilled workers have someone at the point of decision when a meddler breaks in and upsets the whole work. On the other hand, do not let others interrupt you. Just a little word plainly but courteously spoken will usually prevent it.

12. Don't be in a hurry.

One of the great faults of Christian work today is haste. We are too anxious for immediate results and therefore do superficial work. Many of those who followed Christ came to Him slowly. Nicodemus, Joseph of Arimathea, Peter, and even Paul—although the final step in Paul's case seems very sudden—are cases in point. Three days after Jesus appeared to Paul on the way to Damascus, Paul came out into the light and openly confessed Christ. (See Acts 22:5–16.) One man with whom slow but thorough work has been done, and who at last has committed his life to Christ, is better than a dozen who are rushed through the sinner's prayer and think they have accepted Christ when in reality they have not. It is often wise to plant a truth in a man's heart and leave it to work. The seed on rocky ground springs up quickly, but it withers just as quickly.

13. Whenever possible, ask the person to pray with you.

Difficulties can disappear in prayer, and many stubborn people yield when they are brought into the presence of God. I remember talking with a young woman for two hours and making no apparent headway. At last we knelt in prayer, and she was rejoicing in her Savior in less than five minutes.

14. Whenever you seem to fail, go home, pray about it, and find out why you failed.

If you did not know what Scripture verse to use, study the portion of this book that describes the different types of people we meet and how to deal with them. See where your particular case belongs and how you should have responded. Then go back, if you can, and try again. In any case, you will be better prepared the next time. The greatest successes in Christian work come through many apparent defeats. Study these hints and suggestions often to see if your failures come from a lack of preparation.

15. Before parting from the one who has accepted Christ, be sure to give him definite instructions as to how to succeed in the Christian life. The following points should always be insisted upon:

(a) Confess Christ openly before men every opportunity you get (Romans 10:9–10; Matthew 10:32–33).

(b) Be baptized and partake regularly of the Lord's Supper (Acts 2:38–42; Luke 22:19; 1 Corinthians 11:24–26).

(c) Study the Word of God daily (1 Peter 2:2; Acts 20:32; 2 Timothy 3:13–17; Acts 17:2).

(d) Pray daily, often, and in times of temptation (Luke 11:9–13; 22:40; 1 Thessalonians 5:17).

(e) Put every sin, even the smallest, and every doubt out of your life and obey every word of Christ (1 John 1:6–7; Romans 14:23; John 14:23).

(f) Seek the fellowship of other Christians (Ephesians 4:12–16; Acts 2:42, 44–47; Hebrews 10:24–25).

(g) Go to work for Christ (Matthew 25:14–29).

(h) When you fall into sin, don't be discouraged but confess it at once and believe it is forgiven because God says so. Then get up and go on with God (1 John 1:9; Philippians 3:13–14).

You should give these instructions to the one you have led to Christ. You can write them out or give a little tract or book that lists these and other helpful points for living the Christian life.

16. When you have led anyone to Christ, help him grow in his Christian life.

Many who are led to Christ are then neglected, and their Christian growth is poor. The work of following up on those who are converted is as important as the work of leading them to Christ. As a rule, no one can do it as well as the person God used in their conversion.

12

POWER FOR SOULWINNING

One important condition for successful soulwinning demands a separate chapter. In Acts 1:5, Luke 24:49, and Acts 2:4 we have three expressions: "*baptized with the Holy Ghost* [Spirit]," "*endued with power from on high,*" and "*filled with the Holy Ghost* [Spirit]." By a careful comparison of these and related passages, we will find that these various expressions refer to one and the same experience. This experience is an absolutely necessary condition of acceptable and effective service for Christ.

Filled with the Spirit

The infilling of the Holy Spirit is a definite and distinct experience. A Christian will know whether he has received the Spirit or not. Jesus commanded His disciples to wait in Jerusalem until they received power from on high. (See Luke 24:49 and Acts 1:8.) If this were not a definite and distinct experience, the disciples would not know whether they had complied with Christ's command.

The baptism in the Holy Spirit is separate from His regenerating work. The disciples were told in Acts 1:5, "*Ye shalt be baptized with the Holy Ghost* [Spirit] *not many days hence.*" In Acts 8:14–16, we are told that some followers of Christ had already believed and been baptized with water, but the Holy Spirit had not yet fallen upon them. Again in Acts 19:1–6, some of the disciples had not received the Holy Spirit since they believed.

A believer may be regenerated by the Holy Spirit without being baptized with the Holy Spirit. Such a soul is saved but is not yet ready for service. Although every believer has the Holy Spirit according to Romans 8:9, not every believer has the baptism of the Holy Spirit. (See Acts 8:12–16; 19:1–6.) Nevertheless, the baptism is available to everyone who has been born again.

The baptism of the Holy Spirit is always connected with testimony or service. (See 1 Corinthians 12:4–13; 2:4; Acts 4:8, 31; 7:55; 9:17, 20; 10:45–46; 19:6.) The baptism of the Holy Spirit has no direct reference to cleansing from sin. Some teaching on this subject leads men to expect that, if they receive the baptism of the Holy Spirit, the old carnal nature will be eradicated. No Scripture supports this position. If you examine all the passages in which the baptism of the Holy Spirit is mentioned, you will see that it is always connected with testimony and service. A great moral and spiritual uplifting accompanies the baptism and often brings about an entire surrender of the will to Christ, but its primary purpose is for service.

We will get a better understanding of the baptism of the Holy Spirit if we consider its manifestations and results recorded in the Bible. Let us look first at the passage that goes into the most detail on this subject—1 Corinthians 12:4–14. The manifestations or results of the baptism of the Holy Spirit are not precisely the same in every person. For example, the baptism of the Holy Spirit will not make everyone who receives it a successful evangelist or teacher. A different gift may be imparted instead. This fact is often overlooked, resulting in disappointment and doubt. The manifestations or results vary with the lines of service to which God has called different individuals. One may receive the gift of being an evangelist, another a teacher, and another a helper. (See 1 Corinthians 12:28–31; Ephesians 4:8, 11–13.) Some gift will be given in every case. (See 1 Corinthians 12:7, 11.) It may not be the same gift as another person receives, but there will be a gift.

The Holy Spirit is the One who decides what gift or gifts will be imparted to each individual. (See 1 Corinthians 12:7, 11.) It is not for us to select some place of service and then ask the Holy Spirit to qualify us for that service. We should not select some gift and then ask the Spirit to impart to us that gift. We are called to put ourselves entirely at the disposal of the Holy Spirit to send us where He will, into what line of service He will, and to impart what gift He will. He is absolutely sovereign, and our rightful position is one of absolute and unconditional surrender to Him.

Many fail to allow God to choose how He will use them, and they meet with disappointment. I know a sincere and self-sacrificing man who gave up a prosperous business and began the work of an evangelist. He had heard of the baptism of the Holy Spirit and supposed that if he received it, he would be qualified to be an evangelist. The man traveled more than four thousand miles to another country, but the work did not open up for him. He was confused and in doubt until he was led to see that it was not for him to select the work of an evangelist, as good as that work was, and then expect the Holy Spirit to qualify him for it. He gave himself up to be used in whatever work the Spirit would choose. The power of the Spirit came upon him, and he received the gift of an evangelist that he had coveted.

Power for Bold Service

The baptism of the Holy Spirit always imparts power for the service God calls us to fulfill. In a large American city, an uneducated boy was led to Christ. In his humble occupation, he began witnessing for Jesus. He grew one step at a time in Christ's work. A gentleman told me about him and said he would like me to meet him. The gentleman brought him to Chicago, and I invited him to speak one night in one of our tent meetings. The meeting was in a rough neighborhood, and it was usually difficult to hold the audience's attention for very long.

The young man began his message in a simple way. I was afraid I had made a mistake in asking him to speak, but I prayed and watched the audience. There was nothing remarkable in his address as he continued. But I noticed that all the people were listening. They continued to listen to the end. When I asked if there was anyone who wished to accept Christ, people stood in different parts of the tent to signify that they did. A man who had known the speaker before whispered to me, "It is the same wherever he goes." What was the explanation? This uneducated boy had received the baptism of the Holy Spirit and had received power.

One night at the close of a message on the baptism of the Holy Spirit, a minister came to me on the platform and said, "I need this power. Please pray for me."

"Let us kneel right now," I replied, and we did. A few weeks later, I met a gentleman who had been standing near us. "Do you remember," he said, "the minister with whom you prayed at New Britain? He went back to his church, and it is now packed every Sunday. People are being converted right and left." He had received the baptism of the Holy Spirit and power.

The baptism of the Holy Spirit always imparts boldness in testimony and service. (See Acts 4:29–31.) Contrast Peter in Acts 4:8–12 with Peter in Mark 14:66–72. Perhaps you have a great desire to speak to others and win them to Christ, but an insurmountable timidity stands in the way. If you receive the baptism of the Holy Spirit, all of your shyness and fear will be overcome.

We are now ready to define the baptism of the Holy Spirit. The baptism of the Holy Spirit is the Spirit of God falling on the believer, taking possession of his faculties, and imparting to him gifts not naturally his own but which qualify him for the service to which God has called him.

Who Needs the Baptism?

In Luke 24:49, Jesus told the apostles to remain in Jerusalem until they were filled with power from on high. These men had been appointed to be witnesses of the life, death, and resurrection of Christ. (See Luke 24:45–48; Acts 1:22; 10:39–41.) They had received what would seem to be splendid and sufficient training for this work. For more than three years, they were instructed by Jesus Himself. They saw His miracles, death, burial, resurrection, and ascension.

But one thing was still needed. Jesus would not permit them to begin their appointed work until they were baptized in the Holy Spirit. The apostles, with their unparalleled qualifications for service, were not permitted to begin their work until they received the baptism of the Holy Spirit. What presumption it is for any of us with our inferior training to attempt service without it. Even Jesus did not begin His ministry until He was anointed with the Holy Spirit and power. (See Acts 10:38; Luke 3:21–22; 4:1, 14.)

This baptism is an absolutely essential preparation for Christian work. Only ignorance of the requirements of God's Word or daring presumption on our part would cause us to try to work for Christ before being baptized with the Holy Spirit.

It is the privilege of every believer to be baptized with the Holy Spirit. *"For the promise is unto you, and to your children, and to all that are afar off, even as many as the Lord our God shall call"* (Acts 2:39). The *"promise"* of this verse means the promise of the baptism of the Holy Spirit. The verse tells us that this promise is for everyone in all ages of the church's history whom God calls to Himself. If we do not have this baptism, it is our own fault. The baptism of the Holy Spirit is for us. We are responsible before God for all the work we could have done and all the souls we could have won if we would have received the baptism.

13

OBTAINING THE BAPTISM IN THE HOLY SPIRIT

We now come to the practical question: How can we obtain this baptism of the Holy Spirit that is absolutely necessary in our service for Christ? Fortunately, the answer is plainly stated in the Bible.

"Repent, and be baptized every one of you in the name of Jesus Christ for the remission of sins, and ye shall receive the gift of the Holy Ghost [Spirit]" (Acts 2:38). The first step toward obtaining this baptism is repentance. Repentance means a change of mind—a change of mind about sin, about God, and in this case especially (as the context shows), a change of mind about Christ. A

real change of mind leads to action. We turn away from all sin and turn to God. We turn away from rejecting Jesus Christ to accepting Him.

The second step is the rejection of our sin and acceptance of Jesus Christ by baptism in His name. The baptism with the Holy Spirit, in at least one instance, preceded the baptism with water, but this was apparently an exceptional case. (See Acts 10:44–48.)

How to Surrender All

"*The Holy Ghost* [Spirit], *whom God hath given to them that obey him*" (Acts 5:32). The condition of the gift of the Holy Spirit stated here is that we obey Him. Obedience means more than the mere performance of some of the things God commands us to do. It means the entire surrender of our wills, ourselves, and everything we have to Him. We come to Him and say from the heart, "Here I am, Lord. I am Yours. You bought me with a price, and I acknowledge Your ownership. Take me and do with me whatever You desire. Send me wherever You want. Use me as You wish." This entire yielding of ourselves to God is the condition of our receiving the baptism of the Holy Spirit.

At the close of a revival service, a gentleman hurried to the platform and said there was a lady in great distress who wished to speak with me. It was an hour before I could get to her, and she was anxious to receive the baptism of the Holy Spirit. Others had talked to her, but it seemed to do no good. I sat down beside her and said, "Is your will completely surrendered?" She did not know.

"Do you want to work for Jesus?" I asked.

"Yes."

"Are you willing to go back home and be a servant girl if it is God's will?"

"No!"

"You will never receive this blessing until your own will is completely laid down."

"I cannot lay it down."

"Would you like to have God lay it down for you?"

"Yes."

"Well, let us ask Him to do it." We did, and God heard her prayer. She received the baptism of the Holy Spirit and went from the church rejoicing.

Obedience means following the will of God as revealed in His Word or by His Spirit in every circumstance. Any refusal to do what God tells us to do, any conscious doing of what He tells us not to do—even in very little matters—will shut us out of this blessing. If even the smallest thing troubles us as we pray over this matter, we should set it right with God at once.

Asking and Receiving

We must make a definite request for the Father to fill us with the Holy Spirit. *"How much more shall your heavenly Father give the Holy Spirit to them that ask him?"* (Luke 11:13). Ministers often say that because the Holy Spirit is already here and every believer has the Spirit, we do not need to pray for Him to come. This argument overlooks the distinction between having the Holy Spirit and being baptized in the Holy Spirit. It also contradicts the plain teaching of God's Word that He gives the Holy Spirit to *"them that ask him."* Furthermore, the baptism of the Holy Spirit in the book of Acts was constantly given in connection with and in answer to prayer. (See Acts 1:14; 2:1–4; 4:31; 8:15, 17.)

Prayer implies desire. There is no real prayer for the baptism of the Spirit unless there is a deep desire for it. As long as a man thinks he can get along somehow without this blessing, he is not likely to obtain it. But when he reaches the place where he feels he must have this, no matter what it costs, he is on his way toward receiving it. Many ministers of the Gospel have realized that they could not go on with their ministry without this gift. The gift soon came in answer to prayer, and the character of their work was entirely transformed.

For prayer to be effective, it must be given in faith. (See Mark 11:24.) James says this in regard to the prayer for wisdom:

> *Let him ask in faith, nothing wavering. For he that wavereth is like a wave of the sea driven with the wind and tossed. For let not that man think that he shall receive any thing of the Lord.* (James 1:6–7)

The same principle holds true regarding the prayer for the Holy Spirit.

Many miss the blessing at this point. The way to approach God in faith is clearly taught in 1 John 5:14–15:

> *This is the confidence that we have in him, that, if we ask any thing according to his will, he heareth us: and if we know that he hear us, whatsoever we ask, we know that we have the petitions that we desired of him.*

When we ask the Father for the baptism of the Holy Spirit, we know that we have asked something according to His will because it is definitely promised in His Word. Therefore, when I ask God in faith, I have a right to count this blessing as mine. The prayer is heard, and I have the petition that I asked of Him. I can get up and begin my work, assured that the Spirit's power will be with me.

You may ask, "Should I expect any evidence of the Spirit's presence?" The answer is yes, but only in your service to Him. When I know on the authority of God's Word that my prayer is heard, I have the right to begin any service to which He calls me. I can confidently expect the manifestation of the Spirit's power in that service. It is a mistake to wait—as so many do—for the manifestation in peculiar emotional experiences. These may and often do accompany the baptism of the Holy Spirit. But the Bible clearly teaches in 1 Corinthians 12:4–11 that the place to look for manifestation is in service. The most important, reliable, and scriptural manifestations are found in our work.

The Word on Waiting

"Must we not wait," it may be asked, "until we know that we have received the baptism of the Holy Spirit?" The answer is yes, but how are we to know? We know in the same way we know we are saved—by the testimony of God's Word. When I have met His conditions and have asked for this gift that is according to His will, I know by God's Word in 1 John 5:14–15 that my prayer is heard and that I have received the answer. I have a right to proceed with no other evidence than the all-sufficient evidence of God's Word. I can enter into the service to which God calls me.

The disciples waited ten days, and the reason is clearly given in Acts 2:1: *"When the day of Pentecost was fully come."* In the Old Testament types, the Day of Pentecost had been appointed as the day for the first giving of the Holy Spirit and the offering of the firstfruits (the church). Therefore, the Holy Spirit could not be given until that day. (See Leviticus 23:9–21.) But after the Spirit was given, we find no lengthy period of waiting on the part of those who sought this blessing. (See Acts 4:31; 8:15, 17; 9:17, 20; 19:6.) Men are obliged to wait today, but it is only because they have not met the conditions or do not believe and claim the blessing simply on the Word of God. The moment we meet the conditions and claim the blessing, it is ours. (See Mark 11:24.) Any child of God may lay down this book, meet the conditions, ask for the blessing, claim it, and have it.

A student came to talk with me about the baptism of the Holy Spirit. He said he had heard of this before and had been seeking it for months but could not get it. I found that his will was not surrendered, but we soon settled the matter. I said, "Let us kneel down and ask God for the baptism of the Holy Spirit." After we prayed, I asked the student, "Was that petition according to God's will?"

"Yes."

"Was the prayer heard?"

After some hesitation he replied, "It must have been."

"Have you received what you asked of Him?"

"I do not feel it."

I read 1 John 5:15 from the Bible that lay open before us: *"If we know that he hear us, whatsoever we ask, we know that we have the petitions that we desired of him."*

"Now, have you received what you asked?"

A smile spread over his face, and he said, "I must have, for God says so." He left a few minutes later. When I went back to the school in a few days, I met the young man again. His face was all aglow. He knew he had received what at first he took on the Word of God alone.

We must be filled continually with the Spirit to work for God. Many Christians who once experienced the baptism of the Holy Spirit are today trying to work in the power of that old experience and are working without God. A constant fellowship must be maintained so that the Spirit is allowed to work in and through the believer. By the power that works within us, we will be able to do mighty exploits for the kingdom of God.

HEAVEN OR HELL

CONTENTS

1

COME OUT OF HIDING

The first question that God ever asked of man is recorded in Genesis 3:9: *"Where art thou?"* God asked the question of Adam on the evening of that awful day of the first sin. The voice of God in its majesty rolled down the avenues of the Garden of Eden. Until that day, the voice of God had been the sweetest music to Adam. He knew no greater joy than that of glad communion with his Creator and his heavenly Father. But now all was different. As the voice of God was heard in the Garden, Adam was filled with fear and tried to hide himself.

This is the history of every son of Adam from that day until now. Every sinner is trying to hide from the presence and the all-seeing eyes of God.

This accounts for a large share of the skepticism, agnosticism, and atheism of our day. It is sinful man trying to hide from a holy God.

True Reasons for Unbelief

People will give many reasons why they are skeptics, agnostics, or atheists. But in the majority of cases, the real reason is this: they hope to hide themselves from the discomfort of God's presence by denying that He exists. This also accounts for much of the neglect of the Bible. People will tell you that they do not read their Bibles because they have so much else to read or because they are not interested in the Bible. They declare that it is a dull and boring book to them. But the true cause of man's neglect of Bible study is this: the Bible brings God near to us as no other book does, and men are uneasy when they become conscious of the presence of God. Therefore, they neglect the book that brings God near.

This also accounts for much of the absenteeism from the house of God and its services. People give many reasons why they do not attend church. They will tell you they cannot dress well enough to attend church or that they are too busy and too tired. They will complain that the services are dull and uninteresting. But the reason why men and women, old and young, are habitually absent from church is because the house of God brings God near and makes them uncomfortable in their sin.

No one ever succeeded in hiding from God. God said to Adam, "*Where art thou?*" Adam had to come from his hiding place to meet God face-to-face and make full confession of his sin. Sooner or later, no matter how carefully they hide themselves from God, all men and women will have to come from their hiding places and meet Him face-to-face. They will have to make a full declaration of where they stand in His presence.

God puts this question to every Christian and to everyone who is not a Christian: "*Where art thou?*" Where do you stand concerning spiritual and eternal things? Where do you stand concerning God, heaven, righteousness, Christ, and eternity? "*Where art thou?*"

Knowing Where You Stand

Every truly intelligent person desires to know just where he is. Every wise businessman desires to know where he stands financially. In our country, every careful businessman periodically takes an inventory of his stock, examines his accounts, finds out precisely what are his credits and debits, and how much his assets exceed or fall below his liabilities.

He may discover as a result of his scrutiny that he does not stand as well as he thought he did. If that is true, he wants to know it in order that he may conduct his business accordingly. Many have failed in business through unwillingness to face facts and find out just where they stood.

I knew a very brilliant businessman who was truly gifted in a certain type of business enterprise. But his affairs got into a tangled condition.

His wise business friends came to him and advised him to go through his books and find out just where he stood. They said to him, "If you are in bad shape, we will help you out."

But the man was too proud to take their advice. He was too proud to admit that his business was in danger of failure, so he refused to look into it. He resolutely tried to plunge through. But instead of plunging through, he sunk into utter financial ruin. Although he was an exceptionally brilliant man in some areas, he experienced complete financial shipwreck. He never got on his feet again. When he died, he did not have enough money to pay for his funeral expenses, simply because he was not willing to humble his pride and face facts.

Many people are too proud to confess that they are morally and spiritually bankrupt. So they are going to grit their teeth and plunge through. They will fall into utter and eternal ruin. Everyone wants to know where he stands physically. He wants to know the condition of his lungs, heart, stomach, and nerves. He may be worse off than he thinks he is. He may think his heart is sound when it is defective. But he wants to know it, because then he will not subject it to the strain that otherwise he would. Many lie in a premature grave who might be doing good work on earth if they had been willing to find out what their real condition was and to act accordingly.

Every man at sea wishes to know where his vessel is, its exact latitude and longitude. When crossing the Atlantic Ocean some years ago, I sailed for days beneath clouds and through fogs. The sailors were unable to take an observation by the sun and had been sailing blindly. One night I happened to be on deck, when suddenly there was a rift in the clouds, and the North Star appeared. Word was sent below, and the captain of the vessel hurried on deck. I remember how he nearly laid across the compass as he carefully took an observation by the North Star in order to know exactly where we were.

In life, we are all sailing across a perilous sea toward an eternal port. All intelligent men and women will desire to know just where they are—their exact spiritual longitude and their exact spiritual latitude.

How to Evaluate the Question

Let us consider this weighty question of where we are. We should consider it seriously. It is not a question to trifle with. It is amazing that men and women may be sensible about everything else and would not think of trifling with the great financial questions of the day or with great social problems. But they treat this great question of eternity as a joke.

One evening I bought a paper from a little newsboy on the street. As he handed me my change, I asked him, "My boy, are you saved?" The boy treated it as a joke. That might be all you could expect of a poor, uneducated newsboy on the street. But it is not what you would expect of thinking men and women when you come to these great eternal problems of God, eternity, salvation, heaven, and hell.

Anyone who trifles with questions like these is a fool. I don't care about your culture, social position, or reputation. Unless you face the great question of your spiritual condition with the most profound earnestness and seriousness, you are playing the part of a fool.

We should consider this question honestly. Many people today try to deceive themselves, others, and even God. They know in their innermost hearts that they are wrong, but they try to persuade themselves, others, and God that they are right.

You cannot deceive God. It will do you no good to deceive anybody else, and it is the height of folly to deceive yourself. The biggest fool on earth is the man who fools himself. Be honest. If you are lost, admit it; if you are on the road to hell, acknowledge it; if you are not a Christian, say so. If you are an enemy of God, face the facts. If you are a child of the devil, realize it. Be honest with yourself, honest with your fellowmen, and honest with God.

We should consider the question thoroughly. Many people are honest and serious to a certain point, but they don't go to the bottom of things. They are superficial. They give these tremendous questions a few moments' thought, and then their weak minds grow weary. They say, "I guess I am all right; I will take my chances."

No one can afford to guess on questions like these. We must be absolutely certain. It will not satisfy me to hope I am saved; I must know that I am saved. It will not satisfy me to hope that I am a child of God; I must know that I am a child of God. It will not satisfy me to hope that I am bound for heaven; I must know that I am bound for heaven. Do not lay these questions down until you have gone to the bottom of them and know for certain just where you stand.

We should consider these questions prayerfully. God tells us in His Word, and we know from experience, that *"the heart is deceitful above all things, and desperately wicked"* (Jeremiah 17:9). There is nothing that the human heart is as deceitful about as our moral and spiritual conditions. Every man and woman is by nature sharp-sighted to the faults of others and blind to their own faults. We need to face this question in prayer. You will never know where you stand until God shows you.

We must pray like David, *"Search me, O God, and know my heart: try me, and know my thoughts: and see if there be any wicked way in me"* (Psalm 139:23–24). Only when God sheds the light of His Holy Spirit into our hearts and shows us ourselves as He sees us will we ever know ourselves as we truly are. To see ourselves in the light of God's presence, as God sees us, will only be in answer to definite and earnest prayer.

Are You a Religious Person?

One morning I met the minister of a church that formerly I had pastored. He said to me, "Brother Torrey, I had an awful experience this morning."

I said, "What was it, Brother Norris?" He mentioned a member of the church.

"You know she is dying. She sent for me to come and see her this morning. I hurried to her home. The moment I opened the door and entered the room she cried from her bed, 'Oh, Brother Norris, I have been a professing Christian for forty years. I am now dying and have just found out that I was never saved at all.'"

The horror of it! To be a professing Christian for forty years and never find out until your life is at an end that you have never really been a Christian at all. It is better to find it out today than in eternity.

Many men and women have been professing Christians for years but were never saved. In a paper edited by a clergyman, I read a letter complaining about our meetings. The writer said, "These men produced the impression that some of our church members are not saved." Well, that is the impression we tried to produce, for that is the truth of God. In churches throughout the world, you will find many men and women who are unsaved.

Once more we should consider this question scripturally, according to the Book. God has given to you and me only one safe chart and compass to guide us on our voyages through life toward eternity. That chart and compass is the Bible. If you steer your course according to the Book, you will steer safely. If you steer according to your own feelings, according to the speculation of the petty philosopher or the theologian, according to anything but the clear declaration of the Word of God, you steer your course to shipwreck. Any hope that is not founded on the clear, unmistakable teaching of God's Word is absolutely worthless.

You Can Be Sure

In one of my pastorates, a young married couple had a sweet little child entrusted to them by the heavenly Father. Then one day, that little child went home to be with the Lord. In the hour of their sorrow, I went to call on the grieving parents. Taking advantage of their tenderness of heart, I pointed them to the Savior with whom their child was safely at home. They promised to accept Jesus as their Savior.

After some days and weeks had passed and the first shock of the sorrow had gone, they began to drift back into the world again. I called on them to speak with them. Only the wife was at home. I began by talking about the little child and how safe and happy he was in the arms of Jesus. She gladly assented to all of this. Then I turned the topic a little bit and said to her, "Do you expect to see your child again?"

"Oh," she said, "certainly. I have no doubt that I will see my child again."

I said, "Why do you expect to see your child again?"

"Because the child is with Jesus, and I expect when I die I will go to be with Him, too."

I said, "Do you think you are saved?"

"Oh, yes," she replied, "I think I am saved."

"Why do you think you are saved?"

"Because I feel so," she said.

"Is that your only ground of hope?"

"That is all."

I said, "Your hope is not worth anything." That seemed cruel, didn't it? But it was kind. I asked her, "Can you put your finger on anything in the Word of God that proves you have everlasting life?"

"No," she said, "I cannot."

"Well, then," I said, "your hope is absolutely worthless." Then she turned on me, which she had a perfect right to do. It is quite right to talk back to preachers. I believe in it, and she began to talk back.

"Do you expect to go to heaven when you die?"

I responded, "Yes, I know I will."

"When you die, do you expect to be with Christ?"

"Yes," I said, "I know I will."

"Do you think you have everlasting life?"

"Yes," I said, "I know I have."

"Can you put your finger on anything in the Word of God that proves you have eternal life?"

I said, "Yes, thank God, John 3:36: '*He that believeth on the Son hath everlasting life.*' I know I believe in the Son of God. On the sure ground of God's Word, I know I have everlasting life."

2

WHERE DO YOU STAND?

Choose you this day whom ye will serve.
—Joshua 24:15

A few suggestions will help you in considering this question: Where are you? Are you saved or are you lost? You are one or the other. Unless you have been definitely saved by a deliberate acceptance of Jesus Christ, you are definitely lost. Only two classes exist—lost sinners and saved sinners. To which class do you belong?

Are you on the road to heaven or the road to hell? You are on one or the other. The Lord Jesus tells us that there are only two roads—the broad road that leads to destruction and the narrow road that leads to life everlasting. (See Matthew 7:13–14.) Which road are you on? Are you on the road that leads to God, heaven, and glory? Or are you on the road that leads to Satan, sin, shame, and hell?

Some years ago, an English sailor came into a mission in New York City. As he left the church not very much affected, a worker at the door put a little card into his hand. These words were printed on this card: "If I would die tonight, I would go to ________." The place was left blank, and underneath was written, "Please fill in the blank and sign your name."

The sailor, without even reading the card, put it in his pocket and went down to the steamer. During the journey back to England, he was thrown from the rigging and broke his leg. His fellow sailors took him down to his berth, and as he lay there day after day, that card stared him in the face. "If I would die tonight, I would go to ________."

"Well," he said, "if I filled that out honestly, I would have to write *hell*. If I would die tonight, I would go to hell. But I won't fill it out that way." Lying there in his berth, he accepted Jesus Christ as his Lord and Savior and filled out the card: "If I would die tonight, I would go to heaven." One day he went back to New York. He walked into the mission and handed in the card with his name signed to it.

Suppose you had such a card to complete. "If I would die tonight, I would go to ________." What would you answer? Are you a child of God or a child of the devil?

We live in a day in which many superficial thinkers are telling us that all men are the children of God. That is not the teaching of the Bible, and it is not the teaching of Jesus Christ. Jesus Christ said distinctly in John 8:44, talking to certain Jews, *"Ye are of your father the devil."* We are told in 1 John 3:10, *"In this the children of God are manifest, and the children of the devil: whosoever doeth not righteousness is not of God."* And we are told distinctly in John 1:12, *"As many as received him, to them gave he power to become the sons of God."* Every one of us is either a child of God or a child of the devil. Which are you?

When I was speaking in Ballarat, Australia, a large group of educated men sat listening to the sermon. I was preaching on the difference between the children of God and the children of the devil. The next night when I gave the invitation, almost the entire group of educated men came to the front. When they got up to give their testimony, one of them said, "The reason I came tonight and accepted Christ was this: I was here last night and heard Dr. Torrey say that everyone was a child of God or a child of the devil. I knew I was not a child of God; therefore, I knew I must be a child of the devil. I made up my mind I would be a child of the devil no longer. I have come forward tonight to take Jesus Christ."

Are you a Christian in name only, or are you a real Christian? You know there are two kinds. Are you one of these people who call themselves Christians, go to the house of God on Sunday, take Communion, and perhaps even teach a Sunday school class? But the rest of the week, do you run around drinking, carousing, and participating in all the frivolity and foolishness of the world?

Are you one of these Christians who are trying to hold on to Jesus Christ with one hand and the world with the other? Or are you a real Christian who has renounced the world with your whole heart and given yourself to Jesus Christ, a Christian who can sing and mean it, "I surrender all"? What kind of a Christian are you?

Are you for Christ or against Him? You are either one or the other. We read Jesus' words in Matthew 12:30: *"He that is not with me is against me."* Either you are with Jesus wholeheartedly and openly, or you are against Him. Are you for Christ or against Him?

Taking a Stand

In my first pastorate, year after year, there came an outpouring of God's Spirit. In one of these gracious outpourings, many of the leading businessmen of the area were converted. It was a small town, but one of the businessmen would not take a stand. He was one of the most exemplary men in the community. He was an amiable, upright, regular attender at church. He was a member of my Bible class and the choir, but he was one of those men who wanted to please both sides. He was identified with friends in business, in community action groups, and elsewhere, who were not committed Christians. He was afraid that he would offend them if he came out boldly and honestly for Christ.

The weeks passed by. One Sunday morning, he was leaving my Bible class and passed by the superintendent of the Sunday school, who was his intimate friend. They had been in the army together. As he passed by, his friend turned to him and said, "George?"

"Well, what is it, Porter?" said the other, calling him by his first name.

"George, when are you going to take a stand?"

He said, "Ring the bell."

Promptly the superintendent stepped up to the bell and rang it. The congregation turned in surprise, wondering what was going to happen. George stepped to the front of the platform. It was a community where everybody knew everybody else by their first name, and everybody was curious.

"Friends," he said, "I have heard it said time and time again during these meetings that a man must either be for Jesus Christ or against Him. I want you all to know that from this time on, my wife and I are for Christ."

Many people have been involved in a church for years, but they have never taken an open stand for Christ. Take it now. Say, *"As for me and my house, we will serve the Lord"* (Joshua 24:15).

It is important to face the question, "Where are you?" Where you are today may determine where you will spend eternity.

Meeting the Chief Physician

A story is told of Dr. Forbes Winslow, an eminent pathologist in diseases of the mind. A young French nobleman came to London bringing letters of introduction from leading Frenchmen. The letters introduced him to Dr. Winslow and requested the doctor's best care for the young man. He presented his letters, and Dr. Winslow said, "What is your trouble?"

"Dr. Winslow, I cannot sleep. I have not had a good night's sleep for two years. Unless something is done for me, I will go insane."

Dr. Winslow said, "Why can't you sleep?"

"Well," said the young man, "I can't tell you."

Dr. Winslow said, "Have you lost any money?"

"No," he said, "I have lost no money."

"Have you lost friends?"

"No, I have lost no friends recently.

"Have you suffered in honor or reputation?"

"Not that I know of."

"Well then," said the doctor, "why can't you sleep?"

The young man said, "I would rather not tell you."

"Well," said Dr. Winslow, "if you don't tell me, I can't help you."

"Well," he said, "if I must tell you, I will. I am an agnostic. My father was an agnostic before me. Every night when I lie down to sleep, I am confronted with the question, 'Where will I spend eternity?' All night that question rings in my ears. If I succeed in getting off to sleep, my dreams are worse than my waking hours, and I awaken again."

Dr. Winslow said, "I can't do anything for you."

"What!" said the young Frenchman. "Have I come all the way over here from Paris for you to help me, and you dash my hopes to the ground? Do you mean to tell me that my case is hopeless?"

Dr. Winslow repeated, "I can do nothing for you, but I can tell you about a Physician who can." He walked across his study, took up his Bible from the center of the table, and opened it to Isaiah 53:5–6. He began to read:

> *He was wounded for our transgressions, he was bruised for our iniquities: the chastisement of our peace was upon him; and with his stripes we are healed. All we like sheep have gone astray; we have turned every one to his own way; and the Lord hath laid on him the iniquity of us all.*

Looking at the Frenchman, he said, "He is the only Physician in the world who can help you."

There was a curl of scorn on the man's lips. He said, "Dr. Winslow, do you mean to tell me that you, an eminent scientist, believe in that worn-out superstition of the Bible and Christianity?"

"Yes," said Dr. Winslow. "I believe in the Bible. I believe in Jesus Christ. And believing in the Bible and believing in Jesus Christ has saved me from becoming what you are today."

The young fellow thought for a moment. Then he said, "Dr. Winslow, if I am an honest man, I should at least be willing to consider it, correct?"

"Yes, sir."

"Well," he said, "will you explain it to me?"

The eminent physician sat down with his open Bible, and for several days, he showed the young Frenchman the way of eternal life. He saw Christ as his divine, atoning Savior, put his trust in Him, and went back to Paris with peace of mind. He had solved the great question of eternity and where he would spend it, for he would spend it with Christ in glory. Where will you spend eternity?

3

WHY DO YOU NOT BELIEVE?

He that believeth on him is not condemned: but he that believeth not is condemned already, because he hath not believed in the name of the only begotten Son of God.
—John 3:18

The failure to put faith in Jesus Christ is not a mere misfortune. It is a sin—a grievous sin, an appalling sin, a damning sin. Men will tell you very lightly, as if it were something of which they were quite proud, "I do not believe in Jesus Christ." Few men are foolish, blind, or utterly depraved enough to tell you proudly, "I am a murderer" or "I am an adulterer" or "I am a habitual liar." Yet none of these is a sadder or darker confession than "I am an unbeliever in Jesus Christ."

Believing or not believing in Jesus Christ is largely a matter of the will. Some people imagine it is wholly a matter of intellectual conviction. The one who assumes this is a very superficial thinker. Few people do not have sufficient evidence that Jesus is the Son of God and the Savior of those who believe in Him. They must only be willing to yield themselves to the evidence.

Men and women who believe in Jesus Christ have decided to yield to the truth. They believe in Him who is clearly proven to be God's Son. Those who do not believe because of the love of sin, or for some other reason, will not yield to the truth and accept Him as Savior and Lord.

Your refusal to accept Jesus Christ is not because you have honest reasons for believing that He is not who He claims to be. You know it is because you do not want to accept Him and surrender your life to Him. This is a great sin—greater than any sin you can commit against any person by lying to him, stealing from him, or killing him.

Facing the Truth

Don't try to ignore the truth. If you do, you will do it to your eternal ruin. If I am right in this matter, and if the Bible is right, it is infinitely important that you know it. Therefore, read carefully and be honest with yourself.

Unbelief in Jesus Christ is an appalling sin because of the dignity of the person of Jesus Christ. Jesus is the Son of God in a sense that no other person is the Son of God. Consider these Scriptures: "*Who being the brightness of his glory, and the express image of his person*" (Hebrews 1:3); "*For in him dwelleth all the fulness of the Godhead bodily*" (Colossians 2:9); "*when he bringeth in the firstbegotten into the world, he saith, And let all the angels of God worship him*" (Hebrews 1:6); "*That all men should honour the Son, even as they honour the Father*" (John 5:23).

A dignity belongs to Jesus Christ that belongs to no angel or archangel and to none of the "*principalities and powers in heavenly places*" (Ephesians 3:10). His is the "*name which is above every name: that at the name of Jesus every knee should bow…and that every tongue should confess that Jesus Christ is Lord"* (Philippians 2:9–11).

An injury done to Jesus Christ is a sin of vastly greater magnitude than a sin done to man. A mule has rights, but its rights are unimportant when compared with the rights of a man. The law recognizes the rights of a mule, but the killing of a mule is not regarded as serious as the putting out of a man's eye. But the rights of a man, even of the purest, noblest, greatest of men, pale into insignificance before the rights of the infinite God and His Son, Jesus Christ.

God's Majesty and Our Sin

To realize the enormity of a sin committed against Jesus Christ, we must strive for an adequate understanding of His dignity and majesty. When we do, we see that our unbelief robs this infinitely glorious Person of the honor due Him.

What was it that struck conviction into the hearts of three thousand men on the Day of Pentecost and made them cry out in agony, *"Men and brethren, what shall we do?"* (Acts 2:37). It was this: Peter, filled with the Spirit, told them who Jesus was. He said, *"Therefore let all the house of Israel know assuredly, that God hath made the same Jesus, whom ye have crucified, both Lord and Christ"* (verse 36). Their eyes were opened at last to see the glory, dignity, and majesty of the Person they had so outrageously wronged. All the sins of their lifetime instantly seemed to be nothing in comparison with this sin.

If you permit God to open your eyes to see who Jesus is, to see His infinite dignity, glory, and majesty, you will see that every wrong done to any mere man is nothing compared to the wrong done to this holy and majestic Person. You may refuse to let God open your eyes to the infinite glory of Jesus. You may say, "I don't see that He is essentially greater than other men or that His rights are more sacred than those of Longfellow, Lincoln, Washington, or my next-door neighbor." But the day will come when you will have to see.

The full glory of Jesus will be unveiled to the whole universe. If you will not repent now and receive pardon for your awful sin of unbelief, you will be overwhelmed with eternal shame. You will cry for the rocks and the hills to fall on you and hide you from the wrath of the One who sits upon the throne of the universe. (See Revelation 6:15–17.) You will wish to run from the presence of glory into eternal darkness if only you could escape the presence of Him whom you have so grievously wronged. On and on you will wish to flee from the outraged Son of God.

One night God gave me a vision of the glory of Jesus Christ. I saw the appalling nature of sin against Him, this infinitely glorious One. You may not have had such a vision, and you do not need to have it. You know what God's testimony regarding Jesus is. That testimony is in His Word. In that testimony, you will find that the most grievous wrongs against man—theft, adultery, murder—are as nothing. For this reason our text says, *"He that believeth on him is not condemned: but he that believeth not is condemned already, because he hath not believed in the name of the only begotten Son of God"* (John 3:18).

Unbelief in Jesus Christ is an appalling sin because faith is the supreme thing He is entitled to receive. Jesus is worthy of many things. He is worthy of our admiration, our attention, our obedience, our service, and our love—all these things are His due. Not to give Him these things is to rob Him of what is rightly His.

Above all else, Jesus Christ is worthy of faith. Man's confidence belongs in Jesus Christ. He is infinitely worthy of the surrender of our intellects, our feelings, and our wills. It is right for you to go to Him and say, "Lord Jesus, infinite Son of God, I surrender to You my faith, the confidence of my heart, and my will." If you refuse to do that, you have robbed Jesus Christ. You have robbed this glorious, divine Person of His first and greatest right, robbed a divine Person of His supreme due. So it is written in our text, *"He that believeth on him is not condemned: but he that believeth not is condemned already, because he hath not believed in the name of the only begotten Son of God"* (John 3:18).

Unbelief in Jesus Christ is an appalling sin because He is the incarnation of all the infinite moral perfections of God's own being. *"God is light, and in him is no darkness at all"* (1 John 1:5). This infinite, absolute light and this infinite holiness, love, and truth are incarnate in Jesus Christ. The refusal to accept Him is the refusal of light and the choice of darkness. The one who rejects Him loves darkness rather than light. Nothing more clearly reveals a man's heart than what he chooses and what he rejects. A man who chooses dirty books, indecent pictures, and worldly friends is a foul man despite what he pretends to be. A man who rejects the good, the pure, and the true is bad, impure, and false. To reject Christ is to reject the infinite light of God. It reveals a corrupt heart that loves darkness rather than light.

Unbelief in Jesus Christ is an appalling sin because it is trampling underfoot the infinite love and mercy of God. Jesus Christ is the supreme expression of God's love and mercy to sinners. The Bible tells us: *"For God so loved the world, that he gave his only begotten Son, that whosoever believeth in him should not perish, but have everlasting life"* (John 3:16).

Although we have all broken God's holy laws and brought the wrath of the Holy One upon ourselves, God still loves us. Instead of banishing us forever from His presence into the darkness where there is only agony and despair, He provided salvation for us at infinite cost to Himself. His saving love had no limit, and it stopped at no sacrifice. He gave His best—His only begotten Son—to redeem us. All that we need to do to be saved is to believe in God's Son and put our trust in the pardoning mercy and love of God.

But instead of believing and obtaining eternal life, what are you doing? You are not believing; you are rejecting the love and its provision. You are despising and trampling underfoot the salvation that God purchased with the blood of His Son and offered to you. Unbelief in Jesus Christ scorns and insults infinite pardoning love. Men and women, young and old, who do not place the faith of their whole beings in Jesus Christ and receive Him as their Lord and Savior are guilty of scorning and insulting the infinite, pardoning love of God.

Some even go beyond that. They try to make themselves believe that Jesus is not the Son of God and that there is no need for an atonement.

They laugh at the sacrifice the loving Father has made in order that His guilty, hell-deserving subjects might be saved. One sometimes wonders why the love of God does not turn to blazing wrath and why God does not blast the world of Christ-rejecting men with the breath of His mouth.

There are other reasons why unbelief in Jesus Christ is an appalling sin, but these four significant reasons are enough:

1. Because of the infinite dignity of His person.

2. Because faith is rightly His, and withholding it robs a divine Person of His supreme due.

3. Because Jesus Christ is the incarnation of all the infinite moral perfection of God's own being.

4. Because it tramples underfoot the infinite love and mercy of God.

Unbelief in Jesus Christ is an appalling sin. Theft is a gross sin, adultery is worse, and murder is shocking. But all these are nothing compared to the violation of the dignity and majesty of Jesus Christ, the only begotten Son of God, by our unbelief. How God must abhor the sin of unbelief! How all holy men and women must despise the sin of unbelief!

Not only the agnostic and the skeptic are guilty of this sin, but also everyone who holds back from the wholehearted surrender of his mind, affections, and will. All who fail to gladly welcome Jesus as Savior and Lord are guilty of this appalling sin. Do you cry out as the three thousand at Pentecost did, "*What shall we do?*" (Acts 2:37). Soften your hearts of stone; publicly confess your awful sin, and forsake it forever. Don't rest another day under such awful guilt.

We see why unbelief leads to eternal doom. No matter how many good things a person may do, he must forever perish if he refuses to believe in Jesus Christ. Give up your unbelief in Jesus Christ and receive Him now.

4

THE REALITY OF HELL

If thy right eye offend thee, pluck it out, and cast it from thee: for it is profitable for thee that one of thy members should perish, and not that thy whole body should be cast into hell.
—Matthew 5:29

If I were able to choose my own subject to write about, I certainly would never choose hell. It is an awful subject, but a minister of God has no right to choose his own subjects. He must go to God for them and faithfully teach what God has commanded.

I wish that I could believe that there was no hell. That is, I wish that I could believe that all men would repent and accept Christ, and that hell would therefore be unnecessary. Of course, if men persist in sin and persist in the rejection of Christ, it is right that there should be a hell.

If men choose sin, it is for the good of the universe and the glory of God that there is a hell to confine them in. But I wish with all my heart that all men would repent and render hell unnecessary. But I cannot believe it if it is not true. I would rather believe unpleasant truth than to believe pleasant error. As awful as the thought is, I have been driven to the conclusion that there is a hell.

Once, I honestly believed and taught that all men, and even the devil, would ultimately come to repentance, and that hell would one day cease to be. But I could not honestly reconcile this position with the teaching of Christ and the apostles. I finally decided that I must either give up my Bible or give up my eternal hope.

I could not give up the Bible. I had become thoroughly convinced that the Bible, beyond a doubt, was the Word of God. I could not twist and distort the Scriptures to make them agree with what I wanted to believe. As an honest man, there was only one thing left for me to do: give up my opinion that all men would ultimately come to repentance and be saved.

The Painful Truth

I know that if a man stands squarely on the teachings of Christ and the apostles and declares it without fear, he will be called narrow, harsh, and cruel. But I have no desire to be any broader than Jesus Christ was. Is it cruel to tell men the truth? The kindest thing that one can do is to declare the whole counsel of God (see Acts 20:27) and show men the full measure of their danger.

Suppose I was walking down railroad tracts knowing that far behind me there was a train coming loaded with happy travelers. I come to a place where I had supposed that there was a bridge across the chasm. But to my horror, I find that the bridge is out. I say to myself, "I must go back at once, as far as possible up the tracks and stop that oncoming train."

My awful warning that the bridge is out and that the passengers are in peril of a frightful disaster spoils the merriment of the evening. Would that be cruel? Would it not be the kindest thing that I could do?

Suppose when I found the bridge out, I had said, "These people are so happy. I cannot bear to disturb their lightheartedness and pleasure. That would be too cruel. I will sit down here and wait until the train comes." Then I sit down while the train comes rushing on and leaps unwarned into that awful abyss. Soon I would hear the despairing shrieks and groans of the wounded and mangled as they crawl out from among the bodies of the dead. Would that be kind? Would it not be the cruelest thing that I could do? If I acted that way, I would be arrested for manslaughter.

I have been down the tracks of life. I thought that there was a bridge across the chasm, but I have found that the bridge is out. Many of you who are now full of laughter are rushing on unaware of the awful fate that awaits you. I have come back up the track to warn you. I may destroy your present merriment, but by God's grace, I will save you from the awful doom. Is that cruel?

I would much rather be called cruel for being kind than be called kind for being cruel. The cruelest man on earth is the man who believes the stern things we are told in the Word of God about the future penalties of sin but avoids declaring them because they are unpopular.

The Danger of Man's Philosophies

I will not give you my own speculations about the future destiny of those who refuse to repent. Man's speculations on such a subject are absolutely worthless. God knows; we don't. But God has told us much of what He knows about it. Let us listen to Him. One ounce of God's revelation about the future is worth a hundred tons of man's speculation. What difference does it make what you or I think? The question is this: What does God say? His Word says, *"If thy right eye offend thee, pluck it out, and cast it from thee: for it is profitable for thee that one of thy members should perish, and not that thy whole body should be cast into hell"* (Matthew 5:29).

It is absolutely certain that there is a hell. People will tell you that all scholarly ministers and clergymen have given up their belief in hell. This simply is not so. This kind of argument is a favorite with those who know that they have a weak case. They try to bolster it with strong assertions.

It is true that some scholarly ministers have given up belief in hell, but they never gave it up for reasons of Greek or New Testament scholarship. They give it up for purely sentimental and speculative reasons. If a person goes to the New Testament to find out the truth and not to see how he can twist it into conformity with his speculations, he will find the reality of hell in the New Testament.

But suppose that every scholarly minister had given up belief in hell. It would not prove anything. Everybody who is familiar with the history of the world and the history of the church knows that time and time again some scholars have given up belief in doctrines that in the final outcome proved to be true.

There were no scholars in Noah's day who believed there would be a flood. But the flood came just the same. No scholars in Lot's day believed that God would destroy Sodom and Gomorrah, but He did. Jeremiah and one friend were the only leading men in all of Jerusalem who believed what Jeremiah taught about the coming destruction of Jerusalem under Nebuchadnezzar. But history outside the Bible, as well as history in the Bible, tells us that it came true to the very letter.

Every leading school of theological thought in the days of Jesus Christ—the Pharisees, the Sadducees, the Herodians, and the Essenes—every one of the four scoffed at Jesus Christ's prediction about the coming judgment of God upon Jerusalem. But secular history tells us that, in spite of the dissent of all the scholars, it came true just as Jesus predicted.

Nearly every leading scholar in the days of Luther and Huss had given up faith in the doctrine of justification by faith. Luther and his colleagues had to establish a new university to stand for the truth of God. But today we know that Martin Luther was right, and every university of Germany,

France, England, and Scotland was wrong. So even if it every scholarly preacher on earth had given up belief in the doctrine of hell, it would not prove anything.

What the Bible Says

Hell is certain. Why? First of all, because Jesus Christ said so, the apostles said so, and God says so.

Jesus Christ said, "*Then shall he say also unto them on the left hand, Depart from me, ye cursed, into everlasting fire, prepared for the devil and his angels*" (Matthew 25:41).

Paul wrote:

> *The Lord Jesus shall be revealed from heaven with his mighty angels, in flaming fire taking vengeance on them that know not God, and that obey not the gospel of our Lord Jesus Christ: who shall be punished with everlasting destruction from the presence of the Lord, and from the glory of his power.* (2 Thessalonians 1:7–9)

John recorded in Revelation 20:15, "*Whosoever was not found written in the book of life was cast into the lake of fire.*"

Peter wrote:

> *God spared not the angels that sinned, but cast them down to hell, and delivered them into chains of darkness, to be reserved unto judgment;... the Lord knoweth how to deliver the godly out of temptations, and to reserve the unjust unto the day of judgment to be punished.*
> (2 Peter 2:4, 9)

And in Jude, we read:

> *Behold, the Lord cometh with ten thousands of his saints, to execute judgment upon all, and to convince all that are ungodly among them of all their ungodly deeds which they have ungodly committed, and of all*

> *their hard speeches which ungodly sinners have spoken against him.*
> (Jude 14–15)

After Jesus had died and come up again from the abode of the dead, He ascended to the right hand of His Father. He said:

> *The fearful, and unbelieving, and the abominable, and murderers, and whoremongers, and sorcerers, and idolaters, and all liars, shall have their part in the lake which burneth with fire and brimstone: which is the second death.* (Revelation 21:8)

Hell is certain because Jesus Christ and the apostles said it is and because God says it is through them. The only thing against it is the speculation of theologians and dreams of poets. The words of Christ have stood the test of the centuries and always prove true in the final outcome. When I have Christ on one side and speculative theologians on the other, it doesn't take me long to decide which to believe.

Experience, observation, and common sense prove that there is a hell. One of the most certain acts of every man's experience is this: where there is sin, there must be suffering. We all know that. The longer a man continues in sin, the deeper he sinks into ruin, shame, agony, and despair. There are hundreds and thousands of men and women in the world living in a very real hell, and the hell is getting worse every day. You may not know how to reconcile what these men and women suffer with the doctrine that God is love. But no intelligent man gives up facts because he cannot explain the philosophy behind them.

Now, if this process keeps going on, sinking ever deeper into ruin, shame, and despair, when the time of possible repentance has passed, what is left but an everlasting hell? The only thing against it are the dreams of poets and the speculations of would-be philosophers. But the speculations of philosophers have proven to be misleading from the dawn of history. When we have the sure teaching of the Word of God, the case is settled.

There is a hell. It is more certain that there is a hell than that you will wake again tomorrow morning. You probably will; you may not. But it is absolutely certain that there is a hell. The next time you buy a book, no matter how skillfully it is written, and that author wants to prove to you that there is no hell, you will have paid to be made a fool of. There is a hell.

5

A PICTURE OF HELL

Fear him which is able to destroy both soul and body in hell.
—Matthew 10:28

We know that hell is a real place, but what is it like? What kind of people are there? Will they really remain in hell forever? Hell is a place of extreme bodily suffering. This is plain from the teaching of the New Testament. The words commonly used to express the doom of unrepentant sinners are *death* and *destruction*.

What do death and destruction mean? God has carefully defined His terms. In Revelation 17:8, we are told that the beast will go into "*perdition*." The word translated *perdition* is translated elsewhere *destruction*.

In Revelation 19:20, you will read that the beast and the false prophet *"were cast alive into a lake of fire burning with brimstone."* One thousand years after the beast and the false prophet have been thrown into the lake of fire, the devil also is cast in. They will be *"tormented day and night for ever and ever"* (Revelation 20:10). By God's definition, *perdition* or *destruction* is a place in a lake of torment forever.

Now let us took at God's definition of death. *"The fearful, and unbelieving, and the abominable, and murderers, and whoremongers, and sorcerers, and idolaters, and all liars, shall have their part in the lake which burneth with fire and brimstone: which is the second death"* (Revelation 21:8). God's definition of *death* is a portion in the *"lake of fire burning with brimstone"* (Revelation 19:20), the same as His definition of *perdition.*

"Oh," you may respond, "that is all highly figurative." Remember God's descriptions stand for facts. When some people come to something unwelcome in the Bible, they will say it is figurative and imagine that they have done away with it. You cannot do away with God's Word by calling it figurative. God is no liar, and God never overstates the facts. Hell means at least this much: bodily suffering of the most intense kind.

Furthermore, in the next life, we do not exist as disembodied spirits. This theory is man's philosophy and not New Testament teaching. According to the Bible, in the world to come, the spirit has a radically different body, but it is the perfect counterpart of the spirit that inhabits it and partakes in punishment or reward.

Even in this life, inward spiritual sin often causes outward bodily pain. Many are suffering the most severe pain because of inward sin. Hell is the place of punishment for the incurables of the universe, where people exist in awful and perpetual pain.

Painful Memories

But physical pain is the least significant feature of hell. Hell is a place of memory and remorse. In the picture Christ gave us of the rich man in hell, Abraham said to the rich man, *"Remember"* (Luke 16:25). The rich man brought little that he had on earth with him, but he had taken one thing—his memory.

If you choose to go on in sin and spend eternity in hell, you won't take much with you that you own, but you will take your memory. Men will remember the women whose lives they have ruined, and women will remember the time squandered in frivolity, fashion, and foolishness, when they might have been living for God. They will remember the Christ they rejected and the opportunities for salvation they despised.

There is no torment like the torment of an accusing memory. I have seen strong men weeping like children. What was the matter? Memory. One of the strongest, most intelligent men I ever knew threw himself on the floor of my office and sobbed hysterically. What was the matter? Memory. I have had men and women hurry to me at the close of a service with pale faces and haunted eyes, begging for a private conversation. What was the matter? Memory.

You will take your memory with you. The memory and the conscience that are not set at peace in this life by the atoning blood of Christ and the pardoning grace of God never will be. Hell is the place where men remember and suffer.

When D. L. Moody was a boy, one day he was hoeing corn along with an elderly man. Suddenly the man stopped hoeing and began striking a stone with his hoe. Young Moody stared at him. Tears were rolling down the man's cheeks, and he said, "Dwight, when I was a lad like you, I left home to make a living for myself. As I came out of the front gate, my mother handed me a Bible and said, 'My boy, *"Seek ye first the kingdom of God, and his righteousness; and all these things shall be added unto you"'* (Matthew 6:33)."

He took a deep breath and continued, "I went to the next town. I went to church on Sunday, and the minister got up to preach. He announced his text: Matthew 6:33. He looked right down at me pointed his finger at me and said, 'Young man, *"Seek ye first the kingdom of God, and his righteousness; and all these things shall be added unto you."'* I went out of the church and had an awful struggle! It seemed as if the minister was talking to me. I decided, 'No; I will get settled in life first and then I will become a Christian.' I found no work in that town, but I went to another town and found a job. I went to church, as was my custom, Sunday after Sunday. After a few Sundays, the minister stood up in the pulpit and announced his text: Matthew 6:33. '*Seek ye first the kingdom of God, and his righteousness; and all these things shall be added unto you.*'"

The old man began to tremble violently. "Dwight, that minister seemed to look right at me and point his finger right at me. I got up and went out of the church. I went to the cemetery behind the church and sat down on a tombstone. I had an awful fight, but at last I said, 'No, I will not become a Christian until I get settled in life.'" He paused for a moment and then said, "Dwight, from that day to this the Spirit of God has left me, and I have never had the slightest inclination to be a Christian."

Mr. Moody said, "I did not understand it then. I was not a Christian myself. I went to Boston and was converted. Then I understood. I wrote to my mother to ask her what had become of the old man. She answered, "Dwight, he has gone insane, and they have taken him to the Brattleboro Insane Asylum."

I went to Brattleboro and called on him there. As I went into his cell, he glared at me, pointed his finger at me, and said, "Young man, '*Seek ye first the kingdom of God, and his righteousness.*'"

I could do nothing with him. I went back to Boston. After some time, I came home again. I asked my mother where he was now. "Oh!" she said, "he is home, but he is a helpless imbecile."

I went up to his house. There he sat in a rocking chair, a white-haired man. As I went into the room, he pointed his finger at me and said, "Young man, '*Seek ye first the kingdom of God, and his righteousness.*'" He had gone crazy with memory. Hell is the madhouse of the universe, where men and women remember.

Desires Forever Denied

Hell is a place of insatiable and tormenting desire. Remember what Jesus told us of the rich man in hell. The rich man said, *"Send Lazarus, that he may dip the tip of his finger in water, and cool my tongue; for I am tormented in this flame"* (Luke 16:24).

You will carry into the next world the desires that you build up here. Hell is the place where desires and passions exist in their highest potency, and where there is nothing to gratify them. Men and women who are living in sin and worldliness are developing passions and desires for which there is no gratification in hell. Happy are those people who set their affections on things above. Those who cultivate power, passions, and desires for which there is no gratification in the next world will spend eternity in severe torment.

Hell is a place of shame. Oh, the awful, heartbreaking agony of shame! It can cause depression, illness, and even death. A bank cashier was in a hurry to get rich, so he appropriated the funds of the bank and invested them, intending to pay them back. But his investment failed. For a long time, he managed to conceal his theft from the bank examiner. One day the embezzlement was discovered. The cashier had to acknowledge his crime. He was arrested, tried, and sent to prison.

He had a beautiful wife and a lovely child, a sweet little girl. Some time after his arrest and imprisonment, the little child came home sobbing. "Oh," she said, "Mother, I can never go back to that school again. Send for my books."

Thinking it was some childish whim, the mother said, "Of course you will go back."

"No," the child insisted, "I can never go back. Send for my books."

"Darling, what is the matter?"

She said, "Another little girl said to me today, 'Your father is a thief.'"

Oh, the cruel stab! The mother saw that her child could not go back to school. The wound was fatal. That fair blossom began to fade. A physician was called, but her illness surpassed all the capacities of his skill. The child grew weaker every day until they laid her on her bed. The physician said, "Madam, I am powerless in this case. The child's heart has given way with the agony of the wound. Your child will probably die."

The mother went in and said to her dying child, "Darling, is there anything you would like to have me do for you?"

"Oh yes, Mother, send for Father. Let him come home and lay his head down on the pillow beside mine as he used to do."

But the father was behind iron bars. They spoke to the governor, and he said, "I have no power in the matter." They spoke to the warden of the prison. He said, "I have no power in the matter."

But hearts were touched by the girl's condition. The judge and the governor made an arrangement so that the father was permitted to come home under a deputy-warden. He reached his home late at night and entered his house. The physician was waiting. He said, "I think you had better go in tonight, for I am afraid your child will not live until morning."

The father went to the door and opened it. The child looked up quickly. "Oh," she said, "I knew it was you, Father. I knew you would come. Come and lay your head beside mine on the pillow just as you used to do."

The strong man went and laid his head on the pillow. The child lovingly patted his cheek and died. She was killed by shame. Hell is the place of shame, where everybody is dishonored.

No Parties in Hell

Hell is a place of vile companionships. The society of hell is described in Revelation 21:8: "*The fearful, and unbelieving, and the abominable, and murderers, and whoremongers, and sorcerers, and idolaters, and all liars, shall have their part in the lake which burneth with fire and brimstone: which is the second death.*" Some may say, "Many who are brilliant and gifted are going there." It may be, but how long will it take the most gifted man or woman to sink in such a world as that? I can take you to skid row and show you men who were once physicians, lawyers, congressmen, college professors, leading businessmen, and even ministers of the gospel. But now they are living with thugs, prostitutes, and everything that is vile and bad. How did they get there? They began to sink.

Many years ago, my father was one of the delegates to the presidential convention in Chicago. We then lived in New York. He took us children to a quiet country town in Michigan and went on to the convention. On the way home, we got on a Hudson River ferry, filled with the leading Democratic politicians. Many gifted orators stood up and spoke to the crowd, but there was one man who eclipsed everyone else. Everybody was spellbound by the power of his eloquence.

Years passed. One day I saw someone lying on our front lawn, covered with vomit, sleeping heavily, snoring like an overfed hog. When I went up to him, I found it was the same man whose gift of speaking had carried away everyone on that ferry. He died in a psychiatric ward from alcoholism.

During the World's Fair, there was a women's commission appointed to receive the dignitaries and the members of the royalty of other countries. A woman stood near the chairman of the commission, dazzling people by her beauty and wit.

Several years later, some friends of mine were in the slums of Chicago hunting for forlorn people that they might help. They found a poor creature with nails grown like claws, with long, tangled hair twisted full of filth, a face that had not been washed for weeks, clad in a single filthy garment—a wreck! When they began to talk with her, they found it was that woman who had belonged to the women's commission during the World's Fair. She had destroyed herself with cocaine.

A Place without Hope

Finally, hell is a world without hope. There are those who tell you that the Greek word *aionios*, translated "everlasting," does not always means everlasting. The meaning must be determined by the context. In Matthew 25:46, we read: *"And these shall go away into everlasting punishment: but the righteous into life eternal."* If it means everlasting in one part of the verse, it must mean the same in the other part of the verse. In other words, those who are cast into hell because of their sins will receive eternal or everlasting punishment while those who are redeemed will receive eternal or everlasting reward. Scriptures must be carefully interpreted in their context with an honest attempt to discover their true meaning, and not to make them fit a theory.

There is another expression used often in the Bible: "To the ages of the ages." It is used twelve times in one book—eight times describing the existence of God and the duration of His reign, once referring to the duration of the blessedness of the righteous, and in every remaining instance referring to the punishment of the beast, the false prophet, and the unrepentant. It is the strongest known expression for absolute endlessness.

I have searched my Bible for one ray of hope for those who die without repentance. I have failed to find one after years of searching. The New Testament does not contain one ray of hope for men and women who die without Christ. "Forever and ever" is the endless wail of that restless sea of fire. Hell is a place of bodily anguish, a place of agony of conscience, a place of insatiable torment and desire, a place of evil companionship, a place of shame, and a place without hope.

Escape from Hell

There is only one way to escape hell—accept Jesus Christ as your personal Savior, surrender to Him as your Lord and Master, confess Him openly before the world, and live obediently according to His Word. The Bible is perfectly plain about this. Examine the following verses:

> *There is none other name under heaven given among men, whereby we must be saved.* (Acts 4:12)

> *He that believeth on the Son hath everlasting life: and he that believeth not the Son shall not see life; but the wrath of God abideth on him.* (John 3:36)

> *Whosoever therefore shall confess me before men, him will I confess also before my Father which is in heaven. But whosoever shall deny me before men, him will I also deny before my Father which is in heaven.*
> (Matthew 10:32–33)

> *The Lord Jesus shall be revealed from heaven with his mighty angels, in flaming fire taking vengeance on them that know not God, and that obey not the gospel of our Lord Jesus Christ: who shall be punished with everlasting destruction from the presence of the Lord, and from the glory of his power.* (2 Thessalonians 1:7–9)

The question is this: Will you accept Christ now? Hell is too awful to risk it for a year, a month, or even a day. Your eternal destiny may be settled right now.

I know what the devil is whispering to you. He is saying, "Don't be a coward; don't be frightened into repentance." Is it cowardice to be moved by rational fear? Is it heroism to rush into unnecessary danger? Suppose I looked up and saw a building on fire. A man is sitting near an upper window, reading a book carelessly. I see his peril, and I call out, "Flee for your life! The house is on fire!" Then suppose that man leans out of the window and shouts back, "I am no coward. You can't frighten me." Would he be a hero or a fool?

One night I went to see my parents at home. As I stepped off the train, I stepped on to another track. Unknown to me, an express train was coming down that other track. A man saw my peril and cried, "Mr. Torrey, there is a train coming! Get off the track!" I did not shout back, "I am no coward. You can't scare me." I was not such a fool. I got off the track, or I would not be telling you the story.

If you are on the track toward hell, listen to the thunder and rumble of the wrath of God as it comes hurrying on. I beg you to get off the track! Receive Christ now!

6

OBSTACLES ON THE ROAD TO HELL

The Lord is…not willing that any should perish,
but that all should come to repentance.
—2 Peter 3:9

If any man or woman is lost and goes to hell, it won't be God's fault. If God had His way, every man and woman in the world would be saved at once. God is doing everything in His power to bring you to repentance.

Of course, He cannot save you if you will not repent. You can have salvation if you want to be saved from sin, but sin and salvation can never go together. There are people who talk about a scheme of salvation where man can continue in sin and yet be saved. It is impossible. Sin is damnation, and if a man will go on everlastingly in sin, he will be everlastingly lost.

But God is doing everything in His power to turn you away from the path of sin and destruction toward the path of righteousness and everlasting life. God has filled the path of sin, which leads to hell, with obstacles. He has made it hard and bitter.

A great many people are saying today, "The Christian life is so hard." It is not. Jesus said, *"For my yoke is easy, and my burden is light"* (Matthew 11:30). God tells us in His Word, *"The way of transgressors is hard"* (Proverbs 13:15). God has filled it full of obstacles, and you cannot go on in it without surmounting one obstacle after another.

The Power in God's Word

The first obstacle is the Bible. You cannot get very far in the path of sin without finding the Bible in your way. The Bible is one of the greatest hindrances to sin in the world. It contains warnings, invitations, and descriptions of the character and consequences of sin. It gives us representations of righteousness, its beauty and its reward. With its pictures of God and God's love, the Bible always stands as a great hindrance to sin. This is the reason many people hate the Bible. They are determined to sin, and the Bible makes them uneasy in sin, so they hate the Book.

People sometimes say to me, "I object to the Bible because of its immoral stories." But when I look into their lives, I find that their lives are immoral. The Bible paints sin in its true colors with stories that make sin hideous. Their objections are not to the stories but to the uneasiness the Bible causes them in their sinful ways.

People have often been turned back from the path of sin by a single verse in the Bible. Hundreds have been turned from the path of sin by Romans 6:23: *"For the wages of sin is death; but the gift of God is eternal life through Jesus Christ our Lord."* Thousands have been turned away from sin by Amos 4:12: *"Prepare to meet thy God."* Tens of thousands have been turned from the path of sin by John 3:16, *"For God so loved the world, that he gave his only begotten Son, that whosoever believeth in him should not perish, but have everlasting life.*" John 6:37 contains the promise, "*Him that cometh to me I will in no wise cast out.*"

Several years ago a man who had not been in a house of worship for fifteen years came into our church in Chicago. He was a strong agnostic and proud of it. I don't know why he came in that night. I suppose he saw the crowd coming and was curious to know what was going on. He sat down, and I began to preach. In my sermon, I quoted John 6:37: "*Him that cometh to me I will in no wise cast out.*" It went like an arrow into that man's heart.

When the meeting was over, he got up and went out and tried to forget that verse, but could not. He went to bed but could not sleep. "*Him that cometh to me I will in no wise cast out*" kept ringing in his mind. The next day it haunted him at work; for days and weeks, that verse troubled him, but he refused to come to Christ. He came back to the street where our church stands, walked up and down the sidewalk, stamped his foot, and cursed the text, but he could not get rid of it.

Six weeks had passed when he came into our prayer meeting. He stood up and said, "I was here six weeks ago and heard your minister preach. I heard the text, John 6:37, and I have tried to forget it, but it has haunted me night and day. I have walked up and down the sidewalk in front of your church and cursed the text, but I can't get rid of it. Pray for me." We did, and he was saved. One text from God's Word turned him from the path of sin and ruin.

The Miracle of a Mother's Prayers

The second obstacle that God has put in the path of sin is a mother's holy influence and teaching. Hundreds of men and women who are not yet Christians have tried to be unbelievers and plunge into sin. But their mother's holy influence and Christian teaching won't let them go. Sometimes it is years later that a mother's teaching does its work.

A young fellow went west to Colorado to work in the mines. He worked during the day and gambled at night, but he spent more money gambling than he made in the mines. One night he was at the gambling table. He lost his last cent. Then he used some of his employer's money and lost that. He felt he was ruined. He rose from the table, went up into the mountains, drew his revolver, and held it to his temple. He was about to pull the trigger when the words that his mother had spoken to him years before came to his mind: "My son, if you are ever in trouble, think of God." And there, standing in the moonlight, with a revolver pressed against his temple, and his finger on the trigger, he remembered what his mother had said and dropped on his knees. He cried to God and was saved.

In the desperate hardness of our hearts, we often trample our mothers' teachings underfoot, but we find it very hard to get over their prayers. Often at the last moment, people are saved because of their mothers' prayers.

In my church in Chicago, a man used to stand outside with a container of beer. As the people came out of the meeting, he offered them a drink. He was hard, desperate, and wicked, but he had a praying mother in Scotland.

One night after he went home from the meeting where he had caused trouble, he was awakened and saved without getting out of bed. He went back to Scotland to see his mother. He had a brother who was a sailor in the China seas, and the mother and the saved son knelt down and prayed for the wandering boy. That same night while they prayed, the Spirit of God came upon that sailor, and he was saved. He later became a missionary to India—a man saved by a mother's prayers.

When I was rushing headlong in the path of sin and ruin, my mother's prayers arose, and I could not get over them. I used to think that nobody had anything to do with my salvation. I had gone to bed one night with no more thought of becoming a Christian than I had of jumping over the moon. In the middle of the night, I climbed out of bed and decided to end my miserable life, but something came upon me. I dropped on my knees. In five minutes from the time I got out of bed to take my life, I had surrendered to God.

I thought no one had anything to do with it. But I found out later that my mother was four hundred twenty-seven miles away praying. Although I had gotten over sermons, arguments, churches, and everything else, I could not get over my mother's prayers. Do you know why some people are not in hell right now? Their mothers' prayers have kept them out of hell.

Faithful Preaching and Teaching

Another obstacle on the road to hell is the sermons we hear. Many thousands of people are turned from sin to God by sermons that they hear or read. Sometimes the sermon does its work years later.

In my first pastorate, I prepared a sermon on the parable of the ten virgins. There was one member of my congregation who was very much on my heart. I prayed she might be saved by that sermon. I went and preached; but when I gave the invitation, she never made a sign. I went home and did not know what to make of it. I said, "I prayed for her conversion by that sermon and fully expected her conversion, but she is not converted."

Years later, when I had gone to another pastorate, I heard that this woman was converted. I revisited the place, called on her, and said, "I am very glad to hear you have been converted."

She said, "Would you like to know how I was converted?" I said I would.

"Do you remember preaching a sermon years ago on the ten virgins? I could not get your words out of my mind. I felt I must accept Christ that night, but I would not. That sermon followed me, and I was converted years later by it."

Another obstacle is a Sunday school teacher's influence and teaching. A faithful Sunday school teacher is one of God's best instruments on earth for the salvation of the perishing. In Mr. Moody's first Sunday school in Chicago, he had a class of very unruly girls. Nobody could manage them. Finally, he found a young man who could keep the class under control. One day this young man came to Mr. Moody and said, "Mr. Moody," as he suddenly burst into tears.

Mr. Moody said, "What is the matter?"

"The doctor says I have tuberculosis and that I must go to California at once or die." He sobbed as if his heart would break.

Mr. Moody tried to comfort him and said, "Suppose that is true, you have no reason to feel so bad. You are a Christian."

"It is not that, Mr. Moody; I am perfectly willing to die, but I have had this Sunday school class all these years and not one of them is saved. I am going off to leave them, every one unsaved." He sobbed like a child.

Mr. Moody said, "Wait, I will get a carriage, and we will drive around and visit them. One by one you can lead them to Christ."

He took the sickly teacher in the carriage, and they drove around to the homes of the girls. He talked to them about Christ until he was so tired that he had to be taken home. The next day they went out again, and they went out every day until every one of these women but one was saved. They met for a prayer meeting before he went away. One after another led in prayer, and at last the one unsaved girl prayed too and accepted Christ.

He left by the early train the next morning, and Mr. Moody went to see him off. As they were waiting, one by one the girls came to say goodbye. He spoke a few words of farewell to them. As the train pulled out of the station, he stood on the back platform of the car with his finger pointing heavenward, telling his Sunday school class to meet him in heaven.

Kindness Is Never Wasted

Sometimes God throws a kind word or act as an obstacle to sin. A lady, standing at a window looking out on a New York street, saw a drunkard. He had been the mayor of a Southern city, but now he was a penniless drunkard on the streets of New York. He had made up his mind to commit suicide. He started for the river, but then he thought, "I will go into a bar and have one more drink. I have spent a lot of money in that bar, and I can certainly get one drink without paying for it."

He went in, asked for a drink, and told the man he had no money. The man came around from behind the bar and threw him out into the street. The woman who was looking out of the window saw the poor man picking himself up out of the gutter. She hurried over to him, wiped the mud off his face with her handkerchief, and said, "Come over to our meeting. It is bright and warm, and you will be welcome." He followed her over and sat on the bench. The meeting began, and one after another gave his testimony. After the meeting, that lady came and spoke to him about his soul. His heart was touched, and he was saved.

He got a job, and then a better one, and finally was made manager of one of the largest publishing houses in New York City. One day he came to the woman who had found him in the gutter and said, "I have some friends at a hotel who I want you to meet." She went to the hotel, and he introduced her to a fine-looking, middle-aged woman and a lovely young lady. He said, "This is my wife and daughter." They were beautiful, refined, cultured ladies whom he had left when he had gone down to the gates of hell. But a kind act and a word of invitation to Christ reached him and placed him on the path that leads to glory. Oh, let us go as missionaries of God's grace and block the path of sinful men and women with kind deeds and turn them to righteousness and to God!

The Voice of the Spirit

Another obstacle that God puts in the path of sin and ruin is the Holy Spirit. You and I have experienced the Holy Spirit's working, perhaps without realizing it. Perhaps we were right in the midst of a party, when a strange feeling came into our hearts. It was a feeling of unrest, dissatisfaction with the life we were living, or a longing for something better. The feeling would be accompanied by memories of home, church, mother, Bible, and God.

One night a man was at a gambling table. He was a wild, reckless spendthrift. Suddenly the voice of God's Spirit spoke to his heart. He thought he was about to die. He sprang up from the table, threw down his cards, and rushed to his room. There was someone in the room. He thought at first, "I won't pray while the maid is in the room." But he was so much in earnest that he did not care what anybody might think. He dropped down by his bed and called on God for Christ's sake to forgive his sins. The man was Brownlow North. He did a great work for God in Ireland and Scotland in the 1800s.

If you have ever been in a nightclub when there came into your heart a wretchedness, a sense of disgust, a longing for something better, a calling to a purer life, that was God's Spirit. If you have ever felt a stirring in your heart, you might have said to yourself, "I wonder if I had better become a Christian now?" God is sending His Spirit to block the road to hell. Listen to God's Spirit. Yield and accept Christ.

Facing the Cross

God has put one other obstacle in the road as blockade in the path to hell: the cross of Christ. No man can get very far down the path of sin and ruin before he sees the cross looming before him. On that cross hangs a Man, the Son of Man, the Son of God. You see Him hanging with nails in His hands and feet, and a voice says, "It was for you. I bore this for you. I died for you." In the pathway of every man and woman stands the cross with Christ upon it. If you choose to continue in sin, you will have to step over the cross and over the crucified form of the Son of God.

I heard of a godly old man who had a worthless son. That son was more anxious to make money than he was for honor or anything else. He decided to go into the liquor business.

Anyone who is willing to make money out of selling alcoholic beverages will profit from the tears of brokenhearted wives and the groans and sighs of an alcoholic's sons and daughters. The abuse of liquor is sending thousands of people every year to premature graves. It causes more sorrow, more ruined homes, more wretchedness than perhaps anything else on earth. Every tavern owner, bartender, barmaid, and professed Christian who holds stocks in breweries or distilleries is a part of the crime.

Once I knew of a man who was going to open a tavern. His father was deeply grieved and tried to reason with his son. He said, "My boy, you bear an honorable name that has never been disgraced before. Don't disgrace it by putting it up over a bar." But the son was so determined to get rich that he would not listen to his father.

The day came to open the bar. The father was one of the first on hand. He stepped up to every man who approached the door and told him of the miseries that come from alcohol. One after another, they turned away. The son looked out of the window to see why he was getting no customers. He saw his father outside, turning his customers away. He came outside and said, "Father, go home. You are ruining my business."

He said, "I can't help it, my boy. I won't have my name dishonored by this business. If you are determined to go on with it, I will stand here and warn every man that comes to enter your door.

Finally, the son lost his temper. He struck his old father in the face. The father turned to him without any anger. He said, "My son, you can strike me if you will. You can kill me if you will, but no man will enter your bar unless he goes over my dead body."

No man or woman will ever enter hell unless they go over the dead body of Jesus Christ. No man or woman can refuse Christ and persist in sin without trampling underfoot the One who was crucified on the cross of Calvary for us.

God has piled the obstacles high in His patient love. Don't try to surmount them. Turn back. Turn away from the path of sin; turn toward the path of faith in Jesus Christ. Turn now!

7

CATCHING A GLIMPSE OF HEAVEN

He looked for a city which hath foundations,
whose builder and maker is God.
—Hebrews 11:10

For here have we no continuing city, but we seek one to come.
—Hebrews 13:14

Heaven was the city Abraham sought, the *"city which hath foundations."* This is the *"continuing city"* that we are seeking instead of the fleeting and perishable cities and homes of earth. What sort of a place is this city? What sort of a place is heaven?

In answer to the question, I am not going to discuss the sort of a place I imagine heaven to be. I care very little about my speculations or any other man's speculations and fancies on this point. I am going to tell you something that is certain. I am going to tell you what God plainly teaches in His Word.

Many think we know nothing about heaven and that it is all guesswork. This is not so. God has revealed much about it. What He has revealed is very encouraging. It will awaken in every wise and true heart a desire to go there.

If we thought more about heaven, it would help us to bear our burdens here more bravely. We would want to live holier lives and be delivered from the power of greed and lust that often attacks us. Our lives would be filled with joy and sunshine.

Shallow philosophers tell us that our business is to live this present life and let the future take care of itself. You might as well tell the schoolboy that his business is to live today without considering his future. True thoughts of the life that is to come clothe the life that now is with new beauty and strength.

The Reality of Heaven

Jesus said, *"I go to prepare a place for you"* (John 14:2). Some will tell you that heaven is merely a state or condition. Doubtless it is more important to be in a heavenly state or condition than in a heavenly place. But heaven is a real place. We are not to be merely in a heavenly state of mind, but in a heavenly city as well, *"city which hath foundations,"* a *"continuing city."*

Christ has already entered into heaven to appear in the presence of God for us. (See Hebrews 9:24.) He has gone to prepare a place for us and is coming back to take us there. We will not be disembodied spirits in the world to come, but redeemed spirits, in redeemed bodies, in a redeemed universe.

Heaven is a place of incomparable beauty. This is obvious from the description we have in Revelation 21 and 22. The God of the Bible is a God of beauty. He made this world beautiful. Its beauty has been marred by sin. The weed, the thorn, and the brier spring up. The insect devours the roses, and the lilies fade. Decay and death bring loathsome sights and foul smells.

All of creation, together with fallen man, *"groaneth and travaileth in pain together until now"* (Romans 8:22). But enough is left of the original creation to show us how intensely God loves beauty. He has told us in His Word that the creation will be delivered from the bondage of corruption into the glorious liberty of the children of God. (See verses 21–23.)

There will be perfection of beauty in heaven. Perfection of form, color, and sound will be combined into a beauty that will be indescribable. All earthly comparisons fail. Every sense of perception in our present state is clouded by sin. But in our redemption bodies, every sense will be enlarged and exist in perfection.

Some of us have seen beautiful visions on earth. We have seen the mountains rearing their snowcapped heads through the clouds, the vista of rolling hills and verdant valleys, winding rivers and forests with their changing colors, lakes and oceans dancing and tossing and rolling in the moonlight, the heavens in the clear wintry night jeweled with countless stars. We have caught the fragrances that float through the summer night in parks and gardens. We have listened to the indescribable harmonies of piano and violin as they responded to the touch of the master's hand and the more matchless music of the human voice. But all these are nothing compared to the beauty of sight and sound and fragrance that will greet us in that fair city of eternity.

The Best Companions

But the beauty of heaven, as good and attractive as it is, will be its least important characteristic. Heaven will be a place of high and holy companionships. The best, wisest, and noblest people of all ages, such as Abraham,

Isaac, and Jacob, will be there: *"I say unto you, That many shall come from the east and west, and shall sit down with Abraham, and Isaac, and Jacob, in the kingdom of heaven"* (Matthew 8:11). Heaven is the home of Moses, Elijah, Daniel, Paul, John, Rutherford, and Brainerd. All the purest, noblest, most unselfish people the world has ever known are there because they have trusted in the atoning blood of Christ.

"For we know that if our earthly house of this tabernacle were dissolved, we have a building of God, an house not made with hands, eternal in the heavens" (2 Corinthians 5:1). All the dear ones who believed in and loved the Lord Jesus will be there.

Many desire to get into the most exclusive social circles. That is all right if it is not merely the society of wealth, fashion, and foolishness that is so strangely called "the best society." But the most select group of this world will be nothing compared to the society of heaven. The joys we find in the companionship of noble, unselfish, thoughtful people here give only the faintest conception of the joys of heaven's companionships.

The angels are there. *"The angel answering said unto him, I am Gabriel, that stand in the presence of God; and am sent to speak unto thee, and to shew thee these glad tidings"* (Luke 1:19). *"I say unto you, that likewise joy shall be in heaven over one sinner that repenteth, more than over ninety and nine just persons, which need no repentance....Likewise, I say unto you, there is joy in the presence of the angels of God over one sinner that repenteth"* (Luke 15:7, 10). We will enjoy the companionship of these lofty beings—Gabriel, Michael, and the whole angelic host.

God Himself is there, too. In a sense, He is everywhere, but heaven is the place of His unique presence and manifestation of Himself. Scripture says, *"Then hear thou from heaven thy dwelling place"* (2 Chronicles 6:30); *"Thy kingdom come, Thy will be done in earth, as it is in heaven"* (Matthew 6:10).

We will hold communion with Him. Jesus Christ is there. Stephen said, *"Behold, I see the heavens opened, and the Son of man standing on the right hand of God."* (Acts 7:56). *"Seeing then that we have a great high priest, that is passed into the heavens, Jesus the Son of God, let us hold fast our profession"* (Hebrews 4:14). *"Now of the things which we have spoken this is the sum:*

We have such an high priest, who is set on the right hand of the throne of the Majesty in the heavens" (Hebrews 8:1).

To Paul, being with Jesus was one of the most attractive thoughts about heaven. He wrote, *"I am in a strait betwixt two, having a desire to depart, and to be with Christ; which is far better: Nevertheless to abide in the flesh is more needful for you"* (Philippians 1:23–24).

There will be no unpleasant or degrading companions in heaven. The devil will not be there. The lewd, the vulgar, and the obscene will not be there. The greedy, the scheming, and the selfish will not be there. The liar, the slanderer, the backbiter, the meddler, and the gossip will not be there. The mean, the contemptible, and the hypocrite will not be there. The profane, the blasphemer, and the scoffer will not be there . No money, influence, or cunning will get them in. *"There shall in no wise enter into it any thing that defileth, neither whatsoever worketh abomination, or maketh a lie: but they which are written in the Lamb's book of life"* (Revelation 21:27).

There are limitations to the joys of the dearest earthly companionships. It will not be so in heaven. We can perfectly open our hearts to one another there, as we often long to do here but are unable. *"For now we see through a glass, darkly; but then face to face: now I know in part; but then shall I know even as also I am known"* (1 Corinthians 13:12).

Heaven will be a place of glad reunions. *"Then we which are alive and remain shall be caught up together with them in the clouds, to meet the Lord in the air: and so shall we ever be with the Lord"* (1 Thessalonians 4:17). The bereaved wife will meet again the husband she has missed so long, and the son will see the mother whose departure left his life so desolate. What glad days those coming days will be when we meet again, never to part!

The Most Glorious Freedom

Heaven will be a place that is free from everything that curses or mars our lives here. The world we live in would be a happy place if there were no sin, sickness, pain, poverty, or death. But these things ruin the present world.

There will be none of these things in heaven. There will be no sin. Everyone will perfectly obey the will of God. There will be no poverty. Everyone will have all the inexhaustible wealth of God at his disposal. "*And if children, then heirs; heirs of God, and joint-heirs with Christ; if so be that we suffer with him, that we may be also glorified together*" (Romans 8:17).

There will be no grinding labor. When I see the men and women who rise at dawn and go forth to another day of backbreaking labor, I rejoice that there is a place where the weary can rest. "*There remaineth therefore a rest to the people of God*" (Hebrews 4:9).

There will be no sickness or pain. "*God shall wipe away all tears from their eyes; and there shall be no more death, neither sorrow, nor crying, neither shall there be any more pain: for the former things are passed away*" (Revelation 21:4). There will be no more aching limbs, no more throbbing temples, and no more darting pains. Weakness, sighs, groans, nights of tossing in sweltering rooms, and tears will become vague memories from a distant past. There will be no death in heaven.

Heaven will be a place of universal and perfect knowledge. On this earth, the wisest of us sees through a glass darkly, but there, we will see face-to-face. Here we know in part, but there we will know even as we are known. (See 1 Corinthians 13:12.) The wisest scientist or philosopher on earth knows very little. Sir Isaac Newton, the famous physicist, said to one who praised his wisdom, "I am as a child on the seashore picking up a pebble here and a shell there, but the great ocean of truth still lies before me."

In heaven, the most uneducated of us will have fathomed that great ocean of truth. We will have perfect knowledge of all things. The great perplexing problems of God and man, of time and eternity, will be solved. No doubts, questions, uncertainties, or errors will trouble us. Faith will be swallowed up in sight.

Heaven will be a place of universal love. "*Beloved, now are we the sons of God, and it doth not yet appear what we shall be: but we know that, when he shall appear, we shall be like him; for we shall see him as he is"* (1 John 3:2). We will be like our God, and He is love. *"He that loveth not knoweth not God; for God is love"* (1 John 4:8).

What a place to live, where everyone loves each other with a perfect love! Happy is the home where love is triumphant. It may be a very plain place, but it is a happy place. *"Better is a dinner of herbs where love is, than a stalled ox and hatred therewith"* (Proverbs 15:17).

All is love in heaven. And the love there will not be like that of earth—hesitating, suspicious, selfish, now so cold and then so warm. It will be pure, unbounded, unfaltering, unchanging, and Christlike. What a world that will be! The universal brotherhood of which we read and talk so much and see so little will find its perfect realization there.

Heaven will be a place of praise:

> *After this I beheld, and, lo, a great multitude, which no man could number, of all nations, and kindreds, and people, and tongues, stood before the throne, and before the Lamb, clothed with white robes, and palms in their hands; and cried with a loud voice, saying, Salvation to our God which sitteth upon the throne, and unto the Lamb. And all the angels stood round about the throne, and about the elders and the four beasts, and fell before the throne on their faces, and worshipped God, saying, Amen: Blessing, and glory, and wisdom, and thanksgiving, and honour, and power, and might, be unto our God for ever and ever. Amen.* (Revelation 7:9–12)

Men will have open eyes to see God as He is. Souls will burst forth with praise. Suppose we were to catch one glimpse of God as He is, one view of Jesus Christ as He is. A burst of song like the world has never heard would be our response.

Melody will ring out all day long in heaven. Some people ask me in a critical way, "Why do you have so much music in your evangelistic meetings?" I answer, "Because we wish them to be as much like heaven as possible." Heaven will be a very musical place. There will be far more singing than preaching there.

Heaven will be a *"city which hath foundations,"* a *"continuing city."* Earth's greatest cities and fairest homes do not endure; they crumble into dust. The so-called "eternal city" of the past is trodden underneath the feet of the beggars of modern Rome.

The world itself does not abide. *"The world passeth away"* (1 John 2:17). Heaven does abide. Eternity rolls on, but heaven abides in its beauty, glory, joy, and love; and we abide with it.

The Way to Heaven

Is your heart stirred with a longing for that abiding city? Who would not rather have an entrance there than have the fleeting possessions of any of earth's millionaires? If I had my choice between having everything that money could buy and then missing heaven in the end or living in the most wretched tenement but gaining heaven at last, it would not take long to decide which to choose.

When we reach that fair home, the trials of earth will seem small and trifling indeed. *"I reckon that the sufferings of this present time are not worthy to be compared with the glory which shall be revealed in us"* (Romans 8:18).

We may all gain an entrance there. There is only one way, but it is simple and open to all. In John 14:6, *"Jesus saith unto* [Thomas], *I am the way, the truth, and the life: no man cometh unto the Father, but by me."* In John 10:9, Jesus said, *"I am the door: by me if any man enter in, he shall be saved, and shall go in and out, and find pasture."*

Christ is the door to heaven; Christ is the way to God. Accept Christ as your Savior, your Master, and your Lord. Do it now. If you stood outside the door of some beautiful mansion where all inside was beauty and love, and the owner said cordially, "Come in," would you risk waiting for a second invitation? Jesus swings heaven's door open wide and says, "Come in." Accept Him at once and gain a right to enter and live forever in heaven.

A godless father had a sweet little child who was an earnest Christian. The young daughter became ill and died. The father was angry at God. After the funeral, he raged about his room, cursing God and blaming Him for taking his beloved child. At last, utterly worn out, he threw himself on the bed and fell asleep.

In his slumber, he dreamed that he stood beside a dark river. He saw a beautiful land on the far side. As he gazed across the river, he saw children coming toward him. One fair child came forth, whom he recognized as his little daughter. She was beckoning to him and calling, "Come over here, Father! Come over here."

He awoke and burst into tears. He gave up his rebellion against God, accepted Christ, and prepared to meet his child in the fair land beyond the river.

Voices of loved ones who have gone before are calling, "Come over here, Father." "Come over here, Son." "Come over here, Husband." "Come over here, Wife." Accept Christ at once and gain the right to enter heaven and live there forever.

8

THE NEW BIRTH

Ye must be born again.
—John 3:7

No one can be saved unless he is born again by the power of God's Holy Spirit. Jesus said, "*Ye must be born again.*" The necessity is absolute. He did not merely say, "You may be born again if you think that you want to be," but "*Ye must be born again.*"

Nothing else will take the place of the new birth. Neither baptism nor confirmation can be substituted for it. Simon, in the eighth chapter of Acts, was baptized and taken into the early church. But when Peter and John came down and saw his heart, Peter said to him, "*Thou hast neither part nor lot in this matter: for thy heart is not right in the sight of God....For I perceive that thou art in the gall of bitterness, and in the bond of iniquity*" (Acts 8:21, 23). He was a baptized, lost sinner!

I often ask people to come to Christ, but they say, "I have been baptized; I have been confirmed." Have you been born again? "*Ye must be born again.*"

No performance of religious duties will take the place of the new birth. Many people are depending on the fact that they say their prayers, read their Bibles, go to church, receive Communion, and perform other duties. But all of that will not take the place of the new birth. "*Ye must be born again.*"

No Substitutes

Strict adherence to faith will not take the place of the new birth. Many people are saying, "I believe the Apostles' Creed; I hold the right views about Christ, the right views about the Bible, the right views about the Atonement."

You can be orthodox regarding every doctrine and still be lost forever. The devil is as orthodox a person as there is. The devil knows the truth about the Bible. He hates it and loves to get others to believe something else, but he believes it himself. The devil knows the truth about Christ. He believes in the divinity of Christ. He tries to keep others from believing in it, but he believes in it himself. The devil believes the truth about hell. No one knows better than the devil that there is an everlasting hell. The devil is perfectly orthodox, but he is lost. "*Ye must be born again.*" Culture, refinement, and outward morality will not take the place of the new birth. The trouble with us is not merely in our outward lives. The trouble is in the heart. The corruption is in the heart, in the very depths of our inner lives. Merely to reform your outward life will not save you. The change does not go deep enough.

Suppose I had a rotten apple. I could take that apple to an artist and have him put a coating of wax around it, and then paint it until it was beautiful in appearance. But it would be just as rotten as ever. If you would take one bite of it, you would bite into the decay.

Without Christ, people are rotten at the heart. Culture, refinement, respectability, and reform simply put a coating of wax on the outside. We must be changed down to the depths of our beings. We need the power of God going down to the deepest depths of our souls, banishing death and bringing in life, banishing corruption and bringing in the holiness of God.

Without holiness, no one will see God. (See Hebrews 12:14.) It is only by the regenerating power of the Spirit of God that any man or woman can become holy. "*Ye must be born again.*"

The necessity of the new birth is universal. No one will ever see the unless he is born again. There is no exception. I do not care how refined, how highly educated, how amiable, or how attractive you are. You will never see the kingdom of God unless you are born again.

If anybody could have entered the kingdom of God without the new birth, it was Nicodemus. He was an upright man, honored by everyone. He moved in the best society as a man of wealth and culture. He belonged to the orthodox party. He was a man of deep religious earnestness, sincerely desiring to know the right way. He prayed and studied his Bible and went to the synagogue several times a week. The Lord Jesus looked him right in the face, and He said, "Nicodemus, '*Ye must be born again.*'" No exceptions.

Have you been born again? I do not ask if you are a church member or if you believe the truth. I do not ask if you say your prayers or read your Bible. I do not ask if you go to church. I do not ask if you have a liberal heart toward the poor or if you give to missions. Have you been born again?

Born Again *Defined*

What does it mean to be born again? A good definition is given in 2 Corinthians 5:17: "*If any man be in Christ, he is a new creature: old things are passed away; behold, all things are become new."* The new birth is a new creation. It involves a radical transformation by the power of the Spirit of God in the depths of our beings. We receive a new will, new desires, and new thoughts. We were born with a perverted will, corrupted affections, and a blinded mind. By the power of the Holy Spirit, in regeneration, God transforms our wills, our affections, and our tastes. He transforms our way of looking at things.

Every man and woman by nature has a perverted will that is set on pleasing self. What pleases us may not be evil in itself. Perhaps we do not get drunk or swear or lie or do anything vicious or vulgar. But our minds are bent on pleasing ourselves.

When God, by His Spirit, imparts to us His nature and life, our wills are changed along with the whole purpose of our lives. Instead of pleasing self, our wills are surrendered to God, and we live to please Him. We may do a great many of the things we did before, but now we do them because they please God.

Our desires are corrupt by nature. We love the things we should not love and hate the things we should love. For example, many women love to read romantic novels more than they love to read the Bible. If a great many Christian women told the truth they would say, "I would rather read a good love story any day of the week than read the Bible."

You love to go to nightclubs, which God hates. I don't say God hates the people in the nightclubs—He loves them, but He hates the nightclubs. Perhaps you would rather go to the theater than to the gathering of God's children. If you had your choice between going to a first-class opera or to a place where God's Spirit was present in power, would you choose the opera? Would you go to a card party rather than to a quiet meeting of God's people where they knelt down and prayed for the outpouring of the Holy Spirit?

When God, through the power of the Spirit, gives you a new nature, you will love the Bible more than any other book in the world. You will love the places where God manifests Himself better than any places of worldly entertainment. You will love the company of God's people better than you love the pleasures of this world. The beautiful thing is that in a moment of time, by the power of God's Holy Spirit, the change comes. New tastes and new desires take the place of old tastes and old desires.

All Things Become New

Nobody loves worldly entertainment more than I once did. I used to attend four to six dances a week. I played cards every day of my life except on Sundays. You could not pay me to do those things today. I would never go to a nightclub unless I went there to get some poor soul out. I love the things I once hated, and I hate the things I once loved. In those days, I would rather have read any novel than read the Bible. Today I have more joy in reading this Book than in any other book on earth. I love it. My greatest intellectual joy is to study the wonderful pages of this Book of God.

Many people are blind to the divine authority of the Bible. They believe all the nonsense that people try to tell them about the contradictions in it. When you are born again, your mind will be so in tune with the mind of God that you will believe everything His Word says, in spite of what others might say.

Some people cannot believe that Jesus took our sins in His own body on the cross. (See 1 Peter 2:24.) The preaching of this doctrine is *"to them that perish foolishness"* (1 Corinthians 1:18). But when you are born again, the doctrine that the Son of God died on the cross of Calvary will be one of the sweetest doctrines to you in all the universe.

Being born again means having a new will set on pleasing God instead of pleasing self. You will have a new desire to love the things that God loves and to hate the things that God hates. Your mind and heart will believe the truth of God.

Have you been born again? If not, you are not saved. *"Verily, verily, I say unto thee, Except a man be born again, he cannot see the kingdom of God"* (John 3:3).

How can we tell whether we have been born again or not? *"If ye know that he is righteous, ye know that every one that doeth righteousness is born of him"* (1 John 2:29). If you have been born of God, you will do as God does. God does righteousness. If you are born of God, righteousness will be the practice of your life.

To do righteousness means to do the things that are right in God's sight. A man who is born of God will study the Word of God to find out what God's will is as revealed in His Word. When he finds out, he will do it. Are you studying the Word of God daily to find out what God wants you to do? When you find out what God wants you to do, are you doing it?

"Whosoever is born of God doth not commit sin; for his seed remaineth in him: and he cannot sin, because he is born of God" (1 John 3:9). That is, he does not make a practice of sin. To commit sin is to do something you know to be contrary to God's will. The man of God will not, when he knows God's will, disobey it. He may make mistakes. He may do something that he did not think was against God's will. But when he learns that it was wrong, he will confess it as sin. Or he may be overtaken by a sudden temptation and fall. But as soon as he sees it, he will confess it. He will not go on day after day doing what he knows to be contrary to the will of God. Anybody who is making a practice of something that he knows is contrary to the will of God has reason to doubt whether he is born again.

A young man stopped me on the street and asked, "If a man is born again and lives and dies in sin, will he be saved?"

"Why," I said, "a man who is born again will not live in sin. He may fall into it, but he will not stay there."

Do you know the difference between a hog and a sheep? A hog will fall into the mud, and he will stay there. A sheep may fall into the mud, but he gets up as quickly as he can. Many people who we think are Christ's sheep are only washed hogs. A hog that is washed will return to the mire, but a sheep will not stay in the mud. (See 2 Peter 2:22.)

If you are only outwardly reformed and externally converted, in a few weeks you will go back to your sin and your worldliness. You are only a washed hog. The person who is outwardly converted, but not inwardly transformed, will give up after a little while. But if you have been born again, you are transformed from a hog into a sheep, and you will never wallow in sin again.

The Test of Love

Proof of regeneration is the love of the brethren. *"We know that we have passed from death unto life, because we love the brethren. He that loveth not his brother abideth in death"* (1 John 3:14). Our love should include everybody who belongs to Christ, regardless of his social position, race, or color. The nature of God is love, and if God has imparted His nature to you, you have a heart full of love.

I once went to a Communion service where the church was receiving new members. When the people stood up to receive the new members, a lady near me remained seated. When the meeting was over, I said to her, "Why didn't you stand up to receive the new members?"

She replied, "I was not going to stand up for them. They are our charity cases. I am not going to love and watch over and care for them."

They were poor, and she was rich. She loved rich Christians. A child of God will love the poorest person who is born of God just as much as if he were a millionaire.

Practical love shows itself by reaching into the pocket. People will get up in a prayer meeting sometimes and say, "I know I have passed from death to life because I love the brethren." After the meeting, someone says, "Mrs. Smith is in trouble. She needs a little help, and we are taking up a collection for her. Won't you give something?" The reply is, "I cannot do it. Christmas is coming, and I have to get presents for my sisters, children, and cousins, and I cannot give to everybody." You can if you are a child of God.

The proof of the new birth is love. If you have a penny left in your pocket, you will go and share it with your poor brothers and sisters, if you are born again.

"Whosoever believeth that Jesus is the Christ is born of God" (1 John 5:1). You say, "I believe that Jesus is the Christ." Do you? It is not mere religion; it is true belief. *Christ* means King. If you believe in Christ as King, you will set Him up as King in your heart. Does Christ sit upon the throne of your heart? Does Christ rule your life? If He does, you are born of God. If He doesn't, you are not.

"For whatsoever is born of God overcometh the world" (verse 4). There are two classes of people in the world—those who are overcoming the world, and those who are being overcome by the world. To which class do you belong? Are you getting the victory over the world, or is the world getting the victory over you?

A great many people come to me and say, "I know this is not right, but it is what everybody does, and so I do it." The world is getting the victory over you. If you are born of God, you will get the victory over the world. You won't ask what the world does. You will ask what Christ says, and you will obey Christ, your King, and get the victory over the world, even if you have to stand alone.

How to Be Born Again

God tells us exactly what we must do to be born again. *"But as many as received him, to them gave he power to become the sons of God, even to them that believe on his name"* (John 1:12). We are born again by God's Holy Spirit, through His Word, the moment we receive Christ. When you take Christ into your heart, you take the life of God into your heart. Christ comes and reigns and transforms you completely in a moment. It does not matter how worldly you are, how sinful you are, or how unbelieving you are. Anyone can throw his heart open and let Jesus come in to rule and reign. Anyone can take Christ as his Savior and Deliverer from the power of sin. The moment you surrender the control of your life to Him, God, by the power of His Holy Spirit, will make you a new creature.

Let us compare two people: one who has been carefully taught to observe the outward forms of Christianity, and another who has gone down into the depths of sin. We may look at the religious person and say, "She will surely be easily led to accept Christ. But this person who has gone down into the depths of sin probably won't be saved right now."

Why not? If that moral, refined, beautiful girl takes Christ, God by His Holy Spirit will impart His nature to her and make her a child of God. But if the most immoral woman takes Christ, God by His Holy Spirit will impart His nature to her and make her His child in exactly the same way.

The most highly educated, most upright, most attractive person will never be saved until the Holy Spirit makes him a new creation in Christ. The most hopeless, abandoned person can be born again and made a new creature the moment he accepts Christ.

We are all saved the same way—by the acceptance of Christ and the power of the Holy Spirit. Have you been born again? If not, will you receive Jesus right now and be born again?

9

REFUGES OF LIES

The hail shall sweep away the refuge of lies.
—Isaiah 28:17

Every one of us needs a refuge from four things: the accusations of our own conscience, the power of sin, the displeasure of God, and the wrath to come. The trouble is not that people have no refuge, but that they have a false one. Our text characterizes it as a refuge of lies.

God announces to us that there is a day coming for testing the refuges of men. In that day of testing, the hail will sweep away the refuge of lies. Is your refuge a true one or a false one? Is it a refuge that will stand the test of the hour that is coming, or is it a refuge that will go down in a day of storm?

There are four tests that you can apply to every hope that will show clearly whether it is a true hope or a refuge of lies. First, a true refuge must meet the highest demands of your conscience. If it is not a refuge from the accusations of your conscience, it is probably not a refuge from the displeasure of God. *"For if our heart condemn us, God is greater than our heart, and knoweth all things"* (1 John 3:20).

Second, trust in your refuge must make you a better person. If that refuge you trust in is not making you a better person from day to day, it is not a refuge from the power of sin or from the wrath to come. Any hope that does not save you from the power of sin in this life can never save you from the consequences of sin in the life that is to come.

Third, it must stand the test of the dying hour. A refuge that only comforts you when you are well and strong, but fails when you are face-to-face with death, is absolutely worthless.

Finally, it must be a refuge that will stand the test of the Judgment Day. You may say you have a refuge that satisfies you, but will it satisfy God on Judgment Day? That's the question.

Our Own Righteousness

The first refuge of lies is trust in our own morality, our own goodness, or our own character. When you approach a person on the subject of becoming a Christian, he may reply, "No, I don't feel any need of Christ. I am trusting in my own character. Of course, I am not perfect, but I believe that the good in my life will more than make up for the evil. I am trusting in my own good deeds."

Let us apply our four tests. Does your goodness meet the highest demands of your conscience? In talking with highly moral people, I have met only two men who maintained that their own goodness came up to the highest demands of their consciences. You may think that they must have been remarkably good men. No, they had remarkably poor consciences.

I met one of these men when crossing the Atlantic Ocean. I started to talk to him one day about becoming a Christian, and he said to me, "I feel no need of a Savior."

I said, "Do you mean to tell me that you have never sinned?"

"Never," he said.

"Never fallen below the highest demand of your own conscience?"

"Never."

"Never done anything that you regretted afterward?"

"Never."

"Well," you say, "he must have been a good man indeed." Far from it. He was so mean that before we reached New York City, he was the most unpopular man on the ship.

Apply the second test: Is trust in your own goodness making you a better person? As you go on talking about your own morality and trusting in it, do you find that you are growing more unselfish, more kind, more considerate of others, more helpful, and more humble? I have known a great many men who trusted in their own morality. Every one of them grew more cross, critical, self-centered, and proud.

Apply the third test: Will it stand the test of the dying hour? In days of health and strength, a man will boast of his own goodness. But when he comes near death, he wishes that he had a living faith in Christ.

In one of my pastorates, there was the most self-righteous man I ever knew. He had no use for the church, the Bible, Jesus Christ, or ministers. He had a particular grudge against me because of something I had once done that he misunderstood. But he was perfectly confident that he was the best man in the community.

After many years, a cancer appeared on that man's scalp. It spread and ate its way through the scalp until it reached the skull. Little by little, it ate its way through the skull until there was only a thin film of skull between the cancer and the brain. He knew he would soon die. In that hour he said, "Send for Mr. Torrey. I must speak to him."

I hurried to his home at once, sat down beside his bed, and he said, "Oh, Mr. Torrey, tell me how to be saved. Tell me how to become a Christian."

I took my Bible and explained to him as simply as I knew how what to do to be saved. But somehow, he could not grasp it. I sat with him hour after hour. When night came, I said to his wife and family, "You have sat up with him night after night. You go to bed, and I will sit up with him all night and minister to him." They gave me instructions what to do and retired for the night.

All night long I sat by him, except when I had to go into the other room to get something for him to eat or drink. Every time when I returned to the room where he was lying, there came a constant groan from his bed, "Oh, I wish I was a Christian!" And so the man died.

Will your own goodness stand the test of the Judgment Day? Someday you will stand face-to-face with God. That all-seeing, holy eye will look you through and through, the eye of the One who knows all your past, all your secret thoughts, and every hidden imagination. Will you look into His face and say, "O God, Holy One, All-seeing One, I stand here today confident that my own righteousness will satisfy You"? Never!

See if it will stand the test of the Word of God. We know that it will not. Paul warned us about trying to be saved by our own doings. *"As many as are of the works of the law are under the curse: for it is written, Cursed is every one that continueth not in all things which are written in the book of the law to do them"* (Galatians 3:10). We are told in Romans 3:20, *"By the deeds of the law there shall no flesh be justified in his sight."*

Looking Good by Comparison

The second refuge of lies is trust in other people's badness. Some people make their boast in their own goodness; others make their boast in the badness of others. When you urge someone like this to come to Christ, he says, "No, I don't pretend to be very good, but I am just as good as a lot of other folks who are your church members."

Does it satisfy your conscience to say, "Well, I am not very good, but I am no worse than somebody else"? If it does, you must have an insensitive conscience. Is trust in other people's badness making you a better person? I have known many people who talked much of other people's badness, but I have yet to find anyone who was made better by the practice.

Show me a man who is always talking about the faults of others, and I will show you a man who is rotten at the heart. Show me a man who calls every other man a thief, and I will show you a man you can't trust with your wallet. Show me a man who thinks every other man is impure, and I will show you an adulterer. Show me a man or woman who is always talking about others' faults, and I will show you a man or woman who you cannot trust. It never fails.

In one of my Bible classes, I had a woman who was notoriously dishonest in business. One day she said to me, "Brother Torrey"—she loved to use the word *brother*—"Brother Torrey, don't you think that everybody in business is dishonest?"

I looked at her and replied, "When anybody in business accuses everybody in business of being dishonest, he or she convicts at least one person." She was furious! But why should she be? I only told her the truth.

Will you stand the test of the Judgment Day? Face-to-face with God who knows you, will you look into His face and say, "I have never been good, but I am no worse than others"? Never! In that day, God tells us distinctly, *"Every one of us shall give account of himself to God"* (Romans 14:12).

God's Mercy and Judgment

The third refuge of lies is universalism, the belief that God is too good to condemn anyone, that there is no hell, and no future punishment for sin. How common a refuge this is today! When you urge people to come to Christ, they answer, "I believe in the mercy and goodness of God. I believe God is love and too good to condemn anyone. I don't believe in hell."

Does that satisfy the demands of your own conscience? When your conscience points out your sin and demands a change in your life, does it satisfy you to say, "Yes, I know my life is not right, but God is love; therefore, I am going right on trampling His laws underfoot, because He is so good and so loving." Is that the kind of conscience you have? Shame on you! Don't ever do it again. God's infinite love gave His Son to die for you on the cross of Calvary.

Will your misinterpretation of God's goodness stand the test of the dying hour? A certain young man who was not a Christian became suddenly and seriously ill. His family saw that the illness might result in death, and they sent for their pastor. When he came into the room, this young fellow was tossing on a bed of sickness. The pastor hurried to his side and tried to present to him the consolation of the gospel.

He said, "Pastor, I can't listen to you. I have heard it over and over again. I would not listen to it in times of health and strength. I am now very ill. I will die soon. I can't repent in my last hour."

His father paced the room in great anxiety. Finally, he said, "My son, there is nothing for you to be so anxious about. You have not been a bad boy, and there is no hell. You have nothing to fear."

His dying son turned to him and said, "Father, you have deceived me all through my life. If I had listened to Mother instead of to you, I would not be here now. She tried to get me to go to church and Sunday school, but you took me fishing instead. You told me that there was no hell, and I believed you. You have deceived me up to this time, but you can't deceive me any longer. I am dying and going to hell, and my blood is on your soul." Then he turned his face to the wall and died.

Fathers, you who are undermining the teaching of godly wives, the day is coming when your sons will curse you. Will your universalism stand the test of the dying hour?

Is universalism making you a better man? Oh, with many it is simply an excuse for sin! In many of our churches, the world is sweeping in like a flood! All separation is gone, and professed Christians are running after the world, the flesh, and the devil. They have accepted the eternal hope nonsense that is robbing the church of its devotion and beauty. The church is becoming so like the world that you can't tell the two apart. People have grown comfortable in a life of sin, giving up their separation to God.

Will universalism stand the test of the Judgment Day? When you meet God, will you look into His face and say, "O God, I know my life has not been right, but I thought that You were a God of love. I thought You were too good to punish sin. I did not think there was any hell, so I didn't bother to obey Your laws"?

The Danger of Unbelief

The next refuge of lies is infidelity. Let us apply the tests. Does your unbelief meet the highest demands of your own conscience? When conscience points out your sin and demands a new life, do you reply, "Well, I don't believe in the Bible, and I don't believe in God. I don't believe that Jesus Christ is the Son of God"? If that satisfies your conscience, you are not fit to be called a human being.

Is your unbelief making you a better person? My ministry has been largely a ministry to skeptics and agnostics. I have yet to meet the first unbeliever who was made better by his unbelief, but I have known many whose characters have been undermined by a lack of faith. I have had young men come to me with breaking hearts and with sad confessions of immorality and ruin. They tell me that the first step was listening to some ungodly lecturer or reading an ungodly book. Trifling with spiritual matters undermines the foundations of sound character. Unbelief is filling the world with wickedness.

In my own church in Chicago, to which a good many infidels come, one of them said to me, "We come over here to hear you. You don't spare us, but we like men who take a stand. That is the reason we come." There are always a lot of them every Sunday. Thank God, many of them become converted.

Will unbelief stand the test of the dying hour? How often it fails! A friend of mine who was in the army said that in the same company with him was a man who was a very outspoken unbeliever. On the second day of battle, he said to his fellow soldiers, "I have a strange feeling that I am going to be shot today."

"Nonsense," they said. "It is nothing but superstition. You are not going to be shot."

"Well," he said, "I feel very strange. I feel as if I am going to be shot."

At last they were lined up waiting for the word of command. "Forward, march!" They went up the hill, and just as they reached the summit, a volley came from the enemy's guns. A bullet pierced this man near the heart. He cried as they carried him to the rear, "O God, just give me time to repent." It only took one bullet to take the doubt out of that man. It should take less than that to take the nonsense out of you.

Will it stand the test of the Judgment Day? Will you go into God's presence and be ready to say, "God, my answer is this: I was an unbeliever; I was an agnostic; I was a skeptic; I was an atheist"? Do you think you will? Get down on your knees and try to tell Him. You can talk nonsense to your fellowmen, but when you talk to God, it will take the nonsense out of you.

Hiding behind Religion

One more refuge of lies is religion. It may surprise you that religion is as much a refuge of lies as morality, other people's badness, universalism, or infidelity. Religion never saved anybody. It is one thing to trust in religion; it is something entirely different to trust in the living Christ.

You may tell people about Christ, and they may say, "Oh, I am very religious. I go to church. I say my prayers every morning and night. I read my Bible. I go to Communion. I have been baptized. I have been confirmed. I give a tenth of my income to the poor. I am very religious." Well, you can do every bit of that and go straight to hell. Religion never saved anybody.

Is your religion making you a better man or woman? A great deal of religion will not make men or women one bit better. Many religious people will lie as fast as anybody. They will go around slandering their neighbors. Men who are prominent religious businessmen will cut you as wide open in a business deal as any man in town. They turn a deaf ear to the cry of the aged and the needy, unless it is going to get into the papers that they gave them something. Many men are very religious and are perfect scoundrels.

I met a man who seemed to be most religious. He made his employees gather together at a certain hour every day for prayer, and he held religious services with them every Sunday so that they would not have to go to church. But this pious hypocrite was paying the women who worked for him starvation wages. His employees were the palest, most sickly crowd of women I have ever seen. That kind of religion will send a man to the deepest part of hell.

Will your religion stand the test of the dying hour? A great many religious people are as badly scared as anybody when they come to die. I have heard them groan and sigh and weep in the dying hour. Their hollow religion doesn't stand the test of great crisis.

Will it stand the test of the Judgment Day? The Lord Jesus Christ said:

> *Many will say to me in that day, Lord, Lord, have we not prophesied in thy name? and in thy name have cast out devils? and in thy name done many wonderful works? and then will I profess unto them, I never knew you: depart from me, ye that work iniquity.* (Matthew 7:22–23)

Religion is a refuge of lies, and if that is what you are trusting in, you will be lost forever.

The Sure Foundation

Is there no true refuge? Yes, there is. God says, "*Behold, I lay in Zion for a foundation a stone, a tried stone, a precious corner stone, a sure foundation: he that believeth shall not make haste*" (Isaiah 28:16).

This sure foundation stone is Jesus Christ. *"For other foundation can no man lay than that is laid, which is Jesus Christ"* (1 Corinthians 3:11). It is one thing to trust in religion and something entirely different to trust with a living faith in a crucified and risen Christ.

Will this refuge stand the test of our own consciences? When my conscience points to my sin, I have an answer that satisfies it. Jesus bore my sins on the cross. Will it make people better people? Yes. A living faith in a crucified and living Christ will make everyone who has it more like Christ every day. If you have a faith that is not making you like Christ, you do not have a real faith.

Will it stand the test of the Judgment Day? Yes. If it is God's will, I am willing to face Him tonight in judgment. You say, "What! Have you never sinned?" Certainly I have. You will never know how deeply I have sinned. But when God asks for my answer, I will say one word—*Jesus*—and this answer will satisfy God. *"The hail shall sweep away the refuge of lies"* (Isaiah 28:17). Throw them all away, and come to Christ. Be ready for life, ready for death, and ready for eternity.

10

FOUND OUT

Be sure your sin will find you out.
—Numbers 32:23

No one can escape his sins. Every sin we commit will find us out, call us to account, and make us pay. No man ever committed a sin that he did not pay for in some way. The most serious folly of which a man can be guilty is for him to imagine that he can ever gain anything by doing wrong. Whether you hurt anyone else by your own wrongdoing or not, you are sure to hurt yourself.

If a man puts his hand in the fire, he will be burned. If a man sins, he will certainly suffer for each sin he commits. You may escape the laws of men, but you cannot escape the law of God. No man can hide where his sin will not find him.

Men's sins find them out by the execution of human laws. The execution of law in society is necessarily imperfect, yet it is astonishing how often men who break the laws are sooner or later punished for their crimes. A man may successfully elude the meshes of the law for months or even years, but he is all the time weaving a net that will almost certainly entrap him at last. It is a marvelous thing how crime comes to light. A man's sin finds him out and exposes him at last to the contempt of the whole world.

Men's sins find them out in their own bodies. When a man does not pay the penalty of his sin in human courts, he pays it in a court where there is no possibility of bribery—the court of physical retribution for moral offenses. In a general way, there is an intimate connection between morality and health. All sins have physical consequences. The consequences of some sins are often not immediate or definitely traceable to specific sins, but it remains true that every sin has some physical consequences.

Young men see others suffering the terrible consequences of transgressing God's law, yet they go right on as an ox to the slaughter. They suppose that they will be an exception. There are no exceptions to physical law. Any action that is unnatural or immoral is bound to be visited with penalty. Why are there so many men with broken bodies and shattered intellects? Why so many broken-down women? The answer is the violation of God's law: their sins are finding them out.

Of course, disease may be hereditary or the result of accident or misfortune. But if we were to eliminate all the sickness that is the direct or indirect result of our own sins, we would be surprised at the relatively small amount of sickness left.

Consider a sin such as anger. Does it affect an individual's body? It causes disorders in the blood, stomach, brain, and nerves. It is obviously unhealthy in every case and may even lead to paralysis and death. It is amazing the many ways, some direct and some indirect, in which our sins find us out in our own bodies. If you are contemplating sin, just stop and think of this: *"Be sure your sin will find you out."*

Damaging to Character and Conscience

For every sin you commit, you will suffer in character. Sin breeds a moral ulcer. A diseased character is worse than a diseased body. You can't tell a lie without your moral blood being poisoned by it and your moral health undermined.

Do you think you can cheat a man in business and not suffer in your character more than he suffers in his pocket? Do you think you can wrong an employee in his wages and not suffer more in what you become than he suffers in what he gets? Do you think you can wrong a man regarding his wife and not have a deadly cancer develop in your own character? Do you think you can read an impure book or listen to an obscene story and not breed corruption in your own moral nature? Do you think you can violate those laws of purity that God has written in His Word and on your heart and not reap the consequences in your own character? Sin always finds people out in their characters—in what they become.

Again, your sin will find you out in your own conscience. You can hide your sin from everyone but yourself. You are so constructed by God that to know you are a sinner means self-condemnation and agony. Many suffer from the bitter consciousness of sins that no one else knows anything about. No physical torments can match the torments of an accusing conscience. An accusing conscience means hell on earth. No earthly prosperity, no human love, no mirth, music, fun, or intoxication can dispel its clouds or assuage the agony of its gnawing tooth. That sin you are contemplating looks inviting and harmless. It won't look so tempting or innocent after it is committed. It will find you out, and you will suffer.

Your sin will find you out in the lives of your children. One of the most awful things about sin is that its curse falls not only on us, but also on our children. You may complain about this as much as you like, but it is an unquestionable fact.

I remember a man who was a constant, but moderate drinker. He had three sons. I don't think that man was ever drunk in his life. He despised a drunkard, but he laughed at total abstainers. Each one of his three sons became alcoholics. A wise friend of mine says he never has known a man in the liquor business where the curse sooner or later did not strike his own home.

Facing Eternity

There is one more place where your sin will find you out: your sin will find you out in eternity. This present life is not all that there is. Our acts and their consequences will follow us into our future life. If your sin does not find you out here, it will there. You may be absolutely sure of that. In eternity, we will reap the consequences of every sin we sowed here on earth.

Life sometimes seems to go on here to the end without justice. Men defraud their employees, they rob the needy, they condemn other men and their families to poverty in order to increase their already enormous wealth. No one seems to call them to account. It will not always be so. God will call them to strict account. A few thousands or millions of their ill-gotten wealth given to charity will not blind the eyes of a holy God. They will suffer.

Men sometimes lay traps for foolish girls, bringing ruin to their reputations. Yet no one seems to hold the man accountable. He continues to be accepted in the "best society" and is loaded with honors. His sin will find him out, however, if not in this world, then, in the next. He will stand before the universe exposed, dishonored, and condemned to everlasting contempt.

Men despise God, laugh at His Word, and trample underfoot His Son (see Hebrews 10:29), yet God still lets them live. He does not seem to call them to account. But it will not be always so. *"Be sure your sin will find you out."*

You cannot sin without suffering for it. Your sin will find you out in the court of law, in your own body, in your character, in your conscience, in your children, in eternity, or in all of these put together. You will suffer. You will pay an awful price.

> *The Lord Jesus shall be revealed from heaven with his mighty angels, in flaming fire taking vengeance on them that know not God, and that obey not the gospel of our Lord Jesus Christ: who shall be punished with everlasting destruction from the presence of the Lord, and from the glory of his power.* (2 Thessalonians 1:7–9)

All of us have sinned (see Romans 3:23), and for some, our sins are finding us out now. What shall we do? There is only one way of escape from the penalties of the law—the grace of the gospel. "*Christ hath redeemed us from the curse of the law, being made a curse for us*" (Galatians 3:13). He calls, "*Come unto me, all ye that labour and are heavy laden, and I will give you rest*" (Matthew 11:28).

11

SALVATION IS FOR YOU

Who then can be saved?
—Mark 10:26

The disciples asked Jesus this question. Jesus had just told them how hard it was for a rich man to enter the kingdom of heaven. The disciples seem to have held the same opinion that most men do today—a rich man can get anywhere. But Jesus said, *"It is easier for a camel to go through the eye of a needle, than for a rich man to enter into the kingdom of God"* (Mark 10:25).

"Who then can be saved?" Jesus went on to tell them that although it was impossible through man's power for a rich man to be saved, God, with

whom all things are possible, could save even a rich man. But only God could.

We come, then, to the question again: "*Who then can be saved?*" The Bible answers the question clearly. The Bible tells us that there are some people who cannot be saved, and that there are some people who can be saved.

Who Cannot Be Saved?

No one can be saved who will not give up his sin. We read in Isaiah 55:7: "*Let the wicked forsake his way, and the unrighteous man his thoughts: and let him return unto the Lord, and he will have mercy upon him; and to our God, for he will abundantly pardon.*"

Every man and woman has to choose between sin and salvation. You cannot have both. If you won't give up sin, you must give up salvation. Absurd schemes of salvation propose to save a man while he continues in sin. We read in Matthew 1:21 concerning our Savior: "*Thou shalt call his name Jesus: for he shall save his people from their sins.*" Sin is damnation; holiness is salvation. The reason some people are not saved is that they do not want to give up sinning. Some will not give up drunkenness or adultery or profanity or lying or bad tempers. You cannot be saved if you want to sin. If you persist in sinning, you will be lost forever.

No man can be saved who trusts in his own righteousness and is not willing to admit that he is a lost sinner. Thousands of lost sinners are proud of their own morality. They are not willing to humble themselves and say, "I am a poor, vile, worthless, miserable sinner." You can never be saved while you trust in your own righteousness.

Jesus told us that two men went up to the temple to pray. One was a Pharisee, one of the most respectable religious men in the community. The other was a tax collector, a man whom everybody looked down on. The Pharisee talked about his own goodness when he prayed. He looked up and said, "*God, I thank thee, that I am not as other men are, extortioners, unjust, adulterers, or even as this publican*" (Luke 18:11). His contempt for the tax collector was obvious. The Pharisee continued in his prayer: *"I fast twice in the week, I give tithes of all that I possess"* (Luke 18:12). Jesus said that this man went out of the temple an unforgiven, hopelessly lost sinner.

But the tax collector, the outcast, the man everybody looked down on, would not so much as lift his eyes to heaven. He felt he was a miserable, worthless sinner. He beat his breast and said, *"God be merciful to me a sinner"* (verse 13). Jesus said that *"this man went down to his house justified"* (verse 14). Anybody can be saved who will take the sinner's place and cry for mercy.

The World's Largest Family

One day a friend of mine, an old Scotsman, was walking through the country when a man came along and stopped beside him. The man started up a conversation with the old Scotsman, curious about his background. My friend said, "I will tell you who I am, and I will tell you what my business is. I have a very strange business. I am hunting for heirs."

The other man said, "What?"

"I am hunting for heirs to a great estate. I represent a very great estate, and I am hunting heirs for it. There are a good many in this neighborhood."

The other said, "Do you mind telling me their names?"

"No," he said. "It is a very large family. Their name begins with *S*."

"Oh," said the man. "Smith, I suppose?"

"No," the old man replied, "a much larger family than the Smith family."

"Larger than the Smith family! Who are they?"

The old Scotsman said, "They are the sinner family. The estate I represent is the kingdom of God; the inheritance is incorruptible, undefiled, and does not fade away. The heirs to it are the sinners who are willing to take the family name, admit that they are sinners, and look to God for pardon."

Do you belong to the sinner family? If you do, you can be saved. If you are not willing to admit that you do, you cannot be saved. You are lost forever.

No man or woman can be saved who is not willing to accept salvation as a free gift. We are told in Ephesians 2:8, *"For by grace are ye saved through faith; and that not of yourselves: it is the gift of God." "The gift of God is eternal life through Jesus Christ our Lord"* (Romans 6:23).

Salvation is a free gift. Anybody can have it for nothing; nobody can have it any other way. If you are not willing to take it as a free gift, you cannot have it at all.

My wife was talking to a young man, a son of the richest man in the neighborhood. There seemed to be some difficulty about his accepting Christ. Finally my wife said to him, "The trouble with you is you are not willing to accept salvation as a free gift."

"Mrs. Torrey, that is just it. I am not willing to accept salvation as a free gift. If I could earn it, if I could work for it, if I could deserve it, then it would be different. I am willing to earn it, but I am not willing to take it as a free gift."

Nobody can earn it; nobody can merit it; nobody can deserve it. Unless you are willing to take it as a free gift, you will never get it at all. The richest man on earth who gets saved will have nothing more to boast about when he reaches heaven than the lowliest beggar who is saved.

Sincerely Wrong

Nobody can be saved who will not accept Jesus Christ as his Savior. *"There is none other name under heaven given among men, whereby we must be saved"* (Acts 4:12). Anybody can be saved in Christ; nobody can be saved in any other way. An infidel once said to a friend of mine, "If I cannot be saved without accepting Christ, I won't be saved." Well, then, he won't be saved. That is all there is to it.

If you ever go to Sydney, Australia, you will soon find that every citizen in that city is very proud of the harbor. You won't be in Sydney long before somebody will ask you, "What do you think of our harbor?" They should be proud of it. It is one of the finest harbors in the world, but it has only one entrance. There is one enormous rock called the North Head and another called the South Head. The only channel, wide and deep, is between these two heads. A little south of the South Head is another promontory, called Jacob's Ladder.

One night, many years ago, a vessel called the *Duncan Dunbar,* with hundreds of people on board, came outside of Sydney harbor after dark. The captain saw the South Head and thought it was the North Head. He saw Jacob's Ladder and thought it was the South Head. He steered, put on full speed, steamed in between the two lights, and ran onto the rocks. Every one of the hundreds on board perished, except one man who was thrown up into a cave on the face of the rock.

That captain was perfectly sincere. There never was a more sincere man on earth, but he was mistaken, and he was lost. People say it does not make any difference what you believe if you are only sincere. But the more sincerely you believe error, the worse off you are. There is just one channel into salvation, and that is Christ. Try to go any other way, no matter how sincere you are, and you will be wrecked and lost eternally.

Who Can Be Saved?

Sinners can be saved, even the most depraved. Paul wrote, "*This is a faithful saying, and worthy of all acceptation, that Christ Jesus came into the world to save sinners; of whom I am chief*" (1 Timothy 1:15). He has already saved the chief of sinners, and He is able to do it again.

In the city where I used to live, a young girl of thirteen became pregnant. Her father and mother disowned her. Her brothers rejected her, and I doubt if they were any better than she. They cast this poor girl of only thirteen years of age into the streets to fend for herself. She soon became the companion of thieves, robbers, murderers, of everything that was disreputable. She lost the baby because of her poor health and became a member of two of the worst gangs, at different times, in New York and Chicago.

A friend of mine met her one night and said, "If you are ever sick of this life, come to me, and I will help you out of it." A time came when she was thoroughly sick of it, and she went to this gentleman's house. He was a very wealthy man, who used all his money for God. He showed her the way of life, and she was saved. That young woman went on to occupy a high position of great responsibility and honor in her city. There is scarcely anyone who even knows her past life. God has covered it up, though she still has the same name.

A few years ago I was in her town. She came to me and said, "I hope, Mr. Torrey, that you won't think it necessary to tell the people here my story." My wife and I were the only ones there that knew her past record. She had been in our house in the days of her trouble.

I said, "Most assuredly, we shall not." Why should you tell a saved woman's story, when it is underneath the blood of Jesus? It is no longer her story. It is blotted out. Jesus Christ not only saved her out of the depths of sin, but He covered up her past as well.

Depending on His Power

Any person who is too weak to resist sin in his own strength can be saved. It is not a question of human strength, but of Christ's strength. "*Now unto him that is able to keep you from falling, and to present you faultless before the presence of his glory with exceeding joy*" (Jude 24). "*Who are kept by the power of God through faith unto salvation ready to be revealed in the last time*" (1 Peter 1:5). Jesus Christ can keep the weakest man or woman just as well as the strongest.

I have seen men start out in the Christian life who talk this way in testimony meetings: "Friends, you know me; I am a man with great strength of character. When I make up my mind to do anything, I always follow through. I have started out in this Christian life, and I want you to understand that I am not going to backslide as so many do. I am going through." Whenever I hear a man talking that way, I know he is going to backslide within six weeks.

Another man will stand up trembling, hesitant, and he will say, "You all know me. You know I have no willpower left. I have tried to quit my sin time and time again. As you know, I have failed every time. I have absolutely no confidence in myself. But God says in Isaiah 41:10, '*Fear thou not; for I am with thee: be not dismayed; for I am thy God: I will strengthen thee; yea, I will help thee; yea, I will uphold thee with the right hand of my righteousness.*' I am trusting in Him." When I hear a man talking that way, I know he is going to stand every time.

One day somebody came to me in Chicago and said, "We have to find a place for this woman to stay. Her husband got drunk last night and tried to kill her with a knife. It is not safe for her or her child, so she has left him. We must do something to provide for her."

I said, "You are right to provide for her; that is just what we should do."

A few days later, her husband came to me and said, "Mr. Torrey, do you know where my wife is?"

I said, "I do."

"Will you please tell me where she is?"

"I will not. You tried to kill her. You do not deserve to have a wife. I am not going to tell you where she is so that you may go and kill her."

He said, "If you do not tell me, I will commit suicide."

"Very well," I said. "You will go to hell if you do." A man like him never commits suicide. He kept getting drunk instead. He could not help it, poor fellow. Every now and then, he would come to me for a few dollars, saying that he was going to get a job in a shoe factory. I always knew that the money was going for whiskey. He was always saying that he was going to quit drinking. I knew he was not. He meant to. He would say that he was hunting for work. But I knew he was looking for another drink.

That went on for years. One day I said to God, "Heavenly Father, if you will give me this man, I will never despair of the salvation of another man as long as I live." Very soon afterward, he got his feet on the Rock, Christ Jesus, and never fell again.

Years passed, and he became an honored member of that church. When I returned for a visit, among those who came to welcome me was this man, his wife, and a child, a happy family in Jesus Christ. The Christ who saved the lying, habitual, hopeless drunkard can save anyone who will trust in Him.

Power for Deliverance

Anyone can be saved who thinks he has committed the unpardonable sin, if he is willing to come to Jesus Christ. Jesus said, *"All that the Father giveth me shall come to me; and him that cometh to me I will in no wise cast out"* (John 6:37). I think I have never gone anywhere in my life where somebody has not said, "I have committed the unpardonable sin." Almost every one, if not every one, has gone away rejoicing in Jesus.

One time I received a brokenhearted letter from a father who was a Presbyterian minister. He wrote that he had a son who was in deep spiritual darkness. The son thought that he had committed the unpardonable sin, and he was plunged into absolute despair. Would I take him into the Bible Institute? I replied that, though I had every sympathy for him in his sorrow, the Bible Institute was not for the purpose of helping cases like this one, but to train men and women for Christian service.

The father continued to write, begging me to take his son, and he got other friends to plead for him. Finally, I consented to take the young man. He was sent to me under guard, to prevent him from doing something rash on the way.

When he was brought to my office, I showed him to a seat. As soon as the others had left the room, he began the conversation by saying, "I am possessed of the devil."

"I think quite likely you are," I replied, "but Christ is able to cast out devils."

"You do not understand me," he said. "I mean that the devil has entered into me as he did into Judas Iscariot."

"That may be," I answered, "but Christ came to destroy the works of the devil. He says in John 6:37, *'Him that cometh to me I will in no wise cast out.'* If you will just come to Him, He will receive you and set you free from Satan's power."

The conversation went on in this way for some time. He constantly asserted the absolute hopelessness of his case, and I constantly claimed the power of Jesus Christ and His promise, *"Him that cometh to me I will in no wise cast out."*

Days and weeks passed, and we had many conversations, always on the same line. One day I met him in the hall of the Institute and made up my mind that the time had come to have the battle out. I invited him to my office and told him to sit down. "Do you believe the Bible?" I asked.

"Yes," he replied, "I believe everything in it."

"Do you believe that Jesus Christ told the truth when He said, *'Him that cometh to me I will in no wise cast out'?"*

"Yes, I do. I believe everything in the Bible."

"Well, then, will you come to Christ?"

"I have committed the unpardonable sin."

I replied, "Jesus does not say, 'The one who has not committed the unpardonable sin who comes to Me I will in no wise cast out.' He says, *'Him that cometh to me I will in no wise cast out.'"*

"But I have sinned willfully after I have received the knowledge of the truth."

"Jesus does not say, 'The one who has not sinned willfully after he received the knowledge of the truth who comes to Me I will in no wise cast out.' He says, *'Him that cometh to me I will in no wise cast out.'"*

"But I have been enlightened and tasted the heavenly gift and have fallen away. It is impossible to renew me again unto repentance."

"Jesus does not say, 'The one who has not tasted of the heavenly gift, and has not fallen away, if he comes to Me I will in no wise cast him out.' He says, *'Him that cometh to me I will in no wise cast out.'"*

He continued with his excuses. "But I am possessed of the devil. The devil has entered into me as he did into Judas Iscariot. My heart is hard as a millstone."

I answered every one of his protests with the same Scripture, John 6:37, until his excuses were exhausted. I looked him square in the face and said, "Now, will you come? Get down on your knees, and quit your nonsense." He knelt, and I knelt by his side. "Now," I said, "follow me in prayer."

"Lord Jesus," I said, and he repeated, "Lord Jesus." "My heart is as hard as a millstone. I have no desire to come to You. But You said in Your Word, '*Him that cometh to me I will in no wise cast out.*' I believe this statement of Yours. Therefore, though I don't feel it, I believe You have received me."

When he had finished, I said, "Did you really come to Jesus?"

He replied, "I did."

"Has He received you?"

"I do not feel it," he replied.

"But what does He say?"

"Him that cometh to me I will in no wise cast out."

"Is this true? Does Jesus tell the truth, or does He lie?"

"He tells the truth."

"What, then, must He have done?"

"He must have received me."

"Now," I said, "go to your room. Stand firmly on this promise of Jesus Christ. The devil will give you an awful conflict, but just answer him every time with John 6:37. Stand right there, believing what Jesus says in spite of your feelings, in spite of what the devil may say, in spite of everything."

He went to his room. The devil did give him an awful conflict, but he stood firmly on John 6:37 and came out of his room triumphant and radiant.

Years have passed since then. Though the devil tried again and again to plunge him into despair, he stood firmly on John 6:37. He was used of God to do larger work for Christ than almost any man I know. He is the author of that hymn:

Years I spent in vanity and pride,
Caring not my Lord was crucified,
Knowing not it was for me He died On Calvary.
Mercy there was great, and grace was free,
Pardon there was multiplied to me,
There my burdened soul found liberty,
At Calvary.

Anyone can be saved who will come to Jesus. *"The Spirit and the bride say, Come. And let him that heareth say, Come. And let him that is athirst come. And whosoever will, let him take the water of life freely"* (Revelation 22:17).

12

HOW TO FIND REST

Come unto me, all ye that labour and are heavy laden, and I will give you rest. Take my yoke upon you, and learn of me; for I am meek and lowly in heart: and ye shall find rest unto your souls.
—Matthew 11:28–29

What this world needs is rest. What every person who is not already in Christ needs is rest. Millions of people work hard for small pay and go home night after night to wretched homes, worn out, without any fit place to sleep. Millions more have no rest for their hearts, no rest for their souls.

There is One who can give rest to every tired heart. His name is Jesus Christ. He stands with extended hands and says, "*Come unto me, all ye that labour and are heavy laden, and I will give you rest.*"

Those are either the words of a divine Being or the words of a lunatic. If the Lord Jesus Christ offers rest and gives it, He is a divine Being. If He offers rest and cannot give it, He is a lunatic. If any man, even the greatest and the best that the world ever saw, held out his hands to this sorrowing, grief-stricken, burdened world of ours and said, "Come to me, and I will give you rest," you would know at once that the man had gone crazy, for no man could do it. But Jesus offers to do it, and He does it. Millions throughout the centuries have accepted Christ's offer. Nobody who ever accepted it failed to find rest.

Whom Did Jesus Call?

There was a great throng when the Lord Jesus spoke that day. That crowd represented lives filled with misery. Multitudes of the poor were there—the penniless, the sick, the demonic, and the outcast—a mass of misery. The Lord Jesus Christ cast His loving eyes over that great multitude that represented so much misery, and His great heart went out to them. He said, "Come, come to Me, every one of you who has a burden, every one who has a sorrow, every one who has a broken heart. Come to Me, and I will give you rest."

He extends His hands to all men and all women in all ages who are burdened, downtrodden, oppressed, wretched, brokenhearted, and filled with despair. He invites all who labor and are heavy laden to come to Him.

Some commentators have tried to tone down the words of our Lord. They tell us that He meant all who were burdened with the many requirements of the Mosaic law. Others tell us He meant all who were burdened by a consciousness of sin, a sense of guilt. Jesus means just what He says. *"Come unto me, all ye that labour"*—every person who has a burden, a sorrow, a heartache, a trouble, a problem of any kind; Jesus invites you to come.

He invites all who are burdened with a sense of sin and shame. Perhaps you feel that your life is disgraceful. You are ashamed of yourself, and you can hardly lift up your head. You are saying to yourself, "My life is simply shameful," and you are crushed by the sense of your sin. Jesus says to you, *"Come unto me...and I will give you rest."*

A Woman Transformed

That day when our Lord Jesus spoke these words in Capernaum, on the outskirts of the crowd, there was a woman who was a prostitute, an outcast despised by everyone. As she stood there, I have no doubt many women who prided themselves on their morality turned and looked at her with scorn. But soon Jesus looked at her, too—not with scorn, but with pity, with compassion, with tenderness, with yearning, and with love. She saw that He was speaking directly to her. He seemed to lose sight of everybody else as He stretched His hands out toward her and said, *"Come unto me, all ye that labour and are heavy laden, and I will give you rest."*

That woman said in amazement, "He means me!" When the crowd broke up, she followed at a distance to see where Jesus went. Jesus went to the house of Simon, the Pharisee, who had invited Him to dinner. She hurried to her home, took a very costly box of ointment, the most expensive thing that she had, and hurried back to Simon's house. As Jesus reclined there, she came up behind Him, bent over His feet, and began to bathe them with her tears.

The other guests looked on in scorn. They grumbled, "This man pretends to be a prophet. He is no prophet, or He would not allow that woman to touch Him. If He were a prophet, He would know what kind of woman she is. She is a sinner."

Well, He did know. He knew better than any of them did, not only that she was a sinner, but also that she was a repentant sinner. While His feet were still wet with her tears, she wiped them with the long tresses of her beautiful hair. Then she broke open her alabaster box of precious ointment and anointed His feet with the fragrant oil. The Lord Jesus turned to her and said, *"Thy sins are forgiven"* (Luke 7:48). Then He spoke again to her and said, *"Thy faith hath saved thee; go in peace"* (Luke 7:50). That woman, who stood on the outskirts of the crowd with a breaking heart, left that house with the peace of God in her soul. (See Luke 7:36–50.)

Freedom from Bondage

The Lord Jesus invites every man and woman who is burdened by the bondage of sin. Some of you are in bondage to alcohol. You want to be sober and to lead an upright life. You have tried again and again to give up drinking but have failed. Others are burdened with the desire for drugs. You have tried to be free from your bondage. The Lord Jesus says to you, *"Come unto me…and I will give you rest."*

You may be burdened with impurity or some disgusting sin. You have tried to break away time and time again, until at last you have given up. You are utterly discouraged, crushed by the power of your sin. If you could read the secret sorrow of every heart, you would find hundreds of people crushed to the earth by the power of sin. The Lord Jesus says to everyone, *"Come unto me, all ye that labour and are heavy laden, and I will give you rest."*

I have a dear friend who was carefully reared by a godly mother. His father had been an alcoholic. His mother was afraid that her son would become a drunkard, so she made him promise that he would never touch a drop of liquor. He lived for eighteen years without tasting it.

One day he was on a business trip with a friend. On the way back, the man bought some alcohol and asked him to have a drink. "No," he said, "I promised my mother never to drink."

"Well," he said, "if you don't drink you will insult me." That elderly man worked on that boy until he got him to drink his first glass of whiskey. It was as though a demon in him was set on fire. From that time on, he became a drunkard. He lost one job after another and at last was a wrecked man in New York City. He wrote one hundred and thirty-eight bad checks against his last employer, and the officers of the law were looking for him.

One awful night, he went into a bar and for a long time sat there in a drunken stupor. He suddenly began to feel all the horrors of delirium tremens coming over him. He thought he was going to die. He went up to the bar and ordered a drink. Then he threw down the glass and said, "Men, hear me, hear me; I shall never drink another glass of whiskey, even if it kills me."

They all laughed at him. He went out of the bar and down to the police station. He said to the sergeant at the desk, "Lock me up; I am going to have the tremors; lock me up!" The sergeant took him down to the cell and locked him up.

He spent a night and a day in awful agony. The next evening, somebody said to him, "Why don't you go to the city mission?" In an awful condition, he went down to the mission and listened to one man after another give his testimony of how he was saved. When the minister asked all who wanted to receive Christ to come to the front, he went up to the front, knelt down, and said, "Pray for me."

The minister responded, "Pray for yourself."

"Oh," he said, "I don't know how to pray. I have forgotten how to pray."

The minister softly repeated, "Pray for yourself." That wrecked and ruined man lifted up his broken heart to Jesus. Jesus met him and took the bondage of alcohol from him that same night. That man became one of the most respected men in New York City.

Are you burdened? Have you fought again and failed? Have you tried again and again, perhaps signed pledge after pledge, only to break it? Are you burdened with the weight of an overcoming sin? Jesus holds out His hand to you. "*Come unto me, all ye that labour and are heavy laden, and I will give you rest.*"

There is a cure for every sorrow at the feet Jesus. I have a beautiful family Bible that my mother gave to my grandmother at the time of my grandfather's death. On the flyleaf of the Bible in my mother's own beautiful handwriting are the words, "Earth hath no sorrow that heaven cannot heal." That is true, but something better is that earth has no sorrow that Jesus cannot heal right now, before we get to heaven.

Lifting the Burden of Doubt

The Lord Jesus invites all who are burdened by doubt and unbelief. To some men, doubt and unbelief are not a burden. They are glad that they are skeptics. They are proud of their doubts. But to a man of any real moral earnestness, doubt is a burden, a heavy load. He is never proud of doubt. An earnest-minded man wants truth, not uncertainty, and knowledge of God to replace agnosticism.

There are some who honestly doubt, and their doubt is a burden. Jesus says, *"Come unto me, all ye that labour and are heavy laden, and I will give you rest."*

Am I suggesting that a skeptic should come to Christ, an unbeliever come to Christ, an agnostic come to Christ? Certainly; He is the best One you can come to.

Thomas was a skeptic. 'The other disciples had seen our Lord after His resurrection. Thomas was not present. When Thomas came back, the other disciples said, *"We have seen the Lord"* (John 20:25). He said, "I don't believe it. I don't believe you have seen the Lord, and I won't believe it unless I see Him with my own eyes, put my fingers into the prints of the nails in His hands, and thrust my hand into His side."

But Thomas was an honest doubter. When he thought that perhaps the Lord Jesus would be around the next Sunday evening, He was there. He came to Jesus with his doubts. Jesus scattered every one of them, and Thomas cried, *"My Lord and my God"* (verse 28).

Nathaniel was an honest doubter and a thorough skeptic. Philip came to him and said, *"We have found him, of whom Moses in the law, and the prophets, did write, Jesus of Nazareth, the son of Joseph"* (John 1:45).

Nathaniel said, "I don't believe He is the Messiah. He came from Nazareth. *'Can there any good thing come out of Nazareth?'* (verse 46)."

Philip said, "You come and see." This is the thing to do—come and see. Nathaniel said, "I will come." He came along with Philip. He met the Lord, and he had not been with the Lord ten minutes when all his doubts were gone. Nathaniel cried, *"Thou art the Son of God; thou art the King of Israel"* (verse 49).

If you are burdened with doubt, bring your doubts to Jesus. Whatever your burden is, Jesus invites you, every burdened one, every heavyhearted one, to come to Him.

Come Only to Jesus

Jesus says, *"Come unto me,"* not, "Come to the church." The church cannot give you rest. I believe in the church; I believe every converted person should be a member of some church, but the church never gave anybody rest. The church is full of people who have never found rest. They have come to the church instead of coming to Jesus Himself.

Jesus does not say, "Come to a creed." I believe in creeds. I think every person should have a creed. A creed is simply an intelligent, systematic statement of what a person believes. A man should believe something and be able to state intelligently what he believes. If he is an intelligent, studious man, his creed will be getting longer all the time. But there was never a creed written or printed that would give anybody rest. It is not going to a creed that brings peace and forgiveness; it is going to the personal Savior.

The Lord Jesus does not say, "Come to the priest" or "Come to the preacher" or "Come to the evangelist" or "Come to any other man." He says, *"Come unto me."* No preacher can give you rest; no priest can give you rest; no man can give you rest. Jesus says, *"Come unto me."*

I have sometimes asked people if they have come to Jesus, and they say, "Oh, I am a Protestant." Well, that never saved anybody. There will be lots of Protestants in hell. Others say, "I am a Roman Catholic." That never saved anybody either. There will be lots of Roman Catholics in hell. When a man says, "I am a Roman Catholic," I say, "I am not asking you that. Have you come to Jesus?" It is not a question of whether you are a Roman Catholic or a Protestant. Have you come to Jesus? If you have not, will you come now?

Come to Jesus, take His yoke, and surrender absolutely to Him. Commit all your sins to Him to pardon; commit all your doubts to Him to remove; commit all your thoughts to Him to teach; commit yourself to believe in Him, to learn from Him, to obey Him, to serve Him. The moment you come to Him with all your heart and cast yourself upon Him, He will give you rest. You can have rest right now.

One night in my church in Chicago, one of the officers of my church went to the upper balcony after I was through preaching. He stepped up to a gentleman and said, "Are you saved?"

"Yes, sir," he said, "I am saved." He was very positive about it.

"How long have you been saved?"

He said, "About five minutes."

"When were you saved?"

He motioned toward the platform and said, "While that man was preaching." He did not wait until I had finished my sermon. He came to Jesus right then, and Jesus saved him right there.

Will you come? Lose sight of everyone else, and see the Lord Jesus standing there, holding out His hands to you with a heart bursting with love, breaking with pity and compassion. He says to every heavyhearted man and woman, "*Come unto me, all ye that labour and are heavy laden, and I will give you rest.*" Will you come?

13

JOY UNSPEAKABLE

Though now ye see him not, yet believing, ye rejoice with joy unspeakable and full of glory.
—1 Peter 1:8

Christians are the happiest people in the world. According to our text they *"rejoice with joy unspeakable and full of glory,"* and nobody else does. Why are Christians so happy?

First of all, Christians are happy because they know that their sins are all forgiven. *"All that believe are justified from all things"* (Acts 13:39). Christians know their sins are forgiven because the Holy Spirit bears witness of forgiveness in their hearts.

The apostle Peter preached about Jesus in the household of Cornelius. He said, *"To him give all the prophets witness, that through his name whosoever believeth in him shall receive remission of sins"* (Acts 10:43). Cornelius and his whole household believed it, and the Spirit of God came upon them immediately.

When you and I believe in Jesus, His Spirit comes into our hearts, bearing witness with our spirits that our sins are all forgiven and that we are children of God. There is no joy on earth like the joy of knowing that God has forgiven and blotted out every sin you ever committed.

Suppose a person was in prison for some crime, and someone brought him a pardon. Don't you think he would be happy? But that is nothing compared to knowing that God has forgiven all your sins. Oh, the joy that comes into the heart when a man knows that every sin he ever committed is blotted out and that God has absolutely nothing against him!

A great king wrote a song of joy that has lived through the centuries. That king had been a great sinner, and God had forgiven his sin. He had much to be happy about. He was the greatest king of his day. He had great wealth and great armies. He was the greatest general of the time, and he had a great palace. But when he wrote his song of joy he did not say, "Happy is the man who has a beautiful palace" or "Happy is the man who has great armies" or "Happy is the man who is loved by his people." He said, *"Blessed is he whose transgression is forgiven, whose sin is covered. Blessed is the man unto whom the LORD imputeth not iniquity, and in whose spirit there is no guile"* (Psalm 32:1–2). Every man who receives the Lord Jesus as his Savior will have his sins forgiven and will have the joy of knowing that every sin is blotted out.

Sons of the King

Christians are happy because they are set free from sin's power. Everybody who sins is a slave to sin. (See John 8:34.) Since ancient times, many nations and races have been subject to the harshness of slavery. Some of the masters were kind, and some were cruel. But there was never a slaveholder who was such a cruel master as Satan, and there was never a bondage as awful as the bondage of sin.

Every person who is not in Christ is a slave. But when you come to Jesus Christ, He sets you free. *"If ye continue in my word, then are ye my disciples indeed; and ye shall know the truth, and the truth shall make you free.... If the Son therefore shall make you free, ye shall be free indeed"* (John 8:31–32, 36). The Lord Jesus Christ takes every man and woman who believes in Him and sets him or her free from the power of every sin.

Christians are happy because they know that they are children of God. It is a wonderful thing to know that you are a child of God. No one knows it but the Christian, for only the Christian is a child of God.

How does the Christian know that he is a child of God? Because God says so. *"As many as received him, to them gave he power to become the sons of God, even to them that believe on his name"* (John 1:12).

The moment you accept the Lord Jesus Christ, you will be a child of God and know that you are a child of God. Isn't that enough to be happy about? Suppose you knew that you were the son of some great man or the son of a millionaire or the son of a king. Don't you think you would be happy? But being the son of any king is nothing compared to being the son of God, the King of Kings.

One day, many years ago, an English duke lay dying. He called his younger brother to his bedside and said, "Brother, in a few hours you will be a duke, and I will be a king." He was a Christian. He was a child of the King, and he knew that when he left this world, he would get a kingdom in heaven. The moment anyone receives Jesus Christ, even if he is the poorest man on earth, he can lift up his head and say, "I am a child of the King. I know I am a child of God."

Sometimes, as I travel around the world, people will point out a man to me and say, "That man is the son of a great man." What of it? Suppose he is a child of a king? I am a child of God. That is better than being a child of a king.

We read in the Bible that the gospel was preached to the poor. I believe in preaching to the rich. They need it as much as anybody. But I would rather be a poor man who is a child of God than a rich man who is a child of the devil.

Nothing to Fear

Christians are happy because they are delivered from all fear. A Christian who believes the Bible, studies it, and remembers it is not afraid of anything or anybody. A great many wealthy people have all their joy spoiled because they are constantly thinking that some calamity may overtake them. People who have all the comforts of life do not enjoy them because they fear that some calamity may come and sweep the comforts away. Those with very little, who are perhaps barely getting by, do not enjoy what they have because they fear they may be thrown out of work and not be able to make a living. The true Christian is delivered from all those fears.

There is one verse in the Bible that will take away all anxiety as long as you live. *"And we know that all things work together for good to them that love God"* (Romans 8:28).

If a person believes the Bible and keeps it in mind, he is not afraid of calamity; nor is he afraid of any man. Many people are afraid of men and tormented by the fear of men. They want to take a stand as a Christian, but they are afraid of being laughed at or persecuted at home or on their jobs. But a Christian is not afraid of man. The Christian reads Romans 8:31 and says, *"If God be for us, who can be against us?"* A Christian does not fear any man or woman on earth.

In Chicago a man came to me and said, "You had better look out. There is a man who says he has it in for you." He told me who the man was—a very desperate man, a man willing to do almost anything. I was not troubled a bit. I did not lie awake a single night. I was not worried for two seconds. I said, "That is all right. I know he is quite powerful, and I have reason to believe he will do anything, but I know that I am right with God.

God is on my side, and that man can't touch me." A living faith in Jesus Christ takes away all fear of man forever.

It takes away the fear of death. People's lives are shadowed and darkened by the fear of death. Right in the middle of health and strength they say, "Oh, what if I have some terrible disease!" But death has lost all its terror for the Christian. A Christian knows that what men call death is for him simply to depart and be with Christ.

There is one word that fills the heart of the Christian with joy but fills the heart of the unsaved with terror. That word is *eternity*. In eternity, sorrow, separation, sickness, and death are over forever. All is eternal sunshine. A Christian is delivered from fear of eternity. To people who do not know Christ, eternity is a dreadful thing to think about. But for people in Christ, eternity is the sweetest thing there is to think about.

Write out a card with these words, "Where will you spend eternity?" If you hand it to a person who is not a Christian, it will make him mad. But hand it to a Christian, and he will rejoice. He will answer, "Why, I will spend eternity with Christ in glory!"

The Joy of Everlasting Life

Christians are happy because they know they will live forever. It is a wonderful thing to know that you will never die, that throughout the endless ages you will live on and on. "*The world passeth away, and the lust thereof: but he that doeth the will of God abideth for ever*" (1 John 2:17). "*He that believeth on the Son hath everlasting life: and he that believeth not the Son shall not see life; but the wrath of God abideth on him*" (John 3:36).

Before I was a Christian, I did not like to look into the future, but how I love to look into the future now! It is a great joy to preach, but oh, what joy it is to be able to stand and look down through the coming ages and see them roll on, age after age, and know that I am going to live for all eternity in happiness and joy ever increasing! I am not surprised that Christians are happy. I don't wonder that they have "*joy unspeakable and full of glory*" (1 Peter 1:8).

Christians know that they are "*heirs of God, and joint-heirs with Christ*" (Romans 8:17). They know that they have "*an inheritance incorruptible, and undefiled, and that fadeth not away, reserved in heaven for* [them]" (1 Peter 1:4). When someone rides down beautiful country roads and looks out at the beautiful mansions and sees the lakes, forests, parks, and the gardens, he may say, "It must be very pleasant to live there." I suppose it is, but how long will those people live there? They will soon be gone. But every man, woman, and child who takes Jesus will have an inheritance that will last forever. Every earthly inheritance soon fails. Even the richest man on earth won't keep his property very long. But the poorest man who will take Jesus Christ will receive an inheritance that will last forever.

One day a poor English girl was traveling by train and looking out the window. The train passed by beautiful farms and mansions. Every once in a while the poor girl said with a smile, "That belongs to my Father." She would come to a farm and would say, "That belongs to my Father"; to a beautiful mansion, "That belongs to my Father, too"; then she would pass a castle and would say, "That belongs to my Father."

Finally, the man who was listening turned to her and said, "Well, Miss, you must have a rich father."

She said, "He is. I am a child of God." She was very rich.

You may be having a hard time in this world. You may have to work long hours for small pay. Perhaps your home is not very comfortable. Well, you won't have to live here very long. If you receive Christ, you are going to a mansion such as this earth never saw and to an inheritance like none ever inherited on this earth. If you will accept Jesus Christ as your Savior, you will know that you are an heir to all that God has. The whole world belongs to Him—even "*the cattle upon a thousand hills*" (Psalm 50:10). If you are a child of God, if you will take Christ, you will be heir to all that He is and all that He has.

The Holy Spirit Living Within

Christians are happy because God gives them the Holy Spirit to dwell in their hearts. When the Holy Spirit dwells in the heart, He fills it with sunshine, gladness, and joy unspeakable.

One Monday morning a woman came to my door, rang the bell, and said she wanted to see me. My daughter said, "You know he sees no one on Monday." She said, "I know it, but I have got to see him." When I came down, I saw one of the members of my church, a poor woman who had to work hard for her living.

"Oh," she said, "Mr. Torrey, I knew you didn't see anybody on Monday, and I didn't like to trouble you, but I received the Holy Spirit last night. I could not sleep all night, and I made up my mind that I was going to give up one day's work and just come and tell you how happy I was. I just had to. I can't very well afford to give up a day's work, but my heart is so full of joy I could not keep still. I had to tell somebody, and I didn't know anybody else I wanted to tell as much as I wanted to tell you. Though I knew you didn't see anybody on Monday, I thought you would be glad to have me come and tell you."

"Yes," I said, "I am glad." That woman was so happy that she could not work; her heart was full of joy.

I don't care how discouraged your heart is today or how full of sadness you are. I don't care if you think your situation is hopeless. If you will take Jesus as your Savior and surrender your whole heart and your whole life to Him, your heart will be filled with a sweetness above anything to be known this side of heaven.

A Christian can *"rejoice with joy unspeakable and full of glory"* (1 Peter 1:8). But you have to be a true Christian. Just going to church won't do it; just saying your prayers won't do it; just reading the Bible or a prayer book won't do it; just being baptized and confirmed won't do it; just going to the Lord's Supper won't do it. But if you take Jesus into your heart to be your Savior to rule and reign there and surrender all to Him, you will get a joy that is heaven on earth.

People say to me, "Do you expect to go to heaven?" Yes, I know I am going to heaven, but I am in heaven now. I now have a present heaven to live in until I go to the future heaven. Thank God, I feel like singing all the time. I used to be one of the most depressed men on earth. I was despondent; I was gloomy; I used to sit and have the blues by the hour. But I never have had the blues since I accepted the Lord Jesus. I have had trouble. I have had trials. I have seen the time when I had a wife and four children and not a penny to buy them another meal. But it came in time, for I knew where to go—right to God, and He provided. I knew whom I trusted. (See 2 Timothy 1:12.) I knew He could get me out somehow, and He did.

If you want darkness turned into sunshine, if you want sadness turned into joy, if you want despair turned into glory, if you want defeat turned into victory, if you want all that is bad turned into all that is good, receive the Lord Jesus Christ, and receive Him right now.

14

THE FEAR OF MAN

The fear of man bringeth a snare:
but whoso putteth his trust in the LORD shall be safe.
—Proverbs 29:25

Two paths extend before us: one of ruin, the other of salvation. "*The fear of man bringeth a snare: but whoso putteth his trust in the LORD shall be safe.*" The way of salvation is trust in Jehovah. Even if you do not believe another verse in the Bible, you know this verse is true. I don't care how much of an unbeliever a man may be, he knows that the fear of what others will think brings a snare.

Once a young fellow came to Chicago who was too much of a man to gamble. But he liked an occasional innocent game of cards. One night, he was playing cards with his friends, and someone suggested that they put up a dollar to make it interesting. "Oh," they said, "we don't care for the money, but it is just to lend interest to the game."

"No," he said. "I never gamble. I think gambling is stealing." He is right, for gambling is stealing. No self-respecting man wants another man's money. I don't see how a man who has taken another man's money by gambling can look in the mirror.

He insisted, "No. Gambling is rank dishonesty; I never gamble."

"Oh," they said, "it is not gambling; it is just for a little amusement. You better go home and go to Sunday school. Go and sit with your mother." They ridiculed him into his first game of cards for money. The gambler's passion—a harder passion to overcome then the appetite for drink ever was—seized him. He ended up behind prison bars because he gambled until he took his employer's money to gamble with. The fear of man brought snare that landed him in prison.

Afraid to Take a Stand

The fear of man ensnares Christians into a denial of their Lord. It did Peter. He told his Lord, *"Though I should die with thee, yet will I not deny thee"* (Matthew 26:35). But when the servant girl accused him of being a follower of Jesus of Nazareth, he said, *"I do not know the man"* (verse 72). A few moments later, he repeated his denial, and an hour after, with oaths and cursings, frightened by what a servant girl might do or say, he denied his Lord. (See Matthew 26:69–75.)

Many of you are doing the same every day. In your office or shop or factory, Jesus Christ is ridiculed. Hard things are said about the Bible; the name of the Lord who died upon the cross of Calvary for you is taken in blasphemy, and you are not man enough or woman enough to stand up and say, "I am a Christian. I believe in that Christ whom you are ridiculing. I believe in that Bible you are laughing at." You are afraid to be laughed at, and the fear of man has ensnared you into a denial of the Lord who died on the cross for you.

The fear of man ensnares professed Christians into a guilty compromise with the world. Are you doing things in your family life, social life, or business life that you know are wrong? Your best moral judgment condemns you every time you do them, but you say, "Well, everybody does them. I will be considered odd if I don't do them."

A Christian man living in one of the suburbs of Chicago said to me, "My daughter is practically ostracized because she won't drink." Thank God, she was woman enough, though she was still a young girl, to be willing to be ostracized rather than compromise. Many people are not.

Would you rather not participate in worldly entertainment? You know you don't feel happy or comfortable there. But you are not brave enough to stand for modesty, purity, and God. The fear of man has entangled you in a snare that has robbed you by your compromise of every bit of real power for Jesus Christ.

Slothful Silence

The fear of man ensnares Christians into a guilty silence and inactivity. When the invitation is given for Christians to go to work and speak to the unsaved, few want to do it. Oh, you would like to lead someone to Christ. What a joy it would be to you! But you say, "Suppose I talk to somebody and they don't like it; suppose they laugh at me; suppose they say some hard things to me." The fear of man in your home, in your shop, in your hotel, everywhere you go, is shutting your mouth and robbing you of the joy of leading others to Jesus Christ.

Suppose they do laugh at you. They spat in your Master's face. They won't spit in yours. They struck Him with their fists. They probably won't strike you. They nailed Him to the cross. Are you not willing to be laughed at for a Master like that?

I believe that the fear of man that keeps Christians from giving their testimony for Christ and working to bring others to Christ does far more to hinder the work of God than any other cause. Men are being saved by the thousands, but if Christians would abandon their fears and have the boldness to witness and work for their Master, people would be saved by the tens of thousands.

The fear of man ensnares those who are not Christians into the rejection of Jesus Christ. Hundreds of men and women would like to be Christians. They see the joy of it. But they are afraid that if they accept Christ, somebody will ridicule them. The fear of man shuts them out of the acceptance of Jesus Christ. I believe that more people are kept from accepting Christ by the fear of what someone will say or do than by any other cause. If we could get rid of this fear, there would be thousands saved every night at evangelistic crusades instead of two or three.

The fear of man ensnares those who think they have accepted Christ into not making a public confession of Him. Jesus says distinctly, "*Whosoever therefore shall confess me before men, him will I confess also before my Father which is in heaven. But whosoever shall deny me before men, him will I also deny before my Father which is in heaven*" (Matthew 10:32–33).

Paul said distinctly, "*With the heart man believeth unto righteousness; and with the mouth confession is made unto salvation*" (Romans 10:10). Yet a host of men and women are trying to be Christians and never stand up to say so. "I don't believe in this publicity. I don't believe in this standing-up business. I believe in doing things more quietly. I don't believe in excitement." You can give a thousand and one reasons, but if you were honest with yourself, as you will have to be honest with God some day, you would say, "It is because I am afraid to do it."

A fine looking young fellow came to me one day and said, "I am a fool."

I said, "What is the matter?"

He said, "I thought I accepted Christ here the other night, and I have not been man enough to tell another man in the office what I have done. I am a fool."

Well, he was. So are you. You professed to receive Jesus Christ, but to this day you have not told the other people in your office, in your home, in your hotel, in your shop. The fear of man has sealed your mouth, made you a coward, and robbed you of all the joy that there is in a bold Christian experience.

The fear of man ensnares those who start out in the Christian life from going on in it, because somebody says something discouraging. One night two young men both professed to accept Christ at a crusade meeting. One of the men went to his pastor and told him what he had done. His pastor encouraged him in his new walk with Christ.

The other man's pastor was one of those convivial pastors, a man whose chief function is to serve as a figurehead at large banquets where he joins in and encourages the frivolity. The young convert went to this preacher and told him what he had done. His preacher said, "Don't you believe a word they are saying up there." He discouraged him. There must be a deep spot in hell for the man who bears the name of minister and dares to discourage a young convert in his first aspirations toward God.

The poor young fellow was discouraged entirely. A minister of the gospel had laughed at him and snared him into wretched backsliding and maybe even into hell. If you are starting out in the Christian life, no matter who approves or disapproves, you are on the right track. Go on in spite of everybody.

Eternal Consequences

The fear of man ensnares people to their eternal ruin. Many men and women lie in Christless graves and will spend a Christless eternity because the fear of man kept them from the acceptance of Christ. One night after speaking, I gave the altar call. Among those who were moved by the Spirit of God was a young woman. She rose to her feet and started to come to the front. The young man who sat beside her touched her arm. He was engaged to marry her. He said, "Don't go tonight. If you will wait for a few days, I may go with you." For fear of offending her fiancé, she sat down.

I went back the next week to speak at the same place. At the close of the meeting two young women came and said, "Oh, Mr. Torrey, just as soon as you can get away from the meeting here, come with us. There is a young lady who was going to come forward the other night, but the young man to whom she is engaged asked her to wait. She did wait, and now she has scarlet fever. She probably won't live until morning. Come to see her just as soon as you can get away from the meeting."

I left as soon as I could. I entered her home and went into the room where the poor girl lay dying, hardly recognizable as the same person, but perfectly conscious. I urged her to accept Christ. "No," she said, "I was about to receive Him the last time you were here. I didn't repent then. I am dying; I can't repent now."

I begged her. I knew it was her last hour. I did everything, but she would not yield. When I left that room of awful darkness, a young man in the hallway grasped me by the hand. He was shaking like a leaf. "Oh," he said, "Mr. Torrey, I am engaged to marry that girl. Now she is dying without Christ. She is lost, and I am to blame. I am to blame."

The Spirit of God is moving on this earth with mighty power. Many of you are on the verge of a decision for Christ. Don't let the fear of man frighten you from taking your stand now.

Trusting the Lord

Our text in Proverbs 29:25 promises, "*Whoso putteth his trust in the* LORD *shall be safe.*" He will be safe from all danger of yielding to sin and temptation. If you trust God, temptation has no power over you. A man cannot yield to temptation without distrusting God. Every act of sin is an act of distrust of God. He who trusts God will do right even though the heavens fall.

I knew a businessman who lost nearly everything he owned and had to sell everything else in order to pay his debts. He paid all his debts, but it left him practically penniless. Then he was offered a job with a manufacturing firm. He came to me and said, "What should I do? This is an excellent company to work for. They said they will promote me quickly, but if I take this post, I must work on Sundays. What should I do?"

I said, "Well, you will have to decide for yourself, but if you can't do it with a clear conscience, you can't afford to do it."

He said, "I can't do it with a clear conscience." He refused the position, although he did not know what he was to do to support himself and his wife and family of three children. A day or two later, he got a job at very low wages. A few weeks after that, he got a position at several hundred dollars per month. He went on to become the controller of one of the biggest mercantile establishments in the Northwest—all because he trusted God.

When I was home one summer, I found that a young Jewish woman had been converted while I was away. She was a very talented woman, but she had to work hard for her living to support the family. After she was converted, she was full of love for Christ. She went out to the place where she worked, a very large company, and she began talking about Christ to the other employees. Some of them did not like it. They went to the head of the firm and said, "She is constantly talking to us about Christ. We don't like it."

The managers called her in and said, "We have no objection to Christianity, and no objection to your being a Christian. It is a good thing, but you must not talk about it at this company."

"Very well," she said. "I won't work where I can't take Christ with me and talk for my Master."

"Well, then," they said, "you will have to lose your job."

"Very well," she said, "I will give up my position before I will be disloyal to Jesus Christ."

They said, "Go back to work, and we will tell you our decision later." She went back to work.

At the end of the week, she got a letter from the firm. She said, "Here is my discharge," and she tore it open. The letter read: "We have a position with great responsibility, with a much larger salary than you are getting. We think you are the woman for the position, and we offer it to you." They saw she could be trusted. Businessmen are looking for men and women whom they can trust.

Facing Persecution

Whoever trusts in the Lord will be safe from danger of every kind. We read in Romans 8:31: *"If God be for us, who can be against us?"* Men will persecute you. They will ridicule you. They will do all they can to harm you. Jesus said in John 15:20, *"If they have persecuted me, they will also persecute you."* But it won't do you any harm.

Some people are frightened at the thought of being persecuted. But it is one of the greatest privileges on earth for converts to be persecuted for Jesus Christ. Jesus said:

> *Blessed are ye, when men shall revile you, and persecute you, and shall say all manner of evil against you falsely, for my sake. Rejoice, and be exceeding glad: for great is your reward in heaven: for so persecuted they the prophets which were before you.* (Matthew 5:11–12)

When I was in Australia, an organized gang came to break up our meeting. I had said some rather plain things about living a holy life before God that angered a number of people. This gang that came to break up the meetings was seated in the far balcony. The power of God came down, and two ringleaders walked right up from that balcony the whole length of the hall and came down to the front. They turned and faced the crowd and said, "We accept Jesus Christ."

The next day, some friends of the ringleader of the gang met him on the street. They knocked him down and pounded him to make him swear and curse God. But God had taken all the swearing out of him. Instead of swearing, he wrote one of the most beautiful letters to a friend of his, who sent it to me. He wrote about the joy of suffering for Jesus' sake.

They may persecute you. They may pound you, they may hound you, but they can't hurt you if you are right with God. The man who trusts in the Lord is eternally safe.

Jesus said in John 10:28–29:

> *I give unto them eternal life; and they shall never perish, neither shall any man pluck them out of my hand. My Father, which gave them me, is greater than all; and no man is able to pluck them out of my Father's hand.*

If you trust in the Lord, God Almighty's hand is underneath you and around you; Christ the Son's hand is over you and around you. You are in between the almighty hand of God the Father and God the Son, and all the devils in hell can't get you.

Throw away your fear of man. In place of it, put trust in Jehovah. You compromising Christians, throw away your compromise. Be radical for Jesus; be a clean, straight Christian for God. Throw away your guilty silence. Go to work to bring others to Christ, and keep it up tomorrow, the next day, and the day after that. Throw away your guilty silence about unpopular truth, and declare the whole counsel of God, even though some say you are old-fashioned because you tell the truth. Don't worry about what anybody says, but stand up boldly and confess Christ before the world.

The Time for Harvest

In the early days of Mr. Moody's work in Chicago, there was a man who regularly attended the church. He seemed to be on the point of decision for Christ. At last Mr. Moody went to him and urged him to decide at once. He replied that he could not take a stand for Christ. There was a man with whom he worked who would ridicule him, and he could not endure his ridicule. As Mr. Moody kept urging him to make a decision, the man at last became irritated and ceased attending the church.

Some months later, when the man had quite dropped out of sight, Mr. Moody received an urgent call to go and see the man. He found him very ill, apparently dying, and in great anxiety about his soul. Mr. Moody showed him the way of life, and the man professed to accept Christ. His soul seemed at rest. To everyone's surprise, he took a turn for the better, and full recovery seemed sure.

Mr. Moody called on him one day and found him sitting out in the sunshine. Mr. Moody said, "Now that you have accepted Christ, and God has raised you up, you must come and confess Him publicly as soon as you are able to come to church."

To Mr. Moody's astonishment, the man replied, "No, not now. I don't dare admit I am a Christian in Chicago. But I intend to move to Michigan soon. As soon as I get over there, I will come out publicly and take my stand for Christ." Mr. Moody told him that Christ could protect him in Chicago as well as in Michigan, but the man's fear of his friend held him back. Mr. Moody was greatly disappointed and left.

One week from that day, the man's wife called Mr. Moody and begged him to come at once and see her husband. He had suffered a relapse, was worse than ever, and a council of physicians agreed that there was no possibility of recovery.

"Did he send for me to come?" asked Mr. Moody.

"No. He says that he is lost, and that there is no hope for him. He does not wish to see you or speak to you, but I cannot let him die this way. You must come."

Mr. Moody hastened to the house and found the man in a state of utter despair. To all Mr. Moody's pleas for him to take Christ, he would reply that it was too late, that he was lost, that he had thrown away his day of opportunity, and that he could not be saved now. Mr. Moody said, "I will pray for you."

"No," said the man, "don't pray for me. It is useless. I am lost. Pray for my wife and children. They need your prayers."

Mr. Moody knelt down by his side and prayed, but his prayers did not seem to go higher than his head. He could not get hold of God for this man's salvation. When he arose, the man said, "There, Mr. Moody, I knew that prayer would do no good. I am lost."

With a heavy heart, Mr. Moody left the house. All afternoon the man kept repeating, "The harvest is past, the summer is ended, and I am not saved." (See Jeremiah 8:20.) Just as the sun was setting behind the western prairies, the man passed away. In his last moment, they heard him murmuring, "The harvest is past, the summer is ended, and I am not saved." Another soul went out into eternity unprepared, snared into eternal perdition by the fear of man. Throw away your fear of man, and put your trust in the Lord and be saved.

15

HOW GOD LOVES THE WORLD

For God so loved the world,
that he gave his only begotten Son,
that whosoever believeth in him should not perish,
but have everlasting life.
—John 3:16

Thousands of people have been saved by this wonderful verse, tens of thousands, hundreds of thousands—by simply reading it in the Bible. This one verse tells us some very important things about the love of God. It tells us that our salvation begins in God's love. We are not saved because we love God; we are saved because God loves us. Our salvation begins in God's loving us, and it ends in our loving God.

The first thing our text teaches us about the love of God is that the love of God is universal. *"God so loved the world"*—not some part of it, not some elect people or some select class. God loves the rich, but God loves the poor, too. The rich need to hear the gospel just as much as the poor, and they are not nearly as likely to. If some poor man who did not even know where he was going to sleep tonight stood up to receive Christ, many people would not think it amounted to much. But God would be just as pleased to see the poorest man or woman accept Christ as He would be to see the richest millionaire come to Him. God loves the man who can't read or write as much as He loves the most brilliant scientist or philosopher on earth.

If some university professor were converted, some people would be delighted. They would say, "Oh, a wonderful thing happened. One of our learned professors was converted." But if an illiterate person accepted Christ, some people would not be nearly as impressed. The most wonderful thing of all is this: God loves the poor as much as the rich, the uneducated as much as the educated, and the unrighteous as much as the righteous.

One night I was visiting one of the members of my church, and his little girl was playing in the room. The child did something naughty, and her father called out, "Don't be naughty. If you are a good girl, God will love you, but if you are not, God won't love you."

I said, "Charlie, what nonsense are you teaching that child of yours? That is not what my Bible teaches. It teaches that God loves the sinner just as truly as He loves the saint."

It is hard to make people believe that God loves the sinner and the outcast. The Bible emphasizes this truth the most.

Christ Died for Sinners

I was preaching one hot summer's night; it was so hot that the windows were all opened at the back to let in the fresh air. The room was packed. At the back of the room, a man sat on the windowsill. When I asked for all who wished to be saved that night to hold up their hands, that man raised his hand. But as soon as I pronounced the benediction, he started for the door. I forgot about the meeting to follow. All I saw was that man starting for the door, and I went after him. I caught him just as he turned to descend the stairway. I laid my hand on his shoulder and said to him, "My friend, you held up your hand to say you wanted to be saved."

"Yes, I did."

"Why didn't you stay, then, for the second meeting?"

He said, "It is no use."

I said, "God loves you."

"You don't know who you are talking to. I am the worst thief in this town."

"Well, even if you are, I can prove to you from the Bible that God loves you." I opened my Bible to Romans 5:8, and I read: *"But God commendeth his love toward us, in that, while we were yet sinners, Christ died for us."*

I said, "If you are the worst thief in town, you are certainly a sinner, and that verse says that God loves sinners."

It broke the man's heart, and he began to weep. I took him to my office where we sat down, and he told me his story. He said, "I was released from prison this morning. I had started out this evening with some companions to commit one of the most daring burglaries ever committed in this city. By tomorrow morning, I would either have had a big stake of money or a bullet in my body.

"But as we were going down the street together, we passed the corner where you were holding that open-air meeting. A Scotsman was speaking. My mother was Scotch, and when I heard that familiar accent, it reminded me of my mother.

"I had a dream about her the other night in prison. I dreamed that she came to me and begged me to give up my wicked life. When I heard that

Scotsman talk, I stopped to listen. My two pals said, 'Come along,' and cursed me. I said, 'I am going to listen to what this man says.' Then they tried to drag me across the street, but I would not go. What that man said touched my heart. When he invited everyone to this meeting, I came, and that is why I am here."

I opened my Bible and showed him that God loves sinners, that Christ had died for sinners, and that he could be saved by simply accepting Christ. He did accept Christ. We knelt down side by side, and that man offered the most wonderful prayer I ever heard in all my life.

Are you a thief? God loves you. Are you an unbeliever? God loves you. Are you a blasphemer? God loves you. You can't find in all the earth anyone whom God doesn't love.

The Character of God's Love

The second thing our text teaches about the love of God is that God's love is a holy love. *"God so loved the world, that he gave his only begotten Son"* (John 3:16). A great many people cannot understand that. They say, "If God loves me, I cannot see why He doesn't forgive my sins outright without His Son dying in my place. I cannot see the necessity of Christ's death. If God is love, and if God loves me and everybody else, why doesn't He take us to heaven right away without Christ dying for us?"

The text answers the question, *"God so loved."* That *so* brings out the character of God's love. God could not and would not pardon sin without an atonement. God is a holy God. God's holiness must manifest itself in some way. It must either manifest itself in the punishment of the sinner, that is, in our eternal banishment from His presence, or it must manifest itself in some other way.

The death of Jesus Christ on the cross of Calvary was God providing atonement for sinful man. But some people say, "That is not fair. Are you saying that God took the sin of man and laid it on Jesus Christ, an innocent third person? That is not fair."

But Jesus Christ was not a third person. "*God was in Christ, reconciling the world unto himself*" (2 Corinthians 5:19). The atoning death of Jesus Christ on the cross is not God taking my sin from me and laying it on a third person. It is God the Father taking the penalty of my sin into His own heart and dying in His Son, in my place. Jesus Christ was not merely the first Person. He was the second Person, too. Jesus Christ was the Son of Man, the Second Adam, the representative Man. No ordinary man could have died for you and me. It would have been of no value. But Jesus Christ was the Second Adam, your representative and mine. When Christ died on the cross of Calvary, I died in Him, and the penalty of my sin was paid.

If you do not believe in the deity of Christ, the Atonement becomes irrational. If you remove the humanity of Christ and believe He is merely divine, the Atonement becomes irrational. But take all that the Bible says—that God was in Christ, and that in Christ the Word became God manifest in the flesh—and the Atonement is the most profound and wonderful truth the world has ever seen.

God's love is a holy love. In His perfect righteousness, perfect justice, perfect holiness, and perfect love, Christ, through His atoning death, provided pardon to save the vilest of sinners. When you are awakened to a proper sense of your sinfulness, when you see yourself as you really are and see God as He really is, nothing will satisfy your conscience but the doctrine that God, the Holy One, substituted His atoning action for His punitive action. In the death of Jesus Christ on the cross of Calvary, your sins and mine were perfectly settled forever.

Thank God, the law of God has no claim on me. I broke it, I admit, but Jesus Christ kept it. He satisfied its punitive claim by dying for those who had not kept it. On the ground of that atoning death, there is pardon for the vilest sinner.

You may have gone deeper into sin than you realize yourself, but while your sins are as high as the mountains, the Atonement that covers them is as high as the heavens. While your sins are as deep as the ocean, the Atonement that swallows them up is as deep as eternity. On the ground of Christ's atoning death, there is pardon for the vilest sinner on earth.

God's Infinite Love

The third thing our text teaches us about the love of God is the greatness of that love. We see His love in the greatness of the gift He offers us—eternal life. It means a life that is perfect and divine in its quality as well as endless in its duration. "*God so loved the world, that he gave his only begotten Son, that whosoever believeth in him should not perish, but have everlasting life.*"

I thank God for a life that is perfect in quality and that will never end. Most of us will have to die before long, as far as our physical life is concerned. Eighty years from now, you and most of your family and friends will be gone, unless the Lord comes back first. You may say that eighty years is a long time. No, it is not. It sounds long to young people, but when you get to be older, it looks very short. When the eighty years are up, what then? Suppose I had a guarantee that I was going to live two hundred years in perfect health, strength, and prosperity. Would that satisfy me? No, it would not. For when the two hundred years are up, what then? I want something that never ends, and thank God, in Christ, I have something that never ends—eternal life! Who can have it? Anybody. "*Whosoever believeth in him should not perish, but have everlasting life.*"

Somebody asked a little boy, "What does *whoever* mean?" The little fellow answered, "It means you and me and everybody else." When I read that "*God so loved the world, that he gave his only begotten Son, that whosoever believeth in him should not perish, but have everlasting life,*" I know that means me. Thank God it does, and that it includes everybody else.

The Measure of Love

The text tells us a second way in which the greatness of the love of God shows itself: in the sacrifice that God made for us. "*God so loved the world, that he gave his only begotten Son.*" The measure of love is sacrifice. You can tell how much anybody loves you by the sacrifice that he is willing to make for you. God has shown the measure of His love by the sacrifice He made. He gave His very best, the dearest that He had.

No earthly father ever loved his son as God loved Jesus Christ. I have an only son; how I love him! But suppose some day I should see that boy of mine arrested by the enemies of Christ; and suppose they blindfolded him, spat in his face, beat him, and then made a crown of big, cruel thorns and put it on his brow, causing the blood to pour down his face on either side. How do you suppose I would feel?

Then suppose they stripped his garments from him, tied him to a post, and beat him with a stick that had long lashes of leather twisted with bits of brass and lead, until his back was all torn and bleeding. How do you think I would feel?

Suppose they threw him down on a cross laid on the ground, stretched his right hand out on the arm of the cross, put a nail in the hand, lifted the heavy hammer, and drove the nail through the hand; then they stretched his left arm on the other arm of the cross, put a nail in the palm of that hand, lifted the heavy hammer, and sent the nail through that hand; then they drove the nail through his feet. Finally, they took that cross and plunged it into a hole and left him hanging there while the agony grew worse every minute. Suppose they left him to die beneath the burning sun. How do you suppose I would feel if I stood and looked on as my only boy died in awful agony on a cross?

That is just what God saw. He loved His only begotten Son, as you and I never imagined loving our sons. He saw His Son hanging there, aching, all His bones out of joint, tortured in every part of His body! God looked on. Why did He permit it? Because He loves you and me, and it was the only way by which we could be saved.

Your Response to God's Love

How are you going to repay this love? Some people will repay it with hatred. They hate God. They have never said it, but it is true.

A friend of mine was preaching one time in Connecticut. He was staying with a physician who had a beautiful, amiable daughter. She had never made a profession of faith, but she was such a beautiful person that people thought she was a Christian. One night, after the meetings had been going on for some time, my friend said to this young lady, "Are you going up to the meeting tonight?"

She said, "No, I am not."

He said, "I think you had better go."

"I will not go."

"Why," he said, "don't you love God?"

She said, "I hate God." She had never realized it before. I think she would have said she loved God up to that time, but when the demands of God were pressed home by the Holy Spirit, she was not willing to obey. She found out that she hated God.

Some of you have never found out that you hate God, but it is true. How have you used the name of God today? You have used it many times. In prayer? No, in profanity. Why? Because you hate God.

If a woman receives Christ, she may find that her husband makes her life unbearable. Why? Because he hates God, and he wants to make his wife miserable for accepting His Son. If someone in your business accepts Christ, do you laugh at him? If you do, it is because you hate God. Some people will read every heretical book they can get and go to every ungodly lecture. They are trying to convince themselves that the Bible is not God's Word. If anybody comes along and brings up some smart objection to the

Bible, they laugh and rejoice in it. Why? Because they hate God and want to get rid of God's Book.

Some people love to hold up their heads and say, "I don't believe in the divinity of Christ. I don't believe He is the Son of God." Why? Because they hate God, and if they can rob His divine Son of the honor that belongs to Him, they will do it. They are repaying the wondrous love of God with hatred.

Perhaps you refuse to accept Christ. You heard God's message of salvation many times. When people speak to you about committing your life to the Lord, you get angry. You say, "I wish you would not talk to me. It is none of your business whether I am a Christian or not." Why do you respond like this? Because you hate God.

Some people so bitterly hate God that they try to find fault with the doctrine of the Atonement. They try to make themselves believe that Christ did not die on the cross for their salvation. They say, "I cannot understand the philosophy of it." A person who loved God would not stop to ask the philosophy of it. He would lift his heart in simple gratitude and praise to God for His great love and mercy.

Conquered by Love

There is one other thing that our text teaches us about the love of God: the conquering power of God's love. The love of God conquers sin, death, and wrong, and gives everlasting life. The love of God conquers where everything else fails.

The first time I ever preached in Chicago, I noticed a young woman who did not come forward when the rest came. I went down to where she was standing and urged her to come forward. She laughed and said, "No, I am not going forward," and sat down again.

The next night was not an evangelistic service, but a convention meeting. I was president of the convention. As I looked over the audience, I saw that young woman sitting in the back. She was elegantly dressed. I called somebody else to the platform and slipped around to the back part of the building. When the meeting was dismissed, I made my way to where that young lady was sitting. I sat down beside her and said, "Won't you accept Christ tonight?"

"No," she said. "Would you like to know the kind of life I am living?" She was living in the best society, honored and respected. Then she told me a sad story of immorality and laughed as if it were a good joke.

I simply took my Bible and opened it to John 3:16. I passed it over to her and said, "Won't you please read that?" She had to hold it very near her eyes to see the small print, and she began in a laughing way. *"God so loved*—her laughter subsided—*the world"*—there was nothing like a laugh now—*"that he gave his only begotten Son."* She burst into tears, and the tears flowed down on the elegant silk dress she was wearing. Hardened and shameless as she was, trifling as she was, one glimpse of Jesus on the cross of Calvary for her had broken her heart.

One night I was preaching, and we had an after-meeting. The leading soprano in the choir was not a Christian. She was a respectable girl, but very worldly and frivolous. She decided to stay for the after-meeting. Her mother stood up in the congregation and said, "I wish you would all pray for the conversion of my daughter." I did not turn to took at the choir, but I knew perfectly well how that young woman looked. I knew her cheeks were burning, I knew her eyes were flashing, and I knew that she was angry from the crown of her head to the soles of her feet.

As soon as the meeting was over, I hurried down to the door. As she came along, I walked toward her, held out my hand, and said, "Good evening, Cora." Her eyes flashed, and her checks burned. She did not take my hand. She stamped her foot and said, "Mr. Torrey, my mother knows better than to do what she has done tonight. She knows it will only make me worse."

I said, "Cora, sit down." The angry girl sat down, and I opened my Bible to Isaiah 53:5 and handed it to her. I said, "Won't you please read it?" She read: *"He was wounded for our transgressions, he was bruised for our iniquities: the chastisement of our peace was upon him."* She did not get any further; she burst into tears. The love of God revealed in the cross of Christ had broken her heart, and she received Christ into her life.

Let the love of God conquer your stubborn, wicked, foolish, sinful, worldly, careless heart. *"God so loved the world, that he gave his only begotten Son, that whosoever believeth in him should not perish, but have everlasting life."* Yield to that love now.

16

TODAY AND TOMORROW

The Holy Ghost saith, To day if ye will hear his voice.
—Hebrews 3:7

Boast not thyself of to morrow.
—Proverbs 27:1

Today is the wise man's day; tomorrow is the fool's day. The wise man sees what ought to be done and does it today. The foolish man says, "I will do it tomorrow." Those who always do the thing that should be done today are successful for time and for eternity. Those who put off until tomorrow what should be done today will fail for time and eternity. "*The Holy Ghost saith, To day.*" Man, in the folly of his heart, says, "Tomorrow."

I have no doubt that thousands of men and women intend to be Christians at some time, but they keep saying, "Not yet, not today." I am going to tell you not merely why you should become a Christian, but why you should become a Christian today.

The sooner you come to Christ, the sooner you will find the wonderful joy that is found in Him. In Jesus, there is an immeasurably better joy than there is in the world, a purer joy, a holier joy, a more satisfying joy.

This fact is not open to dispute. Everyone knows that it is true. Go to any person who followed the ways of the world and then tried Christ, and ask him, "Which joy is better—the joy that the world gave or the joy that you have found in Christ?" You will get the same answer every time. The joy found in the world cannot for a moment compare to the joy that is found in Christ.

If ever a person had an opportunity to try what this world can give, I had it, and I tried it. I tried all that could be found in the world; then I turned to Christ and tried Him. My testimony is the testimony of millions of others who have found that the joy of the world is not real joy. The joy of Christ is everything.

Anyone who has really found Christ will tell you there is a joy in Christ that is higher, deeper, broader, wider, and more wonderful in every way than the joy that the world gives. The sooner you come to Christ, the sooner you will have that joy.

Deep and Abiding Peace

The sooner you come to Christ, the sooner you will escape the wretchedness and misery that there is away from Christ. First of all, there is the misery of an accusing conscience. No one out of Christ has peace of mind.

One night I was preaching to an audience of men and women to whom twenty dollars would have been a great help. As I was preaching, I took out the money and held it up and said, "Now, is there a anyone in this audience who does not know Christ who has peace in his heart, deep, abiding satisfaction and rest? If he will come up here and say so, I will give him this twenty-dollar bill."

Nobody came up. When the meeting was over, I went down and stood at the door with the twenty dollar bill, for I thought some might be timid about coming up in front for it. I said, "If anybody can claim this twenty dollars by saying, 'I have peace of conscience and heart. My heart is satisfied without Christ,' he can have this twenty dollar bill." They filed out, and nobody claimed the money. Finally, a man came along, and I said, "Don't you want this money?" He answered, "I cannot claim it on those conditions." Neither can you.

Another night I was preaching in Chicago, and I asked everybody in the building who had found rest and perfect satisfaction through the acceptance of Christ to stand up. More than a thousand men and women rose to their feet. I asked them to sit down, and then I said, "If there is an unbeliever in this house who can say he has found rest, peace, and perfect satisfaction of heart, will he please stand?" Many agnostics and skeptics were there. One man stood up in the balcony, and I said, "I see there is a gentleman up there. I am glad that he has the courage of his convictions, and I would like to speak with him after the meeting."

He came to the after-meeting. I said, "You stood up in the meeting tonight to say that you had perfect rest and peace of heart without Christ, and that your soul was satisfied with your unbelief. Is that true?"

"Oh," he said, "Mr. Torrey, that will have to be qualified." I guess it will. *"There is no peace, saith the Lord, unto the wicked"* (Isaiah 48:22).

There is slavery in sin. *"Whosoever committeth sin is the servant of sin"* (John 8:34). Away from Christ is apprehension of what may happen, fear of disaster, fear of what man may do, fear of what may be found beyond the grave. When you come to Christ, you get rid of the fear of man. You have no fear of misfortune, for you are able to say,

"All things work together for good to them that love God" (Romans 8:28). You have no fear of death, for what men call death is simply to depart and be with Christ. The moment you accept Christ, you get rid of the accusations of conscience, the slavery of sin, all fear of disaster, and the dread of death.

Why not get rid of it all right now? Suppose you were on the seashore and saw in the distance a wreck of a ship and a man clinging to a piece of board. If you went to rescue him, do you think he would say, "I think I can hold on until morning. Come out again then, and I will get into the boat and come ashore." You would say, "Man, are you mad? Will you stay out here tonight when you can come ashore now?"

Men and women, out on the wreck of life, the cold waves break over you with all the wretchedness of an accusing conscience, the bondage of sin, the fear of death, and all the multiplied wretchedness of the soul away from God. Why cling to the wreck another night? You can come ashore to safety and joy now, if you will climb right into the lifeboat.

Working for the Lord

The moment a person is saved he can begin to do something for the Master. The sooner you come to Christ, the more you can do for Him. If you are saved a year from now, you can begin to work for Christ, but there will be one year gone that will never come back. You are associated with friends now whom you can lead to Christ. A year from now, they may be past your reach. I had a friend who lived in the same building as I before I was converted. Had I been a Christian then, I could have led him to Christ. Three years later, after I had accepted Christ, we had gone our separate ways.

One day, I picked up the *New York Times* and began to read about a young man who was out playing ball. The man in center field threw the ball in. This young man's back was toward center field, and he was struck at the base of the brain. He never regained consciousness. My father said, "Isn't that your old friend?" I took the paper and read it and said, "Yes, it is my old friend." He was called into eternity without a moment's warning, and my opportunity of bringing him to Christ was gone forever! In the years that have come since, God has used me to lead others to Christ, but I have often thought of Frank. In spite of all those who are now coming to Christ, Frank has gone, and my opportunity of leading him to Christ is lost forever. If you postpone accepting Christ for thirty days, people whom you might have reached during those thirty days will have passed beyond your reach forever.

In my first pastorate, a woman a little over fifty years of age, who had been a backslider, recommitted her life to the Lord. She became the best worker in the community. But her two sons had grown up during the years that she was far from God. They had both married and passed beyond her reach. Although she has been used to bring many to Christ, she was never able to bring these sons to her Lord. Her day of opportunity for them was while she was living in the world. Fathers and mothers living far from God, if you are not saved now, you may be some other day. But your sons and daughters will very likely have passed beyond your reach forever. The sooner you come to Christ, the more people you can bring with you.

The sooner you come to Christ, the richer will be your eternity. We are saved by grace, but we are rewarded according to our works. Every day after a man is saved, he lays up treasures in heaven. (See Matthew 6:20.) Every day you live for Christ, you will be that much richer for all eternity.

Some people have an idea that a man can be saved on his deathbed and have just as abundant an entrance into the kingdom of God as he could have if he had been saved forty years. Neither common sense nor the Bible supports that thought. A man may be saved on his deathbed, but he is saved *"so as by fire"* (1 Corinthians 3:15). His works are all burned up, and he enters heaven penniless. The man who is saved forty years before he dies and serves Christ for those years makes his deposits for which he will be richer throughout all eternity. *"Lay up for yourselves treasures in heaven"* (Matthew 6:20).

If you come to Christ while you are still young, you can enter the kingdom of God with much fuller hands. I thank God I was converted when I was young, but what would I give for those wasted years while I deliberately resisted the Spirit of God! But I can't call them back.

The Day of Salvation

The sooner you come to Christ, the surer you are to come to Christ. If you are not saved today, you may be saved tomorrow, but you may not be saved. I believe there are scores of people who will be saved now or never. People think they can turn to Christ when they decide that they want to, but when the Spirit of God is moving on your heart, it is a solemn moment. To say yes, means life; to say no, means death. To say yes, means heaven; to say no, means hell.

Often a man will be near the kingdom, and he will say, "I am so interested now that I will certainly be just as interested tomorrow." But the critical hour has come, and if he does not yield now, he will have no interest tomorrow.

I once received a message from a wealthy young fellow saying that he wished to see me that night at Mr. Moody's meeting. I went and met him at the close of the meeting. He was on the verge of a decision. As we stood talking on the sidewalk, a bell rang out a late hour. I said to myself, "He is so near a decision, I can leave him safely until tomorrow morning." So I said, "Good night, Will. I will be around to your room tomorrow morning at ten."

It was one of the most fatal mistakes I have ever made. I was there at ten and he was there, but his convictions had all left him. He was hard as stone. His opportunity had come and gone. You may be very near a decision at this moment, on the very borders of the kingdom, but if you say no, tomorrow will be forever too late. Who of us can tell who will be called out of the world into eternity in a moment?

You have a chance now. Don't throw it away. The sooner you accept Christ, the surer you will be to receive Him. Ask Him into your heart now.

You can have the joy of salvation at this moment; why wait a week? You can be saved from a life of wretchedness at once; why bear it another hour? The sooner you come to Christ, the more you can do for Him, and the richer you will be throughout all eternity.

Come to Him today and begin to lay up treasures in the bank of heaven. The sooner you come to Christ, the surer it is that you will come. Come now. "*The Holy Ghost saith, To day if ye will hear his voice, harden not your hearts*" (Hebrews 3:7–8). "*Boast not thyself of to morrow; for thou knowest not what a day may bring forth*" (Proverbs 27:1). "*Behold, now is the accepted time; behold, now is the day of salvation*" (2 Corinthians 6:2).

YOUR LIFE IN GOD

CONTENTS

INTRODUCTION

New Christians need a book that will outline basic principles of their faith so they will enjoy complete success in their new life. Since I could not find such a book, I wrote one myself. This book aims to tell the new convert just what he needs to know most. I hope that pastors, evangelists, and other Christian workers will find it a good book to give young converts. I hope it will also prove helpful to many who have been Christians for a long time but have not made the headway they desire in their Christian life.

1

BEGINNING RIGHT

Beginning the Christian life with a solid, correct foundation influences the success of the remainder of a Christian's life. However, if someone has started life with Jesus, yet is unsure of his foundation, it is simple for him to strengthen it with solid Christian principles.

Receive Jesus as Savior

We are told the right beginning for the Christian life in John 1:12, *"But as many as received him, to them gave he power to become the sons of God, even to them that believe on his name."* The right way to begin the Christian life is by receiving Jesus Christ. He immediately gives power to become a child of God to anyone who receives Him.

If the reader of this book was the most wicked man on earth, and then he received Jesus Christ, that very instant he would become a child of God. God promises this in the most unqualified way in the verse quoted above. No one can become a child of God any other way. No man, no matter how carefully he has been raised, no matter how well he has been sheltered from the vices and evils of this world, is a child of God until he receives Jesus Christ. We are *"children of God by faith in Christ Jesus"* (Gal. 3:26) and in no other way.

What does it mean to receive Jesus Christ? It means to accept Christ as all God offers Him to be for everybody. Jesus Christ is God's gift. *"For God so loved the world, that he gave his only begotten Son, that whosoever believeth in him should not perish, but have everlasting life"* (John 3:16).

Some accept this wondrous gift of God. Everyone who does accept this gift becomes a child of God. Many others refuse this wondrous gift of God, and everyone who refuses this gift perishes. They condemn themselves. *"He that believeth on him is not condemned: but he that believeth not is condemned already, because he hath not believed in the name of the only begotten Son of God"* (John 3:18).

Jesus Is Our Sin-Bearer

What does God offer His Son to be to us?

First of all, God offers Jesus to us to be our Sin-Bearer. We all have sinned. There is not a man or woman, a boy or girl, who has not sinned. *"Even the righteousness of God which is by faith of Jesus Christ unto all and upon all them that believe: for there is no difference: for all have sinned, and come short of the glory of God"* (Rom. 3:22–23). If any of us say that we have not sinned, we are deceiving ourselves and giving the lie to God. *"If we say that we have no sin, we deceive ourselves, and the truth is not in us.... If we say that we have not sinned, we make him a liar, and his word is not in us"* (1 John 1:8, 10). Each of us must bear our own sin, or someone else must bear it in our place. If we were to bear our own sins, it would mean we must be banished forever from the presence of God, for God is holy. *"God is light, and in him is no darkness at all"* (1 John 1:5).

But God Himself has provided another to take responsibility for our sins so that we do not need to bear them ourselves. This Sin-Bearer is God's own Son, Jesus Christ, *"For he hath made him to be sin for us, who knew no sin; that we might be made the righteousness of God in him"* (2 Cor. 5:21).

When Jesus Christ died upon the cross of Calvary, He redeemed us from the curse of the law by being made a curse in our stead. *"Christ hath redeemed us from the curse of the law, being made a curse for us: for it is written, Cursed is every one that hangeth on a tree"* (Gal. 3:13). To receive Christ, then, is to believe this testimony of God about His Son, to believe that Jesus Christ did bear our sins in His own body on the cross. *"Who his own self bare our sins in his own body on the tree, that we, being dead to sins, should live unto righteousness: by whose stripes ye were healed"* (1 Peter 2:24). We know we can trust God to forgive all our sins because Jesus Christ has borne them in our place.

"All we like sheep have gone astray; we have turned every one to his own way; and the LORD hath laid on him the iniquity of us all" (Isa. 53:6). Our own good works—past, present, or future—have nothing to do with the forgiveness of our sins. Our sins are forgiven, not because of any good works we do, but because of the atoning work of Christ on the cross of Calvary in our place. If we rest in this atoning work, we will do good works. But our good works will be the outcome of our being saved and our believing on Christ as our Sin-Bearer. Our good works will not be the ground of our salvation, but the result of our salvation and the proof of it.

We must be very careful not to believe in our good works as the basis of salvation. We are not forgiven because of Christ's death *and our good works;* we are forgiven solely and entirely because of Christ's death. To see this clearly is the right beginning of the true Christian life.

Our Deliverer from Sin

God offers Jesus to us as our Deliverer from the power of sin. Jesus not only died, He rose again. Today He is a living Savior. He has all power in heaven and on earth. *"And Jesus came and spake unto them, saying, All power is given unto me in heaven and in earth"* (Matt. 28:18). He has the power to keep the weakest sinner from falling. *"Now unto him that is able to keep you from falling, and to present you faultless before the presence of his glory with exceeding joy"* (Jude 24). He is able to save not only from the worst but also elevate to the highest all who come unto the Father through Him. *"Wherefore he is able also to save them to the uttermost that come unto God by him, seeing he ever liveth to make intercession for them"* (Heb. 7:25). *"If the Son therefore shall make you free, ye shall be free indeed"* (John 8:36).

To receive Jesus is to believe what God tells us in His Word about Him: to believe that He did rise from the dead; to believe that He now lives; to believe that He has the power to keep us from falling; and to believe that He has the power to keep us from sin day by day. Then, we must trust Him to do what He has said.

This is the secret of daily victory over sin. If we try to fight sin with our own strength, we are bound to fail. If we look up to the risen Christ to keep us every day and every hour, He will keep us. Through the crucified Christ, we get deliverance from the guilt of sin, our sins are all blotted out, and we are free from all condemnation. But it is through the risen Christ that we get daily victory over the power of sin.

Some receive Christ as Sin-Bearer and thus find pardon, but they do not get beyond that. Thus their life is one of daily failure. Others receive Him as their risen Savior also, and they experience victory over sin. To begin right, we must take Him not only as our Sin-Bearer, and thus find pardon; we must also take Him as our risen Savior and our daily Deliverer from the power of sin.

Jesus Is Lord

God offers Jesus to us, not only as our Sin-Bearer and our Deliverer from the power of sin, but He also offers Him to us as our Lord and King.

We read in Acts 2:36, *"Therefore let all the house of Israel know assuredly, that God hath made that same Jesus, whom ye have crucified, both Lord and Christ."* Lord means divine Master, and Christ means anointed King.

To receive Jesus is to take Him as our divine Master, as the One to whom we yield the absolute confidence of our intellects. Believe He is the One in whose Word we can believe absolutely, the One in whom we will believe though many of the wisest men may question or deny the truth of His teachings. Because He is our King, we gladly yield absolute control of our lives to Him, so that the question from this time on is: What would my King Jesus have me do? A correct beginning involves an unconditional surrender to the lordship and kingship of Jesus.

The failure to realize that Jesus is Lord and King, as well as Savior, has led to many a false start in the Christian life. We begin with Him as our Savior, our Sin-Bearer, and our Deliverer from the power of sin. We must not end with Him merely as Savior; we must know Him as Lord and King. There is nothing more important in a right beginning of Christian life than an unconditional surrender, both of thoughts and conduct, to Jesus. Say from your heart and say it again and again, "All for Jesus."

Surrender Your Life to Jesus

Many fail because they shrink back from this entire surrender. They wish to serve Jesus with half their heart, part of themselves, and part of their possessions. To hold back anything from Jesus means a wretched life of stumbling and failure.

The life of entire surrender is a joyous life all along the way. If you have never done it before, go alone with God today, get down on your knees, and say, "All for Jesus," and mean it. Say it very earnestly; say it from the bottom of your heart. Stay there until you realize what it means and what you are doing. It is a wondrous step forward when one really takes it.

If you have taken it already, take it again, and take it often. It always has fresh meaning and brings fresh blessing. In this absolute surrender is found the key to all truth. *"If any man will do his will, he shall know of the doctrine, whether it be of God, or whether I speak of myself"* (John 7:17). In this absolute surrender is found the secret of power in prayer. (See 1 John 3:22.) In this absolute surrender is found the supreme condition of receiving the Holy Spirit. *"And we are his witnesses of these things; and so is also the Holy Ghost, whom God hath given to them that obey him"* (Acts 5:32).

Taking Christ as your Lord and King involves obedience to His will as far as you know it in each small detail of life. There are those who tell us they have taken Christ as their Lord and King who at the same time are disobeying Him daily. They disobey Him in business, domestic life, social life, and personal conduct. These people are deceiving themselves. You have not taken Jesus as your Lord and King if you are not striving to obey Him in everything each day. He Himself says, *"Why call ye me, Lord, Lord, and do not the things which I say?"* (Luke 6:46).

To sum it all up, the right way to begin the Christian life is to accept Jesus Christ as your Sin-Bearer. Trust God to forgive your sins because Jesus Christ died in your place. You must accept Him as your risen Savior who lives to make intercession for you and who has complete power to keep you. Trust Him to keep you from day to day, and accept Him as your Lord and King to whom you surrender absolute control of your thoughts and life.

This is the right beginning, the only right beginning of the Christian life. If you have made this beginning, all that follows will be comparatively easy. If you have not made this beginning, make it now.

2

CONFESSING CHRIST

Once you have begun the Christian life correctly by taking the proper attitude toward Christ in a private transaction between Himself and yourself, your next step is to make an open confession of the relationship that now exists between you and Jesus Christ. Jesus says in Matthew 10:32, "*Whosoever therefore shall confess me before men, him will I confess also before my Father which is in heaven.*" He demands a public confession. He demands it for your sake. This is the path of blessing.

Many attempt to be disciples of Jesus without telling the world. No one has ever succeeded in that attempt. To be a secret disciple means to be no disciple at all. If one really has received Christ, he cannot keep it to himself. *"For out of the abundance of the heart the mouth speaketh"* (Matt. 12:34).

Are You a Closet Christian?

The public confession of Christ is so important that Paul put it first in his statement of the conditions of salvation. He said, *"That if thou shalt* ***confess with thy mouth*** *the Lord Jesus, and shalt believe in thine heart that God hath raised him from the dead, thou shalt be saved. For with the heart man believeth unto righteousness; and with the mouth confession is made unto salvation"* (Rom. 10:9–10, emphasis added).

The life of confession is the life of full salvation. Indeed, the life of confession is the life of the only real salvation. When we confess Christ before men on earth, He acknowledges us before the Father in heaven. Then the Father gives us the Holy Spirit as the seal of our salvation.

It is not enough that we confess Christ just once—for example, when we are confirmed, unite with the church, or come forward in a revival meeting. We should confess Christ constantly. We should not be ashamed of our Lord and King. In our home, church, work, and play, we should let others know where we stand. Of course, we should not parade our Christianity or our piety, but we should leave no one in doubt whether we belong to Christ. We should let it be seen that we honor Him as our Lord and King.

Backsliding

The failure to confess Christ is one of the most frequent causes of backsliding. Christians get into new relationships where they are not known as Christians and where they are tempted to conceal the fact. They yield to the temptation and soon find themselves drifting.

The more you make of Jesus Christ, the more He will make of you. It will save you from many temptations if the fact is clear that you are one who acknowledges Christ as Lord in all things.

3

ASSURANCE OF SALVATION

If one is to have the fullest measure of joy and power in Christian service, one must know that his sins are forgiven, that he is a child of God, and that he has eternal life. It is the believer's privilege to *know* he has eternal life. John said in 1 John 5:13, "*These things have I written unto you that believe on the name of the Son of God;* ***that ye may know*** *that ye have eternal life, and that ye may believe on the name of the Son of God*" (emphasis added). John wrote this first epistle for the express purpose that anyone who believes on the name of the Son of God *will know* he has eternal life.

Eternal Life for His Children

There are those who tell us no one can know he has eternal life until he is dead and has been before the judgment seat of God. But God Himself tells us we may know. To deny the possibility of the believer's knowledge that he has eternal life is to say that the first epistle of John was written in vain, and it is to insult the Holy Spirit who is its real author.

Again Paul told us in Acts 13:39, *"And by him* [that is, by Christ] *all that believe* ***are justified*** *from all things"* (emphasis added). So everyone who believes in Jesus can know that he is justified from all things. He knows it because the Word of God says so. John told us in John 1:12, *"But* ***as many as received him*** [Jesus Christ], *to them gave he power to become the sons of God, even to them that believe on his name"* (emphasis added).

Here is a definite and unmistakable declaration that everyone who receives Jesus becomes a child of God. Therefore, every believer in Jesus may know that he is a child of God. He may know it on the surest of all grounds—the Word of God asserts that he is a child of God.

Faith in Fact, Not Feeling

But how can any individual know he has eternal life? He can know it on the very best authority, through the testimony of God Himself as given in the Bible. The testimony of Scripture is the testimony of God. What the Scriptures say is absolutely true. What the Scriptures say, God says. Now in John 3:36 the Scriptures say, *"He that believeth on the Son* ***hath*** *everlasting life"* (emphasis added). We know whether we believe on the Son or not. We know whether we have that real faith in Christ that leads us to receive Him. If we have this faith in Christ, we have God's own written testimony that we have eternal life, our sins are forgiven, and we are the children of God. We may feel forgiven, or we may not feel forgiven, but that does not matter. It is not a question of what we feel but of what God says. God's Word is always to be believed.

Our own feelings are often to be doubted. There are many who doubt their sins are forgiven, who doubt they have everlasting life, who doubt they are saved. They can have doubts because they do not feel forgiven or feel that they have everlasting life or feel that they are saved. Not feeling forgiven is no reason to doubt.

Suppose you were sentenced to prison and your friends secured a pardon for you. The legal document announcing your pardon would be brought to you. You would read it and know you were pardoned because the legal document said so. But the news would be so good and so sudden that you would be dazed by it. You would not realize you were pardoned. Someone could come to you and say, "Are you pardoned?" What would you reply? You might say, "Yes, I am pardoned." Then he might ask, "Do you feel pardoned?" You may reply, "No, I do not feel pardoned. It is so sudden, so wonderful that I cannot comprehend it."

Then he would say to you, "But how can you know that you are pardoned if you do not feel it?" You would hold out the document and say, "This says so." The time would come, after you read the document over and over again and believed it, when you would not only know you were pardoned, but you would feel it.

The Bible is God's authoritative document declaring that everyone who believes in Jesus is justified. It declares that everyone who believes on the Son has everlasting life. It declares that everyone who receives Jesus is a child of God. If anyone asks you if all your sins are forgiven, reply, "Yes, I know they are because God says so." If anyone asks you if you know you are a child of God, reply, "Yes, I know I am a child of God because God says so." If they ask you if you have everlasting life, reply, "Yes, I know I have everlasting life because God says so."

God says, *"Every one which seeth the Son, and believeth on him, may have everlasting life"* (John 6:40). Then you can say, "I know I believe on the Son, and therefore I know I have eternal life—because God says so." You may not feel it yet, but if you keep meditating on God's statement and believe what God says, the time will come when you will feel it.

God Is Not a Liar

If one who believes on the Son of God doubts he has eternal life, he makes God a liar.

> *He that believeth on the Son of God hath the witness in himself: he that believeth not God hath made him a liar; because he believeth not the record that God gave of his Son. And this is the record, that God hath given to us eternal life, and this life is in his Son. He that hath the Son hath life; and he that hath not the Son of God hath not life.*
>
> (1 John 5:10–12)

Anyone who does not believe God's testimony—that He has given us eternal life, His Son, and that he who has the Son has the life—makes God a liar.

It is sometimes said, "It is presumptuous for anyone to say that he knows he is saved or to say he knows he has eternal life." But is it presumptuous to believe God? Is it not rather presumptuous not to believe God, to claim God is a liar? When you believe on the Son of God and yet doubt that you have eternal life, you make God a liar.

When Jesus said to the woman who was a sinner, "*Thy sins are forgiven*" (Luke 7:48), was it presumptuous for her to go out and say, "I know my sins are forgiven"? Would it not have been presumptuous for her to have doubted for a moment that all her sins were forgiven? Jesus said that they were forgiven. For her to doubt it would have been for her to give the lie to Jesus. Is it then any more presumptuous for the believer today to say, "All my sins are forgiven; I have eternal life," when God says in His written testimony to everyone who believes, "You are justified from all things" (Acts 13:39), "You have eternal life" (John 3:36; 1 John 5:13)?

Be very sure first of all that you really do believe on the name of the Son of God, that you really have received Jesus. If you are sure of this, then never doubt for a moment that all your sins are forgiven. Never doubt for a moment that you are a child of God. Never doubt for a moment that you have everlasting life.

Your Sins Are Forgiven

If Satan comes and whispers, "Your sins are not forgiven," point Satan to the Word of God and say, "God says my sins are forgiven, and I know they are." If Satan whispers, "Well, perhaps you don't believe on Him," then say, "Well, if I never did before, I will now." And then go out rejoicing, knowing your sins are forgiven, knowing you are a child of God, and knowing you have everlasting life.

There are, without a doubt, many who say they know they have eternal life who really do not believe on the name of the Son of God. This is not true assurance. It has no sure foundation in the Word of God, which does not lie. If we wish to get assurance of salvation, we must first become saved.

The reason many do not have the assurance they are saved is they are *not* saved. They need *salvation* before they need *assurance*. But if you have received Jesus in the way described in the first chapter, *you are saved*, you are a child of God, and your sins are forgiven. Believe it. Know it. Rejoice in it.

Having settled the question, let it remain settled. Never doubt it. You may make mistakes; you may stumble; you may fall. Even if you do, if you have really received Jesus, you know that your sins are forgiven. You can rise from your fall and go forward in the glad assurance that there is nothing between you and God.

4

RECEIVING THE HOLY SPIRIT

When the apostle Paul came to Ephesus, he found a small group of Christians. There was something about these disciples that struck Paul unfavorably. We are not told what it was. It may be that he did not find in them that overflowing joy one learns to expect in all Christians who have really entered into the fullness of blessing there is for them in Christ. It may be that Paul was troubled by the fact that there were so few of them. He may have thought that if these disciples were what they ought to be, there would certainly be more by this time.

The Holy Spirit Is Available

Whatever struck Paul as unfavorable, he went right to the root of the difficulty at once by asking them, *"Have ye received the Holy Ghost since ye believed?"* (Acts 19:2). It came out at once that they had not received the Holy Spirit; in fact, they did not know the Holy Spirit was available to them.

Then Paul told them the Holy Spirit had been given. He also showed them what they had to do to receive the Holy Spirit. Before that gathering was over, the Holy Spirit came upon them. From that day on there was a different state of affairs in Ephesus. A great revival began at once so that the whole city was shaken, *"So mightily grew the word of God and prevailed"* (Acts 19:20).

Paul's question to these young disciples in Ephesus should be put to young disciples everywhere, *"Have ye received the Holy Ghost?"* Receiving the Holy Spirit is the great secret of joyfulness in our own hearts, victory over sin, power in prayer, and effective service.

The Spirit Dwells in Every Christian

Everyone who has truly received Jesus has the Holy Spirit dwelling in him in some sense. In many believers, though the Holy Spirit dwells within, He is back in some hidden sanctuary of their being, not a part of their consciousness. It is something quite different, something far better, to receive the Holy Spirit in the sense that Paul meant in his question. To receive the Holy Spirit in such a way that one knows without a doubt that he has received Him is to become conscious of the joy with which He fills our hearts. This joy is different from any joy we have ever known in the world. We can receive the Holy Spirit in such fullness that He rules our lives and produces within us, in ever increasing measure, the fruit of the Spirit. *"The fruit of the Spirit is love, joy, peace, longsuffering, gentleness, goodness, faith, meekness, temperance"* (Gal. 5:22–23).

Paul wanted all Christians to receive the Holy Spirit in such a sense that we are conscious of His drawing our hearts out in prayer in a way that is not of ourselves. He wanted us to receive the Holy Spirit in such a way that we are conscious of His help when we witness for Christ. We are conscious of His aid when we speak to others individually and try to lead them to accept Christ and when we teach a Sunday school class, speak in public, or do any other work for the Master. Have you received the Holy Spirit? If you have not, this is how you may.

Steps for Holy Spirit Filling

1. First of all, in order to receive the Holy Spirit, one must acknowledge the death of Christ on the cross for us as the only and all-sufficient ground upon which God pardons all our sins.

2. In order to receive the Holy Spirit, we must put away every known sin. We must go to our heavenly Father and ask Him to search us through and through, bringing to light anything in our outward life or inward life that is wrong in His sight. If He does bring anything to mind that is displeasing to Him, we should put it away, no matter how dear it is to us. There must be a complete renunciation of all sin in order to receive the Holy Spirit.

3. Third, in order to receive the Holy Spirit, we must openly confess Christ before the world. The Holy Spirit is not given to those who are trying to be disciples in secret, but to those who obey Christ and publicly confess Him before the world. "*Whosoever shall confess me before men*" (Luke 12:8).

4. Fourth, in order to receive the Holy Spirit, there must be absolute surrender of our lives to God. You must go to Him and say, "Heavenly Father, here I am. You have bought me with a price. I am Your property. I renounce all claim to do my own will, all claim to govern my own life, all claim to have my own way. I give myself up unreservedly to You—all I am and all I have. Send me where You want, use me as You like, do with me what You want—I am Yours."

If we hold anything back from God, no matter how small it may seem, that spoils everything. But if we surrender all to God, then God will give all He has to us. There are some who shrink from this absolute surrender to God, but absolute surrender to God is simply absolute surrender to infinite love. It is surrender to the Father—the Father whose love is not only wiser than any earthly father's, but more tender than any earthly mother's.

5. In order to receive the Holy Spirit there should be definite asking for the Holy Spirit. Our Lord Jesus says in Luke 11:13, *"If ye then, being evil, know how to give good gifts unto your children: how much more shall your heavenly Father give the Holy Spirit to them that ask him?"* Just ask God to give you the Holy Spirit and expect Him to do it. He says He will.

6. Finally, in order to receive the Holy Spirit, there must be faith. Simply take God at His Word. No matter how positive any promise of God's Word may be, we enjoy it personally only when we believe. Our Lord Jesus says, *"What things soever ye desire, when ye pray, believe that ye receive them, and ye shall have them"* (Mark 11:24).

When you pray for the Holy Spirit, you have prayed for something according to God's will. Therefore, you know that your prayer is heard and that you have what you asked of Him. *"And this is the confidence that we have in him, that, if we ask any thing according to his will, he heareth us: and if we know that he hear us, whatsoever we ask, we know that we have the petitions that we desired of him"* (1 John 5:14–15). You may feel no different, but do not look at your feelings, but at God's promise. Believe the prayer is heard, believe that God has given you the Holy Spirit, and you will then have in actual experience what you have received in simple faith—on the bare promise of God's Word.

Give the Spirit Control

It is good to kneel down alone and look up to Jesus, putting into His hands anew the entire control of your life. Ask Him to take control of your thoughts, imaginations, affections, desires, ambitions, choices, purposes, words, and actions. In other words, ask Him to take control of everything. Then expect Him to do it. The whole secret of victory in the Christian life is letting the Holy Spirit, who dwells within you, have undisputed right-of-way in the entire conduct of your life.

5

LOOKING TO JESUS

If we are to run with patience the race that is set before us, we must always keep looking to Jesus.

Wherefore seeing we also are compassed about with so great a cloud of witnesses, let us lay aside every weight, and the sin which doth so easily beset us, and let us run with patience the race that is set before us, looking unto Jesus the author and finisher of our faith; who for the joy that was set before him endured the cross, despising the shame, and is set down at the right hand of the throne of God. For consider him that

> *endured such contradiction of sinners against himself, lest ye be wearied and faint in your minds.* (Heb. 12:1–3)

One of the simplest, yet mightiest, secrets of abiding joy and victory is to never lose sight of Jesus.

Focus on Jesus, Not Your Sins

First of all, we must keep looking at Jesus as the reason for our acceptance before God. Over and over again, Satan will attempt to discourage us by recalling our sins and failures. He tries to convince us that we are neither children of God nor saved. If he succeeds in getting us to keep looking at and brooding over our sins, he will soon coax us to become discouraged. Discouragement means failure.

But if we keep looking at what God sees—the death of Jesus Christ in our place that completely atoned for every sin we ever committed—we will never be discouraged because of the greatness of our sins. We will see that, while our sins are very great, they all have been erased. Every time Satan brings up one of our sins, we will see that Jesus Christ has redeemed us from its curse by being made a curse in our place. "*Christ hath redeemed us from the curse of the law, being made a curse for us: for it is written, Cursed is every one that hangeth on a tree*" (Gal. 3:13).

We will see that "*he hath made him to be sin for us, who knew no sin; that we might be made the righteousness of God in him*" (2 Cor. 5:21). In short, whenever Satan taunts us about our sins, we will know they have been washed away forever. "*Who his own self bare our sins in his own body on the tree, that we, being dead to sins, should live unto righteousness: by whose stripes ye were healed*" (1 Pet. 2:24).

If you are troubled right now about any sin you have ever committed, either past or present, just look at Jesus on the cross. Believe what God tells you about Him, that this sin that troubles you was laid upon Him (Isa. 53:6). Thank God that the sin is all settled. Be full of gratitude to Jesus who bore it in your place, and do not worry about your sins anymore.

It is an act of base ingratitude toward God to brood over sins that He in His infinite love has cancelled. Keep looking at Christ on the cross and always walk in the sunlight of God's favor. This favor has been purchased for you at a high cost. Gratitude demands that you always believe in Jesus' gift and walk in the light of it.

Jesus Keeps Us Every Day

Second, we must keep looking at Jesus as our risen Savior, who has all power in heaven and on earth and is able to keep us every day and every hour. Are you tempted to do some wrong at this moment? If you are, remember that Jesus rose from the dead. Remember that at this moment He is living at the right hand of God in glory. Remember He has all power in heaven and on earth, and He can give you victory right now.

Believe what God tells you in His Word, that Jesus has power to save you this moment *"to the uttermost"* (Heb. 7.25). Believe He has power to give you victory over this sin that now attacks you. Ask Him to give you victory and expect Him to do it. In this way, by looking to the risen Christ for victory, you will have victory over sin every day, every hour, every minute. *"Remember that Jesus Christ...was raised from the dead"* (2 Tim. 2:8).

God called every one of us to a victorious life. The secret of this victorious life is always looking to the risen Christ for victory. Through looking to Christ's sacrifice, we obtain pardon and enjoy peace. By looking to the risen Christ, we obtain present victory over the power of sin.

If you have lost sight of the risen Christ and have yielded to temptation, confess your sin and know that it is forgiven because God says so. *"If we confess our sins, he is faithful and just to forgive us our sins, and to cleanse us from all unrighteousness"* (1 John 1:9). Look to Jesus, the Risen One, to give you victory now; then keep looking to Him.

Jesus Is Our Example

Third, we must keep looking to Jesus as the One whom we should follow in our daily conduct. Our Lord Jesus says to us, His disciples today, as He said to His early disciples, *"Follow me"* (Matt. 9:9). The whole secret of true Christian conduct can be summed up in these two words: "Follow Me." *"He that saith he abideth in him ought himself also so to walk,* ***even as he walked****"* (1 John 2:6, emphasis added).

One of the most common causes of failure in Christian life is found in the attempt to follow a good man whom we greatly admire. No man or woman, no matter how good, can be safely followed. If we follow any man or woman, we are bound to go astray. There has been only one absolutely perfect Man on this earth—the man Christ Jesus. If we try to follow any other man, we are more sure to imitate his faults than his virtues. Look to Jesus, and only Jesus, as your guide.

If you are ever perplexed as to what to do, simply ask, "What would Jesus do?" Ask God through His Holy Spirit to show you what Jesus would do. Study your Bible to find out what Jesus did do, and follow His example. Even though no one else seems to be following Jesus, be sure you follow Him.

Do not spend your time or thought criticizing others because they do not follow Jesus. See that you follow Him yourself. When you are wasting your time criticizing others for not following Jesus, Jesus is always saying to you, *"What is that to thee? follow* ***thou*** *me"* (John 21:22, emphasis added). The question for you is not what following Jesus may involve for other people. The question is, "What does following Jesus mean for you?"

This is the life of a disciple—the life of simply following Jesus. Many perplexing questions will come to you, but the most perplexing question will soon become crystal clear if you determine with all your heart to follow Jesus in everything. Satan will always be ready to whisper to you, "Such and such a good man does it." But all you need to do is answer, "It does not matter to me what this or that man does." The only question should be, "What would Jesus do?"

There is wonderful freedom in this life of simply following Jesus. This path is straight and clear. But the path of the one who tries to shape his conduct by observing the conduct of others is full of twists, turns, and pitfalls. Keep looking at Jesus. Follow on with trust wherever He leads. *"The path of the just is as the shining light, that shineth more and more unto the perfect day"* (Prov. 4:18). He is the Light of the World. Anyone who follows Him will not walk in darkness, but will have the light of life all along the way (John 8:12).

6

CHURCH MEMBERSHIP

No Christian can have real success in the Christian life without the fellowship of other believers. The church is a divine institution, built by Jesus Christ Himself. It is the one institution that endures. Other institutions come and go. They do their work for their day and disappear. But the church will continue to the end. *"The gates of hell shall not prevail against it"* (Matt. 16:18). The church is made up of men and women, imperfect men and women; consequently it is an imperfect institution. Nonetheless, it is of divine origin, and God loves it. Every believer should realize that he belongs to it, openly take his place in it, and shoulder his responsibilities regarding it.

The church consists of all believers who are united to Jesus Christ by a living faith in Him. In its outward organization today, it is divided into many sects and local congregations. In spite of these divisions, the church is one. It has one Lord, Jesus Christ. It has one faith, faith in Him as Savior, divine Lord, and only King. All believe in one baptism, the baptism in one Spirit into one body. *"For by one Spirit are we all baptized into one body, whether we be Jews or Gentiles, whether we be bond or free; and have been all made to drink into one Spirit"* (1 Cor. 12:13). *"There is one body, and one Spirit, even as ye are called in one hope of your calling; one Lord, one faith, one baptism"* (Eph. 4:4–5).

Join a Body of Believers

But each individual Christian needs the fellowship of individual fellow believers. The outward expression of this fellowship is membership in some organized body of believers. If we remain aloof from all organized churches, hoping to have a broader fellowship with all believers belonging to all churches, we deceive ourselves. We will miss the helpfulness that comes from intimate union with a local congregation.

I have known many well-meaning people who have neglected membership in any specific organization. I have never known a person to do this whose spiritual life has not suffered. On the Day of Pentecost the three thousand who were converted were baptized at once and were added to the church. *"They continued stedfastly in the apostles' doctrine and fellowship, and in breaking of bread, and in prayers"* (Acts 2:42). Their example is the one to follow. If you have really received Jesus Christ, as soon as possible find a group of people who have also received Him and unite yourself with them.

There Is No Perfect Church

In many communities there may be no choice of churches, because there is only one. In other communities, one will be faced with the question, "Which body of believers should I join?" Do not waste your time looking for a perfect church. There is no perfect church. A church in which you are the only member is the most imperfect church of all. I would rather belong to the most faulty Christian body of believers I ever knew than not belong to any church group at all.

The local churches in Paul's day were very imperfect institutions. Read the epistles to the Corinthians and see how imperfect the church in Corinth was. See how much evil was in it. Yet Paul never dreamed of advising any believer in Corinth to get out of this imperfect church. He did tell them to come out of heathenism and to come out from fellowship with infidels.

> *Be ye not unequally yoked together with unbelievers: for what fellowship hath righteousness with unrighteousness? and what communion hath light with darkness? and what concord hath Christ with Belial? or what part hath he that believeth with an infidel? and what agreement hath the temple of God with idols? for ye are the temple of the living God; as God hath said, I will dwell in them, and walk in them; and I will be their God, and they shall be my people. Wherefore come out from among them, and be ye separate, saith the Lord, and touch not the unclean thing; and I will receive you, and will be a Father unto you, and ye shall be my sons and daughters, saith the Lord Almighty.* (2 Cor. 6:14–18)

He never advised coming out of the imperfect church in Corinth. Though he told the Corinthian church to separate from membership certain persons whose lives were wrong, he never advised anyone to leave the body because these people were not yet separated.

> *But now I have written unto you not to keep company, if any man that is called a brother be a fornicator, or covetous, or an idolater, or a railer, or a drunkard, or an extortioner; with such an one no not to eat.*
> (1 Cor. 5:11)

Guidelines for Finding a Church

Since you cannot find a perfect church, find the best church possible. Unite with a church where they believe in the Bible and where they preach the Bible. Avoid the churches where words, whether open or veiled, are spoken that have a tendency to undermine your faith in the Bible as a reliable revelation from God Himself. The Bible is the all-sufficient rule of faith and practice.

Unite with a church where there is a spirit of prayer, where the prayer meetings are well maintained. Unite with a church that has an active interest in the salvation of the lost, where young Christians are looked after and helped, where the minister and the people have a love for the poor and the destitute. Consider a church that regards its mission in this world to be the same as the mission of Christ, *"to seek and to save that which was lost"* (Luke 19:10).

As to denominational differences, other things being equal, unite with that denomination whose ideas of doctrine, government, and ordinances are most closely related to your own. It is better to join a living church of another denomination than to unite with a dead church of your own. We live in a day when denominational differences are becoming less and less important. Often they have no practical value whatever. One can often feel more at home in a church of another denomination than in a church of his own denomination. The things that divide the denominations are insignificant compared with the great fundamental truths, purposes, and faith that unite them.

If you cannot find a church that agrees with the pattern set forth above, find a church that comes nearest to it. Go into that church, and by prayer and work try to bring that church, as nearly as you can, to be what a church of Christ should be. Do not waste your strength in criticism against either the church or minister. Focus on what is good in the church and in the minister, and do your best to strengthen it. Keep a firm but unobtrusive distance from what is wrong while seeking to correct it.

Do not be discouraged if you cannot correct problems in a day, a week, a month, or a year. Patient love, prayer, and effort will show in time. Withdrawing by yourself, complaining, and grumbling will do no good. Grumbling will simply make you and the truths for which you stand repulsive.

7

BIBLE STUDY

There is nothing more important for the development of a Christian's spiritual life than regular, systematic Bible study. It is as true in the spiritual life as in the physical life that health depends on what we eat and how much we eat. *"Man shall not live by bread alone"* (Matt. 4:4). The soul's proper food is found in one book, the Bible.

Of course, a true minister of the Gospel will feed us the Word of God, but that is not enough. He feeds us only one or two days in the week, and we need to be fed every day. Furthermore, do not depend on being fed by others. We must learn to feed ourselves. If we study the Bible for ourselves as we should study it, we will be, in large measure, independent of human teachers. We will always be safe from spiritual harm, even if we are so unfortunate as to have a man who is ignorant of God's truth for our minister. We live in a day in which false doctrine is everywhere, and the only Christian who is safe from being led into error is the one who studies his Bible for himself, daily.

The Word Keeps Us Safe

The apostle Paul warned the elders of the church in Ephesus that the time was soon coming when vicious wolves would join them and not spare the flock. They would speak perverse things of their own creation, trying to draw disciples away from Jesus. But Paul told them how to be safe even in such perilous times as these. He said, *"I commend you to God, and to the word of his grace, which is able to build you up, and to give you an inheritance among all them which are sanctified"* (Acts 20:32).

Through meditation on the Word of God's grace, they would be safe even in the midst of flourishing error on the part of leaders in the church.

> *For I know this, that after my departing shall grievous wolves enter in among you, not sparing the flock. Also of your own selves shall men arise, speaking perverse things, to draw away disciples after them. Therefore watch, and remember, that by the space of three years I ceased not to warn every one night and day with tears.* (Acts 20:29–31)

Writing later to the bishop of the church in Ephesus, Paul said, *"But evil men and seducers shall wax worse and worse, deceiving, and being deceived"* (2 Tim. 3:13). But he went on to tell Timothy how he and his fellow believers could remain safe even in the times of increasing peril that were coming. This could be done through the study of the Holy Scriptures, which gives readers wisdom, drawing them to salvation.

> *But continue thou in the things which thou hast learned and hast been assured of, knowing of whom thou hast learned them; and that from a*

child thou hast known the holy scriptures, which are able to make thee wise unto salvation through faith which is in Christ Jesus.

(2 Tim. 3:14–15)

Bible Study Brings Success

"All scripture," he added, *"is given by inspiration of God, and is profitable for doctrine, for reproof, for correction, for instruction in righteousness: that the man of God may be perfect, thoroughly furnished unto all good works"* (2 Tim. 3:16–17). Through the study of the Bible, one will be sound in doctrine and led to see his sins and to put them away. He will find discipline in the righteous life and be equipped for all good works. Our spiritual health, growth, strength, victory over sin, soundness in doctrine, joy, and peace in Christ come from study of God's Word. Cleansing from inward and outward sin and fitness for service depend on daily study of the Bible.

The one who neglects his Bible is bound to be a failure in the Christian life. The one who studies his Bible in the right spirit and by a constant method is bound to make a success of the Christian life. This brings us face-to-face with the question, "What is the right way to study the Bible?"

How to Study Your Bible

First of all, we should study it daily. *"These were more noble than those in Thessalonica, in that they received the word with all readiness of mind, and searched the scriptures daily, whether those things were so"* (Acts 17:11). This is of prime importance. No matter how solid the methods of Bible study or how much time one may put into Bible study now and then, the best results can be secured only when one never lets a single day go by without earnest Bible study. This is the only safe course. Any day that is allowed to pass without faithful Bible study is a day that opens our hearts and lives to error and sin. I have been a Christian for more than a quarter of a century, and yet today I would not dare allow even a single day to pass without listening to God's voice as He speaks through the pages of His Book.

It is with this responsibility that many fall away. They grow careless and let a day pass, or even several days, without spending time alone with God or letting Him speak to them through His Word. Mr. Moody once wisely said, "In prayer we talk to God. In Bible study, God talks to us, and we had better let God do most of the talking."

A regular time should be set aside each day for Bible study. I do not think it is wise, as a rule, to say that we will study so many chapters a day, because that leads to undue haste, skimming, and thoughtlessness. But it is good to set apart a certain length of time each day for Bible study. Some can give more time to Bible study than others, but no one should devote less than fifteen minutes a day.

I set a short time span so that no one will be discouraged in the beginning. If a young Christian planned to spend an hour or two a day in Bible study, there is a strong probability that he would not keep the resolution and would become discouraged. Nevertheless, I know of many very busy people who have taken the first hour of every day for years for Bible study. Some have even given two hours a day.

The late Earl Cairns, Lord Chancellor of England, was one of the busiest men of his day. Lady Cairns told me that no matter how late at night he reached home, he always woke up at the same early hour for prayer and Bible study. She said, "We would sometimes get home from Parliament at two o'clock in the morning, but Lord Cairns would always arise at the same early hour to pray and study the Bible." Lord Cairns is reported as saying, "If I have had any success in life, I attribute it to the habit of giving the first two hours of each day to Bible study and prayer."

It is important that one choose the right time for this study. Whenever possible, the best time for study is immediately after waking up in the morning. The worst time is the last thing at night. Of course, it is good to spend a little time just before we go to bed reading the

Bible so that God's voice will be the last voice we hear. The bulk of our Bible study should be done when our minds are clearest and strongest. Whatever time is set apart for Bible study should be kept sacredly for that purpose.

We should study the Bible systematically. A lot of time is frittered away in random study of the Bible. The same amount of time put into systematic study would yield far greater results. Have a definite place where you study, and have a definite plan of study. A good way for a young Christian to begin the study of the Bible is to read the gospel of John. When you have read it through once, read it again until you have gone over the gospel five times. Then read the gospel of Luke five times in the same way. Then read the Acts of the Apostles five times. Then read the following epistles five times each: 1 Thessalonians, 1 John, Romans, and Ephesians.

By this time you will be ready to take up a more thorough method of Bible study. A profitable method is to begin at Genesis and read the Bible through chapter by chapter. Read each chapter through several times, and then answer the following questions on each chapter:

1) What is the main subject of the chapter? State the principal contents of the chapter in a single phrase or sentence.

2) What is the truth most clearly taught and most emphasized in the chapter?

3) What is the best lesson?

4) What is the best verse?

5) Who are the principal people mentioned?

6) What does the chapter teach about Jesus Christ?

Go through the entire Bible in this way.

Another, and more thorough, method of Bible study will yield excellent results when applied to some of the more important chapters of the Bible. However, it cannot be applied to every chapter in the Bible. It is as follows:

1) Read the chapter for today's study five times, reading it out loud at least once. Each new reading will bring out a new point.

2) Divide the chapter into its natural divisions, and find headings that describe the contents of each division. For example, suppose the chapter studied is 1 John 5. You might divide it this way: first division, verses 1–3, *The Believer's Noble Parentage;* second division, verses 4–5, *The Believer's Glorious Victory;* third division, verses 6–10, *The Believer's Sure Ground of Faith.* Continue through each division this way.

3) Note the important differences between the King James Version and the *Revised Standard Version.*

4) Write down the most important facts of the chapter in their proper order.

5) Make a note of the people mentioned in the chapter and any light shed on their character.

6) Note the principal lessons of the chapter. It is helpful to classify these. For instance, lessons about God, lessons about Christ, lessons about the Holy Spirit, and so on.

7) Find the central truth of the chapter.

8) Find the key verse of the chapter if there is one.

9) Find the best verse in the chapter. Mark it and memorize it.

10) Write down any new truth you have learned from the chapter.

11) Write down any truth you already know that has come to you with new power.

12) Write down what definite thing you have resolved to do as a result of studying this chapter.

A beneficial order of study for you might be all of the chapters in Matthew, Mark, Luke, John, and Acts; the first eight chapters of Romans; 1 Corinthians 12, 13, and 15; the first six chapters of 2 Corinthians; then all the chapters in Galatians, Ephesians, Philippians, 1 Thessalonians, and 1 John. Sometimes you can refresh your study by alternating methods.

Another profitable method of Bible study is *the topical method.* This was D. L. Moody's favorite method. Take such topics as: the Holy Spirit, prayer, the blood of Christ, sin, judgment, grace, justification, the new birth, sanctification, faith, repentance, the character of Christ, the resurrection of Christ, the ascension of Christ, the second coming of Christ, assurance, love of God, love (for God, for Christ, for Christians, for all men), heaven, and hell. Get a Bible concordance and study each one of these topics.

We should *study the Bible comprehensively*—the whole Bible. Many Bible readers make the mistake of confining all their reading to certain portions of the Bible that they enjoy. This way they get no knowledge of the Bible as a whole. They miss altogether many of the most important phases of Bible truth. Go through the Bible again and again—a certain portion each day from the Old Testament and a portion from the New Testament. Read carefully at least one Psalm every day.

It is also beneficial to read a whole book of the Bible through at a single sitting. This lets you see the whole picture. Of course, a few books of the Bible would take one or two hours. But most books can be read in a few minutes. The shorter books of the Bible should be read through again and again at a single sitting.

Study the Bible attentively. Do not hurry. One of the worst faults in Bible study is haste. We benefit from Bible study only by learning its truth. It has no magic power. It is better to read one verse attentively than to read a dozen chapters thoughtlessly. Sometimes you will read a verse that grabs you. Don't hurry on. Stop and think about that verse.

As you read, mark in your Bible what impresses you most. One does not need an elaborate marking system; simply highlight what impresses you. Think about what you mark. God affirms that the man who meditates on God's law day and night is blessed. *"But his delight is in the law of the Lord; and in his law doth he meditate day and night"* (Ps. 1:2).

It is amazing how a verse of Scripture will open one's mind to its exact meaning. Memorize the passages that impress you most. *"Thy word have I hid in mine heart, that I might not sin against thee"* (Ps. 119:11). When you memorize a passage of Scripture, memorize its location as well as the words. A busy but spiritually-minded man who was hurrying to catch a train once said to me, "Tell me in a word how to study my Bible." I replied, "Thoughtfully."

Study your Bible comparatively. In other words, compare Scripture with Scripture. The best commentary on the Bible is the Bible itself. Wherever you find a difficult passage in the Bible, there is always another passage that explains its meaning. The best book to use in this comparison is *The Treasury of Scripture Knowledge*. This book gives a large number of references on every verse in the Bible. You may want to take a particular book of the Bible and go through that book verse by verse. Look up and study every reference given in *The Treasury of Scripture Knowledge* dealing with that book. This is a very fruitful method of Bible study. You will also gain by studying the Bible by chapters and looking up the references on the more important verses in each chapter. One will gain a better understanding of passages of Scripture by looking up the references given in *The Treasury of Scripture Knowledge*.

Study your Bible and believe it. The apostle Paul, in writing to the Christians in Thessalonica, said, "*For this cause also thank we God without ceasing, because, when ye received the word of God which ye heard of us, ye received it not as the word of men, but as it is in truth, the word of God, which effectually worketh also in you that believe*" (1 Thess. 2:13). Happy is the one who receives the Word of God as these believers in Thessalonica received it, as the Word of God. In such a person it is especially effective. The Bible is the Word of God, and we get the most out of any book by acknowledging it for what it really is.

It is often said that we should study the Bible just as we study any other book. That principle contains a truth, but it also contains a great error. The Bible, like other books, has the same laws of grammatical and literary construction. But the Bible is a unique book. It is what no other book is—the Word of God. This can be easily proven to any impartial man. The Bible should be studied, then, specifically as the Word of God. This involves five things.

It involves a greater eagerness and more careful, candid study to find out exactly what the Bible teaches. It is important to know the mind of man. It is absolutely essential to know the mind of God. The place to discover the mind of God is the Bible because it is here that God reveals His mind.

It requires a prompt and unquestioning acceptance of, and submission to, its teachings when definitely ascertained. These teachings may appear unreasonable or impossible. Nevertheless, we should accept them. If this book is the Word of God, it is foolish to submit its teachings to the criticism of our finite reasoning.

A little boy who discredits his wise father's statements simply because to his infant mind they appear unreasonable is not thinking wisely but foolishly. Even the greatest of human thinkers is only an infant compared with God. To discredit God's statements found in His Word because they appear unreasonable to our infantile minds shows our shallow thinking. When we are once satisfied that the Bible is the Word of God, its clear teachings must be the end of all controversy and discussion for us.

Correct Bible study includes absolute reliance on all its promises in all their length, breadth, depth, and height. The one who studies the Bible as the Word of God will say of any promise, no matter how vast and beyond belief it appears, "God who cannot lie has promised this, so I will claim it for myself."

Mark the promise you claim. Each day look for some new promise from your infinite Father. He has put *"his riches in glory"* (Phil. 4:19) at your disposal. I know of no better way to grow rich spiritually than to search daily for promises; and when you find them, take them for yourself.

You must also study God's Word in obedience. *"But be ye doers of the word, and not hearers only, deceiving your own selves"* (James 1:22). Nothing goes farther to help one understand the Bible than resolving to obey it. Jesus said, *"If any man will do his will, he shall know of the doctrine"* (John 7:17). The surrendered will means a clear eye. If our eye is pure (that is, our will is absolutely surrendered to God), our whole body will be full of light. But if our eye is evil (that is, if we are trying to serve two masters and are not absolutely surrendered to one Master, God), our whole body will be full of darkness.

> *The light of the body is the eye: if therefore thine eye be single* [pure], *thy whole body shall be full of light. But if thine eye be evil, thy whole body shall be full of darkness. If therefore the light that is in thee be darkness, how great is that darkness! No man can serve two masters: for either he will hate the one, and love the other; or else he will hold to the one, and despise the other. Ye cannot serve God and mammon.*
> (Matt. 6:22–24)

Many passages that look obscure to you now would become as clear as day if you were willing to obey everything the Bible teaches.

Blessing Comes through Obedience

Each commandment discovered in the Bible that is really intended as a commandment to us should be obeyed instantly. It is remarkable how soon one loses his thirst for the Bible and how soon the mind becomes obscured to its teachings when one disobeys the Bible at any point. I have often known people who loved their Bibles, were useful in God's service, and had clear views of the truth. Then they came to a command in the Bible that they were unwilling to obey. Some sacrifice was demanded that they were unwilling to make. As a result, their love for the Bible rapidly waned, their faith in the Bible weakened, and soon they drifted farther and farther away from clear views of the truth.

Nothing clears the mind like obedience; nothing darkens the mind like disobedience. To obey a truth you see prepares you to see other truths. To disobey a truth you see darkens your mind to all truths.

Cultivate prompt, exact, unquestioning, joyous obedience to every command that clearly applies to you. Be on the lookout for new orders from your King. Blessing lies in the direction of obedience to them. God's commands are guideposts that mark the road to present success and eternal glory.

Personal Companionship with God

Studying the Bible as the Word of God involves studying it as His own voice speaking directly to you. When you open the Bible to study, realize that you have come into the very presence of God and that He is going to speak to you. Realize that it is God who is talking to you as if you were looking at Him face-to-face. Say to yourself, "God is now going to speak to me." Nothing gives more freshness and gladness to Bible study than the realization that as you read, God is actually talking to you.

Bible study then becomes personal companionship with God Himself. What a wonderful privilege Mary had one day, sitting at the feet of Jesus and listening to His voice. If we will study the Bible as the Word of God and as if we were in God's presence, then we will enjoy the privilege of sitting at the feet of Jesus and having Him talk to us every day.

This approach makes what would otherwise be a mere mechanical performance of a duty become a wonderfully joyous privilege. One can say as he opens the Bible, "Now God my Father is going to speak to me." Reading the Bible on our knees helps us to realize we are in God's presence. The Bible became in some measure a new book to me when I took to reading it on my knees.

Study the Bible prayerfully. God, the author of the Bible, is willing to act as interpreter of it. He does so when you ask Him. The one who prays the psalmist's prayer with sincerity and faith, *"Open thou mine eyes, that I may behold wondrous things out of thy law"* (Ps. 119:18), will have his eyes opened to new beauties and wonders in the Word.

Be very definite about this. Each time you open the Bible for study, even though it is only for a few minutes, ask God to give you an open and discerning eye. Expect Him to do it. Every time you come to a difficult passage in the Bible, lay it before God, ask for an explanation, and expect it.

The Holy Spirit as Teacher

How often we think as we puzzle over hard passages, "Oh, if I only had some great Bible teacher here to explain this to me!" God is always present. He understands the Bible better than any human teacher. Take your difficulty to Him, and ask Him to explain it. Jesus said, "*When he, the Spirit of truth, is come, he will guide you into all truth*" (John 16:13). It is the privilege of the humblest believer in Christ to have the Holy Spirit for his guide in his study of the Word.

I have known many very humble people, people with almost no education, who got more out of their Bible study than many great theological teachers. This happened because they learned it was their privilege to have the Holy Spirit for their Bible study teacher. Commentaries on the Bible are usually valuable. But one will learn more from the Bible by having the Holy Spirit for his teacher than from all the commentaries ever published.

Use spare time for Bible study. Time is lost in almost every man's life while waiting for meals, riding planes, going from place to place, and so forth. Carry a pocket Bible with you, and use these golden moments to listen to the voice of God.

Store Scripture in your mind and heart. It will keep you from sin (see Psalm 119:11) and false doctrine. (See Acts 20:29–30, 32; and 2 Timothy 3:13–15.) "*And thy word was unto me the joy and rejoicing of mine heart*" (Jer. 15:16). "*For he will speak peace unto his people*" (Ps. 85:8). It will give you victory over the evil one (see 1 John 2:14), and it will give you power in prayer. "*If ye abide in me, and my words abide in you, ye shall ask what ye will, and it shall be done unto you*" (John 15:7). The Word will make you wiser than the aged and your enemies. "*Thou through thy commandments hast made me wiser than mine enemies: for they are ever with me....I understand more than the ancients, because I keep thy precepts....The entrance of thy words giveth light; it giveth understanding unto the simple*" (Ps. 119:98, 100, 130). It will make you "*thoroughly furnished unto all good works*" (2 Tim. 3:17). Try it.

Do not memorize at random, but memorize Scripture in a connected way. Memorize texts on various subjects. Memorize by chapter and verse so that you will know where to put your finger on the text if anyone disputes it. You should have a good Bible for your study.

8

DIFFICULTIES IN THE BIBLE

Sooner or later every young Christian comes across passages in the Bible that are hard to understand and difficult to believe. To many young Christians, these perplexities become a serious hindrance in the development of their Christian life. For days, weeks, and months, faith suffers a partial or total eclipse. At this point wise counsel is needed. We have no desire to conceal the fact that these difficulties exist. We desire instead to frankly face and consider them. What should we do concerning these paradoxes that every thoughtful student of the Bible will sooner or later encounter?

Expect Difficulties

The first thing we have to say about these difficulties is that, from the very nature of the situation, difficulties are to be expected. Some people are surprised and staggered because there are difficulties in the Bible. I would be more surprised and staggered if there were not. What is the Bible? It is a revelation of the mind, will, character, and being of the infinitely great, perfectly wise, and absolutely holy God.

To whom is this revelation made? To men and women like you and me—finite beings. It comes to men who are imperfect in intellectual development, in knowledge, in character, and, consequently, in spiritual discernment.

Because of our weakness, there must be difficulties in such a revelation. When the finite tries to understand the infinite, there is bound to be difficulty. When the ignorant contemplate the speech of One perfect in knowledge, there will be many things that are hard to understand. Some things will also appear absurd to immature and inaccurate minds. When sinful beings listen to the demands of the absolutely holy Being, they are bound to be staggered at some of His demands. When they consider His works, they are bound to be staggered. These will necessarily appear too severe, stern, and harsh.

It is plain that there must be difficulties for us in such a revelation as the Bible is proven to be. If someone were to hand me a book that was as simple as the multiplication table and say, "This is the Word of God, in which He has revealed His whole will and wisdom," I would shake my head and say, "I cannot believe it. That is too easy to be a perfect revelation of infinite wisdom." There must be in any complete revelation of God's mind, will, character, and being things that are difficult for a beginner to understand. Even the wisest and best of us are only beginners.

The Bible Is God's Revelation

The second thing about these difficulties is that a difficulty in a doctrine, or a grave objection to a doctrine, does not in any way prove the doctrine to be untrue. Many thoughtless people imagine it does. If they come across some difficulty in believing the divine origin and absolute inerrancy and infallibility of the Bible, they immediately conclude that the doctrine is disproved. That is very illogical.

Stop a moment and think. Be reasonable and fair. There is scarcely a doctrine in modern science that has not had some great difficulty gaining acceptance. When the Copernican theory, now so universally accepted, was first proclaimed, it encountered a very serious dilemma. If this theory were true, the planet Venus had to have phases like the moon. But no phases could be discovered using the best telescope then in existence. The positive argument for the theory was so strong, however, that it was accepted in spite of this apparently unanswerable objection. When a more powerful telescope was made, it was discovered that Venus had phases after all.

The whole problem arose, as all those in the Bible arise, from man's ignorance of some of the facts in the case. According to the commonsense logic recognized in many departments of science, if the positive proof of a theory is conclusive, it is believed by rational men in spite of any number of discrepancies in minor details. The positive proof that the Bible is the Word of God is absolutely conclusive: it is an absolutely trustworthy revelation from God Himself of Himself, His purposes, and His will, of man's duty and destiny, of spiritual and eternal realities.

Therefore, every rational man and woman must believe it despite minor discrepancies. He who gives up a well-attested truth because there are some facts that he cannot reconcile with that truth is a shallow thinker. He who gives up the divine origin and inerrancy of the Bible because there are some supposed facts that he cannot reconcile with that doctrine is a very shallow Bible scholar.

The Bible Is Logical and Unified

There are many more difficulties in a doctrine that believes the Bible to be of human origin and hence fallible, than the doctrine that the Bible is of divine origin, hence altogether trustworthy. A man may bring you some apparent error and say, "How do you explain this if the Bible is the Word of God?" Perhaps you may not be able to answer him satisfactorily.

Then he thinks he has you, but not at all. Turn to him and ask him, "How do you account for the fulfilled prophecies of the Bible, if it is of human origin? How do you account for the marvelous unity of the Bible? How do you account for its inexhaustible depth? How do you account for its unique power in lifting men up to God? How do you account for the history of the Book, its victory over all men's attacks, and so on."

For every insignificant objection he can bring to your view, you can bring many deeply significant objections to his view. No impartial man will have any difficulty in deciding between the two views. The discrepancies that must confront one who denies the Bible is of divine origin and authority are far more numerous than those that confront people who do believe it is of divine origin.

We Do Not Know Everything

Do not think that because you cannot solve a difficulty you can prove that the difficulty cannot be solved. The fact that you cannot answer an objection does not prove at all that it cannot be answered. It is strange how often we overlook this very evident fact. There are many who, when they see something in the Bible that does not conform to their truth, give it little thought and promptly jump to the conclusion that a solution is impossible. Then they throw away their faith in the reliability of the Bible and its divine origin. A little more modesty in beings so limited in knowledge, as we all are, would have led them to say, "Though I see no possible solution to this difficulty, someone a little wiser than I might easily find one."

If we would only bear in mind that we do not know everything and that there are a great many things that we cannot solve now but could easily solve if we only knew a little more. Above all, we should never forget that there may be a very easy solution through infinite wisdom that to our finite wisdom—or ignorance—appears absolutely insoluble.

What would we think of a beginner in algebra who, having tried without success for half an hour to solve a difficult problem, declared that there was no possible solution to the problem because he could not find one? A man with a lot of experience and ability once left his work and came a long distance to see me. He discovered what seemed to him to be a flat contradiction in the Bible. It defied all attempts at reconciliation. But in a few moments he saw a very simple and satisfactory solution to the difficulty.

A Beautiful and Wondrous Book

The seeming defects in the Book are exceedingly insignificant when compared with its many, marvelous wonders. It certainly reveals great perversity of both mind and heart that men spend so much time focusing on the insignificant points that they consider defects in the Bible. How sad it is that they never recognize the incomparable beauties and wonders that adorn almost every page.

What would we think of any man who, in studying some great masterpiece of art, concentrated his entire attention on what looked to him like a flyspeck in the corner? A large proportion of what is vaunted as "critical study of the Bible" is a laborious and scholarly investigation of supposed flyspecks and an entire neglect of the countless glories of the Book.

Are You a Superficial Reader?

The puzzles and paradoxes in the Bible have far more weight with superficial readers than with students who read it in depth. Take a man who is totally ignorant of the real contents and meaning of the Bible and devotes his whole strength to discovering apparent inconsistencies in it.

To such superficial Bible students, these difficulties seem to have immense importance; but to the one who has learned to meditate on the Word of God day and night, they have little weight.

That mighty man of God, George Müller, who carefully studied the Bible from beginning to end more than a hundred times, was not disturbed by any discrepancies he encountered. His example can encourage the student who is reading it through carefully for the first or second time and finds many things that perplex him.

The difficulties in the Bible rapidly disappear upon careful and prayerful study. There are many things in the Bible that once puzzled us that have been perfectly cleared up and no longer present any difficulty at all! Is it not reasonable to suppose that the difficulties that still remain will also disappear on further study?

Profitable Approach to Discrepancies

How shall we deal with the difficulties that we do find in the Bible?

First of all, *honestly*. Whenever you find a difficulty in the Bible, frankly acknowledge it. If you cannot give a good, honest explanation, do not attempt as yet to give any at all.

Humbly. Recognize the limitations of your own mind and knowledge, and do not imagine there is no solution just because you have not found one. There is, in all probability, a very simple solution. You will find it someday.

With determination. Make up your mind that you will find the solution, if possible, through necessary study and hard thinking. The difficulties in the Bible are your heavenly Father's challenge to you to set your brain to work.

Fearlessly. Do not be frightened when you find a difficulty, no matter how unanswerable it appears at first glance. Thousands have found such difficulties before you. They were seen hundreds of years ago, and still the

Bible stands. You are not likely to discover any difficulty that was not discovered and probably settled long before you were born, though you do not know just where to find the solution.

The Bible, which has stood eighteen centuries of rigid examination and constant, intense assault, will not fail because of any discoveries you make or any attacks of modern infidels. All modern attacks on the Bible simply revamp old objections that have been disposed of a hundred times in the past. These old objections will prove no more effective in their new clothes than they did in the cast-off garments of the past.

Patiently. Do not be discouraged because you do not solve every problem in a day. If some difficulty defies your best effort, lay it aside for a while. Very likely when you come back to it, it will have disappeared, and you will wonder how you were ever perplexed by it. I often have to smile when I remember how I was perplexed in the past over questions that are now clear as day.

Scripturally. If you find a difficulty in one part of the Bible, look for other Scriptures to shed light on it and dissolve it. Nothing explains Scripture like Scripture. Never let apparently obscure passages of Scripture darken the light that comes from clear passages. Rather, let the light that comes from the clear passage illuminate the darkness that seems to surround the obscure passage.

Prayerfully. It is wonderful how difficulties dissolve when one looks at them on his knees. One great reason some modern scholars have learned to be destructive critics is that they have forgotten how to pray.

9

PRAYER

The one who wishes to succeed in the Christian life must lead a life of prayer. Much of the failure in Christian living today, and in Christian work, results from neglect of prayer. Very few Christians spend as much time in prayer as they should. The apostle James told believers in his day that the secret behind the poverty and powerlessness of their lives and service was neglect of prayer. "*Ye have not,*" said God through the apostle James, "*because ye ask not*" (James 4:2). So it is today. "Why is it," many Christians are asking, "that I make such poor headway in my Christian life? Why do I have so little victory over sin? Why do I accomplish so little by my effort?" God answers, "*Ye have not, because ye ask not.*"

Decide on a Life of Prayer

It is easy enough to lead a life of prayer if one only decides to live it. Set apart some time each day for prayer. The habit of David and Daniel is a good one, three times a day. "*Evening, and morning, and at noon,*" said David, "*will I pray, and cry aloud: and he shall hear my voice*" (Ps. 55:17). Of Daniel we read,

> *Now when Daniel knew that the writing was signed, he went into his house; and his windows being open in his chamber toward Jerusalem, he kneeled upon his knees three times a day, and prayed, and gave thanks before his God, as he did aforetime.* (Dan. 6:10)

Of course, one can pray while walking down the street, riding in the car, or sitting at his desk. And one should learn to lift his heart to God right in the busiest moments of his life. But we also need set times of prayer, times when we go alone with God and talk to our Father in the secret place. "*But thou, when thou prayest, enter into thy closet, and when thou hast shut thy door, pray to thy Father which is in secret; and thy Father which seeth in secret shall reward thee openly*" (Matt. 6:6). God is in the secret place. He will meet with us there and listen to our petitions.

Prayer is a wonderful privilege. It is an audience with the King. It is talking to our Father. How strange it is that people would ask the question, "How much time should I spend in prayer?" When a person is summoned to an audience with his king, he never asks, "How much time must I spend with the king?" His question is rather, "How much time will the king give me?" Any true child of God who realizes that prayer is an audience with the King of Kings will never ask, "How much time must I spend in prayer?" Instead, he will ask, "How much time may I spend in prayer, considering other duties and privileges?"

Prepare with Prayer

Begin the day with thanksgiving and prayer. Offer thanksgiving for the definite mercies of the past and prayer for the definite needs of the present day. Think of the temptations that you are likely to meet during the day. Ask God to show you these temptations, and ask for strength from God for victory over them before they come. Many fail in the battle because they wait until the hour of battle to ask for aid. Others succeed because they have gained victory on their knees long before the battle arrived.

Jesus conquered the awful battles of Pilate's judgment hall and the cross because He prayed the previous night. He anticipated the battle the night before and gained the victory through prayer. He told His disciples to do the same. He instructed them, *"Pray that ye enter not into temptation"* (Luke 22:40), but they slept when they should have prayed. And when the hour of temptation came, they fell. Anticipate your battles, fight them on your knees before temptation comes, and you will always have victory. At the very start of the day, secure counsel and strength from God Himself for the duties of the day.

Prayer Saves Time

Never let the rush of business crowd out prayer. The more work that must be accomplished in any day, the more time must be spent in prayer and preparation for that work. You will not lose time by praying; you will save time. Prayer is the greatest time-saver known to man. The more work crowds you, the more you must take time for prayer.

Stop in the middle of the bustle and temptation of the day for thanksgiving and prayer. A few minutes spent alone with God at noon will go far to keep you calm despite the worries and anxieties of modern life.

Close the day with thanksgiving and prayer. Review all the blessings of the day, and thank God in detail for them. Nothing further increases faith in God and His Word than a calm review at the close of each day of what God has done for you that day. Nothing goes further toward bringing new and larger blessings from God than intelligent thanksgiving for blessings already granted.

Close Your Day with a Clean Slate

As the last thing you do each day, ask God to show you anything that has been displeasing in His sight. Then wait quietly before Him, and give God an opportunity to speak to you. Listen. Do not be in a hurry. If God shows you anything in the day that has been displeasing in His sight, confess it fully and frankly as to a holy and loving Father. Believe that God forgives it all, because He says He does. *"If we confess our sins, he is faithful and just to forgive us our sins, and to cleanse us from all unrighteousness"* (1 John 1:9).

Thus, at the close of each day, all your accounts with God will be settled. You can sleep in the joyful awareness that there is not a cloud between you and God. You can rise the next day to begin life anew with a clean balance sheet.

Do this and you can never backslide for more than twenty-four hours. Indeed, you will not backslide at all. It is very hard to straighten out accounts in business that have been allowed to become disordered over a prolonged period. No bank ever closes its business day until its balance sheet is absolutely correct. No Christian should close a single day until his accounts with God for that day have been perfectly adjusted.

Prayer for Specific Blessings

There should be special prayer in special temptation—when we see the temptation approaching. If you possibly can, immediately find a place to be alone somewhere with God, then fight your battle out. Keep looking to God. *"Pray without ceasing"* (1 Thess. 5:17). It is not necessary to always be on your knees, but the heart should be on its knees all the time. We should often be on our knees, or our faces, literally.

This prayer life is a joyous life, free from worry and care. *"Be careful for nothing; but in every thing by prayer and supplication with thanksgiving let your requests be made known unto God. And the peace of God, which passeth all understanding, shall keep your hearts and minds through Christ Jesus"* (Phil. 4:6–7).

There are three things for which one who desires to succeed in the Christian life must especially pray. The first is wisdom. *"If any of you lack wisdom* [and we all do], *let him ask of God"* (James 1:5). The second is strength. *"But they that wait upon the* Lord *shall renew their strength"* (Isa. 40:31). The third is the Holy Spirit. *"Your heavenly Father* [shall] *give the Holy Spirit to them that ask him"* (Luke 11:13).

Even if you have received the Holy Spirit, you should constantly pray for a new blessing of the Holy Spirit and definitely expect to receive it. We need to be in contact with the Spirit, ready for every new emergency of Christian life and Christian service. The apostle Peter was baptized and filled with the Holy Spirit on Pentecost.

> *And when the day of Pentecost was fully come, they were all with one accord in one place. And suddenly there came a sound from heaven as of a rushing mighty wind, and it filled all the house where they were sitting. And there appeared unto them cloven tongues like as of fire, and it sat upon each of them. And they were all filled with the Holy Ghost, and began to speak with other tongues, as the Spirit gave them utterance.*
>
> (Acts 2:1–4)

After his baptism, the Holy Spirit continued to work through Peter as recorded in Acts 4:8, 31: *"Then Peter, filled with the Holy Ghost, said unto them, Ye rulers of the people, and elders of Israel....And when they had prayed, the place was shaken where they were assembled together; and they were all filled with the Holy Ghost, and they spake the word of God with boldness."*

There are many Christians in the world who had a very definite baptism of the Holy Spirit. They experienced great joy and were wonderfully used. But many have tried ever since to continue with only the power of that baptism received years ago. Today their lives are comparatively joyless and powerless. We constantly need to obtain new supplies of oil for our lamps. We secure these new supplies of oil by asking for them.

Do Not Neglect Fellowship

It is not enough that we have our times of secret prayer alone with God. We also need fellowship with others in prayer. If there is a prayer meeting in your church, attend it regularly. Attend it for your own sake and for the sake of the church. If it is a prayer meeting only in name and not in fact, use your influence quietly and constantly (not obstrusively) to make it a real prayer meeting. Attend the prayer meeting regularly for that purpose. Refuse all social engagements for that night.

A major-general in the United States Army once took command of the forces in a new district. A reception was arranged for him on a certain night of the week. When he was informed of this public reception, he replied that he could not attend since it was the evening of his prayer meeting. Everything had to take second place on that night to his prayer meeting. That general proved he was a man who could be depended upon. Christ's church in America owes more to him than to almost any other officer in the United States Army.

Ministers learn to depend on their prayer meeting members. The prayer meeting is the most important meeting in the church. If your church has no prayer meeting, use your influence to start one. It does not take many members to make a good prayer meeting. You can start with two but aim for many members.

It is wise to have a little group of Christian friends with whom you meet every week simply for prayer. There has been nothing more important in my own spiritual development in recent years than a little prayer meeting of less than a dozen friends who have met every Saturday night for years. We met, and together we waited on God. If my life has been of any use to the Master, I attribute it largely to that prayer meeting. Happy is the young Christian who has a little band of friends who regularly meet together for prayer.

10

WORKING FOR CHRIST

One of the important conditions of growth and strength in the Christian life is work. No man can keep up his physical strength without exercise, and no man can keep up his spiritual strength without spiritual exercise—in other words, without working for the Master. The working Christian is a happy Christian. The working Christian is a strong Christian. Some Christians never backslide because they are too busy with their Master's business. Many professing Christians do backslide because they are too idle to do anything but backslide.

Ask, and Be Fruitful

Jesus said to the first disciples, *"Follow me, and I will make you fishers of men"* (Matt. 4:19). Anyone who is not a fisher of men is not following Christ. Bearing fruit by bringing others to the Savior is the purpose for which Jesus has chosen us, and it is one of the most important conditions for power in prayer. Jesus said in John 15:16, *"Ye have not chosen me, but I have chosen you, and ordained you,* ***that ye should go and bring forth fruit,*** *and that your fruit should remain:* ***that whatsoever ye shall ask of the Father in my name, he may give it you****"* (emphasis added). These words of Jesus are very plain. They tell us that the believer who is bearing fruit is the one who can pray in the name of Christ and receive what he asks in that name.

In the same chapter Jesus tells us that bearing fruit in His strength is the condition of fullness of joy. He says, *"These things have I spoken unto you* [that is, things about living in Him and bearing fruit in His strength], *that my joy might remain in you, and that your joy might be full"* (John 15:11). Our experience more than adequately proves the truth of these words of our Master. Those who are full of activity in winning others to Christ are those who are full of joy in Christ Himself.

If you wish to be a happy Christian, a strong Christian, a Christian who is mighty in prayer, begin now to work for Jesus. Never let a day pass without doing some definite work for Him. But how can a young Christian work for Him? How can a young Christian bear fruit? The answer is very simple and very easy to follow.

You can bear fruit for your Master by going to others and telling them what your Savior has done for you, by urging them to accept this same Savior, and by showing them how. There is no other work in the world that is so easy to do, so joyous, and so fruitful. The youngest Christian can do personal work. Of course, he cannot do it as well as he will after he has had more practice. The way to learn to do it is by doing it.

You Can Start Immediately

I have known thousands of Christians all around the world who have begun to work for Christ, and bring others to Christ, the same day they were converted. How often young men and women, yes, and old men and women, too, have come to me and said, "I accepted Jesus Christ last night as my Savior, my Lord, and my King. Tonight I led a friend to Christ." The next day they would come and tell me of someone else they led to Christ.

There are many books that tell how to do personal work. However, one does not need to wait and read a book on the subject before beginning. One of the greatest and most common mistakes that is made is frittering one's life away preparing to get ready to get ready. Some never do get ready. The way to get ready for Christian work is to begin at once. Make up your mind that you will encourage at least one person to accept Christ every day.

Success Despite Mistakes

Early in his Christian life, D. L. Moody made a resolution that he would never let a day pass without speaking to at least one person about Christ. One night he was returning home late from his work. As he neared home, it occurred to him that he had not spoken to anyone about Jesus that day. He said to himself, "It is too late now. I will not get an opportunity. Here will be one day gone without my speaking to anyone about Christ."

Then, just ahead of him, he saw a man standing under a lamppost. He said, "Here is my last opportunity." The man was a stranger, though he knew of Mr. Moody. Mr. Moody hurried up to him and asked, "Are you a Christian?"

The man replied, "That is none of your business. If you were not a preacher, I would knock you into the gutter."

But Mr. Moody spoke a few Christian words to him and passed on.

The next day this man called on one of Mr. Moody's business friends in Chicago in great indignation. He said, "That man Moody of yours is doing more harm than good. He has zeal without knowledge. He came up to me last night, a perfect stranger, and asked me if I was a Christian. He insulted me. I told him if he had not been a preacher I would have knocked him into the gutter."

Mr. Moody's friend called him in and said, "Moody, you are doing more harm than good. You have zeal without knowledge. You insulted a friend of mine on the street last night." Mr. Moody left somewhat crestfallen, feeling that perhaps he was doing more harm than good, that perhaps he did have zeal without knowledge.

Some weeks after, however, late at night, there was a loud pounding on his door. Mr. Moody got out of bed and rushed to the door, thinking his house was on fire. That same man stood at the door. He said, "Mr. Moody, I have not had a night's rest since you spoke to me that night under the lamppost. I have come here for you to tell me what to do to be saved." That night Mr. Moody had the joy of leading that man to Christ.

Better to Have Zeal

It is better to have zeal without knowledge than to have knowledge without zeal. It is better yet to have zeal with knowledge, and anyone may have this. The way to acquire knowledge is through experience, and the way to gain experience is by doing the work. The man who is so afraid of making blunders that he never does anything also never learns anything. The man who goes ahead and does his best, willing to risk the blunders, is the man who learns to avoid blunders in the future.

Some of the most gifted men I have ever known have never really accomplished anything because they were so afraid of making blunders. Some of the most useful men I have ever known were men who started out as the least promising, but who had a real love for souls and worked to win them in a blundering way. Eventually they learned by experience to do things well.

Do not be discouraged by your blunders. Pitch in and keep plugging away. Every honest mistake is a stepping-stone to future success. Every day, try to lead someone to Christ. Of course, you will not always succeed, but the work will still do you good. Years later, you will often find that, where you thought you made the greatest mistakes, you accomplished the best results. The man who becomes angriest at you will often finally be the man who is most grateful to you. Be patient and hope on. Never be discouraged.

Make a prayer list. Pray alone with God. Write down at the top of a sheet of paper, "God helping me, I promise to pray daily and to work persistently for the conversion of the following people." Then kneel down and ask God to show you who to put on that list. Do not make the list so long that your prayer and work become mechanical and superficial.

Prayer Lists and Tracts

After you have made the list, keep your covenant and really pray for them daily. Watch for opportunities to speak to them—use these opportunities. You may have to wait a long time for your opportunities with some of them, and you may have to speak often, but never give up. I prayed about fifteen years for a man, one of the most discouraging men I had ever met. But I finally saw that man converted, and I saw him become a preacher of the Gospel. Many others were later converted through his preaching.

Learn to use tracts. Procure a few good tracts that will meet the needs of different kinds of people. Then hand these tracts out to the people whose needs they are adapted to meet. Follow your tracts up with prayer and personal effort.

Work for Your Pastor

Go to your pastor and ask him if there is some work he would like to have you do for him in the church. Be a person on whom your pastor can depend. We live in a day in which there are many kinds of work going on outside the church. Many of these ministries are good, and you should take part in them as much as you can. Never forget, however, that your first duty is to the church where you are a member.

Be a person your pastor can count on. It may be that your pastor may not want to use you, but at least give him the chance of refusing you. If he does refuse you, don't be discouraged, but find work somewhere else. There is plenty to do and few to do it. It is as true today as it was in the days of our Savior, "*The harvest truly is plenteous, but the labourers are few*" (Matt. 9:37). "*Pray ye therefore the Lord of the harvest, that he will send forth labourers into his harvest*" (v. 38), and pray that He will send you.

The right kind of men are needed in the ministry. The right kind of men and women are also needed for foreign mission work. You may not be the right kind of man or woman for foreign missionary work, but there is still work for you that is just as important as the work of the minister or the missionary. Be sure you fill your place and fill it well.

11

FOREIGN MISSIONS

In order to have the most success in the Christian life, one must be interested in foreign missions. The last command of our Lord before leaving this earth was, "*Go ye therefore, and teach all nations, baptizing them in the name of the Father, and of the Son, and of the Holy Ghost: teaching them to observe all things whatsoever I have commanded you: and, lo, I am with you alway, even unto the end of the world*" (Matt. 28:19–20). Here is a command and a promise. It is one of the sweetest promises in the Bible.

The enjoyment of the promise is conditioned on obedience to the command. Our Lord commands all His disciples to go and make disciples of all nations. This command was not given to the apostles alone, but to every member of Christ's church in all ages. If we go, then Christ will be with us even until the end of the age. If we do not go, we have no right to count on His companionship. Are you going? How can we go?

There are three ways we can go. We must employ at least two of these ways if we are to enjoy the wonderful privilege of daily personal companionship with Jesus Christ.

You May Be God's Missionary

First, many of us can go personally. Many of us should go. God does not call each of us to go as foreign missionaries, but He does call many of us to go who are *not* responding to the call. Every Christian should offer himself for the foreign field and leave the responsibility of choosing or refusing him to the all-wise One, God Himself. No Christian has a right to stay home until he has offered himself definitely to God for the foreign field.

If you have not already done it, do it today. Spend time alone with God and say, "Heavenly Father, here I am, Your property, purchased by the precious blood of Jesus. I belong to You. If You want me in the foreign field, make it clear to me, and I will go." Then keep watching for God's leading. God's leading is a clear leading. *"God is light, and in him is no darkness at all"* (1 John 1:5). If you are really willing to be led, He will make His will for you clear as day.

Until He does make it obvious, do not worry that perhaps you are staying at home when you should go to the foreign field. If He wants you, He will make it clear in His own way and time.

If He does make it clear, then prepare to go step-by-step as He leads you. When His hour comes, go, no matter what it costs. If He does not make it clear that you should go yourself, stay home and do your duty at home. There are other important possibilities for you.

Go through Your Gifts

We all can and should go to the foreign field with our gifts. There are many who would like to go to the foreign field personally, but whom God providentially prevents. These people are still going via the missionaries they support or help to support. It is possible for you to preach the Gospel in the most remote corners of the earth by supporting or helping to support a foreign missionary or a native worker.

Many who read this book are financially able to support a foreign missionary. If you are able to do so, do it. If you are not able to support a foreign missionary, you may be able to support a native helper—do it. You may be able to support one missionary in Japan, another in China, another in India, another in Africa, and another somewhere else—do it.

Giving Is a Privilege

Oh, the joy of preaching the Gospel in lands we will never see with our own eyes! How few in the church today realize their privilege of preaching the Gospel and saving men, women, and children in distant lands by sending substitute missionaries to them—that is, by sending someone who goes for you, where you cannot go yourself.

They could not go if it were not for your gifts. You may be able to give only a small amount to foreign missions, but every bit counts. Many insignificant streams together make a mighty river. If you cannot be a river, at least be a stream.

Learn to give largely. The generous giver is the happy Christian. "*The liberal soul shall be made fat*" (Prov. 11:25). "*He which soweth sparingly shall reap also sparingly; and he which soweth bountifully shall reap also bountifully....And God is able to make all grace abound toward you; that ye, always having all sufficiency in all things, may abound to every good work*" (2 Cor. 9:6, 8).

Generosity Equals Success

Success and growth in the Christian life depend on only a little more than liberal giving. The stingy Christian cannot be a growing Christian. It is wonderful how a Christian begins to grow when he begins to give. Power in prayer depends on liberal giving. One of the most wonderful statements about prayer and its answers is 1 John 3:22. John said, *"And whatsoever we ask, we receive of him, because we keep his commandments, and do those things that are pleasing in his sight."* He received because he kept God's commandments and did those things that pleased God.

The immediate context shows that the special commandments he was keeping were the commandments about giving. He told us in the twenty-first verse that when our hearts cannot condemn us about our stingy giving, then we can have confidence in our prayers to God.

God's answers to our prayers come in through the same door our gifts go out to others. Some of us open the door such a little bit by our small giving that God is not able to pass in to us any large answers to prayer. One of the most remarkable promises in the Bible is found in Philippians 4:19, which states: *"But my God shall supply all your need* [*"fulfil every need of yours"* (RV)] *according to his riches in glory by Christ Jesus."* This promise, however, was made to believers who distinguished themselves by the size and frequency of their giving. (Refer to verses 14–18.)

Of course, we should not confine our giving to foreign missions. We should give to the work of the home church as well as to rescue work in our large cities. We should do good for all men as we have opportunity, especially to those who are fellow Christians. *"As we have therefore opportunity, let us do good unto all men, especially unto them who are of the household of faith"* (Gal. 6:10). Foreign missions should receive a large part of our gifts.

Give systematically. Set aside a fixed proportion of all the money or goods you receive for Jesus. Be exact and honest about your giving. Don't use that part of your income for yourself under any circumstances.

The Christian is not under law, and there is no law binding the Christian to give a tenth of his income. But as a matter of free choice, a tenth is a good proportion to begin with. Don't let it be less than a tenth. God required the tithe from the Israelites, and Christians should give the same or more than what God required in the law. After you have given your tenth, you will soon learn the joy of giving offerings over and above your tenth.

Participate through Prayer

There is another way in which we can be a part of the foreign field. That is by our prayers. We all can go this way. Any hour of the day or night you can reach any corner of the earth by your prayers. I go to Japan, China, Australia, New Zealand, India, Africa, and to other parts of the world every day by my prayers. Prayer really makes things happen.

Do not make prayer an excuse for not going personally if God asks you. And do not make prayer an excuse for small giving. There is no power in that kind of prayer. If you are ready to go yourself, God willing, and if you are actually going by your gifts as God gives you ability, then you can go dynamically with your prayers also.

Missionaries Need Prayer

The greatest need in the work of Jesus Christ today is prayer. The greatest need of foreign missions today is prayer. Foreign missions are successful, but they are not as successful as they could be. They could be more successful if Christians at home, as well as abroad, were living up to their full potential in prayer.

Be specific in your prayers for foreign missions. Pray first of all that God will send forth laborers into His harvest—the right sort of laborers. There are many men and women in the foreign field who should not be there. There was not enough prayer about it. More foreign missionaries are greatly needed, but only more of the right kind of missionaries. Pray to God daily, believing He will send forth laborers into His harvest field.

Pray for the laborers who are already in the field. No group of men and women need our prayers more than foreign missionaries. No group of men and women are objects of more bitter hatred from Satan than they.

Satan delights in attacking the reputation and character of the brave men and women who are at the battlefront for Christ. No one is subjected to as many subtle and awful temptations as foreign missionaries.

We owe it to them to support them with our prayers. Do not merely pray for foreign missionaries in general. Have a few special missionaries whose work you study so that you can pray intelligently for them.

Pray for the native converts. We Christians at home think we have difficulties, trials, temptations, and persecutions, but the burdens we have are nothing compared to what the converts in heathen lands bear. The obstacles are often enormous, and the discouragements crushing. Christ alone can make them stand, but He works in answer to the prayers of His people.

Pray often, pray earnestly, pray intensely, and pray with faith for native converts. We learn from missionary literature how God has wonderfully answered prayer for native converts. It is best to be specific in your prayers for converts and have a specific geographic area about whose needs you keep yourself informed. Pray for the converts in that area. Do not have so many that you become confused and mechanical.

Pray for conversions in the foreign field. Pray for revivals in specific places. The last few years have been years of special prayer for special revival in foreign fields. From every corner of the earth, news has come of how God is amazingly answering these prayers. But the great things that God is beginning to do are small in comparison with what He will do if there is more prayer.

12

COMPANIONS

Our companions have a great influence on our character. The friendships we form create an intellectual, moral, and spiritual atmosphere where we are constantly breathing. Our spiritual health is helped or hindered by this atmosphere. Every young Christian should have a few wisely chosen, intimate friends with whom he can talk freely.

Choosing Your Friends

Search for a few people around your own age with whom you can associate intimately. Be sure that they are spiritual people in the best sense. Be sure they are people who love to study the Bible, who love to talk about spiritual themes, who know how to pray and do pray, and who are really working to bring others to Christ.

Do not feel at all uneasy about the fact that some Christian people are more compatible with you than others. God has made us that way. Some are attracted to certain people and some to others, and it proves nothing against the others or against you. Cultivate the friendship of those whose friendship you find helpful to your own spiritual life.

On the other hand, avoid the companionships that you find spiritually and morally harmful. Of course, we are not to withdraw ourselves totally from unconverted people or even worldly people. We are often to cultivate the acquaintance of unspiritual people, and even corrupt people, in order to win them for Christ. But we must always be on our guard with such friendships, lifting them up so they do not drag us down.

If you find, in spite of your best efforts, that a particular friendship is harming your spiritual life, then give it up. Some people are surrounded with such an atmosphere of unbelief, cynicism, criticism, impurity, greed, or other evils that it is impossible to remain without being contaminated. In such a case, the path of wisdom is plain; stop associating with those people to any large extent. Stop associating with them at all except where there is some possibility of helping them.

Books Are Influential

But there are other companionships that mold our lives in addition to the companionships of living people. The books we read are our companions. They exert a tremendous influence for good or evil. There is nothing that will help us more than a good book, and nothing that will hurt us more than a bad book. Among the most helpful books are the biographies of good men. Read again and again about the lives of such good and truly great men as Wesley, Finney, and Moody. We live in a day in which there are many good biographies. Read them.

Well-written histories are good companions. No study is more practical and instructive than the study of history. It is not only instructive but spiritually helpful if we watch to see the hand of God in history. We can see His inevitable triumph of right, and the inevitable punishment of wrong, in individuals and nations.

Some fiction is helpful, but here one needs to really be on guard. The majority of modern fiction is wicked and very morally harmful. Fiction that is not absolutely bad often promotes false views of life and prepares one more for a fantasy life rather than for reality. The habitual novel reader ruins his powers of keen and nimble thinking.

Fiction is so fascinating that it always tends to drive out other reading that is more helpful mentally and morally. We should be on our guard, even when reading good literature, that the good does not crowd out the best; in other words, that the best of man's literature does not replace the very best—God's Word. God's Book, the Bible, must always have the first place.

Pictures Can Shape a Life

There is another kind of companionship that has a tremendous influence over our lives. That is the companionship of pictures. The pictures we see every day of our lives, and the pictures we see only occasionally, have a tremendous power in shaping our lives.

A mother had two dearly loved sons. It was her dream and ambition that these sons would enter the ministry, but both of them went to sea. She could not understand why until a friend called her attention to the picture of a magnificent ship in full sail, which hung in the dining room. Every day of their lives, her boys saw that picture and had been thrilled by it. An unconquerable love and longing for the sea was created. This picture strongly influenced their lives.

How many masterpieces with worldly suggestions have sent young people on their road to ruin? Many of our art collections are so polluted with indecent pictures that it is not safe for a young man or woman to view them. The evil thoughts they suggest may only be for a moment, yet Satan will know how to bring that picture back again and again to bring harm. Do not look, even for a moment, at any picture that taints your imagination with evil suggestions—no matter how art critics praise it. Avoid, as you would poison, every painting, engraving, etching, and photograph that leaves a spot of impurity in your mind. Feast your soul on pictures that make you holier, kinder, more sympathetic, and tenderer.

13

ACTIVITIES AND ENTERTAINMENT

Young people need recreation. Our Savior does not frown on wholesome recreation. He was interested in the games of children when He was here on earth. He watched the children at play (see Matthew 12:16–19), and He watches the children at play today. He delights in their play when it is wholesome and elevating.

In the stress and strain of modern life, older people also need recreation if they are to do their very best work. But there are pastimes that are wholesome, and there are amusements that are wicked. It is impossible to discuss amusements one by one, and it is unnecessary. A few principles are enough.

Guidelines for Choosing Recreation

Do not indulge in any form of amusement about whose propriety you have any doubts. When you are in doubt, always give God the benefit of the doubt. There are plenty of distractions that are not at all questionable. "*He that doubteth is damned...for whatsoever is not of faith is sin*" (Rom. 14:23). Many young Christians will say, "I am not sure that this is wrong." Are you sure it is right? If not, leave it alone.

Do not indulge in any amusement that you cannot engage in to the glory of God. "*Whether therefore ye eat, or drink, or whatsoever ye do, do all to the glory of God*" (1 Cor. 10:31). Whenever you are in doubt as to whether you should engage in an activity, ask yourself, "Can I do this to the glory of God?"

Do not engage in any activity that will hurt your influence with anybody. There are amusements that are perhaps all right in themselves, but in which we cannot engage without losing our influence with someone. Every true Christian wishes that his life would show everyone the best. There is so much to be done and so few to do it that every Christian desires every last ounce of power for good that he can have with everybody.

If a particular entertainment will injure your influence for good with anyone, the price is too great. Do not engage in it. Whether justly or unjustly, the world discounts the testimony of those Christians who indulge in certain forms of worldly amusements. We cannot afford to have our witness reduced.

Do not engage in any activity that you cannot make a matter of prayer, asking God's blessing. Pray before your play, just as you would pray before your work.

Do not go anyplace where you cannot take Christ with you and where you do not think Christ would feel at home. Christ went to happy places when He was here on earth. He went to the marriage feast in Cana and contributed to the joy of the occasion. *"And the third day there was a marriage in Cana of Galilee; and the mother of Jesus was there: and both Jesus was called, and his disciples, to the marriage"* (John 2:1–2). But there are many modern places where Christ would not be comfortable. Would the atmosphere of the modern theater be agreeable to that Holy One whom we call Lord? If not, then don't go.

Don't engage in any activity that you would not like to be found enjoying if the Lord should come. He may come at any moment. Blessed is that individual who, when He comes, will be watching and ready, glad to receive to Him immediately. *"And ye yourselves like unto men that wait for their lord, when he will return from the wedding; that when he cometh and knocketh, they may open unto him immediately....Be ye therefore ready also: for the Son of man cometh at an hour when ye think not"* (Luke 12:36, 40).

I have a friend who was walking down the street one day thinking about the return of the Lord. As he thought, he was smoking a cigar. The thought occurred to him, "Would you like to meet Christ now with that cigar in your mouth?" He answered honestly, "No, I would not." He threw that cigar away and never lit another.

Do not engage in any activity, no matter how harmless it would be for yourself, that might harm someone else. Someone may be influenced to maintain or even start a harmful habit because our innocent activity was their inspiration.

For most of us the recreation that is most helpful demands considerable physical energy. These activities take us into the open air, leave us refreshed in body and invigorated in mind. Physical exercise, but not overexertion, is one of the great safeguards of the moral conduct of young people. There is little pleasure gained in watching others play the most vigorous game of football, but there is real health for the body and soul in physical exercise.

14

PERSECUTION

One of the discouragements that meets every true Christian before he has gone very far in the Christian life is persecution. God tells us in His Word that *"all that will live godly in Christ Jesus shall suffer persecution"* (2 Tim. 3:12). Sooner or later everyone who surrenders absolutely to God and seeks to follow Jesus Christ in everything will find this verse is true.

We live in a God-hating world and a compromising age. The world's hatred of God today may be veiled. It often does not express itself the same way it expressed itself in Palestine during the days of Jesus Christ. Nevertheless, the world hates God today as much as it ever did. It also hates anyone who is loyal to Christ. It may not imprison or kill him, but in some way it will persecute him.

Do Not Be Discouraged When Persecuted

Persecution is inevitable for a loyal follower of Jesus Christ. Many young Christians, when they meet with persecution, are surprised and discouraged. Many fall away. Many seem to run well for a few days, but, like those of whom Jesus spoke, they *"have no root in themselves, and so endure but for a time: afterward, when affliction or persecution ariseth for the word's sake, immediately they are offended"* (Mark 4:17). I have seen many apparently promising Christian lives end this way. But if persecution is received correctly, it is no longer a hindrance to the Christian life but a help.

Do not be discouraged when you are persecuted. No matter how fierce and hard the persecution, be thankful for it. Jesus said,

> *Blessed are they which are persecuted for righteousness' sake: for theirs is the kingdom of heaven. Blessed are ye, when men shall revile you, and persecute you, and shall say all manner of evil against you falsely, for my sake. Rejoice, and be exceeding glad: for great is your reward in heaven: for so persecuted they the prophets which were before you.*
> (Matt. 5:10–12)

It is a great privilege to be persecuted for Jesus. Peter found this out and wrote to the Christians of his day:

> *Beloved, think it not strange concerning the fiery trial which is to try you, as though some strange thing happened unto you: but rejoice, inasmuch as ye are partakers of Christ's sufferings; that, when his glory shall be revealed, ye may be glad also with exceeding joy. If ye be reproached for the name of Christ, happy are ye; for the spirit of glory and of God resteth upon you: on their part he is evil spoken of, but on your part he is glorified.* (1 Pet. 4:12–14)

A Bad Disposition Can Cause Persecution

Be very sure that the persecution is really for Christ's sake and not because of your own stubbornness, fault, or eccentricity. There are many who bring the displeasure of others on themselves because they are stubborn and cranky. They then flatter themselves that they are being persecuted for Christ's sake and for righteousness' sake.

Be considerate of the opinions of others, and be considerate of the conduct of others. Be sure that you do not push your opinions on others in an unjustifiable way. Do not make your conscience a rule of life for other people. But never yield one inch of principle. Stand firmly behind what you believe. Do it in love, but do it at any cost.

Return Persecution with Love

If when you are standing for conviction and principle you are disliked, slandered, and treated with all manner of unkindness because of it, do not be sad, but rejoice. Do not speak evil of those who speak evil of you, *"because Christ also suffered for us, leaving us an example, that ye should follow his steps:...Who, when he was reviled, reviled not again; when he suffered, he threatened not; but committed himself to him that judgeth righteously"* (1 Pet. 2:21, 23).

At this point many Christians make their mistake. They stand loyally for the truth, but receive the persecution that comes for the truth with harshness. They grow bitter and start condemning everyone but themselves. There is no blessing in bearing persecution that way.

Persecution should be tolerated lovingly and serenely. Do not talk about your own persecution. Rejoice in it. Thank God for it and go on obeying Him. Do not forget to love and pray for those people who persecute you. *"But I say unto you, Love your enemies, bless them that curse you, do good to them that hate you, and pray for them which despitefully use you, and persecute you"* (Matt. 5:44).

Remember Your Reward

Anytime the persecution seems more than you can bear, remember how great the reward is. *"If we suffer, we shall also reign with him: if we deny him, he also will deny us"* (2 Tim. 2:12). Everyone must enter into the kingdom of God through pain and trouble. *"Confirming the souls of the disciples, and exhorting them to continue in the faith, and that we must through much tribulation enter into the kingdom of God"* (Acts 14:22). But do not turn away from Jesus for this reason.

Always remember, however fiercely the fire of persecution may burn, *"the sufferings of this present time are not worthy to be compared with the glory which shall be revealed in us"* (Rom. 8:18). Remember, too, that your *"light affliction, which is but for a moment, worketh for us a far more exceeding and eternal weight of glory"* (2 Cor. 4:17). Keep looking, *"not at the things which are seen, but at the things which are not seen: for the things which are seen are temporal; but the things which are not seen are eternal"* (2 Cor. 4:18).

When the apostles were persecuted, even suffering imprisonment and whippings, *"they departed from the presence of the council* [that had ordered their terrible punishment], *rejoicing that they were counted worthy to suffer shame for his name. And daily in the temple, and in every house, they ceased not to teach and preach Jesus Christ"* (Acts 5:41–42).

Never More than We Can Bear

The time may come when you think you are being persecuted more than others, but you do not know what others have to endure. Even if it is that you are being persecuted more than anyone else, you should not complain. It is more fitting to humbly thank God that He has given you such an honor.

Keep your eyes fixed on

> *Jesus the author and finisher of our faith; who for the joy that was set before him endured the cross, despising the shame, and is set down at*

> *the right hand of the throne of God. For consider him that endured such contradiction of sinners against himself, lest ye be wearied and faint in your minds.* (Heb. 12:2–3)

I was once talking with an old man who became saved when he was still a slave. His cruel master flogged him again and again for his loyalty to Christ, but he said to me, "I simply thought of my Savior dying on the cross in my place, and I rejoiced to suffer persecution for Him."

15

GUIDANCE

I have met many people who are trying to lead a Christian life, but they are troubled over the question of guidance. They desire to do God's will in all things, but it puzzles them to know that the will of God is possible in every situation. When anyone starts out with determination to obey God in everything and be led by the Holy Spirit, Satan tries to confuse that person from knowing the will of God.

Satan often suggests something is the will of God, and it is not at all. When the believer does not follow the false suggestion, Satan says, "You disobeyed God." Because of this, many conscientious young Christians fall into a morbid and unhappy state of mind, fearing they have disobeyed God and lost His favor. This is one of the most frequent devices the devil uses to keep Christians from being cheerful.

Knowing the Will of God

How can we know the will of God?

First, let me say that a healthy Christian life is not governed by a lot of rules about what one is permitted to eat, drink, do, and not do. A life governed by a lot of rules is a life of bondage. One will sooner or later break some of these man-made rules and feel self-condemnation. Paul told us in Romans 8:15, *"Ye have not received the spirit of bondage again to fear; but ye have received the Spirit of adoption, whereby we cry, Abba, Father."*

The true Christian life is a life of a trusting, glad, fear-free child; not led by rules, but by the personal guidance of the Holy Spirit who dwells within. *"As many as are led by the Spirit of God, they are the sons of God"* (Rom. 8:14). If you have received Jesus Christ, the Holy Spirit dwells within you and is ready to lead you at every turn of life.

A life governed by a multitude of rules is a life of bondage and anxiety. A life surrendered to the control of the Holy Spirit is a life of joy, peace, and freedom. There is no anxiety in such a life; there is no fear in the presence of God. We trust God and rejoice in His presence just as a child trusts his earthly father and rejoices in his presence. If we make a mistake, we can tell Him all about it as trustfully as a child and know that He forgives and restores us instantly to His full favor. *"If we confess our sins, he is faithful and just to forgive us our sins, and to cleanse us from all unrighteousness"* (1 John 1:9).

Five Points in Seeking Wisdom

But how can we detect the Holy Spirit's guidance so that we may obey Him and have God's favor at every turn of life? This question is answered in James 1:5–7,

If any of you lack wisdom, let him ask of God, that giveth to all men liberally, and upbraideth not; and it shall be given him. But let him ask in faith, nothing wavering. For he that wavereth is like a wave of the sea driven with the wind and tossed. For let not that man think that he shall receive any thing of the Lord.

The principle is simple. It includes five points.

Recognize your ignorance and inability to guide your own life—you lack wisdom.

Surrender your will to God and really desire to be led by Him.

Have definite prayer time with Him for guidance.

Have confident expectation that God will guide you. "Ask in faith, doubting nothing."

Follow step-by-step as He guides.

God Guides One Step at a Time

God may show you only a step at a time. That is enough. All you need to know is the next step. It is here that many make a mistake. They wish God to show them the whole way before they take the first step.

A university student once came to me with a question about guidance. He said, "I cannot find the will of God. I have been praying, but God does not show me His will." This was in July.

"What are you seeking to know in the will of God?"

"What I should do next summer."

I replied, "Do you know what you should do tomorrow?"

"Yes."

"Do you know what you should do next autumn?"

"Yes, finish my degree. But what I want to know is what I should do when my university course is over."

He was soon led to see that all he needed to know for the present was what God had already shown him. When he did that, God would show him the next step.

Do not worry about what you ought to do next week. Do what God shows you to do for today. Next week will take care of itself. Indeed, tomorrow will take care of itself. Obey the Spirit of God for today. "*Take therefore no thought for the morrow: for the morrow shall take thought for the things of itself. Sufficient unto the day is the evil thereof*" (Matt. 6:34). It is enough to live a day at a time if we do our very best for that day.

God Gives Clear Guidance

God's guidance is clear guidance, "*God is light, and in him is no darkness at all*" (1 John 1:5). Do not be anxious about obscure leadings. Do not let your soul be ruffled by the thought, "Perhaps this obscure leading is what God wants me to do." Obscure leadings are not divine leadings. God's path is as clear as day. Satan's path is full of obscurity, uncertainty, anxiety, and questioning.

If a leading comes and you are not quite sure whether it is the will of God, simply pray to your heavenly Father and say, "Heavenly Father, I desire to know Your will. I will do Your will if You will make it clear. But You are light, and in You is no darkness at all. If this is Your will, make it crystal clear, and I will do it." Then wait quietly for God and do not act until He makes it clear. But the moment He makes it clear, act at once.

You Need a Surrendered Will

The whole secret of guidance is an absolutely surrendered will, a will that is given up to God and ready to obey Him at any cost. Many of our uncertainties about God's guidance are simply caused by our unwillingness to follow God's guiding. We are tempted to say, "I cannot find out what God's will is." The real trouble is that we have found His will, but, because it is something we do not wish to do, we are trying to make ourselves think God wants us to do something else.

God Does Not Contradict His Word

All supposed leadings of God should be tested by the Word of God. The Bible is God's revealed will. Any leading that contradicts the plain teaching of the Bible is certainly not the leading of the Holy Spirit. The Holy Spirit does not contradict Himself.

A man once came to me and said that God was leading him to marry a certain woman. He said she was a very devoted Christian woman, and they were greatly drawn to one another. They felt that God was leading them to be married.

But I said to the man, "You already have a wife."

"Yes," he said, "but we have never lived happily, and we have not lived together for years."

"But," I replied, "that does not alter the situation. God in His Word has told us distinctly the duty of the husband to his wife and how wrong it is in His sight for a husband to divorce his wife and marry another."

"Yes," said the man, "but the Holy Spirit is leading us to one another."

I indignantly replied, "Whatever spirit is leading you to marry one another is certainly not the Holy Spirit but the spirit of the evil one. The Holy Spirit never leads anyone to disobey the Word of God."

Search the Scriptures

In seeking to know the guidance of the Spirit, always search the Scriptures; study them prayerfully. Do not make a book of magic out of the Bible. Do not ask God to show you His will, then open your Bible at random and put your finger on some text, taking it out of context and pretending you have seen the will of God. This is an irreverent and improper use of Scripture. You may open your Bible at just the right place to find the right guidance. But if you do receive real guidance, it will not be by some fanciful interpretation of the passage you find. It will be by taking the passage in its context and interpreting it to mean just what it says as seen in its context.

All sorts of mischief has arisen from using the Bible in this perverse way. I knew an earnest Christian woman who was concerned about the predictions made by a false prophetess. The prophetess claimed Chicago would be destroyed on a certain day. She opened her Bible at random. It opened to the twelfth chapter of Ezekiel, "*Son of man, eat thy bread with quaking, and drink thy water with trembling and with carefulness....And the cities that are inhabited shall be laid waste, and the land shall be desolate*" (Ezek. 12:18, 20).

This seemed to fit the situation exactly, and the woman was considerably affected. But if the verses were studied in context, it would have been evident at once that God was not speaking about Chicago, and the verses were not applicable to Chicago. This was not an intelligent study of the Word of God and, therefore, led to a false conclusion.

Free from Anxiety and Worry

To sum up, lead a life that is not governed by rules but by the personal guidance of the Holy Spirit. Surrender your will totally to God. Whenever you are in doubt about His guidance, ask Him to show you His will, expect Him to do it, then follow step-by-step as He leads. Test all leadings by the plain and simple teachings of the Bible. Live without anxiety and worry that perhaps in an unguarded moment you have not done the right thing.

After you have done what you think God has led you to do, do not always go back wondering whether or not you did His will. You will become morbid if you do. If you really wished to do God's will, sought His guidance, and did what you thought He guided you to do, you may rest assured you did the right thing, no matter what the outcome has been.

Satan is determined to keep us from being happy, cheerful Christians—if he can. God, on the other hand, wishes us to be happy, cheerful, bright Christians every day and every hour. He does not wish us to brood, but to rejoice. *"Rejoice in the Lord alway: and again I say, Rejoice"* (Phil. 4:4).

An exemplary Christian man came to me one Monday morning, dejected over his apparent work failures of the preceding day. "I made wretched work of teaching my Sunday school class yesterday."

"Did you honestly seek wisdom from God before you went to your class?" I asked.

"I did."

"Did you expect to receive it?"

"I did."

"Then," I reassured him, "in the face of God's promise, what right have you to doubt that God gave you wisdom?" (See James 1:5–7.)

His gloom disappeared. He looked up with a smile and said, "I had no right to doubt." Let us learn to trust God.

Let us remember that, if we surrender to Him, He is more willing to guide us than we are to be guided. Let us trust that He does guide us at every step even though our actions may not bring the results we expect. Never worry, but trust God. This way we will be happy, peaceful, strong, and useful at every turn of life.

THE PRESENCE AND WORK OF THE HOLY SPIRIT

CONTENTS

1

THE PERSONALITY OF THE HOLY SPIRIT

Before one can correctly understand the work of the Holy Spirit, he must first of all know the Spirit Himself. A frequent source of error and fanaticism about the work of the Holy Spirit is the attempt to study and understand His work without first of all coming to know Him as a person.

It is of the highest importance from the standpoint of worship that we decide whether the Holy Spirit is a divine person, worthy to receive our adoration, our faith, our love, and our entire surrender to Himself, or whether it is simply an influence emanating from God or a power or an illumination that God imparts to us. If the Holy Spirit is a divine person and we do not know Him as such, then we are robbing a divine Being of the worship and the faith and the love and the surrender to Himself that are His due.

It is also of the highest importance from a practical standpoint that we decide whether the Holy Spirit is merely some mysterious and wonderful power that we, in our weakness and ignorance, are somehow to get hold of and use, or whether the Holy Spirit is a real person, infinitely holy, infinitely wise, infinitely mighty, and infinitely tender, who is to get hold of and use us. The former conception is utterly heathenish, not essentially different from the thought of the African fetish worshiper who has a god that he uses. The latter conception is sublime and Christian. If we think of the Holy Spirit, as so many do, as merely a power or influence, our constant thought will be, "How can I get more of the Holy Spirit?" But if we think of Him in the biblical way as a divine person, our thought will instead be, "How can the Holy Spirit have more of me?"

The conception of the Holy Spirit as being a divine influence or power that we are somehow to get hold of and use leads to self-exaltation and self-sufficiency. One who so thinks of the Holy Spirit and who at the same time imagines that he has received the Holy Spirit will almost inevitably be full of spiritual pride and strut about as if he belonged to some superior order of Christians. One frequently hears such people say, "I am a Spirit-filled man," or "I am a Spirit-filled woman."

But if we once grasp the thought that the Holy Spirit is a divine person of infinite majesty, glory, holiness, and power, who in marvelous condescension has come into our hearts to make His abode there and take possession of our lives and make use of them, it will put us in the dust and keep us in the dust. I can think of no thought more humbling or more overwhelming than the thought that a person of divine majesty and glory dwells in my heart and is ready to use even me.

It is of the highest importance from the standpoint of experience that we know the Holy Spirit as a person. Thousands and tens of thousands of men and women can testify to the blessing that has come into their own lives as they have come to know the Holy Spirit. They have come to know the Holy Spirit not merely as a gracious influence (emanating, it is true, from God) but as a real person, just as real as Jesus Christ Himself. He is an ever-present, loving Friend and mighty Helper who is not only by their sides at all times but also dwells in their hearts every day and every hour. He is ready to undertake for them in every emergency of life. Thousands of ministers, Christian workers, and Christians in the humblest spheres of life have spoken to me or written to me of the complete transformation of their Christian experience that came to them when they grasped the thought (not merely in a theological but in an experiential way) that the Holy Spirit is a person and consequently came to know Him.

There are at least four distinct proofs in the Bible that the Holy Spirit is a person.

Proof #1—The Character of the Holy Spirit

All the distinctive characteristics of personality are ascribed to the Holy Spirit in the Bible. What are these distinctive characteristics, or marks, of personality? Knowledge, feeling or emotion, and will. Any entity that thinks and feels and wills is a person. When we say that the Holy Spirit is a person, there are those who understand us to mean that the Holy Spirit has hands and feet and eyes and ears and mouth and so on, but these are not the characteristics of personality but of bodily substance. All of these characteristics, or marks, of personality are repeatedly ascribed to the Holy Spirit in the Old and New Testaments.

We read in 1 Corinthians,

> *But God hath revealed them unto us by his Spirit: for the Spirit searcheth all things, yea, the deep things of God. For what man knoweth the things of a man, save the spirit of man which is in him? even so the things of God knoweth no man, but the Spirit of God.*
>
> (1 Corinthians 2:10–11)

Here, knowledge is ascribed to the Holy Spirit. We are clearly taught that the Holy Spirit is not merely an influence that illuminates our minds to comprehend the truth but a Being who Himself knows the truth.

We also read, "*But all these worketh that one and the selfsame Spirit, dividing to every man severally as he will*" (1 Corinthians 12:11). Here, will is ascribed to the Spirit, and we are taught that the Holy Spirit is not a power that we get hold of and use according to our desires but a person of sovereign majesty who uses us according to His will.

This distinction is of fundamental importance in our getting into right relations with the Holy Spirit. It is at this very point that many honest seekers after power and efficiency in service go astray. They are reaching out after and struggling to get possession of some mysterious and mighty power that they can make use of in their work according to their own desires. They will never get possession of the power they seek until they come to recognize that there is not some divine power for them to get hold of and use in their blindness and ignorance but that there is a person, infinitely wise as well as infinitely mighty, who is willing to take possession of them and use them according to His own perfect will.

When we stop to think of it, we must rejoice that there is no divine power that we beings, so ignorant and so liable to err as we are, can get hold of and use. How appalling might be the results if there were. But what a holy joy must come into our hearts when we grasp the thought that there is a divine person, One who never errs, who is willing to take possession of us, impart to us such gifts as He sees best, and use us according to His wise and loving will.

We read in Romans 8:27, "*And he that searcheth the hearts knoweth what is the mind of the Spirit, because he maketh intercession for the saints according to the will of God.*" In this passage, "*mind*" is ascribed to the Holy Spirit. The Greek word translated *mind* is a comprehensive word, including the ideas of thought, feeling, and purpose. It is the same word used in Romans 8:7 where we read that "*the carnal mind is enmity against God: for it is not subject to the law of God, neither indeed can be.*" So in this verse, all the distinctive marks of personality are included in the word *mind* and are ascribed to the Holy Spirit.

We find the personality of the Holy Spirit brought out in a most touching and suggestive way in Romans 15:30: "*Now I beseech you, brethren, for the Lord Jesus Christ's sake, and for the love of the Spirit, that ye strive together with me in your prayers to God for me.*" Here we have "*love*" ascribed to the Holy Spirit. The reader would do well to stop and ponder those five words: "*the love of the Spirit.*"

We dwell often upon the love of God the Father. It is the subject of our daily and constant thought. We dwell often upon the love of Jesus Christ the Son. Who would think of calling himself a Christian if he passed a day without meditating on the love of his Savior? But how often have we meditated upon "*the love of the Spirit*"?

Each day of our lives, if we are living as Christians ought, we kneel down in the presence of God the Father, look up into His face, and say, "I thank you, Father, for Your great love that led You to give Your only begotten Son to die upon the cross of Calvary for me." Each day of our lives we also look up into the face of our Lord and Savior, Jesus Christ, and say, "Oh, glorious Lord and Savior, Jesus the Son of God, I thank You for Your great love that led You not to count it a thing to be on equality with God but to empty Yourself, and forsaking all the glory of heaven, come down to earth with all its shame and take my sins upon Yourself and die in my place upon the cross of Calvary." But how often do we kneel and say to the Holy Spirit, "Oh, eternal and infinite Spirit of God, I thank You for Your great love that led You to come into this world of sin and darkness and to seek me out and to follow me so patiently until You brought me to see my utter ruin and need for a Savior and to reveal to me my Lord and Savior, Jesus Christ, as just the Savior whom I need." Yet we owe our salvation just as truly to the love of the Spirit as we do to the love of the Father and the love of the Son.

If it had not been for the love of God the Father looking down upon me in my utter ruin and providing a perfect atonement for me in the death of His own Son on the cross of Calvary, I would have been in hell today. If it had not been for the love of Jesus Christ, the eternal Word of God, looking upon me in my utter ruin and, in obedience to the Father, putting aside all the glory of heaven for all the shame of earth and taking my place, the place of the curse, upon the cross of Calvary and pouring out His life utterly for me, I would have been in hell today. But if it had not been for the love of the Holy Spirit, sent by the Father in answer to the prayer of the Son (see John 14:16), leading Him to seek me out in my utter blindness and ruin, I would have been in hell today. He followed me day after day, week after week, and year after year when I persistently turned a deaf ear to His pleadings, following me through paths of sin where it must have been agony for that holy One to go until at last I listened. And He opened my eyes to see my utter ruin and then revealed Jesus to me as just the Savior that would meet my every need. He then enabled me to receive this Jesus as my own Savior. If it had not been for this patient, long-suffering, never-tiring, infinitely tender love of the Holy Spirit, I would have been in hell today. Oh, the Holy Spirit is not merely an influence or a power or an illumination but is a person, just as real as God the Father or Jesus Christ His Son.

The personality of the Holy Spirit comes out in the Old Testament as truly as in the New, for we read in Nehemiah 9:20, "*Thou gavest also thy good spirit to instruct them, and withheldest not thy manna from their mouth, and gavest them water for their thirst.*" Here, both intelligence and goodness are ascribed to the Holy Spirit. There are some who tell us that while it is true the personality of the Holy Spirit is found in the New Testament, it is not found in the Old. However, it is certainly found in this passage. While it is true that the doctrine of the personality of the Holy Spirit is not as fully developed in the Old Testament as in the New, the doctrine is nevertheless there.

There is perhaps no passage in the entire Bible in which the personality of the Holy Spirit comes out more tenderly and touchingly than in the following: "*And grieve not the holy Spirit of God, whereby ye are sealed unto the day of redemption*" (Ephesians 4:30). Here, grief is ascribed to the Holy Spirit. The Holy Spirit is not a blind, impersonal influence or power that comes into our lives to illuminate, sanctify, and empower us. No, He is immeasurably more than that. He is a holy person who comes to dwell in our hearts, One who sees clearly every act we perform, every word we speak, every thought we entertain, even the most fleeting fancy that is allowed to pass through our minds. If there is anything in act or word or deed that is impure, unholy, unkind, selfish, mean, petty, or untrue, this infinitely Holy One is deeply grieved by it. I know of no thought that will help a person more than this to lead a holy life and to walk softly in the presence of the Holy One.

How often a young man is kept back from yielding to the temptations that surround young manhood by the thought that if he should yield to the temptation that now assails him, his godly mother might hear of it and would be grieved by it beyond expression. How often some young man has had his hand upon the door of some place of sin that he is about to enter and the thought has come to him, "If I should enter there, my mother might hear of it, and it would nearly kill her," and he has turned his back upon that door and gone away to lead a pure life that he might not grieve his mother.

There is One who is holier than any mother, One who is more sensitive against sin than the purest woman who ever walked this earth and who loves us as even no mother ever loved. This One dwells in our hearts, if we are really Christians, and He sees every act we do by day or under cover of the night. He hears every word we utter in public or in private. He sees every thought we entertain. He beholds every fancy and imagination that is permitted even a momentary lodging in our mind. If there is anything unholy, impure, selfish, mean, petty, unkind, harsh, unjust, or in any way evil in act or word or thought or fancy, He is grieved by it. If we will allow those words, *"grieve not the holy Spirit of God,"* to sink into our hearts and become the motto of our lives, they will keep us from many a sin. How often some thought or fancy has knocked for an entrance into my own mind and was about to find entertainment there when the thought came, "The Holy Spirit sees that thought and will be grieved by it," and then the thought has gone.

Proof #2—The Acts of the Holy Spirit

Many acts that only a person can perform are ascribed to the Holy Spirit, and we deny the personality of the Holy Spirit, many passages of Scripture become meaningless and absurd. For example, we read in 1 Corinthians 2:10, *"But God hath revealed them unto us by his Spirit: for the Spirit searcheth all things, yea, the deep things of God."* This passage sets before us the Holy Spirit not merely as an illumination whereby we are enabled to grasp the deep things of God but as a person who Himself searches the deep things of God and then reveals to us the precious discoveries that He has made.

We read in Revelation 2:7, *"He that hath an ear, let him hear what the Spirit saith unto the churches; to him that overcometh will I give to eat of the tree of life, which is in the midst of the paradise of God."* Here, the Holy Spirit is set before us not merely as an impersonal enlightenment that comes to our mind but as a person who speaks and, out of the depths of His own wisdom, whispers into the ear of His listening servant the precious truth of God.

In Galatians 4:6 we read, *"And because ye are sons, God hath sent forth the Spirit of his Son into your hearts, crying, Abba, Father."* Here, the Holy Spirit is represented as crying out in the heart of the individual believer. The Holy Spirit is not merely a divine influence, producing in our own hearts the assurance of our sonship; no, He is also one who cries out in our hearts, who bears witness together with our spirit that we are sons of God (see Romans 8:16).

The Holy Spirit is also represented in the Scripture as one who prays: *"Likewise the Spirit also helpeth our infirmities: for we know not what we should pray for as we ought: but the Spirit itself maketh intercession for us with groanings which cannot be uttered"* (Romans 8:26).

It is plain from this passage that the Holy Spirit is not merely an influence that moves us to pray, not merely an illumination that teaches us how to pray, but rather a person who Himself prays in and through us.

There is wondrous comfort in the thought that every true believer has two divine persons praying for him. One is Jesus Christ, the Son who was once upon this earth, who knows all about our temptations, who can be touched with the feeling of our infirmities, and who is now ascended to the right hand of the Father and in that place of authority and power ever lives to make intercession for us. (See Hebrews 7:25; 1 John 2:1.) There is another person, just as divine as Christ, who walks by our side each day; who dwells in the innermost depths of our being; who knows our needs even as we do not know them ourselves; and who, from these depths, makes intercession to the Father for us. The position of the believer is indeed one of perfect security with these two divine persons praying for him.

We read in John 15:26, "*But when the Comforter is come, whom I will send unto you from the Father, even the Spirit of truth, which proceedeth from the Father, he shall testify of me.*" Here the Holy Spirit is set before us as a person who gives His testimony to Jesus Christ not merely as an illumination that enables the believer to testify of Christ but rather as a person who Himself testifies. A clear distinction is drawn in this and in the following verse between the testimony of the Holy Spirit and the testimony of the believer to whom He has borne His witness, for we read, "*And ye also shall bear witness, because ye have been with me from the beginning*" (John 15:27). So there are two witnesses: the Holy Spirit bearing witness to the believer and the believer bearing witness to the world.

The Holy Spirit is also spoken of as a teacher: "*But the Comforter, which is the Holy Ghost, whom the Father will send in my name, he shall teach you all things, and bring all things to your remembrance, whatsoever I have said unto you*" (John 14:26). And in a similar way, we read,

> *I have yet many things to say unto you, but ye cannot bear them now. Howbeit when he, the Spirit of truth, is come, he will guide you into all truth: for he shall not speak of himself; but whatsoever he shall hear, that shall he speak: and he will show you things to come. He shall glorify me: for he shall receive of mine, and shall show it unto you.*
>
> (John 16:12–14)

And in the Old Testament, we read, "*Thou gavest also thy good spirit to instruct them*" (Nehemiah 9:20). In all these passages it is perfectly clear that the Holy Spirit is not a mere illumination that enables us to apprehend the truth but a person who comes to us to teach us day by day the truth of God. It is the privilege of the humblest believer in Jesus Christ not merely to have his mind illumined to comprehend the truth of God but to have a divine teacher who daily teaches him the truth he needs to know. (See 1 John 2:20, 27.)

The Holy Spirit is also represented as the leader and guide of the children of God. We read in Romans 8:14, *"For as many as are led by the Spirit of God, they are the sons of God."* He is not merely an influence that enables us to see the way that God would have us go, or merely a power that gives us strength to go that way, but rather a person who takes us by the hand and gently leads us on in the paths in which God would have us walk.

The Holy Spirit also has authority to command men in their service of Jesus Christ. We read of the apostle Paul and his companions,

> *Now when they had gone throughout Phrygia and the region of Galatia, and were forbidden of the Holy Ghost to preach the word in Asia, after they were come to Mysia, they assayed to go into Bithynia: but the Spirit suffered them not.* (Acts 16:6–7)

Here, it is a person who leads and directs Paul and his companions and a person whose authority they recognized and to whom they instantly submitted.

Further still than this the Holy Spirit is represented as the One who is the supreme authority in the church, who calls men to work and appoints them to office. We read in Acts 13:2, *"As they ministered to the Lord, and fasted, the Holy Ghost said, Separate me Barnabas and Saul for the work whereunto I have called them."* And, *"Take heed therefore unto yourselves, and to all the flock, over the which the Holy Ghost hath made you overseers, to feed the church of God, which he hath purchased with his own blood"* (Acts 20:28). There can be no doubt to a candid seeker after truth that it is a person of divine majesty and sovereignty who is here set before us.

From all the passages here quoted, it is evident that many acts that only a person can perform are ascribed to the Holy Spirit.

Proof #3—The Office of the Holy Spirit

An office is asserted by the Holy Spirit that can only be asserted by a person. Our Savior said,

> *And I will pray the Father, and he shall give you another Comforter, that he may abide with you for ever; even the Spirit of truth; whom the world cannot receive, because it seeth him not, neither knoweth him: but ye know him; for he dwelleth with you, and shall be in you.*
>
> (John 14:16–17)

Our Lord had announced to the disciples that He was about to leave them. An awful sense of desolation took possession of them. Sorrow filled their hearts (see John 16:6) at the contemplation of their loneliness and absolute helplessness when Jesus would thus leave them alone. To comfort them, the Lord told them that they would not be left alone, that in leaving them, He was going to the Father and that He would pray that the Father would give them another Comforter to take the place of Himself during His absence.

Is it possible that Jesus Christ could have used such language if the other Comforter who was coming to take His place was only an impersonal influence or power? Still more, is it possible that Jesus could have said as He did in John 16:7, "*Nevertheless I tell you the truth; it is expedient for you that I go away: for if I go not away, the Comforter will not come unto you; but if I depart, I will send him unto you,*" if this Comforter whom He was to send was simply an impersonal influence or power? No, one divine person was going, another person just as divine was coming to take His place. For the disciples, it was necessary that the One go to represent them before the Father because another just as divine and sufficient was coming to take His place. This promise of our Lord and Savior of the coming of the other Comforter and of His abiding with us is the greatest and best of all for the present dispensation. This is the promise of the Father (see Acts 1:4), the promise of promises. We will take it up again when we come to study the names of the Holy Spirit.

Proof #4—The Treatment of the Holy Spirit

A treatment is asserted by the Holy Spirit that could only be asserted by a person. We read in Isaiah 63:10 (ASV), *"But they rebelled and grieved his holy Spirit: therefore he was turned to be their enemy, and himself fought against them."* Here, we are told that the Holy Spirit is rebelled against and grieved. (Compare Ephesians 4:30.) Only a person, and only a person of authority, can be rebelled against. Only a person can be grieved. You cannot grieve a mere influence or power.

In Hebrews we read,

> *Of how much sorer punishment, suppose ye, shall he be thought worthy, who hath trodden under foot the Son of God, and hath counted the blood of the covenant, wherewith he was sanctified, an unholy thing, and hath done despite unto the Spirit of grace?*
> (Hebrews 10:29)

Here, we are told that the Holy Spirit is *"done despite unto"* (treated with contempt). There is but one kind of entity in the universe that can be treated with contempt (or insulted), and that is a person. It is absurd to think of treating an influence or a power or any kind of being, except a person, with contempt.

We also read, *"But Peter said, Ananias, why hath Satan filled thine heart to lie to the Holy Ghost, and to keep back part of the price of the land?"* (Acts 5:3). Here, we have the Holy Spirit represented as one who can be lied to. One cannot lie to anything but a person.

In Matthew we read,

> *Wherefore I say unto you, All manner of sin and blasphemy shall be forgiven unto men: but the blasphemy against the Holy Ghost shall not*

> *be forgiven unto men. And whosoever speaketh a word against the Son of man, it shall be forgiven him: but whosoever speaketh against the Holy Ghost, it shall not be forgiven him, neither in this world, neither in the world to come.* (Matthew 12:31–32)

Here, we are told that the Holy Spirit is blasphemed against. It is impossible to blaspheme anything but a person. If the Holy Spirit is not a person, it certainly cannot be a more serious and decisive sin to blaspheme Him than it is to blaspheme the Son of Man, our Lord and Savior, Jesus Christ Himself.

Here, then, we have four distinctive and decisive lines of proof that the Holy Spirit is a person. Theoretically most of us believe this, but do we, in our real thoughts of Him and in our practical attitudes toward Him, treat Him as if He were indeed a person?

At the close of an address on the personality of the Holy Spirit at a Bible conference some years ago, one who had been a church member many years, a member of one of the most orthodox of our modern denominations, said to me, "I never thought of the Holy Spirit before as a person." Doubtless this Christian woman had often sung,

> Praise God from whom all blessings flow,
> Praise Him all creatures here below,
> Praise Him above, ye heavenly host,
> Praise Father, Son, and Holy Ghost.

Doubtless she had often sung,

> Glory be to the Father,
> and to the Son,
> and to the Holy Ghost.
> As it was in the beginning,
> is now, and ever shall be.
> World without end,
> Amen, Amen.

However, it is one thing to sing words; it is quite another thing to realize the meaning of what we sing. If this Christian woman had been questioned in regard to her doctrine, she would doubtless have said that she believed that there were three persons in the Godhead: Father, Son, and Holy Spirit. But a theological confession is one thing; a practical realization of the truth we confess is quite another. So the question is altogether necessary, no matter how orthodox you may be in your doctrinal statements: Do you indeed regard the Holy Spirit as real a person as Jesus Christ, as loving and wise and strong, as worthy of your confidence and love and surrender as Jesus Christ Himself?

The Holy Spirit came into this world to be to the disciples of our Lord after His departure, and to us, what Jesus Christ had been to them during the days of His personal companionship with them. (See John 14:16–17.) Is He that to you? Do you know Him? Every week in your life you hear the apostolic benediction, *"The grace of the Lord Jesus Christ, and the love of God, and the communion of the Holy Ghost, be with you all"* (2 Corinthians 13:14), but while you hear it, do you take in the significance of it? Do you know the communion of the Holy Spirit? The fellowship of the Holy Spirit? The partnership of the Holy Spirit? The comradeship of the Holy Spirit? The intimate, personal friendship of the Holy Spirit?

Here lies the whole secret of a real Christian life, a life of liberty and joy and power and fullness. To have the Holy Spirit as one's ever-present friend and to be conscious of this fact, and to surrender one's life in all its departments entirely to His control—this is true Christian living. The doctrine of the personality of the Holy Spirit is as distinctive of the religion that Jesus taught as the doctrines of the deity and the atonement of Jesus Christ Himself. But it is not enough to believe the doctrine; one must know the Holy Spirit Himself. The whole purpose of this chapter (God, help me to say it reverently) is to introduce you to my friend, the Holy Spirit.

2

THE DEITY OF THE HOLY SPIRIT

In the preceding chapter, we saw clearly that the Holy Spirit is a person, but what sort of a person is He? Is He a finite person or an infinite person? Is He God? This question also is plainly answered in the Bible. In both the Old and the New Testaments there are five distinct and decisive pieces of evidence of the deity of the Holy Spirit.

Evidence #1—Divine Attributes

Each of the four distinctively divine attributes is ascribed to the Holy Spirit. What are these distinctively divine attributes? Eternity, omnipresence, omniscience, and omnipotence. All of these are ascribed to the Holy Spirit in the Bible. We find eternity ascribed to the Holy Spirit in Hebrews 9:14: "*How much more shall the blood of Christ, who through the eternal Spirit offered himself without spot to God, purge your conscience from dead works to serve the living God?*"

Omnipresence is ascribed to the Holy Spirit in the following verses:

> *Whither shall I go from thy spirit? or whither shall I flee from thy presence? If I ascend up into heaven, thou art there: if I make my bed in hell, behold, thou art there. If I take the wings of the morning, and dwell in the uttermost parts of the sea; even there shall thy hand lead me, and thy right hand shall hold me.* (Psalm 139:7–10)

Omniscience is ascribed to the Holy Spirit in several passages. For example, we read the following passages from Scripture:

> *But God hath revealed them unto us by his Spirit: for the Spirit searcheth all things, yea, the deep things of God. For what man knoweth the things of a man, save the spirit of man which is in him? even so the things of God knoweth no man, but the Spirit of God.* (1 Corinthians 2:10–11)

> *But the Comforter, which is the Holy Ghost, whom the Father will send in my name, he shall teach you all things, and bring all things to your remembrance, whatsoever I have said unto you.* (John 14:26)

> *I have yet many things to say unto you, but ye cannot bear them now. Howbeit when he, the Spirit of truth, is come, he will guide you into all truth: for he shall not speak of himself; but whatsoever he shall hear, that shall he speak: and he will show you things to come.* (John 16:12–13)

We find omnipotence ascribed to the Holy Spirit in Luke 1:35:

> *And the angel answered and said unto her, The Holy Ghost shall come upon thee, and the power of the Highest shall overshadow thee: therefore also that holy thing which shall be born of thee shall be called the Son of God.*

Evidence #2—Divine Works

Three distinctively divine works are ascribed to the Holy Spirit. When we think of God and His work, the first work of which we always think is that of creation. In the Scriptures, creation is ascribed to the Holy Spirit. We read in Job 33:4, "*The spirit of God hath made me, and the breath of the Almighty hath given me life.*" We read still again in Psalm 104:30, "*Thou sendest forth thy spirit, they are created: and thou renewest the face of the earth.*" The activity of the Spirit is also referred to in connection with the creation account in Genesis. (See Genesis 1:1–3.)

The impartation of life is also a divine work, and this is ascribed in the Scriptures to the Holy Spirit. We read in John 6:63, "*It is the spirit that quickeneth; the flesh profiteth nothing.*" We read also in Romans 8:11, "*But if the Spirit of him that raised up Jesus from the dead dwell in you, he that raised up Christ from the dead shall also quicken your mortal bodies by his Spirit that dwelleth in you.*" In the description of the creation of man in Genesis 2:7, it is the breath of God—that is, the Holy Spirit—who imparts life to man so that man becomes a living soul. The exact words are, "*And the Lord God formed man of the dust of the ground, and breathed into his nostrils the breath of life; and man became a living soul.*" Although the Holy Spirit as a person does not come out distinctly in this early reference to Him in Genesis 2:7, this passage, when interpreted in the light of the fuller revelation of the New Testament, clearly refers to the Holy Spirit because the Greek word that is rendered *spirit* means "breath."

The authorship of divine prophecies is also ascribed to the Holy Spirit. We read in 2 Peter 1:21, "*For the prophecy came not in old time by the will of man: but holy men of God spake as they were moved by the Holy Ghost."* Even in the Old Testament, there is a reference to the Holy Spirit as the author of prophecy. We read in 2 Samuel 23:2–3,

> *The spirit of the LORD spake by me, and his word was in my tongue. The God of Israel said, the Rock of Israel spake to me, He that ruleth over men must be just, ruling in the fear of God.*

So we see that the three distinctly divine works—creation, the impartation of life, and prophecy—are ascribed to the Holy Spirit.

Evidence #3—Divine Names

Statements that, in the Old Testament, distinctly name the LORD, or Jehovah, as their subject are applied to the Holy Spirit in the New Testament. Thus, the Holy Spirit occupies the position of deity in New Testament thought. A striking illustration of this is found in a comparison of a passage in Isaiah and one in Acts.

> *Mine eyes have seen the King, the LORD of hosts....And he said, Go, and tell this people, Hear ye indeed, but understand not; and see ye indeed, but perceive not. Make the heart of this people fat, and make their ears heavy, and shut their eyes; lest they see with their eyes, and hear with their ears, and understand with their heart, and convert, and be healed.* (Isaiah 6:5, 9–10)

In verse five we are told that it was Jehovah whom Isaiah saw and who speaks (whenever the word LORD is spelled in capitals in the Old Testament, it stands for *Jehovah* in the Hebrew). But in Acts there is a reference to this statement of Isaiah's; and whereas, in Isaiah, we are told it is Jehovah who speaks, in the reference in Acts, we are told that it was the Holy Spirit who was the speaker. The passage in Acts reads as follows:

> *And when they agreed not among themselves, they departed, after that Paul had spoken one word, Well spake the Holy Ghost by Esaias the*

> *prophet unto our fathers, saying, Go unto this people, and say, Hearing ye shall hear, and shall not understand; and seeing ye shall see, and not perceive: for the heart of this people is waxed gross, and their ears are dull of hearing, and their eyes have they closed; lest they should see with their eyes, and hear with their ears, and understand with their heart, and should be converted, and I should heal them.* (Acts 28:25–27)

So we see that what is distinctly ascribed to Jehovah in the Old Testament is ascribed to the Holy Spirit in the New; thus, the Holy Spirit is identified with Jehovah. It is a noteworthy fact that, in the gospel of John, chapter twelve verses thirty-eight to forty-one, where another reference to this passage in Isaiah is made, this same passage is ascribed to Christ (note carefully John 12:41). So in different parts of Scripture, we have the same passage referred to Jehovah, referred to the Holy Spirit, and referred to Jesus Christ. May we not find the explanation of this in the threefold "*Holy*" of the angelic cry in Isaiah 6:3, where we read, "*And one cried unto another, and said, Holy, holy, holy, is the* L*ORD* *of hosts: the whole earth is full of his glory.*" In this we have a distinct suggestion of the tri-personality of the Jehovah of Hosts and hence the propriety of the threefold application of the vision. A further suggestion of this tri-personality of the Jehovah of Hosts is found in Isaiah 6:8 where the Lord is represented as saying, "*Whom shall I send, and who will go for us? Then said I, Here am I; send me.*"

Another striking illustration of Old Testament passages that distinctly name Jehovah as their subject being applied to the Holy Spirit in the New Testament is found in Exodus 16:7. Here we read, "*And in the morning, then ye shall see the glory of the* L*ORD*; *for that he heareth your murmurings against the* L*ORD*: *and what are we, that ye murmur against us?*" Here the murmuring of the children of Israel is distinctly said to be against Jehovah. But in Hebrews 3:7–9, where this instance is referred to, we read,

> *Wherefore (as the Holy Ghost saith, To day if ye will hear his voice, harden not your hearts, as in the provocation, in the day of temptation*

in the wilderness: when your fathers tempted me, proved me, and saw my works forty years....)

The murmurings that Moses said in the book of Exodus were against Jehovah, we are told, in Hebrews, were against the Holy Spirit. This leaves it beyond question that the Holy Spirit occupies the position of Jehovah (or Deity) in the New Testament. (Compare Psalm 95:8–11.)

Evidence #4—Divine Associations

The name of the Holy Spirit is coupled with that of God in a way it would be impossible for a reverent and thoughtful mind to couple the name of any finite being with that of the Deity. We have an illustration of this in 1 Corinthians:

> *Now there are diversities of gifts, but the same Spirit. And there are differences of administrations, but the same Lord. And there are diversities of operations, but it is the same God which worketh all in all.*
> (1 Corinthians 12:4–6)

Here, we find God and the Lord and the Spirit associated together in a relation of equality that would be shocking to contemplate if the Spirit were a finite being. We have a still more striking illustration of this in Matthew 28:19: "*Go ye therefore, and teach all nations, baptizing them in the name of the Father, and of the Son, and of the Holy Ghost.*" What person who had grasped the biblical conception of God the Father would think for a moment of coupling the name of the Holy Spirit with that of the Father in this way if the Holy Spirit were a finite being or even the most exalted of angelic beings?

Another striking illustration is found in 2 Corinthians 13:14: "*The grace of the Lord Jesus Christ, and the love of God, and the communion of the Holy Ghost, be with you all. Amen.*" Can anyone ponder these words and catch anything like their real importance without seeing clearly that it would be impossible to couple the name of the Holy Spirit with that of

God the Father in the way in which it is coupled in this verse unless the Holy Spirit were Himself a divine Being?

Evidence #5—Divine Title

The Holy Spirit is called God. The final and decisive proof of the deity of the Holy Spirit is found in the fact that He is called "*God*" in the New Testament. We read in Acts 5:3–4,

> *But Peter said, Ananias, why hath Satan filled thine heart to lie to the Holy Ghost, and to keep back part of the price of the land? Whiles it remained, was it not thine own? and after it was sold, was it not in thine own power? why hast thou conceived this thing in thine heart? thou hast not lied unto men, but unto God.*

In the first part of this passage, we are told that Ananias lied to the Holy Spirit. When this is further explained, we are told it was not to men but to God that he had lied in lying to the Holy Spirit; in other words, the Holy Spirit to whom he lied is called "*God.*"

To sum it all up, by the ascription of all the distinctively divine attributes and several distinctly divine works, by comparing statements that clearly name Jehovah, the Lord, or God as their subject in the Old Testament to the Holy Spirit in the New Testament, by coupling the name of the Holy Spirit with that of God in a way that would be impossible to couple that of any finite being with that of deity, and by plainly calling the Holy Spirit *God*—in all these unmistakable ways, God in His own Word distinctly proclaims that the Holy Spirit is a divine person.

3

THE HOLY SPIRIT'S DISTINCTION FROM THE FATHER AND FROM HIS SON

We have seen thus far that the Holy Spirit is a person and a divine person. And now another question arises: Is He, as a divine person, separate and distinct from the Father and from the Son? One who carefully studies the New Testament statements will discover that, beyond a doubt, He is. We read in Luke 3:21–22,

> *Now when all the people were baptized, it came to pass, that Jesus also being baptized, and praying, the heaven was opened, and the Holy*

> *Ghost descended in a bodily shape like a dove upon him, and a voice came from heaven, which said, Thou art my beloved Son; in thee I am well pleased.*

Here, the clearest possible distinction is drawn between Jesus Christ, who was on earth; the Father, who spoke to Jesus from heaven as one person speaks to another person, and the Holy Spirit, who descended in a bodily form as a dove from the Father (who was speaking) to the Son (to whom the Father was speaking) and rested upon the Son as a person separate and distinct from Himself.

We see a clear distinction drawn between the name of the Father and that of the Son and that of the Holy Spirit in Matthew 28:19, where we read, "*Go ye therefore, and teach all nations, baptizing them in the name of the Father, and of the Son, and of the Holy Ghost.*" The distinction of the Holy Spirit from the Father and the Son comes out again with exceeding clearness in John 14:16: "*And I will pray the Father, and he shall give you another Comforter, that he may abide with you for ever.*" Here, we see one person (the Son) praying to another person (the Father) and the Father to whom He is praying giving another person (another Comforter) in answer to the prayer of the second person (the Son). If words mean anything, and certainly in the Bible they mean what they say, there can be no mistaking that the Father and the Son and the Spirit are three distinct and separate persons.

Again in John 16:7, a clear distinction is drawn between Jesus who goes away to the Father and the Holy Spirit who comes from the Father to take His place. Jesus says, "*Nevertheless I tell you the truth; it is expedient for you that I go away: for if I go not away, the Comforter will not come unto you; but if I depart, I will send him unto you.*" A similar distinction is drawn in Acts 2:33, where we read, "*Therefore being by the right hand of God exalted, and having received of the Father the promise of the Holy Ghost,* [Jesus] *hath shed forth this, which ye now see and hear.*" In this passage, the clearest possible distinction is drawn between the Son exalted to the right hand of the Father; the Father to whose right hand He is exalted; and the Holy Spirit whom the Son receives from the Father and sheds forth upon the church.

To sum it all up, again and again the Bible draws the clearest possible distinction between the three persons: the Holy Spirit, the Father, and the Son. They are three separate personalities, having mutual relations to one another, acting upon one another, speaking of or to one another, applying the pronouns of the second and third persons to one another.

4

THE SUBORDINATION OF THE SPIRIT TO THE FATHER AND TO THE SON

From the fact that the Holy Spirit is a divine person, it does not follow that the Holy Spirit is in every sense equal to the Father. While the Scriptures teach that in Jesus Christ dwelt all the fullness of the Godhead in a bodily form (see Colossians 2:9) and that He was so truly and fully divine that He could say, *"I and my Father are one"* (John 10:30) and *"He that hath seen me hath seen the Father"* (John 14:9), they also teach with equal clearness that Jesus Christ was not equal to the Father in every respect but subordinate to the Father in many ways.

In a similar way, the Scriptures teach us that though the Holy Spirit is a divine person, He is subordinate to the Father and to the Son. We are taught that the Holy Spirit is sent by the Father in the name of the Son. Jesus declares very clearly,

> *But the Comforter, which is the Holy Ghost, whom the Father will send in my name, he shall teach you all things, and bring all things to your remembrance, whatsoever I have said unto you.* (John 14:26)

In John 15:26 we are told that it is Jesus who sends the Spirit from the Father. The exact words are, *"But when the Comforter is come, whom I will send unto you from the Father, even the Spirit of truth, which proceedeth from the Father, he shall testify of me."* Just as we are elsewhere taught that Jesus Christ was sent by the Father (see John 6:29; 8:29, 42), we are here taught that the Holy Spirit in turn is sent by Jesus Christ.

The subordination of the Holy Spirit to the Father and the Son comes out also in the fact that He derives some of His names from the Father and from the Son. We read in Romans 8:9, *"But ye are not in the flesh, but in the Spirit, if so be that the Spirit of God dwell in you. Now if any man have not the Spirit of Christ, he is none of his."* Here we have two names of the Spirit: one derived from His relation to the Father, *"the Spirit of God"*; and the other derived from His relation to the Son, *"the Spirit of Christ."* In Acts 16:7 (RV), He is spoken of as *"the Spirit of Jesus."*

The subordination of the Spirit to the Son is also seen in the fact that the Holy Spirit speaks not from Himself but only the words that He hears. We read in John,

> *Howbeit when he, the Spirit of truth, is come, he will guide you into all truth: for he shall not speak of himself; but whatsoever he shall hear, that shall he speak: and he will show you things to come.* (John 16:13)

In a similar way, Jesus said of Himself, *"My doctrine is not mine, but his that sent me"* (John 7:16; see also 8:26, 40).

The subordination of the Spirit to the Son comes out again in the clearly revealed fact that it is the work of the Holy Spirit not to glorify Himself but to glorify Christ. Jesus says in John 16:14, *"He shall glorify me: for he shall receive of mine, and shall show it unto you."* In a similar way, Christ sought not His own glory, but the glory of Him that sent Him, that is, the Father. (See John 7:18.)

From all these passages, it is evident that the Holy Spirit in His present work, while possessed of all the attributes of Deity, is subordinated to the Father and to the Son. On the other hand, we shall see later that in His earthly life, Jesus lived and taught and worked in the power of the Holy Spirit.

5

THE PERSON AND WORK OF THE HOLY SPIRIT AS REVEALED IN HIS NAMES

At least twenty-five different names are used in the Old and New Testaments in speaking of the Holy Spirit. There is the deepest significance in these names. Through a careful study of them, we find a wonderful revelation of the person and work of the Holy Spirit.

1. The Spirit

The simplest name by which the Holy Spirit is mentioned in the Bible is that which stands at the head of this paragraph: "*The Spirit.*" This name is also used as the basis of other names, so we begin our study with this. The Greek and Hebrew words so translated literally mean, "breath" or "wind." Both thoughts are in the name as applied to the Holy Spirit.

The thought of breath is brought out in John 20:22, where we read, "*And when he had said this, he breathed on them, and saith unto them, Receive ye the Holy Ghost.*" It is also suggested in Genesis 2:7: "*And the Lord God formed man of the dust of the ground, and breathed into his nostrils the breath of life; and man became a living soul.*" This becomes more evident when we compare this with Psalm 104:30: "*Thou sendest forth thy spirit, they are created: and thou renewest the face of the earth*"; and with Job 33:4: "*The spirit of God hath made me, and the breath of the Almighty hath given me life.*" What is the significance of this name from the standpoint of these passages? It is that the Spirit is the outbreathing of God, His inmost life going forth in a personal form to enliven.

When we receive the Holy Spirit, we receive the inmost life of God Himself to dwell in a personal way in us. When we really grasp this thought, it is overwhelming in its solemnity. Just stop and think what it means to have the inmost life of that infinite and eternal Being whom we call God dwelling in a personal way in you. How solemn and how awesome and yet unspeakably glorious life becomes when we realize this.

The thought of the Holy Spirit as the Wind is brought out in the following Scripture passage.

> *That which is born of the flesh is flesh; and that which is born of the Spirit is spirit. Marvel not that I said unto thee, Ye must be born again. The wind bloweth where it listeth, and thou hearest the sound thereof, but canst not tell whence it cometh, and whither it goeth: so is every one that is born of the Spirit.* (John 3:6–8)

In the Greek, the same word is translated in one part of this passage as *"Spirit"* and in another part of the passage as *"wind."* It would seem as if the word ought to be translated the same way in both parts of the passage. It would then read, "That which is born of the flesh is flesh; and that which is born of the 'Wind' is wind. Marvel not that I said unto thee, Ye must be born again. The wind bloweth where it listeth, and thou hearest the sound thereof, but canst not tell whence it cometh, and whither it goeth: so is everyone that is born of the 'Wind.'" The full significance of this name as applied to the Holy Spirit (or Holy Wind) may be beyond us to fathom, but we can see at least this much of its meaning through the following sections.

Sovereignty

The Spirit, like the wind, is sovereign. *"The wind bloweth where it listeth"* (John 3:8). You cannot dictate to the wind. It does as it wills. It is the same with the Holy Spirit: He is sovereign; we cannot dictate to Him. He divides *"to every man severally as he will"* (1 Corinthians 12:11). When the wind is blowing from the north, you may long to have it blow from the south. But cry as noisily as you can to the wind, "Blow from the south," and it will keep right on blowing from the north.

Although you cannot dictate to the wind while it blows as it will, you may learn the laws that govern the wind's motions. By bringing yourself into harmony with these laws, you can get the wind to do your work. You can erect your windmill so that, whichever way the wind blows from, the wheels will turn and the wind will grind your grain or pump your water.

In the same way, while we cannot dictate to the Holy Spirit, we can learn the laws of His operations. By bringing ourselves into harmony with those laws—above all, by submitting our wills absolutely to His sovereign will—the sovereign Spirit of God will work through us and accomplish His own glorious work by our instrumentality.

Invisible yet Mighty

The Spirit, like the wind, is invisible but nonetheless perceptible and real and mighty. You hear the sound of the wind (see John 3:8), but the wind itself you never see. You hear the voice of the Spirit, but He Himself is ever invisible. (The word translated *"sound"* in John 3:8 is the word that is translated *"voice"* elsewhere in Scripture and here in other versions.) We not only hear the voice of the wind, but we also see its mighty effects. We feel the breath of the wind upon our cheeks; we see the dust and the leaves blowing before the wind; we see the vessels at sea driven swiftly toward their ports. All along, the wind itself remains invisible. It is the same with the Spirit; we feel His breath upon our souls and see the mighty things He does, but we do not see Him. He is invisible, but He is real and perceptible.

I will never forget a solemn hour in Chicago Avenue Church in Chicago. Dr. W. W. White was making a farewell address before going to India to work among the students there. Suddenly, without any apparent warning, the place was filled with an awesome and glorious Presence. It was very real to me, but the question arose in my mind, "Is this merely subjective, just a feeling of my own, or is there an objective Presence here?" After the meeting was over, I asked different people whether they were conscious of anything and found that, at the same point in the meeting, they too became distinctly conscious of an overwhelming Presence, the Presence of the Holy Spirit, although they saw no one. Though many years have passed, there are those who speak of that hour to this day.

On another occasion in my own home in Chicago, when kneeling in prayer with an intimate friend, it seemed as if an unseen and awesome Presence entered the room as we prayed. I realized what Eliphaz meant when he said, *"Then a spirit passed before my face; the hair of my flesh stood up"* (Job 4:15). The moment was overwhelming but as glorious as it was awesome.

These are but two illustrations of many that might be given. None of us have seen the Holy Spirit at any time, but we have been distinctly conscious again and again and again of His presence. We have witnessed His mighty power, and we cannot doubt His reality. There are those who tell us that they do not believe in anything that they cannot see. Not one of them has ever seen the wind, but they all believe in the wind. They have felt the wind, and they have seen its effects. In the same way, we, beyond a doubt, have felt the mighty presence of the Spirit and witnessed His mighty workings.

Inscrutable

The Spirit, like the wind, is inscrutable. *"Thou...canst not tell whence it cometh, and whither it goeth"* (John 3:8). Nothing in nature is more mysterious than the wind. Even more mysterious still is the Holy Spirit in His operations. We hear of how suddenly and unexpectedly in widely separated communities He begins to work His mighty work. Doubtless there are hidden reasons why He thus begins His work, but often these reasons are completely undiscoverable by us. We know not where He comes from or where He goes. We cannot tell where He will display His mighty and gracious power next.

Indispensable

The Spirit, like the wind, is indispensable. Without wind, that is "air in motion," there is no life, and so Jesus says, *"Verily, verily, I say unto thee, except a man be born of water and of the Spirit, he cannot enter into the kingdom of God"* (John 3:5). If the wind should absolutely cease to blow for a single hour, most of the life on this earth would cease to be.

Time and again, when health reports for different cities of the United States are issued, it is found that the five healthiest cities in the United States were five cities located on the Great Lakes. Many have been surprised at this report when they have visited some of these cities and found that they were far from being the cleanest cities or the most sanitary in their general arrangement. Yet year after year, this fact has been reported. The explanation is simply this: It is the wind blowing from the lakes that has brought life and health to the cities. Just so, when the Spirit ceases to blow in any heart or any church or any community, death ensues; but when the Spirit blows steadily upon the individual or the church or the community, there is abounding spiritual life and health.

Life-Giving

Closely related to the foregoing thought is the fact that, like the wind, the Holy Spirit is life-giving. This thought comes out again and again in the Scriptures. For example, we read in John 6:63 (ASV), *"It is the spirit that giveth life,"* and in 2 Corinthians 3:6 we read, *"The letter killeth, but the spirit giveth life."* Perhaps the most suggestive passage on this point is Ezekiel 37:8–10. (Compare John 3:5.)

> *And when I beheld, lo, the sinews and the flesh came up upon them, and the skin covered them above: but there was no breath in them. Then said he unto me, Prophesy unto the wind, prophesy, son of man, and say to the wind, Thus saith the Lord God; Come from the four winds, O breath, and breathe upon these slain, that they may live. So I prophesied as he commanded me, and the breath came into them, and they lived, and stood up upon their feet, an exceeding great army.*

Israel, in the prophet's vision, was only bones, very many and very dry (see verses 2, 11), until the prophet proclaimed to them the word of God. Then there was a noise and a shaking, and the bones came together; bone joined to bone, and sinews and flesh came upon the bones. But still there was no life. When the wind blew the breath of God's Spirit, however, then they *"stood up upon their feet, an exceeding great army."*

All life in the individual believer, the teacher, the preacher, and the church is the Holy Spirit's work. Perhaps you might make the acquaintance of a man, and as you hear him talk and observe his conduct, you are repelled and disgusted. Everything about him declares that he is a dead man, a moral corpse—and not only dead but also rapidly decaying. You get away from him as quickly as you can. Months afterward you meet him again. You hesitate to speak to him; you want to get out of his very presence. But you do speak to him, and he has not uttered many sentences before you notice a marvelous change. His conversation is sweet and wholesome and uplifting; everything about his manner is attractive and delightful. You soon discover that the man's whole conduct and life has been transformed. He is no longer a decaying corpse but a living child of God. What has happened? The Wind of God has blown upon him; he has received the Holy Spirit, the Holy Wind.

Some quiet Sabbath day, you visit a church. Everything about the outward appointments of the church are all that could be desired. There is an attractive meetinghouse, an expensive organ, a gifted choir, a scholarly preacher. The service is well arranged, but you have not been long at the gathering before you are forced to see that there is no life, that it is all form and that there is nothing really being accomplished for God or for man. You go away with a heavy heart. Months after you have occasion to visit the church again. The outward appointments of the church are much as they were before, but the service has not proceeded far before you note a great difference. There is a new power in the singing, a new spirit in the prayer, a new grip in the preaching; everything about the church is teeming with the life of God. What has happened? The Wind of God has blown upon that church; the Holy Spirit, the Holy Wind, has come.

You go some day to hear a preacher of whose abilities you have heard great reports. As he stands up to preach, you soon learn that almost all of what has been said in praise of his abilities has been from the merely intellectual and rhetorical standpoint. His diction is faultless, his style beautiful, his logic unimpeachable, his orthodoxy beyond criticism. It is an intellectual treat to listen to him. Yet as he preaches, you cannot avoid a feeling of sadness, for there is no real grip, no real power, indeed, no reality of any kind in the man's preaching. You go away with a heavy heart at the thought of this waste of magnificent abilities. Months, perhaps years, pass by. You again find yourself listening to this celebrated preacher, but what a change! The same faultless diction, the same beautiful style, the same unimpeachable logic, the same skillful articulation, the same sound orthodoxy, but now there is something more. There is reality, life, grip, and power in the preaching. Men and women sit breathless as he speaks, sinners bowed with tears of contrition, pricked to their hearts with conviction of sin. Men and women and boys and girls renounce their selfishness, their sin, and their worldliness and accept Jesus Christ and surrender their lives to Him. What has happened? The Wind of God has blown upon that man. He has been filled with the Holy Wind.

Irresistible

Like the wind, the Holy Spirit is irresistible.

We read in Acts 1:8,

> *But ye shall receive power, after that the Holy Ghost is come upon you: and ye shall be witnesses unto me both in Jerusalem, and in all Judaea, and in Samaria, and unto the uttermost part of the earth.*

When this promise of our Lord was fulfilled in Stephen, we read, "*And they were not able to resist the wisdom and the spirit by which he spake*" (Acts 6:10). A man filled with the Holy Spirit is transformed into a cyclone, or tornado. What can stand before the wind? When St. Cloud, Minnesota, was visited with a tornado years ago, the wind picked up loaded freight cars and carried them off the track. It wrenched an iron bridge from its foundations, twisted it together, and hurled it away. When a tornado later visited St. Louis, Missouri, it cut off telegraph poles a foot in diameter as if they had been pipe stems. It cut off enormous trees close to the root, and it cut off the corner of brick buildings where it passed as though they had been cut by a knife. Nothing could stand before it. In the same way, nothing can stand before a Spirit-filled preacher of the Word.

None can resist the wisdom and the Spirit by which he speaks. The Wind of God took possession of Charles G. Finney, an obscure country lawyer, and sent him through New York state, then through New England, then through England, mowing down strong men by his resistless, Spirit-given logic. One night in Rochester, scores of lawyers, led by the justice of the Court of Appeals, filed out of the pews and bowed in the aisles and yielded their lives to God.

The Wind of God took possession of D. L. Moody, an uneducated young businessman in Chicago. In the power of this resistless Wind, men, women, and young people were mowed down before his words, brought in humble confession and renunciation of sin to the feet of Jesus Christ, and filled with the life of God. They have been the pillars in the churches of

Great Britain and throughout the world ever since. The great need today in individuals, in churches, and in preachers is that the Wind of God blow upon us.

Much of the difficulty that many find with John 3:5, *"Jesus answered, Verily, verily, I say unto thee, except a man be born of water and of the Spirit, he cannot enter into the kingdom of God,"* would disappear if we would only bear in mind that *"Spirit"* means "wind" and translate the verse literally: "Except a man be born of water and Wind [there is no *"the"* in the original], he cannot enter the kingdom of God." The thought would then seem to be, "Except a man be born of the cleansing and quickening power of the Spirit," or unless a man be born of the "cleansing Word" (compare John 15:3; Ephesians 5:26; James 1:18; 1 Peter 1:23), "and the quickening power of the Holy Spirit."

2. *The Spirit of God*

The Holy Spirit is frequently spoken of in the Bible as the Spirit of God. For example, *"Know ye not that ye are the temple of God, and that the Spirit of God dwelleth in you?"* (1 Corinthians 3:16). In this name we have the same essential thought as in the former name but with this addition: that His divine origin, nature, and power are emphasized. He is not merely "the Wind" as seen in number one above but rather "The Wind of God."

3. *The Spirit of Jehovah*

This name of the Holy Spirit is used in Isaiah 11:2 (ASV): *"And the Spirit of Jehovah shall rest upon him."* The thought of the name is essentially the same as the preceding with the exception that God is here thought of as the covenant God of Israel. He is thus spoken of in the connection in which the name is found. The Bible, following that unerring accuracy that it always exhibits in its use of the different names for God, thus speaks of the Spirit as the Spirit of Jehovah and not merely as the Spirit of God.

4. The Spirit of the Lord Jehovah

The Holy Spirit is called *"the Spirit of the Lord Jehovah"* in Isaiah 61:1 (ASV):

> *The Spirit of the Lord Jehovah is upon me; because Jehovah hath anointed me to preach good tidings unto the meek; he hath sent me to bind up the broken-hearted, to proclaim liberty to the captives.*

The Holy Spirit is here spoken of not merely as the Spirit of Jehovah but as the Spirit of the Lord Jehovah because of the relation in which God Himself is spoken of in this connection. He is spoken of as not merely Jehovah, the covenant God of Israel, but as Jehovah, Israel's Lord as well as their covenant-keeping God. This name of the Spirit is even more expressive than the name: "the Spirit of God."

5. The Spirit of the Living God

The Holy Spirit is called *"the Spirit of the living God"* in 2 Corinthians 3:3:

> *Forasmuch as ye are manifestly declared to be the epistle of Christ ministered by us, written not with ink, but with the Spirit of the living God; not in tables of stone, but in fleshly tables of the heart.*

What is the significance of this name? It is made clear by the context. The apostle Paul is drawing a contrast between the Word of God written with ink on parchment and the Word of God written on *"fleshly tables of the heart"* by the Holy Spirit. In this connection, the Holy Spirit is called *"the Spirit of the living God"* because He makes God a living reality in our personal experience instead of a mere intellectual concept.

There are many who believe in God and who are perfectly orthodox in their conception of God, but, after all, God is only an intellectual theological proposition to them. It is the work of the Holy Spirit to make God something vastly more than a theological notion, no matter how orthodox. He is the Spirit of the living God, and it is His work to make God a living God to us, a Being whom we know, with whom we have personal acquaintance, a Being more real to us than the most intimate human friend we have. Have you a real God? Well, you may have. The Holy Spirit is the Spirit of the living God, and He is able and ready to give to you a living God, to make God real in your personal experience.

There are many who have a God who once lived and acted and spoke, a God who lived and acted at the creation of the universe, who perhaps lived and acted in the days of Moses and Elijah and Jesus Christ and the apostles, but who no longer lives and acts. If He exists at all, He has withdrawn Himself from any active part in nature and the history of man. He created nature, gave it laws and powers and now leaves it to run itself. He created man and endowed him with his various faculties but has now left him to work out his own destiny. They may go further than this; they may believe in a God who spoke to Abraham and to Moses and to David and to Isaiah and to Jesus and to the apostles but who speaks no longer. We may read in the Bible what He spoke to these various men, but we expect that He will not speak to us.

In contrast with these, it is the work of the Holy Spirit, the Spirit of the living God, to help us to know a God who lives and acts and speaks today, a God who is ready to come as near to us as He came to Abraham, to Moses, to Isaiah, to the apostles, or to Jesus Himself. Not that He has any new revelations to make for He guided the apostles into all the truth (see John 16:13), but though there has been a complete revelation of God's truth made in the Bible, still God lives today and will speak to us as directly as He spoke to His chosen ones of old. Happy is the man who knows the Holy Spirit as the Spirit of the living God, and who, consequently, has a real God, a God who lives today, a God upon whom he can depend today to undertake for him, a God with whom he enjoys intimate personal fellowship, a God to whom he may raise his voice in prayer, and a God who speaks back to him.

6. The Spirit of Christ

"But ye are not in the flesh, but in the Spirit, if so be that the Spirit of God dwell in you. Now if any man have not the Spirit of Christ, he is none of his" (Romans 8:9). The Holy Spirit is called *"the Spirit of Christ." "The Spirit of Christ"* in this passage does not mean a Christlike spirit. It means something far more than that—it is a name of the Holy Spirit. Why is the Holy Spirit called the Spirit of Christ? For several reasons.

He Is Christ's Gift

The Holy Spirit is not merely the gift of the Father but also the gift of the Son. We read in John 20:22 that Jesus *"breathed on them, and saith unto them, Receive ye the Holy Ghost."* The Holy Spirit is therefore the breath of Christ as well as the breath of God the Father. It is Christ who breathes upon us and imparts to us the Holy Spirit.

In John 14:15–26, Jesus teaches us that it is in answer to His prayer that the Father gives to us the Holy Spirit. In Acts 2:33 we read that Jesus, *"being by the right hand of God exalted, and having received of the Father the promise of the Holy Ghost,"* shed Him forth upon believers. That verse says that Jesus, having been exalted to the right hand of God in answer to His prayer, receives the Holy Spirit from the Father and sheds forth upon the church Him whom He has received from the Father. In Matthew 3:11 we read that it is Jesus who baptizes with the Holy Spirit. In John 7:37–39 Jesus bade all who are thirsty to come unto Him and drink, and the context makes it clear that the water that He gives is the Holy Spirit, who becomes a source of life and power flowing out to others, in those who receive Him. It is the glorified Christ who gives to the church the Holy Spirit. In John 4:10, Jesus declares that He is the One who gives the living water, the Holy Spirit. In all these passages, Christ is set forth as the One who gives the Holy Spirit, so the Holy Spirit is called *"the Spirit of Christ."*

He Reveals Christ

There is a deeper reason why the Holy Spirit is called *"the Spirit of Christ"*; it is the work of the Holy Spirit to reveal Christ to us. In John 16:14, we read, "[The Holy Spirit] *shall glorify me: for he shall receive of mine, and shall show it unto you.*" In a similar way it is written, "*But when the Comforter is come, whom I will send unto you from the Father, even the Spirit of truth, which proceedeth from the Father, he shall testify of me*" (John 15:26). This is the work of the Holy Spirit: to bear witness of Christ and reveal Jesus Christ to men. And as the revealer of Christ, He is called "*the Spirit of Christ.*"

He Forms Christ in Us

There is a still deeper reason yet why the Holy Spirit is called "*the Spirit of Christ*"; it is His work to form Christ as a living presence within us. In Ephesians 3:16–17, the apostle Paul prays to the Father,

> *That he would grant you, according to the riches of his glory, to be strengthened with might by his Spirit in the inner man; that Christ may dwell in your hearts by faith.*

This then is the work of the Holy Spirit: to cause Christ to dwell in our hearts, to form the living Christ within us. Just as the Holy Spirit literally and physically formed Jesus Christ in the womb of the Virgin Mary (see Luke 1:35), so the Holy Spirit spiritually but really forms Jesus Christ within our hearts today. Jesus told His disciples that when the Holy Spirit came, He Himself would come; that is, the result of the coming of the Holy Spirit to dwell in their hearts would be the coming of Christ Himself.

> *And I will pray the Father, and he shall give you another Comforter, that he may abide with you for ever; even the Spirit of truth; whom the world cannot receive, because it seeth him not, neither knoweth him: but ye know him; for he dwelleth with you, and shall be in you. I will not leave you comfortless: I will come to you.* (John 14:16–18)

It is the privilege of every believer in Christ to have the living Christ formed by the power of the Holy Spirit in his own heart; therefore, the

Holy Spirit who thus forms Christ within the heart is called the Spirit of Christ. How wonderful! How glorious is the significance of this name. Let us ponder it until we understand it, as far as it is possible to understand it, and until we rejoice exceedingly in the glory of it.

7. *The Spirit of Jesus Christ*

The Holy Spirit is called *"the Spirit of Jesus Christ"* in Philippians 1:19: *"For I know that this shall turn to my salvation through your prayer, and the supply of the Spirit of Jesus Christ."* The Spirit is not merely the Spirit of the eternal Word but the Spirit of the Word incarnate; not merely the Spirit of Christ but the Spirit of Jesus Christ. It is the Man Jesus, exalted at the right hand of the Father, who receives and sends the Spirit. This is why we read in Acts 2:32–33,

> *This Jesus hath God raised up, whereof we all are witnesses. Therefore being by the right hand of God exalted, and having received of the Father the promise of the Holy Ghost, he hath shed forth this, which ye now see and hear.*

8. *The Spirit of Jesus*

The Holy Spirit is called *"the Spirit of Jesus"* in Acts 16:6–7 (ASV),

> *And they went through the region of Phrygia and Galatia, having been forbidden of the Holy Spirit to speak the word in Asia; and when they were come over against Mysia, they assayed to go into Bithynia; and the Spirit of Jesus suffered them not.*

By using the name *"the Spirit of Jesus,"* the thought of the relation of the Spirit to the Man Jesus is still more clear than in the name preceding this, the Spirit of Jesus Christ.

9. The Spirit of His Son

The Holy Spirit is called *"the Spirit of his Son"* in Galatians 4:6: *"And because ye are sons, God hath sent forth the Spirit of his Son into your hearts, crying, Abba, Father."* We see from the context of the preceding verses that this name is given to the Holy Spirit in special connection with His testifying to the sonship of the believer:

> *But when the fulness of the time was come, God sent forth his Son, made of a woman, made under the law, to redeem them that were under the law, that we might receive the adoption of sons.* (Galatians 4:4–5)

It is *"the Spirit of His Son"* who testifies to our sonship. The thought is that the Holy Spirit is a filial Spirit, a Spirit who produces a sense of sonship in us. If we receive the Holy Spirit, we no longer think of God as if we were serving under constraint and bondage but as sons living in joyous liberty. We do not fear God; we trust Him and rejoice in Him. When we receive the Holy Spirit, we do not receive a *"spirit of bondage again to fear"* but *"the Spirit of adoption, whereby we cry, Abba, Father"* (Romans 8:15). This name of the Holy Spirit is one of the most suggestive of all. We do well to ponder it long until we realize the glad fullness of its significance. We will take it up again when we come to study the work of the Holy Spirit.

10. The Holy Spirit

This name occurs frequently and is the name with which most of us are familiar. One of the most well-known passages in which the name is used is Luke 11:13: *"If ye then, being evil, know how to give good gifts unto your children: how much more shall your heavenly Father give the Holy Spirit to them that ask him?"* This name emphasizes the essential moral character of the Spirit. He is holy in Himself. We are so familiar with the name that we neglect to weigh its significance. Oh, if we only realized more deeply and constantly that He is the *Holy* Spirit! We would do well if we, as the seraphim in Isaiah's vision, would bow in His presence and cry, *"Holy, holy, holy"* (Isaiah 6:3). Yet how thoughtlessly we often talk about Him and pray for Him to help us. We pray for Him to come into our churches and into our hearts, but what would He find if He should come there? Would He not find much that would be painful and agonizing to Him?

What would we think if vile women from the lowest den of iniquity in a great city should go to the purest woman in the city and invite her to come and live with them in their disgusting vileness with no intention of changing their evil ways? But that would not be as shocking as you and I asking the Holy Spirit to come and dwell in our hearts when we have no intentions of giving up our impurity or our selfishness or our worldliness or our sin. It would not be as shocking as it is for us to invite the Holy Spirit to come into our churches when they are full of worldliness and selfishness and contention and envy and pride and all that is unholy.

However, if the denizens of the lowest and vilest den of infamy should go to the purest and most Christlike woman asking her to go and dwell with them with the intention of putting away everything that was vile and evil and giving to this holy and Christlike woman the entire control of the place, she would go. And as sinful and selfish and imperfect as we may be, the infinitely holy Spirit is ready to come and take His dwelling in our hearts if we will surrender to Him the absolute control of our lives and allow Him to bring everything in thought and fancy and feeling and purpose and imagination and action into conformity with His will. The infinitely holy Spirit is ready to come into our churches, however imperfect and worldly they may be now, if we are willing to put the absolute control of everything in His hands. But let us never forget that He is the Holy Spirit; when we pray for Him, let us pray for Him as such.

11. The Holy Spirit of Promise

The Holy Spirit is called *"the holy Spirit of promise"* in Ephesians 1:13: *"In whom ye also trusted, after that ye heard the word of truth, the gospel of your salvation: in whom also after that ye believed, ye were sealed with that holy*

Spirit of promise." We have here the same name as that given above with the added thought that this Holy Spirit is the great promise of the Father and of the Son. The Holy Spirit is God's great, all-inclusive promise for the present dispensation. The one thing for which Jesus bade the disciples wait after His ascension before they undertook His work was *"the promise of the Father"* (Acts 1:4), that is the Holy Spirit.

The great promise of the Father until the coming of Christ was the coming atoning Savior and King. When Jesus came and died His atoning death upon the cross of Calvary and arose and ascended to the right hand of the Father, then the second great promise of the Father was the Holy Spirit, to take the place of our absent Lord. (See Acts 2:33.)

12. *The Spirit of Holiness*

The Holy Spirit is called *"the spirit of holiness"* in Romans 1:4: *"And declared to be the Son of God with power, according to the spirit of holiness, by the resurrection from the dead."* At first glance, it may seem as if there were no essential differences between the two names—that is, the Holy Spirit and the Spirit of Holiness—but there is a marked difference. *Holy Spirit,* as already said, emphasizes the essential moral character of the Spirit as holy. *Spirit of Holiness,* however, brings out the thought that the Holy Spirit is not merely holy in Himself but He imparts holiness to others. The perfect holiness that He Himself possesses He imparts to those who receive Him. (Compare 1 Peter 1:2.)

13. *The Spirit of Judgment*

The Holy Spirit is called *"the spirit of judgment"* in Isaiah 4:4: *"When the Lord shall have washed away the filth of the daughters of Zion, and shall have purged the blood of Jerusalem from the midst thereof by the spirit of judgment, and by the spirit of burning."* There are two names of the Holy Spirit in this passage. The first is the Spirit of Judgment. The Holy Spirit is so called because it is His work to bring sin to light, to convict of sin. (Compare John 16:7–9.) When the Holy Spirit comes to us, the first thing He does is open our eyes to see our sins as God sees them. He judges our sin. (We will go into this more at length in studying John 16:7–11 when considering the work of the Holy Spirit.)

14. *The Spirit of Burning*

This name is also used in Isaiah 4:4. This name emphasizes His searching, refining, rubbish-consuming, illuminating, and energizing work. The Holy Spirit is like a fire in the heart in which He dwells, and as fire tests and refines and consumes and illuminates and warms and energizes, so does He. It is the cleansing work of the Holy Spirit that is especially emphasized in this context. (See Isaiah 4:3–4.)

15. *The Spirit of Truth*

The Holy Spirit is called *"the Spirit of truth"* in John 14:17: *"Even the Spirit of truth; whom the world cannot receive, because it seeth him not, neither knoweth him: but ye know him; for he dwelleth with you, and shall be in you."* (Compare John 15:26; 16:13.) The Holy Spirit is called the Spirit of Truth because it is the work of the Holy Spirit to communicate and to impart truth to those who receive Him. This comes out in John 19:14, and, if possible, it comes out even more clearly in John 16:13: *"Howbeit when he, the Spirit of truth, is come, he will guide you into all truth: for he shall not speak of himself; but whatsoever he shall hear, that shall he speak: and he will show you things to come."* All truth is from the Holy Spirit. It is only as He teaches us that we come to know the truth.

16. *The Spirit of Wisdom and Understanding*

The Holy Spirit is called *"the spirit of wisdom and understanding"* in Isaiah 11:2: *"And the spirit of the LORD shall rest upon him, the spirit of wisdom and understanding, the spirit of counsel and might, the spirit of knowledge and of the fear of the LORD."* The significance of the name is so plain as to need no explanation. It is evident, both from the words used and from the context, that it is the work of the Holy Spirit to impart wisdom and understanding to those who receive Him. Those who receive the Holy Spirit receive the Spirit *"of power, and of love, and of a sound mind* [or sound sense]" (2 Timothy 1:7).

17. The Spirit of Counsel and Might

We find this name used of the Holy Spirit in Isaiah 11:2, as well. The meaning of this name is also obvious; the Holy Spirit is called *"the spirit of counsel and might"* because He gives us counsel in all our plans and strength to carry them out. (Compare Acts 1:8; 8:29; 16:6–7.) It is our privilege to have God's own counsel in all our plans and God's strength in all the work that we undertake for Him. We receive them by receiving the Holy Spirit, *"the spirit of counsel and might."*

18. The Spirit of Knowledge and of the Fear of the Lord

This name is also used in Isaiah 11:2. The significance of this name is obvious. It is the work of the Holy Spirit to impart knowledge to us and to beget in us a reverence for Jehovah, a reverence that reveals itself above all in obedience to His commandments. The one who receives the Holy Spirit finds his delight *"in the fear of the LORD"* (Isaiah 11:3). The three suggestive names just given refer especially to the gracious work of the Holy Spirit in the servant of the Lord, that is, Jesus Christ. (See Isaiah 11:1–5.)

19. The Spirit of Life

The Holy Spirit is called *"the Spirit of life"* in Romans 8:2: *"For the law of the Spirit of life in Christ Jesus hath made me free from the law of sin and death."* The Holy Spirit is called the Spirit of Life because it is His work to impart life. (Compare John 6:63 RV; Ezekiel 37:1–10.) In the context of Romans 8:2, beginning back in Romans 7:7, Paul is drawing a contrast between the law of Moses outside a man—holy and just and good, it is true, but impotent—and the living Spirit of God in the heart, imparting spiritual and moral life to the believer and thus enabling him to meet the requirements of the law of God. He draws this contrast to show that what the law alone could not do, in that it was weak through the flesh, the Spirit of God imparting life to the believer and dwelling in the heart enables him to do. Therefore, the righteousness of the law is fulfilled in those who walk not after the flesh but after the Spirit:

> *For the law of the Spirit of life in Christ Jesus hath made me free from the law of sin and death. For what the law could not do, in that it was weak through the flesh, God sending his own Son in the likeness of sinful flesh, and for sin, condemned sin in the flesh: that the righteousness of the law might be fulfilled in us, who walk not after the flesh, but after the Spirit.* (Romans 8:2–4)

The Holy Spirit is therefore called the Spirit of Life because He imparts spiritual life and consequent victory over sin to those who receive Him.

20. The Oil of Gladness

The Holy Spirit is called "*the oil of gladness*" in Hebrews 1:9: "*Thou hast loved righteousness, and hated iniquity; therefore God, even thy God, hath anointed thee with the oil of gladness above thy fellows.*" Someone may ask what reason have we for supposing that "*the oil of gladness*" in this passage is a name of the Holy Spirit. The answer is found in a comparison of Hebrews 1:9 with Acts 10:38 and Luke 4:18. In Acts 10:38, we read, "*How God anointed Jesus of Nazareth with the Holy Ghost and with power.*" In Luke 4:18, Jesus Himself is recorded as saying, "*The Spirit of the Lord is upon me, because he hath anointed me to preach the gospel to the poor.*" In both of these passages, we are told it was the Holy Spirit with which Jesus was anointed. As in the passage in Hebrews, we are told that it was with the oil of gladness that He was anointed; therefore, of course, the only possible conclusion is that the oil of gladness means the Holy Spirit. What a beautiful and suggestive name it is for Him whose fruit is, first, "*love*" and then "*joy*" (Galatians 5:22).

The Holy Spirit becomes a source of boundless joy to those who receive Him. He so fills and satisfies the soul that the soul who receives Him "*shall never thirst*" (John 4:14). No matter how great the afflictions with which the believer receives the Word, still he will have the "*joy of the Holy Ghost*" (1 Thessalonians 1:6).

On the day of Pentecost, when the disciples were baptized with the Holy Spirit, they were so filled with ecstatic joy that others looking on them thought they were intoxicated. They said, "*These men are full of new wine*" (Acts 2:13). Paul draws a comparison between abnormal intoxication that comes through excess of wine and the wholesome exhilaration from which there is no reaction that comes through being filled with the Spirit:

> *And be not drunk with wine, wherein is excess; but be filled with the Spirit; speaking to yourselves in psalms and hymns and spiritual songs, singing and making melody in your heart to the Lord; giving thanks always for all things unto God and the Father in the name of our Lord Jesus Christ.* (Ephesians 5:18–20)

When God anoints one with the Holy Spirit, it is as if He broke a precious alabaster box of oil of gladness above their heads until it ran down to the hem of their garments and the whole person was suffused with joy unspeakable and full of glory.

21. *The Spirit of Grace*

The Holy Spirit is called "*the Spirit of grace*" in Hebrews 10:29:

> *Of how much sorer punishment, suppose ye, shall he be thought worthy, who hath trodden under foot the Son of God, and hath counted the blood of the covenant, wherewith he was sanctified, an unholy thing, and hath done despite unto the Spirit of grace?*

This name brings out the fact that it is the Holy Spirit's work to administer and apply the grace of God. He Himself is gracious, it is true, but the name means far more than that. The name means that He makes the manifold grace of God ours experientially. It is only by the work of the Spirit of Grace in our hearts that we are enabled to appropriate to ourselves that infinite fullness of grace that God has bestowed upon us from the beginning in Jesus Christ. It is ours from the beginning, as far as belonging to us is concerned, but it is only ours experientially as we claim it by the power of the Spirit of Grace.

22. The Spirit of Grace and of Supplication

The Holy Spirit is called *"the spirit of grace and of supplication"* in Zechariah 12:10 (RV):

> *And I will pour upon the house of David, and upon the inhabitants of Jerusalem, the spirit of grace and of supplication; and they shall look unto me whom they have pierced; and they shall mourn for him, as one mourneth for his only son, and shall be in bitterness for him, as one that is in bitterness for his firstborn.*

The phrase *"the spirit of grace and of supplication"* in this passage is beyond a doubt a name of the Holy Spirit.

We have already studied the name *"the Spirit of grace"* in the previous section, but here there is a further thought of that operation of grace that leads us to pray intensely. The Holy Spirit is so called because it is He who teaches us to pray because all true prayer is in the Spirit: *"But ye, beloved, building up yourselves on your most holy faith, praying in the Holy Ghost"* (Jude 1:20). We of ourselves know not how to pray as we ought, but it is the work of the Holy Spirit to make *"intercession for us with groanings which cannot be uttered"* (Romans 8:26) and to lead us out in prayer *"according to the will of God"* (verse 27). The secret of all true and effective praying is knowing the Holy Spirit as the Spirit of Grace and of Supplication.

23. *The Spirit of Glory*

The Holy Spirit is called *"the spirit of glory"* in 1 Peter 4:14: *"If ye be reproached for the name of Christ, happy are ye; for the spirit of glory and of God resteth upon you: on their part he is evil spoken of, but on your part he is glorified."* This name does not merely teach that the Holy Spirit is infinitely glorious Himself, but rather it teaches that He imparts the glory of God to us, just as the Spirit of Truth imparts truth to us. As the Spirit of Life imparts life to us; as the Spirit of Wisdom and Understanding and of Counsel and Might and Knowledge and the Fear of the LORD imparts to us wisdom and understanding and counsel and might and knowledge and the fear of the LORD; and as the Spirit of Grace applies and administers to us the manifold grace of God; so too the Spirit of Glory is the administrator to us of God's glory.

In the immediately preceding verse we read, *"But rejoice, inasmuch as ye are partakers of Christ's sufferings; that, when his glory shall be revealed, ye may be glad also with exceeding joy"* (1 Peter 4:13). It is in this connection that He is called the Spirit of Glory. We find a similar connection between the sufferings that we endure and the glory that the Holy Spirit imparts to us:

> *The Spirit itself beareth witness with our spirit, that we are the children of God: and if children, then heirs; heirs of God, and joint-heirs with Christ; if so be that we suffer with him, that we may be also glorified together.* (Romans 8:16–17)

The Holy Spirit is the administrator of glory as well as grace, or rather, the grace that culminates in glory.

24. *The Eternal Spirit*

The Holy Spirit is called *"the eternal Spirit"* in Hebrews 9:14: *"How much more shall the blood of Christ, who through the eternal Spirit offered himself without spot to God, purge your conscience from dead works to serve the living God?"* The eternity and the deity and infinite majesty of the Holy Spirit are brought out by this name.

25. The Comforter

The Holy Spirit is called *"the Comforter"* over and over again in the Scriptures. For example, in John 14:26 we read, *"But the Comforter, which is the Holy Ghost, whom the Father will send in my name, he shall teach you all things, and bring all things to your remembrance, whatsoever I have said unto you."* And in John 15:26: *"But when the Comforter is come, whom I will send unto you from the Father, even the Spirit of truth, which proceedeth from the Father, he shall testify of me."* (See also John 16:7–16.)

The word translated *"Comforter"* in these passages means just that—"comforter," or "one who comforts"—but it also means much more besides. It is a word difficult to translate into any one word in English. The translators of the Revised Version found difficulty in deciding which word to use. They have suggested *"Advocate"* or *"Helper,"* in the margin, as well as a simple transference of the Greek word into English, *"Paraclete."*

The word translated *"Comforter"* literally means "one called to another's side"—the idea being of a person right at hand to take another's part. It is the same word that is translated "advocate" in 1 John 2:1: *"My little children, these things write I unto you, that ye sin not. And if any man sin, we have an advocate with the Father, Jesus Christ the righteous."* The word *advocate*, as we now understand it, does not give the full force of the Greek word so rendered. Etymologically, *advocate* means nearly the same thing. *Advocate* is from the Latin, *advocatus*, and means "one called to another to take his part." In our modern usage, however, the word has acquired a restricted meaning. The Greek word *parakletos* is translated *comforter* and means "one called alongside," that is, one called to stand constantly by our side and be ever ready to stand by us and take our part in everything in which his help is needed. It is a wonderfully tender and expressive name for the Holy One. Sometimes when we think of the Holy Spirit, He seems to be so far away. But when we think of the Parakletos, or, in plain English, our "Stand-byer" or "Part-taker," how near He is.

Up to the time that Jesus made this promise to the disciples, He Himself had been their *Parakletos*. When they were in any emergency or difficulty, they turned to Him. On one occasion, for example, the disciples were in doubt as to how to pray, and they turned to Jesus and said, *"Lord, teach us to pray"* (Luke 11:1). And the Lord taught them this wonderful prayer that has come down through the ages:

> *And he said unto them, When ye pray, say, Our Father which art in heaven, Hallowed be thy name. Thy kingdom come. Thy will be done, as in heaven, so in earth. Give us day by day our daily bread. And forgive us our sins; for we also forgive every one that is indebted to us. And lead us not into temptation; but deliver us from evil.*
> (Luke 11:2–4)

On another occasion, Peter was sinking in the waves of Galilee and cried, *"Lord, save me"* (Matthew 14:30), and *"immediately Jesus stretched forth his hand, and caught him"* (verse 31) and saved him. In every extremity, they turned to Him. Likewise, now that Jesus is gone to the Father, we have another person just as divine as He is, just as wise as He, just as strong, just as loving, just as tender, just as ready, and just as able to help—and He is always right by our side. Yes, better yet, He dwells in our hearts and will take hold and help if we only trust Him to do it.

If the truth of the Holy Spirit as set forth in the name *Parakletos* gets into our hearts and abides there, it will banish all loneliness forever; for how can we ever be lonely when this best of all friends is ever with us? In the last eight years, I have been called upon to endure what would naturally be a very lonely life. Most of the time I am separated from my wife and children by the calls of duty. For eighteen months consecutively, I was separated from almost all my family by many thousands of miles. The loneliness would have been unendurable were it not for the one all-sufficient Friend, who was always with me.

I recall one night walking up and down the deck of a storm-tossed steamer in the South Seas. Most of my family was eighteen thousand miles away; the remaining member of my family was not with me. The officers were busy on the bridge. I was pacing the deck alone, and the thought came to me, "Here you are all alone." Then another thought came, "I am not alone; by my side, as I walk this deck in the loneliness and the storm, walks the Holy Spirit," and He was enough. I said something like this once at a Bible conference in St. Paul. A doctor came to me at the close of the meeting and gently said, "I want to thank you for that thought about the Holy Spirit always being with us. I am a doctor. Often I have to drive far out in the country in the night and storm to attend a case, and I have often been so lonely, but I will never be lonely again. I will always know that by my side in my doctor's carriage, the Holy Spirit goes with me."

If this thought of the Holy Spirit as the ever-present Paraclete once gets into your heart and abides there, it will banish all fear forever. How can we be afraid in the face of any peril if this divine One is by our side to counsel us and to take our part? There may be a howling mob about us or a lowering storm; it does not matter. He stands between us and both mob and storm.

One night I had promised to walk four miles to a friend's house after an evening session of a conference. The path led along the side of a lake. As I started for my friend's house, a thunderstorm was coming up. I had not counted on this, but as I had promised, I felt I ought to go. The path led along the edge of the lake, oftentimes very near to the edge. Sometimes the lake was near the path and sometimes many feet below. The night was so dark with the clouds, I could not see ahead. Now and then there would be a blinding flash of lightning in which I could see where the path was washed away, and then it would be blacker than ever. I could hear the lake booming below. It seemed a dangerous place to walk. But that very week I had been speaking upon the personality of the Holy Spirit and about the Holy Spirit as an ever-present friend, and the thought came to me, "What was it you were telling the people in the address about the Holy Spirit as an ever-present friend?" And then I said to myself, "Between me and the boiling lake and the edge of the path walks the Holy Spirit," and I pushed on, fearless and glad.

When we were in London, a young lady attended the meeting one afternoon in the Royal Albert Hall. She had an abnormal fear of the dark. It was absolutely impossible for her to go into a dark room alone, but the thought of the Holy Spirit as an ever-present Friend sank into her mind. She went home and told her mother what a wonderful thought she had heard that day and how it had banished forever all fear from her. It was already growing very dark in the London winter afternoon, and her mother looked up and said, "Very well, let us see if it is real. Go up to the top of the house and shut yourself alone in a dark room." She instantly sprang to her feet, bounded up the stairs, went into a room that was totally dark, shut the door, and sat down. All fear was gone, and as she wrote the next day, the whole room seemed to be filled with a wonderful glory, the glory of the presence of the Holy Spirit.

In the thought of the Holy Spirit as the Paraclete there is also a cure for insomnia. For two awful years, I suffered from insomnia. Night after night, I would go to bed apparently almost dead from lack of sleep. It seemed as though I must sleep, but I could not sleep. Oh, the agony of those two years! It seemed as if I would lose my mind if I did not get relief. Relief came at last, and for years I went on without the suggestion of trouble from insomnia. Then one night I retired to my room in the institute and lay down expecting to fall asleep in a moment as I usually did. But scarcely had my head touched the pillow when I became aware that insomnia was back again. If one has ever had it, he never forgets it and never mistakes it. It seemed as if insomnia were sitting on the footboard of my bed, grinning at me and saying, "I am back again for another two years." "Oh," I thought, "two more awful years of insomnia."

However, that very morning, I had been lecturing to our students in the institute about the personality of the Holy Spirit and about the Holy Spirit as an ever-present friend. At once the thought came to me, "What were you talking to the students about this morning? What were you telling them?" And, I looked up and said, "Blessed Spirit of God, You are here. I am not alone. If You have anything to say to me, I will listen," and He began to open to me some of the deep and precious things about my Lord and Savior, things that filled my soul with joy and rest. The next thing I knew I was asleep, and the next thing I knew it was the following morning. So, whenever insomnia has come my way since, I have simply remembered that the Holy Spirit was there, and I have looked up to Him to speak to me and to teach me. He has done so, and insomnia has taken its flight.

In the thought of the Holy Spirit as the Paraclete, there is a cure for a breaking heart. How many aching, breaking hearts there are in this world of ours, so full of death and separation from those we most dearly love. Example after example could be given of a women who, a few months or a few weeks ago, had no care or no worry, for by her side was a Christian husband who was so wise and strong that the wife rested all responsibility upon him and walked carefree through life and was satisfied with his love and companionship. But one awful day, he was taken from her. She was left alone, and all the cares and responsibilities rested upon her. How empty that heart has been ever since; how empty the whole world has been. She has just dragged through her life and her duties as best she could with an aching and almost breaking heart. There is One, if she only knew it, wiser and more loving than the tenderest husband; One willing to bear all the care and responsibilities of life for her; One who is able, if she will only let Him, to fill every nook and corner of her empty and aching heart. That One is the Paraclete.

I said something like this in St. Andrew's Hall in Glasgow. At the close of the meeting a sad-faced Christian woman wearing a widow's garb came to me as I stepped out of the hall into the reception room. She hurried to me and said, "Dr. Torrey, this is the anniversary of my dear husband's death. Just one year ago today he was taken from me. I came today to see if you could not speak some word to help me. You have given me just the word I need. I will never be lonesome again." A year and a half passed by. I was on the yacht of a friend on the lochs of the Clyde. One day a little boat put out from shore and came alongside the yacht. One of the first to come up the side of the yacht was this widow. She hurried to me, and the first thing she said was, "The thought that you gave me that day in St. Andrew's Hall on the anniversary of my husband's leaving me has been with me ever since, and the Holy Spirit does satisfy me and fill my heart."

It is in our work for our Master that the thought of the Holy Spirit as the Paraclete comes with greatest helpfulness. I think it may be permissible to illustrate it from my own experience. I entered the ministry because I was literally forced to. For years I refused to become a Christian because I was determined that I would not be a preacher, and I feared that if I surrendered to Christ I must enter the ministry. My conversion turned upon my yielding to Him at this point. The night I yielded, I did not say, "I will accept Christ" or "I will give up sin," or anything of that sort. I simply cried, "Take this awful burden off my heart, and I will preach the gospel." But no one could be less fitted by natural temperament for the ministry than I.

From early boyhood, I was extraordinarily timid and bashful. Even after I had entered Yale College, when I would go home in the summer and my mother would call me in to meet her friends, I was so frightened that when I thought I was speaking, I actually did not make an audible sound. When her friends had gone, my mother would ask, "Why didn't you say something to them?" I would reply that I supposed I had, but my mother would say, "You did not utter a sound." Think of a young fellow like that entering the ministry. I never mustered courage even to speak in a public prayer meeting until after I was in the theological seminary. Then I felt, if I were to enter the ministry, I must be able to at least speak in a prayer meeting. I learned a little piece by heart to say, but when the hour came, I forgot much of it in my terror. At the critical moment, I grasped the back of the settee in front of me and pulled myself hurriedly to my feet and held on to the settee. My voice faltered. I repeated as much as I could remember and sat down. Think of a man like that entering the ministry.

In the early days of my ministry, I would write my sermons out in full and commit them to memory, stand up and twist a button until I had repeated it as best I could, and then sink back into the pulpit chair with a sense of relief that that was over for another week. I cannot tell you what I suffered in those early days of my ministry. But the glad day arrived when I came to know the Holy Spirit as the Paraclete. The thought got possession of me that when I stood up to preach, there was Another who stood by my side. While the audience saw me, God saw Him. The responsibility was all upon Him. He was abundantly able to meet it and care for it all. All I had to do was to stand back as far out of sight as possible and let Him do the work.

I have no dread of preaching now. Preaching is the greatest joy of my life. Sometimes when I stand up to speak and realize that He is there, that all the responsibility is upon Him, such a joy fills my heart that I can scarcely restrain myself from shouting and leaping. He is just as ready to help us in all our work, in our Sunday school classes, in our personal work, and in every other line of Christian effort.

Many hesitate to speak to others about accepting Christ. They are afraid they will not say the right thing; they fear that they will do more harm than they will good. You certainly will if you do it, but if you will just believe in the Paraclete and trust Him to say it and to say it in His way, you will never do harm but always good. It may seem at the time that you have accomplished nothing, but perhaps years later you will find out you have accomplished much. Even if you do not find it out in this world, you will find it out in eternity.

There are many ways in which the Paraclete stands by us and helps us, which we will examine at length when we come to study His work. He stands by us when we pray (see Romans 8:26–27); when we study the Word (see John 14:26; 16:12–14); when we do personal work (see Acts 8:29); when we preach or teach (see 1 Corinthians 2:4); when we are tempted (see Romans 8:2); and when we leave this world (see Acts 7:54–60). Let us get this thought firmly fixed now and for all time: that the Holy Spirit is One called to our side to take our part.

> Ever present, truest Friend,
>   Ever near, Thine aid to lend.

6

THE WORK OF THE HOLY SPIRIT IN THE MATERIAL UNIVERSE

There are many who think of the work of the Holy Spirit as limited to man, but God reveals to us in His Word that the Holy Spirit's work has a far wider scope than this. We are taught in the Bible that the Holy Spirit has a threefold work in the material universe.

Creation of the Material Universe

The creation of the material universe and of man is effected through the agency of the Holy Spirit. We read in Psalm 33:6, *"By the word of the Lord were the heavens made; and all the host of them by the breath of his mouth."* We have already seen in our study of the names of the Holy Spirit that the Holy Spirit is the breath of Jehovah, so this passage teaches us that all the hosts of heaven, all the stellar worlds, were made by the Holy Spirit. We are taught explicitly in Job 33:4 that the creation of man is the Holy Spirit's work. We read, *"The spirit of God hath made me, and the breath of the Almighty hath given me life."* Here, both the creation of the material frame and the impartation of life are attributed to the agency of the Holy Spirit.

In other passages of Scripture we are taught that creation was in and through the Son of God. For example we read in Colossians 1:16, *"For by him were all things created, that are in heaven, and that are in earth, visible and invisible, whether they be thrones, or dominions, or principalities, or powers: all things were created by him, and for him."* In a similar way we read in Hebrews 1:2, that God *"hath in these last days spoken unto us by his Son, whom he hath appointed heir of all things, by whom also he made the worlds* [ages]." In the passage given earlier (Psalm 33:6), the Word as well as the Spirit are mentioned in connection with creation. In the account of the creation and the rehabilitation of this world to be the abode of man, Father, Word, and Holy Spirit are all mentioned. (See Genesis 1:1–3.) It is evident from a comparison of these passages that the Father, Son, and Holy Spirit are all active in the creative work. The Father works in His Son, through His Spirit.

Maintenance of Living Creatures

The maintenance of living creatures is attributed to the agency of the Holy Spirit in the Bible. The original creation of the material universe is not the only matter attributed to the agency of the Holy Spirit as we can see in the following verses:

> *Thou hidest thy face, they are troubled: thou takest away their breath, they die, and return to their dust. Thou sendest forth thy spirit, they are created: and thou renewest the face of the earth.*
> (Psalm 104:29–30)

The clear indication of this passage is that not only are things brought into being through the agency of the Holy Spirit but that they are maintained in being by the Holy Spirit. Not only is spiritual life maintained by the Spirit of God, but material being is as well. Things exist and continue by the presence of the Spirit of God in them. This does not mean for a moment that the universe is God, but it does mean that the universe is maintained in its being by the immanence of God in it. This is the great and solemn truth that lies at the foundation of the awful and debasing perversions of pantheism in its countless forms.

Development of the Universe

The development of the material universe into higher states of order is attributed to the agency of the Holy Spirit. Not only is the universe created through the agency of the Holy Spirit and maintained in its existence through the agency of the Holy Spirit, but the development of the earlier, chaotic, undeveloped states of the material universe into higher orders of being is effected through the working of the Holy Spirit. We read in Genesis,

> *And the earth was* [or became] *without form, and void; and darkness was upon the face of the deep. And the Spirit of God moved upon the face of the waters. And God said, Let there be light: and there was light.* (Genesis 1:2–3)

We may take this account to refer either to the original creation of the universe, or we may take it as the deeper students of the Word are more and more inclined to take it—as an account of the rehabilitation of the earth after its plunging into chaos through sin after the original creation described in verse one. In either case, we have set before us here the development of the earth from a chaotic and unformed condition into its present highly developed condition through the agency of the Holy Spirit.

We see the process carried still further in Genesis 2:7: "*And the Lord God formed man of the dust of the ground, and breathed into his nostrils the breath of life; and man became a living soul.*" Here again, it is through the agency of the breath of God that a higher thing, human life, comes into being. Naturally, as the Bible is the history of man's redemption, it does not dwell upon this phase of truth, but seemingly each new and higher impartation of the Spirit of God brings forth a higher order of being: first, inert matter; then motion; then light; then vegetable life; then animal life; then man; and, as we shall see later, then the new man; and then Jesus Christ, the supreme Man, the completion of God's thought of man, the Son of Man. This is the biblical thought of development from the lower to the higher by the agency of the Spirit of God as distinguished from the godless evolution that has been so popular in the present generation. It is, however, only hinted at in the Bible. The more important phases of the Holy Spirit's work, His work in redemption, are those that are emphasized and stated and reiterated. The Word of God is even more plainly active in each state of progress in creation. "*God said*" occurs ten times in the first chapter of Genesis.

7

THE HOLY SPIRIT CONVICTS THE WORLD

Our salvation begins experientially with our being brought to a profound sense that we need a Savior. The Holy Spirit is the One who brings us to this realization of our need. We read in John 16:8–11 (ASV),

> *And he, when he is come, will convict the world in respect of sin, and of righteousness, and of judgment: of sin, because they believe not on me; of righteousness, because I go to the Father, and ye behold me no more; of judgment, because the prince of this world hath been judged.*

Conviction of Sin

We see in John 16:8–11 that it is the work of the Holy Spirit to convict men of sin and so convince them of their error in respect to sin as to produce a deep sense of personal guilt. We have the first recorded fulfillment of this promise in Acts:

> *Therefore let all the house of Israel know assuredly, that God hath made that same Jesus, whom ye have crucified, both Lord and Christ. Now when they heard this, they were pricked in their heart, and said unto Peter and to the rest of the apostles, Men and brethren, what shall we do?* (Acts 2:36–37)

The Holy Spirit had come just as Jesus had promised He would, and when He came, He convicted the world of sin. He pricked them in their hearts with a sense of their awful guilt in the rejection of their Lord and their Christ. If the apostle Peter had spoken the same words the day before Pentecost, no such results would have followed. But now Peter was filled with the Holy Spirit (see Acts 2:4), and the Holy Spirit took Peter and his words and, through the instrumentality of Peter and his words, convicted his hearers. The Holy Spirit is the only One who can convince men of sin.

"*The* [natural] *heart is deceitful above all things, and desperately wicked: who can know it?*" (Jeremiah 17:9), and there is nothing in which the inbred deceitfulness of our hearts comes out more clearly than in our estimations of ourselves. We are all of us sharp-sighted enough to the faults of others, but we are all blind by nature to our own faults. Our blindness to our own shortcomings is oftentimes little short of ludicrous. We have a strange power of exaggerating our imaginary virtues and utterly losing sight of our defects. The longer and more thoroughly one studies human nature, the more clearly he will see how hopeless the task is of convincing other men of sin. We cannot do it, nor has God left it for us to do. He has put this work into the hands of One who is abundantly able to do it—the Holy Spirit.

One of the worst mistakes we can make in our efforts to bring men to Christ is to try to convince them of sin in any power of our own. Unfortunately, it is one of the commonest mistakes. Preachers will stand in the pulpit and argue and reason with men to make them see and realize that they are sinners. They make it as plain as day. It is a wonder that their hearers do not see it, but they do not. Personal workers sit down beside an inquirer and reason with him and bring forward passages of Scripture in a most skillful way—the very passages that are calculated to produce the desired effect—and yet there is no result. Why? Because we are trying to do the Holy Spirit's work—the work that He alone can do—to convince men of sin. If we would only bear in mind our own utter inability to convince men of sin and cast ourselves upon Him in utter helplessness to do the work, we would see results.

At the close of an inquiry meeting in our church in Chicago, one of our best workers brought to me an engineer on the Pan Handle Railway with the remark, "I wish that you would speak to this man. I have been talking to him two hours with no result." I sat down by his side with my open Bible, and in less than ten minutes that man, under deep conviction of sin, was on his knees crying to God for mercy.

When the man had gone out, the worker who had brought him to me said, "That is very strange."

"What is strange?" I asked.

"Do you know," the worker said, "I used exactly the same passages in dealing with that man that you did, and though I had worked with him for two hours with no result, in ten minutes, with the same passages of Scripture, he was brought under conviction of sin and accepted Christ."

What was the explanation? Simply this: For once that worker had forgotten something that she seldom forgot, namely, that the Holy Spirit must do the work. She had been trying to convince the man of sin. She had used the right passages; she had reasoned wisely; she had made out a clear case; but she had not looked to the only One who could do the work. When she brought the man to me and said, "I have worked with him for two hours with no result," I thought to myself, "If this expert worker has dealt with him for two hours with no result, what is the use of my dealing with him?" In a sense of utter helplessness, I cast myself upon the Holy Spirit to do the work, and He did it.

While we cannot convince men of sin, there is One who can: the Holy Spirit. He can convince the most hardened and blinded man of sin. He can change men and women from utter carelessness and indifference to a place where they are overwhelmed with a sense of their need for a Savior. How often we have seen this illustrated.

Some years ago, the officers of the Chicago Avenue Church were burdened with the fact that there was so little profound conviction of sin manifested in our meetings. There were conversions, and a good many were being added to the church, but very few were coming with an apparently overwhelming conviction of sin. One night, one of the officers of the church said, "Fellow believers, I am greatly troubled by the fact that we have so little conviction of sin in our meetings. While we are having conversions and many accessions to the church, there is not that deep conviction of sin that I like to see. I propose that we, the officers of the church, meet from night to night to pray that there may be more conviction of sin in our meetings." The suggestion was taken up by the entire committee.

We had not been praying many nights when one Sunday evening, I saw a showily dressed man with a very hard face, sitting in the front seat underneath the gallery. A large diamond was blazing from his shirt-front. He was sitting beside one of the deacons. As I looked at him while preaching, I thought to myself, "That man is a gambling man, and Deacon Young has been fishing today." It turned out that I was right. The man was the son of a woman who kept a gambling house in a Western city. I think he had never been in a Protestant service before. Deacon Young had gotten hold of him that day on the street and had brought him to the meeting. As I preached, the man's eyes were riveted upon me. When we went downstairs to the after-meeting, Deacon Young took the man with him. I was late dealing with the anxious that night. As I finished with the last one about eleven o'clock and almost everybody had gone home,

Deacon Young came over to me and said, "I have a man over here I wish you would come and speak with." It was this big gambler. He was deeply agitated.

"Oh," he groaned, "I don't know what is the matter with me. I never felt this way before in all my life," and he sobbed and shook like a leaf. Then he told me this story: "I started out this afternoon to go down to Cottage Grove Avenue to meet some men and spend the afternoon gambling. As I passed by the park over yonder, some of your young men were holding an open-air meeting, and I stopped to listen. I saw one man testifying whom I had known in a life of sin, and I waited to hear what he had to say. When he finished, I went on down the street. I had not gone far when some strange power took hold of me and brought me back, and I stayed through the meeting. Then this gentleman spoke to me and brought me over to your church, to your Yoke Fellows' Meeting. I stayed for supper with them, and he brought me up to hear you preach. Then he brought me down to this meeting." Here he stopped and sobbed, "Oh, I don't know what is the matter with me. I feel awful. I never felt this way before in all my life," and his great frame shook with emotion.

"I know what is the matter with you," I said. "You are under conviction of sin; the Holy Spirit is dealing with you," and I pointed him to Christ. He knelt down and cried to God for mercy, to forgive his sins for Christ's sake.

Not long after, one Sunday night, I saw another man sitting in the gallery almost exactly above where this man had sat. A diamond flashed from this man's shirtfront as well. I said to myself, "There is another gambling man." He turned out to be a traveling man who was also a gambler. As I preached, he leaned further and further forward in his seat. In the midst of my sermon, without any intention of giving out the invitation, simply wishing to drive a point home, I said, "Who will accept Jesus Christ tonight?" Quick as a flash the man sprang to his feet and shouted, "I will." It rang through the building like the crack of a revolver. I dropped my sermon and instantly gave the invitation; men and women and young people rose all over the building to yield themselves to Christ. God was answering prayer, and the Holy Spirit was convincing men of sin.

The Holy Spirit can convince men of sin. We need not despair of anyone, no matter how indifferent they may appear, no matter how worldly, no matter how self-satisfied, no matter how irreligious. The Holy Spirit can convince men of sin.

A young minister of very rare culture and ability once came to me and said, "I have a great problem on my hands. I am the pastor of the church in a university town. My congregation is largely made up of university professors and students. They are most delightful people. They have very high moral ideals and are living most exemplary lives. Now," he continued, "if I had a congregation in which there were drunkards and outcasts and thieves, I could convince them of sin, but my problem is how to make people like that, the most delightful people in the world, believe that they are sinners—how to convict them of sin."

I replied, "It is impossible. You cannot do it, but the Holy Spirit can." And so He can. Some of the deepest manifestations of conviction of sin I have ever seen have been on the part of men and women of most exemplary conduct and attractive personality. But they were sinners, and the Holy Spirit opened their eyes to the fact.

While it is the Holy Spirit who convinces men of sin, He does it through us. This comes out very clearly in the context of the passage before us (John 16:8–11). Jesus says in the preceding verse, "*Nevertheless I tell you the truth; It is expedient for you that I go away: for if I go not away, the Comforter will not come unto you; but if I depart, I will send him unto you*" (John 16:7). Then He goes on to say, "*And he, when he is come* [unto you], *will convict the world in respect of sin*" (John 16:8 ASV). That is, our Lord Jesus sends the Holy Spirit to us as believers, and when He is come to us believers, through us to whom He has come, He convinces the world. On the day of Pentecost, it was the Holy Spirit who convinced the three thousand of sin, but the Holy Spirit came to the group of believers and through them convinced the outside world.

As far as the Holy Scriptures definitely tell us, the Holy Spirit has no way of getting at the unsaved world except through the agency of those who are already saved. Every conversion recorded in Acts was through the agency of men or women already saved. Take, for example, the conversion of Saul of Tarsus. If there were ever a miraculous conversion, it was that. The glorified Jesus appeared visibly to Saul on his way to Damascus, but before Saul could come out clearly into the light as a saved man, human instrumentality had to be brought in. Prostrate on the ground, Saul cried to the risen Christ asking what he must do, and the Lord told him to go into Damascus, where he would be told what to do. And then Ananias, *"a certain disciple"* (Acts 9:10), was brought on the scene as the human instrumentality through whom the Holy Spirit could do His work. (See Acts 9:17; 22:16.)

Take the case of Cornelius. Here again was a most remarkable conversion through supernatural agency. An angel appeared to Cornelius, but the angel did not tell Cornelius what to do to be saved. The angel rather said to Cornelius, *"Send men to Joppa, and call for Simon, whose surname is Peter; who shall tell thee words, whereby thou and all thy house shall be saved"* (Acts 11:13–14). We may go right through the record of the conversions in Acts, and we will see they were all effected through human instrumentality.

How solemn, how almost overwhelming, is the thought that the Holy Spirit has no way of getting at the unsaved with His saving power except through the instrumentality of those of us who are already Christians. If we realized that, would we not be more careful to offer to the Holy Spirit a more free and unobstructed channel for His all-important work? The Holy Spirit needs human lips to speak through. He needs yours, and He needs lives so clean and so utterly surrendered to Him that He can work through them.

Notice of which sin it is that the Holy Spirit convinces men—the sin of unbelief in Jesus Christ. *"Of sin, because they believe not on me"* (John 16:9), says Jesus. Not the sin of stealing, not the sin of drunkenness, not the sin of adultery, not the sin of murder, but the sin of unbelief in Jesus Christ. The one thing that the eternal God demands of men is that they believe on Him whom He has sent (see John 6:29). The one sin that reveals man's rebellion against God and daring defiance of Him is the sin of not believing in Jesus Christ, and this is the one sin that the Holy Spirit puts to the front and emphasizes and of which He convicts men. This was the sin of which He convicted the three thousand on the day of Pentecost. Doubtless, there were many other sins in their lives, but the one point that the Holy Spirit brought to the front through the apostle Peter was that the One whom they had rejected was their Lord and Christ, attested to be so by His resurrection from the dead. (See Acts 2:22–36.) *"Now when they heard this* [namely, that He whom they had rejected was Lord and Christ], *they were pricked in their heart"* (Acts 2:37). This is the sin of which the Holy Spirit convinces men today.

In regard to the comparatively minor moralities of life, there is a wide difference among men, but the thief who rejects Christ and the honest man who rejects Christ are alike condemned at the great point of what they do with God's Son, and this is the point that the Holy Spirit presses home. The sin of unbelief is the most difficult of all sins of which to convince men. The average unbeliever does not look upon unbelief as a sin. Many an unbeliever looks upon his unbelief as a mark of intellectual superiority. Not infrequently, he is all the more proud of it because it is the only mark of intellectual superiority that he possesses. He tosses his head and says, "I am an agnostic," "I am a skeptic," or "I am an infidel," and assumes an air of superiority on that account. If he does not go so far as that, the unbeliever frequently looks upon his unbelief as, at the very worst, a misfortune. He looks for pity rather than for blame. He says, "Oh, I wish I could believe. I am so sorry I cannot believe," and then appeals to us for pity because he cannot believe. But when the Holy Spirit touches a man's heart, he no longer looks upon unbelief as a mark of intellectual superiority. He does not look upon unbelief as a mere misfortune. He sees it as the most daring, decisive, and damning of all sins and is overwhelmed with a sense of his awful guilt in that he had not believed on the name of the only begotten Son of God.

Conviction of Righteousness

The Holy Spirit not only convicts of sin; He also convicts in respect to righteousness. He convicts the world of righteousness because Jesus Christ has gone to the Father. That is, He convicts (convinces with a convincing that is self-condemning) the world of Christ's righteousness, which is attested to by His going to the Father. The coming of the Spirit is in itself a proof that Christ has gone to the Father (see Acts 2:33), and the Holy Spirit thus opens our eyes to see that Jesus Christ, whom the world condemned as an evil-doer, was indeed the righteous One. The Father sets the stamp of His approval upon His character and claims by raising Him from the dead, exalting Him to His own right hand, and giving Him a name that is above every name.

The world at large today claims to believe in the righteousness of Christ, but it does not really believe in the righteousness of Christ. It has no adequate conception of the righteousness of Christ. The righteousness that the world attributes to Christ is not the righteousness that God attributes to Him but a poor human righteousness, perhaps a little better than our own. The world loves to put the names of other men that it considers good alongside the name of Jesus Christ. But when the Spirit of God comes to a man, He convinces him of the righteousness of Christ. He opens his eyes to see Jesus Christ standing absolutely alone, not only far above all men but *"Far above all principality, and power, and might, and dominion, and every name that is named, not only in this world, but also in that which is to come"* (Ephesians 1:21).

Conviction of Judgment

The Holy Spirit also convicts the world of judgment. The ground upon which the Holy Spirit convinces men of judgment is upon the ground of the fact that *"the prince of this world is judged"* (John 16:11). When Jesus Christ was nailed to the cross, it seemed as if He were judged there; in reality, it was the prince of this world who was judged at the cross. By raising Jesus Christ from the dead, the Father made it plain to all coming ages that the cross was not the judgment of Christ but the judgment of the prince of darkness. The Holy Spirit opens our eyes to see this fact and so convinces us of judgment.

There is a great need today that the world be convinced of judgment. Judgment is a doctrine that has fallen into the background, that has indeed almost sunken out of sight. It is not popular today to speak about judgment, retribution, or hell. One who emphasizes judgment and future retribution is not thought to be quite up-to-date; he is considered medieval or even archaic. But when the Holy Spirit opens the eyes of men, they believe in judgment.

In the early days of my Christian experience, I had great difficulties with the Bible doctrine of future retribution. I came again and again up to what it taught about the eternal penalties of persistent sin. It seemed as if I could not believe it: it must not be true, I thought. Time and again I would back away from the stern teachings of Jesus Christ and the apostles concerning this matter. But one night, I was waiting upon God that I might know the Holy Spirit in a fuller manifestation of His presence and His power. God gave me what I sought that night. With this larger experience of the Holy Spirit's presence and power, there came such a revelation of the glory, the infinite glory, of Jesus Christ that I no longer had any difficulties with what the Book said about the stern and endless judgment that would be visited upon those who persistently rejected this glorious Son of God. From that day to this, while I have had many a heartache over the Bible doctrine of future retribution, I have had no intellectual difficulty with it. I have believed it. The Holy Spirit has convinced me of judgment.

8

THE HOLY SPIRIT BEARING WITNESS TO JESUS CHRIST

When our Lord was talking to His disciples on the night before His crucifixion about the Comforter who was to come and take His place after His departure, He said,

> *But when the Comforter is come, whom I will send unto you from the Father, even the Spirit of truth, which proceedeth from the Father, he shall bear witness of me: and ye also bear witness, because ye have been with me from the beginning.* (John 15:26–27 RV)

When the apostle Peter and the other disciples were strictly commanded by the Jewish council not to teach in the name of Jesus, they said, *"We are his witnesses of these things; and so is also the Holy Ghost"* (Acts 5:32). It is clear from these words of Jesus Christ and the apostles that it is the work of the Holy Spirit to bear witness concerning Jesus Christ.

We find the Holy Spirit's testimony to Jesus Christ in the Scriptures. Besides this, the Holy Spirit also bears witness directly to the individual heart concerning Jesus Christ. He takes His own Scriptures, interprets them to us, and makes them clear to us. All truth is from the Spirit, for He is *"the Spirit of truth"* (John 15:26), but it is especially His work to bear witness to Him who is the truth, that is, Jesus Christ. (See John 14:6.) It is only through the testimony of the Holy Spirit directly to our hearts that we ever come to a true, living knowledge of Jesus Christ. (Compare 1 Corinthians 12:3.) No amount of mere reading the written Word and no amount of listening to man's testimony will ever bring us to a living knowledge of Christ. It is only when the Holy Spirit Himself takes the written Word, or takes the testimony of our fellowmen, and interprets it directly to our hearts that we really come to see and know Jesus as He is.

On the day of Pentecost, Peter gave all his hearers the testimony of the Scriptures regarding Christ, and he also gave them his own testimony. He told them what he and the other apostles knew by personal observation regarding Christ's resurrection. Unless the Holy Spirit Himself had taken the Scriptures that Peter had brought together and taken the testimony of Peter and the other disciples, the three thousand on that day would not have seen Jesus as He really was, nor would they have received Him and been baptized in His name. The Holy Spirit added His testimony to that of Peter and that of the written Word. Mr. Moody used to say in his terse and graphic way that when Peter said, *"Therefore let all the house of Israel know assuredly, that God hath made that same Jesus, whom ye have crucified, both Lord and Christ"* (Acts 2:36), the Holy Spirit said, "Amen," and the people saw and believed. It is certain that unless the Holy Spirit had come that day and, through Peter and the other apostles, borne His direct testimony to the hearts of their hearers, there would have been no saving vision of Jesus on the part of the people.

If you wish men to get a true view of Jesus Christ, such a view of Him that they may believe and be saved, it is not enough that you give them the Scriptures concerning Him. It is not enough that you give them your own testimony. You must seek the testimony of the Holy Spirit for them and put yourself into such a relationship with God that the Holy Spirit may bear His testimony through you. Neither your testimony nor that of the written Word alone will effect this, even though it is your testimony or that of the Word that the Holy Spirit uses. Unless your testimony and that of the Word is taken up by the Holy Spirit and He Himself testifies, they will not believe.

This explains something that every experienced worker probably notices. We sit down beside an inquirer, open our Bibles, and give him those Scriptures that clearly reveal Jesus as the atoning Savior on the cross, a Savior from the guilt of sin, and as a risen Savior, a Savior from the power of sin. It is just the truth the man needs to see and believe in order to be saved, but he does not see it. We go over these Scriptures, which, to us, are as plain as day again and again, and the inquirer sits there in blank darkness. He sees nothing; he grasps nothing. Sometimes we almost wonder if the inquirer is stupid and that's why he cannot see it.

No, he is not stupid, except with that spiritual blindness that possesses every mind unenlightened by the Holy Spirit: *"But the natural man receiveth not the things of the Spirit of God: for they are foolishness unto him: neither can he know them, because they are spiritually discerned"* (1 Corinthians 2:14). We go over it again, and still he does not see it. We go over it again, and his face lightens up as he exclaims, "I see it. I see it." He sees Jesus, believes, is saved, and knows that he is saved there on the spot. What has happened? Simply this: The Holy Spirit has borne His testimony, and what was dark as midnight before is as clear as day now.

This explains also why it is that one who has been long in darkness concerning Jesus Christ so quickly comes to see the truth when he surrenders his will to God and seeks light from Him. When he surrenders his will to God, he has put himself into that attitude toward God where the Holy Spirit can do His work. (See Acts 5:32.) Jesus said in John 7:17,

"If any man will do [God's] *will, he shall know of the doctrine, whether it be of God, or whether I speak of myself."* When a man wills to do the will of God, then the conditions are provided on which the Holy Spirit works, and He illuminates the mind to see the truth about Jesus and to see that His teaching is the very Word of God.

John wrote in John 20:31, *"But these are written, that ye might believe that Jesus is the Christ, the Son of God; and that believing ye might have life through his name."* John wrote his gospel for this purpose: that men might see Jesus as the Christ, the Son of God, through what he recorded; and that they might believe that He is the Christ, the Son of God; and that, thus believing, they might have life through His name. The best book in the world to put into the hands of one who desires to know about Jesus and be saved is the gospel of John. However, many a man has read the gospel of John over and over and over again and has not seen and believed that Jesus is the Christ, the Son of God. But let the same man surrender his will absolutely to God and ask God for light as he reads this gospel and promise God that he will take his stand on everything in the gospel that He shows him to be true, and before the man has finished reading, he will see clearly that Jesus is the Christ, the Son of God; and this same man will believe and have eternal life. Why? Because he has put himself into the place where the Holy Spirit can take the things written in the gospel and interpret them and bear His testimony. I have seen this tested and proven time and time again all around the world.

Men have come to me and said that they did not believe Jesus to be the Christ, the Son of God. Many have gone even further and said they were agnostics and did not even know whether there was a personal God. Then I have told them to read the gospel of John; that, in that gospel, John presented the evidence that Jesus was the Christ, the Son of God. Often, they have told me they have already read it repeatedly and yet were not convinced that Jesus was the Christ, the Son of God. Then I have said to them, "You have not read it the right way," and I have urged them to surrender their wills to God (or in the case where they were not sure there was a God, to take their stand upon the right to follow it wherever it might carry them). Then I have had them agree to read the gospel of John slowly and thoughtfully; and each time before they read, I have had them agree to look up to God, if there were any God, to help them to understand what they were reading and to promise Him that they would take their stand upon whatever He showed them to be true and follow it wherever it would carry them. In every instance, before they had finished the gospel, they had come to see that Jesus was the Christ, the Son of God, and they have believed and been saved. They had put themselves in that position where the Holy Spirit could bear His testimony to Jesus Christ, and He had done it. Through His testimony, they saw and believed.

If you wish men to see the truth about Christ, do not depend upon your own powers of expression and persuasion; instead cast yourself upon the Holy Spirit, seek His testimony for them, and see to it that they put themselves in the place where the Holy Spirit can testify. This is the cure for both skepticism and ignorance concerning Christ. If you yourself are not clear concerning the truth about Jesus Christ, seek for yourself the testimony of the Holy Spirit regarding Christ. Read the Scriptures, read especially the gospel of John, but do not depend upon the mere reading of the Word. Before you read it, put yourself in such an attitude toward God, by the absolute surrender of your will to Him, that the Holy Spirit may bear His testimony in your heart concerning Jesus Christ. What we all most need is a clear and full vision of Jesus Christ, and this comes through the testimony of the Holy Spirit.

One night, a number of our students came back from the Pacific Garden Mission in Chicago and said to me, "We had a wonderful meeting at the mission tonight. There were many drunkards and outcasts at the front who accepted Christ."

The next day, I met Mr. Harry Monroe, the superintendent of the mission, on the street, and I said, "Harry, the boys say you had a wonderful meeting at the mission last night."

"Would you like to know how it came about?" he replied.

"Yes."

"Well," he said, "I simply held up Jesus Christ, and it so pleased the Holy Spirit to illumine the face of Jesus Christ that men saw and believed."

It was a unique way of putting it, but it was an expressive way and true to the essential facts in the case. It is our part to hold up Jesus Christ. We must then look to the Holy Spirit to illuminate His face or to take the truth about Him and make it clear to the hearts of our hearers. He will do it, and men will see and believe. Of course, we need to be so walking toward God that the Holy Spirit may take us as the instruments through whom He will bear His testimony.

9

THE REGENERATING WORK OF THE HOLY SPIRIT

The apostle Paul wrote, *"Not by works of righteousness which we have done, but according to his mercy he saved us, by the washing of regeneration, and renewing of the Holy Ghost"* (Titus 3:5). In these words, we are taught that the Holy Spirit renews men, or makes men new, and that through this renewing of the Holy Spirit, we are saved. Jesus taught the same in John 3:3–5:

> *Jesus answered and said unto him, Verily, verily, I say unto thee, except a man be born again, he cannot see the kingdom of God. Nicodemus*

> *saith unto him, How can a man be born when he is old? can he enter the second time into his mother's womb, and be born? Jesus answered, Verily, verily, I say unto thee, except a man be born of water and of the Spirit, he cannot enter into the kingdom of God.*

What is regeneration? Regeneration is the impartation of life (spiritual life) to those who are dead (spiritually dead) through their trespasses and sins (see Ephesians 2:1). It is the Holy Spirit who imparts this life. It is true that the written Word is the instrument that the Holy Spirit uses in regeneration. We read in 1 Peter 1:23, *"Being born again, not of corruptible seed, but of incorruptible, by the word of God, which liveth and abideth for ever."* We read in James 1:18, *"Of his own will begat he us with the word of truth, that we should be a kind of firstfruits of his creatures."* These passages make it plain that the Word is the instrument used in regeneration, but it is only as the Holy Spirit uses the instrument that the new birth results. *"It is the spirit that giveth life"* (John 6:63 ASV).

In 2 Corinthians 3:6, we are told that *"the letter killeth, but the spirit giveth life"*[1] This is sometimes interpreted to mean that the literal interpretation of Scripture, the interpretation that takes it in its strict grammatical sense and makes it mean what it says, kills. It then means that some spiritual interpretation—an interpretation that "gives the spirit of the passage" by making it mean something it does not say—gives life, and those who insist upon Scripture meaning exactly what it says are called "deadly literalists." This is a favorite perversion of Scripture with those who do not like to take the Bible as meaning just what it says and who find themselves driven into a corner looking about for some convenient way of escape.

If one will read the words in their context, he will see that this thought was utterly foreign to the mind of Paul. Indeed, one who will carefully study the epistles of Paul will find that he himself was a literalist of the literalists. If literalism is deadly, then the teachings of Paul are among the most deadly ever written. Paul built an argument upon the turn of a word, upon a number or a tense. So what does 2 Corinthians 3:6 mean? The way to find out what any passage means is to study the words used in their context. Paul is drawing a contrast between the Word of God outside of us—written with ink upon parchment or engraved on tablets of stone—and the Word of God written within us on tablets that are hearts of flesh with the Spirit of the living God (see 2 Corinthians 3:3). He tells us that if we merely have the Word of God outside us in a book or on parchment or on tablets of stone, that it will kill us, that it will only bring condemnation and death. But if we have the Word of God made a living thing in our hearts, written upon our hearts by the Spirit of the living God, that it will bring us life.[2] No number of Bibles upon our tables or in our libraries will save us, but the truth of the Bible written by the Spirit of the living God in our hearts will save us.

To put the matter of regeneration in another way: Regeneration is the impartation of a new nature, God's own nature, to the one who is born again. (See 2 Peter 1:4.) Every human being is born into this world with a perverted nature; his whole intellectual, emotional, and discretionary nature is perverted by sin. No matter how excellent our human ancestry, we come into this world with a mind that is blind to the truth of God: *"But the natural man receiveth not the things of the Spirit of God: for they are foolishness unto him: neither can he know them, because they are spiritually discerned"* (1 Corinthians 2:14). We come with affections that are alienated from God, loving the things that we ought to hate and hating the things that we ought to love:

> *Now the works of the flesh are manifest, which are these; Adultery, fornication, uncleanness, lasciviousness, idolatry, witchcraft, hatred, variance, emulations, wrath, strife, seditions, heresies, envyings, murders, drunkenness, revellings, and such like: of the which I tell you before, as I have also told you in time past, that they which do such things shall not inherit the kingdom of God.* (Galatians 5:19–21)

We come with a will that is perverted, set upon pleasing itself rather than pleasing God: *"Because the carnal mind is enmity against God: for it is not subject to the law of God, neither indeed can be"* (Romans 8:7).

In the new birth, a new intellectual, emotional, and discretionary nature is imparted to us. We receive the mind that sees as God sees, that thinks God's thoughts after Him. (See 1 Corinthians 2:12–14.) We receive affections in harmony with the affections of God: *"The fruit of the Spirit is love, joy, peace, longsuffering, gentleness, goodness, faith, meekness, temperance: against such there is no law"* (Galatians 5:22–23). We receive a will that is in harmony with the will of God, that delights to do the things that please Him. Like Jesus we say, *"My meat is to do the will of him that sent me, and to finish his work"* (John 4:34; compare John 6:38 and Galatians 1:10). It is the Holy Spirit who creates this new nature in us, or imparts this new nature to us. No amount of preaching, no matter how orthodox it may be, and no amount of mere study of the Word will regenerate unless the Holy Spirit works. It is He and He alone who makes a man a new creature.

The new birth is compared in the Bible to growth from a seed. The human heart is the soil, and *"the seed is the word of God"* (Luke 8:11; compare 1 Peter 1:23; James 1:18; and 1 Corinthians 4:15). Every preacher or teacher of the Word is a sower, but the Spirit of God is the One who quickens the seed that is sown. The divine nature then springs up as the result. There is abundant soil everywhere in which to sow seed in the human hearts that are around. There is abundant seed to be sown; any of us can find it in the granary of God's Word. There are many sowers today, but unless the Spirit of God quickens it as we sow the seed and unless the heart of the hearer closes around it by faith, there will be no harvest. Every sower needs to see to it that he realizes his dependence upon the Holy Spirit to quicken the seed he sows, and he needs to see to it also that he is in such relation to God that the Holy Spirit may work through him and quicken the seed he sows.

The Holy Spirit does regenerate men. He has power to raise the dead. He has power to impart life to those who are morally dead and decaying. He has power to impart an entirely new nature to those whose nature now is so corrupt that to men they appear to be beyond hope. How often I have seen it proven. How often I have seen men and women utterly lost and ruined and vile come into a meeting scarcely knowing why they came.

As they have sat there, the Word has been spoken, the Spirit of God has quickened the Word thus sown in their hearts, and in a moment, that man or woman, by the mighty power of the Holy Spirit, has become a new creation.

I know a man who seemed as completely abandoned and hopeless as men ever become. He was about forty-five years of age. He had gone off in evil courses in early boyhood. He had run away from home, had joined the navy and afterward the army, and had learned all the vices of both. He had been dishonorably discharged from the army because of his extreme dissipation and disorderliness. He had found his companions among the lowest of the low and the vilest of the vile. When he would go up the street of a Western town at night, merchants would hear his yell and would close their doors in fear. This man went one night into a revival meeting in a country church out of curiosity. He made sport of the meeting that night with a boon companion who sat by his side, but he went again the next night. The Spirit of God touched his heart. He went forward and bowed at the altar. He arose a new creation. He was transformed into one of the noblest, truest, purest, most unselfish, most gentle, and most Christlike men I have ever known.

I am sometimes asked, "Do you believe in sudden conversion?" I believe in something far more wonderful than sudden conversion. I believe in sudden regeneration. Conversion is merely an outward thing, the turning around. Regeneration goes down to the deepest depths of the inmost soul, transforming thoughts, affections, will, the whole inward man. I believe in sudden regeneration because the Bible teaches it and because I have seen it countless times. I believe in sudden regeneration because I have experienced it. We are sometimes told that the religion of the future will not teach sudden, miraculous conversion. If the religion of the future does not teach sudden miraculous conversion, if it does not teach meaningful, sudden, and miraculous regeneration by the power of the Holy Spirit, then the religion of the future will not be in conformity with the facts of experience and will not be scientific. It will miss one of the most certain and most glorious of all truths.

Man-devised religions in the past have often missed the truth, and man-devised religions in the future will doubtless do the same. However, the religion God has revealed in His Word and that He confirms in experience teaches sudden regeneration by the mighty power of the Holy Spirit. If I did not believe in regeneration by the power of the Holy Spirit, I would quit preaching. What would be the use in facing great audiences in which there were multitudes of men and women hardened and seared, caring for nothing but the things of the world and the flesh, with no high and holy aspirations, with no outlook beyond money and fame and power and pleasure, if it were not for the regenerating power of the Holy Spirit?

But with the regenerating power of the Holy Spirit, it is worth the commitment, for the preacher can never tell where the Spirit of God is going to strike and do His mighty work. There sits before you a man who is a gambler or a drunkard or a philanderer. There does not seem to be much use in preaching to him. But you can never tell; that very night the Spirit of God may touch that man's heart and transform him into one of the holiest and most useful of men. It has often occurred in the past and will doubtless often occur in the future. There sits before you a woman who is a mere butterfly of fashion. She seems to have no thought above society and pleasure and adulation. Why preach to her? Without the regenerating power of the Holy Spirit, it would be foolishness and a waste of time. But you can never tell; perhaps this very night the Spirit of God will shine in that darkened heart and open the eyes of that woman to see the beauty of Jesus Christ, and she may receive Him. Then and there the life of God will be imparted by the power of the Holy Spirit to her trifling soul.

The doctrine of the regenerating power of the Holy Spirit is a glorious doctrine. It sweeps away false hopes. It comes to the one who is trusting in education and culture and says, "Education and culture are not enough; you must be born again." It comes to the one who is trusting in mere external morality and says, "External morality is not enough; you must be born again." It comes to the one who is trusting in the externalities of religion—in going to church, reading the Bible, saying prayers, being confirmed, being baptized, partaking of the Lord's Supper—and says, "The mere externalities of religion are not enough; you must be born again." It comes to the one who is trusting in turning over a new leaf, in outward reform, in quitting his meanness, and it says, "Outward reform, quitting your meanness is not enough; you must be born again." But in place of the vague and shallow hopes that it sweeps away, it brings in a new hope, a good hope, a blessed hope, a glorious hope. It says, "You may be born again." It comes to the one who has no desire higher than the desire for things animal or selfish or worldly and says, "You may become a partaker of the divine nature and love the things that God loves and hate the things that God hates. You may become like Jesus Christ. You may be born again."

10

THE SATISFACTION THAT COMES FROM THE INDWELLING SPIRIT

The Holy Spirit takes up His abode in the one who is born of the Spirit. The apostle Paul said to the believers in Corinth, *"Know ye not that ye are the temple of God, and that the Spirit of God dwelleth in you?"* (1 Corinthians 3:16). This passage refers not so much to the individual believer as to the whole body of believers, the church. The church as a body is indwelt by the Spirit of God. But in 1 Corinthians 6:19, we read, *"Know ye not that your body is the temple of the Holy Ghost which is in you, which ye have of God, and ye are not your own?"* It is evident in this passage that Paul is not speaking of the body of believers, of the church as a whole, but of the individual believer. In a similar way, the Lord Jesus said to His disciples on the night before His crucifixion,

> *And I will pray the Father, and he shall give you another Comforter, that he may abide with you for ever; even the Spirit of truth; whom the world cannot receive, because it seeth him not, neither knoweth him: but ye know him; for he dwelleth with you, and shall be in you.*
>
> (John 14:16–17)

The Holy Spirit dwells in everyone who is born again. We read in Romans 8:9, *"Now if any man have not the Spirit of Christ, he is none of his."* The Spirit of Christ in this verse, as we have already seen, does not mean merely a Christlike spirit; it is a name of the Holy Spirit. One may be a very imperfect believer, but if he really is a believer in Jesus Christ, if he has really been born again, the Spirit of God dwells in him. It is very evident from the first epistle to the Corinthians that the believers in Corinth were very imperfect believers; they were full of imperfection, and there was gross sin among them. Nevertheless, Paul told them, even when dealing with them concerning gross immoralities, that they are temples of the Holy Spirit. (See 1 Corinthians 6:15–19.)

The Holy Spirit dwells in every child of God. In some, however, He dwells way back, behind consciousness, in the hidden sanctuary of their spirits. He is not allowed to take possession as He desires of the whole man—spirit, soul, and body. Some, therefore, are not distinctly conscious of His indwelling, but He is there nonetheless. What a solemn and yet what a glorious thought, that in me dwells this august person, the Holy Spirit.

If we are children of God, we are not so much to pray that the Spirit may come and dwell in us, for He does that already. We are rather to recognize His presence, His gracious and glorious indwelling, give to Him complete control of the house He already inhabits, and strive to live so as not to grieve this holy One, this divine guest. We shall see later, however, that it is right to pray for the filling or baptism with the Spirit. What a thought it gives of the hallowedness and sacredness of the body to think of the Holy Spirit dwelling within us. How considerately we ought to treat these bodies and how sensitively we ought to shun everything that will defile them. How carefully we ought to walk in all things so as not to grieve Him who dwells within us.

This indwelling Spirit is a source of full and everlasting satisfaction and life. Jesus said in John 4:14, *"Whosoever drinketh of the water that I shall give him shall never thirst; but the water that I shall give him shall be in him a well of water springing up into everlasting life."* Jesus was talking to the woman of Samaria by the well at Sychar. She had said to Him, *"Art thou greater than our father Jacob, which gave us the well, and drank thereof himself, and his children, and his cattle?"* (John 4:12). Then Jesus answered and said to her, *"Whosoever drinketh of this water shall thirst again"* (John 4:13). How true that is of every earthly fountain. No matter how deeply we drink, we will thirst again.

No earthly spring of satisfaction ever fully satisfies. We might drink of the fountain of wealth as deeply as we can, but it will not satisfy for long. We will thirst again. We might drink of the fountain of fame as deeply as any man ever drank, yet the satisfaction is but for an hour. We might drink of the fountain of worldly pleasure, of human science and philosophy, and of earthly learning. We might even drink of the fountain of human love, but none will satisfy for long. We will thirst again.

Jesus went on to say, *"But whosoever drinketh of the water that I shall give him shall never thirst; but the water that I shall give him shall be in him a well of water springing up into everlasting life"* (verse 14). The water that Jesus Christ gives is the Holy Spirit. John tells us this in the most explicit of language:

> *In the last day, that great day of the feast, Jesus stood and cried, saying, If any man thirst, let him come unto me, and drink. He that believeth on me, as the scripture hath said, out of his belly shall flow rivers of living water. (But this spake he of the Spirit, which they that believe on him should receive....)* (John 7:37–39)

The Holy Spirit fully and forever satisfies the one who receives Him. He becomes a well of water within him, springing up, ever springing up, into everlasting life. It is a great thing to have a well that you can carry with you; to have a well that is within you; to have your source of satisfaction not in the things outside yourself but in a well within and that is always within and that is always springing up in freshness and power; to have our well of satisfaction and joy within us. We are then independent of our environment. It matters little whether we have health or sickness, prosperity or adversity; our source of joy is within and is ever springing up. It matters comparatively little even whether we have our friends with us or are separated from them, separated even by what men call death. This fountain within is always gushing up, and our souls are satisfied.

Sometimes this fountain within gushes up with greatest power and fullness in the days of deepest bereavement. At such time, all earthly satisfactions fail. What satisfaction is there in money or worldly pleasure, in the theater or the opera or the dance, in fame or power or human learning, when some loved one is taken from us? But in the hours when those that we loved most dearly upon earth are taken from us, it is then that the spring of joy of the indwelling Spirit of God bursts forth with fullest flow. Sorrow and sighing flee away, and our own spirits are filled with peace and ecstasy. We have *"beauty for ashes, the oil of joy for mourning, the garment of praise for the spirit of heaviness"* (Isaiah 61:3). If the experience were not too sacred to put in print, I could tell of a moment of sudden and overwhelming bereavement and sorrow when it seemed as if I would be crushed, when I cried aloud in an agony that seemed unendurable, when suddenly and instantly this fountain of the Holy Spirit within burst forth, when I knew such a rest and joy as I had rarely known before and my whole being was suffused with the oil of gladness.

The one who has the Spirit of God dwelling within as a well springing up into everlasting life is independent of the world's pleasures. He does not need to run after the theater and the opera and the dance and the cards and the other pleasures without which life does not seem worth living to those who have not received the Holy Spirit. He gives these things up, not so much because he thinks they are wrong as because he has something so much better. He loses all taste for them.

A lady once came to Mr. Moody and said, "Mr. Moody, I do not like you."

He asked, "Why not?"

She said, "Because you are too narrow."

"Narrow! I did not know that I was narrow."

"Yes, you are too narrow. You don't believe in the theater; you don't believe in cards; you don't believe in dancing."

"How do you know I don't believe in the theater?" he asked.

"Oh," she said, "I know you don't."

Mr. Moody replied, "I go to the theater whenever I want to."

"What," cried the woman, "you go to the theater whenever you want to?"

"Yes, I go to the theater whenever I want to."

"Oh," she said, "Mr. Moody, you are a much broader man than I thought you were. I am so glad to hear you say it, that you go to the theater whenever you want to."

"Yes, I go to the theater whenever I want to. I just don't want to." Anyone who has really received the Holy Spirit, and in whom the Holy Spirit dwells and is unhindered in His working, will not want to. Why is it then that so many professed Christians do go after these worldly amusements? For one of two reasons: either because they have never definitely received the Holy Spirit or else because the fountain is choked. It is quite possible for a fountain to become choked. The best well in one of our inland cities was choked and dry for many months because an old rag carpet had been thrust into the opening from which the water flowed. When the rag was pulled out, the water flowed again, pure and cool and invigorating. There are many in the church today who once knew the matchless joy of the Holy Spirit, but some sin or worldly conformity, some act of disobedience, more or less conscious disobedience, to God has come in and the fountain is choked. Let us pull out the old rags today that this wondrous fountain may burst forth again, springing up every day and hour into everlasting life.

11

THE HOLY SPIRIT SETTING THE BELIEVER FREE FROM THE POWER OF INDWELLING SIN

In Romans 8:2, the apostle Paul wrote, *"For the law of the Spirit of life in Christ Jesus hath made me free from the law of sin and death."* We learn from Romans 7:9–24 what the law of sin and death is. Paul wrote that there was a time in his life when he was *"alive without the law"* (verse 9), but the time came when he was brought face-to-face with the law of God. He saw that this law was holy, and the commandment holy and just and good. And he made up his mind to keep this holy and just and good law of God.

But he soon discovered that beside this law of God outside him, which was holy and just and good, there was another law inside him directly contrary to this law of God outside him. While the law of God outside him said, "This good thing" and "this good thing" and "this good thing" and "this good thing thou shalt do," the law within him said, "You cannot do this good thing that you would."

A fierce combat ensued between this holy and just and good law outside him, which Paul himself approved after the inward man, and this other law in his members, which warred against the law of his mind and kept constantly saying, "You cannot do the good that you would." But this law in his members, the law that *"the good that I would I do not: but the evil which I would not, that I do"* (Romans 7:19), gained the victory. Paul's attempt to keep the law of God resulted in total failure. He found himself sinking deeper and deeper into the mire of sin, constrained and dragged down by this law of sin in his members, until at last he cried out, *"O wretched man that I am! who shall deliver me from the body of this death?"* (Romans 7:24).

Then Paul made another discovery. He found that in addition to the two laws that he had already found—the law of God outside of him, holy and just and good; and the law of sin and death within him, the law that the good he would he could not do and the evil he would not he must keep on doing—there was a third law: *"The law of the Spirit of life in Christ Jesus hath made me free from the law of sin and death"* (Romans 8:2). This law is about the righteousness that you cannot achieve in your own strength by the power of your own will approving the law of God, the righteousness that the law of God outside of you, holy and just and good though it is, cannot accomplish in you, in that it is weak through your flesh. The Spirit of Life in Christ Jesus can produce this righteousness in you so *"that the righteousness of the law might be fulfilled in us, who walk not after the flesh, but after the Spirit"* (Romans 8:4). In other words, when we come to the end of ourselves, when we fully realize our own inability to keep the law of God and in utter helplessness look up to the Holy Spirit in Christ Jesus to do for us that which we cannot do for ourselves, and when we surrender our every thought and every purpose and every desire and every affection to His absolute control and thus walk after the Spirit, the Spirit does take control and set us free from the power of sin that dwells in us and brings every hour of our lives into conformity with the will of God. It is the privilege of the child of God in the power of the Holy Spirit to have victory over sin every day and every hour and every moment.

There are many professed Christians today living in the experience Paul described in Romans 7:9–24. Each day is a day of defeat, and at the close of the day, if they review their lives, they must cry as Paul did, "*O wretched man that I am! who shall deliver me from the body of this death?*" (Romans 7:24). There are some who even go so far as to reason that this is the normal Christian life, but Paul tells us distinctly that this was "*when the commandment came*" (Romans 7:9), not when the Spirit came. In other words, it is the experience under law and not in the Spirit. The pronoun "*I*" occurs twenty-seven times in these fifteen verses, and the Holy Spirit is not found once. Whereas in the eighth chapter of Romans, the pronoun "*I*" is found only twice in the whole chapter, and the Holy Spirit appears constantly. Again, Paul tells us in Romans 7:14 that this was his experience as "*carnal, sold under sin.*" Certainly, that does not describe the normal Christian experience.

On the other hand, in Romans 8:9 we are told how not to be in the flesh but in the Spirit. In the eighth chapter of Romans, we have a picture of the true Christian life, the life that is possible to each one of us and that God expects from each one of us. Here, we have a life where not merely the commandment comes but the Spirit comes and works obedience to the commandment and brings us complete victory over the law of sin and death. Here, we have life, not in the flesh but in the Spirit, where we not only see the beauty of the law (see Romans 7:22) but where the Spirit also imparts power to keep it (see Romans 8:4). We still have the flesh, but we are not in the flesh and do not live after the flesh. We "*through the Spirit do mortify the deeds of the body*" (Romans 8:13). The desires of the body are still there, desires that, if made the rule of our lives, would lead us into sin. But day by day, by the power of the Spirit, we put to death the deeds to which the desires of the body would lead us. We walk by the Spirit and therefore do not fulfill the lusts of the flesh (see Galatians 5:16). We have crucified the flesh with the passions and lusts thereof (see verse 24).

It would be going too far to say we still had a carnal nature, for a carnal nature is a nature governed by the flesh. We have the flesh, but in the Spirit's power, and it is our privilege to get daily, hourly, constant victory over the flesh and over sin. But this victory is not in ourselves, nor in any strength of our own. Left to ourselves, deserted of the Spirit of God, we would be as helpless as ever. It is still true that in us—that is, in our flesh—"*dwelleth no good thing*" (Romans 7:18). It is all in the power of the indwelling Spirit, but the Spirit's power may be in such fullness that one is not even conscious of the presence of the flesh. It seems as if it were dead and gone forever, but it is only kept in place of death by the Holy Spirit's power. If for one moment we were to take our eyes off of Jesus Christ, if we were to neglect the daily study of the Word and prayer, down we would go. We must live in the Spirit and walk in the Spirit if we would have continuous victory. (See Galatians 5:16, 25.) The life of the Spirit within us must be maintained by the study of the Word and prayer.

One of the saddest things ever witnessed is the way in which some people who have entered by the Spirit's power into a life of victory become self-confident and fancy that the victory is in themselves and that they can safely neglect the study of the Word and prayer. The depths to which such people sometimes fall is appalling. Each of us needs to take to heart the inspired words of the apostle, "*Wherefore let him that thinketh he standeth take heed lest he fall*" (1 Corinthians 10:12).

I once knew a man who seemed to make extraordinary strides in the Christian life. He became a teacher of others and was a great blessing to thousands. It seemed to me that he was becoming self-confident, and I trembled for him. I invited him to my room, and we had a long heart-to-heart conversation. I told him frankly that it seemed as if he were going perilously near exceedingly dangerous ground. I said that I found it safer at the close of each day not to be too confident that there had been no failures or defeats that day but to go alone with God and ask Him to search my heart and show me if there was anything in my outward or inward life that was displeasing to Him. Very often, failures were brought to light that must be confessed as sin.

"No," he replied, "I do not need to do that. Even if I should do something wrong, I would see it at once. I keep very short accounts with God, and I would confess it at once."

I said it seemed to me as if it would be safer to take time alone with God for Him to search us through and through. While we might not know anything against ourselves, God might know something against us (see 1 Corinthians 4:4), and He would bring it to light. Our failure could be confessed and put away.

"No," he said. He did not feel that was necessary. Satan took advantage of his self-confidence. He fell into most appalling sin, and though he has since confessed and professed repentance, he has been utterly set aside from God's service.

In John 8:32, we read, *"Ye shall know the truth, and the truth shall make you free."* In this verse, it is the truth, or the Word of God, that sets us free from the power of sin and gives us victory. In Psalm 119:11, we read, *"Thy word have I hid in mine heart, that I might not sin against thee."* Here again, it is the indwelling Word that keeps us free from sin. In this matter as in everything else, what in one place is attributed to the Holy Spirit is elsewhere attributed to the Word. The explanation, of course, is that the Holy Spirit works through the Word, and it is futile to talk of the Holy Spirit dwelling in us if we neglect the Word. If we are not feeding on the Word, we are not walking after the Spirit, and we will not have victory over the flesh and over sin.

12

THE HOLY SPIRIT FORMING CHRIST WITHIN US

Paul offered a wonderful and deeply significant prayer in Ephesians for the believers in Ephesus and for all believers who read the epistle. He wrote,

> *For this cause I bow my knees unto the Father of our Lord Jesus Christ, of whom the whole family in heaven and earth is named, that he would grant you, according to the riches of his glory, to be strengthened with might by his Spirit in the inner man; that Christ may dwell in your hearts by faith; that ye, being rooted and grounded in love, may be able*

> *to comprehend with all saints what is the breadth, and length, and depth, and height; and to know the love of Christ, which passeth knowledge, that ye might be filled with all the fulness of God.*
>
> (Ephesians. 3:14–19)

We have here an advance in thought over that which we just studied in the last chapter. It is the carrying out of the former work to its completion. Here the power of the Spirit manifests itself, not merely in giving us victory over sin but in four things: in Christ dwelling in our hearts; in our being rooted and grounded in love; in our being made strong to comprehend and know, with all the saints, the breadth, and length, and depth, and height of the love of Christ, which passeth knowledge; and in our being *"filled with all the fulness of God"* (Ephesians 3:19).

Christ Dwelling in Our Hearts

The word translated *"dwell"* in Ephesians 3:17 is a very strong word. It means literally, "to dwell down," "to settle," "to dwell deep." It is the work of the Holy Spirit to form the living Christ within us, dwelling deep down in the deepest depths of our being. We have already seen that this was a part of the significance of the name sometimes used of the Holy Spirit, *"the Spirit of Christ"* (Romans 8:9). In Christ on the cross of Calvary, making an atoning sacrifice for sin, bearing the curse of the broken law in our place, we have Christ *for* us. But by the power of the Holy Spirit bestowed upon us by the risen Christ, we have Christ *in* us. Herein lies the secret of a Christlike life.

We hear a great deal in these days about doing as Jesus would do. Certainly we ought, as Christians, to live like Christ. *"He that saith he abideth in him ought himself also so to walk, even as he walked"* (1 John 2:6). But any attempt on our part to imitate Christ in our own strength will only result in utter disappointment and despair. There is nothing more futile that we can possibly attempt than to imitate Christ in the power of our own will. If we imagine that we succeed, it will be simply because we have a very incomplete knowledge of Christ. The more we study Him, and the more perfectly we understand His conduct, the more clearly we will see how far short we have come from imitating Him. But God does not demand the impossible of us; He does not demand of us that we imitate Christ in our own strength. He offers to us something infinitely better. He offers to form Christ in us by the power of His Holy Spirit. And when Christ is thus formed in us by the Holy Spirit's power, all we have to do is let this indwelling Christ live out His own life in us, and then we will be like Christ without struggle and effort of our own.

A woman, who had a deep knowledge of the Word and a rare experience of the fullness that there is in Christ, stood one morning before a body of ministers as they plied her with questions. "Do you mean to say, Mrs. H——," one of the ministers asked, "that you are holy?" Quickly but very meekly and gently, the elect lady replied, "Christ in me is holy." No, we are not holy. To the end of our lives, in and of ourselves, we are full of weakness and failure, but the Holy Spirit is able to form the Holy One of God within us, the indwelling Christ. He will live out His life through us in all the humblest relations of life, as well as in those relations of life that are considered greater. He will live out His life through the mother in the home, through the day-laborer in the pit, through the businessman in his office—everywhere.

Our Being Rooted and Grounded in Love

In Ephesians 3:17, Paul multiplied figures here. The first figure is taken from the tree shooting its roots down deep into the earth and taking fast hold upon it. The second figure is taken from a great building with its foundations laid deep in the earth on the rock. Paul therefore tells us that, by the strengthening of the Spirit in the inward man, we send the roots of our life down deep into the soil of love and also that the foundations of the superstructure of our character are built upon the rock of love. Love is the sum of holiness, *"the fulfilling of the law"* (Romans 13:10). Love is what we all most need in our relations to God, to Jesus Christ, and to one another, and it is the work of the Holy Spirit to root and ground our lives in love.

There is the most intimate relation between Christ being formed within us, or made to dwell in us, and our being rooted and grounded in love, for Jesus Christ Himself is the absolutely perfect embodiment of divine love.

Our Being Made Strong to Know

It is not enough that we love; we must know the love of Christ. But that love passes knowledge. It is so broad, so long, so high, so deep, that no one can comprehend it. But we can *"apprehend"* (Ephesians 3:18 RV) it; we can lay hold upon it; we can make it our own; we can hold it before us as the object of our meditation, our wonder, and our joy. But it is only in the power of the Holy Spirit that we can thus apprehend it. The mind cannot grasp it at all in its own native strength. A man untaught and unstrengthened by the Spirit of God may talk about the love of Christ; he may write poetry about it; he may go into rhapsodies over it—but it is only words, words, words. There is no real apprehension. But the Spirit of God makes us strong to really apprehend it in all its breadth, in all its length, in all its depth, and in all its height.

Our Being "Filled unto All the Fulness of God"

There is a very important change between the Authorized (KJV) and Revised Version (RV). The King James Version reads, *"filled with all the fulness of God"* (Ephesians 3:19). The Revised Version reads more exactly, *"filled unto all the fulness of God."* It is no wonder that the translators of the KJV staggered at what Paul said and sought to tone down the full force of his words. To be filled with all the fullness of God would not be so wonderful. It is an easy matter to fill a pint cup with all the fullness of the ocean; a single dip will do it. But it would be an impossibility indeed to fill a pint cup unto all the fullness of the ocean until all the fullness that there is in the ocean is in that pint cup. It is seemingly a more impossible task that the Holy Spirit undertakes to do for us, to fill us *"unto all the fulness"* of the infinite God, to fill us until all the intellectual and moral fullness that there is in God is in us.

This is the believer's destiny; we are *"heirs of God, and joint-heirs with Christ"* (Romans 8:17). In other words, we are heirs of God to the extent that Jesus Christ is an heir of God; that is, we are heirs to all God is and all God has. It is the work of the Holy Spirit to apply to us that which is already ours in Christ. It is His work to make all God has and all God is experientially ours until the work is consummated in our being: *"filled unto all the fulness of God."* This is not the work of a moment, or a day, or a week, or a month, or a year; but the Holy Spirit day by day puts His hand, as it were, into the fullness of God and conveys to us what He has taken from there and puts it into us. Then again, He puts His hand into the fullness that there is in God and conveys to us what is taken from there and puts it into us. And this wonderful process goes on day after day, and week after week, and month after month, and year after year, and never ends until we are *"filled unto all the fulness of God."*

13

THE HOLY SPIRIT BRINGING FORTH CHRISTLIKE GRACES OF CHARACTER IN THE BELIEVER

There is a singular charm, a charm that one can scarcely explain, in the words of Paul in Galatians 5:22–23: *"But the fruit of the Spirit is love, joy, peace, longsuffering, gentleness* [or *"kindness"* (RV)], *goodness, faith, meekness, temperance: against such there is no law."* What a catalog we have here of lovely moral characteristics. Paul tells us that these are the fruit of the Spirit; that is, if the Holy Spirit is given control of our lives, this is the fruit that He will bear in them. All real beauty of character, all real Christlikeness in us, is the Holy Spirit's work; it is His fruit. He produces it. He bears it; we do not. It is well to notice that these graces are not said to be the *fruits* of the Spirit but the *fruit*. In other words, if the Spirit is given control of our lives, He will not bear one of these as fruit in one person and another as fruit in another person; instead, this will be the one fruit of many flavors that He produces in each one of us.

There is also a unity of origin running throughout all the multiplicity of manifestation. The life set forth in these verses is a beautiful one. Every word is worthy of earnest study and profound meditation. Think of these words one by one: "*love*," "*joy*," "*peace*," "*longsuffering*," "*kindness*" (RV), "*goodness*," "*faith*,"[1] "*meekness*," "*temperance*" (or a life under perfect control by the power of the Holy Spirit). We have here a perfect picture of the life of Jesus Christ Himself. Is not this the life that we all long for, the Christlike life? However, this life is not natural to us and is not attainable by us through any effort of our own. The life that is natural to us is set forth in the three preceding verses:

> *Now the works of the flesh are manifest, which are these; adultery, fornication, uncleanness, lasciviousness, idolatry, witchcraft, hatred, variance, emulations, wrath, strife, seditions, heresies, envyings, murders, drunkenness, revellings, and such like: of the which I tell you before, as I have also told you in time past, that they which do such things shall not inherit the kingdom of God.* (Galatians 5:19–21)

All these works of the flesh will not manifest themselves in each individual. Some will manifest themselves in one, others in others, but they have one common source: the flesh. If we live in the flesh, this is the kind of life that we will live. It is the life that is natural to us. But when the indwelling Spirit is given full control in the one He inhabits; when we are brought to realize the utter badness of the flesh and give up in hopeless despair of ever attaining to anything in its power; when, in other words, we come to the end of ourselves and just give over the whole work of making us what we ought to be to the indwelling Holy Spirit, then and only then are these holy graces of character, which are set forth in Galatians 5:22–23, evident as His fruit in our lives. Do you wish these graces in your character and life? Do you really wish them? Then renounce self utterly and all its strivings after holiness, give up any thought that you can ever attain to anything really morally beautiful in your own strength, and let the Holy Spirit, who already dwells in you if you are a child of God, take full control and bear His own glorious fruit in your daily life.

We get very much the same thought from a different point of view in Galatians 2:20:

> *I am crucified with Christ: nevertheless I live; yet not I, but Christ liveth in me: and the life which I now live in the flesh I live by the faith of the Son of God, who loved me, and gave himself for me.*

We hear a great deal in these days about the ethical culture, which usually means the cultivation of the flesh until it bears the fruit of the Spirit. It cannot be done, no more than thorns can be made to bear figs and the bramble bush grapes. (See Luke 6:44 and Matthew 12:33.)

We also hear a great deal about character building. That may be all very well if you bear constantly in mind that the Holy Spirit must do the building, and even then it is not so much building as fruit-bearing. (See, however, 2 Peter 1:5–7.)

We also hear a great deal about cultivating graces of character, but we must always remember that the way to cultivate true graces of character is by submitting ourselves utterly to the Spirit to do His work and bear His fruit. This is "*sanctification of the Spirit*" (1 Peter 1:2; 2 Thessalonians 2:13). There is a sense, however, in which cultivating graces of character is right; namely, we look at Jesus Christ to see what He is and what we therefore ought to be, then we look to the Holy Spirit to make us this, and thus, "*beholding as in a glass the glory of the Lord, are changed into the same image from glory to glory, even as by the Spirit of the Lord*" (2 Corinthians 3:18). Settle it, however, clearly and forever, that the flesh can never bear this fruit, that you can never attain to these things by your own effort, that they are "*the fruit of the Spirit.*"

14

THE HOLY SPIRIT GUIDING THE BELIEVER INTO LIFE AS A SON

The apostle Paul wrote in Romans 8:14, *"For as many as are led by the Spirit of God, they are the sons of God."* In this passage we see the Holy Spirit taking the conduct of the believer's life. A true Christian life is a personally conducted life, conducted at every turn by a divine person. It is the believer's privilege to be absolutely set free from all care and worry and anxiety as to the decisions that we must make at any turn of life. The Holy Spirit undertakes all that responsibility for us. A true Christian life is not one governed by a long set of rules outside of us, but rather one led by a living and ever-present person within us.

It is in this connection that Paul said, *"For ye have not received the spirit of bondage again to fear"* (Romans 8:15). A life governed by rules outside of one's self is a life of bondage. There is always fear that we haven't made quite enough rules, and there is always the dread that, in an unguarded moment, we may have broken some of the rules that we have made. The life that many professed Christians lead is one of awful bondage, for they have put upon themselves a yoke more grievous to bear than that of the ancient Mosaic law, concerning which Peter said to the Jews of his time, that *"neither our fathers nor we were able to bear"* (Acts 15:10).

Many Christians have a long list of self-made rules: "Thou shalt do this," and "Thou shalt do this," and "Thou shalt do this," and "Thou shalt not do that," and "Thou shalt not do that," and "Thou shalt not do that." If, by any chance, they break one of these self-made rules, or forget to keep one of them, they are at once filled with an awful dread that they have brought upon themselves the displeasure of God (and even sometimes imagine that they have committed the unpardonable sin). This is not Christianity; this is legalism. *"For ye have not received the spirit of bondage again to fear"* (Romans 8:15); we have received the Spirit who gives us the place of sons.

Our lives should not be governed by a set of rules outside of us but by the loving Spirit of adoption within us. We should believe the teaching of God's Word that the Spirit of God's Son dwells within us, and we should surrender the absolute control of our lives to Him and look to Him to guide us at every turn of lives. He will do it only if we surrender it to Him and trust Him to do it. If, in a moment of thoughtlessness, we go our own way instead of His, we will not be filled with an overwhelming sense of condemnation and of fear of an offended God; instead we will go to God as our Father, confess our going astray, believe that He forgives us fully because He says so (see 1 John 1:9), and go on light and happy of heart to obey Him and be led by His Spirit.

Being led by the Spirit of God does not mean for a moment that we will do things that the written Word of God tells us not to do. The Holy Spirit never leads men contrary to the Book of which He Himself is the Author. If there is some spirit that is leading us to do something that is contrary to the explicit teachings of Jesus or the apostles, we may be perfectly sure that this spirit leading us is not the Holy Spirit. This point needs to be emphasized in our day, for there are not a few who give themselves over to the leading of some spirit whom they say is the Holy Spirit but who is leading them to do things explicitly forbidden in the Word. We must always remember that many false spirits and false prophets are out in the world. (See 1 John 4:1.) There are many who are so anxious to be led by some unseen power that they are ready to surrender the conduct of their lives to any spiritual influence or unseen person. In this way, they open their lives to the conduct and malevolent influence of evil spirits to the utter wreck and ruin of their lives.

A man who made great professions of piety once came to me and said that the Holy Spirit was leading him and "a sweet Christian woman" whom he had met to contemplate marriage.

"Why," I said, in astonishment, "you already have one wife."

"Yes," he said, "but you know we are not congenial, and we have not lived together for years."

"Yes," I replied, "I know you have not lived together for years, and I have looked into the matter, and I believe that the blame for that lies largely at your door. In any event, she is your wife. You have no reason to suppose she has been untrue to you, and Jesus Christ explicitly teaches that if you marry another while she lives, you commit adultery." (See Luke 16:18.)

"Oh, but," the man said, "the Spirit of God is leading us to love one another and to see that we ought to marry one another."

"You lie, and you blaspheme," I replied. "Any spirit that is leading you to disobey the plain teaching of Jesus Christ is not the Spirit of God but some spirit of the devil."

This perhaps was an extreme case, but cases of essentially the same character are not rare. Many professed Christians seek to justify themselves in doing things that are explicitly forbidden in the Word by saying that they are led by the Spirit of God. Not long ago, I protested to the leaders in a Christian assembly where, at each meeting, many professed to speak with tongues in distinct violation of the teaching of the Holy Spirit through the apostle Paul in 1 Corinthians 14:27–28:

> *If any man speak in an unknown tongue, let it be by two, or at the most by three, and that by course; and let one interpret. But if there be no interpreter, let him keep silence in the church; and let him speak to himself, and to God.*

The defense they made was that the Holy Spirit led them to speak several at a time and many in a single meeting and that they must obey the Holy Spirit. In such a case as this, they felt they were not subject to the Word.

The Holy Spirit never contradicts Himself. He never leads the individual to do that which in the written Word He has commanded us all not to do. Any leading of the Spirit must be tested by that which we know to be the leading of the Spirit in the Word. But while we need to be on our guard against the leading of false spirits, it is our privilege to be led by the Holy Spirit and to lead a life free from the bondage of rules and free from the anxiety that we will not go wrong—a life as children whose Father has sent an unerring Guide to lead them all the way. Those who are thus led by the Spirit of God are *"sons of God"* (Romans 8:14). That is, they are not merely children of God—born, it is true, of the Father, but immature—but they are the grown children, the mature children of God. They are no longer babes but sons.

The apostle Paul draws a contrast in Galatians 4:1–7 between the babe under the tutelage of the law who differs little from a servant and the full-grown son who is no more a servant but a son walking in joyous liberty. It sometimes seems as if comparatively few Christians today had really thrown off the bondage of law, or rules outside themselves, and entered into the joyous liberty of sons.

15

THE HOLY SPIRIT BEARING WITNESS TO OUR SONSHIP

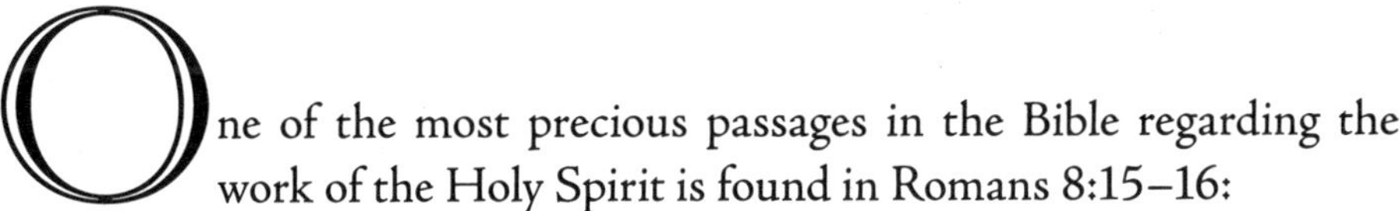

One of the most precious passages in the Bible regarding the work of the Holy Spirit is found in Romans 8:15–16:

> *For ye have not received the spirit of bondage again to fear; but ye have received the Spirit of adoption, whereby we cry, Abba, Father. The Spirit itself beareth witness with our spirit, that we are the children of God.*

There are two witnesses to our sonship. First, our own spirits, taking God at His Word—"*As many as received him, to them gave he power to become the sons of God"* (John 1:12)—bear witness to our sonship. Our own spirits unhesitatingly affirm that what God says—that we are sons of God—is true because God says so.

But there is another witness to our sonship, namely, the Holy Spirit. He bears witness together with our spirit. "Together with" is the force of the Greek used in this passage. It does not say that He bears witness to our spirit but "together with" it. How He does this is explained in Galatians 4:6: *"And because ye are sons, God hath sent forth the Spirit of his Son into your hearts, crying, Abba, Father."* When we have received Jesus Christ as our Savior and accepted God's testimony concerning Christ that, through Him, we have become sons, then the Spirit of His Son comes into our hearts, filling them with an overwhelming sense of sonship and crying through our hearts, *"Abba, Father."*

The natural attitude of our hearts toward God is not that of sons. We may call Him "Father" with our lips as when, for example, we repeat in a formal way the prayer that Jesus taught us, *"Our Father which art in heaven"* (Matthew 6:9), but there is no real sense that He is our Father. Our calling Him so is mere words. We do not really trust Him. We do not love to come into His presence; we do not love to look up into His face with a sense of wonderful joy and trust because we are talking to our Father. We dread God. We come to Him in prayer because we think we ought to and perhaps we are afraid of what might happen if we do not. However, when the Spirit of His Son bears witness together with our spirits to our sonship, then we are filled and thrilled with the sense that we are sons. We trust Him as we never even trusted our earthly fathers. There is even less fear of Him than there was of our earthly fathers. Reverence there is and awe, as well. But oh, such a sense of wonderful childlike trust!

Notice *when* the Spirit bears witness with our spirits that we are the children of God. We have the order of experience in the order of the verses in Romans 8. First, we see the Holy Spirit setting us free from the law of sin and death. Consequently, the righteousness of the law is fulfilled in us who walk not after the law but after the Spirit (see verses 2–4). Next, we have the believer not minding the things of the flesh but the things of the

Spirit (see Romans 8:5). Then, we have the believer, day by day, through the Spirit, putting the deeds of the body to death (see verse 13). Then, we have the believer led by the Spirit of God. Then and only then, we have the Spirit bearing witness to our sonship.

There are many seeking the witness of the Spirit to their sonship in the wrong place. They practically demand the witness of the Spirit to their sonship before they have even confessed their acceptance of Christ and certainly before they have surrendered their lives fully to the control of the indwelling Spirit of God. No, let us seek things in their right order. Let us accept Jesus Christ as our Savior and surrender to Him as our Lord and Master because God commands us to do so. Let us confess Him before the world because God commands that. (See Matthew 10:32–33; Romans 10:9–10.) Let us assert that our sins are forgiven, that we have eternal life, that we are sons of God because God says so in His Word, and we are unwilling to make God a liar by doubting Him. (See John 1:12; 5:24; Acts 10:43; 13:38–39; and 1 John 5:10–13.) Let us surrender our lives to the control of the Spirit of Life, looking to Him to set us free from the law of sin and death. Let us set our minds not upon the things of the flesh but upon the things of the Spirit. Let us, through the Spirit, day by day, put to death the deeds of the body. Let us give our lives up to be led by the Spirit of God in all things. Then, let us simply trust God to send the Spirit of His Son into our hearts, filling us with a sense of sonship, crying, *"Abba, Father,"* and He will do it.

God, our Father, longs that we would know and realize that we are His sons and daughters. He longs to hear us call Him "Father" from hearts that realize what they say and that trust Him without a fear or anxiety. He is our Father; He alone in all the universe realizes the fullness of meaning that there is in that wonderful word *Father,* and it brings joy to Him to have us realize that He is our Father and to call Him so.

Some years ago, there was a father in the state of Illinois who had a child who had been deaf and dumb from her birth. It was a sad day in that home when they came to realize that that little child was deaf and would never hear and, as they thought, would never speak. The father heard of an institution in Jacksonville, Illinois, where deaf children were taught to speak. He took this little child to the institution and put her in the superintendent's charge. After the child had been there some time, the superintendent wrote telling the father that he should come and visit his child. A day was appointed, and the child was told that her father was coming. As the hour approached, she sat up in the window, watching the gate for her father to pass through. The moment he entered the gate, she saw him, ran down the stairs and out on the lawn, met him, looked up into his face, and lifted up her hands and said, "Papa." When that father heard the dumb lips of his child speak for the first time and frame that sweet word, *"Papa,"* such a throb of joy passed through his heart that he literally fell to the ground and rolled upon the grass in ecstasy.

There is a Father who loves as no earthly father, who longs to have His children realize that they are His children. When we look up into His face and, from a heart that the Holy Spirit has filled with a sense of sonship, call Him *"Abba* [Papa], *Father,"* no language can describe the joy of God.

16

THE HOLY SPIRIT AS A TEACHER

"*But the Comforter, which is the Holy Ghost, whom the Father will send in my name, he shall teach you all things, and bring all things to your remembrance, whatsoever I have said unto you*" (John 14:26). Our Lord Jesus said these words in His last conversation with His disciples before His crucifixion.

Here we have a twofold work of the Holy Spirit, teaching and bringing to remembrance the things that Christ had already taught. We will take them in the reverse order.

The Holy Spirit Bringing to Remembrance

The Holy Spirit brings to remembrance the words of Christ. This promise was made primarily to the apostles, and it is the guarantee of the accuracy of their report of what Jesus said. But the Holy Spirit does a similar work with each believer who expects it of Him and who looks to Him to do it. The Holy Spirit brings to our mind the teachings of Christ and of the Word just when we need them for either the necessities of our life or of our service. Many of us could tell of occasions when we were in great distress of soul or great questioning as to duty or great extremity as to what to say to one whom we were trying to lead to Christ or to help, and at that exact moment, the very Scripture we needed—some passage we had not thought of for a long time and quite likely of which we had never thought of in this connection—was brought to mind. Who did it? The Holy Spirit did it. He is ready to do it even more frequently if we only expect it of Him and look to Him to do it. It is our privilege every time we sit down beside an inquirer to point him to the way of life to look up to the Holy Spirit and say, "Just what shall I say to this inquirer? Just what Scripture shall I use?"

There is deep significance in the fact that, in the verse immediately following this precious promise, Jesus said, *"Peace I leave with you, my peace I give unto you"* (John 14:27). It is by the Spirit bringing His words to remembrance and teaching us the truth of God that we obtain and abide in this peace. If we will simply look to the Holy Spirit to bring Scripture to mind just when we need it, and just the Scripture we need, we shall indeed have Christ's peace every moment of our lives.

One who was preparing for Christian work came to me in great distress. He said he must give up his preparation for he could not memorize the Scriptures. "I am thirty-two years old," he said, "and have been in business now for years. I have gotten out of the habit of study, and I cannot memorize anything." The man longed to be in his Master's service, and the tears stood in his eyes as he said it. "Don't be discouraged," I replied. "Take your Lord's promise that the Holy Spirit will bring His words to remembrance. Learn one passage of Scripture, fix it firmly in your mind, then another and then another, and look to the Holy Spirit to bring them to your remembrance when you need them." He went on with his preparation. He trusted the Holy Spirit. Afterward he took up work in a very difficult field, a field where all sorts of error abounded. They would gather around him on the street like bees, and he would take his Bible and trust the Holy Spirit to bring to remembrance the passages of Scripture that he needed. The Holy Spirit did it. His adversaries were filled with confusion as he met them at every point with the sure Word of God, and many of the most hardened were won for Christ.

The Holy Spirit Teaching

The Holy Spirit will teach us all things. There is a still more explicit promise to this effect two chapters further on in John. Here, Jesus said,

> *I have yet many things to say unto you, but ye cannot bear them now. Howbeit when he, the Spirit of truth, is come, he will guide you into all truth: for he shall not speak of himself; but whatsoever he shall hear, that shall he speak: and he will show you things to come. He shall glorify me: for he shall receive of mine, and shall show it unto you.*
>
> (John 16:12–14)

This promise was made in the first instance to the apostles, but the apostles themselves applied it to all believers. (See 1 John 2:20, 27.)

It is the privilege of each believer in Jesus Christ, even the humblest, to be "*taught of God*" (John 6:45). The humblest believer is independent of human teachers: "*Ye need not that any man teach you*" (1 John 2:27). This, of course, does not mean that we may not learn much from others who are taught of the Holy Spirit. If John had thought that, he would never have written this epistle to teach others. The man who is the most fully taught of God is the very one who will be most ready to listen to what God has taught others. Much less does it mean that, when we are taught of the Spirit, we are independent of the written Word of God, for the Word is the very place to which the Spirit, who is the Author of the Word, leads His pupils and the instrument through which He instructs them. (See

John 6:33; Ephesians 5:18–19; 6:17; and Colossians 3:16.) But while we may learn much from men, we are not dependent upon them. We have a divine Teacher, the Holy Spirit.

We shall never truly know the truth until we are thus taught directly by the Holy Spirit. No amount of mere human teaching, no matter who our teachers may be, will ever give us a correct and exact and full apprehension of the truth. Not even a diligent study of the Word, either in English or in the original languages, will give us a real understanding of the truth. We must be taught directly by the Holy Spirit, and we may be thus taught, each one of us. The one who is thus taught will understand the truth of God better, even if he does not know one word of Greek or Hebrew, than the one who knows Greek and Hebrew thoroughly, and all the cognate languages as well, but who is not taught of the Spirit.

The Spirit will guide the one whom He thus teaches *"into all truth"* (John 16:13). The whole sphere of God's truth is for each one of us, but the Holy Spirit will not guide us into all the truth in a single day or in a week or in a year, but step by step.

There are two special areas of the Spirit's teaching mentioned in John 16:

1. *"He will show you things to come"* (verse 13). There are many who say we can know nothing of the future, that all our thoughts on that subject are guesswork. It is true that we cannot know everything about the future. There are some things that God has seen fit to keep to Himself, secret things that belong to Him. (See Deuteronomy 29:29.) For example, we cannot *"know the times or the seasons"* (Acts 1:7) of our Lord's return, but there are many things about the future that the Holy Spirit will reveal to us.

2. *"He shall glorify me* [that is, Christ]*: for he shall receive of mine, and shall show it unto you"* (verse 14). This is the Holy Spirit's special way of teaching the believer, as well as the unbeliever, about Jesus Christ. It is His work, above all else, to reveal Jesus Christ and to glorify Him. His whole teaching centers in Christ. From one point of view or the other, He is always bringing us to Jesus Christ. There are some who fear to emphasize

the truth about the Holy Spirit lest Christ Himself be disparaged and put in the background, but there is no one who magnifies Christ as the Holy Spirit does. We shall never understand Christ, nor see His glory, until the Holy Spirit interprets Him to us. No amount of listening to sermons and lectures, no matter how able, no amount of mere study of the Word even, would ever give us to see the things of Christ. The Holy Spirit must show us, and He is willing to do it and can do it. He is longing to do it. The Holy Spirit's most intense desire is to reveal Jesus Christ to men.

On the day of Pentecost when Peter and the rest of the company were *"filled with the Holy Ghost"* (Acts 2:4), they did not talk much about the Holy Spirit; they talked about Christ. Study Peter's sermon on that day. Jesus Christ was his one theme, and Jesus Christ will be our one theme if we are taught of the Spirit. Jesus Christ will occupy the whole horizon of our vision. We will have a new Christ, a glorious Christ. Christ will be so glorious to us that we will long to go and tell everyone about this glorious One whom we have found. Jesus Christ is so different when the Spirit glorifies Him by taking of His things and showing them to us.

The Holy Spirit Revealing

The Holy Spirit reveals to us the deep things of God, which are hidden from and are foolishness to the natural man.

> *Eye hath not seen, nor ear heard, neither have entered into the heart of man, the things which God hath prepared for them that love him. But God hath revealed them unto us by his Spirit: for the Spirit searcheth all things, yea, the deep things of God. For what man knoweth the things of a man, save the spirit of man which is in him? even so the things of God knoweth no man, but the Spirit of God. Now we have received, not the spirit of the world, but the spirit which is of God; that we might know the things that are freely given to us of God. Which things also we speak, not in the words which man's wisdom teacheth, but which the Holy Ghost teacheth; comparing spiritual things with spiritual.*
>
> (1 Corinthians 2:9–13)

This passage, of course, refers primarily to the apostles, but we cannot limit this work of the Spirit to them. The Spirit reveals to the individual believer the deep things of God, things that human eyes have not seen, nor ears heard, things that have not entered into the heart of man, the things that God has prepared for them who love Him. It is evident from the context that this does not refer solely to heaven or the things to come in the life hereafter. The Holy Spirit takes the deep things of God that God has prepared for us, even in the life that is now, and reveals them to us.

The Holy Spirit Interpreting

The Holy Spirit interprets His own revelation. He imparts power to discern, know, and appreciate what He has taught. In the next verse of 1 Corinthians 2, we read, *"But the natural man receiveth not the things of the Spirit of God: for they are foolishness unto him: neither can he know them, because they are spiritually discerned"* (1 Corinthians 2:14). Not only is the Holy Spirit the author of revelation, the written Word of God; He is also the interpreter of what He has revealed. Any profound book is immeasurably more interesting and helpful when we have the author of the book right at hand to interpret it to us, and it is always our privilege to have the author of the Bible right at hand when we study it. The Holy Spirit is the author of the Bible, and He stands ready to interpret its meaning to every believer every time he opens the Book. To understand the Book, we must look to Him; then the darkest places become clear. We often need to pray with the psalmist of old, *"Open thou mine eyes, that I may behold wondrous things out of thy law"* (Psalm 119:18).

It is not enough that we have the revelation of God before us in the written Word to study; we must also have the inward illumination of the Holy Spirit to enable us to apprehend it as we study. It is a common mistake, but a most palpable mistake, to try to comprehend a spiritual revelation with the natural understanding. It is the foolish attempt to do this that has landed so many in the bog of so-called "higher criticism." In order to understand art, a man must have aesthetic sense as well as the knowledge of colors and of paint, and to understand a spiritual revelation, a man must be taught of the Spirit. A mere knowledge of the languages in which the Bible was written is not enough. A man with no aesthetic sense might as well expect to appreciate the Sistine Madonna, just because he is not color blind, as a man who is not filled with the Spirit can expect to understand the Bible, simply because he understands the vocabulary and the laws of grammar for the languages in which the Bible was written. We might as well think of setting a man to teach art because he understands paints as to set a man to teach the Bible because he has a thorough understanding of Greek and Hebrew. In our day, we need not only to recognize the utter insufficiency and worthlessness before God of our own righteousness, which is the lesson of the opening chapters of the epistle to the Romans, but also the utter insufficiency and worthlessness of our own wisdom when it comes to the things of God, which is the lesson of the first epistle to the Corinthians, especially the first three chapters. (See, for example, 1 Corinthians 1:19–21, 26–27.)

In the same way, the Jews of old had a revelation by the Spirit, but they failed to depend upon the Spirit Himself to interpret it to them, so they went astray. So Christians today have a revelation by the Spirit, and many are failing to depend upon the Him to interpret the revelation to them, and so go astray. The whole evangelical church recognizes, theoretically at least, the utter insufficiency of man's own righteousness. What it needs to be taught in the present hour, and what it needs to be made to feel, is the utter insufficiency of man's wisdom. That is perhaps the lesson that this century of towering intellectual conceit needs most of all to learn.

To understand God's Word, we must empty ourselves utterly of our own wisdom and rest in utter dependence upon the Spirit of God to interpret it to us. We do well to take to heart the words of Jesus Himself in Matthew 11:25: *"I thank thee, O Father, Lord of heaven and earth, because thou hast hid these things from the wise and prudent, and hast revealed them unto babes."*

A number of Bible students were once discussing the best methods of Bible study. One man, who was in point of fact a learned and scholarly man, said, "I think the best method of Bible study is the baby method." When we have entirely put away our own righteousness, then and only then, we get the righteousness of God. (See Romans 10:3; Philippians 3:4–7, 9.) When we have entirely put away our own wisdom, then and only then, we get the wisdom of God. *"Let no man deceive himself,"* said the apostle Paul. *"If any man among you seemeth to be wise in this world, let him become a fool, that he may be wise"* (1 Corinthians 3:18). The emptying must precede filling, the self poured out that God may be poured in.

We must daily be taught by the Spirit to understand the Word. We cannot depend today on the fact that the Spirit taught us yesterday. Each new time that we come in contact with the Word, it must be in the power of the Spirit for that specific occasion. That the Holy Spirit once illumined our minds to grasp a certain truth is not enough. He must do it each time we confront that passage. Andrew Murray has well said, "Each time you come to the Word in study, in hearing a sermon, or in reading a religious book there ought to be a definite act of humility. You must deny your own wisdom and yield yourself in faith to the divine Teacher."[1]

The Holy Spirit Enabling

The Holy Spirit enables the believer to communicate to others, in power, the truth that he himself has been taught. Paul said in 1 Corinthians 2:1–5,

> *And I, brethren, when I came to you, came not with excellency of speech or of wisdom, declaring unto you the testimony of God. For I determined not to know any thing among you, save Jesus Christ, and him crucified. And I was with you in weakness, and in fear, and in much trembling. And my speech and my preaching was not with enticing words of man's wisdom, but in demonstration of the Spirit and of power: that your faith should not stand in the wisdom of men, but in the power of God.*

In a similar way, in writing to the believers in Thessalonica in 1 Thessalonians 1:5, Paul wrote: *"For our gospel came not unto you in word only, but also in power, and in the Holy Ghost, and in much assurance; as ye know what manner of men we were among you for your sake."*

Not only do we need the Holy Spirit to reveal the truth to chosen apostles and prophets in the first place and to interpret the truth He has thus revealed to us as individuals in the second place, but also, in the third place, we need the Holy Spirit to enable us to effectually communicate to others the truth that He Himself has interpreted to us. We need Him all along the line. One great cause of real failure in the ministry, even when there is seeming success—not only in the regular ministry but in all forms of service as well—comes from the attempt to teach what the Holy Spirit has taught us by *"enticing words of man's wisdom"* (1 Corinthians 2:4), that is, by the arts of human logic, rhetoric, persuasion, and eloquence. What is needed is Holy Spirit power, *"demonstration of the Spirit and of power"* (verse 4).

There are three causes of failure in preaching today. First, some other message is taught than the message the Holy Spirit has revealed in the Word. Men preach science, art, literature, philosophy, sociology, history, economics, experience, etc., and not the simple Word of God as found in the Holy Spirit's Book, the Bible.

Second, the Spirit-taught message of the Bible is studied and sought to be apprehended by the natural understanding, that is, without the Spirit's illumination. How common that is, even in institutions where men are being trained for the ministry, even institutions that may be altogether orthodox.

Third, the Spirit-given message, the Word, studied and apprehended under the Holy Spirit's illumination, is given out to others with *"enticing words of man's wisdom"* and not in *"demonstration of the Spirit and of power"* (1 Corinthians 2:4). We need, and are absolutely dependent upon, the Spirit all along the line. He must teach us how to speak as well as what to speak. His must be the power as well as the message.

17

PRAYING, RETURNING THANKS, WORSHIPING IN THE HOLY SPIRIT

Two of the most deeply significant passages in the Bible on the subject of the Holy Spirit and on the subject of prayer are found in Jude 1:20 and Ephesians 6:18. In Jude 1:20, we read, *"But ye, beloved, building up yourselves on your most holy faith, praying in the Holy Ghost,"* and in Ephesians 6:18, *"Praying always with all prayer and supplication in the Spirit, and watching thereunto with all perseverance and supplication for all saints."* These passages distinctly teach us three things.

Lesson 1—Spirit-Led Prayer

The Holy Spirit guides the believer in prayer. The disciples did not know how to pray as they ought so they came to Jesus and said, *"Lord, teach us to pray"* (Luke 11:1). We today do not know how to pray as we ought—we do not know what to pray for, nor how to ask for it—but there is One who is always at hand to help (see John 14:16–17), and He knows what we should pray for. He helps our infirmity in this matter of prayer as in other matters (see Romans 8:26). He teaches us to pray. True prayer is prayer in the Spirit (i.e., the prayer that the Holy Spirit inspires and directs).

The prayer in which the Holy Spirit leads us is the prayer *"according to the will of God"* (Romans 8:27). When we ask anything according to God's will, we know that He hears us, and we know that He has granted the things that we ask. (See 1 John 5:14–15.) We may know it is ours at the moment when we pray, just as surely as we know it afterward when we have it in our actual possession.

But how can we know the will of God when we pray? In two ways. First of all, we know His will by what is written in His Word. All the promises in the Bible are sure, and if God promises anything in the Bible, we may be sure it is His will to give us that thing. But there are many things we need that are not specifically promised in the Word, and still, even in that case, it is our privilege to know the will of God, for it is the work of the Holy Spirit to teach us God's will and to lead us out in prayer along the line of God's will. This is the second way we can know the will of God as we pray.

Some object to the Christian doctrine of prayer, for they say that it teaches we can go to God in our ignorance and change His will and subject His infinite wisdom to our erring foolishness, but that is not the Christian doctrine of prayer at all. The Christian doctrine of prayer is that it is the believer's privilege to be taught by the Spirit of God Himself to know what the will of God is and not to ask for the things that our foolishness would prompt us to ask for but to ask for things that the never-erring Spirit of God prompts us to ask for. True prayer is prayer *"in the Spirit"* (Ephesians 6:18), that is, prayer that the Spirit inspires and directs.

When we come into God's presence, we should recognize our infirmities: our ignorance of what is best for us, our ignorance of what we should pray for, and our ignorance of how we should pray for it. In the consciousness of our utter inability to pray correctly, we should look up to the Holy Spirit to teach us to pray and cast ourselves utterly upon Him to direct our prayers and to discover our desires and guide our utterance of them. There is no place where we need to recognize our ignorance more than we do in prayer. Rushing heedlessly into God's presence and asking the first thing that comes into our minds, or that some other thoughtless one asks us to pray for, is not praying *"in the Holy Ghost"* (Jude 1:20) and is not true prayer. We must wait for the Holy Spirit and surrender ourselves to Him. The prayer that God the Holy Spirit inspires is the prayer that God the Father answers.

The longings that the Holy Spirit creates in our hearts are often too deep for utterance, too deep apparently for clear and definite comprehension on the part of the believer himself in whom the Spirit is working: *"The Spirit itself maketh intercession for us with groanings which cannot be uttered"* (Romans 8:26). God Himself *"searcheth the hearts"* to know what *"the mind of the Spirit"* is (verse 27) in these unuttered and unutterable longings. But God does know what the mind of the Spirit is. He does know what these Spirit-given longings, which we cannot put into words, mean, even if we do not. These longings are *"according to the will of God"* (verse 27), and God grants them. It is in this way that it comes to pass that God *"is able to do exceeding abundantly above all that we ask or think, according to the power that worketh in us"* (Ephesians 3:20). There are other times when the Spirit's leadings are so clear that we pray with the Spirit and with the understanding also (see 1 Corinthians 14:15). We distinctly understand what it is that the Holy Spirit leads us to pray for.

Lesson 2—Spirit-Guided Thanksgiving

The Holy Spirit inspires the believer and guides him in thanksgiving, as well as in prayer.

> *And be not drunk with wine, wherein is excess; but be filled with the Spirit; speaking to yourselves in psalms and hymns and spiritual songs, singing and making melody in your heart to the Lord; giving thanks always for all things unto God and the Father in the name of our Lord Jesus Christ.* (Ephesians 5:18–20)

Not only does the Holy Spirit teach us to pray, He also teaches us to render thanks. One of the most prominent characteristics of the Spirit-filled life is thanksgiving. On the day of Pentecost, when the disciples were filled with the Holy Spirit and spoke as the Spirit gave them utterance, they told the wonderful works of God (see Acts 2:4, 11). Today when any believer is filled with the Holy Spirit, he always becomes filled with thanksgiving and praise. True thanksgiving is *"unto God and the Father,"* through or *"in the name of our Lord Jesus Christ"* (Ephesians 5:20), in the Holy Spirit.

Lesson 3—Spirit-Inspired Worship

The Holy Spirit inspires worship on the part of the believer. We read in Philippians 3:3 (RV), *"For we are the circumcision, who worship by the Spirit of God, and glory in Christ Jesus, and have no confidence in the flesh."* Prayer is not worship; thanksgiving is not worship. Worship is a definite act of the creature in relation to God. Worship is bowing before God in adoring acknowledgment and contemplation of Him and the perfection of His being. Someone has said, "In our prayers, we are taken up with our needs; in our thanksgiving, we are taken up with our blessings; in our worship, we are taken up with Himself."

There is no true and acceptable worship except that which the Holy Spirit prompts and directs. *"God is a Spirit: and they that worship him must worship him in spirit and in truth....for the Father seeketh such to worship him"* (John 4:24, 23). The flesh seeks to intrude into every sphere of life. The flesh has its worship as well as its lusts. The worship that the flesh[1] prompts is an abomination to God. In this, we see the folly of any attempt at a conference of religions where the representatives of radically different religions attempt to worship together.

Not all earnest and honest worship is worship in the Spirit. A man may be very honest and very earnest in his worship and still not have submitted himself to the guidance of the Holy Spirit in the matter, and so his worship is in the flesh. Oftentimes, even when there is great loyalty to the letter of the Word, worship may not be in the Spirit—in other words, inspired and directed by Him. To worship aright, as Paul put it, we must have *"no confidence in the flesh"* (Philippians 3:3); that is, we must recognize the utter inability of the flesh[1] to worship acceptably. And we must also realize the danger that exists of the flesh intruding itself into our worship. In utter self-distrust and self-abnegation, we must cast ourselves upon the Holy Spirit to lead us rightly in our worship. Just as we must renounce any merit in ourselves and cast ourselves upon Christ and His work for us upon the cross for justification, so we must renounce any supposed capacity for good in ourselves and cast ourselves utterly upon the Holy Spirit and His work in us, in holy living, knowing, praying, thanking, worshiping, and all else that we are to do.

18

THE HOLY SPIRIT SENDING MEN FORTH TO DEFINITE LINES OF WORK

As they ministered to the Lord, and fasted, the Holy Ghost said, Separate me Barnabas and Saul for the work whereunto I have called them. And when they had fasted and prayed, and laid their hands on them, they sent them away. So they, being sent forth by the Holy Ghost, departed unto Seleucia; and from thence they sailed to Cyprus.
—Acts 13:2–4

It is evident from this passage that the Holy Spirit calls men into definite lines of work and sends them forth into the work. He not only calls men in a general way into Christian work but selects the specific work and points it out.

Many a Christian is asking today, and many others ought to ask, "Shall I go to China, to Africa, to India?" There is only one person who can rightly settle that question for you, and that person is the Holy Spirit. You cannot settle the question for yourself, much less can any other man settle it rightly for you. Not every Christian man is called to go to China; not every Christian man is called to go to Africa; not every Christian man is called to go to the foreign field at all. God alone knows whether He wishes you in any of these places, but He is willing to show you. In a day such as we live in, when there is such a need for the right men and the right women on the foreign field, every young and healthy and intellectually competent Christian man and woman should definitely offer themselves to God for the foreign field and ask Him if He wants them to go; but they ought not to go until He, by His Holy Spirit, makes it plain.

The great need in all areas of Christian work today is men and women whom the Holy Spirit calls and sends forth. We have plenty of men and women whom men have called and sent forth. We have plenty of men and women who have called themselves, for there are many today who object strenuously to being sent forth by men or by any organization of any kind. But, in fact, these men and women who are sent forth by themselves and not by God are immeasurably worse.

How does the Holy Spirit call? The passage before us, Acts 13:2–4, does not tell us how the Holy Spirit spoke to the group of prophets and teachers in Antioch, telling them to separate Barnabas and Saul to the work for which He had called them. It is presumably purposely silent on this point. Possibly it is silent on this point lest we should think that the Holy Spirit must always call in precisely the same way. There is nothing whatsoever to indicate that He spoke by an audible voice. Much less is there anything to indicate that He made His will known in any of the fantastic ways in which some in these days profess to discern His leading—as for example, by twitchings of the body, by shuddering, by opening the Bible at random and putting a finger on a passage that may be construed into some entirely different meaning than that which the inspired author intended by it. The important point is that He made His will clearly known and that He is willing to make His will clearly known to us today. Sometimes He makes it known in one way and sometimes in another, but He will make it known.

But how do we receive the Holy Spirit's call? First of all, by desiring it; second, by earnestly seeking it; third, by waiting upon the Lord for it; fourth, by expecting it. The record reads, *"As they ministered to the Lord, and fasted"* (Acts 13:2). They were waiting upon the Lord for His direction. For the time being, they had turned their backs utterly upon worldly cares and enjoyments, even upon those things that were perfectly proper in their places.

Many a man, to justify his staying home from the foreign field, is saying today, "I have never had a call." How do you know that? Have you been listening for a call? God usually speaks in a still small voice, and it is only the listening ear that can catch it. Have you ever definitely offered yourself to God to send you where He will? While no man or woman ought to go to China or Africa or other foreign field unless they are clearly and definitely called, they ought each to offer themselves to God for this work and be ready for the call and be listening sharply so that they may hear the call if it comes. Let it be borne distinctly in mind that a man needs no more definite call to Africa than to Boston, or New York, or London, or any other desirable field at home.

The Holy Spirit not only calls men and sends them forth into definite areas of work, but He also guides in the details of daily life and service as to where to go and where not to go, what to do and what not to do. We read in Acts 8:27–29,

> *And* [Philip] *arose and went: and, behold, a man of Ethiopia, an eunuch of great authority under Candace queen of the Ethiopians, who had the charge of all her treasure, and had come to Jerusalem for to worship, was returning, and sitting in his chariot read Esaias* [Isaiah] *the prophet. Then the Spirit said unto Philip, Go near, and join thyself to this chariot.*

Here, we see the Spirit guiding Philip in the details of service into which He had called him. In a similar way, we read in Acts 16:6–7 (RV),

> *And they went through the region of Phrygia and Galatia, having been forbidden of the Holy Ghost to speak the word in Asia; and when they were come over against Mysia, they assayed to go into Bithynia; and the Spirit of Jesus suffered them not.*

Here, we see the Holy Spirit directing Paul where not to go.

It is possible for us to have the unerring guidance of the Holy Spirit at every turn of life. Take, for example, our personal work. It is manifestly not God's intention that we speak to everyone we meet. To attempt to do so would be to attempt the impossible, and we would waste much time in trying to speak to people where we could do no good that might be used in speaking to people where we could accomplish something. There are some to whom it would be wise for us to speak. There are others to whom it would be unwise for us to speak. Time spent on them would be taken from work that would be more to God's glory. Doubtless, as Philip journeyed toward Gaza, he met many before he met the one of whom the Spirit said, "*Go near, and join thyself to this chariot*" (Acts 8:29). The Spirit is as ready to guide us as He was to guide Philip.

Some years ago, a Christian worker in Toronto had the impression that he should go to the hospital and speak to someone there. He thought to himself, "Whom do I know at the hospital at this time?" There came to his mind one whom he knew was at the hospital, and so he hurried there. But as he sat down by his side to talk with him, he realized it was not for this man that he was sent. He got up to lift a window. What did it all mean? There was another man lying across the aisle in the ward from the man he knew, and the thought came to him that this might be the man to whom he should speak. He turned and spoke to this man and had the privilege of leading him to Christ. There was apparently nothing serious in the man's case. He had suffered some injury to his knee and there was no thought of a serious issue, but that man passed into eternity that night.

Many instances of a similar character could be recorded, and they prove from experience that the Holy Spirit is as ready to guide those who seek His guidance today as He was to guide the early disciples. He is ready to guide us, not only in our more definite forms of Christian work but also in all the affairs of life, business, study, and everything we have to do. There is no promise in the Bible more plainly explicit than the following:

> *If any of you lack wisdom, let him ask of God, that giveth to all men liberally, and upbraideth not; and it shall be given him. But let him ask in faith, nothing wavering. For he that wavereth is like a wave of the sea driven with the wind and tossed. For let not that man think that he shall receive any thing of the Lord.* (James 1:5–7)

This passage not only promises God's wisdom but also tells us specifically just what to do to obtain it. There are really five steps stated or implied in the passage.

Step 1—Acknowledge Our Lack

This passage is clear that we "lack wisdom." We must be conscious of and fully admit our own inability to decide wisely. Here is where we often fail to receive God's wisdom. We think we are able to decide for ourselves, or at least we are not ready to admit our own utter inability to decide. There must be an entire renunciation of the wisdom of the flesh.

Step 2—Desire God's Plan

We must really desire to know God's way and be willing, at any cost, to do God's will. This is implied in the word, "*ask*." The asking must be sincere, and if we are not willing to do God's will, whatever it may be, at any cost, the asking is not sincere. This is a point of fundamental importance. There is nothing that goes so far to make our minds clear in the discernment of the will of God as revealed by His Spirit as an absolutely surrendered will. Here, we find the reason why men often do not know God's will and do not have the Spirit's guidance. They are not willing to do whatever the Spirit leads at any cost. The one who wants to do His will who will know not only of the doctrine but his actual daily duty. Men oftentimes come to me and say, "I cannot find out the will of God," but when I put the question to them, "Are you willing to do the will of God at any cost?" they admit that they are not. The way that is very obscure when we hold back from an absolute surrender to God becomes as clear as day when we make that surrender.

Step 3—Ask for Guidance

We must definitely "ask" for guidance, as James 1:5 so clearly says. It is not enough to desire; it is not enough to be willing to obey. We must ask, definitely ask, God to show us the way.

Step 4—Expect Guidance

We must confidently expect guidance. *"Let him ask in faith, nothing wavering"* (James 1:6). There are many who cannot find the way, though they ask God to show it to them, simply because they have not the absolutely undoubting expectation that God will show them the way. God promises to show it if we expect it confidently. When you come to God in prayer to show you what to do, know for a certainty that He will show you. He does not tell how He will show you, but He promises that He will show you and that is enough.

Step 5—Follow Step-by-Step

We must follow step-by-step as the guidance comes. As said before, just how it will come, no one can tell, but it will come. Often, only one step will be made clear at a time; that is all we need to know—the next step. Many are in darkness because they do not know and cannot find what God would have them do next week or next month or next year.

A college man once came to me and told me that he was in great darkness about God's guidance, that he had been seeking to find the will of God and learn what his life's work should be, but he could not find it. I asked him how far along he was in his college course. He said his sophomore year. I asked, "What is it you desire to know?"

"What I shall do when I finish college."

"Do you know that you ought to go through college?"

"Yes."

This man not only knew what he ought to do next year but the year after, but still he was in great perplexity because he did not know what he ought to do when these two years were ended. God delights to lead His children a step at a time. He leads us as He led the children of Israel:

> *And when the cloud was taken up from the tabernacle, then after that the children of Israel journeyed: and in the place where the cloud abode, there the children of Israel pitched their tents. At the commandment of the Lord the children of Israel journeyed, and at the commandment of the Lord they pitched: as long as the cloud abode upon the tabernacle they rested in their tents. And when the cloud tarried long upon the tabernacle many days, then the children of Israel kept the charge of the Lord, and journeyed not. And so it was, when the cloud was a few days upon the tabernacle; according to the commandment of the Lord they abode in their tents, and according to the commandment of the Lord they journeyed. And so it was, when the cloud abode from even unto the morning, and that the cloud was taken up in the morning, then they journeyed: whether it was by day or by night that the cloud was taken up, they journeyed. Or whether it were two days, or a month, or a year, that the cloud tarried upon the tabernacle, remaining thereon, the children of Israel abode in their tents, and journeyed not: but when it was taken up, they journeyed. At the commandment of the Lord they rested in the tents, and at the commandment of the Lord they journeyed: they kept the charge of the Lord, at the commandment of the Lord by the hand of Moses.* (Numbers 9:17–23)

Many who have given themselves up to the leading of the Holy Spirit get into a place of great bondage and are tortured because they have leadings that they fear may be from God but of which they are not sure. If they do not obey these leadings, they are fearful they have disobeyed God and sometimes imagine that they have grieved away the Holy Spirit because they did not follow His leading. This is all unnecessary. Let us settle it in our minds that God's guidance is clear guidance. *"God is light, and in him is no darkness at all"* (1 John 1:5). Any leading that is not perfectly clear is not from Him—that is, if our wills are absolutely surrendered to Him. Of course, the uncertainty may arise from an unsurrendered will. But if our wills are absolutely surrendered to God, we have the right, as God's children, to be sure that any guidance is from Him before we obey it.

We have a right to go to our Father and say, "Heavenly Father, here I am. I desire above all things to do Your will. Now make it clear to me, Your child. If this thing that I have a leading to do is Your will, I will do it, but make it clear as day if it is Your will." If it is His will, the heavenly Father will make it as clear as day. You need not and ought not do that thing until He does make it clear, and you need not and ought not condemn yourself because you did not do it. God does not want His children to be in a state of condemnation before Him. He wishes us to be free from all care, worry, anxiety, and self-condemnation. Any earthly parent would make the way clear to his child who asked to know it, and our heavenly Father will make it much more clear to us. Until He does make it clear, we don't need to have fears that, in not doing it, we are disobeying God. We have no right to dictate to God as to how He should give His guidance—as, for example, by asking Him to shut up every way, by asking Him to give a sign, by guiding us in putting our finger on a text, or in any other way. It is ours to seek and to expect wisdom, but it is not ours to dictate how it will be given. The Holy Spirit divides to *"every man severally as he will"* (1 Corinthians 12:11).

Two things are evident from what has been said about the work of the Holy Spirit: first, how utterly dependent we are upon the work of the Holy Spirit at every turn of Christian life and service; second, how perfect is the provision for life and service that God has made. The fullness of privilege that is open to the humblest believer through the Holy Spirit's work is so wonderful. It is not so much what we are by nature—either intellectually, morally, physically, or even spiritually—that is important. The important matter is what the Holy Spirit can do for us and what we will let Him do. Not infrequently, the Holy Spirit takes the one who seems to have the least natural promise and uses him far beyond those who have the greatest natural promise. Christian life is not to be lived in the realm of natural temperament, and Christian work is not to be done in the power of natural endowment. Christian life is to be lived in the realm of the Spirit, and Christian work is to be done in the power of the Spirit. The Holy Spirit is willing and eagerly desirous of doing for each one of us His whole work, and He will do in each one of us all that we will let Him do.

19

THE HOLY SPIRIT AND THE BELIEVER'S BODY

The Holy Spirit does a work for our bodies as well as for our minds and hearts. We read in Romans 8:11, *"But if the Spirit of him that raised up Jesus from the dead dwell in you, he that raised up Christ from the dead shall also quicken your mortal bodies by his Spirit that dwelleth in you."*

The Holy Spirit quickens the mortal body of the believer. It is very evident from the context that this refers to the future resurrection of the body. (See Romans 8:21–23.) The resurrection of the body is the Holy Spirit's work. The glorified body is from Him; it is *"a spiritual body"* (1 Corinthians 15:44). At the present time, we have only the firstfruits of the Spirit and are waiting for the full harvest, *"the redemption of our body"* (Romans 8:23).

There is, however, a sense in which the Holy Spirit even now quickens our bodies. Jesus told us in Matthew 12:28 that He cast out devils by the Spirit of God. We read in Acts 10:38, *"How God anointed Jesus of Nazareth with the Holy Ghost and with power: who went about doing good, and healing all that were oppressed of the devil."* In James 5:14, the apostle wrote, *"Is any sick among you? let him call for the elders of the church; and let them pray over him, anointing him with oil in the name of the Lord."* The oil in this passage (as elsewhere) is a type of the Holy Spirit, and the truth is set forth that the healing is the Holy Spirit's work.

God, by His Holy Spirit, does impart new health and vigor to these mortal bodies in the present life. To go to the extremes that many do and take the ground that the believer who is walking in fellowship with Christ need never be ill is to go further than the Bible warrants us in going. It is true that the redemption of our bodies is secured by the atoning work of Christ, but until the Lord comes, we only enjoy the firstfruits of that redemption.

We are waiting and sometimes groaning for our full place as sons manifested in the redemption of our bodies (see Romans 8:23). But while this is true, it is the clear teaching of Scripture, as well as a matter of personal experience on the part of thousands, that the life of the Holy Spirit does sweep through these bodies of ours in moments of weakness and of pain and sickness, imparting new health to them, delivering them from pain and filling them with abounding life. It is our privilege to know the quickening touch of the Holy Spirit in these bodies as well as in our minds and affections and will. It would be a great day for the church and for the glory of Jesus Christ if Christians would renounce forever all the devil's counterfeits of the Holy Spirit's work—Christian Science, mental healing, hypnotism, and the various other forms of occultism, and depend upon God by the power of His Holy Spirit to work in these bodies of ours what He, in His unerring wisdom, sees that we most need.

20

THE BAPTISM WITH THE HOLY SPIRIT

One of the most deeply significant phrases used in connection with the Holy Spirit in the Scriptures is "baptized with the Holy Spirit." John the Baptist was the first to use this phrase. In speaking of himself and the coming One, he said,

> *I indeed baptize you with water unto repentance: but he that cometh after me is mightier than I, whose shoes I am not worthy to bear: he shall baptize you with the Holy Ghost, and with fire.*
>
> (Matthew 3:11)

The second *"with"* in this passage is in italics in the KJV text, meaning it is not found in the Greek. There are not two different baptisms spoken of, the one with the Holy Spirit and the one with fire, but rather one baptism with the Holy Wind and Fire. Jesus afterward used the same expression. In Acts 1:5, He said, *"For John truly baptized with water; but ye shall be baptized with the Holy Ghost not many days hence."* When this promise of John the Baptist and of our Lord was fulfilled in Acts 2:3–4, we read, *"And there appeared unto them cloven tongues like as of fire, and it sat upon each of them. And they were all filled with the Holy Ghost."* Here we have another expression, *"filled with the Holy Ghost,"* used synonymously with "baptized with the Holy Spirit."

We read again in Acts,

> *While Peter yet spake these words, the Holy Ghost fell on all them which heard the word. And they of the circumcision which believed were astonished, as many as came with Peter, because that on the Gentiles also was poured out the gift of the Holy Ghost. For they heard them speak with tongues, and magnify God.* (Acts 10:44–46)

Peter himself, later describing this experience in Jerusalem, told the story in this way:

> *And as I began to speak, the Holy Ghost fell on them, as on us at the beginning. Then remembered I the word of the Lord, how that he said, John indeed baptized with water; but ye shall be baptized with the Holy Ghost. Forasmuch then as God gave them the like gift as he did unto us, who believed on the Lord Jesus Christ; what was I, that I could withstand God?* (Acts 11:15–17)

Here, Peter distinctly referred the experience that came to Cornelius and his household, being *"baptized with the Holy Ghost."* We see that the expressions *"the Holy Ghost fell"* and *"the gift of the Holy Ghost"* are practically synonymous expressions with "baptized with the Holy Ghost." Still other expressions are used to describe this blessing, such as *"receive the gift of the Holy Ghost"* (Acts 2:38; see Acts 19:2–6); *"the Holy Ghost came on them"* (Acts 19:6); *"gifts of the Holy Ghost"* (Hebrews 2:4; see 1 Corinthians 12:4, 11, 13); *"I send the promise of my Father upon you;"* and *"endued with power from on high"* (Luke 24:49).

What Is the Baptism of the Holy Spirit?

A Definite Experience

In the first place, the baptism with the Holy Spirit is a definite experience of which one may, and ought, to know whether he has received it or not.

This is evident from our Lord's command to His disciples in Luke 24:49 and in Acts 1:4 that they should not depart from Jerusalem to undertake the work that He had commissioned them to do until they had received this promise from the Father. It is also evident from Acts 8:15–16, where we are distinctly told, *"the Holy Ghost...as yet...was fallen upon none of them."* It is evident also from Acts 19:2 (RV), where Paul put to the little group of disciples at Ephesus the definite question, *"Did ye receive the Holy Ghost when ye believed?"*

It is evident that the receiving of the Holy Spirit was an experience so definite that one could answer yes or no to the question whether they had received the Holy Spirit. In this case, the disciples definitely answered, *"Nay, we did not so much as hear whether the Holy Ghost was given"* (Acts 19:2 RV). They did not say what our King James Version makes them say, which is that they did not so much as hear whether there was any Holy Spirit. They knew that there was a Holy Spirit. They knew furthermore that there was a definite promise of the baptism with the Holy Spirit, but they had not heard that that promise had been as yet fulfilled. Paul told them that it had, and he took steps whereby they were definitely baptized with the Holy Spirit before that meeting closed.

It is equally evident from Galatians 3:2 that the baptism with the Holy Spirit is a definite experience of which one may know whether he has received it or not. In this passage, Paul said to the believers in Galatia, *"This only would I learn of you, Received ye the Spirit by the works of the law, or by the hearing of faith?"* Their receiving of the Spirit had been so definite as a matter of personal consciousness that Paul could appeal to it as a ground for his argument.

In our day, there is much talk about the baptism with the Holy Spirit and prayer for the baptism with the Spirit that is altogether vague and indefinite. Men arise in meetings and pray that they may be baptized with the Holy Spirit. If you should go afterward to the one who offered the prayer and put to him the question, "Did you receive what you asked? Were you baptized with the Holy Spirit?" it is quite likely that he would hesitate and falter and say, "I hope so." But there is none of this indefiniteness in the Bible. The Bible is clear as day on this, as on every other point. It sets forth an experience so definite and so real that one may know whether or not he has received the baptism with the Holy Spirit and can answer yes or no to the question, "Have you received the Holy Spirit?"

A Unique Occurrence

In the second place, it is evident that the baptism with the Holy Spirit is an operation of the Holy Spirit that is distinct from, and additional to, His regenerating work.

This is evident from Acts 1:5: *"For John truly baptized with water; but ye shall be baptized with the Holy Ghost not many days hence."* It is clear then that the disciples had not yet been baptized with the Holy Spirit, that they were to be thus baptized not many days later, but the men to whom Jesus spoke these words were already new men. They had been so pronounced by our Lord Himself. He had said to them in John 15:3, *"Now ye are clean through the word which I have spoken unto you."* What does *"clean through the word"* mean? The question is answered in 1 Peter 1:23: *"Being born again, not of corruptible seed, but of incorruptible, by the word of God, which liveth and abideth for ever."*

A little earlier on the same night, Jesus had said to them in John 13:10, *"He that is washed needeth not save to wash his feet, but is clean every whit:*

and ye are clean, but not all." The Lord Jesus had pronounced that apostolic company *clean*—reborn men—with the exception of the one who never was a reborn man, Judas Iscariot, who should betray Him. (See verse 11.) Jesus Christ had pronounced the remaining eleven reborn men. Yet He told these same men in Acts 1:5 that the baptism with the Holy Spirit was an experience they had not yet realized, that still lay in the future. So it is evident that it is one thing to be born again by the Holy Spirit through the Word and something distinct from this and additional to it to be baptized with the Holy Spirit.

The same thing is evident from Acts 8:12, compared with the fifteenth and sixteenth verses of the same chapter. In the twelfth verse, we read that a large company of disciples had believed the preaching of Philip concerning the kingdom of God and the name of Jesus Christ and *"were baptized in the name of the Lord Jesus"* (Acts 8:16). Certainly, in this company of baptized believers, there were at least some reborn people. Whatever the true form of water baptism may be, they undoubtedly had been baptized by it because the baptizing had been done by a Spirit-commissioned man, but we read,

> *When* [Peter and John] *were come down, prayed for them, that they might receive the Holy Ghost: (for as yet he was fallen upon none of them: only they were baptized in the name of the Lord Jesus.)*
>
> (Acts 8:15–16)

They were baptized believers; they had been baptized into the name of the Lord Jesus. Some of them were most assuredly reborn men, and yet not one of them had received, or been baptized with, the Holy Spirit. So again, it is evident that the baptism with the Holy Spirit is an operation of the Holy Spirit distinct from and additional to His regenerating work. A man may be reborn by the Holy Spirit and still not be baptized with the Holy Spirit. In being reborn, there is the impartation of life by the Spirit's power, and the one who receives it is saved. In the baptism with the Holy Spirit, there is the impartation of power, and the one who receives it is fitted for service.

The baptism with the Holy Spirit, however, may take place at the moment of rebirth. It did, for example, in the household of Cornelius. We read in Acts 10:43 that, while Peter was preaching, he came to the point where he said concerning Jesus, *"To him give all the prophets witness, that through his name whosoever believeth in him shall receive remission of sins."* At that point, Cornelius and his household believed, and we immediately read,

> *While Peter yet spake these words, the Holy Ghost fell on all them which heard the word. And they of the circumcision which believed were astonished, as many as came with Peter, because that on the Gentiles also was poured out the gift of the Holy Ghost.* (Acts 10:44–45)

The moment they believed the testimony about Jesus, they were baptized with the Holy Spirit, even before they were baptized with water. Rebirth and the baptism with the Holy Spirit took place practically at the same moment, and so they do in many experiences today. It would seem as if, in a normal condition of the church, this would be the usual experience. But the church is not in a normal condition today. A very large part of the church is in the place where the believers in Samaria were before Peter and John came and where the disciples in Ephesus were before Paul came and told them of their larger privilege—baptized believers, baptized into the name of the Lord Jesus, baptized unto repentance and remission of sins, but not as yet baptized with the Holy Spirit. Nevertheless, the baptism with the Holy Spirit is the birthright of every believer. It was purchased for us by the atoning death of Christ. When He ascended to the right hand of the Father, He received the promise of the Father and shed Him forth upon the church, and if anyone today has not the baptism with the Holy Spirit as a personal experience, it is because he has not claimed his birthright.

Potentially, every member of the body of Christ is baptized with the Holy Spirit: *"For by one Spirit are we all baptized into one body, whether we be Jews or Gentiles, whether we be bond or free; and have been all made to drink into one Spirit"* (1 Corinthians 12:13). But there are many believers with whom that which is potentially theirs has not become a matter of real, actual, personal experience. All men are potentially justified in the atoning death of Jesus Christ on the cross; that is, justification is provided for them and belongs to them. (See Romans 5:18.) What potentially belongs to every man, each man must appropriate to himself by faith in Christ. Then justification is actually and experientially his; just so, while the baptism with the Holy Spirit is potentially the possession of every believer, each individual believer must appropriate it for himself before it is experientially his. We may go still further than this and say that it is only by the baptism with the Holy Spirit that one becomes, in the fullest sense, a member of the body of Christ, because it is only by the baptism with the Spirit that he receives power to perform those functions for which God has appointed him as a part of the body.

As we have already seen, every true believer has the Holy Spirit (see Romans 8:9), but not every believer has the baptism with the Holy Spirit (though every believer may have, as we have just seen). It is one thing to have the Holy Spirit dwell within us—perhaps dwelling within us way back in some hidden sanctuary of our being, behind definite consciousness—and something far different to have the Holy Spirit take complete possession of the one whom He inhabits. There are those who press the fact that every believer potentially has the baptism with the Spirit to such an extent that they clearly teach that every believer has the baptism with the Spirit as an actual experience. But unless the baptism with the Spirit today is something radically different from what the baptism with the Spirit was in the early church, indeed unless it is something not at all real, then either a very large proportion of those whom we ordinarily consider believers are not believers or else one may be a believer and a reborn man without having been baptized with the Holy Spirit. Certainly, the latter was the case in the early church. It was the case with the apostles before Pentecost; it was the case with the church in Ephesus; it was the case with the church in Samaria. And there are thousands today who can testify to having received Christ and been born again, and then afterward, sometimes long afterward, having been baptized with the Holy Spirit as a definite experience.

This is a matter of great practical importance. There are many who are not enjoying the fullness of privilege that they might enjoy because, by pushing individual verses in the Scriptures beyond what they will bear and against the plain teaching of the Scriptures as a whole, they are trying to persuade themselves that they have already been baptized with the Holy Spirit when they have not. If they would only admit to themselves that they had not, they could then take the steps whereby they would be baptized with the Holy Spirit as a matter of definite, personal experience.

An Evangelistic Purpose

The next thing that is clear from the teaching of Scripture is that the baptism with the Holy Spirit is always connected with, and primarily for the purpose of, testimony and service.

Our Lord, in speaking of this baptism that the disciples were so soon to receive, said in Luke 24:49, *"And, behold, I send the promise of my Father upon you: but tarry ye in the city of Jerusalem, until ye be endued with power from on high."* And again He said,

> *For John truly baptized with water; but ye shall be baptized with the Holy Ghost not many days hence....But ye shall receive power, after that the Holy Ghost is come upon you: and ye shall be witnesses unto me both in Jerusalem, and in all Judaea, and in Samaria, and unto the uttermost part of the earth.* (Acts 1:5, 8)

In the record of the fulfillment of this promise of our Lord, we read, *"And they were all filled with the Holy Ghost, and began to speak with other tongues, as the Spirit gave them utterance"* (Acts 2:4). Then follows the detailed account of what Peter said and of the result. The result was that Peter and the other apostles spoke with such power that three thousand people that day were convicted of sin, had renounced their sin, had confessed their acceptance of Jesus Christ in baptism, and had continued steadfastly in the apostles' doctrine and fellowship and in the breaking of bread and in prayer ever afterward. (See Acts 2:41–42.)

In Acts 4:31–33, we read that, when the apostles on another occasion were filled with the Holy Spirit, the result was that they *"spake the word of God with boldness"* (verse 31) and that *"with great power gave the apostles witness of the resurrection of the Lord Jesus"* (verse 33). The following is a description of Paul being baptized with the Holy Spirit:

> *And Ananias went his way, and entered into the house; and putting his hands on him said, Brother Saul, the Lord, even Jesus, that appeared unto thee in the way as thou camest, hath sent me, that thou mightest receive thy sight, and be filled with the Holy Ghost. And immediately there fell from his eyes as it had been scales: and he received sight forthwith, and arose, and was baptized. And when he had received meat, he was strengthened....And straightway he preached Christ in the synagogues, that he is the Son of God.* (Acts 9:17–20)

And in the twenty-second verse, we read that he *"confounded the Jews which dwelt at Damascus, proving that this is very Christ."*

In 1 Corinthians 12 we have the fullest discussion of the baptism with the Holy Spirit found in any passage in the Bible. This is the classic passage on the whole subject. The results there recorded are gifts for service. The baptism with the Holy Spirit is not primarily intended to make believers happy but to make them useful. It is not intended merely for the ecstasy of the individual believer; it is intended primarily for his efficiency in service. I do not say that the baptism with the Holy Spirit will not make the believer happy, for part of the fruit of the Spirit is "joy." If one is baptized with the Holy Spirit, joy must inevitably result. I have never known one to be baptized with the Holy Spirit into whose life there did not come, sooner or later, a new joy, a higher and purer and fuller joy than he had ever known before.

But this is not the prime purpose of the baptism nor the most important and prominent result. Great emphasis needs to be laid upon this point, for there are many Christians who, in seeking the baptism with the Spirit, are seeking personal ecstasy and rapture. They go to conventions and conferences for the deepening of the Christian life and come back and tell what a wonderful blessing they have received, referring to some new ecstasy that has come into their hearts. However, when you watch them, it is difficult to see that they are any more useful to their pastors or their churches than they were before, and one is compelled to think that whatever they have received, they have not received the real baptism with the Holy Spirit.

Ecstasies and raptures are all right in their places. When they come, thank God for them—I know something about them—but in a world such as we live in today, where sin and self-righteousness and unbelief are so triumphant, where there is such an awful tide of men, women, and young people sweeping on toward eternal perdition, I would rather go through my whole life and never have one touch of ecstasy but have power to witness for Christ. I would rather have power to win others for Christ and thus to save them than to have raptures 365 days in the year but have no power to stem the awful tide of sin and bring men, women, and children to a saving knowledge of my Lord and Savior, Jesus Christ.

The purpose of the baptism with the Holy Spirit is not primarily to make believers individually holy. I do not say that it is not the work of the Holy Spirit to make believers holy, for as we have already seen, He is the Spirit of Holiness, and the only way we shall ever attain holiness is by His power. I do not even say that the baptism with the Holy Spirit will not result in a great spiritual transformation and uplifting and cleansing, for the promise is, *"He shall baptize you with the Holy Ghost, and with fire"* (Matthew 3:11). The thought of fire as used in this connection is the thought of searching, refining, cleansing, and consuming. A wonderful transformation took place in the apostles at Pentecost and has taken place in thousands who have been baptized with the Holy Spirit since Pentecost, but the primary purpose of the baptism with the Holy Spirit is efficiency in testimony and service. It has to do more with gifts for service than with graces of character. It is the impartation of spiritual power or gifts in service, and sometimes one may have rare gifts by the Spirit's power and yet manifest few of the graces of the Spirit. (See 1 Corinthians 13:1–3 and Matthew 7:22–23.) In every passage in the Bible in which the baptism with the Holy Spirit is mentioned, it is connected with testimony or service.

21

THE RESULTS OF THE BAPTISM WITH THE HOLY SPIRIT

We shall perhaps get a clearer idea of just what the baptism with the Holy Spirit is if we stop to consider what the results are of the baptism with the Holy Spirit.

Various Manifestations

The specific manifestations of the baptism with the Holy Spirit are not precisely the same in all people. This appears very clearly in 1 Corinthians:

> *Now there are diversities of gifts, but the same Spirit. And there are differences of administrations, but the same Lord. And there are diversities of operations, but it is the same God which worketh all in all. But the manifestation of the Spirit is given to every man to profit withal. For to one is given by the Spirit the word of wisdom; to another the word of knowledge by the same Spirit; to another faith by the same Spirit; to another the gifts of healing by the same Spirit; to another the working of miracles; to another prophecy; to another discerning of spirits; to another divers kinds of tongues; to another the interpretation of tongues: but all these worketh that one and the selfsame Spirit, dividing to every man severally as he will. For as the body is one, and hath many members, and all the members of that one body, being many, are one body: so also is Christ. For by one Spirit are we all baptized into one body, whether we be Jews or Gentiles, whether we be bond or free; and have been all made to drink into one Spirit.*
> (1 Corinthians 12:4–13)

Here, we see one baptism but a great variety of manifestations of the power of that baptism. There are diversities of gifts but the same Spirit. The gifts vary with the different areas of service to which God calls different people. The church is a body, and different members of the body have different functions. The Spirit imparts to the one who is baptized with the Spirit those gifts that fit him for the service to which God has called him. It is very important to bear this in mind. Many have gone entirely astray on the whole subject because of their failure to see this.

In my early study of the subject, I noticed the fact that, in many instances, those who were baptized with the Holy Spirit spoke with tongues (for example, see Acts 2:4; 10:46; 19:6), and I wondered if everyone who was baptized with the Holy Spirit would speak with tongues. I did not know of anyone who was speaking in tongues today, and so I wondered still further whether the baptism with the Holy Spirit was for the present age. But one day as I was studying 1 Corinthians 12, I noticed what Paul said to the believers in that wonderfully gifted church in Corinth, all of whom had been pronounced to be baptized with the Spirit (see verse 13):

> *And God hath set some in the church, first apostles, secondarily prophets, thirdly teachers, after that miracles, then gifts of healings, helps, governments, diversities of tongues. Are all apostles? are all prophets? are all teachers? are all workers of miracles? have all the gifts of healing? do all speak with tongues? do all interpret?*
>
> (1 Corinthians 12:28–30)

So I saw it was clearly taught in the Scriptures that one might be baptized with the Holy Spirit and still not have the gift of tongues. I saw furthermore that the gift of tongues, according to the Scripture, was the last and the least important of all the gifts and that we were urged to desire earnestly the greater gifts. (See 1 Corinthians 12:31; 14:5, 12, 14, 18–19, 27–28.)

A little later, I was tempted to fall into another error—more specious but in reality just as unscriptural as this—namely, that if one were baptized with the Holy Spirit, he would receive the gift relating to an evangelist. I had read the story of D. L. Moody, of Charles G. Finney, and of others who were baptized with the Holy Spirit and of the power that came to them as evangelists. The thought was suggested that if anyone is baptized with the Holy Spirit, he should also obtain power as an evangelist. This was also unscriptural. If God has called a man to be an evangelist and is baptized with the Holy Spirit, he will receive power as an evangelist, but if God has called him to be something else, he will receive power to become something else. Three great evils come from the error of thinking that everyone who is baptized with the Holy Spirit will receive power as an evangelist.

The first evil is the evil of disappointment. There are many who seek the baptism with the Holy Spirit expecting power as an evangelist, but God has not called them to that work. Though they really meet the conditions of receiving the baptism with the Spirit and do receive the baptism with the Spirit, power as an evangelist does not come. In many cases, this results in bitter disappointment and sometimes even in despair. The one who has expected the power of an evangelist and has not received it sometimes even questions whether he is a child of God. If he had properly understood the matter, he would have known that the fact that he had not received power as an evangelist is no proof that he has not received the baptism of the Spirit, and much less is it a proof that he is not a child of God.

This second evil is graver still, namely, the evil of presumption. A man whom God has not called to the work of an evangelist or a minister often rushes into it because he has received, or imagines he has received, the baptism with the Holy Spirit. He thinks all a man needs to become a preacher is the baptism with the Holy Spirit. This is not true. In order to succeed as a minister, a man needs a call to that specific work, and furthermore, he needs the knowledge of God's Word that will prepare him for the work. If a man is called to the ministry and studies the Word until he has something to preach and he is then baptized with the Holy Spirit, he will have success as a preacher. But if he is not called to that work, or if he does not have the knowledge of the Word of God that is necessary, he will not succeed in the work, even though he receives the baptism with the Holy Spirit.

The third evil is greater still, namely, the evil of indifference. There are many who know that they are not called to the work of preaching. If then they think that the baptism with the Holy Spirit simply imparts power as an evangelist, or power to preach, the matter of the baptism with the Holy Spirit is one of no personal concern to them. For example, consider a mother with a large family of children. She knows perfectly well, or at least it is hoped that she knows, that she is not called to do the work of an evangelist. She knows that her duty lies with her children and her home. If she reads or hears about the baptism with the Holy Spirit and gets the impression that the baptism with the Holy Spirit simply imparts power to do the work of an evangelist or to preach, she will think, "The evangelist needs this blessing, my minister needs this blessing, but it is not for me." But if she understands the matter as it is taught in the Bible, that, while the baptism with the Spirit imparts power, the way in which the power will be manifested depends entirely upon the area of work to which God calls us; if she understands that no efficient work can be done without it and sees still further that there is no function in the church of Jesus Christ today more holy and sacred than that of sanctified motherhood, she will say, "The evangelist may need this baptism, my minister may need this baptism, but I must have as well it to bring up my children in the nurture and admonition of the Lord."

A Gift Given to All

While there are diversities of gifts and manifestations of the baptism with the Holy Spirit, there will be some gift to everyone thus baptized. We read in 1 Corinthians 12:7, *"But the manifestation of the Spirit is given to every man to profit withal."* Each most insignificant member of the body of Christ has some function to perform in that body. The body grows by that *"which every joint supplieth"* (Ephesians 4:16), and to each least significant joint, the Holy Spirit imparts power to perform the function that belongs to him.

The Gift Chosen by the Spirit

The Holy Spirit decides how the baptism with the Spirit will manifest itself in any given case. We read in 1 Corinthians 12:11, *"But all these worketh that one and the selfsame Spirit, dividing to every man severally as he will."* The Holy Spirit is absolutely sovereign in deciding how—that is, in what special gift, operation, or power—the baptism with the Holy Spirit will manifest itself. It is not for us to pick out some field of service and then ask the Holy Spirit to qualify us for that service. It is not for us to select some gift and then ask the Holy Spirit to impart to us this self-chosen gift. It is for us to simply put ourselves entirely at the disposal of the Holy Spirit to send us where He will, to select for us what kind of service He will, and to impart to us what gifts He will. He is absolutely sovereign, and our position is that of unconditional surrender to Him. I am glad that this is so. I rejoice that He, in His infinite wisdom and love, is to select the field of service and the gifts, and that this is not to be left to me in my shortsightedness and folly. It is because of the failure to recognize this absolute sovereignty of the Spirit that many fail to obtain the blessing and meet with disappointment. They are trying to select their own gift and so get none.

I once knew an earnest child of God in Scotland who, after hearing of the baptism with the Holy Spirit and the power that resulted from it, gave up, at a great sacrifice, his work as a ship plater for which he was receiving large wages. He heard that there was a great need of ministers in the Northwest in America. He came to the Northwest. He met the conditions of the baptism with the Holy Spirit, and I believe he was really baptized with the Holy Spirit. But God had not chosen him for the work of an evangelist, and the power as an evangelist did not come to him. No field seemed to open, and he was in great despondency. He even questioned his acceptance before God.

One morning he came into our church in Minneapolis and heard me speak upon the baptism with the Holy Spirit. As I pointed out that the baptism with the Holy Spirit manifested itself in many different ways and the fact that one did not have power as an evangelist was no proof that he had not received the baptism with the Holy Spirit, light came into his heart. He put himself unreservedly into God's hands for Him to choose the field of labor and the gifts. An opening soon came to him as a Sunday school missionary. Then, when he had given up choosing for himself and left it with the Holy Spirit to divide to him as He would, a strange thing happened; he did receive power as an evangelist and went through the country districts in one of our northwestern states with mighty power as an evangelist.

Power Always Present

While the power may be of one kind in one person and of another kind in another person, there will always be power, the very power of God, when one is baptized with the Holy Spirit.

> *For John truly baptized with water; but ye shall be baptized with the Holy Ghost not many days hence. When they therefore were come together, they asked of him, saying, Lord, wilt thou at this time restore again the kingdom to Israel? And he said unto them, It is not for you to know the times or the seasons, which the Father hath put in his own*

power. But ye shall receive power, after that the Holy Ghost is come upon you: and ye shall be witnesses unto me both in Jerusalem, and in all Judaea, and in Samaria, and unto the uttermost part of the earth.
(Acts 1:5–8)

As truly as anyone who reads these pages and who has not already received the baptism with the Holy Spirit and who seeks it in God's way, he will obtain it. Then, there will come into his service a power that was never there before, power for the very work to which God has called him. This is not only the teaching of Scripture. This truth is also demonstrated by religious experiences throughout the centuries. Religious biographies abound in instances of men who have worked as best they could until one day they were led to see that there was such an experience as the baptism with the Holy Spirit and to seek it and obtain it. From that hour, there came into their service a new power that utterly transformed its character.

In this matter, one thinks first of such men as Finney and Moody and Brainerd, but cases of this nature are not confined to a few exceptional men. They are common. I have personally met and corresponded with hundreds and thousands of people around the globe who could testify definitely to the new power that God has granted them through the baptism with the Holy Spirit. These thousands of men and women are in all branches of Christian service; some of them are ministers of the gospel, some evangelists, some mission workers, some YMCA secretaries, Sunday school teachers, fathers, mothers, personal workers, etc. Nothing could possibly exceed the clearness and the confidence and the joyfulness of many of these testimonies.

I will not soon forget a minister whom I met some years ago at a State Convention of the Young People's Society of Christian Endeavor at New Britain, Connecticut. I was speaking upon the subject of personal work, and as I drew the address to a close, I said that, in order to do effective personal work, we must be baptized with the Holy Spirit. In a very few sentences, I explained what I meant by that.

At the close of the address, this minister came to me on the platform and said, "I do not have this blessing you have been speaking about, but I want it. Will you pray for me?"

I said, "Why not pray right now?"

He said, "I will."

We put two chairs side by side and turned our backs upon the crowd as they passed out of the armory. He prayed, and I prayed that he might be baptized with the Holy Spirit. Then we separated. Some weeks after that, one who had witnessed the scene came to me at a convention in Washington and told me how this minister had gone back to his church a transformed man, that now his congregations filled the church, that it was largely composed of young men, and that there were conversions at every service. Some years after that, this minister was called to another field of service. His most spiritually minded friends advised him not to go because all the ruling elements in the church to which he had been called were against aggressive evangelistic work, but for some reason or other, he felt it was the call of God and accepted it. In six months, there were sixty-nine conversions, and thirty-eight of them were businessmen of the town.

After attending an Interprovincial Convention of the Young Men's Christian Association (YMCA) of the Provinces of Canada in Montreal some years ago, I received a letter from a young man. He wrote, "I was present at your last meeting in Montreal. I heard you speak upon the baptism with the Holy Spirit. I went to my room and sought that baptism for myself and received it. I am chairman of the Lookout Committee of the Christian Endeavor Society of our church. I called together the other members of the committee. I found that two of them had been at the meeting and had already been baptized with the Holy Spirit. Then we prayed for the other members of the committee, and they were baptized with the Holy Spirit. Now we are going out into the church, and the young people of the church are being brought to Christ right along."

A lady and gentleman once came to me at a convention and told me how, though they had never seen me before, they had read the report of an address on the baptism with the Holy Spirit delivered in Boston at a

Christian workers' convention and that they had sought this baptism and had received it. The man then told me the blessing that had come into his service as superintendent of the Sunday school. When he had finished, his wife broke in and said, "Yes, and the best part of it is, I have been able to get into the hearts of my own children, which I was never able to do before."

Here were three distinctly different areas of service, but there was power in each case. The results of that power may not, however, be manifest at once in conversions. Stephen was filled with the Holy Spirit, but as he witnessed in the power of the Holy Spirit for his risen Lord, he saw no conversions at the time. All he saw was the gnashing of teeth, the angry looks, and the merciless rocks, and so it may be with us. However, there was a conversion, even in that case, though it was a long time before it was seen, and that conversion, the conversion of Saul of Tarsus, was worth more than hundreds of ordinary conversions.

Boldness for Service

Another result of the baptism with the Holy Spirit will be boldness in testimony and service. We read in Acts 4:31, "*And when they had prayed, the place was shaken where they were assembled together; and they were all filled with the Holy Ghost, and they spake the word of God with boldness.*" The baptism with the Holy Spirit imparts to those who receive it new liberty and fearlessness in testimony for Christ. It converts cowards into heroes.

Upon the night of our Lord's crucifixion, Peter proved himself a craven coward. He denied with oaths and curses that he knew the Lord. But after Pentecost, this same Peter was brought before the very council that had condemned Jesus to death, and he himself was threatened. However, filled with the Holy Spirit, he said,

> *Ye rulers of the people, and elders of Israel, if we this day be examined of the good deed done to the impotent man, by what means he is made whole; be it known unto you all, and to all the people of Israel, that by the name of Jesus Christ of Nazareth, whom ye crucified, whom God raised from the dead, even by him doth this man stand here before you*

> *whole. This is the stone which was set at nought of you builders, which is become the head of the corner. Neither is there salvation in any other: for there is none other name under heaven given among men, whereby we must be saved.* (Acts 4:8–12)

A little later, when the council commanded him and his companion, John, not to speak or teach in the name of Jesus, they answered, "*Whether it be right in the sight of God to hearken unto you more than unto God, judge ye. For we cannot but speak the things which we have seen and heard*" (Acts 4:19–20). On a still later occasion, when they were threatened and commanded not to speak and when their lives were in jeopardy, Peter told the council to their faces,

> *We ought to obey God rather than men. The God of our fathers raised up Jesus, whom ye slew and hanged on a tree. Him hath God exalted with his right hand to be a Prince and a Saviour, for to give repentance to Israel, and forgiveness of sins. And we are his witnesses of these things; and so is also the Holy Ghost, whom God hath given to them that obey him.* (Acts 5:29–32)

The natural timidity of many a man today vanishes when he is filled with the Holy Spirit. With great boldness and liberty, with utter fearlessness of consequences, he gives his testimony for Jesus Christ.

Occupation with Things Above

The baptism with the Holy Spirit causes the one who receives it to be occupied with God and Christ and spiritual things.

In the record of the day of Pentecost, we read,

> *They were all filled with the Holy Ghost, and began to speak with other tongues, as the Spirit gave them utterance....And they were all amazed and marvelled, saying one to another, Behold, are not all these which speak Galilaeans? And how hear we every man in our own tongue,*

> *wherein we were born?...we do hear them speak in our tongues the wonderful works of God.* (Acts 2:4, 7–8, 11)

Then followed Peter's sermon, a sermon that, from start to finish, is entirely taken up with Jesus Christ and His glory:

> *Then Peter, filled with the Holy Ghost, said unto them, Ye rulers of the people, and elders of Israel, if we this day be examined of the good deed done to the impotent man, by what means he is made whole; be it known unto you all, and to all the people of Israel, that by the name of Jesus Christ of Nazareth, whom ye crucified, whom God raised from the dead, even by him doth this man stand here before you whole.* (Acts 4:8–10)

An account of a later day reads,

> *And when they had prayed, the place was shaken where they were assembled together; and they were all filled with the Holy Ghost, and they spake the word of God with boldness....And with great power gave the apostles witness of the resurrection of the Lord Jesus: and great grace was upon them all.* (Acts 4:31, 33)

We read of Saul of Tarsus, that when he had been filled with the Holy Spirit, "*straightway in the synagogues he proclaimed Jesus*" (Acts 9:20 RV). We read of the household of Cornelius:

> *While Peter yet spake these words, the Holy Spirit fell on all them which heard the word. And they of the circumcision which believed were astonished, as many as came with Peter, because that on the Gentiles also was poured out the gift of the Holy Ghost. For they heard them speak with tongues, and magnify God.* (Acts 10:44–46)

Here we see the whole household of Cornelius, as soon as they were filled with the Holy Spirit, magnifying God.

In Ephesians 5:18–19, we are told that the result of being filled with the Spirit is that those who are thus filled will speak to one another in psalms and hymns and spiritual songs, singing and making melody in their hearts to the Lord. Men who are filled with the Holy Spirit will not be singing sentimental ballads, not comic ditties, nor operatic airs while the power of the Holy Spirit is upon them. If the Holy Spirit should come upon anyone while listening to one of the most innocent of the world's songs, he would not enjoy it and would long to hear something about Christ. Men who are baptized with the Holy Spirit do not talk much about self but much about God and especially much about Christ. This is necessarily so, as it is the Holy Spirit's office to bear witness to the glorified Christ. (See John 15:26; 16:14.)

To sum up everything that has been said about the results of the baptism with the Holy Spirit: The baptism with the Holy Spirit is the Spirit of God coming upon the believer, filling his mind with a real apprehension of truth, especially of Christ, taking possession of his faculties, and imparting to him gifts not otherwise his but that qualify him for the service to which God has called him.

22

THE NECESSITY OF THE BAPTISM WITH THE HOLY SPIRIT

The New Testament has much to say about the necessity for the baptism with the Holy Spirit. When our Lord was about to leave His disciples to go to be with the Father, He said, "*And, behold, I send the promise of my Father upon you: but tarry ye in the city of Jerusalem, until ye be endued with power from on high*" (Luke 24:49). He had just commissioned them to be His witnesses to all nations, beginning at Jerusalem (see verses 47–48), but He tells them here that before they undertake this witnessing, they must wait until they receive the promise of the Father. They were thus endued with power from on high for the work of witnessing that they were to undertake. There is no doubt as to what Jesus meant by *"the promise of my Father,"* for which they were to wait before beginning the ministry that He had laid upon them, for in Acts we read,

> *And, being assembled together with them,* [He] *commanded them that they should not depart from Jerusalem, but wait for the promise of the Father, which, saith he, ye have heard of me. For John truly baptized with water; but ye shall be baptized with the Holy Ghost not many days hence.* (Acts 1:4–5)

It is evident then that *"the promise of the Father"* through which the endowment of power was to come was the baptism with the Holy Spirit. He went on to tell His disciples,

> *Ye shall receive power, after that the Holy Ghost is come upon you: and ye shall be witnesses unto me both in Jerusalem, and in all Judaea, and in Samaria, and unto the uttermost part of the earth.* (Acts 1:8)

Now who were the men to whom Jesus said this? The men were the disciples whom He Himself had trained for the work. For more than three years, they had lived in the closest intimacy with Him; they had been eyewitnesses of His miracles, of His death, of His resurrection, and in a few moments were to be eyewitnesses of His ascension as He was taken up right before their eyes into heaven. And what were they to do? Simply go and tell the world what their own eyes had seen and what their own ears had heard from the lips of the Son of God. Were they not equipped for the work? With our modern ideas of preparation for Christian work, we should say that they were thoroughly equipped. But Jesus said, "No, you are not equipped. There is another preparation in addition to the preparation already received, so absolutely necessary for effective work that you must not stir one step until you receive it. This other preparation is the promise of the Father, the baptism with the Holy

Spirit." If the apostles with their altogether exceptional fitting for the work that they were to undertake needed this preparation for work, how much more do we?

In light of what Jesus required of His disciples before undertaking the work, does it not seem like the most daring presumption for any of us to undertake to witness and work for Christ until we also have received the promise of the Father, the baptism with the Holy Spirit? There was apparently an imperative need that something be done at once. The whole world was perishing, and they alone knew the saving truth. Nevertheless, Jesus strictly charged them to "wait." Could there be a stronger testimony to the absolute necessity and importance of the baptism with the Holy Spirit as a preparation for work that should be acceptable to Christ?

But this is not all. In Acts 10:38, we read, *"How God anointed Jesus of Nazareth with the Holy Ghost and with power: who went about doing good, and healing all that were oppressed of the devil; for God was with him."* To what does this refer in the recorded life of Jesus Christ? If we will turn to Luke 3:21–22, and Luke 4:1, 14, 17–18, we will get our answer. In Luke 3:21–22, we read that, after Jesus had been baptized and was praying, *"The heaven was opened, and the Holy Ghost descended in a bodily shape like a dove upon him, and a voice came from heaven, which said, Thou art my beloved Son; in thee I am well pleased."*

Then, the next thing that we read, with nothing intervening but the human genealogy of Jesus, is the following: *"And Jesus being full of the Holy Ghost returned from Jordan, and was led by the Spirit into the wilderness"* (Luke 4:1). Then follows the story of His temptation. Then we read, *"And Jesus returned in the power of the Spirit into Galilee: and there went out a fame of him through all the region round about"* (Luke 4:14). Further, we read,

> *And there was delivered unto him the book of the prophet Esaias* [Isaiah]. *And when he had opened the book, he found the place where it was written, The Spirit of the Lord is upon me, because he hath anointed me to preach.* (Luke 4:17–18)

Evidently then, it was at the Jordan, in connection with His baptism, that Jesus was anointed with the Holy Spirit and power, and He did not enter upon His public ministry until He was thus baptized with the Holy Spirit. And who was Jesus? It is the common belief of Christendom that He had been supernaturally conceived through the Holy Spirit's power, that He was the only begotten Son of God, that He was divine, very God of very God, and yet truly man. If such a One, *"leaving us an example, that ye should follow his steps"* (1 Peter 2:21), did not venture upon His ministry for which the Father had sent Him until he was definitely baptized with the Holy Spirit, what is it for us to dare to do it? If in the light of these recorded facts, we dare to do it, does it not seem like the most unpardonable presumption? Doubtless it has been done in ignorance by many of us, but can we plead ignorance any longer?

It is evident that the baptism with the Holy Spirit is an absolutely necessary preparation for effective work for Christ along every line of service. We may have a very clear call to service—as clear, it may be, as the apostles had—but the charge is laid upon us as upon them: that before we begin that service, we must tarry until we are clothed with power from on high. This endowment of power is through the baptism with the Holy Spirit.

Even yet, this is not all. We read in Acts 8:14–16,

> *Now when the apostles which were at Jerusalem heard that Samaria had received the word of God, they sent unto them Peter and John: who, when they were come down, prayed for them, that they might receive the Holy Ghost: (for as yet he was fallen upon none of them: only they were baptized in the name of the Lord Jesus.)*

There was a great company of happy converts in Samaria, but when Peter and John came down to inspect the work, they evidently felt that there was something so essential that these young disciples had not received that, before they did anything else, they must see to it that they received it.

In a similar way we read,

> *And it came to pass, that, while Apollos was at Corinth, Paul having passed through the upper coasts came to Ephesus: and finding certain disciples, he said unto them, Have ye received the Holy Ghost since ye believed? And they said unto him, We have not so much as heard whether there be any Holy Ghost.* (Acts 19:1–2)

When he found that they had not received the Holy Spirit, the first thing that he saw to was that they should receive the Holy Spirit. He did not go on with the work with the outsiders until that little group of twelve disciples had been equipped for service. So we see that when the apostles found believers in Christ, the first thing that they always did was to demand whether they had received the Holy Spirit as a definite experience, and if not, they saw to it at once that the steps were taken whereby they should receive the Holy Spirit.

It is evident then that the baptism with the Holy Spirit is absolutely necessary in every Christian for the service that Christ demands and expects of him. There are certainly few greater mistakes that we are making today in our various Christian enterprises than that of appointing men to teach Sunday school classes and do personal work and even to preach the gospel because they have been converted and received a certain amount of education, including perhaps a college and seminary course, but have not as yet been baptized with the Holy Spirit. We think that, if a man is hopefully pious and has had a college and seminary education and comes out of it reasonably orthodox, he is now ready for our hands to be laid upon him and to be ordained to preach the gospel. But Jesus Christ says, "No." There is another preparation so essential that a man must not undertake this work until he has received it. "*Tarry ye* [literally 'sit ye down'],*...until ye be endued with power from on high*" (Luke 24:49).

A distinguished theological professor has said that the question, "Have you met God?" ought to be put to every candidate for the ministry. Yes, but we ought to go farther than this and be even more definite. To every candidate for the ministry, we should put the question, "Have you been baptized with the Holy Spirit?" and if not, we should say to him, as Jesus said to the first preachers of the gospel, "Sit down until you are endued with power from on high."

Not only is this true of ordained ministers; it is also true of every Christian, for all Christians are called to ministry of some kind. Any man who is in Christian work and who has not received the baptism with the Holy Spirit ought to stop his work right where he is and not go on with it until he has been *"endued with power from on high"* (Luke 24:49).

What will our work do while we are waiting? The question can be answered by asking another, "What did the world do during these ten days while the early disciples were waiting?" They knew the saving truth, and they alone knew it; yet in obedience to the Lord's command they were silent. The world was no loser. Beyond a doubt, when the power came, they accomplished more in one day than they would have accomplished in years if they had gone on in self-confident defiance and disobedience to Christ's command.

We, too, after we have received the baptism with the Spirit, will accomplish more real work for our Lord in one day than we ever would in years without this power. Even if it were necessary to spend days in waiting, they would be well spent, but we will see later that there is no need that we spend days in waiting, that the baptism with the Holy Spirit may be received today.

Someone may say that the apostles had gone on missionary tours during Christ's lifetime, even before they were baptized with the Holy Spirit. This is true, but that was before the Holy Spirit was given and before the command was given, *"Tarry ye...until ye be endued with power from on high"* (Luke 24:49). After that, it would have been disobedience and folly and presumption to have gone forth without this endowment, and we are living today after the Holy Spirit has been given and after the charge has been given to tarry until clothed.

Who Can Be Baptized with the Holy Spirit?

We come now to the question of first importance, namely, who can be baptized with the Holy Spirit? At a convention some years ago, a very intelligent Christian woman, a well-known worker in educational as well as Sunday school work, sent me this question: "You have told us of the necessity of the baptism with the Holy Spirit, but who can have this baptism? The church to which I belong teaches that the baptism with the Holy Spirit was confined to the apostolic age. Will you not tell us who can have the baptism with the Holy Spirit?" Fortunately, this question is answered in the most explicit terms in the Bible:

> *Then Peter said unto them, Repent, and be baptized every one of you in the name of Jesus Christ for the remission of sins, and ye shall receive the gift of the Holy Ghost. For the promise is unto you, and to your children, and to all that are afar off, even as many as the Lord our God shall call.* (Acts 2:38–39)

What is the promise to which Peter referred in the thirty-ninth verse? There are two interpretations of the passage: One is that the promise of this verse is the promise of salvation; the other is that the promise of this verse is the promise of the gift of the Holy Spirit (or the baptism with the Holy Spirit—a comparison of Scripture passages will show that the two expressions are synonymous).

Which is the correct interpretation? There are two laws of interpretation universally recognized among Bible scholars. These two laws are the law of usage (or *usus loquendi,* as it is called) and the law of context. Many a verse in the Bible standing alone might have two or three or even more possible interpretations, but when these two laws of interpretation are applied, it is settled to a certainty that only one of the various possible interpretations is the true interpretation.

The law of usage is this: When you find a word or phrase in any passage of Scripture and you wish to know what it means, do not go to a dictionary, but go to the Bible itself. Look up the various passages in which the word is used and especially how the particular writer being studied uses it and also how it is used in that particular book in which the passage is found. Thus, you can determine what the precise meaning of the word or phrase is in the passage in question.

The law of context is this: When you study a passage, you should not take it out of its context but should look at what goes before it and what comes after it. While it might mean various things if it stands alone, it can only mean one thing in the context in which it is found.

Now let us apply these two laws to the passage in question. First of all, let us apply the law of usage. We are trying to discover what the expression "*the promise*" means in Acts 2:39. Turning back to Acts 1:4–5, we read,

> [He] *commanded them that they should not depart from Jerusalem, but wait for the promise of the Father, which, saith he, ye have heard of me. For John truly baptized with water; but ye shall be baptized with the Holy Ghost not many days hence.*

It is evident, then, that here, the promise of the Father means the baptism with the Holy Spirit.

Turn now to Acts 2:33: "*Therefore being by the right hand of God exalted, and having received of the Father the promise of the Holy Ghost, he hath shed forth this, which ye now see and hear.*" In this passage, we are told in so many words that the promise is the promise of the Holy Spirit. If this peculiar expression means the baptism with the Holy Spirit in Acts 1:4–5, and the same thing in Acts 2:33, by what same law of interpretation can it possibly mean something entirely different six verses farther down in Acts 2:39? So the law of usage establishes that the promise of Acts 2:39 is the promise of the baptism with the Holy Spirit.

Now let us apply the law of context, and we will find that, if possible, this is even more decisive. Read the following verses:

> *Then Peter said unto them, Repent, and be baptized every one of you in the name of Jesus Christ for the remission of sins, and ye shall receive the gift of the Holy Ghost. For the promise is unto you, and to your children, and to all that are afar off, even as many as the Lord our God shall call.* (Acts 2:38–39)

It is evident here that the promise is the promise of the gift of the baptism with the Holy Spirit. It is settled then by both laws that the promise of Acts 2:39 is that of the gift of the Holy Spirit or baptism with the Holy Spirit. Let us then read the verse in that way, substituting this synonymous expression for the expression *"the promise,"* "For the baptism with the Spirit is unto you, and to your children, and to all that are afar off, even as many as the Lord our God shall call."

"It is unto you," said Peter, that is, to the crowd assembled before him. There is nothing in that for us. We were not there. That crowd was all Jews, and we are not Jews. But Peter did not stop there. He went further and said, *"And to your children,"* that is, to the next generation of Jews or all future generations of Jews. Still there is nothing in it for us, for we are not Jews. But Peter did not stop even there. He went further and said, *"And to all that are afar off."* That does take us in. We are the Gentiles who were once *"far off"* but now *"made nigh by the blood of Christ"* (Ephesians 2:13). Lest there be any mistake about it whatever, Peter added *"even as many as the Lord our God shall call"* (Acts 2:39). So, on the very day of Pentecost, Peter declared that the baptism with the Holy Spirit is for every child of God in every coming age of the church's history.

Some years ago, at a ministerial conference in Chicago, a minister of the gospel from the Southwest came to me after a lecture on the baptism with the Holy Spirit and said, "The church to which I belong teaches that the baptism with the Holy Spirit was for the apostolic age alone."

"I do not care," I replied, "what the church to which you belong teaches or what the church to which I belong teaches. The only question with me is, what does the Word of God teach?"

"That is right," he said.

I then handed him my Bible and asked him to read Acts 2:39, and he read, *"For to you is the promise, and to your children, and to all that are afar off, even as many as the Lord our God shall call unto him"* (RV).

"Has He called you?" I asked.

"Yes, He certainly has."

"Is the promise for you then?"

"Yes, it is." He took it, and the result was a transformed ministry.

Some years ago, at a students' conference, the gatherings were presided over by a prominent Episcopalian minister, a man greatly honored and loved. I spoke at this conference on the baptism with the Holy Spirit and dwelt upon the significance of Acts 2:39. That night, as we sat together after the meetings were over, this servant of God said to me, "Mr. Torrey, I was greatly interested in what you had to say today on the baptism with the Holy Spirit. If your interpretation of Acts 2:39 is correct, you have your case, but I doubt your interpretation of Acts 2:39. Let us talk it over." We did talk it over. Several years later, in July, 1894, I was at the students' conference at Northfield. As I entered the back door of Stone Hall that day, this Episcopalian minister entered the front door. Seeing me, he hurried across the hall and held out his hand and said, "You were right about Acts 2:39 at Knoxville, and I believe I have a right to tell you something better yet—that I have been baptized with the Holy Spirit."

I am glad that I was right about Acts 2:39, not that it is of any importance that I should be right, but the truth thus established is of immeasurable importance. It is glorious to be able to go literally around the world and face audiences of believers all over the United States, in the Sandwich Islands, in Australia and Tasmania and New Zealand, in China and Japan and India, in England and Scotland, Ireland, Germany, France, and Switzerland and to be able to tell them (and to know that I have God's sure Word under my feet when I do tell them), "You may all be baptized with the Holy Spirit." But that unspeakably joyous and glorious thought has its solemn side. If we may be baptized with the Holy Spirit, then we must be. If we are baptized with the Holy Spirit, then souls will be saved through our instrumentality who will not be saved if we are not thus baptized. If then we are not willing to pay the price of this baptism and therefore are not thus baptized, we will be responsible before God for every soul that might have been saved who was not saved because we did not pay the price and therefore did not obtain the blessing.

I often tremble for myself and for my peers in the ministry, and not only for my peers in the ministry, but for my peers in all forms of Christian work, even the most humble and obscure. Why? Because we are preaching error? No, alas, there are many in these dark days who are doing that, and I do tremble for them, but that is not what I mean now. Do I mean that I tremble because we are not preaching the truth? It is quite possible not to preach error and yet not preach the truth; many a man has never preached a word of error in his life but still is not preaching the truth. I do tremble for them, but that is not what I mean now. I mean that I tremble for those of us who are preaching the truth, the very truth as it is in Jesus, the truth as it is recorded in the written Word of God, the truth in its simplicity, its purity, and its fullness, but who are preaching it in *"enticing words of man's wisdom"* and not *"in demonstration of the Spirit and of power"* (1 Corinthians 2:4), preaching it in the energy of the flesh and not in the power of the Holy Spirit. There is nothing more death dealing than the gospel without the Spirit's power. *"The letter killeth, but the spirit giveth life"* (2 Corinthians 3:6). It is awfully solemn business preaching the gospel either from the pulpit or in more quiet ways. It means death or life to those who hear, and whether it means death or life depends very largely on whether we preach it with or without the baptism of the Holy Spirit.

Repeated Refilling

We need repeated refilling with the Holy Spirit. Even after one has been baptized with the Holy Spirit, no matter how definite that baptism may be, he needs to be filled again and again with the Spirit. This is the clear teaching of the New Testament. We read in Acts 2:4, *"And they were all filled with the Holy Ghost, and began to speak with other tongues, as the Spirit gave them utterance."* Now, one of those who was present on this occasion and who therefore was filled at this time with the Holy Spirit was Peter. Indeed, he stands forth most prominently in the chapter as a man baptized with the Holy Spirit. We read in Acts 4:8, *"Then Peter, filled with the Holy Ghost, said unto them...."* Here, we read again that Peter was filled with the Holy Spirit. Further down, we read that, being assembled together and praying, *"they were all filled with the Holy Ghost, and they spake the word of God with boldness"* (Acts 4:31). We are expressly told in the context that two of those present were John and Peter. Here, then, was a third instance in which Peter was filled with the Holy Spirit.

It is not enough that one be filled with the Holy Spirit once. We need a new filling for each new emergency of Christian service. The failure to realize this need of constant refillings with the Holy Spirit has led to many a man, who at one time was greatly used by God, being utterly laid aside. There are many today who once knew what it was to work in the power of the Holy Spirit who now have lost their unction and their power. I do not say that the Holy Spirit has left them—I do not believe He has—but the manifestation of His presence and power has gone.

One of the saddest sights among us today is that of the men and women who once toiled for the Master in the mighty power of the Holy Spirit who are now practically of no use, or may even be a hindrance to the work, because they are trying to go in the power of the blessing received a year or five years or twenty years ago. For each new service that is to be conducted, for each new soul that is to be dealt with, for each new work for Christ that is to be performed, for each new day, and for each new emergency of Christian life and service, we should seek and obtain a new filling with the Holy Spirit. We must not *"neglect"* the gift that is in us (1 Timothy 4:14) but on the contrary *"stir into flame"* this gift (2 Timothy 1:6 RV, margin). Repeated fillings with the Holy Spirit are necessary for continuance and increase of power.

The question may arise, Should we call these new fillings with the Holy Spirit "fresh baptisms" with the Holy Spirit? To this we would answer that the expression "baptism" is never used in the Scriptures to refer to a second experience, and there is something of an initiatory character in the very thought of baptism. So, if one wishes to be precisely biblical, it would seem to be better not to use the term "baptism" to refer to a second experience, but to limit it to the first experience. On the other hand, *"filled with the Holy Ghost"* is used in Acts 2:4 to describe the experience promised in Acts 1:5, where the words used are *"ye shall be baptized with the Holy Ghost."* And it is evident from this and from other passages that the two expressions are to a large extent practically synonymous. However, if we confine the expression "baptism with the Holy Spirit" to our first experience, we will be more exactly biblical. It would be well to speak of one baptism but many fillings.

However, I would much prefer that one should speak about new or fresh baptisms with the Holy Spirit, standing for the all-important truth that we need repeated fillings with the Holy Spirit, than that he should so insist on exact phraseology that he loses sight of the truth that repeated fillings are needed. In other words, I would rather have the right experience by a wrong name than the wrong experience by the right name. This much is as clear as day: that we need to be filled again and again and again with the Holy Spirit. I am sometimes asked, "Have you received the second blessing?" Yes, and the third and the fourth and the fifth and hundreds beside, and I am looking for a new blessing today.

23

OBTAINING THE BAPTISM WITH THE HOLY SPIRIT

We come now to the question of first practical importance, namely, what a person must do in order to be baptized with the Holy Spirit. This question is answered in the plainest and most positive way in the Bible. A plain path is laid down in the Bible consisting of a few simple steps that anyone can take, and it is absolutely certain that anyone who takes these steps will enter into the blessing. This is, of course, a very positive statement, and we would not dare be so positive if the Bible were not equally positive. But what right have we to be uncertain when the Word of God is positive? There are seven steps in this path.

Accepting Jesus Christ as Our Lord and Savior

The first step is that we accept Jesus Christ as our Savior and Lord. We read in Acts 2:38 (RV), *"Repent ye, and be baptized every one of you in the name of Jesus Christ unto the remission of your sins; and ye shall receive the gift of the Holy Ghost."* Isn't this statement as positive as the one made above regarding blessings? Peter said that, if we do certain things, the result will be, *"Ye shall receive the gift of the Holy Ghost."* All seven steps are in this passage, but we will also refer to other passages to throw light upon this.

The first two steps are in the word *"repent." "Repent,"* said Peter. What does it mean to repent? The Greek word for repentance means "an afterthought" or "change of mind." To repent, then, means to change your mind. But change your mind about what? About three things: about God, about Jesus Christ, and about sin. What the change of mind is about in any given instance must be determined by the context. The context in the present case tells us that the change of mind referred to here is primarily about Jesus Christ. Peter had just said,

> *Let all the house of Israel know assuredly, that God hath made that same Jesus, whom ye have crucified, both Lord and Christ. Now when they heard this, they were pricked in their heart, and said unto Peter and to the rest of the apostles, Men and brethren, what shall we do?*
> (Acts 2:36–37)

It was here that Peter said, *"Repent ye,"* or "Change your mind about Jesus; change your mind from that attitude of mind that rejected Him and crucified Him to that attitude of mind that accepts Him as Lord and King and Savior." This, then, is the first step toward receiving the baptism of the Holy Spirit. Receive Jesus as Savior and Lord; first of all, receive Him as your Savior. Have you done that?

What does it mean to receive Jesus as Savior? It means to accept Him as the One who bore our sins in our place on the cross (see 2 Corinthians 5:21; Galatians 3:13) and to trust God to forgive us because Jesus Christ died in our place. It means to rest all our hope of being accepted by God upon the finished work of Christ on the cross of Calvary. There are many who profess to be Christians who have not done this.

When you go to many who call themselves Christians and ask them if they are saved, they reply, "Yes." Then, if you put to them the question: "What are you resting upon as the ground of your salvation?" they will reply something like this: "I go to church, I say my prayers, I read my Bible, I have been baptized, I have united with the church, I partake of the Lord's Supper, I attend prayer meetings, and I am trying to live as near right as I know how." If you are resting upon these things as the ground of your acceptance before God, then you are not saved, for all these things are your own works (all proper in their places, but still your own works), and we are distinctly told in Romans 3:20 that *"by the deeds of the law there shall no flesh be justified in his sight: for by the law is the knowledge of sin."*

However, if you go to others and ask them if they are saved, they will reply "Yes." And, then, if you ask them what they are resting upon as the ground of their acceptance before God, they will reply something to this effect, "I am not resting upon anything I ever did, or upon anything I am ever going to do; I am resting upon what Jesus Christ did for me when He bore my sins in His own body on the cross. I am resting in His finished work of atonement." If this is what you are really resting upon, then you are saved. You have accepted Jesus Christ as your Savior and have taken the first step toward the baptism with the Holy Spirit.

The same thought is taught elsewhere in the Bible, for example in Galatians 3:2. Here, Paul asked of the believers in Galatia, *"Received ye the Spirit by the works of the law, or by the hearing of faith?"* Just what did he mean? On one occasion, when Paul was passing through Galatia, he was detained there by some physical infirmity. We are not told what it was, but at all events, he was not so ill that he could not preach the gospel, or glad tidings, to the Galatians, that Jesus Christ had redeemed them from the curse of the law by becoming a curse in their place through dying on the cross of Calvary. These Galatians believed this testimony. This was the hearing of faith, and God set the stamp of His endorsement upon their faith by giving them the Holy Spirit as a personal experience.

But after Paul had left Galatia, certain Judaizers came down from Jerusalem, men who were substituting the law of Moses for the gospel, and taught them that it was not enough that they simply believe in Jesus Christ. In addition to this, the Judaizers taught that they must keep the law of Moses, especially the law of Moses regarding circumcision, and that without circumcision, they could not be saved. In other words, they could not be saved by simple faith in Jesus. (Compare Acts 15:1.) These young converts in Galatia became upset. They did not know whether they were saved or not. They did not know what they ought to do, and all was confusion. It was just as when modern Judaizers come around and get after young converts and tell them that, in addition to believing in Jesus Christ, they must keep the Mosaic seventh day Sabbath or they cannot be saved. This is simply the old controversy breaking out at a new point.

When Paul heard what had happened in Galatia, he was very indignant and wrote the epistle to the Galatians, simply for the purpose of exposing the utter error of these Judaizers. He showed them how Abraham himself was justified *before* he was circumcised by simply believing God (see Galatians 3:6), and how he was circumcised *after* he was justified as a seal of the faith that he already had while he was in uncircumcision. In addition to this proof of the error of the Judaizers, Paul appeals to their own personal experience. He asked them if they had received the Holy Spirit, and they replied that they had. He then asked them how they had received the Holy Spirit—by keeping the law of Moses or by the hearing of faith, the simple accepting of God's testimony about Jesus Christ that their sins were laid upon Him and that they were thus justified and saved. The Galatians had had a very definite experience of receiving the Holy Spirit, and Paul appealed to it and recalled to their minds how it was by the simple hearing of faith that they had received the Holy Spirit.

The gift of the Holy Spirit is God's seal upon the simple acceptance of God's testimony about Jesus Christ—that our sins were laid upon Him—while trusting God to forgive us and justify us. This, then, is the first step toward receiving the Holy Spirit. But we must not only receive Jesus as Savior; we must also receive Him as Lord. Of this we will speak further in connection with another passage in the fourth step.

Renunciation of Sin

The second step in the path that leads into the blessing of being baptized with the Holy Spirit is renunciation of sin. Repentance, as we have seen, is a change of mind about sin as well as a change of mind about Christ: a change of mind from that attitude of mind that loves sin and indulges sin to that attitude of mind that hates sin and renounces sin. This, then, is the second step—renunciation of sin. The Holy Spirit is a *Holy* Spirit, and we cannot have both Him and sin. We must make our choice between the Holy Spirit and unholy sin. We cannot have both. He who will not give up sin cannot have the Holy Spirit. It is not enough that we renounce one sin or two sins or three sins or many sins; we must renounce all sin. If we cling to one single known sin, it will shut us out of the blessing.

Here, we find the cause of failure in many people who are praying for the baptism with the Holy Spirit, going to conventions and hearing about the baptism with the Holy Spirit, reading books about the baptism with the Holy Spirit, perhaps spending whole nights in prayer for the baptism with the Holy Spirit, and yet obtaining nothing. Why? Because there is some sin to which they are clinging. People often say to me or write to me, "I have been praying for the baptism with the Holy Spirit for a year (five years, ten years, one man said twenty years). Why do I not receive?" In many such cases, I feel led to reply, "It is sin, and if I could look down into your heart this moment as God looks into your heart, I could put my finger on the specific sin." It may be what you are pleased to call a *small* sin, but there are no small sins. There are sins that concern small things, but every sin is an act of rebellion against God. Therefore no sin is a small sin.

A controversy with God about the smallest thing is sufficient to shut one out of the blessing.

Mr. Finney tells of a woman who was greatly in earnest about the baptism with the Holy Spirit. Every night after the meetings, she would go to her room and pray way into the night. Her friends were afraid she would go insane, but no blessing came. One night as she prayed, some little matter of head adornment, a matter that would probably not trouble many Christians today, but a matter of controversy between her and God, came up (as it had often come up before) as she knelt in prayer. She put her hand to her head and took the pins out of her hair and threw them across the room and said, "There go!" Instantly the Holy Spirit fell upon her. It was not so much the matter of head adornment as the matter of controversy with God that had kept her out of the blessing.

If there is anything that always comes up when you get nearest to God, that is the thing to deal with. Some years ago, at a convention in a southern state, the presiding officer, a minister in the Baptist church, called my attention to a man and said, "That man is 'the pope' of our denomination in ———; everything he says goes. But he is not at all with us in this matter, but I am glad to see him here." This minister kept attending the meetings. At the close of the last meeting, where I had spoken about the conditions for receiving the baptism with the Holy Spirit, I found this man awaiting me in the vestibule.

He said, "I did not stand up on your invitation today."

I replied, "I saw you did not."

"I thought you said," he continued, "that you only wanted those to stand who could say they had absolutely surrendered to God?"

"That is what I did say," I replied.

"Well, I could not say that."

"Then you did perfectly right not to stand. I did not want you to lie to God."

"Say," he continued, "you hit me pretty hard today. You said if there was anything that always comes up when you get nearest to God, that is the thing to deal with. Now, there is something that always comes up when I get nearest to God. I am not going to tell you what it is. I think you know."

"Yes," I replied. (I could smell it.)

"Well, I simply wanted to say this to you."

This was on Friday afternoon. I had occasion to go to another city, and returning through that city the following Tuesday morning, the minister who had presided at the meeting was at the station. "I wish you could have been in our Baptist ministers' meeting yesterday morning," he said. "That man I pointed out to you from the north part of the state was present. He got up in our meeting and said, 'Fellow Christians, we have been all wrong about this matter,' and then he told what he had done. He had settled his controversy with God, had given up the thing that had always come up when he got nearest to God. Then he continued and said, 'Fellow Christians, I have received a more definite experience than I had when I was converted.'"

Just such an experience is awaiting many others, both minister and layman, just as soon as he will judge his sin, just as soon as he will put away the thing that is a matter of controversy between him and God, no matter how small the thing may seem. If anyone sincerely desires the baptism with the Holy Spirit, he should go alone with God and ask God to search him and bring to light anything in his heart or life that is displeasing to Him; and when He brings it to light, he should put it away. If, after sincerely waiting on God, nothing is brought to light, then we may proceed to take the other steps. But there is no use praying, no use going to conventions, no use reading books about the baptism with the Holy Spirit, no use doing anything else, until we judge our sins.

Open Confession

The third step is an open confession of our renunciation of sin and our acceptance of Jesus Christ. After telling his hearers to repent in

Acts 2:38, Peter continued and told them to *"be baptized every one of you in the name of Jesus Christ for the remission of sins."* Heart repentance alone was not enough. There must be an open confession of that repentance, and God's appointed way of confessing of repentance is baptism. None of those to whom Peter spoke had ever been baptized, and, of course, what Peter meant in that case was water baptism. But suppose one has already been baptized, what then? Even in that case, there must be that for which baptism stands, namely, an open confession of our renunciation of sin and our acceptance of Jesus Christ. The baptism with the Spirit is not for the secret disciple but for the openly confessed disciple.

Undoubtedly, there are many today who are trying to be Christians in their hearts, many who really believe that they have accepted Jesus as their Savior and their Lord and have renounced sin, but they are not willing to make an open confession of their renunciation of sin and their acceptance of Christ. Such a person cannot have the baptism with the Holy Spirit. Someone may ask, "Do not the Friends (Quakers), who do not believe in water baptism, give evidence of being baptized with the Holy Spirit?" Undoubtedly, many of them do, but this does not alter the teaching of God's Word. God doubtless condescends in many instances where people are misled as to the teaching of His Word by their ignorance, if they are sincere; but that fact does not alter His Word. Even with a member of the congregation of Friends, who sincerely does not believe in water baptism, there must be that for which baptism stands before the blessing is received, namely, the open confession of acceptance of Christ and of renunciation of sin.

Absolute Surrender to God

The fourth step is absolute surrender to God. This comes out in what has already been said, namely, that we must accept Jesus as Lord as well as Savior. It is stated explicitly in Acts 5:32: *"And we are his witnesses of these things; and so is also the Holy Ghost, whom God hath given to them that obey him."* That is the fourth step: *"obey him,"* or obedience.

But what does *obedience* mean? Someone will say, "doing as we are told." Right, but doing how much that we are told? Not merely one thing or two things or three things or four things, but obedience is doing all things. The heart of obedience is in the will; the essence of obedience is the surrender of the will to God. It is going to God our heavenly Father and saying, "Heavenly Father, here I am. I am your property. You have bought me with a price. I acknowledge your ownership and surrender myself and all that I am absolutely to you. Send me where you will; do with me what you will; use me as you will." This is, in most instances, the decisive step in receiving the baptism with the Holy Spirit.

In the Old Testament typology, it was when the whole burnt offering was laid upon the altar—with nothing kept back within or without the sacrificial animal—that the fire came forth from the Holy Place where God dwelt and accepted and consumed the gift upon the altar. So it is today, in the fulfillment of that type, when we lay ourselves, a whole burnt offering, upon the altar, keeping nothing within or without back, so that the fire of God, the Holy Spirit, descends from the real Holy Place, heaven (of which the Most Holy Place in the tabernacle was simply a type), and accepts the gift upon the altar. When we can truly say, "My all is on the altar," then we will not have long to wait for the fire. The lack of this absolute surrender is shutting many out of the blessing today. People turn the keys of almost every closet in their heart over to God, but there is some small closet of which they wish to keep the key themselves. Then the blessing does not come.

At a convention in Washington, D.C., on the last night, I had spoken on how to receive the baptism with the Holy Spirit. The Spirit Himself was present in mighty power that night. The chaplain of one of the houses had said to me at the close of the meeting, "It almost seemed as if I could see the Holy Spirit in this place tonight."

There were many to be dealt with. About two hours after the meeting closed (about eleven o'clock), a worker came to me and said, "Do you see that young woman over to the right with whom Miss W——— is speaking?"

"Yes."

"Well, she has been dealing with her for two hours, and she is in awful agony. Won't you come and see if you can help?"

I went into the seat behind this woman in distress and asked her her trouble. "Oh," she said, "I came from Baltimore to receive the baptism with the Holy Spirit, and I cannot go back to Baltimore until I have received Him."

"Is your will laid down?" I asked.

"I am afraid not."

"Will you lay it down now?"

"I cannot."

"Are you willing that God should lay it down for you?"

"Yes."

"Ask Him to do it."

She bowed her head in prayer and asked God to empty her of her will, to lay it down for her, to bring it into conformity to His will, in absolute surrender to His own. When the prayer was finished, I asked, "Is it laid down?"

She said, "It must be. I have asked something according to His will. Yes, it is done."

I said, "Ask Him for the baptism with the Holy Spirit."

She bowed her head again in brief prayer and asked God to baptize her with the Holy Spirit, and in a few moments, she looked up with peace in her heart and in her face. Why? Because she had surrendered her will. She had met the conditions, and God had given the blessing.

An Intense Desire for the Baptism with the Holy Spirit

The fifth step is an intense desire for the baptism with the Holy Spirit. Jesus said in John 7:37–39:

> *If any man thirst, let him come unto me, and drink. He that believeth on me, as the scripture hath said, out of his belly shall flow rivers of living water. (But this spake he of the Spirit, which they that believe on him should receive.)*

Here, again, we have belief in Jesus as the condition of receiving the Holy Spirit, but we also have this: "*If any man thirst.*" Doubtless, when Jesus spoke these words, He had in mind the Old Testament promise in Isaiah 44:3: "*For I will pour water upon him that is thirsty, and floods upon the dry ground: I will pour my spirit upon thy seed, and my blessing upon thine offspring.*" In both of these passages, thirst is the condition of receiving the Holy Spirit. What does it mean to thirst? When a man really thirsts, it seems as if every pore in his body has just one cry: "Water! Water! Water!" Apply this to the matter in question; when a man thirsts spiritually, his whole being has but one cry: "The Holy Spirit! The Holy Spirit! The Holy Spirit!"

As long as one fancies he can get along somehow without the baptism of the Holy Spirit, he is not going to receive that baptism. As long as one is casting about for some new kind of church, machinery, new style of preaching, or anything else by which he hopes to accomplish what the Holy Spirit only can accomplish, he will not receive the baptism of the Holy Spirit. As long as one tries to find some subtle system of interpretation to read out of the New Testament what God has put into it—namely, the absolute necessity that each believer receive the baptism of the Holy Spirit as a definite experience—he is not going to receive the baptism of the Holy Spirit. As long as a man tries to persuade himself that he has received the baptism with the Holy Spirit when he really has not, he is not going to receive the baptism with the Holy Spirit. But when one gets to the place where he sees the absolute necessity of being baptized with the Holy Spirit as a definite experience, and desires this blessing at any cost, he is far on the way toward receiving it.

At a state YMCA convention, where I had spoken on the baptism with the Holy Spirit, two ministers went out of the meeting side by side. One said to the other, "That kind of teaching leads either to fanaticism or despair." He did not attempt to show that it was unscriptural. He felt condemned and was not willing to admit his deficiency of the baptism and seek to have it supplied. So, he tried to avoid the condemnation that came from the Word by this bright remark: "That kind of teaching leads either to fanaticism or despair." Such a man will not receive the baptism with the Holy Spirit until he is brought to himself, honestly acknowledges his need, and intensely desires to have it supplied.

How different was another minister of the same denomination who came to me one Sunday morning at Northfield. I was to speak that morning on how to receive the baptism with the Holy Spirit. He said to me, "I have come to Northfield from ——— for just one purpose, to receive the baptism with the Holy Spirit, and I would rather die than go back to my church without receiving it."

I said, "My brother, you are going to receive it."

The following morning, he came very early to my house. He said, "I have to go away on the early train, but I came around to tell you before I went that I have received the baptism with the Holy Spirit."

Definite Prayer for the Baptism with the Holy Spirit

The sixth step is definite prayer for the baptism with the Holy Spirit. Jesus said in Luke 11:13, *"If ye then, being evil, know how to give good gifts unto your children: how much more shall your heavenly Father give the Holy Spirit to them that ask him?"* This is very explicit. Jesus taught us that the Holy Spirit is given in answer to definite prayer—just ask Him. There are many who tell us that we should not pray for the Holy Spirit, and they reason it out very inaccurately. They say that the Holy Spirit was given as an abiding gift to the church at Pentecost, and why pray for what is already given? To this, the late Reverend Dr. A. J. Gordon well replied that Jesus Christ was given as an abiding gift to the world at Calvary (see John 3:16), but what was given to the world as a whole, each individual in the world must appropriate for himself. In the same way, the Holy Spirit was given to the church as an abiding gift at Pentecost, but what was given to the church as a whole, each individual in the church must appropriate for himself. God's way of appropriation is prayer.

Those who say we should not pray for the Holy Spirit go further still than this. They tell us that every believer already has the Holy Spirit (which we have already seen is true in a sense), and why pray for what we already have? To this, the very simple answer is that it is one thing to have the Holy Spirit dwelling way out of consciousness in some hidden sanctuary of the being and something quite different, and vastly more, to have Him take possession of the whole house that He inhabits. But against all these inaccurate arguments, we place the simple word of Jesus Christ: *"How much more shall your heavenly Father give the Holy Spirit to them that ask him?"* (Luke 11:13).

It will not do to say, as has been said, that this promise was for the time of the earthly life of our Lord, and to go back to the promise of Luke 11:13 is to forget Pentecost and to ignore the truth that now every believer has the indwelling Spirit. We find that, after Pentecost as well as before, the Holy Spirit was given to believers in answer to definite prayer. For example, we read in Acts 4:31, *"When they had prayed, the place was shaken where they were assembled together; and they were all filled with the Holy Ghost, and they spake the word of God with boldness."* Again, in Acts 8:15–16, we read that when Peter and John had come down and saw the believers in Samaria, they *"prayed for them, that they might receive the Holy Ghost: (for as yet he was fallen upon none of them: only they were baptized in the name of the Lord Jesus.)"* Again, in the epistle of Paul to the Ephesians, Paul told the believers in Ephesus that he was praying for them that they might be strengthened with power through His Spirit. (See Ephesians 3:16.) So right through the New Testament after Pentecost, as well as before, by specific teaching and illustrative example, we are taught that the Holy Spirit is given in answer to definite prayer.

At a Christian workers' convention in Boston, a believer came to me and said, "I notice that you are on the program to speak on the baptism with the Holy Spirit."

"Yes."

"I think that is the most important subject on the program. Now be sure and tell them not to pray for the Holy Spirit."

I replied, "My friend, I will be sure and not tell them that: for Jesus says, '*How much more shall your heavenly Father give the Holy Spirit to them that ask him?*'" (Luke 11:3).

"Yes, but that was before Pentecost."

"How about Acts 4:31? Was that before Pentecost or after?"

He said, "It was certainly after."

"Well," I said, "take it and read it."

"'*And when they had prayed, the place was shaken where they were assembled together; and they were all filled with the Holy Ghost, and they spake the word of God with boldness.*'"

"How about Acts 8:15–16? Was that before Pentecost or after?"

"Certainly, it was after."

"Take it and read it."

"'*Who, when they were come down, prayed for them, that they might receive the Holy Ghost: (for as yet he was fallen upon none of them: only they were baptized in the name of the Lord Jesus.)*'"

He had nothing more to say. What more was there to say? But with me, it is not a matter of mere interpretation that the Holy Spirit is given in answer to definite prayer. It is a matter of personal and certain experience. I know that God gives the Holy Spirit in answer to prayer just as well as I know that water quenches thirst and food satisfies hunger. My first experience of being baptized with the Holy Spirit was while I waited upon God in prayer. Since then, time and again, as I have waited on God in prayer, I have been definitely filled with the Holy Spirit. Often, as I have knelt in prayer with others, as we prayed, the Holy Spirit has fallen upon us just as perceptibly as the rain ever fell upon and fructified the earth.

I shall never forget one experience in our church in Chicago. We were holding a noon prayer meeting of the ministers at the YMCA auditorium, in preparation of an expected visit to Chicago by Mr. Moody. At one of these meetings, a minister sprang to his feet and said, "What we need in Chicago is an all-night meeting of the ministers."

"Very well," I said. "If you will come up to Chicago Avenue Church on Friday night at ten o'clock, we will have a prayer meeting, and if God keeps us all night, we will stay all night."

At ten o'clock on Friday night, four or five hundred people gathered in the lecture rooms of the Chicago Avenue Church. They were not all ministers. They were not all men.

Satan made a mighty attempt to ruin the meeting. First of all, three men got down by the door and knelt down by chairs and pounded and shouted until some of our heads seemed almost splitting. Some felt they must retire from the meeting, and when a brother went to expostulate with them and urge them that things be done decently and in order, they swore at the brother who made the protest. Still later, a man sprang up in the middle of the room and announced that he was Elijah. The poor man was insane. These things were distracting, and there was more or less confusion until nearly midnight. Some thought they would go home. But it is a poor meeting that the devil can spoil, and some of us were there for a blessing and were determined to remain until we received it. About midnight, God gave us complete victory over all the discordant elements. Then, for two hours, there was such praying as I have rarely heard in my life.

A little after two o'clock in the morning, a sudden hush fell upon the whole gathering; we were all on our knees at the time. No one could speak; no one could pray; no one could sing; all you could hear was the subdued sobbing of joy, unspeakable and full of glory. The very air seemed trembling with the presence of the Spirit of God. It was now Saturday morning. The following morning, one of my deacons came to me and said, with bated breath, "I shall never forget yesterday morning until the last day of my life." But it was not by any means all emotion. There was solid reality that could be tested by practical tests.

A man went out of that meeting in the early morning hours and took a train for Missouri. When he had transacted his business in the town that he visited, he asked the proprietor of the hotel if there was any meeting going on in the town at the time. The proprietor said, "Yes, there is a protracted meeting going on at the Cumberland Presbyterian Church." The man was himself a Cumberland Presbyterian. He went to the church, and when the meeting was opened, he arose in his place and asked the minister if he could speak. Permission was granted, and with the power of the Holy Spirit upon him, he spoke so that fifty-eight or fifty-nine people professed to accept Christ on the spot.

A young man went out of the meeting in the early morning hours and took a train for a city in Wisconsin, and I soon received word from that city that thirty-eight young men and boys had been converted while he spoke. Another young man, one of our students in the Institute, went to another part of Wisconsin, and soon I began to receive letters from ministers in that neighborhood inquiring about him and telling how he had gone into the schoolhouses and churches and soldiers' home, and how there were conversions wherever he spoke.

In the days that followed, men and women from that meeting went out over the earth, and I doubt if there was any country that I visited in my tour around the world—Japan, China, Australia, New Zealand, India, etc.—in which I did not find someone who had gone out from that meeting with the power of God upon them. For me to doubt that God fills men with the Holy Spirit in answer to prayer would be thoroughly unscientific and irrational. I know He does. And in a matter like this, I would rather have one ounce of believing experience than ten tons of unbelieving interpretation.

Faith

The seventh and last step is faith. We read in Mark 11:24, *"Therefore I say unto you, What things soever ye desire, when ye pray, believe that ye receive them, and ye shall have them."* No matter how definite God's promises are, we only realize these promises experientially when we believe. For example, we read in James 1:5, *"If any of you lack wisdom, let him ask of God, that giveth to all men liberally, and upbraideth not; and it shall be given him."* Now, that promise is as positive as a promise can be, but we read in the following verses:

> *But let him ask in faith, nothing wavering. For he that wavereth is like a wave of the sea driven with the wind and tossed. For let not that man think that he shall receive any thing of the Lord. A double minded man is unstable in all his ways.* (James 1:6–8)

The baptism with the Spirit, as we have already seen, is for those believers in Christ who have put away all sin and surrendered absolutely to God and who ask for it. But, even though we ask, there will be no receiving if we do not believe. There are many who have met the other conditions of receiving the baptism with the Holy Spirit and yet do not receive simply because they do not believe. They do not expect to receive, and they do not receive.

But there is a faith that goes beyond expectation, a faith that puts out its hand and takes what it asks on the spot. This comes out in the Revised Version of Mark 11:24: "*Therefore I say unto you, All things whatsoever ye pray and ask for, believe that ye have received them, and ye shall have them.*" When we pray for the baptism with the Holy Spirit, we should believe that we have received (that is, that God has granted our prayer, and therefore it is ours), and then we will have the actual experience of what we have asked.

When the Revised Version came out, I was greatly puzzled about the rendering of Mark 11:24. I had begun at the beginning of the New Testament and gone right through, comparing the King James Version with the Revised Version, and comparing both with the best Greek text; but when I reached this passage, I was greatly puzzled. I read in the King James Version, "*What things soever ye desire, when ye pray, believe that ye receive them, and ye shall have them,*" and that seemed plain enough. Then I turned to the Revised Version and read, "*All things whatsoever ye pray and ask for, believe that ye have received them, and ye shall have them.*" I said to myself, "What a confusion of the tenses.

Believe that ye have already received (past), and ye shall have afterward (future). What nonsense."

Then I turned to my Greek Testament and found, whether sense or nonsense, the Revised Version was the correct rendering of the Greek, but what it meant I did not know for years. Then, one time, I was studying and expounding to my church the first epistle of John. I came to 1 John 5:14–15 (RV), and I read,

> *And this is the boldness which we have toward him, that, if we ask anything according to his will, he heareth us: and if we know that he heareth us whatsoever we ask, we know that we have the petitions which we have asked of him.*

Then I understood Mark 11:24. Do you see it? If not, let me explain it a little further. When we come to God in prayer, the first question to ask is, "Is that which I have asked of God according to His will?" If it is promised in His Word, of course, we know it is according to His will. Then we can say with 1 John 5:14, "I have asked something according to His will, and I know He hears me." Then we can go further and say with the fifteenth verse, "Because I know He hears what I ask, I know I have the petition that I asked of Him. I may not have it in actual possession, but I know it is mine because I have asked something according to His will and He has heard me and granted that which I have asked. What I thus believe, that I have received because the Word of God says so; and I will afterward have it in actual experience."

Now, apply this to the matter before us. When I ask for the baptism with the Holy Spirit, I have asked something according to His will, for Luke 11:13 and Acts 2:39 say so; therefore, I know my prayer is heard. Still further, I know that, because the prayer is heard, I have the petition that I have asked of Him; in other words, I know I have the baptism with the Holy Spirit. I may not feel it yet, but I have received it. What I thus count mine, resting upon the naked word of God, I will afterward have in actual experience.

Some years ago, I went to the students' conference at Lake Geneva, Wisconsin, with Mr. F. B. Meyer of London. Mr. Meyer spoke that night on the baptism of the Holy Spirit. At the conclusion of his address, he said, "If any of you wish to speak with Mr. Torrey or myself after the meeting is over, we will stay and speak with you." A young man came to me who had just graduated from one of the Illinois colleges. He said, "I heard of this blessing thirty days ago and have been praying for it ever since but do not receive. What is the trouble?"

"Is your will laid down?" I asked.

"No," he said, "I am afraid it is not."

"Then," I said, "there is no use praying until your will is laid down. Will you lay down your will?"

He said, "I cannot."

"Are you willing that God should lay it down for you?"

"I am."

"Let us kneel and ask Him to do it."

We knelt side by side, and I placed my Bible open at 1 John 5:14–15 (RV) on the chair before him. He asked God to lay down his will for him and empty him of his self-will and to bring his will into conformity with the will of God. When he had finished the prayer, I said, "Is it done?"

He said, "It must be. I have asked something according to His will, and I know He hears me, and I know I have the petition I have asked. Yes, my will is laid down."

"What is it you desire?"

"The baptism with the Holy Spirit."

"Ask for it."

Looking up to God, he said, "Heavenly Father, baptize me with the Holy Spirit now."

"Did you get what you asked?" I enquired.

"I don't feel it," he replied.

"That is not what I asked you," I said. "Read the verse before you." So he read, "'*This is the boldness which we have toward him, that, if we ask anything according to his will, he heareth us.*'"

"What do you know?" I asked.

He said, "I know that, if I ask anything according to His will, He hears me."

"What did you ask?"

"I asked for the baptism with the Holy Spirit."

"Is that according to His will?"

"Yes, Acts 2:39 says so."

"What do you know then?"

"I know He has heard me."

"Read on."

"'*And if we know that he heareth us whatsoever we ask, we know that we have the petitions which we have asked of him.*'"

"What do you know?" I asked.

"I know I have the petition I asked of Him."

"What was the petition you asked of Him?"

"The baptism with the Holy Spirit."

"What do you know?"

"I know I have the baptism with the Holy Spirit. I don't feel it, but God says so."

We arose from our knees and, after a short conversation, separated. I left Lake Geneva the next morning but returned in a few days. I met the young man and asked if he had really received the baptism with the Holy Spirit. He did not need to answer. His face told the story, but he did answer. He went into a theological seminary the following autumn, was given a church his junior year in the seminary, and had conversions from the outset. The next year, on the Day of Prayer for Colleges, there came a mighty outpouring of the Spirit upon the seminary largely through his influence. The president of the seminary wrote to a denominational paper that it was a veritable Pentecost, and it all came through this young man who received the baptism with the Holy Spirit through simple faith in the Word of God.

Anyone who will accept Jesus as his Savior and his Lord, put away all sin out of his life, publicly confess his renunciation of sin and acceptance of Jesus Christ, surrender absolutely to God, ask God for the baptism with the Holy Spirit, and take it by simple faith in the naked Word of God, can receive the baptism with the Holy Spirit right now. There are some who so emphasize the matter of absolute surrender that they ignore, or even deny, the necessity of prayer. It is always unfortunate when one so emphasizes one side of truth that he loses sight of another side, which may be equally important. In this way, many lose the blessing that God has provided for them.

The seven steps given above lead with absolute certainty into the blessing. However, several questions arise.

1. *Must we not wait until we know we have received the baptism with the Holy Spirit before we take up Christian work?*

Yes, but how will we know? There are two ways of knowing anything in the Christian life. First, by the Word of God; second, by experience or feeling. God's order is to know things first of all by the Word of God. How one may know by the Word of God that he has received the baptism with the Holy Spirit has just been told. We have a right when we have met the conditions and have definitely asked for the baptism with the Holy Spirit to say, "It is mine," and to get up and go on in our work, leaving the matter of experience to God's time and place. We get assurance that we have received the baptism with the Holy Spirit in precisely the same way that we get assurance of our salvation.

When an inquirer comes to you, whom you have reason to believe really has received Jesus but who lacks assurance, what do you do with him? Do you tell him to kneel down and pray until he gets assurance? Not if you know how to deal with a soul. You know that true assurance comes through the Word of God, that it is through what is "*written*" that we are to know that we have eternal life. (See 1 John 5:13.) So, you take the inquirer to the written Word. For example, you take him to John 3:36. You tell him to read it.

He reads, "'*He that believeth on the Son hath everlasting life.*'"

You ask him, "Who has everlasting life?"

He replies from the passage before him, "'*He that believeth on the Son.*'"

"How many who believe on the Son have everlasting life?"

"Everyone that believes on the Son."

"Do you know this to be true?"

"Yes."

"Why?"

"Because God says so."

"What does God say?"

"God says, '*He that believeth on the Son hath everlasting life.*'"

"Do you believe on the Son?"

"Yes."

"What have you then?"

He ought to say, "Everlasting life," but quite likely he will not. He may say, "I wish I had everlasting life." You point him again to the verse and, by questions, bring out what it says; and you hold him to it until he sees that he has everlasting life, sees that he has everlasting life simply because God says so. After he has assurance on the ground of the Word, he will have assurance by personal experience, by the testimony of the Spirit in his heart.

Now you should deal with yourself in precisely the same way about the baptism with the Holy Spirit. Hold yourself to the word found in 1 John 5:14–15, and know that you have the baptism with the Spirit simply because God says so in His Word, whether you feel it or not. Afterward, you will know it by experience.

God's order is always: first, His Word; second, belief in His Word; third, experience or feeling. We desire to change God's order and have first, His Word, then feeling, then we will believe, but God demands that we believe on His naked Word. *"Abraham believed God, and it was accounted to him for righteousness"* (Galatians 3:6; compare Genesis 15:6). Abraham had as yet no feeling in his body of new life and power. He just believed God, and feeling came afterward. God demands of us today, as He did of Abraham of old, that we simply take Him at His Word and count the thing ours that He has promised simply because He has promised it. Afterward, we get the feeling and the realization of that which He has promised.

2. *Will there be no manifestation of the baptism with the Spirit that we receive?*

Will everything be just as it was before? If so, where is the reality and use of the baptism? Yes, there will be manifestation, very definite manifestation, but bear in mind what the character of the manifestation will be and when the manifestation is to be expected. When is the manifestation to be expected? After we believe, after we have received by simple faith in the naked Word of God.

And what will be the character of the manifestation? Here many go astray. They have read the wonderful experiences of Charles G. Finney, John Wesley, D. L. Moody, and others. These men tell us that, when they were baptized with the Holy Spirit, they had wonderful sensations. Finney, for example, described it as great waves of electricity sweeping over him so that he was compelled to ask God to withhold His hand lest he die on the spot. Mr. Moody, on rare occasions, described a similar experience. That these men had such experiences, I do not for a moment question. The word of such men as Charles G. Finney, D. L. Moody, and others is to be believed; yet there is another reason why I cannot question the reality of these experiences. While these men doubtless had these experiences, there is not a passage in the Bible that describes such an experience. I am inclined to think the apostles had them, but if they had, they kept them to themselves. It is well that they did, for if they had put them on record, that is what we would be looking for today.

But what are the manifestations that actually occurred in the case of the apostles and the early disciples? New power in the Lord's work. We read at Pentecost that they were *"all filled with the Holy Ghost, and began to speak with other tongues, as the Spirit gave them utterance"* (Acts 2:4). Similar accounts are given of what occurred in the household of Cornelius and what occurred in Ephesus. All we read in the case of the apostle Paul is that Ananias came in and said, *"Brother Saul, the Lord, even Jesus, that appeared unto thee in the way as thou camest, hath sent me, that thou mightest receive thy sight, and be filled with the Holy Ghost"* (Acts 9:17). Then Ananias baptized him, and the next thing we read is that Paul went straight down to the synagogue and preached Christ so mightily in the power of the Spirit that he *"confounded the Jews which dwelt at Damascus, proving that this is very Christ"* (Acts 9:22).

So, right through the New Testament, the manifestation that we are taught to expect, and the manifestation that actually occurred, was new power in Christian work, and that is the manifestation that we may expect today. We need not look too carefully for that. The thing for us to do is to claim God's promise and let God take care of the mode of manifestation.

3. *May we not have to wait for the baptism with the Holy Spirit?*

Didn't the apostles have to wait ten days, and may we not have to wait ten days also, or even more? No, there is no necessity that we wait. We are told distinctly in the Bible why the apostles had to wait ten days. In Acts 2:1, we read, *"And when the day of Pentecost was fully come"* (literally, *"when the day of Pentecost was being fulfilled"* [RV margin]). Way back in the Old Testament, and back of that in the eternal counsels of God, the day of Pentecost was set for the coming of the Holy Spirit and the gathering of the church, and the Holy Spirit could not be given until the day of Pentecost was fully come. Therefore, the apostles had to wait until the day of Pentecost was fulfilled, but there was no waiting after Pentecost.

There was no waiting, for example, in Acts 4:31. Scarcely had they finished the prayer when the place where they were gathered together was shaken, and *"they were all filled with the Holy Ghost."* There was no waiting in the household of Cornelius. They were listening to their first gospel sermon, and Peter said as the climax of his argument, *"To* [Jesus] *give all the prophets witness, that through his name whosoever believeth in him shall receive remission of sins"* (Acts 10:43). No sooner had Peter spoken these words than they believed, and *"the Holy Ghost fell on all them which heard the word"* (Acts 10:44). There was no waiting in Samaria after Peter and John came down and told them about the baptism with the Holy Spirit and prayed with them. There was no waiting in Ephesus after Paul came and told them that there was not only the baptism of John unto repentance but the baptism of Jesus in the Holy Spirit. It is true that they had been waiting some time until then, but it was simply because they did not know that there was such a baptism for them.

Many may wait today because they do not know that there is the baptism with the Spirit for them, or they may have to wait because they are not resting in the finished work of Christ or because they have not put away sin or because they have not surrendered fully to God or because they will not definitely ask and believe and take. But the reason for the waiting is not in God; it is in ourselves. Anyone who will lay this book down at this point and take the steps that have been stated can immediately receive the baptism with the Holy Spirit.

I would not say a word to dissuade men from spending much time in waiting upon God in prayer for *"they that wait upon the LORD shall renew their strength"* (Isaiah 40:31). There are few of us indeed in these days who spend as many hours as we should in waiting upon God. I can bear joyful testimony to the manifest outpourings of the Spirit that have come time and again as I have waited upon God through the hours of the night with fellow believers, but the point I would emphasize is that the baptism with the Holy Spirit may be had at once. The Bible proves this; experience proves it.

There are many waiting for feeling who ought to be claiming by faith. In these days, we hear of many who say they are "waiting for their Pentecost." Some have been waiting weeks, some have been waiting months, some have been waiting years. This is not scriptural, and it is dishonoring to God. These Christians have an unscriptural view of what constitutes Pentecost. They have fixed it in their minds that certain manifestations are to occur. Since these particular manifestations, which they themselves have prescribed, do not come, they think they have not received the Holy Spirit. There are many who have been led into the error, already refuted in this book, that the baptism with the Holy Spirit always manifests itself in the gift of tongues. They have not received the gift of tongues; therefore, they conclude that they have not received the baptism with the Holy Spirit. But as already seen, one may receive the baptism with the Holy Spirit and not receive the gift of tongues. Others still are waiting for some ecstatic feeling. We do not need to wait at all. We may meet the conditions; we may claim the blessing at once on the ground of God's sure Word.

There was a time in my ministry when I was led to say that I would never enter my pulpit again until I had been definitely baptized with the Holy Spirit and knew it or until God in some way told me to go. I shut myself up in my study and, day by day, waited upon God for the baptism with the Holy Spirit. It was a time of struggle. The thought would arise, "Suppose you do not receive the baptism with the Holy Spirit before Sunday. How will it look for you to refuse to go into your pulpit." But I held fast to my resolution. I had a more or less definite thought in my mind of what might happen when I was baptized with the Holy Spirit, but it did not come that way at all. One morning as I waited upon God, one of the quietest and calmest moments of my life it was just as if God said to me, "The blessing is yours. Now go and preach."

If I had known my Bible then as I know it now, I might have heard that voice the very first day speaking to me through the Word. But I did not know it, and God, in His infinite condescension, looking upon my weakness, spoke it directly to my heart. There was no particular ecstasy or emotion, simply the calm assurance that the blessing was mine. I went into my work, and God manifested His power in that work. Some time passed—I do not remember just how long—and I was sitting in that same study. I do not remember that I was thinking about this subject at all, but suddenly it was just as if I had been knocked out of my chair onto the floor. I lay upon my face crying, "Glory to God! Glory to God!" I could not stop. Some power, not my own, had taken possession of my lips and my whole person. I am not of an excitable, hysterical, or even emotional temperament, but I lost control of myself absolutely. I had never shouted before in my life, but I could not stop. When, after a while, I got control of myself, I went to my wife and told her what had happened. I tell this experience, not to magnify it, but to say that the time when this wonderful experience (which I cannot really fully describe) came was not the moment when I was baptized with the Holy Spirit. The moment when I was baptized with the Holy Spirit was in that calm hour when God said, "It is yours. Now go and preach."

There is an afternoon that I will never forget. It was July 8, 1894. It was at the Northfield Students' Convention. I had spoken that morning in the church on how to receive the baptism with the Holy Spirit. As I drew to a close, I took out my watch and noticed that it was exactly twelve o'clock. Mr. Moody had invited us to go up on the mountain that afternoon at three o'clock to wait upon God for the baptism with the Holy Spirit. As I looked at my watch, I said, "Gentlemen, it is exactly twelve o'clock. Mr. Moody has invited us to go up on the mountain at three o'clock to wait upon God for the baptism with the Holy Spirit. It is three hours until three o'clock. Some of you cannot wait three hours, nor do you need to wait. Go to your tent, go to your room in the hotel or in the buildings, go out into the woods, go anywhere where you can get alone with God; meet the conditions of the baptism with the Holy Spirit, and claim it at once."

At three o'clock, we gathered in front of Mr. Moody's mother's house, four hundred fifty-six of us in all, all men from the eastern colleges. (I know the number because Mr. Paul Moody counted us as we passed through the gates down into the lots.) We commenced to climb the mountainside. After we had gone some distance, Mr. Moody said, "I do not think we need to go further. Let us stop here." We sat down, and Mr. Moody said, "Have any of you anything to say?" One after another, perhaps seventy-five men, arose and said words to this effect, "I could not wait until three o'clock. I have been alone with God, and I have received the baptism with the Holy Spirit." Then Mr. Moody said, "I can see no reason why we should not kneel down here right now and ask God that the Holy Spirit may fall on us as definitely as He fell on the apostles at Pentecost. Let us pray." We knelt down on the ground; some of us lay on our faces on the pine needles.

As we had gone up the mountainside, a cloud had been gathering over the mountain. As we began to pray, the cloud broke, and the raindrops began to come down upon us through the overhanging pine trees. However, another cloud, big with mercy, had been gathering over Northfield for ten days, and our prayers seemed to pierce that cloud allowing the Holy Spirit to fall upon us. It was a wonderful hour. There are many who will never forget it.

Anyone who reads this book may have a similar hour alone by himself now. He can take the seven steps one by one, and the Holy Spirit will fall upon him.

24

THE WORK OF THE HOLY SPIRIT IN PROPHETS AND APOSTLES

The Holy Spirit's Distinctive Work

The work of the Holy Spirit in apostles and prophets is an entirely distinctive work. He imparts to apostles and prophets a special gift for a special purpose.

> *Now there are diversities of gifts, but the same Spirit....For to one is given by the Spirit the word of wisdom; to another the word of knowledge by the same Spirit; to another faith by the same Spirit; to another the gifts of healing by the same Spirit; to another the working of miracles; to another prophecy; to another discerning of spirits; to another divers kinds of tongues; to another the interpretation of tongues: but all these worketh that one and the selfsame Spirit, dividing to every man severally as he will....And God hath set some in the church, first apostles, secondarily prophets, thirdly teachers, after that miracles, then gifts of healings, helps, governments, diversities of tongues. Are all apostles? are all prophets? are all teachers? are all workers of miracles? have all the gifts of healing? do all speak with tongues? do all interpret?*
>
> (1 Corinthians 12:4, 8–11, 28–30)

It is evident from these verses that the work of the Holy Spirit in apostles and prophets is of a distinctive character.

The doctrine is becoming very common and very popular in our day that the work of the Holy Spirit in preachers and teachers and ordinary believers, illuminating them and guiding them into the truth and opening their minds to understand the Word of God, is the same in kind and differs only in degree from the work of the Holy Spirit in prophets and apostles. It is evident from the passage just cited that this doctrine is thoroughly unscriptural and untrue. It overlooks the fact so clearly stated and carefully elucidated that, while there is *"the same Spirit,"* there are *"diversities of gifts," "diversities of administrations," "diversities of operations"* (1 Corinthians 12:4–6), and that not all are prophets and not all are apostles. (See 1 Corinthians 12:29.)

A very scholarly and brilliant preacher seeking to minimize the difference between the work of the Holy Spirit in apostles and prophets and His work in other men calls attention to the fact that the Bible says of Bezaleel that God *"filled him with the spirit of God"* (Exodus 31:3) to devise the work of the tabernacle. (See Exodus 31:1–11.) The preacher gives this as a proof that the inspiration of the prophet does not differ from the inspiration of the artist or architect. However, in doing this, he loses sight of the fact that the tabernacle was to be built after the *"pattern of the tabernacle....which was showed thee* [Moses] *in the mount"* (Exodus 25:9, 40), and that, therefore, it was itself a prophecy and an exposition of the truth of God. It was not mere architecture. It was the Word of God done into wood, gold, silver, brass, cloth, skin, etc. And Bezaleel needed as much special inspiration to reveal the truth in wood, gold, silver, brass, etc., as the apostle or prophet needs it to reveal the Word of God with pen and ink on parchment.

There is much reasoning in these days about inspiration that appears at first sight very learned but that will not bear much rigid scrutiny or candid comparison with the exact statements of the Word of God. There is nothing in the Bible more inspired than the tabernacle, and if the destructive critics would study it more, they would give up their ingenious but groundless theories as to the composite structure of the Pentateuch.

The Holy Spirit's Revealing Work

Truth hidden from man for ages, and which they had not discovered, and could not discover by the unaided processes of human reasoning has been revealed to apostles and prophets in the Spirit.

> *By revelation he made known unto me the mystery; (as I wrote afore in few words, whereby, when ye read, ye may understand my knowledge in the mystery of Christ) which in other ages was not made known unto the sons of men, as it is now revealed unto his holy apostles and prophets by the Spirit.* (Ephesians 3:3–5)

The Bible contains truth that men had never discovered before the Bible stated it. It contains truth that men never could have discovered if left to themselves. Our heavenly Father, in great grace, has revealed this truth to us, His children, through His servants—the apostles and the prophets. The Holy Spirit is the agent of this revelation.

There are many who tell us today that we should test the statements of Scripture by the conclusions of human reasoning or by the "Christian consciousness." The folly of all this is evident when we bear in mind that the revelation of God transcends human reasoning, and that any consciousness that is not the product of the study and absorption of Bible truth is not really a Christian consciousness.

We know the fact that the Bible does contain truth that man has never discovered, not merely because it is so stated in the Scriptures; but we know it also as a matter of fact. There is not one of the most distinctive and precious doctrines taught in the Bible that men have ever discovered apart from the Bible. If our consciousness differs from the statements of this Book, which is so plainly God's Book, it is not yet fully Christian, and the thing to do is not to try to pull God's revelation down to the level of our consciousness but to tone our consciousness up to the level of God's Word.

Revelation from the Spirit Above

The revelations made to the prophets were independent of their own thinking and were made to them by the Spirit of Christ that was in them. These revelations were subjects of inquiry even to their own minds. They were not their own thoughts, but His.

> *Of which salvation the prophets have inquired and searched diligently, who prophesied of the grace that should come unto you: searching what, or what manner of time the Spirit of Christ which was in them did signify, when it testified beforehand the sufferings of Christ, and the glory that should follow. Unto whom it was revealed, that not unto themselves, but unto us they did minister the things, which are now reported unto you by them that have preached the gospel unto you with the Holy Ghost sent down from heaven; which things the angels desire to look into.* (1 Peter 1:10–12)

These words make it plain that a person both *in* the prophets and *independent* of the prophets—that person being the Holy Spirit—revealed truth that was independent of their own thinking, which they did not altogether understand themselves, and regarding which it was necessary that they make diligent search and study. Another person than themselves was thinking and speaking, and they were seeking to comprehend what He said.

Not from Prophet's Own Will

No prophet's utterance was of the prophet's own will, but he spoke from God, and the prophet was carried along in his utterance by the Holy Spirit.

We read in 2 Peter 1:21 (RV), "*For no prophecy ever came by the will of man: but men spake from God, being moved by the Holy Ghost.*" Clearly then, the prophet was simply an instrument in the hands of another. As the Spirit of God carried him along, so he spoke.

It was the Holy Spirit who spoke in the prophetic utterances. It was His word that was upon the prophet's tongue. We read in Hebrews 3:7, "*Wherefore (as the Holy Ghost saith, To day if ye will hear his voice...).*" Further, we read,

> *Whereof the Holy Ghost also is a witness to us: for after that he had said before, This is the covenant that I will make with them after those days, saith the Lord, I will put my laws into their hearts, and in their minds will I write them.* (Hebrews 10:15–16)

We read again in Acts 28:25, "*And when they agreed not among themselves, they departed, after that Paul had spoken one word, Well spake the Holy Ghost by Esaias* [Isaiah] *the prophet unto our fathers.*" Still again, we read in 2 Samuel 23:2, "*The spirit of the* LORD *spake by me, and his word was in my tongue.*"

Over and over again in these passages, we are told that it was the Holy Spirit who was the speaker in the prophetic utterances and that it was His word, not theirs, that was upon the prophet's tongue. The prophet was simply the mouth by which the Holy Spirit spoke. As a man—that is, without the Spirit teaching him and using him—the prophet might be as fallible as other men are. However, when the Spirit was upon him and he was taken up and borne along by the Holy Spirit, he was infallible in his teachings, for his teachings in that case were not his own but the teachings of the Holy Spirit. When thus borne along by the Holy Spirit, it was God who was speaking and not the prophet.

For example, there can be little doubt that Paul had many mistaken notions about many things, but when he taught as an apostle in the Spirit's power, he was infallible. Rather, the Spirit who taught through him was infallible, and the consequent teaching was infallible, as infallible as God Himself. We do well, therefore, to carefully distinguish what Paul may have thought as a man and what he actually did teach as an apostle. In the Bible, we have the record of what he taught as an apostle. There are those who think that Paul said he was not sure if he had the word of the Lord in 1 Corinthians 7:6, 25: *"But I speak this by permission, and not of commandment....yet I give my judgment, as one that hath obtained mercy of the Lord."* If this is the true interpretation of the passage (which is more than doubtful), we see how careful Paul was when he was not sure to note the fact, and this gives us additional certainty in all other passages.

It is sometimes said that Paul taught in his early ministry that the Lord would return during his lifetime, and that in this he was, of course, mistaken. But Paul never taught anywhere that the Lord would return in his lifetime. It is true he says in 1 Thessalonians 4:17, *"Then we which are alive and remain shall be caught up together with them in the clouds, to meet the Lord in the air: and so shall we ever be with the Lord."* As he was still living when he wrote the words, he naturally and properly did not include himself with those who had already fallen asleep in speaking of the Lord's return. However, this is not to assert that he would remain alive until the Lord came. Quite probably, at this period of his ministry, he entertained the hope that he might remain alive and consequently lived in an attitude of expectancy. But the attitude of expectancy is the true attitude in all ages for each believer. It is quite probable that Paul expected that he would be alive at the coming of the Lord, but if he did so expect, he did not so teach. The Holy Spirit kept him from this as from all other errors in his teachings.

Exact Words Chosen by the Spirit

The Holy Spirit in the apostles taught not only the thoughts (or "concepts") but the words in which the thoughts were to be expressed. We read in 1 Corinthians 2:13 (ASV), "*Which things also we speak, not in words which man's wisdom teacheth, but which the Spirit teacheth; combining spiritual things with spiritual words.*" This passage clearly teaches that the words, as well as the thoughts, were chosen and taught by the Holy Spirit. This is also a necessary inference from the fact that thought is conveyed from mind to mind by words, and it is the words that express the thought. If the words were imperfect, then the thought expressed in these words would necessarily be imperfect and, to that extent, be untrue. Nothing could be plainer than Paul's statement "*in words... which the Spirit teacheth.*" The Holy Spirit has Himself anticipated all the modern ingenious and wholly unbiblical and false theories regarding His own work in the apostles.

The more carefully and minutely we study the wording of the statements in this wonderful Book, the more we will become convinced of the marvelous accuracy of the words used to express the thought. Very often, the solution of an apparent difficulty is found in studying the exact words used. The accuracy, precision, and inerrancy of the exact words used is amazing. To the superficial student, the doctrine of verbal inspiration may appear questionable or even absurd. Any regenerated and Spirit-taught person who ponders the words of the Scripture day after day and year after year will become convinced that the wisdom of God is in the very words, as well as in the thought that the words endeavor to convey. A change of word or letter or tense or case or number in many instances would land us into contradiction or untruth, but when taking the words exactly as written, difficulties disappear and truth shines forth. The divine origin of nature shines forth more clearly in the use of a microscope as we see the perfection of form and adaptation of means to an end of the minutest particles of matter. In a similar manner, the divine origin of the Bible shines forth more clearly under the microscope as we notice the perfection with which the turn of a word reveals the absolute thought of God.

Someone may ask, "If the Holy Spirit is the Author of the words of Scripture, how do we account for variations in style and diction? How do we explain, for instance, that Paul always used Pauline language and John Johannine language, etc.?" The answer to this is very simple. If we could not account at all for this fact, it would have but little weight against the explicit statement of God's Word with anyone who is humble enough and wise enough to recognize that there are a great many things that he cannot account for at all, which could be easily accounted for if he knew more. However, these variations are easily accounted for. The Holy Spirit is quite wise enough and has quite enough facility in the use of language to reveal truth to and through any given individual to use words, phrases, forms of expression, and idioms in that person's vocabulary and forms of thought and to make use of that person's peculiar individuality. Indeed, it is a mark of the divine wisdom of this Book that the same truth is expressed with absolute accuracy in such widely variant forms of expression.

Prophetic Words Are the Words of God

The utterances of the apostles and the prophets are the Word of God. When we read these words, we are listening not to the voice of man, but to the voice of God. We read in Mark 7:13, "*Making the word of God of none effect through your tradition, which ye have delivered: and many such like things do ye.*" Jesus had been setting up the law given through Moses against the Pharisaic traditions. In doing this, He expressly says in this passage that the law given through Moses was "*the word of God.*" In 2 Samuel 23:2, we read, "*The spirit of the* Lord *spake by me, and his word was in my tongue.*" Here again, we are told that the utterance of God's prophet was the word of God. In a similar way, God said in 1 Thessalonians 2:13,

For this cause also thank we God without ceasing, because, when ye received the word of God which ye heard of us, ye received it not as the word of men, but as it is in truth, the word of God, which effectually worketh also in you that believe.

Here, Paul declared that the word that he spoke, taught by the Spirit of God, was the very word of God.

25

THE WORK OF THE HOLY SPIRIT IN JESUS CHRIST

Jesus Christ Himself is the one perfect manifestation in history of the complete work of the Holy Spirit in man.

Begotten of the Spirit

Jesus Christ was begotten of the Holy Spirit.

And the angel answered and said unto her, The Holy Ghost shall come upon thee, and the power of the Highest shall overshadow thee: therefore

> *also that holy thing which shall be born of thee shall be called the Son of God.* (Luke 1:35)

As we have already seen, in regeneration, the believer is begotten of God; but Jesus Christ was begotten of God in His original generation. He is the only begotten Son of God. (See John 3:16.) It was entirely by the Spirit's power working in Mary that the Son of God was formed within her. The regenerated man has a carnal nature received from his earthly father and a new nature imparted by God. Jesus Christ had only the one holy nature, that which, in man, is called the new nature. Nevertheless, He was a real man as He had a human mother.

Spotless Life

Jesus Christ led a holy and spotless life and offered Himself without spot to God through the working of the Holy Spirit. We read in Hebrews 9:14, *"How much more shall the blood of Christ, who through the eternal Spirit offered himself without spot to God, purge your conscience from dead works to serve the living God?"* Jesus Christ met and overcame temptations, as other men may meet and overcome them, in the power of the Holy Spirit. He was tempted and suffered through temptation (see Hebrews 2:18). He was tempted in all points like we are (see Hebrews 4:15), but never once in any way did He yield to temptation. He was tempted entirely apart from sin (see Hebrews 4:15), but He won His victories in a way that is open for all of us to win victory in the power of the Holy Spirit.

Fitted for Service

Jesus Christ was anointed and fitted for service by the Holy Spirit. We read in Acts 10:38, *"How God anointed Jesus of Nazareth with the Holy Ghost and with power: who went about doing good, and healing all that were oppressed of the devil; for God was with him."* In a prophetic vision of the coming Messiah in the Old Testament we read,

> *The spirit of the Lord God is upon me; because the Lord hath anointed me to preach good tidings unto the meek; he hath sent me to bind up the brokenhearted, to proclaim liberty to the captives, and the opening of the prison to them that are bound.* (Isaiah 61:1)

In Luke's record of the earthly life of our Lord in Luke 4:14, we read, "*And Jesus returned in the power of the Spirit into Galilee: and there went out a fame of him through all the region round about.*" In a similar way, Jesus said of Himself when speaking in the synagogue in Nazareth,

> *The Spirit of the Lord is upon me, because he hath anointed me to preach the gospel to the poor; he hath sent me to heal the brokenhearted, to preach deliverance to the captives, and recovering of sight to the blind, to set at liberty them that are bruised, to preach the acceptable year of the Lord.* (Luke 4:18–19)

All these passages contain the one lesson that it was by the special anointing with the Holy Spirit that Jesus Christ was qualified for the service to which God had called Him. As He stood in the Jordan after His baptism, "*the Holy Ghost descended in a bodily shape like a dove upon him*" (Luke 3:22). It was then and there that He was anointed with the Holy Spirit, baptized with the Holy Spirit, and equipped for the service that lay before Him. Jesus Christ received His equipment for service in the same way that we receive ours—by a definite baptism with the Holy Spirit.

Led by the Spirit

Jesus Christ was led by the Holy Spirit in His movements here upon earth. We read in Luke 4:1, "*And Jesus being full of the Holy Ghost returned from Jordan, and was led by the Spirit into the wilderness.*" Living as a man here upon earth and setting an example for us, each step of His life was under the Holy Spirit's guidance.

Taught by the Spirit

Jesus Christ was taught by the Spirit who rested upon Him. The Spirit of God was the source of His wisdom in the days of His flesh. In the Old Testament prophecy of the coming Messiah, we read,

> *And the spirit of the* Lord *shall rest upon him, the spirit of wisdom and understanding, the spirit of counsel and might, the spirit of knowledge and of the fear of the* Lord*; and shall make him of quick understanding in the fear of the* Lord*: and he shall not judge after the sight of his eyes, neither reprove after the hearing of his ears.*
>
> (Isaiah 11:2–3)

Further on, in Isaiah 42:1 (RV), we read, *"Behold my servant, whom I uphold; my chosen, in whom my soul delighteth: I have put my spirit upon him; he shall bring forth judgment to the Gentiles."* Matthew told us in Matthew 12:17–18 that this prophecy was fulfilled in Jesus of Nazareth.

Jesus' Words from the Holy Spirit

The Holy Spirit abode upon Jesus in all His fullness, and the words He spoke, consequently, were the very words of God. We read in John 3:34, *"For he whom God hath sent speaketh the words of God: for God giveth not the Spirit by measure unto him."*

Apostles Chosen through the Holy Spirit

After His resurrection, Jesus Christ gave commandments to His apostles, whom He had chosen through the Holy Spirit. We read in Acts 1:2, *"Until the day in which he was taken up, after that he through the Holy Ghost had given commandments unto the apostles whom he had chosen."* This relates to the time after His resurrection, and so we see Jesus still working in the power of the Holy Spirit, even after His resurrection from the dead.

Miracles Done through the Holy Spirit

Jesus Christ wrought His miracles here on earth in the power of the Holy Spirit. In Matthew 12:28, we read, *"I cast out devils by the Spirit of God."* It is through the Spirit that miracle-working power was given to some in the church after our Lord's departure from this earth (see 1 Corinthians 12:9–10), and in the power of the same Spirit, Jesus Christ wrought His miracles.

Resurrection through the Holy Spirit

It was by the power of the Holy Spirit that Jesus Christ was raised from the dead. We read in Romans 8:11, *"But if the Spirit of him that raised up Jesus from the dead dwell in you, he that raised up Christ from the dead shall also quicken your mortal bodies by his Spirit that dwelleth in you."* The same Spirit who is to quicken our mortal bodies and is to raise us up in some future day raised up Jesus.

Undisputable Facts

The following things are plainly evident from this study of the work of the Holy Spirit in Jesus Christ. First of all, we see the completeness of His humanity. He lived, He thought, He worked, He taught, He conquered sin, and He won victories for God in the power of that very same Spirit whom it is our privilege also to have.

In the second place, we see our own utter dependence upon the Holy Spirit. If it was in the power of the Holy Spirit that Jesus Christ, the only begotten Son of God, lived and worked, achieved and triumphed, how much more dependent are we upon Him at every turn of life and in every phase of service and every experience of conflict with Satan and sin?

The third thing that is evident is the wondrous world of privilege, blessing, victory, and conquest that is open to us. The same Spirit through whom Jesus was originally begotten is at our disposal for us to be begotten again of Him. The same Spirit through whom Jesus offered Himself without spot to God is at our disposal that we also may offer ourselves without spot to Him. The same Spirit by which Jesus was anointed for service is at our disposal that we may be anointed for service. The same Spirit who led Jesus Christ in His movements here on earth is ready to lead us today. The same Spirit who taught Jesus and imparted to Him wisdom and understanding, counsel and might, and knowledge and the fear of the Lord is here to teach us.

Jesus Christ is our pattern: *"He that saith he abideth in him ought himself also so to walk, even as he walked"* (1 John 2:6), *"the firstborn among many brethren"* (Romans 8:29). Whatever He realized through the Holy Spirit is for us also to realize today.

ABOUT THE AUTHOR

Reuben Archer Torrey was born in Hoboken, New Jersey, on January 28, 1856. He graduated from Yale University in 1875 and from Yale Divinity School in 1878.

Upon his graduation, Dr. Torrey became a Congregational minister. A few years later, he joined Dwight L. Moody in his evangelistic work in Chicago and became the pastor of the Chicago Avenue Church. He was selected by D. L. Moody to become the first dean of the Moody Bible Institute of Chicago. Under Torrey's direction, Moody Institute became a pattern for Bible institutes around the world.

Torrey is respected as one of the greatest evangelists of modern times. At the turn of the century, he began his evangelistic tours and crusades. He spent the years of 1903–1905 in a worldwide revival campaign, along with the famous song leader Charles McCallon Alexander. Together they ministered in many parts of the world and reportedly brought nearly one hundred thousand souls to Jesus. Torrey continued worldwide crusades for the next fifteen years, eventually reaching Japan and China. During those same years, he served as Dean of the Bible Institute of Los Angeles and pastored the Church of the Open Door in that city.

Torrey longed for more Christian workers to take an active part in bringing the message of salvation through Christ to a lost and dying world. His straightforward style of evangelism has shown thousands of Christian workers how to become effective soulwinners.

R. A. Torrey died on October 26, 1928. He is well remembered today for his inspiring devotional books on the Christian life, which have been translated into many different languages. The evangelistic message that sent Torrey around the world is still ministering through his teachings to all whose hearts yearn to lead men, women, and children to salvation through Jesus Christ.